Cyberspace Sovereignty

Binxing Fang

Cyberspace Sovereignty

Reflections on Building a Community of Common Future in Cyberspace

Science Press
Beijing

Springer

Binxing Fang
China Electronic Corporation
Beijing
China

The published book is sponsored by Chinese Academy of Engineering, Cyber Security Association of China, Group of Research on Cyberspace Sovereignty, and ShenZhen Cyberspace Laboratory.

ISBN 978-981-13-0319-7 ISBN 978-981-13-0320-3 (eBook)
https://doi.org/10.1007/978-981-13-0320-3

Jointly published with Science Press, Beijing, China

The print edition is not for sale in China Mainland. Customers from China Mainland please order the print book from: China Science Publishing & Media Ltd (Science Press).
ISBN of the China Mainland edition: 978-7-03-053906-9

Library of Congress Control Number: 2018939939

Printed on acid-free paper

This Springer imprint is published by the registered company Springer Nature Singapore Pte Ltd.
part of Springer Nature
The registered company address is: 152 Beach Road, #21-01/04 Gateway East, Singapore 189721, Singapore

Preface I

President Xi Jinping advocated "respect to cyber sovereignty" in the first World Internet Conference in 2014. He was the first state head who initiated the principle of *Cyber Sovereignty*. This reflects the clear stance of our country in global Internet governance: sovereign countries should participate in the governance of the Internet on an equal footing, combat in concert cybercrime, and jointly promote the construction, utilization, and development of cyberspace by abiding by the principle of respecting other nations' cyber sovereignty, the principle of cyber sovereign equality among nations, the principle of noninterference in other nations' internal affairs of cyberspace and the principle of all nations being equal and benefiting each other in cyberspace.

Cyberspace is a man-made electromagnetic space within the Internet, various telecommunication networks and communication systems, various transmission systems and radio and television networks, various computer systems, and ICT infrastructures such as embedded processors and controllers in key industrial facilities, as the carrier, over which people create, store, change, transmit, use, and display data and do other things with data to accomplish specific communication technology activities.

International Co-governance of Telecommunication Networks

In the case of telecommunication networks, the international community has effectively carried out sovereign state-based co-governance of international telecommunication networks using the International Telecommunication Union (ITU) as a platform for global governance of telecommunication networks. The reason why the international community reached a consensus on co-governance of telecom space derived from the evolution of telecommunication networks.

In the nineteenth century, the telegraph technology was invented, which enabled countries to establish their national telegraph networks. With the need for cross-border communication arising, some European countries signed the "International Telegraph Convention" in 1865 and announced the establishment of an international co-governance institution of sovereign states—the International Telegraph Union, referred to as ITU. With the use and development of the radio and broadcast, in 1906 more than 20 countries signed the "International Wireless Telegraph Convention", managed by the ITU on its behalf. In 1932, more than 70 states agreed to merge the International Telegraph Convention with the International Wireless Telegraph Convention, enacted the International Telecommunication Convention and decided to have the International Telegraph Convention renamed the International Telecommunication Union as from 1934, still referred to as ITU. In 1947, the ITU became a specialized agency of the United Nations.

Obstacles in the International Co-governance of the Internet

Objectively speaking, the Internet has become not only an infrastructure on which countries in the world are highly dependent, but also a basic environment in which people all over the world reply for existence. Hundreds of millions of Internet users are concerned with even the slightest disturbance or trouble in the Internet. It should have been natural that such international space for coexistence is managed in an international co-governance mode. In fact, however, such a mode, in which telecommunication networks is managed, did not find a replication in the Internet space. The reason is that the evolution of the Internet makes it difficult for the fairness of co-governance thereof to benefit all the nations.

The Internet originated from the US military's Advanced Research Projects Agency Network (ARPANET) in the late 1960s. In the early 1980s, part of the ARPANET was used for civilian purposes and was built by the National Science Foundation (NSF) using TCP/IP protocol into the NSFNET. Because the TCP/IP protocol was accessible for free, some countries also used it to build their own parts of the Internet. At that time, the United States also encouraged other countries to get access to the NSFNET, the core of the US Internet. In 1987, some US companies were commissioned by the NSF to manage the NSFNET backbone networks. In 1993, the NSF set up a network information center managed by a number of corporate entities to serve Internet companies and users. In 1997, the United States set up an Internet number registration agency responsible for address allocation. By then, the US private sector had taken a leading role in the management of the Internet. In 1998, the US Department of Commerce withdrew the right to manage the Internet by signing an agreement with the Internet Corporation for Assigned Names and Numbers (ICANN). The Internet has become a network solely managed by the United States ever since.

The great difference between the developing history of the Internet and that of telecommunication networks makes it natural that they are managed in different modes. In the case of telecommunication networks, some countries first built their own telecommunication networks and then linked their respective networks to each other on agreements, thereby forming a sovereign state-led management mode. For the Internet, the United States first built it, and then other countries were allowed to get access to it, thereby forming a US-led centralized management mode. In other words, it is the US that has the right to speak in the management of the Internet.

In October 2016, the US government officially stopped managing the ICANN, making it an international organization, but the prerequisite is that governments do not interfere with the ICANN and it is managed solely by "stakeholders". The so-called stakeholders refer to organizations who "live with the Internet", such as Google, Cisco, and other Internet-related businesses. Managed by such organizations, the Internet is bound to benefit. However, because only a few organizations have the opportunity to participate in the management of the Internet, the "stakeholder" management mode has objectively led to "the law of the jungle": the strong rule and the weak blindly follow.

Conflicts Between Stakeholder Management Mode and International Co-governance

Although the Internet is a gift of the United States dedicated to the world, other countries have invested a lot of human, material, and financial resources in the Internet, and it has become an infrastructure which people all around the world cannot live without. Therefore, the Internet is no longer space on which only "stakeholders" reply for existence, but rather is a platform for each country's political, military, economic, cultural, and social affairs and is an important pillar of an information country. From that point of view, countries should not let the Internet be unorganized, and they cannot give up their right to engage in the management of the Internet.

The first goal of "Stakeholders" is to maximize their interests, whereas providing universal service is one of the attributes of the Internet as an infrastructure benefitting the livelihood of the vast majority of the public. Obviously, the Internet is not only a platform for stakeholders' profit-earning, but also serves the public—free access and use is not in line with the stakeholders' value system. Hence, the stakeholder-based management mode has the risk of polarization: the backward becomes more backward, and the advanced becomes more advanced. Take IP address allocation, for example. The idea that he who first applies for an address gets the address first follows the value system of the market economy, but that makes countries that awake late lose opportunities. On the contrary, if the sovereign state-based ITU management mode is followed, the distribution mode of the planning economy is likely to take care of the future needs of the underdeveloped countries. Besides, sovereign states as spokespersons for those countries can even help them enter the information age as soon as possible. That is the difference between the stakeholder management and the sovereign state management, which also reflects the conceptual difference between market competition and fair distribution.

The debate over whether to choose the stakeholder management mode or the mode of co-governance by sovereign states, in essence, disregards the existence of Cyberspace Sovereignty. Since there is sovereignty in the telecommunication space, the ITU management mode becomes a natural choice. However, the global communication over the Internet, which makes the Internet like a single network, is not an acceptable ground for the argument that no sovereignty exists in cyberspace. After all, people likewise communicate globally over the sovereign telecommunication networks. The neglect of Internet sovereignty arises from the fact that the other countries accepted the technology and standard gifts from the United States, thus ignoring their own rights. In fact, as the US cyberspace security coordinator Michelle admitted, "cyberspace is carried by a series of servers that are facilities located in a country, so cyberspace is not an independent existence." Since a country has sovereignty over ICT facilities, it is derivable that the country has sovereignty over cyberspace carried by the facilities located in its territory. If there is no cyberspace sovereignty, there is no basis for cyberspace legislation; if there is no cyberspace sovereignty, there is no way to combat cybercrime; if there is no cyberspace sovereignty, there is no right to clear harmful information such as child pornography on the Internet; and so on. Those legal and administrative acts that have been incorporated into individual countries' administration systems showcase the objective existence of cyberspace sovereignty.

Cyberspace Sovereignty, the Determinant of International Co-governance of the Internet

There is cyberspace sovereignty in the Internet space, but the international community does not follow the sovereignty principle to govern the Internet together. It is argued that the driving force behind Internet innovation comes from stakeholders, and that advancing the technology of the Internet should also rely on those stakeholders who have mastered the Internet and new technologies. Undeniably, however, the Internet's public policy issues concern the power of sovereign states and are related to national policies and even international political issues, and they have had nothing to do with earning profits from the Internet. In December 2003, the Declaration of Principles, published at the United Nations World Summit on the Information Society, stressed that "Policy authority for Internet-related public policy issues is the sovereign right of States. They have rights and responsibilities for international Internet-related public policy issues." Suppose an extreme example. If someone wants to register the domain name ".ISIS", the stakeholders are likely to ignore the possible harmfulness of the domain name and even unlikely to consider from a perspective other than the economic benefits. The sovereign state-based mode probably prevents, within a consensus reached by the states, the so-called Islamic State of Iraq and Syria (ISIS) from using the Internet to express their ideas.

In short, after we make clear the objectiveness and necessity of the existence of cyberspace sovereignty, the next thing is to manage the Internet based on the sovereignty principle. The international community should deepen its commitment to international cooperation in cyberspace and work together to build a cyberspace-destined community, make proper use of, promote the development of, and govern the Internet. An international organization similar to the ITU should be built to govern the Internet in a "multi-stakeholder" mode. When it comes to Internet policies, they should be made by sovereign countries, and for technology innovation, the stakeholders should play a greater role.

We should adhere to the concept of cyberspace sovereignty, advance the global governance of the Internet toward a more just and reasonable direction, promote cyberspace to achieve the goals of equality, respect, innovation, development, openness, sharing, safety, and orderliness.

Beijing, China Binxing Fang
June 2017

Preface II

At the end of 2014, President Xi Jinping as the first state head voiced "respect to cyber sovereignty". Following that, more than 30 researchers from different units, including Fang Binxing, took the assignment "Research on Cyberspace Sovereignty" from the Office of the Central Leading Group for Cyberspace Affairs and the Chinese Academy of Engineering in 2015. The research is focused on the generation, development, conflict, security, and other issues of cyberspace sovereignty. Chen Zuoning, the Vice President of the Chinese Academy of Engineering, attached great importance to the study and gave their advice.

In 1994, China formally got access to the Internet. Two years later China's Internet began to enter a wide popularity stage, and the National State High-Tech Development Plan ("863" Plan) included the Internet technology into the research guides. In 1998, the Ministry of Electronics Industry and the Ministry of Posts and Telecommunications were combined to form the Ministry of Information Industry, which allowed the Internet and telecommunications business to be independent of the government functions and be run by enterprises. The Ministry of Information Industry, unlike the former Ministry of Electronics Industry and Ministry of Posts and Telecommunications, no longer undertook the management activities, but served as the government to regulate the operation of various types of network services. With the functions of the government becoming clear, the Ministry of Information Industry began to make more efforts in the management of security problems and introduced a series of management systems and policies.

In 1996, the Internet activist John Perry Barlow published the famous "A Declaration of the Independence of Cyberspace", claiming that cyberspace belongs to the "future world" in which there is no government, no sovereignty, and it is global social space where its own social contract is forming and people deal with what happened in cyberspace in their own ways. As can be seen from the declaration, some people regard cyberspace as a "virtual world" independent of the physical world and thus resist governmental management from the physical world.

With the Chinese government strengthening the management of the Internet, the Western governments began to criticize China's Internet management and mobilized those identifying the Internet as being independent of the physical world to join the attack on the Chinese government. "Noninterference in each other's internal affairs" was originally a practice of international exchanges, but in cyberspace, it seems to be discarded by the Western countries. Astonishingly, the basic principle for international exchanges can be easily trampled. The reason is that there is a debate over whether cyberspace is sovereign space. To this end, since 2009, our research group has concentrated our study on whether cyberspace is a "global public domain", as some people imaged, and whether countries around the world really gave up the power to exercise sovereignty in cyberspace. Our research shows that the answer is NO. To take how the countries deal with bad information, for example, the countries, including the Western countries, have put forward their own bad information standards, enacted corresponding laws, setting up corresponding management departments, mobilized social organizations to engage in the management in various forms, developed various technical means to assist in the management, and carried out a series of special campaigns to combat cybercrime. We compiled the research results and wrote the book "*How Foreign Countries Supervise Bad Information on the Internet: Methods and Technology*", published by the Law Press in January 2016. It has been proved that cyberspace sovereignty is an objective reality and it is necessary to increase publicity of cyberspace sovereignty and demonstrate the reasonableness, legitimacy, and necessity of cyberspace sovereignty.

On October 18, 2011, Fang Binxing delivered a lecture on *Cyberspace Sovereignty* at "The First International Symposium on Cyberspace and the Third Internet Governance and Law Forum" held in Beijing, discussing the concept of cyberspace sovereignty. On October 25 the same year, Fang Binxing delivered a lecture on "Countries' 'Cyber Sovereignty' in the Information Age" at the "International Information Security Symposium", held in Changsha, expounding on the international status of cyber sovereignty. That same year, on the November 11, Fang Binxing made a speech on "'Five-Four Rules' of Cyberspace Security of the Future Networks" at the "2011 China's Future Network Development and Innovation Forum", held in Nanjing, putting forward the four basic rights of cyber sovereignty. On December 16, the same year, Fang Binxing as the representative of the 11th National People's Congress, submitted the "Suggestions on China Popularizing the Idea of 'Cyber Sovereignty'", coming up with the importance of advocating cyber sovereignty. On April 28, 2012, Fang Binxing's suggestions were compiled and published on page 3 of "Guangming Daily" with the title "Advocating Cyber Sovereignty Extremely Important". On May 3, the same year, Fang Binxing was at Central South University and made a speech entitled "Talking about National Cyber Sovereignty in the Information Age", putting forward the basic means of safeguarding the four basic rights of cyber sovereignty.

Fang Binxing, accompanying members of the Department of Arms Control of the Ministry of Foreign Affairs, took part in a group of governmental experts' three sessions of the United Nations' third discussion on Developments in the Field of Information and Telecommunications in the Contest of International Security, held on August 6–10, 2012, January 14–18, 2013, and June 3–7, 2013. Recommended by Fang Binxing, through the efforts of the Department of Arms

Control and with the support of some countries, including Russia, the contents about cyberspace sovereignty were included in the Report of the Group of Governmental Experts on Developments in the Field of Information and Telecommunications in the Context of International Security as Item 20, which states: "State sovereignty and international norms and principles that flow from sovereignty apply to State conduct of ICT-related activities, and to their jurisdiction over ICT infrastructure within their territory." The fruits of the three sessions were published on June 28, 2013 in the form of United Nations document A/68/98.

Subsequent to President Xi Jinping's initiative of "respecting cyber sovereignty" made at the end of 2014, our research group undertook the projects "Research on Strategies for Cyberspace Security" and "Research on Cyberspace Sovereignty" in 2015. In 2016, 1 year later, the group wrote a report on results of the research on cyberspace sovereignty and thus gave this book.

This book focuses on the interpretation of what cyberspace is and how the international community views cyberspace. It analyzes what cyberspace sovereignty is, how the international community views cyberspace sovereignty, why there is uncertainty about cyberspace sovereignty, what the focus of international conflicts on cyberspace sovereignty is, what the significance of advocating cyberspace sovereignty in our country is, and how cyberspace sovereignty can be safeguarded.

The following people participated in the writing of this book (listed alphabetically): Chen Xiaohua, Chu Chengyuan, Cui Xiang, Du A'ning, He Jun, Jia Yan, Jin Shuyuan, Li Aiping, Li Fenghua, Li Yuxiao, Lin Peng, Wang Bai Ling, Wang Bin, Wang Xuan, Wang Zhongru, Xie Yongjiang, Xiong Dapeng, Xu Jin, Zhai Lidong, Zhang Hongli, Zhang Weizhe, Zhang Zhaoxin, Zhao Hongrui, Zou Hongxia, Zou Peng et al. The author's foreword was written by Fang Binxing; Chap. 1 "Definition of Fundamental Concepts" was written by Fang Binxing, Jia Yan, Lin Peng, Xu Jin, Zhang Zhaoxin, and Zhao Hongrui; Chap. 2 "Understanding of Traditional Sovereignty Concept", by Zhao Hongrui; Chap. 3 "Interpretation of the Concept of 'Cyberspace Sovereignty'", by Fang Binxing, Wang Bin and Zhang Weizhe; Chap. 4 "Necessities for Advocating Cyberspace Sovereignty", by Fang Binxing, Lin Peng, Wang Bailing, Wang Xuan, Zhang Hongli, and Zhang Weizhe; Chap. 5 "The Relationship between Cyberspace Sovereignty and Internet Stakeholders", by Jin Shuyuan and Li Yuxiao; Chap. 6 "China's Declaration of Cyberspace Sovereignty", by Fang Binxing and Wang Zhongru; Chap. 7 "Objective Existence of Cyberspace Sovereignty in Countries' Affairs", by Fang Binxing and Zhai Lidong; Chap. 8 "Positions of States toward Cyberspace and Cyber-Relating Regulations", by Fang Binxing, Li Yuxiao, and Zhao Hongrui; Chap. 9 "Scientific Basis for Maintaining Cyberspace Sovereignty", by Chen Xiaohua, Fang Binxing, He Jun, and Jia Yan; Chap. 10 "Extension of Cyberspace Sovereignty", by Fang Binxing and Li Fenghua; Chap. 11 "Conflicts of Cyberspace Sovereignty Concept", by Fang Binxing, Jin Shuyuan, and Li Aiping; Chap. 12 "Main Initiatives to Safeguard Cyberspace Sovereignty", by Chu Chengyuan, Cui Xiang, Du A'ning, Fang Binxing, Guo Li, Xie Yongjiang, Zhang Hongli, and Zou Peng; and Chap. 13 "Conclusion", by Fang Binxing. Fang Binxing developed this book's writing frame and was responsible for editing. Zou Peng, Zou Hongxia, Xiong Da Peng, et al. were responsible for proofreading.

We are grateful for the guidance, correction, and help of the following people: Chen Zuoning, Vice President of the Chinese Academy of Engineering; Fu Cong, Ambassador, Deputy Director-General Long Zhou, Director Dai Huai Cheng, Section Chief Zhao Li, and Section Chief Xu Feng from the Ministry of Foreign Affairs; Director Zhao Zeliang and Deputy Director Hu Xiao from the Cyber Security Coordination Department of the Office of the Central Leading Group for Cyberspace Affairs; Gu Jian, the Deputy Director of the Department of Cyber Security Defense of the Ministry of Public Security; President Hu Chuanping and Director Zou Xiang from the Third Research Institution of the Ministry of Public Security; Liu Xinran, the Deputy Director of the National Internet Emergency Center of the Ministry of Industry and Information Technology; Li Yongzhi, the Vice President of the Donghua University; Du Yuejin, the Vice President of the Security Department of Alibaba; Deputy Director Fan Guimei and Chen Lei from the Chinese Academy of Engineering; Director Han Yi from China Electronics Corporation; Lu Hui, an Associate Professor from the Institute of Microelectronics of the Chinese Academy of Sciences; and Long Chaoze from the Chinese Academy of Cyberspace. We also appreciate guidance from the following academics in the Chinese Academy of Engineering: Shen Changxiang, Cai Jiren, Li Youping, Lu Xicheng, He Xingui, Wang Tianran, Wu Jiangxing, Liu Yunjie, Lv Yueguang, and Ding Wenhua.

Beijing, China
June 2017

Binxing Fang
Group of Research on Cyberspace Sovereignty

Contents

About the Author

Binxing Fang is an academician of the Chinese Academy of Engineering and an expert in cyberspace security. He is the Chief Scientist of the China Electronics Corporation, the Chief Academic Adviser of the Computer School of Harbin Institute of Technology (Shenzhen), the Honorary Dean of the Cyberspace Institute of Advanced Technology of the Guangzhou University, the Director of the National Engineering Laboratory for Information Security Technologies, and the Director of the Key Laboratory of Trustworthy Distributed Computing and Service, Ministry of Education. He is the Chairman of Cyber Security Association of China, the Chairman of Chinese Information Processing Society of China, the Chairman of the China Security Alliance of Cloud and Emerging Technology Innovation, the Chairman of Network and Information Security Technical Committee of China Communications Standards Association.

Since 1999, Fang has put forward the idea of building the national Network and Information Security infrastructure, and has organized and implemented the corresponding system, and has made great achievements in international leading.

At present, he is mainly engaged in research of cloud security, Internet of Things security, artificial intelligence security, IoT search, and big search, cyber range, and cyberspace security education methods and other aspects of research work.

Abbreviations

ACM	Association for Computing Machinery
ACPA	Anticybersquatting Consumer Protection Act
ACPO	Association of Chief Police Officers
AfriNIC	African Network Information Centre
AOL	American Online
APC	Association for Progressive Communications
APNIC	Asia-Pacific Network Information Centre
APP	Applications Area
ARPA	Advanced Research Projects Agency
AS	Autonomous System
AT&T	American Telephone and Telegraph Company
BBC	British Broadcasting Corporation
BBN	Bolt, Beranek and Newman Inc.
BGPsec	Border Gateway Protocol Security
BSkyB	British Sky Broadcasting
BSS	Broadcast Satellite Service
C2M	Customer to Manufactory
CA	Certificate Authority
CBM	Confidence Building Measures
CCITT	International Telegraph and Telephone Consultative Committee
ccTLD	country code Top-Level Domain
CDA	Communications Decency Act
CEE	Center for Excellence in Education
CENTDR	Council of European National Top-Level Domain Registries
CERN	Conseil European Pour la Recherche Nuclear
CERNET	China Education and Research Network
CERT	Computer Emergency Response Team
CNCERT	National Computer Network Emergency Response Technical Team/Coordination Center

CNN	Cable News Network
CNNIC	China Internet Network Information Center
CNP	Card Not Present
CNVD	China National Vulnerability Database
COTS	Commercial off-the-shelf
CPR	International Institute for Conflict Prevention and Resolution
CSD	Canal Satellite Digital
CSNET	Computer Science Network
CTIRU	Counter Terrorism Internet Referral Unit
CTSS	Compatible Time Sharing System
DARPA	Defense Advanced Research Projects Agency
DBS	Direct Broadcast Satellite
DDoS	Distributed Denial-of-Service
DISA	Defense Information Systems Agency
DNS	Domain Name System
DNSMON	DNS Monitoring Service
DNSSEC	Domain Name System Security Extensions
DoD	Department of Defense of the United States
DoT	Department of Telecommunications
DRAM	Dynamic Random Access Memory
EFF	Electronic Frontier Foundation
EMI	Electric and Musical Industries Ltd.
FCC	Federal Communications Commission
FIRST	Forum for Incident Response and Security Teams
FISC	Foreign Intelligence Surveillance Court
GDPR	General Data Protection Regulation
GDS	Global Distribution System
GEN	General Area
GGE	Group of Governmental Experts on Developments in the Field of Information and Telecommunications in the Context of International Security
gTLD	generic Top-Level Domain
HTC	High Tech Computer Corporation
IaaS	Infrastructure as a Service
IAB	Internet Architecture Board
IANA	Internet Assigned Numbers Authority
IBM	International Business Machines Corporation
ICANN	The Internet Corporation for Assigned Names and Numbers
ICSA	インターネットコンテンツセーフティ協会, Internet Content Security Association
ICT	Information and Communications Technology
IDC	Internet Data Center
IEC	International Electrotechnical Commission

IEEE	Institute of Electrical and Electronic Engineers
IESG	Internet Engineering Steering Group
IETF	Internet Engineering Task Force
IFCC	Internet Fraud Complaint Center
IFIP	International Federation for Information Processing
IGF	Internet Governance Forum
IIKK	InterCon International KK
INFORMS	Institute for Operations Research and the Management Sciences
INT	Internet Area
InterNIC	Internet Network Information Center
IoT	Internet of Things
IP	Internet Protocol
IRTF	Internet Research Task Force
ISIL	Islamic State of Iraq and the Levant
ISIS	Islamic State of Iraq and al-Sham
ISO	International Organization for Standardization
ISOC	Internet Society
ISP	Internet Service Provider
ITI	Information Technology Infrastructure
ITRs	International Telecommunications Regulations
ITU	International Telecommunication Union
KMI	Key Management Infrastructure
LACNIC	Latin America and Caribbean Network Information Centre
LIR	Local Internet Registry
LISP	List Processor

Microsoft Corporation

MOU	Memorandum of Understanding
MX	Mail Exchanger
NAC	Network Analysis Company
NAF	National Arbitration Forum
NCFC	The National Computing and Networking Facility of China
NCP	Network Control Protocol
NCSS	The National Cyber Security Strategy
NDSS	Network and Distributed System Security
NIR	National Internet Registry
NNTP	Network News Transfer Protocol
NORSAR	Norwegian Seismic Array
NSF	The National Science Foundation
NSI	Network Solutions Inc.
NSRC	Network Startup Resource Center

NTIA	National Telecommunications and Information Administration
O2O	Online to Offline
OECD	Organization for Economic Co-operation and Development
OPS	Operations and Management Area
PDA	Personal Digital Assistant
PKI	Public Key Infrastructure
PMI	Privilege Management Infrastructure
QoS	Quality of Service
Radio HK	Radio Hong Kong
RFC	Request for Comments
RFID	Radio-Frequency Identification
RIPE	The Réseaux IP Européens (French)
RIR	Regional Internet Registry
RIS	Routing Information Service
RSS	Really Simple Syndication
RTG	Routing Area
SBA	Singapore Broadcasting Authority
SCO	Shanghai Cooperation Organization
SEC	Security Area
SFNB	Security First Network Bank
SIGCOMM	Special Interest Group on Data Communication
SIP	Session Initiation Protocol
SMTP	Simple Mail Transfer Protocol
SQL	Structured Query Language
SUB	Sub-IP Area
TCP	Transmission Control Protocol
TIA	Telecommunications Industry Association
TIC	Trusted Internet Connections
TPS	Television Par Satellite
TSC	Technical service contract
TSV	Transport Area
TVWF	Television Without Frontiers Directive
UARS	Universal Anycast Root Server
UCLA	University of California at Los Angeles
UNCITRAL	United Nations Commission on International Trade Law
USAID	United States Agency for International Development
UUCP	Unix-to-Unix Copy Protocol
VoIP	Voice over Internet Protocol
WAIS	Wide Area Information Servers
WARC	World Administration Radio Conference
WCIT	World Conference on International Telecommunications
WGIG	Working Group on Internet Governance

WIPO	World Intellectual Property Organization
WSIS+10	World Summit on Information Society Review Process + 10
WTDC	World Telecommunication Development Conference
WTO	World Trade Organization
XMPP	Extensible Messaging and Presence Protocol
XSF	XMPP Standards Foundation

Introduction

This book is the first one that comprehensively discusses *Cyberspace Sovereignty* in China, reflecting China's clear attitude in the global Internet governance: respecting every nation's right to independently choose a development path, cyber management modes, and Internet public policies and to participate in the international cyberspace governance on an equal footing.

At present, the concept of cyberspace sovereignty is still very strange to many people, so it needs to be thoroughly analyzed. This book will not only help scientific and technical workers in the field of cyberspace security, law researchers, and the public understand the development of cyberspace sovereignty at home and abroad, but also serve as reference basis for the relevant decision-making and management departments in their work.

Chapter 1
The Definitions of Fundamental Concepts

Abstract The concept of Cyberspace can be regarded as the combination of Cyber and Space. Among them, Cyber involves technical attributes and focuses on its various forms in the information technology level. Space involves social attributes and focuses on the people who use the Cyber and the ways to use the Cyber. Therefore, Cyberspace is not only involved in the digital world because of the flow of information, but also in the physical world because of the people who use the Cyber and their behavior.

Keywords Network · Infrastructure · Data · User · Operation

To study cyberspace sovereignty, the concept of cyber space must be clarified; and thus, the notation and denotation of the term "cyber" must be made explicit.

In fact, the term "cyber", when not particularly referring to cyber space, sometimes can be simply defined as the network. That is, merely the part of technical system is emphasized, so as to focus on the infrastructure. Moreover, the definition of cyber space changes along with time.

Daniel T. Kuehl listed the following evolution[1] of the definition of cyber space in Chap. 2 of his work From Cyber space to Cyber power: Defining the Problem.[2]

- Greece: kybernetes (the steersman) or cybernetics, the study of control processes, which was the basis for Tom Rona's concept (1976) of "information warfare."
- William Gibson, Neuromancer (1984): "a consensual hallucination."

The above definitions are substantially the literal meaning of the word "cyber", strengthening its meaning "controlling" and "reactive" as a root word.

- Edward Waltz, Information Warfare: Principles and Operations (1998): The "cyberspace dimension" refers to the middle layer—the information infras-

[1]Chapter 2 From Cyberspace to Cyberpower: Defining the Problem, Table 2.1. Definitions of Cyberspace. http://ctnsp.dodlive.mil/files/2014/03/Cyberpower-I-Chap-02.pdf [2016-9-6].
[2]Kuehl DT (2009) From cyber space to cyber power: defining the problem. Cyberpower and National Security, National Defense University Press.

B. Fang, *Cyberspace Sovereignty*,
https://doi.org/10.1007/978-981-13-0320-3_1

tructure—of the three realms of the information warfare battlespace. These three realms are the physical (facilities, nodes), the information infrastructure, and the perceptual.
- Dorothy Denning, Information Warfare and Security (1999): "The information space consisting of the sum total of all computer networks."
- New world Encyclopaedia: "Cyberspace is a global domain within the information environment consisting of the interdependent network of information technology infrastructures (ITI) including the Internet, telecommunication networks, computer systems, and embedded processors and controllers."

In these definitions, cyberspace concentrates on the cyber itself, stressing on the components of cyber.

- Winn Schwartau, Information Warfare: Chaos on the Electronic Superhighway (2nd ed., 1996): "[National] cyberspaces are distinct entities, with clearly defined electronic borders… Small-C cyberspaces consist of personal, corporate or organizational spaces… Big-C cyberspace is the National Information Infrastructure… add [both] and then tie it all up with threads of connectivity and you have all of cyberspace."
- Merriam Webster Third New International Dictionary(2002): "The on-line world of computer networks."
- Oxford English Dictionary (2014): "The notional environment in which communication over computer networks occurs."
- National Military Strategy for Cyberspace Operations(2006): "A domain characterized by the use of electronics and the electromagnetic spectrum to store, modify and exchange information via networked systems and physical infrastructures."

In these definitions, cyber space also focuses on the cyber itself, while strengthening the capability of cyber for information transmission.

- Winn Schwartau, Information Warfare: Chaos on the Electronic Superhighway (1994): "That intangible place between computers where information momentarily exists on its route from one end of the global network to the other… the ethereal reality, an infinity of electrons speeding down copper or glass fibers at the speed of light… Cyberspace is borderless… [but also] think of cyberspace as being divided into groups of local or regional cyberspace - hundreds and millions of smaller cyberspaces all over the world."

"Space" is emphasized in these definitions of cyber space. That is, the subject of activities in cyberspace (individual, company or organization) is highlighted.

- Google: "The electronic medium of computer networks, in which online communication takes place… a metaphor for the non-physical terrain created by computer systems… the impression of space and community formed by computers, computer networks, and their users… the place where a telephone conversation appears to occur… the place between the phones."

These definitions give a complete expression of cyberspace, covering the characteristics of both cyber and space. The characteristics of cyber relate to the components of cyber (electronic medium) and the capability of cyber (online communication); and the characteristics of space relate to people (user) and the space of their activities (place for conversations).

The above-listed definitions merely include cyber and the function and the subject of activities thereof, but fail to explicitly mention human activities. However, activity is the most important attribute for space. This problem is soon solved. For example, the work Cyberspace: Definition and Implications[3] provides a definition of cyber space as follows: "cyberspace is a time-dependent set of inter-connected information systems and the human users that interact with these systems." This definition emphasizes human interactive activities.

Some say that merely discussing cyber infrastructure is just as merely caring about the human body below the neck, which falls within the "cyber" focusing on the technical level; the discussion on human activities is like the discussion on the human body above the neck, which falls within the "space" focusing on the social level; only when the above two aspects are both included in the discussion, the term "cyberspace" is truly in discussion. Therefore, only if the definitions of cyber and space are made clear, cyberspace can be studied further.

1.1 Basic Definition of Cyber

Generally, cyber is deemed as an inter-connecting system consisting of nodes and connected edges for displaying a plurality of objects and the interconnection there between. The cyber is a model abstracting problems of the same category from the reality, and studying these problems using mathematic methods based on graphic theory. It is denoted as a directed (or undirected) weighted graph consisting of a vertex and arcs (or edges), which is widely used for optimization in the fields of engineering technology and scientific production management and the like. Nodes in the cyber may represent people, objects, places, etc. in the real world. Thus, with people as the nodes, human relation network, information network, social network and the like are formed; with objects as the nodes, biological network, neural network, genetic network, etc. are formed; and with places as the nodes, urban network, transportation network and water supply network are formed.

Cyber according to the loads can be divided into information network and non-information network. Information network refers to information communication technology networks with information communication technical system as the carrier and electromagnetic information as the load, such as telecommunication networks, computer networks, broadcast and television networks, and so on.

[3]Ottis R, Lorents P (2011) Cyberspace: definition and Implications. https://ccdcoe.org/multimedia/cyberspace-definition-and-implications.html [2016-9-5].

Non-information network may be a communication system existing in a physical space, which is featured by physical existence and intercommunication, such as road network, waterway network and the like. Non-information network may otherwise mean conceptive correlation. This is an intangible connection, such as human relation network (social network in a physical society) and so on. The cyberspace sovereignty discussed in this book is sovereignty over the information network. Thus, this book only concerns the information network.

In the reality, information network can be generalized into the following abstract concept: a system connecting each isolated "end node" (producer and consumer of information) via "connecting edges" (physical or virtual links) realize transit between each end node via "switching nodes", thereby realizing exchange of "load" between the end nodes. Thus, cyber contains four fundamental elements: end node, switching node, connecting edge, and load. The end node is the node for receiving and sending the load. The switching node is the node for transiting the load, which enables interconnection among several end nodes. The connecting edge is the link between end nodes and switching nodes, used for carrying and transmitting the load. The load refers to signal, data, information and the like, such as electromagnetic signal, quantum signal, network data, platform information, etc.

Under the above-described cyber, the load is via the connecting edges transmitted from an end node as a source point to the switching node and then transmitted from the switching node to an end node as a destination node.

1.2 Various (Electromagnetic) Information Networks

From the perspective of specific (electromagnetic) information network application, the cyber configurations in the current cyberspace mainly include: telecommunication networks, broadcast and television networks, the Internet, mobile Internet, social networks (overlay network), Internet of Things, Sensor Networks, industrial control networks, quantum communication networks, etc.

1.2.1 Telecommunication Networks

Telecommunication network is a communication system supporting intercommunication between users and formed by several telecommunication systems interconnecting with each other. It is an important infrastructure for people to realize long-distance communication. It uses cables, radio waves, optical fibers and other electromagnetic transmission systems to transit, transmit and receive identifications, characters, images, sounds or other signals. The Telecommunication network consists of a terminal apparatus for transmission and exchange, signalling process and agreements, and corresponding operation supporting systems.

The Telecommunication network in its concept can be divided into transmission network and service network. The transmission network is the carrier for multiple service networks. It can be copper wire transmission, microwave transmission, satellite transmission, optical fiber transmission, and many others. Generally, transmission network comprises a terminal device, a transmission device, an exchange device, and some other components. It focuses on the transmission of signals. Service network focuses on services in various forms, such as voice, data, image, broadcast and television.

According to the nature of the telecommunication services, telecommunication network can be further divided into telephone network, public telegraph network, telex network, data communication network, fax communication network, image communication network, videotext communication network, mobile communication network, etc.

1. The telephone network

The telephone network is a network conveying telephone information, which enables interactive voice communication and open telephone service. Telephone network is an automatic voice communication system consisting of end offices, interoffice trunk, satellite communication system, optical fibers, undersea cable, long relay wireless communication system, tandem exchange, International Switching Center, International Transit Center, long distance trunk, and subscriber lines, phone sets and private exchange in a closed numbering area. The voice is conveyed from one phone set terminal to another via a system platform such as the end office, the tandem exchange, local telephone exchange, transmission system and the like. In the telephone network, a phone set terminal is equivalent to an end node, the end office, the tandem exchange, the International Switching Center, and the International Transit Center equivalent to the switching nodes, the subscriber lines at the phone set terminal, the interoffice trunk, the long distance trunk, the long relay wireless communication system, the satellite communication system, the optical fibers and the undersea cable equivalent to the connecting edges, and the voice stimulation signal equivalent to the load.

2. Public telegraph network

Public telegraph network is a network for providing public telegraph service including text telegraphing and delivery to a predetermined address. The addresser sends the telegram to the respective addressing office; the latter sends the text message to the recipient. Local post office transmits information via transmission links through telegraph switching equipment, telegram collecting and diverting machine, and process control automatic switching system, etc. In this network, the forwarding office and the office of destination are the end nodes, the telegraph switching equipment, the telegram collecting and diverting machine and the process control automatic switching system are the switching nodes, the transmission links are the connecting edges, and the telegram is the load.

3. Telex network

Telex network refers to a communication network with which a subscriber sends a telegram to a recipient by connecting the communication circuit with a telegraphing machine. It uses a telex mounted in the office or home of the subscriber and exchanges telegraphs by temporarily communicating with recipients at home or abroad. It is different from the public telegraph network in the aspect that the nodes in the telex network are teletypewriter sets while the nodes of a public telegraph network are the forwarding office and the office of destination.

4. Data communication network

Data communication network is a communication network for providing data communication service, including the following three forms of data transmission service: circuit exchange, packet switching and rental circuit. It is a communication network that sends a 0, 1 digital stream through the transmission line and the exchange equipment to a receiving end via digital input and output devices such as a modem. When a voice message is converted into a 0, 1 digital stream by a modulation device, the voice message can be transmitted by the data communication network. The 0, 1 digital stream is demodulated to voice message at the receiving node. In this network, the modem is equivalent to an end node, the transmission line equivalent to the connecting edges, the exchange equipment equivalent to the switching node, and the 0, 1 digital stream equivalent to the load.

5. Fax communication network

Fax communication network can be deemed as a data communication network with a fax machine as the terminal device. The fax machine is equivalent to the end nodes. The rest components of the fax communication network are the same with the data communication network.

6. Image communication network

Image communication network is a data communication network with video equipment (such as a videophone) as a terminal device, wherein the video device is equivalent to the end node and the rest components are the same with the data communication network.

7. Videotext communication network

Videotext communication network emerged in the 20th century. It is an interactive telecom service that provides videotext information services to society by means of information stored in databases. The graphic information provided is called "visual data". Videotext communication network, also known as interactive videotext, is a communication method using two-way images and text retrieval, which achieves interactive sessions between the user terminal and the database through data communication network. It is convenient for the user to access various information required. In the videotext communication networks, the user terminals, databases and editing terminals are equivalent to the end nodes while the rest components are the same with the data communication network.

8. Mobile communication network

Mobile communication network is a way of communication between a mobile subscriber and a fixed subscriber or another mobile subscriber. According to the coverage and the operation manner of the system, the current mobile communication network, can be divided into: two-way interactive cellular public mobile communication, one-way or two-way interactive dedicated mobile communication, one-way radio paging, home cordless telephone and wireless local loop, etc.

Mobile communication network usually uses cellular topology, so as to improve the spectrum utilization, reduce mutual interference, and increase system capacity. Generally, a cellular system is used, which covers hexagonal structures having a radius of 10 km, together with a composite structure of micro cells and Pico cells. The radius of the current operating cell reaches thousands of meters while the radius of the micro cell ranges from meters to hundreds of meters. In the mobile communication network, the mobile terminal (cell phone) is equivalent to the end node, the cellular base station and the switching equipment equivalent to the switching nodes, the cell phone signal equivalent to the load, and the wireless carrier equivalent to the connecting edges.

1.2.2 Broadcast and Television Networks

Broadcast and television networks use electromagnetism to emit signals, and use radio wave as a carrier for transmitting programs. The radio wave can be received by a conventional electronic receiver (such as a radio, a television set, or a set-top box) within the signal coverage of the electromagnetic transmitter. Broadcast and television network is a point-to-multipoint network. Conventional broadcast and television network is point-to-multipoint unilateral network while modern cable network becomes point-to-multipoint bilateral network. The radio, the television set, the set-top box and the broadcast platform of the television program are the end nodes, with the broadcast platform of the television program being a "super end node", while the radio, the television set and the set-top box being common end nodes. The information exchange relationship is between the super end node and the common end node. Theoretically, there is no interactive channel between common end nodes. In addition, the radio wave and the optical fiber are equivalent to the connecting edges; the deconcentrator and the emission tower are equivalent to the switching node; and the program signal is equivalent to the load.

1.2.3 The Internet

The Internet is a huge network formed by interrelating networks. Usually, Internet refers to computer networks based on TCP/IP protocols. These networks are connected by a group of universal protocols (TCP/IP) and form a logically single huge international network. Data transmission of the Internet is complete by packets. Generally, underlying transport is performed by means of data communication network, and the upper layer performs addressing by means of routers. The subscriber terminal in the Internet is the end node; the routers of each level are the switching nodes; the transmission lines are the connecting edges; and the packets and the data transmitted are the load.

1.2.4 Mobile Internet

Mobile Internet is in its nature Internet with intelligent mobile terminal as the access. The smart phone, tablet computer, e-book, personal digital assistant (PDA) and the like on the Internet are the end nodes. The rest components are the same with the mobile communication network, only the digital telex being the load.

1.2.5 Social Networks

In terms of information networks, social networks refer to online social network services, or social network services. Online social network originates from social networking, which is a social structure consisting of the connecting relations among social individual groups and individuals on the information network. Online social network can be divided into 4 categories: ① instant messaging application, i.e., a platform that provides online real-time communication service, such as QQ, Wechat, MiTalk, Whatsapp and the like; ② online social application, which is a platform that provides online social relation service, such as Facebook, Google+, Renren.com, and so on; ③ micro blog application, which is a platform providing two-way short message releasing service, such as Twitter, Sina Microblog, Tecent Microblog, and so on; ④ other applications such as shared space, which is the rest Web 2.0 applications capable of intercommunication without close relations, such as forums, blogs, video sharing, social bookmarking, online shopping, and many others,[4] wherein, the user accounts are the end nodes, the friend relation in the instant messaging applications and online social applications are the connecting edges; the following relationship, forwarding and responding relationships in micro blog applications are the connecting edges; groups in the instant messaging applications and online social applications are the switching nodes; the platform of the micro blog applications and the shared space applications are the switching nodes; information (e.g., blogs) released by the subscribers are the load.

---

[4]Huijboom N, Broek TVD, Frissen V et al (2009) Public services 2.0: key areas in the public-sector impact of social computing, Vol 6. Joint Research Centre, Institute for Prospective Technological Studies.

1.2.6 Internet of Things

Internet of Things (IoT) is the Internet interconnecting things. The concept has two levels of meanings: first, the core and the foundation of IoT is still the Internet; i.e., IoT is a network extending and expanding from the Internet; second, the subscriber terminal is expanded and extends among various objects to support information exchange and communication among objects, forming the interconnection between things. Thus, the Internet of Things is a network which interconnecting things via the Internet.

Internet of Things in its nature is a network consisting of things or objects having identifications and virtual characteristics that are interconnected. It connects various things to the Internet via information sensor devices according to agreed protocols, thereby realizing intelligent identifying, locating, tracking, monitoring and managing functions through information exchange and communication. The sensor devices and the things having identifications are the end nodes; the rest three factors use signal transmission means, and thus are the same with the telecommunication network, the Internet and the mobile Internet.

1.2.7 Sensor Networks

Sensor networks can be regarded as a distributed information system composed of large-scale randomly distributed sensor nodes (terminals), base stations and information monitoring center. According to the change of demand and sensing objects, it can sense and collect information of various objects in the network distribution area in a dynamic self-organizing manner. It is used to serve the purpose of decision-making and monitoring. The network structure of the sensor networks can be divided into a sensing domain, a network domain and an application domain. The sensing domain is mainly used to realize the collection and processing of the information in the sensor networks, the technologies used currently including radio frequency identification (RFID), ZigBee and Bluetooth, and so on. The network domain is mainly used for carrying and transmission of the information in the sensor networks. The application domain is mainly used to realize the representation and application of information. The sensor nodes are the end nodes. The radio frequency signal, the ZigBee signal and the Bluetooth signal are the connecting edges. The forwarding nodes in a self-organizing network and the network domain are the switching nodes. The application signal is the load.

1.2.8 Industrial Control Networks

Industrial control networks refer to the network consisting of measurement and control instruments and controllers that have digital communication capabilities and are scattered in the production site in a large number. For example, the industrial control network may be configured by connecting field devices such as controller, sensor, actuator, etc. via a fieldbus; or, the Ethernet may be applied in the field of industrial control to form the levels of field equipment, control and management. The field devices such as controller, sensor and actuator are the end nodes. The bus and the Ethernet are the switching nodes. The wire for accessing the bus or the Ethernet is the connecting edge. The control signal and the measurement signal are the loads.

1.2.9 Quantum Communication Networks

Quantum communication network is a communication network in which quantum information including single quantum bits and multi-particle entanglement bits are transmitted between nodes through quantum channels. Quantum communication is performed based on quantum state transmission. The existing quantum communication usually uses photons as the quantum state carrier, of which the pattern of manifestation is photon state transmission, and thus, uses optical fiber network to perform the quantum communication. The communication is realized by first producing quantum bits (photons) with quantum optical devices, then realizing long-distance transmission by using quantum repeater for entanglement swapping and entanglement purification, and at last using a single photon detector to detect the photons so as to extract information by analysis.

The photon generating device, the quantum repeater and the single photon detector are the end nodes. The optical wave and the optical fiber are equivalent to the connection edges. Key information distributed in the key of quantum communication and the quantum state in the quantum state invisible transmission is the load.

Free-space quantum communication can be distributed using low-orbit satellites and free-space entangled photons, which is realized by a quantum signal being emitted from the ground to pass through the atmosphere, a satellite receiving the quantum signal and forwarding the signal to another specific satellite as needed, and at last the quantum signal travelling through the atmosphere from the specific satellite to arrive at a predetermined receiving location somewhere on the earth. In this case, the satellite is equivalent to the switching node.

However, in some circumstances, quantum communication does not need an exchange center. It can be performed by direct point-to-point transmission. In such cases, lacking switching nodes, the network is an information network without a center.

1.3 The Concept of Space

Space in mathematics refers to a multi-dimensional collection having a special nature and some additional structures. "Dimension" shows a direction in space. A space determined by multiple directions is called a multi-dimensional space.

For example, a linear mode determined by one direction is a one-dimensional space; a plane mode established by the two directions is a two-dimensional space; and a stereo mode composed of three directions is called a three-dimensional space; a flowing space determined the three-dimensional direction and the time direction is a four-dimensional space, also known as the space-time.

Modern physics usually holds the idea that the space we are facing is relative. The space constitutes the abstract concept of things and is also the carrier of the abstract concept. Ancient Greek atomists define the space as "void (vacant space)", which was considered the opposite of material completeness. Material is dynamic while space is static. In the universe, the space we are facing is not pure vacuum, and is filled with material. This is the traditional sense of relative space. Relative space changes along with the movement of material. In fact, it is material, not space that moves. Newton argues that absolute space is essentially not associated with anything in the outside world and is always invariant and static. He believes that relative space is a movable part or a measurement of absolute space.

Space in philosophy usually refers to four-dimensional space-time having the property of material existence and movement. First, space is an integral part of a specific thing. Any specific thing that can be seen by eye and can be touched by hand is located at a certain spatial location. Since abstract things exist in specific things, space is also an expression of the existence of abstract things. Second, space is the form of existence and the manifestation of movement. Movement has two kinds of manifestation: behavior and existence. Behavior is a relatively obvious movement while existence is a relatively static movement. Specific things can merely exist in a certain space. Even a drop of water, a grain of sand, an atom, or a ray of light exists in a certain space and has a certain spatial location as the manifestation. All specific behavior, phenomena, and things happen, develop and come to an end in a specific space, with a specific spatial requirement as the manifestation. Finally, space is the unity of opposites composed by absolute abstract things and relatively abstract things and meta-ontology and meta-entity. Everything can be divided into two sides. Therefore, space can be divided into specific space and general space. Specific space is an object of cognition with a specific limit of amount, a space body having determined three-dimensional requirements for the length, width and height. It is the manifestation of general space. General space is an object of cognition without a specific limit of amount, a space body without determined three-dimensional requirements for the length, width and height. It is the nature and content of specific space.

Space in philosophy solves the problem of the universality and ontology of space. Yet it cannot be applied in society, life and practice. Space is considered a production having social and historical significance and cannot be simplified as geometry. It must be further given its political, economic, cultural and social significance. In social theory, the understanding of what people understand about space goes beyond the discussion of its ontology. People pay more attention to the social practice of space and give more importance to the subjective behavior of people in space and space production and regeneration.

Henri Lefebvre, a critical Marxist philosopher of France, has integrated the material and social dimensions of space. He takes human practice as the domain of material space. People's perception, creation and use of material space are deeply rooted in daily practices. The core of Henri Lefebvre's idea of space lies in production in space.[5] He proposed the three-dimensional analytical framework of space, namely "spatial practice", "spatial manifestation" and "manifestation space", which is a spatial practice on the perceived level, involving human action to produce, use, control and reconstruct this space, the production and reproduction of space in social spatial practice, and spatial position and configuration combination.

Regarding the discussion on theories of spatial social practice, David Havey, a British geographer, points out that[6] the question "what is the space" should be replaced by "how different human practices create and use different spatial concepts". Space is contained in the object. The object only exists when it contains and displays in itself the relationship with other objects.

To sum up, the understanding of space should be based on the reality of human behavior and practice. The significance of space should be searched from the interaction of a certain space and human. Specific things (referred to as subject) and the movements of the subject are two core attributes of the connotation of space.

1.4 Introduction of the Concept of Cyberspace

The word "cyber" came from Norbert Wiener's work. Wiener defined cybernetics in his Cybernetics or Control and Communication in the Animal and the Machine in 1948.[7] His basic idea is that people can dock with a machine, and that the resulting system can provide an alternative environment for the interaction, which lays a foundation for the formation of the concept of cyberspace.

People considered the word "cyber" as a prefix later. For example, Finland's Cyber Security Strategy Government Resolution[8] issued by Finland in January 2013 described cyber as follows: "The word 'cyber' is almost invariably the prefix for a term or the modifier of a compound word, rather than a stand-alone word. Its inference usually relates to electronic information (data) processing, information technology, electronic communications (data transfer) or information and computer systems.

[5]Levebvre H. Space: social product and use value. http://wenku.baidu.com/link?url=ZA2cgpMcuNbGkctPnRU00VEqj4EvDHsE0AV124Jn4CkMHGReLhlWIL_v-RsRW7erLqRhev0qUs4iWpHEh9-GrTFqCpRfam1O4iGoGfLudKK [2016-11-30].

[6]David H. Time-space compression and the postmodern condition. http://fields.eca.ac.uk/disruptivetechnologies/wp-content/uploads/2011/10/Harvey-David-Time-space-compression-and-the-postmodern-condition.pdf [2016-11-30].

[7]Wiener N (1948) Cybernetics or control and communication in the animal and the machine, Vol 25. MIT press. http://www.allen-riley.com/utopia/cybernetics.pdf [2016-9-24].

[8]Finland's Cyber Security Strategy Government Resolution 24 Jan 2013. https://ccdcoe.org/cyber-definitions.html [2016-9-10].

Only the complete term of the compound words (modifier + head) can be considered to possess actual meaning. The word cyber is generally believed to originate from the Ancient Greek verb 'κυβερεω (kybereo)' 'to steer, to guide, to control'."

The word cyberspace was initiated by a science fiction author William Gibson,[9] who coined this word in his novel Burning Chrome[10] in 1981, and this word was then emerged. Later, Gibson kept using the word cyberspace in his 1984 novel Neuromancer,[11] and this word swept the world as the novel Neuromancer won three major science fiction awards. Gibson admitted that he was inspired from Wiener's "cybernetics" when coining cyberspace. He described cyberspace in his book as "a consensual hallucination experienced daily by billions of legitimate operators, in every nation, by children being taught mathematical concepts …" This definition focuses on people's perception of a new environment, and when it reveals the potential to develop a real-world cyberspace experience, it makes people feel the characteristics of cyberspace.

Cyberspace, a concept coined in 1980s, was viewed initially as a space fundamentally separated from the physical world. Some theorists went so far as to assert that cyberspace transcends geographic and national boundaries, and therefore strains traditional notions of sovereignty and security. Similarly, Abraham M. Denmark proposed the following contents in Contested Commons: the Future of American Power in a Multi-polar World[12]: today there are four major global commons: maritime, air, space and cyberspace; each commons is fundamentally different from the others; the global commons share four broad characteristics: (1) they are not owned or controlled by any single entity; (2) their utility as a whole is greater than if broken down into smaller parts; (3) states and non-state actors with the requisite technological capabilities are able to access and use them for economic, political, scientific and cultural purposes; and (4) states and non-state actors with the requisite technological capabilities are able to use them as a medium for military movement and as a theatre for military conflict; cyberspace is now an integral part of modern life; people around the world interact, cooperate and compete through a series of networked linkages that span the world.

The ability to provide essential services by private and public institutions can be enhanced through cyberspace formed by a combination of simple web-based communications and more complex infrastructure networks. Modern militaries also employ cyberspace facilities as a key enabler of military operations, using

[9]Discussion on origin and translation of cyberspace. http://www.360doc.com/content/16/0115/19/21966267_528220372.shtml [2016-12-31].

[10]William G. BURNING CHROME. http://dinhe.net/~aredridel/.notmine/www.digipromo.com/vruz/ebooks/scifi/William%20Gibson-Burning%20Chrome.rtf [2016-11-30].

[11]William G (1984) Neuromancer, Vol 4. Phantasia Press Edition, Bloomfield, MI. http://www.taodocs.com/p-4046079.html [2016-12-31].

[12]Denmark A, Mulvenon J (2010) Contested commons. Contested commons: the future of american power in a multi-polar world, pp 3–48. https://s3.amazonaws.com/files.cnas.org/documents/CNAS-Contested-Commons_1.pdf [2016-12-31].

commercial and private networks for everything from command and control to logistics support.

However, Greg Rattray mentioned in American Security in the Cyber Commons that cyberspace is fundamentally a physical environment, created by connecting physical systems and networks, and managed by rules set in software and communications protocols—all of which are located in the sovereign boundaries of nation-states, and that while much of the information in cyberspace is considered public, the physical elements of the cyberspace—the desktops, the laptops, the servers, the Internet-enabled refrigerators, the routers, the telephones, the mobile phones, the LAN cables, the fiber optic cables—have clear owners.[13] Wolff Heintschel von Heinegg, who is from Institute for European Law of Goethe University Frankfurt, pointed out the following contents in Territorial Sovereignty and Neutrality in Cyberspace[14]: cyberspace requires a physical architecture to exist; the equipment connected to a proprietary transmission network is usually located within the territory of a State; it is owned by the government or by corporations; the integration of physical components of cyber infrastructure located within a State's territory into the "global domain" of cyberspace cannot be interpreted as a waiver of the exercise of territorial sovereignty; States have continuously emphasized their right in cyberspace, including those to exercise control over the cyber infrastructure located in areas in its sovereign territory, to assert their jurisdiction over cyber activities on their territory and to protect their cyber infrastructure against trans-border interference by other States or by individuals; in fact, States have exercised, and will continue to exercise, their criminal jurisdiction over cybercrimes and they continue to regulate activities in cyberspace.

Many scholars have tried to explain the essential meaning of cyberspace since 1984, but most of their definitions tend to describe how to use cyberspace. In 1999, Lance Strate proposed a three-level taxonomy to describe cyberspace.[15] He divided cyberspace into three levels: a "zero level" referring to ontology and cyberspace-time; a "first level" referring to physical, conceptual and perceptual cyberspace; and a "second level" referring to synthesis of network media space, which enriches the connotation and extension of cyberspace.

In Official Definition of the United States Department of Defense Military Term,[16] cyberspace is defined as "The notional environment in which digitized information is communicated over computer networks". In 2006, United States Department of Defense and Joint Chiefs of Staff first put forward a general

[13]Rattray G, Evans C, Healey J. Chapter V: American security in the cyber commons. https://s3.amazonaws.com/files.cnas.org/documents/CNAS-Contested-Commons_1.pdf [2016-12-31].

[14]Wolff HVH (2013) Territorial sovereignty and neutrality in cyberspace. Intl L Stud Ser US Naval War 89:i. https://www.usnwc.edu/getattachment/ff9537ce-94d6-49a8-a9ef-51e335126c1e/von-Heinegg.aspx [2016-9-24].

[15]Strate L (1999) The varieties of cyberspace: problems in definition and delimitation. Western J Commun 63(3):382–412.

[16]U.S. DoD Terminology: cyberspace. http://www.militaryfactory.com/dictionary/military-terms-defined.asp?term_id=1464 [2016-9-5].

definition of cyberspace for operations, wherein National Military Strategy for Cyberspace Operations[17] defined cyberspace as "a domain characterized by the use of electronics and the electromagnetic spectrum to store, modify, and exchange data via networked systems and associated physical infrastructures …"; Technogeopolitics of Militarization and Security in Cyberspace[18] defined cyberspace as "… a scope of using electronics and the electromagnetic spectrum to store, modify and exchange information via networked information systems and physical infrastructure"; thereafter, Gordon England, assistant minister from the Department of Defense, redefined cyberspace[19] as "a global domain within the information environment, consisting of the interdependent network of information technology infrastructures, including the Internet, telecommunications networks, computer systems, and embedded processors and controllers". These definitions involve the hardware technology component. It is worth noting, however, that these definitions lack human component, but human is an important element in the definitions of Norbert Wiener and William Gibson.

The cyberspace in Cyber space: Definition and Implications[20] defined by Rain Ottis, ambassador from NATO Cooperative Cyber Defense Center of Excellence, includes a human factor: "Cyberspace is a time-dependent set of interconnected information systems and the human users that interact with these systems." Ottis stressed that "Please note that we also include human users in the definition. Cyberspace is a man-made space and is created by people to serve for human use." In International Telecommunication Union ITU-T-REC-X.1205-200804-I Standard[21] (Series X: Data Networks, Open System Communications and Security. Telecommunication security. Overview of cyber security), cyberspace is represented by cyber environment, and it is defined as the one "including users, networks, devices, all software, processes, information in storage or transit, applications, services, and systems that can be connected directly or indirectly to networks". The International Organization for Standardization ISO/IEC27032:2012 Standard[22] (Information technology-Security techniques-Guidelines for cyber security) defines cyberspace with a slightly different expression by emphasizing human interaction, that is, "the cyberspace is a complex environment resulting from

[17]Pace P (2009) National military strategy for cyberspace operations. Unclassified memo, December 2009. http://nsarchive.gwu.edu/NSAEBB/NSAEBB424/docs/Cyber-023.pdf [2016-9-24].

[18]Yannakogeorgos P (2009) Technogeopolitics of militarization and security in cyberspace. https://rucore.libraries.rutgers.edu/rutgers-lib/26118/PDF/1/ [2016-9-24].

[19]26 Years After Gibson, Pentagon Defines 'Cyberspace'. https://www.wired.com/2008/05/pentagon-define/ [2016-9-7].

[20]Cyber space: Definition and Implications. https://ccdcoe.org/multimedia/cyberspace-definition-and-implications.html [2016-9-6].

[21]Series X: Data Networks, Open System Communications and Security. Telecommunication security. Overview of cybersecurity. http://www.itu.int/rec/T-REC-X.1205-200804-I [2016-12-31].

[22]International Organization for Standardization, ISO/IEC27032:2012, Information technology-Security techniques-Guidelines for cybersecurity. https://www.iso.org/obp/ui/#iso:std:iso-iec:27032:ed-1:v1:en [2016-9-19].

the interaction of people, software and services on the Internet, supported by technology devices and networks connected to the Internet without any physical form".

Hence, cyberspace boasts a definition comprising both technology component, human component (accessed to and used by human) and communication and control component, as if it were back to Norbert Wiener's cybernetic definition. Therefore, academic Wang Chengwei had strongly advocated translating "cyberspace" to "控域(Controlled Doman)" to face up to Norbert Wiener's contribution to this field.

Even if the definitions are omnifarious, most of them are consistent in one aspect, that is, the core of cyberspace is composed of worldwide interconnected hardware, software and data thereof. Furthermore, another importance is that people can dock with the cyberspace, and people and cyberspace are integrated when using the Internet.

1.5 Diversified Description Methods for Cyberspace

In fact, countries have explicitly defined "cyberspace" in their National Cyberspace (Security) Strategy in accordance with their strategic intention. In January 2014, the New America's Open Technology Institute submitted a report entitled Compilation of Existing Cybersecurity and Information Security Related Definitions,[23] which was compiled by Tim Maurer and Robert Morgus. In the report, they summarized the definitions of cyberspace from many countries.

The definitions offered by respective countries can be roughly classified into the following five cases that reflect their intentions in formulating strategies: the first case is to simply define cyberspace as an information and communication infrastructure, that is, concerning only about the technology level; the second case is to define cyberspace as an information and communication infrastructure and resident data, which also concerns only about the technology level; the third case is to define cyberspace as a collection of facilities, data and people, which concerns about people while concerning about the technology level; the fourth case is to define cyberspace as a collection of facilities, data and operations, which concerns about activities while concerning about the technology level; and the fifth case is to define cyberspace as a complete set of various factors of facilities, data, people and operations in such a cyberspace, that is, concerning about both levels of technology and society.

---

[23]Compilation of Existing Cybersecurity and Information Security Related Definitions. https://na-production.s3.amazonaws.com/documents/compilation-of-existing-cybersecurity-and-information-security-related-definitions.pdf [2016-9-10].

1.5.1 Simply Defining Cyberspace as Information and Communication Infrastructure

Countries that hold such an opinion focus their attention of cyberspace only on infrastructure itself, so their focus of protection is also infrastructure alone.

1. National Cyber Security Strategy of Afghanistan

In Afghanistan's *"National Cyber Security Strategy of Afghanistan"*,[24] the cyberspace is defined as below: "Cyber space: The environment, which consists of information systems that span across the world including the networks that interconnect these systems."

2. French Information Systems Defence and Security: France's Strategy

In France's *"Information Systems Defence and Security: France's Strategy"*,[25] the cyberspace is defined as below: "The communication space created by the worldwide interconnection of automated digital data processing equipment."

3. National Security Strategy of Japan

In Japan's *"National Security Strategy"*,[26] the cyberspace is defined as "a global domain comprised of information systems, telecommunications networks and others, provides a foundation for social, economic, military and other activities".

4. On the Approval of the Programme for the Development of Electronic Information Security (Cyber-Security) for 2011–2019 of Lithuania

In Lithuania's "On the Approval of the Programme for the Development of Electronic Information Security (Cyber-Security) for 2011–2019",[27] the cyberspace is defined as follows: "Cyberspace is a global space which has no national boundaries, hence, the rapid spread of threats across cyberspace."

[24]National Cyber Security Strategy of Afghanistan, 2014. http://nic.af/Content/files/National%20Cybersecurity%20Strategy%20of%20Afghanistan%20(November2014).pdf [2016-9-25].

[25]Information Systems Defence and Security: France's Strategy, 2011: 21. http://www.ssi.gouv.fr/uploads/IMG/pdf/2011-02-15_Information_system_defence_and_security_-_France_s_strategy.pdf [2016-9-24].

[26]Japan, National Security Strategy, 2013: 9. http://japan.kantei.go.jp/96_abe/documents/2013/__icsFiles/afieldfile/2013/12/17/NSS.pdf [2016-9-24].

[27]Government of the Republic of Lithuania Resolution No. 796 of 29 June 2011 on the approval of the programme for the development of electronic information security (cyber-security) for 2011-2019, 2011: 3. https://www.itu.int/en/ITU-D/Cybersecurity/Documents/National_Strategies_Repository/Lithuania_2011_EIS(KS)PP_796_2011-06-29_EN_PATAIS.pdf [2016-9-24].

5. New Zealand's Cyber Security Strategy

In "New Zealand's Cyber Security Strategy",[28] the cyberspace is defined as "the global network of interdependent information technology infrastructures, telecommunications networks and computer processing systems in which online communication takes place".

6. Developing the National Information Security Strategy for the Kingdom of Saudi Arabia, NISS, DRAFT 7

In Saudi Arabia's "Developing National Information Security Strategy for the Kingdom of Saudi Arabia, NISS, DRAFT 7",[29] the cyberspace is defined as "a global domain within the information environment consisting of the interdependent networks of information systems infrastructures including the internet, telecommunications networks, computer systems, embedded processors and controllers".

7. National Strategy for the Protection of Switzerland Against Cyber Risks

In Switzerland's "National Strategy for the Protection of Switzerland Against Cyber Risks",[30] the cyberspace is defined as follows: "The state, the private sector and society make use of information and communication infrastructure and access to cyberspace (Internet, mobile networks and applications, e-business, e-government, computer based control programmes)."

8. National Cyber Security Strategy and 2013–2014 Action Plan of Turkey

In Turkey's "National Cyber Security Strategy and 2013–2014 Action Plan",[31] the cyberspace is defined as "the environment which consists of information systems that span across the world including the networks that interconnect these systems".

9. The National Strategy to Secure Cyberspace of the United States

In America's "National Strategy to Secure Cyberspace",[32] the cyberspace is defined as follows: "Cyberspace is composed of hundreds of thousands of interconnected computers, servers, routers, switches, and fiber optic cables that allow our critical infrastructures to work."

---

[28]New Zealand's Cyber Security Strategy, 2011: 12. http://www.dpmc.govt.nz/sites/all/files/publications/nz-cyber-security-strategy-june-2011_0.pdf [2016-9-24].

[29]Developing National Information Security Strategy for the Kingdom of Saudi Arabia, NISS, DRAFT 7: A-2. http://www.itu.int/en/ITU-D/Cybersecurity/Documents/National_Strategies_Repository/SaudiArabia_NISS_Draft_7_EN.pdf [2016-12-31].

[30]National strategy for the protection of Switzerland against cyber risks, 2012: 5. https://www.enisa.europa.eu/topics/national-cyber-security-strategies/ncss-map/National_strategy_for_the_protection_of_Switzerland_against_cyber_risksEN.pdf [2016-9-24].

[31]Turkey, National Cyber Security Strategy and 2013–2014 Action Plan, 2013: 8. https://www.enisa.europa.eu/topics/national-cyber-security-strategies/ncss-map/national-cybersecurity-strategy-and-2013-2014-action-plan/at_download/file [2016-9-24].

[32]White House, and United States of America. The National Strategy to Secure Cyberspace. https://www.us-cert.gov/sites/default/files/publications/cyberspace_strategy.pdf [2016-9-17].

10. National Initiative for Cybersecurity Careers and Studies of the United States

In the Explore Terms: A Glossary of Common Cyber Security Terminology of "National Initiative for Cybersecurity Careers and Studies"[33] of the United States, the cyberspace is defined as "The interdependent network of information technology infrastructures, that includes the Internet, telecommunications network, computer systems, and embedded processors and controllers."

11. Cyberspace Policy Review: Assuring a Trusted and Resilient Information and Communications Infrastructure of the United States

In America's "Cyberspace Policy Review: Assuring a Trusted and Resilient Information and Communications Infrastructure",[34] the cyberspace is defined as "The globally-interconnected digital information and communications infrastructure known as 'cyberspace' underpins almost every facet of modern society and provides critical support for the U.S. economy, civil infrastructure, public safety, and national security."

1.5.2 *Defining Cyberspace as an Information and Communication Infrastructure and Resident Data*

Countries that hold such an opinion focus their attention of cyberspace not only on infrastructure, but also on data that cyberspace carries, so their focus of protection includes network infrastructure and resident data.

1. Cyber Security Strategy of Belgium

In Belgium's "Cyber Security Strategy",[35] the cyberspace is defined as follows: "Cyberspace is the global environment for the interconnection of information and communication systems. Cyberspace is wider than the computer world and also contains computer networks, computer systems, digital media and digital data, whether physical or virtual."

---

[33]National Initiative for Cybersecurity Careers and Studies, Explore Terms: A Glossary of Common Cybersecurity Terminology. https://definedterm.com/a/download/document/11128 [2016-9-24].

[34]Cyberspace Policy Review: Assuring a Trusted and Resilient Information and Communications Infrastructure, 2009: III. https://www.smartgrid.gov/files/Cyberspace_Policy_Review_Assuring_Trusted_Resilient_Informat_200908.pdf [2016-9-24].

[35]Belgium, Cyber Security Strategy, 2012: 12. https://www.enisa.europa.eu/topics/national-cyber-security-strategies/ncss-map/belgian-cyber-security-strategy/at_download/file [2016-9-24].

2. Canada's Cyber Security Strategy, for a Stronger and More Prosperous Canada

In "Canada's Cyber Security Strategy, for a Stronger and More Prosperous Canada",[36] the cyberspace is defined as follows: "Cyberspace is the electronic world created by interconnected networks of information technology and the information on those networks. It is a global commons where more than 1.7 billion people are linked together to exchange ideas, services and friendship."

3. Cyber Security Strategy for Germany

In Germany's "Cyber Security Strategy for Germany",[37] the cyberspace is defined as follows: "Cyberspace is the virtual space of all IT systems linked at data level on a global scale. The basis for cyberspace is the Internet as a universal and publicly accessible connection and transport network which can be complemented and further expanded by any number of additional data networks. IT systems in an isolated virtual space are not part of cyberspace."

4. National Cyber Security Strategy of Hungary

In "National Cyber Security Strategy of Hungary",[38] the cyberspace is defined as follows: "Cyberspace means the combined phenomenon of globally interconnected, decentralised and ever-growing electronic information systems as well as the societal and economic processes appearing in and through these systems in the form of data and information."

5. 2013 National Strategic Framework for Cyberspace Security of Italy

In Italy's "2013 National Strategic Framework for Cyberspace Security",[39] the cyberspace is defined as follows: "Cyberspace is a man-made domain essentially composed of ICT nodes and networks, hosting and processing an ever-increasing wealth of data of strategic importance for States, firms, and citizens alike, and for all political, social and economic decision-makers."

---

[36]Canada's Cyber Security Strategy, For a Stronger and More Prosperous Canada, 2010: 2. http://www.publicsafety.gc.ca/cnt/rsrcs/pblctns/cbr-scrt-strtgy/index-eng.aspx [2016-9-24].

[37]Cyber Security Strategy for Germany, 2011: 9. http://www.cio.bund.de/SharedDocs/Publikationen/DE/Strategische-Themen/css_engl_download.pdf?__blob=publicationFile [2016-9-24].

[38]Annex 1 to Government Decision No. 1139/2013 National Cyber Security Strategy of Hungary, 2013: 3. https://www.enisa.europa.eu/topics/national-cyber-security-strategies/ncss-map/HU_NCSS.pdf [2016-9-24].

[39]Annex 1 to Government Decision No. 1139/2013 National Cyber Security Strategy of Hungary, 2013: 3. https://www.enisa.europa.eu/topics/national-cyber-security-strategies/ncss-map/HU_NCSS.pdf [2016-9-24].

6. The Defence Cyber Strategy of the Netherlands

In the Netherlands' "Defence Cyber Strategy of the Netherlands",[40] the cyberspace is defined as follows: "For the purposes of this strategy, 'cyberspace' is understood to cover all entities that are or may potentially be connected digitally. The domain includes permanent connections as well as temporary or local connections, and in all cases relates in some way to the data (source code, information, etc.) present in this domain."

7. Department of Defense Dictionary of Military and Associated Terms of the United States

In America's "Department of Defense Dictionary of Military and Associated Terms",[41] the cyberspace is defined as follows: "Cyberspace: the global domain within the information environment consisting of the interdependent networks of information technology infrastructures and resident data, including the Internet, telecommunications networks, computer systems, and embedded processors and controllers."

1.5.3 Defining Cyberspace as a Collection of Facilities, Data and People

Countries that hold such an opinion focus their attention not only on cyberspace infrastructures and resident data, but also on users in the cyberspace, so their objects of protection include infrastructures, resident data and users in the cyberspace.

1. Cybersecurity Strategy: Towards a World-leading, Resilient and Vigorous Cyberspace of Japan

In Japan's "Cybersecurity Strategy: Towards a World-leading, Resilient and Vigorous Cyberspace",[42] the cyberspace is defined as "global virtual spaces such as the internet, composed of information systems, information communications networks and similar systems and which circulate large quantities of a large variety of information, have rapidly expanded and begun permeating real-space".

[40]Netherlands, The Defence Cyber Strategy, 2012: 4. https://ccdcoe.org/strategies/Defence_Cyber_Strategy_NDL.pdf [2016-9-24].

[41]Joint Publication 3-12(R): Cyberspace Operation. http://www.dtic.mil/doctrine/new_pubs/jp3_12R.pdf [2016-9-5].

[42]Cybersecurity Strategy: Towards a world-leading, resilient and vigorous cyberspace, 2013: 5. http://www.nisc.go.jp/active/kihon/pdf/cybersecuritystrategy-en.pdf [2016-9-24].

2. Resolution No. 3611: Advancing National Cyberspace Capabilities of Israel

In Israel's "Resolution No. 3611: Advancing National Cyberspace Capabilities",[43] the cyberspace is defined as "the physical and non-physical domain that is created or composed of part or all of the following components: mechanized and computerized systems, computer and communications networks, programs, computerized information, content conveyed by computer, traffic and supervisory data and those who use such data".

3. Qatar National Cyber Security Strategy

In "Qatar National Cyber Security Strategy",[44] the cyberspace is defined as "a virtual or electronic environment that results from the interdependent network of information and communications technology (e.g., the Internet, telecommunications networks, computer systems, and embedded processors and controllers) that links people with services and information".

4. Notice of Intention to Make South African National Cybersecurity Policy

In South African's "Notice of Intention to Make South African National Cybersecurity Policy",[45] the cyberspace is defined as follows: "Cyberspace means a physical and non-physical terrain created by and/or composed of some or all of the following: computers, computer systems, networks, and their computer programs, computer data, content data, traffic data, and users."

5. National Cyber Security Strategy of Spain

In Spain's "National Cyber Security Strategy",[46] the cyberspace is defined as "Cyberspace, the name given to the global and dynamic domain composed of the infrastructures of information technology-including the Internet-networks and information and telecommunications systems, has blurred borders, involving their users in an unprecedented globalisation that provides new opportunities but also entails new challenges, risks and threats."

[43]Israel, Resolution No. 3611: Advancing National Cyberspace Capabilities, 2011: 1. http://www.itu.int/en/ITU-D/Cybersecurity/Documents/National_Strategies_Repository/Israel_2011_Advancing%20National%20Cyberspace%20Capabilities.pdf [2016-9-24].

[44]Qatar National Cyber Security Strategy, 2014: 23. https://www.itu.int/en/ITU-D/Cybersecurity/Documents/National_Strategies_Repository/Qatar_2014_national_cyber_security_strategy.pdf [2016-9-25].

[45]Department of Communications, Notice of Intention to Make South African National Cybersecurity Policy, 2010: 12. http://www.gov.za/sites/www.gov.za/files/32963_118_0.pdf [2016-9-24].

[46]Spain, National Cyber Security Strategy, 2013: 9. https://www.enisa.europa.eu/topics/national-cyber-security-strategies/ncss-map/NCSS_ESen.pdf [2016-9-24].

1.5.4 Defining Cyberspace as a Collection of Facilities, Data and Operations

Countries that hold such an opinion focus their attention not only on cyberspace infrastructures and resident data, but also on operations of data, so their objects of protection include infrastructures, resident data and corresponding operations in the cyberspace.

1. Draft Act on Cyber Security and Change of Related Acts of Czech Republic

In Czech Republic's "Draft Act on Cyber Security and Change of Related Acts",[47] the cyberspace is defined as follows: "Cyber space means digital environment, enabling to create, process, and exchange information, created by information systems and services and electronic communication networks."

2. Finland's Cyber Security Strategy

In "Finland's Cyber Security Strategy",[48] the cyberspace is defined as follows: "Cyber domain (cyber environment) means an electronic information (data) processing domain comprising of one or several information technology infrastructures. Note 1: Representative to the environment is the utilisation of electronics and the electromagnetic spectrum for the purpose of storing, processing and transferring data and information via telecommunications networks. Note 2: Information (data) processing means collecting, saving, organizing, using, transferring, disclosing, storing, modifying, combining, protecting, removing, destroying and other similar actions on information (data)."

3. Government of Kenya Cybersecurity Strategy

In Kenya's "Government of Kenya Cybersecurity Strategy",[49] the cyberspace is defined as follows: "Cyberspace is more than just the Internet and information and communications technology (ICT). It is a domain similar to the domains of land, air, sea, and space, but with its own distinct characteristics and challenges. The cyber domain is characterized by the digital storage, modification, and exchange of data via networked systems and supported by critical information infrastructures. It has national and international dimensions that include industry, commerce, intellectual property, security, technology, culture, policy, and diplomacy. As such, cyberspace plays a critical role in the global economy."

---

[47]Czech Republic, Draft Act on Cyber Security and Change of Related Acts (Act on Cyber Security), 2014: 2. https://www.govcert.cz/download/legislativa/container-nodeid-1168/draft-actcybersecurity-130415.pdf [2016-12-31].

[48]Finland's Cyber Security Strategy. http://www.yhteiskunnanturvallisuus.fi/en/materials/doc_download/40-finlandas-cyber-security-strategy [2016-9-25].

[49]Government of Kenya Cybersecurity Strategy, 2014: 2. http://www.icta.go.ke/wp-content/uploads/2014/03/GOK-national-cybersecurity-strategy.pdf [2016-9-25].

4. Tallinn Manual on the International Law Applicable to Cyber Warfare of NATO

In NATO's "Tallinn Manual on the International Law Applicable to Cyber Warfare",[50] the cyberspace is defined as "the environment formed by physical and non-physical components, characterized using computers and electro-magnetic spectrum, to store, modify, and exchange data using computer networks".

5. Cyber Security Strategy of the United Kingdom: Safety, Security and Resilience in Cyber Space

In UK's "Cyber Security Strategy of the United Kingdom: Safety, Security and Resilience in Cyber Space",[51] the cyberspace is defined as follows: "Cyber space encompasses all forms of networked, digital activities; this includes the content of and actions conducted through digital networks."

6. The UK Cyber Security Strategy: Protecting and Promoting the UK in a Digital World

In 'The UK Cyber Security Strategy: Protecting and Promoting the UK in a Digital World",[52] the cyberspace is defined as follows: "Cyberspace is an interactive domain made up of digital networks that is used to store, modify and communicate information. It includes the internet, but also the other information systems that support our businesses, infrastructure and services."

1.5.5 Defining Cyberspace as a Complete Set of Facilities, Data, People and Operations

Countries that hold such an opinion clearly provide facilities, data, people and their operations (activities) to fully depict the essence of cyberspace. Therefore, these countries focus more on activities occurring in the cyberspace, and they will focus on protection and management of activities in the cyberspace in addition to the protection of infrastructures, resident data and users in the cyberspace.

---

[50]The NATO Cooperative Cyber Defence Centre of Excellence, Tallinn Manual on the International Law Applicable to Cyber Warfare, 2013: 211. http://www.jku.at/intlaw/content/e275831/e275836/e276629/Tallinn_Manual_CW.pdf [2016-9-8].

[51]Cyber Security Strategy of the United Kingdom: Safety, Security and Resilience in Cyber Space, 2009:7. https://www.gov.uk/government/uploads/system/uploads/attachment_data/file/228841/7642.pdf [2016-9-24].

[52]United Kingdom, The UK Cyber Security Strategy: Protecting and Promoting the UK in a Digital World, 2011:11. https://www.gov.uk/government/uploads/system/uploads/attachment_data/file/60961/uk-cyber-security-strategy-final.pdf [2016-9-24].

1. Austrian Cyber Security Strategy

In "Austrian Cyber Security Strategy",[53] the cyberspace is defined as follows: "Cyber space is the virtual space of all IT systems interconnected at data level on a global scale. The basis for cyber space is the Internet as a universal and publicly accessible connection and transport network, which may be supplemented and expanded through other data networks. In common parlance, cyber space also refers to the global network of different independent IC infrastructures, telecommunication networks and computer systems. In the social sphere the use of this global network allows individuals to interact, exchange ideas, disseminate information, give social support, engage in business, control action, create art and media works, play games, participate in political discussions and a lot more."

2. China's National Cyberspace Security Strategy

China officially released "National Cyberspace Security Strategy"[54] on December 27, 2016. However, cyberspace is not clearly defined in the Strategy, but is merely described as below: "In the wake of the flying development of the information revolution, a cyberspace composed of the Internet, telecommunications networks, computer systems, automatized control systems, digital equipments and the applications, services and data they carry, is currently comprehensively changing people's ways of production and life, and is profoundly influencing humankind's social historical development process." The description contains facilities (the Internet, telecommunications networks, computer systems, automatized control systems, digital equipments), data (data they carry), users (humankind) and operation (the applications and services they carry). Hence, China's description of cyberspace contains all four factors of the cyberspace.

3. Columbia's Policy Guidelines for Cybersecurity and Cyberdefense

In Columbia's Policy Guidelines for Cybersecurity and Cyberdefense,[55] the cyberspace is defined as "the physical and virtual environment composed of computers, computer systems, computer programs (software), and telecommunications, data and information networks, in which users interact with each other".

---

[53]Austrian Cyber Security Strategy, 2013: 21. https://www.enisa.europa.eu/topics/national-cyber-security-strategies/ncss-map/AT_NCSS.pdf [2016-9-24].

[54]National Cyberspace Security Strategy. http://www.cac.gov.cn/2016-12/27/c_1120195926.htm [2016-12-28].

[55]Republic of Colombia, National Planning Department, Policy Guidelins for Cybersecurity and Cyberdefense, 2011: 34. https://www.sites.oas.org/cyber/Documents/Colombia%20-%20National%20Cybersecurity%20and%20Cyberdefense%20Policy.pdf [2016-9-24].

4. India's National Cyber Security Policy

In India's National Cyber Security Policy,[56] the cyberspace is defined as follows: "Cyberspace is a complex environment consisting of interactions between people, software, and services, supported by worldwide distribution of information and communications technology (ICT) devices and networks."

5. Cyber Security Strategy of Latvia 2014–2018

In Latvia's "Cyber Security Strategy of Latvia 2014-2018",[57] the cyberspace is defined as follows: "Cyber space is an interactive environment that includes users, networks, computing technology, software, processes, and information in transit or storage, applications, services, and systems that can be connected directly or indirectly to the Internet, telecommunications and computer networks. Cyber space has no physical boarders."

6. National Cyber Security Strategy for Montenegro 2013–2017

In Montenegro's "National Cyber Security Strategy for Montenegro 2013-2017",[58] "Cyber" is defined as: "anything relating to, or involving computers or computer networks (such as Internet). Cyberspace is more than Internet; it includes not only hardware, software and information systems, but also the people, social interaction within these networks."

7. Cyberspace Protection Policy of the Republic of Poland

In "Cyberspace Protection Policy of the Republic of Poland",[59] the cyberspace is defined as "a space of processing and exchanging information created by the ICT systems, together with links between them and the relations with users".

8. Cyber Security Strategy of Romania and Action Plan on Nationwide Deployment of National Information Security System

In Romania's "Strategiei de Securitate Cibernetică a României şi a Planului de Acţiune la Nivel Naţional Privind Implementarea Sistemului Naţional de Securitate

[56]Ministry of Communication and Information Technolory, India, National Cyber Security Policy-2013 (NCSP-2013), 2013: 1. http://meity.gov.in/sites/upload_files/dit/files/National%20Cyber%20Security%20Policy%20(1).pdf [2016-9-24].

[57]Cyber Security Strategy of Latvia 2014-2018, 2014. https://www.enisa.europa.eu/topics/national-cyber-security-strategies/ncss-map/lv-ncss [2016-9-24].

[58]National Cyber Security Strategy for Montenegro 2013-2017, 2013: 5. http://www.mid.gov.me/ResourceManager/FileDownload.aspx?rid=165416&rType=2&file=Cyber%20Security%20Strategy%20for%20Montenegro.pdf [2016-9-24].

[59]Cyberspace Protection Policy of the Republic of Poland, 2013: 5. https://www.enisa.europa.eu/topics/national-cyber-security-strategies/ncss-map/copy_of_PO_NCSS.pdf [2016-9-24].

Cibernetică"[60] (Cyber Security Strategy of Romania and Action Plan on Nationwide Deployment of National Information Security System), the cyberspace is defined as "spaţiul cibernetic-mediul virtual, generat de infrastructurile cibernetice, incluzând conţinutul informaţional procesat, stocat sau transmis, precum şi acţiunile derulate de utilizatori în acesta" (the virtual environment generated by cyber infrastructures, including processing, storage or transmission of content information and operations executed by users thereon).

9. Conceptual Views Regarding the Activities of the Armed Forces of the Russian Federation in the Information Space

The Russian Federation usually opposes the use of "cyberspace", only uses "information and communications technology (ICT)", or "information space" if necessary. In "Conceptual Views Regarding the Activities of the Armed Forces of the Russian Federation in the Information Space",[61] the cyberspace is defined as follows: "Information Space: area of activity related to the formation, creation, transformation, transmission, use and storage of the information affecting inter alia the individual and social consciousness, information infrastructure and the information per se."

10. Conceptual Strategy for Cyber Security of the Russian Federation

In Russia's "Концепция Стратегии Кибербезо- пасности Российской Федерации"[62] (Conceptual Strategy for Cyber Security of the Russian Federation), the cyberspace is defined as follows: "Киберпространство—сфера деятельности в информационном пространстве, образованная совокупностью коммуникацио нных каналов. Интернета и других телекоммуникационных сетей, технологичес кой инфраструктуры, обеспечивающей их функционирование, и любых форм осуществляемой посредством их использования человеческой активности (личности, организации, государства)." (Cyberspace: an area of activity in the information space, formed by communication channels of Internet and other telecommunication networks, and technology infrastructures that ensure its functioning and any [data] form of human [individual, organization, nation] activities occurring thereon).

[60]Hotărârea nr. 271/2013 pentru aprobarea Strategiei de securitate Cibernetică a României şi a Planului de Acţiune la Nivel Naţional Privind Implementarea Sistemului Naţional de Securitate Cibernetică, 2013:7. https://www.enisa.europa.eu/topics/national-cyber-security-strategies/ncss-map/StrategiaDeSecuritateCibernetica%20ARomaniei.pdf [2016-12-31].

[61]Conceptual Views Regarding the Activities of the Armed Forces of the Russian Federation in the Information Space, p. 5. https://ccdcoe.org/strategies/Russian_Federation_unofficial_translation.pdf [2016-9-24].

[62]Концепция Стратегии Кибербезопасности Российской Федерации, p. 2. http://council.gov.ru/media/files/41d4b3dfbdb25cea8a73.pdf [2016-9-24].

1.6 Analyses on the Four Elements of Cyberspace

In the article named Some Principles of Cyber Strategy—Analysis—Eurasia Review,[63] cyberspace is also called "The cyber domain", being expressed in the article in the following way: "The cyber domain, or cyberspace, has been defined by Andrew Krepinevich as…" In this sense, Cyberspace can be decomposed into such two levels as "Cyber" and "Space [or "Domain"]", wherein the substance of Cyber is realized through computer infrastructure and communication lines. However, the true sense lies in what kind of information is contained in the computer and how to use the information, which is the meaning of Space. "Space" means to reflect characteristics of human and activities over the Cyber. Due to the specialty of network, the main body on the cyber can be either a person or an agent of the person, or even pure machine behaviors (e.g. the artificial intelligent system AlphaGo). Therefore, "Cyber role" can be used to represent the main body, which is a concept of "User" and can be human, software, objects, labels or the like. As a result, the significance of "User" and "Role" is specifically stressed in the definition of Cyberspace, and these "Users" and "Roles" are participating for interaction.

Cyberspace includes four basic elements: Facility (Carrier, i.e. Infrastructure), Data (Objects, Payload), Roles (Subjects, i.e. User), and Operations (Activities/Behaviors).

The "Facility" of the four elements is corresponding to an integration of "end node", "connecting side" and "switching node" in the definition of "Network"; it can be understood that the forms of all types of carriers for carrying all kinds of payloads (signals, data, information and so on) are right the "Facility", because the attributes presented by these facilities in Cyberspace are identical, all of which are shown as the characteristic of "carrying". Even though that it is the "Interaction" behaviors that are supported by the "Channel", both the node facility and the channel facility (Terminal, Server, Router, Cable) are merely regarded as platforms for reflecting information carrying, which shows the characteristic of "leading the net" in cyberspace sovereignty.

The "Data" of the four elements refers to digital signs expressing such informations as light, electricity, sound, magnetism, quantum (and even smaller particles that may appear in the future) and so on in the cyberspace, and it is corresponding to "Payload" in the definition of "Network". Being operated, Data are passive and in a position as the object; in addition, Data are processed results, and are representative reflections of a certain activity intention. Data is defined in such a way so that the "Cyberspace" being discussed can be limited within the virtual space "Electro-Magnetic Cyberspace", excluding physical spaces such as "Traffic Network Space" (road network, air transportation network and so on).

---

[63]Some Principles of Cyber Strategy—Analysis—Eurasia Review. ISN Security Watch, 2014. http://maritimesecurity.asia/free-2/sea-lines-of-communication/some-principles-of-cyber-strategy-analysis-eurasia-review/ [2016-9-6].

Apparently, "Facility" and "Data" belong to the technology level, reflect the attributes of "Network", and are usually the action points being managed.

The "Roles" of the four elements generally refers to all roles and users in the Cyberspace. In the cyberspace, humans are roles; besides, organizations, equipments, softwares, websites, virtual humans (robots), network equipments (Router) and so on may also be the main body roles capable of producing information. Therefore, relative to Data, "Cyber roles" are positive and are in the position as the subject. In addition, the "Cyber roles" here relate to "human" in physics society, wherein the connection may be direct or reflective, and may be indirect sometimes —e.g. robots—the robots are not immediately operated by humans, but humans exist behind the tasks executed by the robots, for instance, the operation algorithms or operation rules are provided by humans.

The "Operations" of the four elements refers to various data activities and behaviors in the cyberspace, and is substantively all kinds of behaviors of processing data.

Apparently, both "Roles" and "Operations" belong to the social levels, and reflect the attributes of "Space", the social feature of which is usually the "managed" main object. For the cyberspace, "Roles" and "Operations" are prominently important, and the management rules for the cyberspace usually lie in the restrictions on "Roles" and "Operations". Therefore, it is necessary to know both the "Link" and "Interaction" attributes of "Roles" and "Operations", and, more importantly, the characteristics of being restricted by certain rules.

1.7 The History of Cyberspace

In its primary development and application phase, Cyberspace was simply used for exchanging information and supporting physical space. As the special status of cyberspace is more and more prominent, activities of human society are highly dependent on the cyberspace. As a result, issues of cyberspace rights are also highlighted.

1.7.1 The History of Radio Broadcast

Radio and television are multi-functional modern communication tools using radios and electronic equipments. In the field of news communication, they share the features of being rapid, widespread and immediate. Research on radio and television started from the second half of the 19th century. During the first half of the 20th century, radio and television appeared and were rapidly developed. The history of radio broadcast can be generally divided into four phases.

1. Phase 1: Background for the appearance of broadcast

In the second half of the 19th century, radio and television were proved to be feasible. In 1864, James Clerk Maxwell of Britain predicted that electro-magnetic field is spread in the form of waves[64]; in 1888, Heinrich Rudolf Hertz of Germany verified the existence of electro-magnetic waves[65]; at the end of the 19th century, Guglielmo Marconi of Italy and Александр Степанович Попов of Russia invented the technology of radio communication on the basis of former researches[66]; in 1906, Telefunken of Germany succeeded in its wireless telephone experiments[67]; in 1907, Lee de Forest of the US performed experiments for music and language radio broadcast in New York.[68]

2. Phase 2: Appearance of broadcast and its primary development

On November 2, 1920, KDKA, which is the first radio station in the world, began to broadcast in Pittsburg, US[69]; in 1921, the Ministry of Posts and Telecommunications of France established the first radio station of France, and broadcast regularly through the Eiffel Tower.[70] In 1922, France built Radio France, and private radio stations began to emerge two years later.[71] In 1922, London ZLO Radio Station officially started to broadcast daily programs in UK, and then was changed to be British Broadcasting Corporation (BBC) in 1927[72]; by 1925, more than 20 countries

[64]Baidu baike, James Clerk Maxwell. http://baike.baidu.com/view/15809.htm?fromtitle=James+Clerk+Maxwell&type=syn [2016-9-27].

[65]Baidu baike, Heinrich Rudolf Hertz. http://baike.baidu.com/link?url=ggKdfMkZX-FkYaWFRqRle7rIZLz-h6fn9zR9vIDHZD1M7docJAn4xvW_1mw-hNF1xW0j-JVGV42cBNqlqlCip5eaHZzMWXWGJz0lXqeMIyQLj0YsaVHjB2ik3ilIr1YcnNI-RkKD1WNdhnLGL6tywW7hiqBlBwS7yZNiUmHh0kjG [2016-9-27].

[66]History of Radio Communication. http://bglxx.zje.net.cn/mysxd/ShowArticle.asp?ArticleID=2800 [2016-9-28].

[67]Baidu baike, History of World Radio and Television. http://baike.baidu.com/link?url=eTRUZXxdYV6csKfpyypJBVCIUGNHH9NtA2Oru4G8b-x6BVaqDL_wcStEy79VwZlgm4yVhB3u8VnhchTQEVsn-YA9zkQjRSMtCRK3JOYduAZ0_vCLuIBnSa1x9iNeCUULhcDO7Bk4nkVir09foEX7Ia [2016-9-27].

[68]History of Radio Broadcast-BCL. http://www.imbcl.com/docs/61-bcl.html [2016-9-28].

[69]Baidu baike, KDKA Radio Station. http://baike.baidu.com/link?url=a8S8oSe-TYq-DTKYi51cZEh5BSAEQXM70QwzULH_d9UNVtqviOP6FXZuoe-Kbpk3X58U0uNGA9mV9DgGgir-0_59QXSvWCkZeo65Y5xykVfyUTjdH2EHH2WchxnjjQiFi73dHivKG_4RxxlUoRE6f4K [2016-9-27].

[70]Introduction to Modern Broadcasting. http://www.wxphp.com/wxd_03mta8a6w462a888ee59_1.html [2016-9-27].

[71]Historical Stages and System Reform of French Radio and Television. http://www.mediaeconomy.com.cn/node/371 [2016-9-28].

[72]Baidu baike, Radio Stations. http://baike.baidu.com/link?url=jJbzsd5nQ5FhsWvrbG9uWxmzUWtdt5qZfBroFXaiLwv-BmeS8i3ZK8RQYcOOiyJNxS-C4OFyoZ8J5Smz6uLJ2a5Ak5CVK_01RFZ8MTuiQCGFqtkyRuDaHnMXpJDyg2zmx [2016-9-22].

had officially begun to broadcast, and broadcasting had been rapidly developed thereafter all over the world.[73] In this phase, broadcasts were played mainly within the country, and showed extreme advantages in information transmission.

3. Phase 3: Development of international broadcasting

In order to maintain its colonial rules, the Netherlands began to broadcast in Dutch to its distant overseas colony of East India and some other areas in 1927, and the Netherlands became the first country in the world performing overseas broadcasting.[74] Soon, Germany (1929), France (1931), UK (1932), Japan (1934) and other countries began to broadcast to their overseas territories one after another, aiming to strengthen ties with overseas expatriates and serve their agents, soldiers and merchants in colonies, so the broadcasts were mostly in their native languages.[75] In 1929, the former Soviet Union also started overseas broadcasting in Germany, and the languages of overseas broadcasting had expanded to French, English, Hungarian, Spanish, Italian, Swedish, Czech and Polish by 1933; moreover, the former Soviet Union also performed unscheduled broadcasting in Portuguese and Turkish.[76] International broadcasting had been greatly developed during the World War II. Before the war broke out in 1939, 27 countries had started overseas broadcasting; when the war was over in 1945, there were as many as 55 countries performing overseas broadcasting. The representative of news broadcast was BBC of UK, which had been using altogether 39 languages in its overseas broadcasting and was broadcasting accumulatively for 763 h per week by 1944, and BBC was the largest one of all countries.[77]

4. Phase 4: Broadcast started to be used for political purposes

After World War II, international radio stations all over the world tended to be increasingly strengthened, particularly in that the maximum power of a single broadcast transmitter had been enhanced from 50–100 kW to 500–1000 kW. In the middle of the 1980s, 78 countries had started overseas broadcasting, and the international broadcasting of this moment had been regarded as a huge communication tool and started to show obvious political intentions.[78] In February, 1939,

---

[73] Baidu baike, History of World Radio and Television. http://baike.baidu.com/link?url=zURj1VUUPzen9yS2RdexYKzbEtmKBQ9sJSXqs3GPIL-YCcaXqyR_LAvddh9O3WtVdLy9R8wU2eFTB-nabCq2OT1iDVLNXPtoCDrp592KNt1dOWgL3vGFdksrCeGHONlL2JHwvj55aILC-BkuaJT5zq [2016-9-27].

[74]Introduction to Radio and Television (1). http://3y.uu456.com/bp_2zail0g4wh55mbv22qny_1.html [2016-9-27].

[75]Zhao SF, Guo BP (1986) Overview of international broadcasting. J Int Comm 4:27–31.

[76]Hudong.com, the former Radio Moscow. http://www.baike.com/wiki/%E5%8E%9F%E8%8E%AB%E6%96%AF%E7%A7%91%E5%B9%BF%E6%92%AD%E7%94%B5%E5%8F%B0 [2016-9-27].

[77]Baidu baike, International broadcasting. http://baike.baidu.com/link?url=uwXgOXlNY7tWKhtgkogrKlAA-a8VajpVv8BiRs9A15-sLi9dChZ7l1TgkH0Z38ensQz_8JmcUbMBT-vsCANYGZ44Wxn-K2GnEqWTfqOPE826Dbkg1_sbkeNpaIHsy9F2 [2016-9-27].

the General Electric Company (GE, also called Qiyi Company in China) of America started to broadcast to China for one hour each day, mainly in Cantonese and occasionally in Mandarin; after the outbreak of World War II, the Pacific Branch of the News Coordination Bureau of the US government requisitioned the equipment of GE, and started to broadcast in Cantonese and Mandarin, each for half an hour every day; in June, 1942, this broadcast was incorporated into VOA, and started to broadcast in Minnan dialect and Teochew dialect.[79] After the U.S.A. launched the Korea War, VOA strengthened Chinese broadcasting by adding programs in Tibetan, Teochew dialect and Hakka dialect. During the cold war, VOA had performed abundant naked propaganda against communists, the Soviet Union and China; in the late 60s and early 70s, VOA and some other radio stations adopted the report technique of "Balance", hoping to gain the reputation of being "frank" and "objective" by revealing some "family scandal" and reporting perspectives of both sides. As the cold war came to an end, VOA showed a prominently hostile tendency to our regime in its Chinese shortwave broadcast, and therefore was regarded as the top "Radio Enemy" by our country.[80] From 1970s to the end of 1980s, the influences of VOA over the society of China peaked. As the reform and opening-up began, the public demands on information, entertainment and education "erupted like a volcano", so the government roughly acquiesced in the activities of listening to radios, and VOA greatly improved its influences by taking advantage of this opportunity. In addition, since many young students used VOA as one of the important channels for English learning, the influence of VOA was further enhanced. In the 21st century, due to rapid popularization of internet and mobile terminals, the public can get information more conveniently and rapidly. In March 2011, Chinese Broadcasting of BBC, who would be 70 years old 55 days later, "passed away peacefully" in the Scottish folk music of "Auld Lang Syne".[81] Deutsche Welle, which was the only German radio station for overseas broadcasting, also stopped the Chinese shortwave programs on January 1, 2013, 47 years after its debut.[82]

As a communication form, broadcasting has a stable position in consensus and propaganda. However, following the appearance of the almighty internet, it is historically inevitable that the broadcasting will be replaced by the internet. As a result, the development of broadcasting is going downhill. Broadcasting is used for

---

[78]Comparison and Analysis of Quantities of Broadcasting from International Broadcasting of Modern Countries. http://www.cnki.com.cn/Article/CJFDTOTAL-GDXK607.032.htm [2016-9-8].

[79]Guan SJ, Wen JH (2011) The past and present VOA. Party & Government Forum: Cadre Digest 5:44–46. http://theory.people.com.cn/GB/14776106.html [2016-9-28].

[80]72 Years' Chinese Broadcasting of VOA: Decoding the "Unfailing Radio Wave". http://www.360doc.com/content/16/0629/18/4137846_571719403.shtml [2016-9-8].

[81](Vision Extension) The "Radio Enemy" in Memory: The disappearing radio wave. http://news.xinhuanet.com/mrdx/2013-01/18/c_132112142.htm [2016-9-8].

[82]Financial News, Those disappearing Overseas "Radio Enemies". http://paper.zbnews.net/xb/content/20130125/Articel22002IP.htm [2016-9-22].

ideological propagandas to other countries, so it directly challenges regime stability, as well as the electro-magnetic space sovereignty, of other countries. Facing this problem, concerned countries will usually take interference measures so as to limit the spread of overseas broadcasting in the cyberspace of the country.

1.7.2 History of Direct Broadcasting Satellite

By using geosynchronous satellites located in the high altitude space of 35,800 km, Direct Broadcasting Satellite (DBS) performed node-to-face broadcasting for such programs as videos, photos and articles, and sound, so that each family can receive the programs by using a tiny antenna and extremely simple equipment. According to the International Telecommunication Union (ITU), satellite broadcasting belongs to Broadcast Satellite Service (BSS). The development of satellite broadcasting can be roughly divided into three phases.

1. Phase 1: Experimental phase of the broadcast satellite service

In 1974, the US launched "Application Technology Satellite" ATS-6 and performed the world's first broadcasting experiment by using the geosynchronous satellite on a delicate satellite orbit; in 1976, Canada and America jointly launched a communication technology satellite CTS (Hermes), and experimented the launching of direct satellite broadcasting by using a high power of 12 GHz.[83] In the World Administration Radio Conference-77 (WARC-77) in 1977,[84] the first BSS planning was established, BSS downlink and uplink planning was respectively made on the frequency bands of 11.7–12.2 GHz (downlink), 14.5–14.8 GHz and 17.3–18.1 GHz (uplink), and some broadcast satellite orbits and frequency resources were comparatively distributed to countries all over the world, as a result of which the application of broadcast satellites entered into an experimental phase. In 1979, the WARC amended the frequency division table, improved the means for frequency division, and brought up methods for notification, examination and registration (i.e. the principle of "First registration, first occupation").[85]

2. Phase 2: Development phase of the broadcast satellite service

Approved by the Federal Communications Commission of America in 1983, the Satellite Television Company of America was permitted to manufacture, launch and operate two TV broadcast satellites, became the first company approved to

---

[83]Development Overview of Direct Broadcasting Satellite. http://www.doc88.com/p-9092357688790.html [2016-9-27].

[84]Documents of the World Administrative Radio Conference for the Planning of the Broadcasting-Satellite Service. http://www.itu.int/dms_pub/itu-s/oth/02/01/S020100003C4815PDFE.PDF [2016-9-27].

[85]Final Acts of World Administration Radio Conference, Geneva, 1979. http://www.itu.int/dms_pub/itu-s/oth/02/01/S02010000394002PDFE.PDF [2016-9-27].

manufacture broadcast satellites, and planned to provide TV service for the USA Eastern Time zone.[86] In January 1984, Japan launched the first practical broadcast satellite "Lily"-II (BS-2).[87] In November 1987, the first TV broadcast satellite of the former West Germany was successfully launched by European "Ariane" II carrier rocket, marking the beginning of the TV services new era in Western Europe.[88] In October 1988, the first TV broadcast satellite of France was also launched by an Ariane II rocket, and the five TV channels on the satellite were available for Television Francais 1 (TF1), TF4, TF7, Radio France and Radio France Internationale, and a former West Germany TV station.[89] Digital broadcast satellite has the advantages of high quality, large capacity, and providing multimedia services, so the development flourished all over the world. Since spectrum resources and satellite orbit resources are limited, some developed countries were not satisfied of being restricted by the BSS Planning of 1977, and accelerated their development. In order to prevent the few developed countries from plundering the precious resources without limitation, and to maintain its own sovereignty and interests, WARC re-planed BSS in 2000, and formulated new rules and provisions for radio. In this way, some flaws existing in radio rules and planning part were made up to some extent, and the current BSS planning was formed. As a result, the countries advanced in aerospace technology turned over to use their technological advantages and seek loopholes in ITU radio rules, and reported the broadcast satellite system in advance to ITU on the basis of "First registration, first occupation" principle; meanwhile, they took advantage of the flaws of some rules, and reported new BSS resources via the so-called planning amendment procedure, thereby "lawfully" plundering the broadcast satellite space resources.[90] Since then, the struggle for broadcast satellite resources, mostly for satellite orbits and radio frequencies, began among countries all over the world.

At the same time, countries were alert of the enormous propaganda roles played by radio and TV, and restrictions were made by laws. Take England as an example, according to England's Independent Television Act of 1954, an Independent Television Company needed to be set up, commercial television system was to be introduced, and the Independent Television Company was in charge of managing and monitoring commercial television; Independent Broadcasting Company Act of 1973 was passed in 1973, which was systemized and centralized to be the

[86]American Broadcasting Satellite. http://xuewen.cnki.net/CJFD-ZKDJ198005003.html [2016-9-27].

[87]Zhang YH (1984) "Lily"-II (BS-2) Broadcasting Satellite of Japan. Foreign Missiles Aerosp 7. http://mall.cnki.net/magazine/article/ZGHT198407001.htm [2016-9-27].

[88]On November 21, 1987, the first European TV broadcasting satellite was successfully launched. http://agzy.youth.cn/qsnag/lsjt/201311/t20131122_4252605.htm [2016-9-27].

[89]France launched its first TV broadcasting satellite on October 28, 1988. http://www.todayonhistory.com/10/28/d5673.htm [2016-9-27].

[90]International Scramble of Satellite Frequency and Orbit Resources. http://www.360doc.com/content/13/0524/14/3245043_287756472.shtml [2016-9-8].

Broadcasting Act of 1981 after being revised for several times and then turned into the Broadcasting Act of 1990.[91] Based on the Broadcasting Act of 1990, England established two new organizations—the Independent Television Commission and the Radio Agency, replacing the original Independent Broadcasting Bureau and the original Cable Television Authority; the original contract management system for commercial radios and televisions was replaced with the license system, each license will be issued based on corresponding punishment provisions for violators, and the license for each kind of service will be issued to the highest bidder after the competitive bidding; the commercial broadcasting communication function in the charge of the original Independent Broadcasting Bureau was shifted into the charge of the independent national communication companies. The Broadcasting Act of 1990 triggered a series of reforms for British radio and television.[92]

3. Phase 3: Competition phase of the Broadcast Satellite Service

DirecTV Japan was established in September 1995 and used the communication satellite SUPERBIRD-C capable of providing 90 television channels, 29 broadcasting channels and 16 data channels.[93] The first digital satellite TV station (Canalsat) of France was established in April 1996 by Canal Plus, and the second one was started also in April jointly by Luxemburg Radio Group, TF1, the Public Television Company and so on; early in 1997, 6 publicly-operated or privately-operated companies including TF1, TF6 or the like established the "Satellite Television Corporation of France" (TV Par Satellite), owning as many as 350,000 users in that very year.[94] By using 14 transponders on the satellite Astra 2E launched in October 1997, the British Sky Broadcasting (BSkyB) started digital satellite direct broadcasting service, and could provide programs on 100 channels at the very beginning; by the midmonth of August 1998, the number of US satellite broadcasting users was more than 7 million; TV Par Satellite of France started its business in January 1997, and had developed 170,000 users by July; the sub-company AB Sat of AB Group of France was set up at the end of December 1996 and provided digital broadcast satellite services on altogether 18 channels; the Canal Satellite Digital of Spain was started in 1997, developed 85,000 users within 6 months, and provided TV and voice broadcast programs on 35 channels.[95]

[91]Zhang Y (2006) Glimpse of british radio and television management system. Lanzhou J 10:176–177. http://www.docin.com/p-511663282.html [2016-9-27].

[92]Exploration of the Media Regulation System of China from British Television Act and Ofcom. http://media.people.com.cn/n/2015/0323/c395002-26737117.html [2016-9-27].

[93]Current Development Situation of Broadcast Satellites and Satellite Broadcast in the World. https://www.cc362.com/article/8095066.html [2016-9-8].

[94]History of Journalism and Communication of France—Development and Current Situation from 1950s to Nowadays. http://ejm.ruc.edu.cn/readnews.aspx?nid=334 [2016-9-21].

[95]Evilzhang, Tencent. Current Development Situation of Broadcast Satellite and Satellite Broadcast in the World. http://tech.qq.com/a/ 20061025/ 000473.htm [2016-9-21].

For stopping some few developed countries from racing to control broadcasting satellite orbits, frequency resources and damaging political and economic interests of other countries, some developing countries, mainly in the first and third zones, called for a new planning on WARC in 1995 so as to fairly and rationally distribute corresponding resources to each country.[96] ITU set up a BSS re-planning policy steering group and a re-planning technology expert group in 1997 so as to get prepared for re-planning the Broadcast Satellite Service. After the Direct Broadcasting Satellites were officially used, countries all around the world, especially the developed countries, started the fights for satellite orbit resources and frequency resources. Following the rapid development of the Broadcast Satellite Service, some countries began to infringe the economy, culture, religion, sovereignty and so on of other countries by using satellite broadcast. For fighting against these infringing activities, ITU has made clear provisions. For example, Article 196 in the Constitution of ITU stipulates the principle that the radio and satellite channel resources should be fairly used by each country so as to prevent all of the radio and satellite channel resources from being divided by the few developing countries.[97] A special clause, i.e. Article 23.13, was formulated in Radio Regulations Articles[98] for Broadcast Satellite Service (BSS): Unless being permitted by these countries in advance, all of the available technical means should be adopted during the process of designing each characteristic of BSS space station so as to feasibly reduce the radiation to territories of other countries to the greatest extent.

1.7.3 History of Cable Television

Opposite to radio TV (or terrestrial TV) and satellite TV, Cable TV is a broadcasting system directly transmitting, by using coaxial cable as a medium, TV and FM radio programs to users' televisions. In 1949 in mountainous areas of Pennsylvania and Oregon of America, operators set up antennas on the mountain tops to receive programs, then the program signals were transmitted to local families by using cables.[99]

The key of cable TV lies in the landing of satellite TV stations. China issued Regulation Provisions on Ground Receiving Equipments of Satellite TV

---

[96]Peng SC (1996) Summary of WACR in 1995. Space Int 2:8–15. http://www.cnki.com.cn/Article/CJFDTotal-GJTK199602005.htm [2016-9-27].

[97]http://www.chinalawedu.com/. ITU Institution. http://www.chinalawedu.com/falvfagui/fg23155/176611.shtml [2016-9-22].

[98]Radio Regulations Articles. http://www.itu.int/dms_pub/itu-s/oth/02/02/S02020000244501PDFE.PDF [2016-9-27].

[99]Chapter IX Television Section1 Invention and Development of TV. http://www.docin.com/p-17264074.html [2016-9-27].

Broadcasting[100] on October 5, 1993 and Regulations on Broadcasting and Television[101] on September 1, 1997, clearly prescribing that any individual is not allowed to install or use satellite ground-receiving equipments, and that TV stations, cable TV stations and TV relay stations in all regions are forbidden to rebroadcast overseas TV programs transmitted by satellites.

European Council passed European Agreement on Transnational TVs and Radios in May 1993 and passed European Agreement on Problems including Copyrights, Neighboring Right and so on in Transnational Satellite Broadcasting in May 1994; as a result, a comparatively complete legal framework about European transnational radios and TVs was gradually formed. According to the Agreement, when re-broadcasting satellite programs, the cable systems of all countries have the right to adopt different disposing principles and to make exclusive choices of receiving or rejecting.[102]

The landing of foreign TV stations triggered relevant problems about cyberspace sovereignty competition, so countries began to be concerned about the concept of cyberspace sovereignty. Following are the provisions about "restrictions on license holding and transferring" in the Telecommunications Action of 1996[103]: ① Radio and TV licenses cannot be issued to or held by foreign governments, and representatives of foreign governments; ② licenses for broadcasting, public transmission, satellite communication, and satellite radio stations cannot be issued or held in case of any of the following situations: (a) any foreigner or representative; (b) any company established on the basis of laws of foreign governments; (c) any company more than 1/5 share of which was held by foreigners or representatives, or by foreign governments or representatives, or the company established on the basis of foreign laws; (d) if the Federal Communications Commission finds out that over 25% of the shares of the radio and TV, public communication, satellite transmission and satellite radio station are directly or indirectly owned by any foreign natural person, legal person, government or other organization who violates public interests.[104]

In China, citizens (except hotels leveled above three stars and a part of foreigner residence zones) are forbidden to install satellite TV; meanwhile, there are

---

[100]Regulation Provisions on Ground Receiving Equipments of Satellite TV Broadcasting. http://www.gov.cn/fwxx/bw/gjgbdydszj/content_2262992.htm [2016-9-27].

[101]Regulations on Broadcasting and Television. http://www.people.com.cn/item/faguiku/wh/F46-1020.html [2016-9-28].

[102]Major Project supported by National Social Science Fund: research findings of "Research on Communication Strategies and Influences of Multilingual International Channels", emphasis should be laid on foreign laws and regulations for international TV communications. http://www.17zhadui.com/html/2013/guojimaoyi_0920/18689.html [2016-9-21].

[103]Telecommunications Act of 1996. https://www.gpo.gov/fdsys/pkg/PLAW-104publ104/pdf/PLAW-104publ104.pdf [2016-9-20].

[104]Li Y (2016) Simple analysis of American TV monitoring system and legal regulations. China Radio $ TV Acad J 2:92–95. http://www.cnki.com.cn/Article/CJFDTotal-GDXK201602029.htm [2016-9-27].

restrictions on playing overseas TV channels on cable TV. After entering into WTO, in order to follow the rule that the entrance of foreign media are open in China, the State Administration of Radio, Film and Television (SARFT) officially allowed the public broadcasting of some overseas entertainment satellite channels on the Cable TV Network of Guangdong: in 2001, Phoenix Satellite Television of Hong Kong was officially permitted to be played in Guangdong; in February 2002, China Entertainment Television owned by America Online/Time Warner was played in Guangdong; in April 2002, Star TV owned by American News Corporation was officially played in Guangdong; in July, two channels of STAR of Hong Kong, i.e. ATV Home and ATV World, were officially permitted to be played in Guangdong; in 2004, the MTV channel owned by US Viacom Company officially landed in Guangdong. Together with TVB Jade and TVB Pearl, which had already been actually input into the Cable TV net of Guangdong, there are as many as 8 overseas TV channels open to the public in Guangdong.[105]

In 2002, the overseas channels that were allowed to land China by the "State Administration of Radio, Film and Television (SARFT)", must be broadcast through the satellites specified by China. In July 2002, satellite signals from BBC World Channel were shielded by SARFT due to the report containing scenes of Fanlungong.[106] In March 2003, Star TV was once again permitted by SARFT to land on the whole nation with restrictions.[107] On October 28, 2004, Temporary Provisions on Enterprises Producing and Operating Sino-Foreign Joint Venture & Cooperation Radio and TV Programs (No. 44) issued by SARFT and the Ministry of Commerce came out, including a series of rules specific to foreign-owned enterprises, e.g. no exclusively foreign-owned enterprises producing and operating radio and TV programs can be established, legal representatives must be entrusted by the Chinese Part, the Chinese-part in joint venture must hold at least 51% of the stock of the joint venture, and joint ventures have no right to make political news and special subject or column programs of the same type.[108] Unsatisfied with the situation that the Star TV was restricted to land only in Guandong, and hotels leveled above three stars and communities for foreigners in China, the American News Group cooperated with Qinghai Television[109] in 2005 and bought out, without permission, the time frame after the re-broadcasting of CCTV News on

[105]Xie Y, Luo WG, Chen GL. Influences of overseas TV channels on local TV news media and programs of Guangdong. http://www.doc88.com/p-3137551585805.html [2016-9-27].

[106]China blacks out BBC. 2002-07-05. http://news.bbc.co.uk/2/hi/entertainment/2097890.stm [2016-9-13].

[107]China Network. Landing of Star TV was Approved. http://www.china.com.cn/chinese/jingji/288022.htm [2016-9-21].

[108]Temporary Provisions on Enterprises Producing and Operating Sino-Foreign Joint Venture & Cooperation Radio and TV Programs. http://govinfo.nlc.gov.cn/jssnjfz/xxgk/njstzcjwyh/201301/t20130121_3341451.shtml?classid=401 [2016-9-22].

[109]Secret Business of News Group: Suspected of being involved in smuggling contents from overseas channels. http://finance.people.com.cn/GB/1039/3600233.html [2016-9-28].

Qinghai Television each day, aiming to indirectly land all over the mainland of China. SARFT called an emergency stop to this illegal action.[110] By 2008, 31 overseas TV channels had been approved by China to broadcast TV programs to special inland areas through the platform of Sino satellite. These overseas TV channels having lawful landing qualifications must follow the rules of Administrative Measures for Landing of Overseas Satellite Television Channels (No. 27)[111] issued by SARFT in June 2004, and the supervision and administration of the institution appointed by SARFT must be accepted.[112]

As for Taiwan's TV, any TV program from Taiwan area had not been approved by the government to be landed in any mainland region, and had not been approved to be re-broadcasted on the overseas platform of Apstar-6 satellite. In 2012, after being approved by the government, Taiwan's TV channels landed onto Pingtan's comprehensive pilot area.[113]

1.7.4 History of the Internet

The Internet can also be called the INTERNET when it refers specifically to the Transmission Control Protocol/Internet Protocol (TCP/IP) as the protocol. The method of interconnecting computer networks is called "Network Interconnection". On such a basis, a global interconnected network covering the whole world was developed, and is called Internet, which is an interconnected network structure form. World Wide Web (WWW) is the most important form of service to promote the rapid development of Internet. It is a global access system based hypertext links.

Different from other computer networks, Internet is a computer network dominated by the US, and the development history of the international Internet is basically the development process of American Internet, the order of which is as follows: the Internet was first for military use, then the Internet for military use and that for civil use were separated, and finally the Internet for civil use is regulated by the government. The US government started to control the Internet when it was being developed by leaps and bounds all around the world, and the US government's control over Internet manifested its Internet sovereignty. Prior to this, there were roughly four phases for the Internet development.

---

[110]Star TV denied evacuation from mainland market, and alleged normal operation of the company. http://sh.sina.com.cn/news/20080410/100689921.shtml [2016-9-21].

[111]Decree from State Administration of Radio, Film and Television (No. 27). http://www.sarft.gov.cn/art/2004/8/1/art_1583_26284.html [2016-9-22].

[112]Zhang JH (2008) Impacts of the landing of overseas satellite television on Chinese culture. In: Satellite TV and IP Multimedia, p 21. http://shdm500.cn/asdaqw70.html [2016-9-28].

[113]Zhang RH (2013) Reflections on the landing of Taiwan's TV channels onto Pingtan comprehensive pilot area. News World 1:142–144. http://epaper.anhuinews.com/html/xwsj/20130123/article_2880809.shtml [2016-9-28].

1. Phase 1: The initial Phase of the Internet

The predecessor of Internet was started from the World Area Network project ARPANET that was started to be developed by the original Advanced Research Projects Agency (ARPA) of America in 1969.[114] ARPANET then was only to ensure the information transmission and the disaster recovery of information system during the Cold War and was not open.

In 1970, the first 56kbps communication line, which ran across the American border and was used for ARPANET transmission, was built up by American Telephone and Telegraph Company (AT&T), and connected the University of California at Los Angeles (UCLA) and the BBN Company (Bolt Beranek and Newman Inc.)[115] of America.[116]

In 1972, Raymond Tomlinson of BBN Company invented an E-mail program capable of sending messages in the distributed network.[117]

In 1972, the host of ARPANET began to use the first "host-host" transmission protocol, i.e. the Network Control Protocol (NCP).[118] At the end of the same year, the University of Hawaii successfully developed ALOHAnet, and connected it into ARPANET. By using the gateway, it is possible for people in Hawaii to access to the Rutherford and Appleton Laboratory (RAL) in England.[119]

2. Phase 2: The development phase of the Internet

In 1973, the American Advanced Research Projects Agency was renamed to be the American Defense Advanced Research Projects Agency (DARPA); ARPANET solved the problem that computer interconnection was possible only within the Home Network, and it was supportive for inter-network interconnection. The University College of London in England took the lead in connecting into ARPANET via NORSAR[120] in Norway, and became the first international connections to the ARPANET.[121]

---

[114]ARPAnet: The World's First Internet. https://www.techopedia.com/definition/27856/network-control-protocol-ncp [2016-12-31].

[115]BBN Technologies is a high-tech company located in Cambridge, Massachusetts, and was established in 1948. Because of the contract with the Advance Research Projects Agency for US defense, it joined in the initial development of ARPANET and Internet. Now, it's a subsidiary of Raytheon Company.

[116]The History of the Internet. http://www.thocp.net/reference/internet/internet1.htm [2016-9-27].

[117]The First Network Email. https://openmap.bbn.com/~tomlinso/ray/firstemailframe.html [2016-9-30].

[118]Network Control Protocol (NCP). https://www.techopedia.com/definition/27856/network-control-protocol-ncp [2016-9-27].

[119]Gateways: Historical Underpinnings of a Single Internet. https://www.ideals.illinois.edu/bitstream/handle/2142/73453/223_ready.pdf [2016-9-30].

[120]NORSAR is an internationally-accepted independent non-profit research foundation. http://www.norsar.no/norsar/about-us/ [2016-9-27].

[121]The History of the Internet. http://www.thocp.net/reference/internet/internet1.htm [2016-9-27].

In 1974, Vinton G. Cerf and Robert E. Kahn working for DARPA published a paper named A Protocol for Packet Network Intercommunication[122] on IEEE Transactions on Communications, and made detailed description about the Transmission Control Protocol (TCP) therein.

In 1976, the Bell Laboratory of AT&T developed the Unix-Unix File-copying Protocol (Unix-Unix Copy Protocol, UUCP), which was published in the following year together with the UNIX operation system.[123]

In 1978, Vinton G. Cerf, Jon Postel and Danny Cohen discussed and decided to break TCP down into two independent parts, i.e. TCP function and Internet Protocol (IP), wherein TCP was responsible for decomposing complete information into several independent data packets, and then to complete information after receiving them; IP was in charge of transmitting each data gram to its respective destination.[124]

In 1979, DARPA began to fund the experiments of the Packet Radio Network (PRNET) so as to support communications among moving trucks.[125]

In 1981, BITNET became the first collaboration network connecting the City University of New York and Yale University, and was mainly used for providing functions such as listing service of e-mail and distributed information, and document transmission.[126] In the same year, computer scientists, the University of Delaware, the University of Purdue, the University of Wisconsin, Rand Corporation and BBN Company started to build up the Computer Science NETwork (XSNET). The National Science Foundation of America funded the establishment of CSNET by using the seed fund, which was prepared for providing network services (particularly mail service) for the college/university scientists having no access to ARPANET. CSNET connected the research and education institutions of America.[127]

In 1982, the American Defense Communications Agency (DCA) and the American Defense Advanced Research Projects Agency made Transmission Control Protocol (TCP) and Internet Protocol (IP), which are collectively called as

[122](1974) A protocol for packet network intercommunication. IEEE Trans Comm 22(5):637–648. http://www.signallake.com/innovation/CerfKahnMay74.pdf [2016-9-28].

[123]The UUCP System. https://www.mhprofessional.com/downloads/products/0072263369/0072263369_uucp.pdf [2016-9-27].

[124]History of the Internet, TCP/IP. http://www.securenet.net/members/shartley/history/tcp_ip.htm [2016-9-28].

[125]The DARPA Packet Radio Network Protocols. http://morse.colorado.edu/~timxb/5520/ho/JubinDARPA.pdf [2016-9-30].

[126]BITNET referred to the abbreviation of "Because It's There NETwork" at first, but then was changed into the abbreviation of "Because It's Time Network". http://www.computerhope.com/jargon/b/bitnet.htm [2016-9-29].

[127]CSNET (Computer Science Network). https://sites.google.com/site/internettechnologys/Home/road-map-of- internet-events/csnet-computer-science- network [2016-9-30].

TCP/IP Protocol Suite, for ARPANET[128]; Norway adopted TCP/IP protocols, and connected to the Internet through SANNET.[129] As a result, the definition of interconnection network came out for the first time, namely, Internet is an internet connected through TCP/IP Protocols. The Department of Defense of the United States (DoD) announced to use TCP/IP Protocols as the DoD standard network protocols, which was called DoD TCP/IP at the beginning.[130]

3. Phase 3: The growth phase of the Internet

In 1983, ARPANET was switched from Network Control Protocol (NCP) to TCP/IP Protocol.[131] In the same year, ARPANET was split into two parts including ARPANET and MILNET, wherein MILNET was for the military service. 68 of the 113 nodes at that time entered MILNET, which was later incorporated into the Defense Data Network (DDN) established in 1983. This famous MILNET evolved into the current Non-Secure Internet Protocol Router Network (NIPRNET) of the American Military Network, which is used by US military to transmit sensitive but non-secure internal user data.[132] At the same time, the divided ARPANET was submitted to computer researchers as the research network, but its development was slow due to fund shortage. Following the civilization of ARPANET, NSF decided to build a new NSFNET by using software of ARPANET and TCP/IP protocols on the strength of the technology basis of CSNET.

In 1984, JUNET (Japan Unix network) using UUCP Protocol was built up[133]; in the same year, the Joint Academic Network (JANET) using Colored Book Protocol was built up and operated in England.[134]

In 1985, after one year's efforts of university networking, the NetNorth established by Canada accessed the city of Ithaca in New York of America from Toronto of Canada through BITNET.[135] In the same year NSFNET was completed and operated, and became leader of civil internet ever since. ARPANET was gradually eliminated, and quit running in 1989.[136] CSNET connected more than 170

[128]Introduction to TCP/IP. https://technet.microsoft.com/en-us/library/bb726991.aspx [2016-9-28].

[129]Hobbes' Internet Timeline v4.1. https://tcf.ua.edu/Classes/Jbutler/T389/HobbesInternetTimeline.htm [2016-9-28].

[130]What is TCP/IP (Internet Protocol Suite). http://www.internet-guide.co.uk/tcp-ip.html [2016-9-28].

[131]NSFNET. http://www.internet-guide.co.uk/NSFNET.html [2016-9-29].

[132]What was MILNET? http://www.wisegeek.com/what-was-milnet.htm [2016-9-29].

[133]Broadband Internet Deployment in Japan. http://cn.bing.com/search?q=1984+UUCP+JUNET+japan&go=%E6%90%9C%E7%B4%A2&qs=n&form=QBRE&pq=1984+uucp+junet+japan&sc=0-21&sp=-1&sk=&cvid=D538462CB16146E693C5C5866F57079F [2016-9-29].

[134]The U.K. JANET Network and Its Use by Libraries. http://docs.lib.purdue.edu/cgi/viewcontent.cgi?article=1148&context=iatul [2016-9-29].

[135]Networking in Canada. https://www.questia.com/magazine/1G1-12500741/networking-in-canada [2016-9-29].

[136]Baidu baike. ARPANET. http://baike.baidu.com/view/196838.htm [2016-9-28].

universities, enterprises, research institutions and numerous portal websites of other countries in 1985; CSNET merged together with BITNET in 1987; CSNET and BITNET were combined to form CREN Organization in 1989[137]; CSNET was out of service in 1991.[138]

In 1986, for enabling non-IP networks to have domain addresses, Craig Partridge of CSNET submitted specifications for mail routing and domain systems and brought up the realization method of mail exchanger (MX) records.[139] For improving news transmission efficiency of USENET on TCP/IP network, Phil Lapsley of Berkeley started his researches on Network News Transfer Protocol (NNTP) as a personal project, and officially issued NNTP specification in March 1986.[140]

In 1987, NSF signed a cooperation contract with Merit Network Company, and entrusted the Merit Network Company[141] to regulate the NSFNET backbone network; later, IBM Corporation and MCI Company[142] signed agreements with Merit Network Company and took part in the management of the NSFNET backbone network.

In 1988, Morris worm, the first computer virus, appeared on the internet of America, and influenced 10% of more than 60,000 hosts on the internet. This event prompted the establishment of Computer Emergency Response Team (CERT), which is the first international CERT organization established by DARPA.[143] In the same year, the regional network of Canada first accessed via NSFNET: ONet accessed via Cornell, RISO accessed via Princeton, and BCNET accessed via the

[137]CREN (Corporation for Research and Educational Networking) is a non-profit organization with members in research and education field, and its commission is to support higher education and research organizations with strategic IT knowledge services and communication tools. http://www.cren.net/ [2016-9-29].

[138]1980S: ARPANET to Internet: CSNET. http://www.cybertelecom.org/notes/internet_history80s.htm [2016-9-29].

[139]RFC 974, Mail Routing and the Domain System. http://www.uazone.org/inet/docs/rfc974.html [2016-9-29].

[140]1986: NNTP. http://fr.giganews.com/usenet-history/nntp.html [2016-9-29].

[141]Merit (Michigan educational research information triad) Network Corporation was created in 1996 by Michigan State University, Wayne State University, and the University of Michigan, and established networking as early as in 1972. https://www.merit.edu/about-us/merits-history/ [2016-9-29].

[142]MCI (Microwave Communications Inc.) is the predecessor of Verizon Corporation, and was the second largest long-distance call operator of America; its predecessor is the American World-Com Corporation collapsed due to accounting scandal, which was purchased by Verizon on May 8, 2005 at the price of 8.4 billion dollars. http://gb.cri.cn/3821/2005/02/17/153@451844.htm [2016-9-29].

[143]The Morris Worm: Internet malware turns 25. http://www.zdnet.com/article/the-morris-worm-internet-malware-turns-25/ [2016-9-29].

University of Washington; countries that had accessed NSFNET at that period include: Canada (CA), Denmark (DK), Finland (FI), France (FR), Iceland (IC), Norway (NO), Sweden (SE) and so on.[144]

4. Phase 4: The market-entering phase of the Internet

With the permission given by the Federal Networking Council, Corporation for the National Research Initiative (CNRI) successfully interconnected the commercial MCI e-mail system to the Internet as part of a general e-mail interconnection experiment in 1989, giving birth to two for-profit companies—UUNET[145] and PSINET[146] dependent on the Internet services.[147]

In 1990, Tim Berners-Lee from Conseil Europeen pour la Recherche Nucleaire (CERN) in Geneva implemented a hypertext system capable of providing efficient information access for members of international high-energy physics,[148] and triggered the development of World Wide Web (WWW).

In 1991, Thinking Machines published the Wide Area Information Servers (WAIS) invented by Brewster Kahle[149]; Mark P. McCahill and so on published the GOPHER[150] system used for information searching[151]; CERN published the WWW developed by Berners-Lee.[152]

In 1992, the Internet Society (ISOC) was registered[153]; the website of World Bank (http://www.worldbank.org/) came online. Network Coordination Center (NCC) for the network registries in European area was established, then started to provide address registration and coordination services for European Internet users.[154] The countries and regions connected to NSFNET in that period are as follows: Antarctica (AQ), Cameroon (CM), Cyprus (CY), Ecuador (EC), Estonia

[144]Network Working Group RFC 2235, Hobbes' Internet Timeline. https://www.rfc-editor.org/rfc/pdfrfc/rfc2235.txt.pdf [2016-9-29].

[145]It was set up in 1987 and has been one of the largest Internet service providers and one of the early single-layer networks. Its headquarters is in north Virginia and has been one of the first commercial Internet service providers. http://www.bing.com/knows/search?q=uunet&mkt=zh-cn [2016-9-30].

[146]PSINET is one of the first Internet connection service providers. https://en.wikipedia.org/wiki/PSINet [2016-9-30].

[147]What is the Internet (And What Makes It Work). https://www.cnri.reston.va.us/what_is_internet.html [2016-9-30].

[148]The History of HTML. http://inventors.about.com/od/computersoftware/a/html.htm [2016-9-30].

[149]Wide area information server. http://www.seomastering.com/wiki/Wide_area_information_server [2016-9-30].

[150]GOPHER. http://www.bing.com/knows/search?q=gopher&mkt=zh-cn [2016-9-30].

[151]Mark P. McCahill. http://www.digplanet.com/wiki/Mark_P._McCahill [2016-9-30].

[152]Longer Biography. https://www.w3.org/People/Berners-Lee/Longer.html [2016-9-30].

[153]ICANN WIKI. https://icannwiki.com/Internet_Society [2016-9-30].

[154]Réseaux IP Européens Network Coordination Centre. https://en.wikipedia.org/wiki/Middle_East [2016-9-30].

(EE), Kuwait (KW), Latvia (LV), Luxembourg (LU), Malaysia (MY), Slovenia (SK), Slovakia (SI), Thailand (TH), and Venezuela (VE).[155]

In 1993, NSF established the Internet Network Information Center (InterNIC) to provide Internet services[156]; NSF established the Internet Network Information Center (InterNIC) formed by many entities to provide services for users: AT&T was in charge of catalog and database services; the Network Solutions Inc. (NSI) provided registration service[157]; the General Atomics Inc. and the California Education and Research Federation Network (CERFnet) provided information services.[158] The website of the White House (http://www.whitehouse.gov/) came online. The IIKK Company (InterCon International KK) of Japan provided commercial Internet access for the first time.[159] Internet Talk Radio started broadcasting as the first radio station on the Internet.[160]

In 1994, commercial activities began to move onto the Internet, which enabled Americans to order Pizza over Pizza Hut.[161] Traditional banks began to move onto the Internet.[162] China completed the first fully-functional TCP/IP connection to Internet, then became a member of the Internet family.[163] In the same year, the early search engine "infoseek" came onto the market.[164]

In 1995, the world's first internet bank "Security First Network Bank" of America was started.[165] Radio HK, which is the first non-stop commercial radio station only available on Internet, was on the air.[166] Registration of top level

---

[155]Network Working Group RFC 2235, Hobbes' Internet Timeline. https://www.rfc-editor.org/rfc/pdfrfc/rfc2235.txt.pdf [2016-9-29].

[156]Li T (1996) Milestones of internet. Modern Telecomm Technol (6):41–43.

[157]In 1991, the US Defense Department decided to pay for entrusting NSI Company to take charge of domain registration and regulation (see RFC 1261). Funded by the US government, registration of all of the general top-level domains including .com, .org, .mil, .gov, .edu, and .net or the like is free. In 1992, the network of NSFNET operated by NSF replaced DAPARNET, and became the backbone of Internet, and NSI Company was still entrusted with domain registration. Apparently, NSI had always been in charge of domain regulation, the US government withdrawed the right of internet administration till Internet grew into an international internet, and ICANN was entrusted with the domain regulation.

[158]What is InterNIC. http://www.wisegeek.com/what-is-internic.htm [2016-10-1].

[159]Building On-Ramps to the Information Superhighway. http://www.japaninc.com/cpj/magazine/issues/1994/jun94/06infohi.html [2016-10-1].

[160]Video killed the radio star. http://museum.media.org/radio/ [2016-10-1].

[161]Pizza Hut Offers Big Discount to Celebrate 20th Anniversary of the World's First Online Purchase. https://www.entrepreneur.com/article/230620 [2016-10-1].

[162]Company News. A Credit Card for On-Line Sprees. http://www.nytimes.com/1994/10/15/business/company-news-a-credit-card-for-on-line-sprees.html [2016-10-1].

[163]http://hb.qq.com. Review over 1994–2015: China's 21 years of entrance into international Internet. http://hb.qq.com/a/20151217/031075.htm [2016-9-22].

[164]Baidu baike. Infoseek. http://baike.baidu.com/view/1450341.htm [2016-9-22].

[165]Baidu baike. SFNB. http://baike.baidu.com/view/4882734.htm [2016-9-22].

[166]Radio Oz. http://www.radiooz.com.au/ [2016-10-1].

domains was not free any more, and 50 dollars would be charged every year since September 14,[167] wherein.edu domain registration fees have always been paid by NSF.

In 1996, the highly controversial Communications Decency Act, (CDA) of America came out to prevent people from diffusing pornographic materials on the Internet, while this act was unanimously regarded by the Supreme Court as violation to the constitution several months later[168]; China's Temporary Provisions for International Network Regulation of Computer Information Networks came out to set rules for Internet usage[169]; the Military Government of Burma imposed restrictions on Internet access, and the State Law and Order Restoration Council (SLORC) forbid un-authorized computer internet usage.[170] Netscape and Microsoft started the browser wars on WWW, and both fought for network users with each other.[171]

In 1997, the American Registry for Internet Numbers (ARIN) was set up,[172] and took back from NSI the regulation and registration right of the IP number specific to geographic areas.[173]

In 1998, US Department of Commerce and the Internet Corporation for Assigned Names and Numbers (ICANN) reached an agreement, that was to shift the management of the Domain Name System (DNS) to ICANN managed by US Department of Commerce.[174] ICANN started to sign "Sponsor" agreements with countries so as to entrust relevant department of the countries to regulate the country code Top-Level Domain (ccTLD) of their own.

Internet is not limited to information transmission any more; instead, it demonstrates information, especially to the unknown users. Therefore, Internet plays the media role of radio, TV and news publications, and results in ideological conflicts. However, control measures equivalent to those for radio, TV and news publications were not taken among countries, so some countries including China were forced to take firewall measures, so that to take the lead in implementing internet sovereignty of the country.

---

[167]Amendment 4 to Cooperative Agreement Between NSI and U.S. Government. https://archive.icann.org/en/nsi/coopagmt-amend4-13sep95.htm [2016-10-1].

[168]Communications Decency Act (CDA). https://www.britannica.com/topic/Communications-Decency-Act [2016-10-1].

[169]Temporary Provisions for International Network Regulation of Computer Information Networks of PRC. http://www.weiweikl.com/JA2.htm [2016-10-1].

[170]The BurmaNet News: October 9, 1996. http://scholarworks.lib.csusb.edu/cgi/viewcontent.cgi?article=1164&context=ciima[2016-10-1].

[171]History of the Internet–the Browser wars. http://www.nethistory.info/History%20of%20the%20Internet/browserwars.html [2016-10-1].

[172]ARIN Overview. http://lists.arin.net/pipermail/clew/2000-July/000023.html [2016-10-1].

[173]Amendment 7 to Cooperative Agreement Between NSI and U.S. Government. http://fanyi.baidu.com/#en/zh/ [2016-10-1].

[174]ICANN. https://icannwiki.com/ICANN [2016-10-1].

1.7.5 Change of Focuses During Cyberspace Development

Traditional telephones, telegrams, radios, TVs, movies, and satellites and so on are self-built, and have respective features, users, regions and control of their own, so the builders naturally have jurisdiction. In the digital era, traditional media information is connected due to the development of global internet, which gradually changed the properties of the traditional media information. The main characteristic lies in that information is transmitted by using the transmission channels of others, so it is no longer possible to control the whole process of information transmission.

According to statistics,[175] over 80% of online information and over 95% of service information were provided by America at the beginning of the 21st century. China only took respectively 0.1% and 0.05% of the information input and output flow of the whole Internet. As a result, the weakness of Chinese traditional media in international communication, which was caused by language, was further amplified in network communication. In 1997, according to a article written by Rothkopf from Columbia University of America in No. 107 of Foreign Policy, "For the United States, a central objective of an Information Age foreign policy must be to win the battle of the world's information flows, dominating the airwaves as Great Britain once ruled the seas", "The United States dominates this global traffic in information and ideas. American music, American movies, American televisions, and American software are so dominant that they are now available literally everywhere on the Earth. They influence the tastes, lives, and aspirations of virtually every nation."[176]

According to Alvin Toffler of America in his Power shift[177] published in 1990, "The world had left the era controlled by violence and money, and the magic power of world politics in the future will be in the hands of powerful people having access to information. They will achieve their aims that cannot be conquered by violence and money by using the mastered power for network control and information publishing and by using the powerful culture and language advantage of English." In the opinion of Former French President Chirac, "The world today is faced with the threat of monoculture", which is a "new form of colonialism", and "global informatization" now is faced with the great risk of "global Americanization".[178]

[175]People's Daily Online. Promotion of the International Communication Ability of China's Military Media. http://media.people.com.cn/GB/22114/52789/207738/13381713.html [2016-9-21].

[176]Foreign Policy, No. 107, Summer, 1997. http://www.jstor.org/stable/1149331?seq=1#page_scan_tab_contents [2016-9-13].

[177]Toffler. Power shift[M]. Beijing: Press of Central Party School of CPC, 1991.

[178]Guangming Daily. Network—A double-edged sword of culture. 1999-5-26. http://www.gmw.cn/01gmrb/1999-05/26/GB/18068^GM10-210.HTM [2016-9-21].

1.8 The Reality of Cyberspace

Cyberspace is called virtual space, but with cyberspace developing and human activities carried out in large quantity, it is getting more and more realistic.

1.8.1 The Authenticity from the Perspective of Virtual-Real Mapping

The authenticity of cyberspace can be understood from the perspective of the virtual-real "mapping". At present, for any kind of specific cyberspace, its manifestation is invariably a projection of a physical society. Without physical space, there will be no corresponding cyber virtual space. Likewise, all things in cyberspace serve the physical space and are projected onto it.

The online social network is social platforms of virtual space, where most of the roles completely conceal their own physical identities, many of them have nothing to do with their social identities, and what's more, some of them even have people confused about their genders and ages, so people completely travel in the virtual space. However, the ideologies, the way of understanding the objective world, the outlook on life and the world view, among other things—which those roles reflect in essence—are surely embodied in a certain form in the physical world. Therefore, public opinions from the online social networks, as virtual space, might cause ripples in the real world.

1.8.2 The Authenticity of Cyberspace from Its Representations

Online to Offline (O2O), on the surface, is a service mode or online-and-offline production mode, but it also reflects, from the other side, the true nature of the cyberspace. Just because of its reality, communication and interaction become possible. That explains why a dream—where interaction is impossible—is really "virtual". The authenticity of the network reflects that the application of the Internet is an interaction with the physical world, that the network is real and practical, and that the data generated by the network is not illusory but real. Admittedly, the authenticity of the network data has also brought about an impact on users' privacy. And the authenticity of network data is also pushing forward a new round of technological innovation, scientific inventions, and other endeavors.

To sum up, the authenticity of cyberspace exists objectively in the framework of state sovereignty and international public space. At the same time, it is also the objective basis for cyberspace sovereignty. Network authenticity is the equal basis to realize cyberspace governance. Facing up to the authenticity of the network is legal progress in the network world. Expounding the authenticity of the network is necessary for building cooperation and consensus, promoting the network justice and sharing the fruits of civilization among all countries around the world, especially developing countries.

1.9 The Definition of Cyberspace

Based on the preceding sections of this chapter, including the four elements of cyberspace, the description of cyberspace, the history of cyberspace evolution and the authenticity of cyberspace, we will define the cyberspace in order to deepen the research of follow-up problems. This section will describe cyberspace's definition from three perspectives: a perspective from which the public can understand cyberspace with ease, a normative perspective, and an international perspective.

1.9.1 The Definition from the Public Point of View

People are familiar with the traditional physical space. For example, the ocean space is the vast, connected water space on the surface of the earth that is composed of salt water. The salt water is the carrier of the ocean space. People can enter the ocean space by means of ships and other tools. There are underground resources at the bottom of the ocean and marine resources in its middle part. The water surface can provide convenient resources for transportation at sea. The ocean's water center is an internationally public area. The ocean near the land is the sea, with its resources belonging to the bordering land/country. For the ocean space, people pay their attention to the carrier (salt water), resources (underground resources, seafood), activities (transportation) and activity subjects (ship).

Based on that thinking habit, we can simply describe cyberspace as below:

"Cyberspace is man-made electromagnetic space with terminals, computers, network equipments as the carrier, over which people create, store, change, transmit, use and display data and do other things with data to accomplish specific activities. In such space, people, machines and objects can be organically connected together to interact and produce various kinds of information that affects people's lives, including content information, business information, control information, and so on."

That is, this special "space" is not the traditional, natural, physical space such as land, ocean, airspace, but specifically refers to special, man-made space that is specifically in support of electromagnetic signal activities; and it is a dedicated space which people create by relying on electromagnetism-related theories, using relevant technical facilities (a network platform formed with terminals, computers, network equipments, etc.) so as to generate, process and transmit electromagnetic signals. Just like seawater carrying ships, people enter cyberspace through the relevant information and communication technology (ICT) facilities as carriers. Data, which human beings process, is analog to the layers of ocean resources. Activities carried out by people in cyberspace, including data creation, storage, modification, exchange, use and display, are like activities in the ocean. People who conduct activities, as users, in the cyberspace are comparable to ships in the ocean.

The material basis for constructing cyberspace is networked, ICT-based infrastructure, including the networked, various information systems and information equipments. Hence, networking is the basic characteristic and the necessary premise of cyberspace. Since this space is of high value, internationally interacted and easy to cause the conflict of state interests, there is naturally the problem of cyberspace sovereignty.

1.9.2 The Definition from an Academic Point of View

In order to further analyze the cyberspace, we need to give a more exact definition from an academic perspective on the basis of the above vivid description. Cyberspace can be academically defined as below:

"Cyberspace is a man-made space for human beings to carry out 'generalized signals' 'operations' by relying on the 'ICT system' through the 'cyber role'. The 'cyber role' refers to the subject that generates and transmits the generalized signal, reflecting human's will. The 'ICT system' includes the Internet, various telecommunication networks and communication systems, various communication systems and radio and television networks, various computer systems, optical, electromagnetic or digital information processing facilities among various key industrial facilities—such as embedded processors and controllers. The 'generalized signal' means various electromagnetic signals usable for expression, storage, processing and transmission that are created based on optical, electrical, acoustic, magnetic and other principles, and other forms of signals—e.g., quantum signals and biological signals—that are capable of interaction with electromagnetic signals. Those signals lead to the results of generating, storing, processing, transmitting and displaying 'information' after being processed in the ICT system. The 'operation' refers to the behavior of expressing human will that the user accomplishes by relying on the generalized signal and using the ICT as means, including signal generation, data storage, status modification, information transmission and content display, collectively referred to as 'ICT activities'."

In such definition, the ICT system, generalized signal, cyber role and operation together reflect the four elements of cyberspace: "facilities, data, roles, operations." It also reflects the facilities' extensiveness and the data's broad spectrum, and it reflects the cyber role's generalization, subjectiveness, initiative, and purpose in operation.

1.9.3 The Presentation from the International Perspective

Cyberspace has attracted more and more attention and research in the international community. The definition of cyberspace terminology has also been varying, with arguments concerning it arising. From the perspective of the United Nations, the UN's relevant organizations generally do not use the term "cyberspace" when discussing cyberspace problems, but rather highlights the use of ICT. Because the countries represented by the European Union and Russia believe that "cyberspace" is so illusory and impractical that it fails to accurately express the specific things they care about. Of course, because the United States opposes the UN involvement in Internet governance, it likewise does not want the UN to care about cyberspace—which means watching the Internet. Therefore, the UN uses "ICT" more frequently.

Here is an example. The UN document A/70/174, entitled "Report of the Group of Governmental Experts on Developments in the Field of Information and Telecommunications in the Context of International Security", refers to cyberspace sovereignty in this way: "State sovereignty and international norms and principles that flow from sovereignty apply to the conduct by States of ICT-related activities and to their jurisdiction over ICT infrastructure within their territory".

There is no direct definition of cyberspace in the above sentence, but the meaning of cyberspace is actually expressed in the following two technical and social aspects: "ICT-related activities" and "ICT infrastructure".

As is evident from the above, the UN highlights the perspective of "ICT-related activities". We therefore define cyberspace from another point of view:

"Cyberspace is an artificial space built on ICT infrastructure to support people in carrying out various ICT-related information activities in the space. The ICT infrastructure includes the Internet, various telecommunication networks and communication systems, various communication systems and radio and television networks, various computer systems, and embedded processors and controllers among various key industrial facilities. The information activities include the creation, storage, change, transmission, use, display and other operations directed to information."

1.10 The Definition of Cyberspace Security

Cyberspace security is naturally the most important topic when we discuss cyberspace. Traditionally, people have only defined information security, expressing it as below: "Information security is an ability obtained by performing a set of suitable controls. The controls can be policies, conventions, procedures, organizational structures, and software functions. Building those controls aims to ensure that users' specific safety objectives can be met. The specific objectives show up in the protection aimed at the four core security attributes of confidentiality, identifiability, control and availability of information systems, information itself and information utilization—that is, ensuring that the information and information system is not grasped by the unauthorized, the information and operation on the information can be identified, the information and systems are controllable, and the information and system services are available to the authorized at any time. Information security is reflected on the four levels of physical security, operational security, data security, content security."

However, the traditional definition of information security is only around the information system, information itself and its use, which has not extended to the cyberspace. Besides, due to being limited by the technology itself, the definition's extension is not wide enough to cover social properties. Thus, to define cyberspace security, the four core security attributes and four levels of information security should firstly be taken into consideration. And then, it is necessary to consider cyberspace's domain specifics and activity specifics so as to fully express cyberspace security's non-technical extension.

The definition of cyberspace security is as follows:

"Cyberspace security involves security issues that exist in electromagnetic equipments, information communication systems, operating data and system applications in cyberspace. It must not only protect the ICT system—including the Internet, various telecommunication networks and communication systems, various communication systems and radio and television networks, various computer systems, and embedded processors and controllers among various key industrial facilities—and data carried by it from being attacked, but also prevent against and cope with risks concerning political security, national defense security, economic security, cultural security, social security and the like, which result from the use or abuse of the ICT system. Dealing with those risks needs comprehensive means such as law, management, technology and self-discipline, so as to guarantee confidentiality, identifiability (including integrity, authenticity, and non-repudiation), availability and control of the ICT system and the data carried by it."

Chapter 2
Understanding of the Traditional Sovereignty Concept

Abstract Todays, there is a convergence of high-tech evolution and the traditional sovereignty evolution. Cyberspace sovereignty is a natural extension of state sovereignty in the cyberspace. And the state sovereignty is also gradually formed in the evolution of the world order. The precondition for the existence of sovereignty is to possess territories, citizens, and regime due to its attributes in territory, citizens and politics. At the same time, the state sovereignty has its connotation and extension, that is, the right of independence, the right of equality, the right of self-defense and the right of jurisdiction. All the legal "Pillars" produced the modern cyberspace sovereignty. This Chapter's author is Prof. Dr. Zhao Hongrui.

Keywords State sovereignty · The right of independence · The right of equality The right of self-defense · The right of jurisdiction

The modern sovereignty concept reflects the ancient Chinese concept of "maintaining internal security and resisting foreign aggression", the national coordination is used as the supreme exercising means; western countries experienced the gambling and honing of patriarchy, theocracy, monarchical power, civil rights and sovereignty; in the international community, an international consensus about the modern sovereignty concept has been reached.

The legal meaning of the modern sovereignty concept is contained in *The Charter of the United Nations of 1945*.[1] In the last 20 years, UN has formed some international consensus about cyberspace and cyberspace sovereignty, and domestic legislation activities about internet regulation have been carried out all over the world. Generally, the modern sovereignty concept has naturally introduced think-

Prof. Dr. Zhao Hongrui, The Dean of Hunanities, Social Sciences & Law School of Harbin Institute of Technology, China, published *China Monetaory Aggregate Approach* (2013), *World Civilization Aggregate Approach* (2015), *On Cyber Soverignty* (2018) in Chinese. In English version, this chapter modified by Prof. Dr. Fang Binxing.

[1]The Charter of the United Nations. http://www.un.org/zh/sections/un-charter/introductory-note/index.html [2016-10-1].

B. Fang, *Cyberspace Sovereignty*,
https://doi.org/10.1007/978-981-13-0320-3_2

ing, legislation and practice about cyberspace, both in the level of UN and in the level of national laws. Cyberspace sovereignty theory and practice vary in the international community, but they have been a hot field catching more and more attention.

2.1 The Origin of Sovereignty

National cyberspace sovereignty shares some similarities with territorial sovereignty, popular sovereignty, political sovereignty, monetary sovereignty and genetic sovereignty in their basic connotation; in other words, element features of national cyberspace sovereignty are the same as those of the national sovereignty in both internal (connotation) and external aspects (denotation).

In 1912, Liang Qichao brought up in his *Discussion about Founding Principles of China* that "Everyone is longing for an integral new country"[2] and "make China an international country".[3] Liao Zhongkai mentioned in 1919: "It is a recently common theory from country scholars that the most crucial elements for making up a modern country lie in the following three things: people, territory and sovereignty."[4]

Looking through *The Charter of the United Nations of 1945*, both the theory of modern national sovereignty from Liang Qichao, and the theory of national sovereignty elements, including territory, people and government (or political system), from Liao Zhongkai are element features of modern national sovereignty. The connotation of modern national sovereignty is mutually dependent and inseparable, and none of them can be omitted. The people, territory (and its resources), and regime (and its governance) within a country together form the three basic connotations of national sovereignty.

Before the United Nations was founded in 1945, sovereignty theories were mainly from Europe. Ever since European countries signed *The Peace of Westphalia*[5] in 1648, theories about national sovereignty have been brought up, practiced, rethought and amended till a global consensus had been reached.

[2]Simple Analysis about the Democracy and Republicanism Theory of Liang Qichao Before and After the Revolution of 1911. http://www.doc88.com/p-9973955782365.html [2016-10-1].

[3]Founding Principles of China (Excerpt). http://www.my285.com/xdmj/lqc/047.htm [2016-10-1].

[4]Liao ZK. The Relationship between Chinese People and Territory in the Construction of A New Country, Series of Republic of China, Part II. Liao Zhongkai Collection. http://www.doc88.com/p-9009316582753.html [2016-10-1].

[5]Leo Gross. The peace of Westphalia, 1648–1948.http://www.jstor.org/stable/pdf/2193560.pdf [2016-12-1].

2.1.1 400-Year History of the Western Sovereignty Concept

Western scholars usually regard *Politics* of Aristotle and *Classical Roman Law* as the source of the sovereignty concept.[6] This viewpoint theoretically gave sovereignty the meaning of domestic "Supreme Right of Administration", but it failed to make clear whether the national sovereignty should be "equal" or "dominating" to foreign countries. The national sovereignty theory was first brought up by Jean Bodin,[7] who is a French thinker, jurist and politician of the 16th century. In 1576, Bodin published *On Sovereignty,*[8] and brought up the sovereignty concept and statism of "supreme" "**Monarchical Sovereignty**" for the first time. However, it was only a theory, and the national sovereignty had not been widely accepted and internationally practiced by the countries in the world.

The modern practice of national sovereignty began only 400 years ago in Europe. It originated from the gambling of international political order in Europe since the Thirty Years' War in 1618. Usually, the countries would reach a constitutional consensus on national territory (resources), people and regime by establishing the constitution and basic law within the country. Based on current consensus of the international community, national sovereignty is domestically constitutional to its own constitution, and is internationally approved and constitutional to *The Charter of the United Nations*.

1. Westphalia Sovereignty Practice

During the European "Thirty Years' War" of 1618-1648, European belligerents signed *The Peace of Westphalia*[9] based on *The Rights of War and Peace*[10] of Hugo Grotius, and started to acknowledge, commit and fulfill the national sovereignty theory in domestic political order and international relationship practices. Since then, the national sovereignty theories had truly become the core element of modern national system running.

---

[6] Merriam (2006) History of sovereignty theory since Rousseau (trans: Honghai BI). Law Press, Beijing, p 1. http://item.jd.com/1199363161.html [2016-10-1].

[7] Jean Bodin. http://plato.stanford.edu/entries/bodin/ [2016-10-1].

[8] Jean B (1994) On sovereignty: four books of six books on commonwealth. Cambridge University Press, Cambridge. https://book.douban.com/subject/2361924/ [2016-10-1].

[9] Simple Analysis of The Peace of Westphalia. http://wenku.baidu.com/link?url=0Vc0yFUdA3aSzWx0IwgTeSy_DfFF5nR72sxsbWVWVYnIHiC81Q-EaFUJ0jNrsdIUkPHJ2yKhkriSVZzM6tL2jrtWH_B7jbeAWxyGCIawSc8G [2016-10-1].

[10] Grotius H (1625) The rights of war and peace, http://detail.dangdang.com/23277751.html [2016-10-1].

2. Sovereignty Theories before the Foundation of the United Nations[11]

Prior to the three waves of independence of modern nations and countries, early sovereignty theories focused on the national sovereignty's attribute of "maintaining internal security".[12] In this era of "National Sovereignty 1.0", from "Monarchical Sovereignty" of Bodin, to "National Sovereignty" of Niccolò Machiavelli,[13] till "Popular Sovereignty" of Jean-Jacques Rousseau,[14] "Utility Sovereignty" of Jeremy Bentham,[15] and "History Sovereignty" of Henry Maine,[16] the cognition of traditional sovereignty theories in modern times comes down to two points: one is the inseparability of sovereignty, and the other is the ultimate power of sovereignty. These theories of national sovereignty are all restricted to internal absoluteness.

2.1.2 Three Waves of Independence by Sovereign Nations of the World

Modern sovereignty is based on the independence of all countries. National sovereignty is first primarily on the territory of the country, but there is no boundary line on earth. As the first element of sovereignty, territorial space did not clearly exist at the very beginning. Boundary lines of all countries were artificially drawn, and those were determined by national states during the independence of "Three waves".

1. The first wave of national independence

In 1648, *The Peace of Westphalia* came out to determine the international order of Europe; besides, it delimited national boundaries on the continent of Europe,

[11]Simple Analysis of The Peace of Westphalia. http://wenku.baidu.com/link?url=0Vc0yFUdA3aSzWx0IwgTeSy_DfFF5nR72sxsbWVWVYnIHiC81Q-EaFUJ0jNrsdIUkPHJ2yKhkriSVZzM6tL2jrtWH_B7jbeAWxyGCIawSc8G [2016-10-1].

[12][US] Samuel P Huntington. The Third Wave The Wave of Democratization in Late 20th Century, translated by Jinggen OU-YANG. Beijing: China Renmin University Press, issued in 2013. http://item.jd.com/11218509.html [2016-10-1].

[13]Machiavelli. The Prince. The Chapter about Properties of "Ragione di Stato". http://www.docin.com/p-825087644.html [2016-10-1].

[14]On Rousseau's Theory of Popular Sovereignty. http://wenku.baidu.com/link?url=tIY9v0njKOvpOdiDALSMebnNYlgP4yuFiFIDTWsAvnbKmTKA6-w0VXMHml3CYse0sxicft335gzdQbNQcvjUO72O1X8f96hfpt2YLb6izSP_ [2016-10-1].

[15]Bentham. An Introduction to the Principles of Morals and Legislation. The Commercial Press, 2000: 60. Yunjing CHE, The application of Bentham's Utilizatism in His Sovereignty Theory—After Reading Jeremy Bentham's A Fragment on Government, Journal of Chongqing University of Science and Technology, 2009(11): 20. http://wenku.baidu.com/link?url=XF2F6kxQrc2UTsKXdbqzQmT_ZPox7KcnDorsPq0Hyd2-S2whaKbovoG3JaEnBHkrhvZsbx06-qeqxNbB-M5xO3LYH962X9iA5NtpiUyMqV7 [2016-10-1].

[16][UK] Maine. Ancient Law. Translated by Jingyi SHEN. The Commercial Press, 1959: 7. http://www.360doc.com/content/12/0911/17/99504_235572412.shtml [2016-9-28].

acknowledged independence and sovereignty of nations, and showed that national sovereignty, national territory and national independence had become principles to be followed in international relationships. As a result, diplomatic envoys were established among countries so as to perform activities in foreign affairs.

2. The second wave of national independence

Major events, such as American Independence, the French Revolution, the postwar 1814 Vienna System of Napoleon, the Independence Movement of Latin America in the 19th century, Versailles Balance of 1919, and Yalta Balance of 1943 and so on successively occurred in the international community, as a result, the "sovereignty ripple" in the world map was further expanded and strengthened.[17]

3. The third wave of national independence

In the 20th century, following the end of World War II and the beginning of the Cold War, the European colonial system triggered worldwide national independence movements, as a result of which plenty of new national countries were born in Asia, Africa and Latin America, then the former Soviet Union disassembled, Yugoslavia divided, Crimea joined into Russia, till the Syria civil war and the chaos caused by wars among "Islamic States" happened nowadays, separation, reunion and evolution of sovereignty in the world map are still fermented in the international community.[18]

2.1.3 The Internally Relative Constitutionality of Sovereignty: Postwar Iraq

Sovereignty is permanent, so is the right to use resources. Domestically, sovereignty comforts to the constitution of the country, but changes of constitution, government or head of state do not necessarily mean the change of sovereignty. For instance, before the war in Iraq, Saddam broke through the constitution bans and respectively transferred the cooperation and development rights of three oil fields, so as to gain supports from Russia, China and France. China acquired the cooperation and exploitation right of al-Ahdab oil field[19] and singed the cooperation

[17]Zhao HR (2015) World civilization aggregate approach. China Legal Publishing House, (029): 113. http://item.jd.com/1657437195.html [2016-10-1].

[18]Historical origin and review of global hegemony of modern America. http://bbs.tianya.cn/post-worldlook-1364157-1.shtml [2016-4-21].

[19]Discovered in 1979, the al-Ahdab oil field is located in central and southern Iraq and is 160 kms away from Baghdad; its structural area is about 200 km^2, and its oil reserves are about one billion barrels. In June 1997, Petro China and the Iraq government signed the agreement for exploiting the al-Ahdab oil field, but the agreement was then suspended due to the political environment changes in Iraq. http://baike.baidu.com/link?url=BR8EGkTknC8eaQtyo7hi-JqT-KmbDDln44vj-BKeLT7f3LElqkjxhAUOZega6aqFzVm-sILoMB8pPa2m-7wA_a [2016-4-28].

contract. However, as the Iraq War broke out, America intervened in the war and overturned the Iraq Saddam regime, led to a series of events occurred in Iraq, such as regime changes, constitution amendment, the change of president and so on. In the postwar Iraq, the president had been changed, the constitution was amended, the government was regrouped, and the US army was stationed, which then raised the question, whether the cooperation and development contract of oil fields with China was still valid? This is a resource inheritance problem beyond the rules of laws and reaching the supreme national sovereignty.

In November 2008, after multilateral negotiations, the Oasis Oil Company of China eventually signed a new al-Ahdab oil field development and service contract in Baghdad with the state-owned North Oil Company of Iraq, and officially started the project on March 11, 2009. The al-Ahdab oil field project is the first foreign oil cooperation project after the Iraq War, in which China invested about 3 billion US dollars in the form of the Technical Service Contract (TSC). The contract term is also 23 years and can be extended according to actual situations. The Chinese party is supposed to get a service charge of 6 US dollars per barrel at the beginning, and then the service charge would gradually be reduced to 3 US dollars per barrel. The daily output of crude oil can reach as much as 25,000 barrels at the first three years, and would get a production capacity of 115,000 barrels per day within 6 years. This example shows that China's rights and interests in oil field cooperation and exploitation transferred by Iraqi sovereignty have been effectively inherited, although the invasion of the U.S. into Iraq is a violation against *The Charter of the United Nations*.

2.1.4 The Externally Relative Constitutionality of Sovereignty: Switzerland and the Tax Haven

Sovereignty is externally in compliance with *The Charter of the United Nations* so as to be widely accepted by the international community. However, beyond the current 193 state members[20] of the UN, autonomous entities having relative sovereignty still exist because of historical reasons.

Switzerland has always been called "the stable oasis", and has escaped from 400 years' of European war, including two world wars, due to its status of permanent neutrality. In 1934, Switzerland issued the *Bank Secrecy Act,* so as to improve modern rule by law of financial shelter.[21] It's guessed by some scholars that the establishment of Switzerland may have been founded by some Northern European forces for financial safes. In history, Switzerland has always been regarded as a safe for depositing fortune by countries in war, and Switzerland has

[20]http://www.un.org/zh/member-states/index.html. [2016-12-31].

[21]Whole Story of the Bank Secrecy Act of Switzerland. http://history.huanqiu.com/world/2015-02/5711180.html [2016-9-20].

evolved to be the largest financial offshore centre in the world. Nowadays, since the international community is fighting against oversea tax evasion with full strength, Switzerland has to wave the white flag. Switzerland tried to cooperate with the international community in the fight against money laundering by passing the decree of *Freezing and Return of Illicit Assets of Foreign Sensitive Politicians*, so as to improve its image. On May 6, 2015, Switzerland promised to hand over detailed information of foreigners' accounts.[22] Many UN agencies are set in Geneva of Switzerland, and Switzerland also participated in most activities of UN specialized agencies, however, Switzerland did not apply to join the UN until September 10, 2002 when most citizens were supportive in the national referendum. For quite a long time, it is deemed by Swiss that Switzerland would inevitably have to take orders from a great power or would get involved into international disputes once Switzerland joined into UN, which would influence the neutrality status of Switzerland.

Beyond the UN, there are lots of islands all over the world which were set for tax evasion during England's colonial period, such as the Virgin Islands, Cayman Islands, Bermuda, and Mauritius and so on. In the name of autonomous sovereignty or national sovereignty, these famous offshore financial centers and "tax havens" usually formulate company laws with hardly no tax restrictions, namely, no taxation on profits, extreme confidentiality of accounts, anonymous shareholders, full circulation of foreign currencies. Generally speaking, nations or areas identified as tax havens are all characterized in zero-taxation or extremely-low taxation (particularly for income tax and capital gains tax), strict bank or business secrecy law, open foreign currency with no restrictions (free channels for capital), no cooperation with foreign tax authorities (signing no or very few tax treaties), convenient transportation and information (excellent mobility and concealing).

2.2 The Connotation of Sovereignty

As concluded by scholars such as Liang Qichao, Liao Zhongkai and so on, national sovereignty internally includes the following three basic elements: territory (territorial land, territorial waters, territorial airspace and resources), people (including foreigners living in or associated with the territory of the country), and regime (including the political systems that are not yet fully independent and autonomous). The basic principle of national sovereignty is internally required to be following with the spirits of the constitution of the country, and enjoys the territory unity, people unity and regime unity, which constitute the inseparable, sustainable and full sovereignty.

[22]Sina Finance. Swiss Bank is still Tax Haven. http://finance.sina.com.cn/world/20151013/014523453877.shtml [2016-4-22].

2.2.1 The First Natural Attribute of Sovereignty Connotation: Territory Sovereignty

According to Article 78 of *The Charter of the United Nations*,[23] "The trusteeship system shall not apply to territories which have become Members of the United Nations, relationship among which shall be based on respect for the principle of sovereignty equality." In *Oppenheim's International Law*,[24] Territory is described as "a determined part on earth governed by the sovereignty of the country".

The explanation of territory defined by the International Law can be expanded to be territorial land, territorial waters and territorial airspace without including public regions of human beings, such as the outer space, the Polar Regions, and high seas. Out of respect to territory sovereignty, one country is not allowed to encroach, divide or annex territories of other countries, and, unless permitted by other countries, is not permitted to send forces, warships or policemen to enter into or pass through the territory of other countries, or send planes to fly over the territory of other countries, and is not permitted to carry out administration or government activities within the territory of another country, or to perform official enquiries or to incite its citizens to perform secret activities within the territory of other countries; otherwise, it would be a violation of the International Law.[25] If one country is to infringe the sovereignty of another country by initiating different types of network warfare, such as the precise strikes on enemy network by using cyber weapons, electronic-impulse weapons, and electronic-biological weapons or the like, civil network or civil entities will be damaged at the same time as the military strike. Therefore, the cyberspace sovereignty and the territory sovereignty possess natural unity; as either resources or assets of a country, the data sovereignty in the cyberspace sovereignty also shares the natural unity with the territory sovereignty.

2.2.2 The Second Natural Attribute of Sovereignty Connotation: People Sovereignty

It is mentioned in the first sentence in the first paragraph of the preface of *The Charter of the United Nations*[26]: "WE THE PEOPLES OF THE UNITED NATIONS DETERMINED, to save succeeding generations from the scourge of

[23]Chapter XII of The Chapter of the United Nations:International Trusteeship System. http://www.un.org/zh/sections/un-charter/chapter-xii/index.html [2016-9-20].

[24]Sir RJ, Arthur SW (1992) Oppenheim's international Law, 9th edn. 5: 563. http://yuedu.163.com/book_reader/3beba30312b64cf38062e65ac09d4ddb_4/24 [2016-9-28].

[25]Lu L C. On National Territory and Sovereignty. http://www.cermn.com/art202706.aspx [2016-9-28].

[26]The preamble of The Charter of the United Nations. http://www.un.org/zh/sections/un-charter/preamble/index.html [2016-9-20].

war, which twice in our lifetime has brought untold sorrow to **mankind**, and to reaffirm faith in fundamental **human rights**, in **the dignity** and worth of the human person, in the equal rights of men and women and of nations large and small, and to establish conditions under which justice and respect for the obligations arising from treaties and other sources of international law can be maintained, and to promote social progress and better standards of **life** in larger freedom, AND FOR THESE ENDS to practice tolerance and live together in peace with one another as good neighbors, and to unite our strength to maintain international peace and security, and to ensure, by the acceptance of principles and the institution of methods, that armed forces shall not be used, save in the common interest, and to employ international machinery for the promotion of the economic and social advancement of **all peoples**, HAVE RESOLVED TO COMBINE OUR EFFORTS TO ACCOMPLISH THESE AIMS".

The people defined here are THE PEOPLES in English plural form, and "super-sovereignty" people do not exist at all. The viewpoints of popular sovereignty have been clarified as early as in Aristotle and Bodin times, but its core status in national security had not been established until the preface in *The Charter of the United Nations*. Correspondingly, all of the activities of people should be protected by the sovereignty, and all of the activities of people in cyberspace should be protected by the cyberspace sovereignty of this country. As a result, the cyberspace sovereignty and the popular sovereignty of this country enjoy the natural unity.

2.2.3 The Third Natural Attribute of Sovereignty Connotation: Politics Sovereignty

Political sovereignty is a sum of the political system (Regime) and the administrative authorities (Government) of a country, and the government is the exerciser, regulator, vindicator and representative of the national sovereignty. It is mentioned in the first sentence in the paragraph of the preamble of *The Charter of the United Nations*: "Accordingly, our respective Governments, through representatives assembled in the city of San Francisco, who have exhibited their full powers found to be in good and due form, have agreed to the present Charter of the United Nations and do hereby establish an international organization to be known as the United Nations". For another example, it is stipulated in the first item of Article 57[27] of *The Charter of the United Nations*: "The various specialized agencies, established by intergovernmental agreement and having wide international responsibilities, as defined in their basic instruments, in economic, social, cultural, educational, health, and related fields, shall be brought into relationship with the

[27]Chapter IX of The Charters of the United Nations: INTERNATIONAL ECONOMY AND SOCIAL COOPERATION. http://www.un.org/zh/sections/un-charter/chapter-ix/index.html [2016-9-20].

United Nations in accordance with the provisions of Article 63." It proves that, according to the United Nations, the governments of the countries are representatives of the sovereignty of the countries.

2.2.4 *Un-evolved Sovereignty: Sovereignty Protection of Non-self-Governing Territories*

According to Article 73[28] in Chapter XI (Declaration Regarding Non-self-governing Territories) of *The Charter of the United Nations*, "Members of the United Nations which have or assume responsibilities for the administration of territories **whose peoples have not yet attained a full measure of self-government** recognize the principle that the interests of the inhabitants of these territories are paramount, and accept as a sacred trust the obligation to promote to the utmost, within the system of international peace and security established by the present Charter, the well-being of the inhabitants of these territories, and, to this end: to develop self-government, to take due account of the political aspirations of the peoples, and to assist them in the progressive development of their free political institutions, according to the particular circumstances of each territory and its peoples and their varying stages of advancement…." It shows that, instead of discriminating and indulging hegemony, UN fully respects the sovereignty of non-self-governing territories and promotes modernization of self-governing regimes.

2.3 Extensions of Sovereignty

In *The Charter of the United Nations*, each equal country is endowed with the right of international self-defense, the right of international self-independence and the right of international equality in the category of national sovereignty. These three sovereignty rights are advocated and exercised among countries. The countries have reached international rules through equal sovereignty in public sphere such as space, polar, high sea and so on, and jointly constitute the extension of state sovereignty. The basic principles of national sovereignty are supposed to be in accordance with the spirits of domestic constitution as well as the world order managed by *The Charter of the United Nations*.

---

[28]Chapter XI of The Charters of the United Nations: DECLARATION REGARDING NON-SELF-GOVERNINGTERRITORIES. http://www.un.org/zh/sections/un-charter/chapter-xi/index.html [2016-9-20].

2.3.1 The First Natural Attribute of Sovereignty Denotation: The Right of International Self-Defense

Defense is a right of International Law, which is rooted in the International Law and is clearly recognized and supported by Article 51 of *The Charter of the United Nations*. The legal concept of self-defense was derived from domestic laws and then was introduced into the International Law; moreover, it was applicable among countries from the very beginning, and became the reason for proving legitimacy of wars. The right of self-defense in International Law refers to the inherent rights or natural rights for a country to use force so as to fight against foreign armed attacks and protect itself.

According to Article 51 of *The Charter of the United Nations*,[29] "Nothing in the present Charter shall impair the inherent right of individual or collective self-defense if an armed attack occurs against a Member of the United Nations, until the Security Council has taken measures necessary to maintain international peace and security. Measures taken by Members in the exercise of this right of self-defense shall be immediately reported to the Security Council and shall not in any way affect the authority and responsibility of the Security Council under the present Charter to take at any time such action as it deems necessary to maintain or restore international peace and security". Apparently, the right of self-defense is exercised by a state sovereignty to repulse foreign armed attack or to eliminate approaching threats so as to restore or sustain the original legal state.[30]

The right of self-defense is an inherent right of a sovereign nation, but it is strictly restricted when it is specifically exercised. For instance, in the case of network warfare, what kind of technical skills and evidence can prove the existence of "network attack"? How will the UN determine the attack power and "take necessary measures"? It is believed that network warfare can be subdivided into various ways such as network information stealing, system crash, remote control, prewar strikes and composite strikes or the like[31]; however, as for these ways, criteria for judging strike source, strike intensity and loss severity are still missing nowadays. Therefore, whether a sovereign nation can advocate and successfully exercise this inherent right in the cyberspace depends largely on the technical skills of the country involved and the justice determination in the cyberspace. Of course,

---

[29]Chapter VII of The Charter of the United Nations: ACTION WITH RESPECT TO THREATS TO THE PEACE, BREACHES OF THE PEACE, AND ACTS OF AGGRESSION. http://www.un.org/zh/sections/un-charter/chapter-vii/index.html [2016-9-20].

[30]Yu M C. Legal issues about the Application of the Right of Self-defense. JURIST, 2003(3): 154. http://www.doc88.com/p-9079395623944.html [2016-9-28].

[31]Originated from the speech given on October 12-14, 2014 by Professor Hashimoto Yasuaki from the National Security Institute of Japanese Defense Agency, and the speech was given in the law school of Harbin Institute of Technology about CYBER LAW, non-traditional security, and the topic of government by law.

if the domestic governance of a country is unstable, or if the country is not capable to sustain integral territory sovereignty, popular sovereignty and political sovereignty, the exercising of international self-defense will certainly be affected.

2.3.2 The Second Natural Attribute of Sovereignty Denotation: The Right of International Independence

According to paragraph 4 in Article 2[32] of The *Charter of the United Nations*, "All Members shall refrain in their international relations from the threat or use of force against **the territorial integrity or political independence of any state**, or in any other manner inconsistent with the Purposes of the United Nations." Externally political independence and internally political autonomy are two sides of a national sovereignty. However, in the real-world order, many countries are politically independent in name only, and have virtually abandoned the autonomy of national security by means of military alliance.

In this way, the national security autonomy depends on the following 6 indicators including "the possession of nuclear power, industry system, military industry system, the possession of veto, mobilization ability, alliance relation", on such a basis, it is possible to measure "History + Geopolitics + Strength" of a nation, and to analysis and determine the strategic game in the future. Of course, it should be further measured in altogether 10 categories including 5 traditional security fields, such as conventional weapons, chemical weapons, nuclear weapons, frontier defense and international peacekeeping, and 5 non-traditional security fields, such as outer space, cyberspace, energy, monetary market and anti-terrorism. In order to measure the capacity of national security autonomy, the following 6 factors should serve as the criteria for judging whether a country satisfies the security autonomy conditions: one country is regarded to possess independent national security autonomy only when the country possesses the following six characteristics: ① autonomous regime (no civil unrest); ② coordinated military and politics (rather than disconnection between military and politics); ③ independent national defense (anti-aggression capability); ④ independent strategy (the possession of nuclear power); ⑤ complete industries (each of the main industries possesses production and research-development capability); ⑥ international recognition (by permanent members of the UN Security Council). The three standards for judging "half-autonomy of national security" are as follows: instead of possessing all of the 6 criteria, one country may partly possess the security autonomy such as: ① the country possesses nuclear power and is attached to a certain military group; or ② the country possesses nuclear power but is antagonistic to some military groups; or ③ the country possesses nuclear power and is neutral or

[32]Chapter I of The Charter of the United Nations: PURPOSES AND PRINCIPLES. http://www.un.org/zh/sections/un-charter/chapter-i/index.html [2016-9-20].

non-aligned. Generally, the security can be divided as autonomous, half-autonomous and non-autonomous according to the above criteria, and the nations can be divided into "three worlds" on the basis of security autonomy[33]: among the 193 countries who have joined the United Nations and the 2 observer countries (Vatican, Palestine) all over the world, only three of them are totally autonomous, i.e. China, US and Russia, accounting for 1.5%; 14 of them are half-autonomous, accounting for 7.2%, wherein Britain and France possess veto power but are subject to NATO; the rest 178 countries are non-autonomous, accounting for 91.3%, wherein North Korea is suspected to possess nuclear power but has unsatisfactory historical geopolitics, veto power, and capability and so on.

Without territory sovereignty, popular sovereignty and political sovereignty, there would certainly be no international status like independent nations. In the field of non-traditional security, the national cyberspace is substantively both "interconnected" and "autonomous"; the cyberspace security "autonomy" of all nations are not equally divided according to the seats of the five permanent members of UN. America is the only country which has realized cyberspace security autonomy. The overall situation of the national security of China is autonomous, but the cyberspace security field is half-autonomous; in addition, the currency security, space security, energy security and anti-terrorism security of China are also relatively half-autonomous but slightly better than cyberspace security autonomy.[34] Therefore, in order to realize cyberspace security and autonomy, it is necessary to create an objectively feasible and unique top-level designing way for safeguarding national cyberspace sovereignty.

2.3.3 The Third Natural Attribute of Sovereignty Denotation: The Right of International Equality

The right of equality is one of the fundamental rights of a state, and it is a basic representation of a country's sovereignty. According to researches, this term first appeared in *Moscow Declaration* of October 13, 1943.[35] Ian Brownlie once pointed out, "The sovereignty and equality of States represent the basic constitutional doctrine of the law of nations".[36] The international equality right is apparently

---

[33]Zhao HR (2015) World civilization aggregate approach. China Legal Publishing House, Beijing. http://item.jd.com/1657437195.html [2016-10-1].

[34]Zhao HR (2015) World civilization aggregate approach. China Legal Publishing House, Beijing, p 205–262. http://item.jd.com/1657437195.html [2016-10-1].

[35]Moscow Declaration (1943). http://wk.baidu.com/view/a1a2b97701f69e31433294ae [2016-9-28].

[36]Ian Brownlie. Principles of Public International Law (6thed.), 2003: 287. Colin Waarbrick, Brownlie's Principles of Public International Law: An Assessment. http://www.ejil.org/pdfs/11/3/546.pdf [2016-10-1].

important to sovereign states. It is clearly stipulated in paragraph one in Article 2[37] of *The Charter of the United Nations*, "The Organization is based on the principle of the sovereign equality of all its Members". Furthermore, according to paragraph one of Article 18,[38] "Each member of the General Assembly shall have one vote"; and according to paragraph two, "Decisions of the General Assembly on important questions shall be made by a two-thirds majority of the members present and voting." Seen through the appearance, the essence of international equality right is also divided into levels. According to *The Charter of the United Nations*, national sovereignty can be divided into three equal levels.

1. "General sovereignty equality in principle"

According to paragraph 2 of Article 1 in Chapter I[39] of *The Charter of the United Nations*, "To develop friendly relations among nations based on **respect for the principle of equal rights and self-determination of peoples**, and to take other appropriate measures to strengthen universal peace." It is prescribed in paragraph one of Article 2, "The Organization is based on the principle of the sovereign equality of all its Members." "General sovereignty equality in principle" safeguards the universal principle of "one vote for each member state" and "the minority obeying the majority". It is also implemented into concrete stipulations (e.g. *DECLARATION ON PRINCIPLES OF INTERNATIONAL LAW FRIENDLY RELATIONS AND COOPERATION AMONG STATES IN ACCORDANCE WITH THE CHARTER OF THE UNITED NATIONS*).[40] This principle contains the connotation of sovereignty equality and includes the following contents of enjoying equal legal status and full sovereignty, being obliged to respect sovereignty of other countries, no infringement to national territory integrity and political independence, freedom of choosing a political, economical and cultural development system, peaceful coexistence and so on.

2. "Voting right to world peace of 15 UN Security Council members"

The voting right to world peace is represented as the voting power owned by 5 permanent members of the UN Security Council and 10 non-permanent members surpassing other 179 states. Established under *The Charter of the United Nations*, the Security Council of the United Nations is the only UN organization having the right to take military actions for sustaining international peace and security. 15 Security Council members have the right to suggest the United Nations ceasing

---

[37]Chapter I of The Charter of the United Nations: PURPOSES AND PRINCIPLES. http://www.un.org/zh/sections/un-charter/chapter-i/index.html [2016-9-20].

[38]Chapter IV of The Charter of the United Nations: THE GENERAL ASSEMBLY. http://www.un.org/zh/sections/un-charter/chapter-iv/index.html [2016-9-20].

[39]Chapter I of The Charter of the United Nations: PURPOSES AND PRINCIPLES.http://www.un.org/zh/sections/un-charter/chapter-i/index.html [2016-9-20].

[40]DECLARATION ON PRINCIPLES OF INTERNATIONAL LAW FRIENDLY RELATIONS AND COOPERATION AMONG STATES IN ACCORDANCE WITH THE CHARTER OF THE UNITED NATIONS. http://wenku.baidu.com/view/3e15707d5acfa1c7aa00cc58.html [2016-12-31].

or restoring the rights of other member states. Each member state of the Security Council has one vote to security issues. According to paragraph one of Article 12[41] of *The Charter of the United Nations*, "While the Security Council is exercising in respect of any dispute or situation the functions assigned to it in the present Charter, the General Assembly shall not make any recommendation with regard to that dispute or situation unless the Security Council so requests." It can be seen that members of the Security Council take more responsibilities and obligations for international security, and they enjoy the world peace voting power surpassing other 179 state members.

3. "One-vote Veto of 5 permanent members of the UN Security Council to world peace"

One-vote veto means that each permanent member of the Security Council has the right to stop the Security Council from passing proposals for non-procedural matters that is not accepted by the member. According to paragraph 1 of Article 23 of *The Charter of the United States*, the Republic of China, the United States of America, the Soviet Union, the United Kingdom of Great Britain and Northern Ireland and France are permanent members enjoying special status; according to paragraph 3 of Article 27, the 5 permanent members of the Security Council "equally" have a voting power surpassing other countries for non-procedural matters, and have the power to veto.[42] According to Article 108 and paragraph 2 of Article 109 of *The Charter of the United States*, the five permanent members of the Security Council even have veto to the amendments and taking effects of *The Charter of the United Nations*, which is a significant legal source of the International Law.[43] Besides common veto, permanent members of the Security Council can also use veto in the following two ways, one of which is "Double Veto". Before 1950s, permanent members of the Security Council usually broadened the scope of veto, which means they would make any matter be non-procedural and then veto proposals for this matter. Then UN tried to restrain this privilege, namely, the President of the Security Council usually judged a certain matter to be procedural according to Article 30 of *Provisional Rules of Procedure*[44] of the Security Council, and the ruling of the President would be effective unless it is challenged by more than 9 members of the Security Council. The other way is the "Invisible Veto", namely, the permanent members of the Security Council often threatened to use veto so as to make a relevant proposal live up to their will.

---

[41]Chapter IV of The Charter of the United Nations: THE GENERAL ASSEMBLY. http://www.un.org/zh/sections/un-charter/chapter-iv/index.html [2016-9-20].

[42]Chapter V of The Charter of the United Nations: THE SECURITY COUNCIL. http://www.un.org/zh/sections/un-charter/chapter-v/index.html [2016-9-20].

[43]Chapter 18 of The Charter of the United Nations: Amendments. http://www.un.org/zh/sections/un-charter/chapter-xviii/index.html [2016-9-20].

[44]Provisional Rules of Procedure of the UN Security Council, Chapter VI: Conduct of Business. http://www.un.org/zh/sc/about/rules/chapter6.shtml [2016-10-1].

2.4 Applications of Sovereignty

The order of sovereignty equality can be sorted by universality or by logicality. The self-defense, independence and equality of sovereignty are sorted right according to the producing logicality of national sovereignty. One advantage of the discussion sorted in this way is to make clear the following facts: the international equality of national sovereignty is equality of different levels, rather than absolute equality or real equality; the practical utilization of national sovereignty depends more on the geographic history, the world order viewpoint, and the internal and external constitutionality of each country.

2.4.1 Geographic History Determines Endowments of Traditional National Sovereignty

Any system visualized for the world is based on its spatial visualization; any world order would be firstly implemented into a geographic space.

1. "Equilibrium endowment" of European powers surrounding Alps

The most vivid description about European order is a "equilibrium fight" of European powers "surrounding Alps". This equilibrium feature of Europe is largely determined by its geographic feature. Europe is a part of Eurasia. Its northern, western and southern sides are respectively on the brink of Arctic, Atlantic, and Mediterranean and Black Sea, and its eastern and southeastern parts are adjacent to Asia; its horizontal contour is shattered, and population centers distributed everywhere are isolated by numerous mountains and forests. The average height of the entire Europe is 340 m, and the terrain is dominated by plains. A series of mountains stand in the center, they are integrally called the Alps Mountain Range. From Greece, Italy, France, Spain, Portugal, England to German, European powers are all at the foot of the Alps and this geographical situation results in endless wars in Europe dating back to 2500 years, and makes it impossible for Europe to be united, or to generate a single sovereignty. As believed by Paul Kennedy, "The political diversity of Europe is largely caused by its geographical condition."[45] Since the "terrorist incident of 9·11" in 2001, America started the global fight against terrorism and came back to Asia-Pacific named as "Rebalance"; however, seen as a whole, the international security order in recent 70 years since the second World War is still in the era of "intercontinental equilibrium" and "intercontinental containment". It is predicted that the world security order in the future 30 years may

[45]Kennedy P (2006) The rise and fall of the great powers. International Culture Press, Beijing, p 16. http://lz.book.sohu.com/fullscreen-chapter-57606.html [2016-9-28].

still be around and stay in the historical vestige of European "equilibrium".[46] This is the sovereignty destiny under the geographical order of Europe.

2. "Harmony Endowment" of East Asia with high northwest and low southeast geography

Facing the Pacific Ocean, East Asia includes China, Japan, Korea, North Korea and Mongolia, and its terrain in northwest is high and the terrain in southeast is low. Geographically, the terrain of East Asia can be divided into three platforms: the first platform is Qinghai-Tibet Plateau with an altitude of over 4000 km; the second platform is a series of basins and plateaus; the third platform is plains, hills and islands. The largest country in East Asia is China, the geographic feature of which is a typical representative of East Asia. Since the ancient times about 4000 years ago, China has become the most important civilized state in this area from the country established by Chinese civilization originating from the Yellow River Basin (Central Plain).

The concept of "Universe" in ancient China was first popular in Spring and Autumn Period,[47] and refers to the territory centered around Zhou Dynasty more often, e.g. Jiuzhou and Sihai which are poetic names for China. The "Universe View" is a series of views on world order formed by using the spatial concept in the thoughts of ancient China. It influenced policies made by Chinese dynasties in all ages for processing relations with foreign countries. It became the concept basis of the "Universe System". The "Universe" concept constructed by Chinese ideologists forms the largest space unit because it contains "outside" in the space of "Universe". Instead of the outside beyond the "Universe", the word "outside" in ancient China refers to the exterior part of the "Universe", namely, the border part relative to the center. In *China*, Shi Jie mentioned: "The sky is above, and the ground is below; China is the center of the world between the sky and the ground, while the four barbarians are in the remote area. Barbarians are exterior, and China is interior. There are interior and exterior of the Universe, so there are boundaries."[48] The viewpoint of "The universe is one family"[49] was directly brought up in *The Book of Rites-Liyun*, and this "Universe view" finally formed the integral situation that peoples from five areas including "China" and "Yi Man Rong Di" are jointly called "universe" and live together in "Four Seas". Dominated by the Universe view, center dynasties never accepted the political powers of surrounding

[46]Zhao HR (2015) World civilization aggregate approach. China Legal Publishing House, Beijing. http://item.jd.com/1657437195.html [2016-10-1].

[47]He XH (2006) Analysis of Universe view of ancient China. Southeast Asian Studies 1: 50. http://www.mianfeiwendang.com/doc/80fdadc6a878f5c1cd549ab0/1 [2016-9-28].

[48]On National Thought of Shi Jie—Take On China as the center. http://wenku.baidu.com/link?url=yO2Xuo88CIgnpx81N_tGN7tYoj7XPdL-tbo-mqGDGBaLrLtsNYkr4kry5pWiCwX4gF3hbUAGvYjVUQktSFkS_wIbz72lZsz_cU5R8q9BNLC [2016-10-1].

[49]Original text/Translation of The Book of Rites-Liyun. http://www.360doc.com/content/14/1025/18/19764134_419772974.shtml [2016-10-1].

peoples in law, and the borders between them were more like the line of actual control between different regimes, rather than national boundaries. Unlike the coexistence of numerous sovereign states in Europe, the thought of "Universe view" refers to the "Great Unity". Throughout the history of East Asia, it is clear that the unity of "Universe" could be realized as long as the geographic advantage of "high northwest, low southeast" was utilized. Historical evidence includes the First Emperor of Qin, Emperor Wu of Han, Emperor Gaozu of Tang, and the entering of northern Shanxi by the Central Red Army or the like. The "Universe" predestination of East Asia is different from the "Sovereignty" predestination of Europe. The "Sovereignty" predestination of Europe finally determines national boundaries and sovereignties through "balanced fighting" and signing treaties of peace; however, the "Universe" predestination of East Asia does not generate the concept of sovereignty at all, and the people commonly believed that national security can be realized only by "Universe Domination" after the unification. This is the "Universe Endowment" of the geographical order of East Asia.

3. "Hegemony Endowment" of North America: Isolation, Cold War, and Domination

The main object of hegemony is to realize the peaceful interests under its ruling by constructing the geographical order. Even since the Roman Empire, no country is as dominant as America. The geographical characteristics of North America conform to the following three historic stages experienced by its national sovereignty: Isolation, Cold War, and Hegemony. Facing Atlantic in east, Pacific in west, and Arctic Ocean in north, North America is separated from South America in south by Panama Canal, and is separated from Europe by the Denmark Strait in the east, forming its advantageous geographical location. America is the most developed country in the world it is also a typical representative of the sovereignty endowment of "Isolation, Cold War, and Domination". The super-strong strength of America is based on its uniquely advantageous natural conditions: America is the fourth largest country in the world, and 2/3 of its territory is inhabitable; it faces the Atlantic in the east and the Pacific in the west, possesses long coastline and numerous natural harbors, and has accesses to the world's most productive fishing areas; within its borders, there are diverse climates, abundant resources, and various kinds of raw materials and agricultural products. The superior geographical position of America, i.e. "two oceans in west and east, no powerful nation in north and south", played a significant role in the national sovereignty characteristic of "isolationism" and "hegemonism" since the founding of the United States. At the end of the 18th century, US repeatedly concluded treaties with foreign countries while pursuing isolation. The United States was weak and lacked independent defense capability, so the leaders of the US government kept a lukewarm relationship with Europe by taking advantage of the superior geographical position of America, so that America never got involved or isolated and maintained the freedom of action.

After the Second World War, US changed its tradition of isolationism, and respected the diplomatic policy of "global interventionism".[50] By this time, the comprehensive national strength of US had peaked, and isolationism had historically gone downhill; in addition, President Roosevelt, who led America to the way of hegemony, is even more a remarkable genius. The United States was founded late; moreover, it is open, and its vast territory with a thin population required a large number of immigrants. The unique economic development and immigrations of America are crucial to the development of its high and new technologies, sophisticated techniques and advanced weapons. From the latter half of the 20th century up to now, US have established its hegemony in the international system, and one of its large strategic objectives is to avoid the decline of hegemony. As stated by Hans J. Morgenthau,[51] a famous international relationship expert of US, "International politics, like all politics, is a struggle for power. Whatever the ultimate aims of international politics, power is always the immediate aim." Nicolas Spykman also believes, "The competition for right is the essential essence of human relations. This is particularly true in the field of international affairs … Everything else is secondary. Because only power can achieve the purpose of foreign policy in the end."[52] As a result, guided by the hegemonic thought, the post-cold-war American sovereign behavior is embodied as "hegemony endowment".

From the perspective of the Internet, the control over the Internet by the United States not only maintains its advantages as those in the traditional fields, but also eliminates such natural barriers as Europe and Asia have in the traditional fields, so it is easy to form the situation of single strong power.

2.4.2 The World View of "Super-Sovereignty" in History

Hegemonic powers always tend to have territory ambitions, and the differences in geographical endowments of the countries also determine their respective sovereign perceptions and world conceptions. Geopolitics is a combination of geography and politics, especially for the relationship with other countries. Hegemonic states in history have always studied and planned theories beyond their own territory and beyond their own sovereignty. In 1897, *Political Geography* written by a German geographer Friedrich Ratzel was considered as a sign of formation of geopolitical

[50]Liu JZ (1998) Discussion on the interventionism of America after the cold war. International Politics Quarterly, 3: 25–36. http://www.cnki.com.cn/Article/CJFDTotal-GJZY199803003.htm [2016-10-1].

[51]Morgenthau H, Nations PA (1978) The struggle for power and peace. Alfred Kopf, Nova York. http://homepage.univie.ac.at/vedran.dzihic/morgenthau.pdf[2016-9-27].

[52]Spykman NJ (1942) America's strategy in world politics: The United States and the balance of power. Transaction Publishers. https://www.amazon.com/Americas-Strategy-World-Politics-Balance/dp/1412806313 [2016-10-1].

theory.[53] For the first time in history, this book systematically and organically combined politics and geography, and explained details of the relationship between the space occupied by a nation and its geographical position. The word "geopolitics" did not appear yet, but the main ideas and contents of geopolitical theories have been fully expressed. After that, several significant theories influencing national sovereignty and security strategies were formed in the development progress of geopolitics, such as "Sea Power Theory", "Land Power Theory", and "Air Power Theory" and so on. These theories are essentially "Super-sovereignty".

1. "Sea Power Theory" of Mahan

Alfred Thayer Mahan, a US naval officer, is considered as the initiator of "Sea Power Theory". In his book named *The Influence of Sea Power upon History (1660—1783),*[54] which was published in 1890, he mentioned that sea power was crucial to the development, prosperity and security of a country. Any country or alliance, as long as it can control the high seas, can control the trade and wealth of the world, thereby controlling the whole world. The ability for a country to acquire such status depends on its geographical location, land form, territorial limits, population size, characteristics of the public and the government characteristics. If a country intends to be a world power, it must have the ability to act freely on the ocean and, if necessary, monopolize maritime trade. Mahan proposed to focus on the Eurasian continent, arguing that different parts of Eurasian continent should be controlled by using different strategies and ideas. He thought the United States should work together with marginal powers of the Eurasian continent, such as Britain and Japan, so as to compete with powers located at the core area of Europe and Asia, thereby preventing great powers at vital position of Eurasian continent from controlling other marginal areas via their control over the Eurasian continent, and preventing Eurasian continent from forming the strategic posture of enveloping the United States.

2. "Land Power Theory" of Mackinder

Halford John Mackinder is a British geographer and the first scholar who analyses the world political forces as a global strategist. According to Mackinder, the history of the whole world is the history of struggles between land power and maritime power. Due to the abundant human and material resources, and the improving transportation of land powers, the sea powers will finally be suppressed by the land powers. He believes that the development of land transportation technology has changed "the relationship between human and most of the world's reality", and this strengthened the dominant position of Eurasian countries. In his

[53]Zhang HM, Hao CY (2013). See the development trend of Geopolitics from its history and status in quo. Contemporary International Relations, 2: 52–57. http://www.cssn.cn/ddzg/ddzg_ldjs/ddzg_zz/201310/t20131030_786488.shtml [2016-12-31].

[54]Maham (2006) The influence of sea power upon history. Chinese People's Liberation Army Publishing House, Beijing. http://detail.dangdang.com/9137370.html [2016-10-1].

book *The Geographical Hub of History*[55] published in 1904, Mackinder brought up the concept of "hub belt" or "heartland". He named the central inland area of Eurasian continent as a hub belt, and named the peripheral annular area closely surrounding the hub belt as "inner crescent belt" (including Europe, Middle East, India and China) and "outer crescent belt" (including British, Japan and other islands at the margin of Eurasian continent, sub-Saharan Africa, Oceania, and the entire America).

Mackinder asserted that the key to control the heartland was the occupation of Eastern Europe. He concluded his global strategic thoughts into three famous phrases, namely, the one ruling Eastern Europe controls the heartland; the one ruling the heartland controls the world islands; the one ruling the world islands controls the whole world. He also mentioned that, the most likely in control of the heartland was Russia and Germany and warned the west to prevent the expansion of Russia and alliance of Russia and Germany.

3. "Air Power Theory" of Douhet

In 1921, in his book *The Command of the Air,*[56] the Italian general Giulio Douhet brought up the "Air Power Theory". He believes that "Aviation opened up a new activity field for human—the sky field, and necessarily formed a new battlefield." In the sky field, Airplanes have become a new and unique means of human warfare. The acquisition of command of the air is the key to victory. "The mastery of air power represents a situation capable of preventing flight of enemies and maintaining flight of its own". Only rely on an air force capable of capturing air domination, the national defense of a country can be ensured. Therefore, sufficient attention should be paid to the air force and army, and naval forces should be gradually reduced until the air force is strong enough to seize the air domination. At the same time, it is necessary to find out and destroy the enemy aircrafts and all locations for producing them. The air power theory of Douhet and various principles he elaborated greatly influenced the air combat strategies of Italy and Germany during WW II. The influences of Air Power Theory on US "have been confirmed by General Michelle in WWII."[57]

Following the arrival of information era, the control of cyberspace became a unique means for controlling an information country. In particular, in the case of the Internet, its centralized operation mode artificially provides an entry point for super-sovereignty; as a result, it is possible to control the operation of Internet in all countries as long as the root domain name system is controlled.

---

[55][UK] Ha Mackinder (1985) The geographical hub of history. The Commercial Press. http://wenku.baidu.com/link?url=x06t7nR2B7IdlWrvXc8SqU_VoKwxGuCPhBrb6XtXAlBA0WzgeUHqCHhwBtigNFLmnTRmgZ7XTv3CyQDjXtdyMh-dq1isfAQdvtgLJECQ5du [2016-10-1].

[56]Giulio D (2015) The command of the air. Qunyan Press, Beijing. http://item.winxuan.com/1201200902 [2016-10-1].

[57]Geopolitics. https://www.91guoxin.com/baike/geopolitics/ [2016-9-27].

2.4.3 *"Overall Coordination of Two Great Situations" Reflects Constitutionality of Sovereignty*

All the views on sovereignty from "Universe View" of East Asia, "Equilibrium" of Europe and "Hegemony endowment" of the U.S. need to be governed as a whole within the two frames of *The Charter of the United Nations* and the every nation's constitutions. The natural commission of national sovereignty to maintain internal peace and repel external aggression.

1. To make an overall plan of external and internal situations, and to maintain internal peace and resist external aggression

Zhang Zhongjing, a Chinese medical scientist in Han dynasty, wrote in his book named *Treatise on Febrile Diseases Part I of Sun Diseases*: "Liquorice is sweet and neutral, and is capable of maintaining internal peace and repelling external aggression". Since then, this sentence has always been quoted in national strategies. Zhang Juzheng in Ming dynasty stressed in *The Book for Explaining 6 Issues*: "I know that the government of an Emperor is to maintain internal peace firstly before resisting external aggression", which means that it is necessary to stabilize domestic situations before solving the external problems of a country. At present, "overall planning of situations at home and abroad" reflects the rule-by-law principle of exercising sovereignty in accordance with the constitution of one country and *The Charter of the United Nations* by all countries. The "overall planning of situations at home and abroad" by all countries in the background of the great revolution of international community really accomplishes "maintenance of domestic peace and resistance of external aggression"; moreover, it internally conforms to relevant provisions of the constitution of one country, and externally exercises and safeguards its sovereignty according to *The Charter of the United Nations*.

2. All national sovereignties include two aspects of "maintaining domestic peace" and "resisting external aggression"

The internal sovereignty and the external sovereignty, and even the part of sovereignty transferred to some organizations, are all regarded as organic elements of the national sovereignty, and jointly constitute a unified national sovereignty. In *Concise Encyclopedia Britannica*, sovereignty is divided into "internal sovereignty" (which is the ultimate responsibility or authority in a national decision-making process) and "external sovereignty" (which is a nation's freedom from foreign controls, and which stands for the autonomy or independence of the country), and the activities of extraterritoriality and establishing a state within a state are violations to national sovereignty. From the perspective of sovereignty, one state enjoys the right to independently exercise its jurisdiction without interference from other countries and all sovereignties are equal, regardless of the sizes and strength of the nations.

3. The duality of national sovereignty is for the internal and external affairs

The internally and externally double characteristics of national sovereignty are commonly admitted by legal scholars at home and abroad. According to Oppenheim, "Sovereignty is the supreme authority, i.e. an authority independent of any other authority in the world. Therefore, in the strictest and narrowest sense, sovereignty refers to comprehensive independence, whether inside or outside of the territory."[58] Zhou Gengsheng believes that "Sovereignty is the supreme right for one country to independently handle its own internal and external affairs. If it is analyzed, national sovereignty has characteristics of two aspects, namely, it is internally supreme and externally independent."[59]

2.4.4 *Extensions of State Sovereignty into Cyberspace*

The rules of law and doctrines of national sovereignty apply completely to traditional security fields. However, as for non-traditional security, the application of state sovereignty must experience the process of technology support and consensus forming.

In 1999, a British political scientist Tim Jordan systematically elaborated the concept of Cyberpower from the perspectives of politics and sociology for the first time[60]: Cyberpower is the power form of politics and culture in cyberspace and on the Internet.

American scholar Joseph Nigro also noted[61]: "cyberpower depends on a series of resources related to electronics and computers used for information creation, control and communication, including hardware infrastructure, network, software and human skills; defined from the perspective of behavior, cyberpower refers to the ability to obtain desired results by using interconnected information resources in the cyberspace; cyberpower can be used for producing desired results in the cyberspace, or for producing desired results beyond the cyberspace by using network tools."

These definitions of cyberpower show the essence of the intense fighting for cyberspace by the western great powers, i.e. to obtain the novel national power of

---

[58][UK] Revised by Lauterpacht (1981) Oppenheim international law. Translated by Tieya WANG, Tiqiang CHEN. Beijing: Commercial Press, 1(1): 101. http://yuedu.163.com/book_reader/8088907541e44e3d8cc343d94b6c758e_4/119 [2016-9-27].

[59]Chinese Social Sciences Net. "Autonomy" should be distinguished from "Sovereignty". http://www.cssn.cn/zzx/zzxll_zzx/201310/t20131026_616961.shtml [2016-9-27].

[60]Jordan T (1999). Cyberpower. The culture and politics of cyberspace and the Internet. Psychology Press. Tim Jordan. Cyberpower: Politics in Cyberspace. http://www.docin.com/p-687387495.html [2016-9-27].

[61]Nigro Jr LJ (2012) The future of power. Parameters 42(3): 94–96. http://strategicstudiesinstitute.army.mil/pubs/parameters/Articles/2012autumn/BookReviews-IndividualPDFs/Nye_TheFuturePower.pdf [2016-9-28].

network dominance, which can both influence the internet and further have impact on state sovereignty and international community.

In the international political system, cyberpower will determine a country's international status. In the cyber war, the party having greater cyberpower will be more likely to initiatively start a war. For instance, in Russia-Georgia conflict in August 2008, it is reported that Russia initiated a powerful Internet attack on Georgia, which was at a disadvantage in the conflict due to its failure to release accurate information about the war by using networks. Therefore, the frontier issues commonly concerned by military circles of various countries, international political field, network technology field and the people all over the world are to explore and demonstrate in the non-traditional field the natural extension of state sovereignty.

Chapter 3
Interpretation of the Concept of "Cyberspace Sovereignty"

Abstract Cyberspace sovereignty, originating and extending from the state sovereignty, inherits many attributes of the national sovereignty, including the four basic elements of territory, population, resources and regime, the four basic rights of the right of independence, equality, self-defense, jurisdiction, and the four basic principles of respecting national sovereignty, mutual non-aggression, mutual non-interference in internal affairs and sovereignty equality. Cyberspace has different forms of expression, and people hold different views on the sovereignty issues in different forms of cyberspace.

Keywords Cyberspace sovereignty · The four basic elements of the national sovereignty · The four basic rights of the national sovereignty · The four basic principles of the national sovereignty

3.1 Multiple Interpretations About Cyberspace Sovereignty

Now the concept of cyberspace sovereignty has attracted more and more attention. With the evolution of time, there have been various interpretations about the concept of cyberspace sovereignty, but the fundamental ideas of those interpretations are all about determination of the ownership of rights over networks and the space in which networks are involved.

B. Fang, *Cyberspace Sovereignty*,
https://doi.org/10.1007/978-981-13-0320-3_3

3.1.1 "Cyber Sovereignty": A Shortened Form of "Cyberspace Sovereignty"

Most often the cyber sovereignty mentioned by people concerns internet space. For example, Xinhuanet put the following interpretation on cyber sovereignty[1]: "internally, cyber sovereignty refers to independent development, supervision, and management of a state's own internet affairs; and externally, cyber sovereignty refers to preventing a state's internet from external invasion and attack." Even so, it is generally considered that "cyber sovereignty" refers to "cyberspace sovereignty" instead of "internet sovereignty".

At present, in most cases, a traditional and narrowly-defined concept of "cyber" has been gradually used to refer to "cyberspace". The narrowly-defined "cyber" refers to a collection of devices that construct a network, whereas the broadly-defined "network" refers to "cyber", which is short for "cyberspace", namely, various electromagnetic networks and the activities involved therein. The phrase refers to the broadly-defined "cyber", namely, cyberspace that covers various networks and cyber activities. Moreover, the newly-introduced *National Security Law of the People's Republic of China*[2] prescribes that "the State shall establish a network and information security system; improve the capability to secure network and information; strengthen innovation, research, development, and application of network and information technologies; achieve security controllability of network and information key technologies, critical infrastructure, and information system and data in important fields; enhance cyber management; prevent, frustrate, and legally punish any cyber illegal and criminal conduct such as cyber attack, cyber invasion, cyber spying, dissemination of illegal and harmful information, and so on; and maintain the sovereignty, security, and development interest of the State's cyberspace", which also directly indicates that the term cyber therein refers to cyberspace.

President Xi Jinping pointed out in his speech delivered at the opening ceremony of the second World Internet Conference[3] that "Cyber sovereignty shall be respected. The principle of the sovereign equality established by the *Charter of the United Nations* is one of the basic norms guiding international relations and covers every field of state-to-state exchanges, and the principle and spirit of the sovereign equality should also apply to cyberspace." President Xi Jinping's speech at the symposium on cyber security and IT application also includes the following wording: "we advocate

---

[1]Xinhuanet. "What Is 'Cyber Sovereignty'?". http://news.xinhuanet.com/politics/2014-07/10/c_126736910.htm [2016-8-23].

[2]National Security Law of the People's Republic of China, voted through by the Standing Committee of National People's Congress on July 1, 2015. http://www.gov.cn/xinwen/2015-07/01/content_2888316.htm [2016-9-1].

[3]Xi Jinping's Speech at the Opening Ceremony of the 2nd World Internet Conference (Full Text). http://news.xinhuanet.com/fortune/2015-12/16/c_1117481089.htm [2016-10-2].

respect for cyber sovereignty and construction of a cyberspace community with a shared future".[4] In the above speeches, the term "cyber" refers to "cyberspace", and the term "cyber sovereignty" refers to "cyberspace sovereignty".

The *Outline of National Informatization Development Strategy* of China issued on July 27, 2016 mentions the following contents: "Set up correct cyber security concept; insist on active defense and effective response; strengthen cyber security defense capability and deterrence capability; and effectively maintain national cyberspace sovereignty, security and development interest. Safeguard cyber sovereignty and national security. Manage cyber activities within the state sovereignty in accordance with the law, and stoutly defend cyber state sovereignty. Resolutely prevent and fight any conduct that splits the country, incites rebellion, subverts the people's democratic dictatorship, undermines unity, steals and divulges confidential information, and the like." The phrases including "maintain national cyberspace sovereignty" and "defend cyber sovereignty" in the above contents also indicate that "cyberspace sovereignty" and "cyber sovereignty" have the same meaning.

3.1.2 The United Nations' Perspective

Since 2004, the UN established the "Group of Governmental Experts on Developments in the Field of Information and Telecommunications in the Context of International Security, GGE" and organized five sessions respectively in years 2004–2005, 2009–2010, 2012–2013, 2014–2015, and 2016–2017 to continue to study existing threats and potential threats in the field of information security and international cooperation measures which may be adopted to cope with these threats. In June, 2013, the UN published the third outcome report of the working group, i.e., *Report of the Group of Governmental Experts on Developments in the Field of Information and Telecommunications in the Context of International Security,*[5] and article 20 in the report makes it clear that "state sovereignty and international norms and principles that flow from sovereignty apply to state conduct of ICT-related activities, and to their jurisdiction over ICT infrastructure within their territory". According to the above wording, although the above article 20 does not directly mention the term "cyberspace", it indicates that application of state sovereignty is embodied in the following two levels: ① in a technical level, state sovereignty applies to ICT infrastructure, which is located in the level of "cyber" and certainly includes the internet, various telecommunication networks and communication systems, various communication systems and radio and television networks, various

[4]Xi Jinping' Speech at the Symposium on Cybersecurity and IT Application (Published in Full). http://news.cctv.com/2016/04/25/ARTIa8uTHXqX8JF25uz6S7Yh160425.shtml [2016-8-27].

[5]Item 94 of the Provisional Agenda of the Sixty-eighth Session of the General Assembly of the United Nations, Developments in the field of information and telecommunications in the context of international security. http://www.un.org/ga/search/view_doc.asp?symbol=A/68/98&referer=/english/&Lang=C [2016-9-1].

computer systems, and various embedded processors and controllers in key industrial facilities; ② in a social level, state sovereignty applies to ICT activities, which is located in the level of "space", that is, activity forms on the platform of ICT system. According to the description of cyberspace in Chap. 1, "cyber" indicates the ICT infrastructure, and "space" indicates the area of activities, so the above article directly interprets the meaning of state sovereignty applying to cyberspace, that is, it explicitly confirms application of state sovereignty in "cyberspace".

From another perspective, "States' jurisdiction over ICT infrastructure within their territory", on the one hand, defines the limit of a State's "territorial cyberspace", namely, the cyberspace constituted by ICT systems within the territory; and on the other hand, indicates exercise of "jurisdiction" over the infrastructure, namely, exercise of "jurisdiction" over the "territorial cyberspace".

Of course, there are still a lot of problems that need further study. For example, what principles should be applied for information about other countries that flows through one country's information infrastructure? Take as an example the United States. About 70% of the traffic through its backbone switching equipments is information about other countries.[6] How should that information be treated? Moreover, in terms of territorial waters, territorial land, or territorial air space, there is a clear spatial scale definition of sovereignty. Carriers (such as aircraft, ships) which go beyond the territorial limits of a country are deemed as mobile territory, and national sovereignty can still be exercised on those carriers. However, in the cyberspace that goes beyond the spatial boundaries of a country, the carrier and the load may be separated from each other (like the case in which nationals travel abroad), and in that case, how to secure sovereignty? If a carrier (server) of a country is hosted in a machine room of an internet data center (IDC) in another country, should the carrier be deemed as the "mobile territory" of that country or to be within the scope of the sovereignty of the third country? These problems need to be gradually clarified and resolved with the determination of cyberspace sovereignty.

3.1.3 *Geneva Declaration of Principles*

On December 10, 2003, the 1st World Summit on the Information Society was held in Geneva, Switzerland. In the *Geneva Declaration of Principles*[7] approved at the first phase of the World Summit on the Information Society, Article 49 reads as follows:

"The management of the Internet encompasses both technical and public policy issues and should involve all stakeholders and relevant intergovernmental and international organizations. In this respect it is recognized that:

---

[6]Google Public DNS: 70 billion requests a day and counting. http://archive.feedblitz.com/732152/~4140902 [2016-9-13].

[7]Declaration of Principles (2003), Geneva. http://www.itu.int/net/wsis/outcome/booklet/declaration_Bzh.html [2016-9-13].

(1) Policy authority for Internet-related public policy issues is the sovereign right of States. They have rights and responsibilities for international Internet-related public policy issues;
(2) The private sector has had and should continue to have an important role in the development of the Internet, both in the technical and economic fields;
(3) Civil society has also played an important role on Internet matters, especially at community level, and should continue to play such a role;
(4) Intergovernmental organizations have had and should continue to have a facilitating role in the coordination of Internet-related public policy issues;
(5) International organizations have also had and should continue to have an important role in the development of Internet-related technical standards and relevant policies."

The *Declaration of Principles* approved at the Geneva Phase of the Word Summit establishes the basic principles of internet-based information society, makes stipulations about the principles of internet governance, and earnestly requests the UN Secretary General to set up a Working Group on Internet Governance to conduct an in-depth study of internet-related issues and provide reference for the Tunis Phase. The *Plan of Action* proposes, on the basis of the *Declaration of Principles*, some slightly specific requirements for governments, such as developing national e-strategies, including the capacity building before 2005; fostering a pro-competitive and predictable policy, legal and regulatory framework; promoting regional root servers and the use of internationalized domain names; creating policies and laws that preserve cultural and linguistic diversity on the Internet and so on.

As can be derived from the *Geneva Declaration*, the World Summit on the Information Society emphasized the imposition of sovereignty over "space", for example, by formulating internet public policies; and conferred the "network" part on stakeholders, for example, establishment of technical standards and so on was delivered to international organizations.

3.1.4 Perspectives in the International Code of Conduct for Information Security

In September, 2011, China, Russia, Tajikistan and Uzbekistan jointly drew up a draft of the *International Code of Conduct for Information Security*[8] and appealed to the international community to consider the international code within the UN framework, so as to reach an early consensus on the international norms and rules guiding

[8]The UN document A/66/359, a draft for discussion of the International Code of Conduct for Information Security submitted by the Russian Federation, Tajikistan, Uzbekistan and China on September 12, 2011. http://www.un.org/zh/documents/view_doc.asp?symbol=A/66/359 [2016-8-30].

state conduct in the field of information. The *Code of Conduct* proposes 11 major clauses, wherein Clause 5 mentions that "to reaffirm all States' rights and responsibilities to protect, in accordance with relevant laws and regulations, their information space and critical information infrastructure from threats, disturbance, attack and sabotage". At the 4th International Conference on Cyber Conflict in 2012, Keir Giles from the Conflict Studies Research Centre gave the following analysis in the article "Russia's Public Stance on Cyberspace Issue"[9]: "Russia, along with a number of like-minded nations (for example members of the CIS, CSTO and SCO), strongly supports the idea of national control of all internet resources that lie within a state's physical borders, and … each member state is entitled to set forth sovereign norms and manage its information space according to its national laws."[10]

On January 9, 2015, six members of the Shanghai Cooperation Organization (SCO) presented an updated version of the *International Code of Conduct for Information Security* to the UN, which was submitted to the UN Secretary General Ban Ki-moon, and the six members requested that the updated version be circulated as an official document[11] during the 69th session of the UN General Assembly. The 5th statement of the Code is "to endeavour to ensure the supply chain security of information and communications technology goods and services, in order to prevent a State from exploiting its dominant position in information and communications technologies, including dominance in resources, critical infrastructures, core technologies, goods and services in information and communications networks to undermine other States' right to independent control of information and communications goods and services, or to threaten their political, economic and social security". It is emphasized therein that the cyberspace facilities are subject to a States' own cyberspace sovereignty (control).

3.2 Definition of Cyberspace Sovereignty

In an early stage, the constitution of sovereignty emphasizes three elements including people, territory (resources) and regime. However, in fact, resources are a basic element in determining sovereignty, which is specifically embodied by the distinction between "island" and "reef". On an island, sovereignty depends on the people who have historically been living on the island; as for a reef, sovereignty depends on the extension of the bed of territorial waters. The difference between "island" and "reef" is whether natural resources, such as freshwater resources, are

[9]Keir Giles. Russia's Public Stance on Cyberspace Issues. https://ccdcoe.org/publications/2012proceedings/2_1_Giles_RussiasPublicStanceOn-CyberInformationWarfare.pdf [2016-9-13].

[10]Keir Giles. "Information Troops"—A Russian Cyber Command?//Proceedings of 3rd International Conference on Cyber Conflict, Tallinn, Estonia, 2011: 45-60. https://ccdcoe.org/publications/2011proceedings/2011_Proceedings.pdf [2016-12-31].

[11]Cyberspace activities shall be subject to the principle of sovereignty. http://www.npc.gov.cn/npc/xinwen/lfgz/lfdt/2015-07/23/content_1941830.htm [2016-9-13].

available for human survival. Those having resources available for human survival are "islands", whereas those without such resources are "reefs". Ma Ying-jeou advertised for "Taiping water" with a high profile substantially for promoting the idea that the Taiping Island is an "island", thereby highlighting that China has the sovereignty over the island. Thus, the constitution of sovereignty includes four elements: population, territory, resources and regime.

The definition of cyberspace sovereignty can be considered from the following two aspects: a general description and a comprehensive description.

3.2.1 The Basic Elements of Cyberspace Sovereignty

Speaking of sovereignty, it inevitably involves jurisdiction. In accordance with prevailing rules of international law, territory is the space for a state to exercise its sovereignty. A state's network refers to the ICT infrastructure consisting of ICT systems built in its own territory. It is unquestionable that a State can exercise state sovereignty to govern, just as other entities, its own ICT infrastructure.[12] Besides, network behavior occurs in the cyberspace carried by ICT systems, so the cyberspace has a characteristic like that of "fictional parts of territory" formed by ships, aircraft, and the like, that is, in global commons, the jurisdiction over cyberspace comes from the jurisdiction over the ICT system on which the cyberspace depends. As a result, a state's sovereignty naturally extends to cyberspace. The jurisdiction over cyberspace is essentially an extension of the jurisdiction over the ICT infrastructure that hosts the cyberspace. Therefore, cyberspace sovereignty can be described as follows:

"Cyberspace sovereignty is a natural extension of state sovereignty in the cyberspace hosted by the ICT infrastructure located in the territory of a state; namely, a state has jurisdiction (right to interfere in data operation) over ICT activities (in respect of cyber roles and operations) present in cyberspace, ICT systems per se (in respect of facilities), and data carried by the ICT systems (virtual assets)."

In the above description, the ICT activities relate to cyber roles which are equivalent to "network population"; the ICT systems per se relate to facilities which are the platforms carrying the cyberspace and are equivalent to "territorial cyberspace"; the data carried by the ICT systems is similar to "cyber assets"; and jurisdiction refers to the right to interfere in facilities, data and data operation, which is equivalent to "cyber regime".

The above description directly points out that cyberspace sovereignty inherits all four elements of state sovereignty, clarifies the "regime" attribute of cyberspace sovereignty, namely, a regime controls the "territorial cyberspace", the "cyber resources" carried by the "territorial cyberspace", and the population and operations in cyberspace.

---

[12]Cyberspace activities shall be subject to the principle of sovereignty.

3.2.2 Basic Rights of Cyberspace Sovereignty

The basic rights of cyberspace sovereignty also directly come from state sovereignty, namely, the right of cyberspace independence, the right of cyberspace equality, the right of cyberspace self-defense and the right of cyberspace jurisdiction. The right of cyberspace independence is embodied in that networks within a state's territory can independently operate without external interference. That is natural in the clear majority of network models, such as radio and television networks, industrial control networks, but as far as the internet is concerned, the particularity of the centralized operation model of the global internet results in subjection of the internet operation in each state by the centralized control positions of the internet in terms of domain name resolution.

The right of cyberspace equality is embodied in that sovereign states have equal status in respect of network interconnection and network operation, equal power of decision-making in respect of technology evolution and public policy of international cyberspace, and equal right to speak in respect of international cyberspace governance. In the physical society, people have acknowledged that regardless of size, states have equal power to express, but the internet is always an exception, in which states could not be equally expressed in the corresponding links, and the "stakeholder"[13] management model formed a system of "law of the jungle", making the strong become stronger and the weak can only accept the reality.

The right of cyberspace self-defense is embodied in that the network is deemed as a specialized protected area. The US has already implemented the idea. The US not only developed Manhattan Project to support the idea, but also set up a systematic network army to protect the interests of the US in cyberspace. However, China still has a long way to go in this respect.

The right of cyberspace jurisdiction refers to exercise of sovereignty over cyberspace within a state's territory, which exists in all states of the world. Many states oppose the notion of cyberspace sovereignty, but at the practical level, all states, without exception, strictly control their own cyberspace and prevent external interference.

3.2.3 Basic Principles of Cyberspace Sovereignty

The basic principles of cyberspace sovereignty also come from state sovereignty. Respect for cyberspace sovereignty means that the right of cyberspace independence

[13]In Sept., 2005, Zoellick, the US Deputy State Secretary then, delivered a speech on the subject of relations between the US and China. In order to develop the China-US relations and try to resolve differences between the US and China in trade and security, in the speech, Zoellick introduced the concept of "stakeholder", and proposed that the U.S. and China both belong to stakeholders. The introduction of the concept provided a good idea and strategy for the Bush administration and the US mainstream society, and won the international community's praise.

shall be respected, and conduct causing sovereign cyberspace to be unable to autonomously operate shall not be adopted; mutual non-aggression means that cyber attacks shall not be carried out on other states' cyberspace; mutual non-interference in internal cyber affairs means indiscreet remarks or criticisms shall not be made on the jurisdiction over sovereign cyberspace; equal cyberspace sovereignty means that sovereign states have equal rights to co-govern cyberspace, rather than relying on the "stakeholder" model that causes some states to lose their right to participate in co-governance of network, while the others dominate the global cyberspace.

3.2.4 Definition of Cyberspace Sovereignty

Taking account of the above-mentioned three aspects, namely, the four basic elements including territory, resources, population and regime; the four basic rights including the right of independence, the right of equality, the right of self-defense and the right of jurisdiction; and the four basic principles including respect for sovereignty, mutual non-aggression, mutual non-interference in internal affairs and equal sovereignty, we can give a definition of cyberspace sovereignty as follows:

"Cyberspace sovereignty of a state is based on the ICT systems under the state's own jurisdiction; the boundaries thereof consist of a collection of the state's own network device ports directly connected to the network devices of other states; cyberspace sovereignty is exercised for protection of various operations of data by cyber roles. The constituting facilities of cyberspace, the carried data and the operation of data are subject to judicial and administrative jurisdiction of the state to which they belong; each state can equally participate in the governance of international network interconnection; operations of the information and communication infrastructure located in the territory of a state shall not be interfered in by other states; a state has the right to protect its own cyberspace from aggression and to maintain corresponding military capabilities. States shall show mutual respect for cyberspace sovereignty; one state shall not invade the cyberspace of another state; one state shall not interfere in another state's cyberspace management affairs; the cyberspace sovereignty of each state has equal status in international cyberspace governance activities."

The starting points of this definition include defining the "**territorial cyberspace**" by the wording "cyberspace sovereignty of a state is based on the ICT systems under the state's own jurisdiction"; reflecting the elements of "**users, data, and regime**" through the definition of "protection of various operations of data by cyber roles"; and defining the "**border**" by the definition that "the boundaries thereof consist of a collection of the state's own network device ports directly connected to the network devices of other states".

The above definition expresses the attribute of "**the right of cyberspace jurisdiction**" by the wording that "the constituting facilities of cyberspace, the carried data and the operations of data are subject to judicial and administrative jurisdiction of the state to which they belong"; expresses the attribute of "**the right of cyberspace**

equality" by the wording that "each state can equally participate in the governance of international network interconnection"; expresses the attribute of "**the right of cyberspace independence**" by the wording that "operation of the information and communication infrastructure located in the territory of a state shall not be interfered by other states"; and expresses the attribute of "**the right of cyberspace self-defense**" by the wording that "a state has the right to protect its own cyberspace from aggression and to maintain corresponding military capabilities". Lastly, the definition reflects the basic principles of "**respect for sovereignty, mutual non-aggression, non-interference in each other's internal affairs and sovereign equality**".

3.3 The Evolution of Sovereignty in a Variety of Cyberspace

Cyberspace sovereignty is objective existence independent of human will. There are various networks in cyberspace. From the perspective of cyberspace sovereignty, these networks can be divided into five types. (1) A type of networks over which cyberspace sovereignty naturally exists, such as sensor networks, industrial control networks. Activities in this type of networks are undoubtedly local behavior, and the right of jurisdiction over these networks in a state does not overlap that in another state, so it is not necessary to particularly emphasize the existence of cyberspace sovereignty over these networks. (2) A type of networks over which the governments of respective states have already been exercising sovereignty, such as radio space. Each state has been adopting conducts and means to interfere with unauthorized radio broadcast from another state which had permeated into the state's own territory, and the international community has not questioned the de facto conduct of radio space sovereignty. (3) A type of networks over which cyberspace sovereignty has been unanimously acknowledged by the international community, such as telephone network space, telegraph network space, and the like. These cross-border networks include domestic parts which are objectively under the jurisdiction of their governments and cross-border intercommunication parts which are coordinated by the international organization (International Telecommunication Union) in which sovereign states participate, and thus the existence of cyberspace sovereignty is embodied. (4) A type of network forms over which cyberspace sovereignty is a controversial issue, but the objective existence of cyberspace sovereignty cannot be ignored, such as the internet space. From the viewpoint of cyberspace sovereignty, these networks are freaks resulting from historical evolution but really existing. (5) A type of cyberspace over which cyberspace sovereignty has not yet been paid attention to by people, and the sovereignty ownership is not clear, such as satellite networks. This type usually refers to those cyberspace forms whose construction can hardly reply on one state, whose territorial cyberspace cannot be defined, and whose sovereignty has not yet been claimed by people. This book does not deal with the fifth case.

3.3.1 The Type of Networks Over Which Cyberspace Sovereignty Naturally Exists

Over networks having distinct local characteristics such as internet of things, sensor networks, industrial control networks and the like, cyberspace sovereignty naturally exists. This type of network is constructed based on region and population to be served, and there is no cross-regional interaction, so the sovereignty that it is involved in naturally integrates with national sovereignty. There is no obstacle or challenge to exercise of sovereignty over this type of networks, and thus the international community does not have any conflict of interest over this type of networks, so people do not need to emphasize the existence of a state's cyberspace sovereignty over this type of cyberspace.

1. Internet of Things

The internet of things is usually divided into three layers. The bottom layer is an information acquisition layer for obtaining parameter information of objects or applying control information to objects, which usually relies on terminal devices such as mobile terminals, radio frequency tags, wireless card readers, near field communication terminals, etc. The intermediate layer performs remote transmission of information by existing communication means, which usually relies on telecommunication networks, and the internet. The upper layer processes the information from sensors to serve specific applications, which usually relies on information processing systems, cloud computing platforms and the like. From this point of view, the essential attribute of the internet of things per se is mainly manifested in the information acquisition layer, so the internet of things does not have a cross-border attribute. As a result, the right of jurisdiction over the internet of things in a state does not overlap that in another state, and governments directly administer their own internet of things. For example, the US Trade Commission pointed out in the *Internet of Things*: *Privacy & Security in a Connected World* [*FTC staff report*][14] that IoT equipment manufacturing enterprises shall consider data security in production, they are not allowed to collect unnecessary information.

2. Sensor Networks

A sensor network is an information network consisting of several spatially distributed automatic terminal devices which use sensors to collaboratively monitor physical or environmental conditions (such as temperature, sound, vibration, pressure, speed, contaminants, etc.) at different positions. Just like the internet of things, the intermediate layer and the upper layer of a sensor network are also

[14]Internet of Things: Privacy & Security in a Connected World (FTC Staff Report). 2015. https://www.ftc.gov/system/files/documents/reports/federal-trade-commission-staff-report-november-2013-workshop-entitled-internet-things-privacy/150127iotrpt.pdf [2016-8-27].

broadband communication networks (the internet) and application processing systems. Therefore, there is no cross-border issue, and certainly there is no conflict of jurisdiction either.

3. Industrial Control networks

Industrial control networks have long been a kind of production networks confined to specific production entities until the emergence of "Internet+", which creates the need for remote control and incorporates broadband wide area transmission network components into some of the production industrial control networks. Nevertheless, industrial control networks are still limited to a network form in one or several enterprises, so there is no controversial issue in respect of jurisdiction.

3.3.2 *The Type of Networks Over Which Cyberspace Sovereignty Is Not Challenged*

Radio broadcast networks; social networks, cloud computing platforms and the like have a cross-border attribute. However, in specific practice, each state naturally exercises state sovereignty over this type of networks, and it does not cause any conflict over sovereignty claim between states.

1. Radio Broadcast Networks

In the age that satellite communications were underdeveloped, radio broadcasting prevailed. Broadcasts are not only made domestically, but also made abroad through shortwave. However, for political reasons, some states adopt a manner of interference to deal with broadcasts from other unfriendly states, so as to restrict the arrival of those broadcasts in their territories. For example, it is said that North Korea has set up a corresponding interference system in the border area to interfere with international broadcasts from South Korea. That substantially reflects a state's jurisdiction over the radio electromagnetic space, and such an act was not questioned by other states. Therefore, electromagnetic space sovereignty undoubtedly exists.

2. Cloud Storage

Cloud computing is based on the internet (in the future, it will be based on other types of networks), but as a special case of cyberspace, cloud computing has a characteristic of centralized cross-region processing, so it should be considered as a special form of cyberspace. Due to the cross-region characteristic of cloud storage, there are international conflicts of interest over cloud storage. For example, as to the foreign clouds built in China, the cloud security review in China objectively exercises state sovereignty over those cloud storage platforms.[15]

According to the introduction in *The Privacy, Data Protection and Cybersecurity Law Review*,[16] the Japanese *Act on the Protection of Personal Information*[17] prescribes that foreign companies that want to collect Japanese citizens' information shall have an agency in Japan and need to comply with the Japanese laws if the servers thereof are set up abroad; and that a business operator collecting and handling personal information must not provide the collected personal data to a third party without obtaining the prior consent of the data subject. Though the *Act on the Protection of Personal Information* does not contain any explicit provisions about international transmission of information, it is generally believed that if any business operator handling personal information in Japan wants to send data to foreign countries, like providing the data for a third party, he shall be restricted by the Japanese *Act on the Protection of Personal Information*.

The Russian *Personal Data Protection Act*[18] provides that any domestic or foreign company that collects personal information about Russian citizens must use in-country servers when processing (including collecting, accumulating and storing) any personal information-related data.

In the German *Telecoms Data Retention Law*,[19] telecommunications companies and Internet service providers must store sensitive data such as location, telephone number, IP address, traffic, etc. on servers within Germany.

In 2015, the European Court of Justice determined that the agreement about automatic data exchange between European companies and US companies was invalid.[20] The European Court of Justice held that for personal data of the EU citizens, US servers are not "safe harbor".

It is noteworthy that the above laws reflect conflicts between a state's government and transnational companies, but there is no conflict over jurisdiction between states, which indicates that a state in fact exercises sovereignty over cloud storage space. However, the international community has acquiesced to this objective fact,

---

[15]Cloud Computing Network Security Review of the First Batch of Cloud Platforms Is Complete. http://finance.huanqiu.com/roll/2016-09/9465615.html [2016-10-2].

[16]The Privacy, Data Protection And Cybersecurity Law Review. First Edition. 2014-11. http://www.sidley.com/~/media/files/publications/2014/11/the-privacy-data-protection-and-cybersecurity-la__/files/japan/fileattachment/japan.pdf [2016-8-27].

[17]The Japanese Act on the Protection of Personal Information (Law No. 57 of H15). http://www.iolaw.org.cn/showNews.asp?id=12426 [2016-9-27].

[18]Exploration of the Personal Data Protection System in Russia. http://www.cctb.net/llyj/lldt/llqy/201405/t20140521_307367.htm [2016-8-30].

[19]Germany passes data retention law. http://www.freepatentsonline.com/article/Information-Management-Journal/184698633.html [2016-8-27].

[20]The European Court of Justice Declares the US-EU "Safe Harbor" Agreement Invalid. http://dw.com/p/1GjEg [2016-8-30].

which thus demonstrates the regional attribute of cyberspace. In fact, many states have enacted laws on the issue of information collection and storage.

3. Online Social Networks

Online social networks are a kind of virtual networks built on information cyberspace. An online social network is a social structure composed of a collection of social individuals and connection relations between individuals, which can support online social intercourse of human beings. The most well-known online social networks are Twitter, Facebook, WeChat, Sina Weibo, QQ, etc. The core feature of an online social network is that an operator is responsible for construction of a network platform and for operation of the corresponding social network. Because of this feature, a company running a social network is subject to the jurisdiction of a local government according to its registration place, so that the social network is also naturally subject to the jurisdiction of government. Despite the cross-border and globalized features of an online social network, and though users are not subject to territory restriction, the conduct that a government governs an online social networking is in fact accepted by the public; no one challenges the authority of cyberspace sovereignty in this regard.

3.3.3 The Type of Networks Over Which Cyberspace Sovereignty Has Been Widely Acknowledged by the International Community

The ownership of jurisdiction over telegraph networks, telephone networks, telecommunications networks, radio and television networks and other cyberspace forms has been unanimously acknowledged by the international community, and an international co-governance system based on sovereign states has been established. The reason behind this is associated with the history of the development of telegraph, telephone, telecom, radio and television technologies.

In the 19th century, the invention of telegraph technology enabled states to establish their own telegraph networks. As the need for cross-border intercommunication arose, construction of an international interconnected network form was required, which involved coordination between the states. In order to achieve international telegraph communication and ensure international interconnection, on May 17, 1865, representatives from 20 European countries including France signed the *International Telegraph Convention*[21] in Paris, and the 20 countries declared the establishment of an international co-governance organization of sovereign

[21]Convention télégraphique internationale de Paris (1865) et. Règlement de service international (1865). http://www.itu.int/dms_pub/itu-s/oth/02/09/S02090000015201PDFF.PDF [2016-10-3].

states, namely, the International Telegraph Union (ITU).[22] The business scope of the organization has gradually extended to the governance of telephone. Along with the application and development of radio and broadcasting, cross-border conflicts and coordination of interests also got involved. In 1906, representatives from 27 countries including France and Germany signed the *International Radiotelegraph Convention*[23] in Berlin, and the International Telegraph Union took the co-governance responsibility.[24] In 1932, representatives from more than 70 countries, including France, Germany and Spain, convened a conference in Madrid. In the conference, they merged the *International Telegraph Convention* and the *International Radiotelegraph Convention*, developed the *International Telecommunication Convention*,[25] and decided that the International Telegraph Union was to be officially renamed "International Telecommunication Union (ITU)"[26] since January 1, 1934. On October 15, 1947, with the consent of the UN, the International Telecommunication Union became a specialized agency of the UN, and its headquarters was moved from Bern, Switzerland to Geneva, Switzerland.[27] This organization composed of sovereign states embodies cyberspace sovereignty over telecommunications networks, radio and television networks. The international community has reached a consensus over the cyberspace sovereignty of those networks, and sovereign states equally perform international co-governance.

3.3.4 *The Type of Networks Over Which Cyberspace Sovereignty Is a Controversial Issue*

Some people oppose cyberspace sovereignty with a high profile. Essentially, those people oppose internet sovereignty, because the internet sovereignty causes a rather great controversy, and the international community has irreconcilable differences. The reason lies in the particularity of the history of the internet development.

The first chapter gives an introduction of the development history of the internet. The development of the internet is different from the history of telecommunication networks, that is, the telecommunication networks were first built by respective

[22]International Telegraph Union (ITU). http://news.xinhuanet.com/english/2003-04/17/content_837415.htm [2016-10-3].

[23]Convention radiotélégraphique internationale (1906: Berlin, Allemagne). http://www.itu.int/dms_pub/itu-s/oth/02/09/S02090000125201PDFF.PDF [2016-10-3].

[24]International Radiotelegraph Conference (Berlin, 1906). http://www.itu.int/en/history/Pages/RadioConferences.aspx?conf=36&dms=S0201000010 [2016-10-3].

[25]International Telecommunication Convention (Madrid, 1932). http://www.itu.int/dms_pub/itu-s/oth/02/09/S02090000055201PDFE.PDF [2016-10-3].

[26]International Telegraph Conference (Madrid, 1932). http://www.itu.int/en/history/Pages/Plenipotentiary-Conferences.aspx?conf=5&dms=S0201000018 [2016-10-3].

[27]ITU became a United Nations specialized agency in 1947. http://www.itu.int/en/about/Pages/history.aspx [2016-10-3].

states and interconnection thereof was then negotiated by the international community; whereas the Internet is invented and first built by the US alone. Although Japan, Canada and other countries had established internetworks driven by the US during the development period of this time, since 1986, Canada and other countries began to connect to the Internet of the US successively, which was represented by the National Science Foundation Network (NSFNET). Thereafter, Denmark, Finland, France, Iceland, Norway, Sweden also connected to the NSFNET run by the US National Science Foundation one after another. This set-up determines that the international internet is a network in which the core is the Internet in the US, and the operation pattern of international interconnection is that countries of the world connect to the Internet. As a result, the power to manage the international internet is naturally in the hands of the US government.

1. The US's ability to Control the International Internet

As the existing Domain Name System (DNS) has been using a centralized management framework, the hub and key basic resources of the global internet have already been controlled by individual countries such as the US. In special periods, the internet in other countries may be unilaterally disconnected or paralyzed by the US, so that the US has the novel strategic deterrent ability to control the "switch" of the internet. Once this strategic threat is put into practice, great damage will be caused to governments, economy, society and people in the other countries, so it has attracted more and more attention and caused concerns in the rest of the countries around the world.

People often use computers to do activities such as visiting websites, sending and receiving e-mails on the internet. Usually people only need to know the name of a website or a mailbox, and do not need to remember the IP (Internet Protocol) address thereof which is expressed by a string of numbers. This easy use-pattern is owed by the DNS, whose main function is to "translate" the names of websites into IP addresses. For example, the name of the website of the Chinese Academy of Engineering is www.cae.cn, and an IP address of the website on the internet is 119.146.74.35. The DNS can be deemed as an "internet phone book", wherein the contacts are names of websites, and the phone numbers are IP addresses. In the DNS, the server of the highest level is called the "root" server, which is responsible for resolution of the top level domain (such as.com.cn). A root server is equivalent to an international telephone switchboard, and the difference is that all access to the internet basically needs to pass through this "switchboard" first to continue. Data in the "root zone" of a root server is equivalent to a table of international call area codes in the phone book. Hence, if a root server has a problem, the entire DNS will be abnormal or even crash, so that users cannot access the internet.

In the beginning of 1998, the US government issued a green book on management of internet names and addresses, claiming a direct management right of the internet, which was objected by almost all the other countries and organizations. In June, 1998, after soliciting public opinion, the National Telecommunications and Information Administration (NTIA) under the US Department of Commerce issued a revised version of the green paper, namely, the "white paper",[28] which states, at the end, "In order to promote global participation in the Internet business, the core functions associated with DNS should not be managed by the private sector, but should be implemented by the NTIA." The White Paper proposes establishing a non-governmental not-for-profit entity in October 1998 provided that the principles of stability, competition, bottom-up coordination and representation are guaranteed. This non-governmental not-for-profit entity is a nonprofit organization located in California, the US, and is named "The Internet Corporation for Assigned Names and Numbers (ICANN)". It was then one party of the *Memorandum of Understanding* (MOU), which has the function of coordinating and managing the DNS and is under the supervision of the NTIA.

By 2000, the *Memorandum of Understanding* was superseded by the sole supplier contract signed with the ICANN, which contract includes that the ICANN replaces the Internet Assigned Numbers Authority (IANA) to perform all its functions. The IANA's functions include coordinating internet protocol parameters and assigning internet number resources. The ICANN's responsibilities include management of several IANA's registration records, such as the Root Zone WHOIS database, which includes current and verified contact information for all top-level domain operators (e.g., .COM, .ORG, and .NET).[29] The ICANN is the entity that performs these functions and applies policies developed by the customers having the IANA's functions. The ICANN Board is not entitled to make or change policy decisions on its own. The NTIA's interference is authorized by the president instead of the Congress, so from a historical perspective, this internet governance model has no legal rights. The NTIA envisages that it would terminate its contract with the ICANN if the private sector's management of the DNS and the IANA functions had been completed. Such a vision was finally realized in October, 2016.[30]

At present, there are 13 original root servers all over the world. Among them, 10 servers are in the US, 2 servers are in Europe, and 1 server is in Japan. 1 of the 10 servers in the US is the primary server. The other 12 servers, as secondary root servers, regularly download root zone data from the primary root server.[31] With the authorization from the US Department of Commerce, Verisign, Inc. now operates the primary root server, and the ICANN is responsible for management of the root zone data. In order to improve domain name resolution performance and reliability, root server operators have so far built hundreds of root server mirrors all over the world, but those mirrors still entirely use data from the primary root server managed by the ICANN and are directly controlled by the root operators. Therefore, the

[28]MEMORANDUM OF UNDERSTANDING BETWEEN THE U.S. DEPARTMENT OF COMMERCE AND INTERNET CORPORATION FOR ASSIGNED NAMES AND NUMBERS. https://www.icann.org/resources/unthemed-pages/icann-mou-1998-11-25-en [2016-10-3].

[29]Root Zone Database. http://www.iana.org/domains/root/db [2016-10-3].

[30]The US Government Agreed to Transfer the Management Power of Internet Names. http://news.china.com/internationalgd/10000166/20160819/23325782.html [2016-8-27].

[31]The Primary Root Server. http://baike.baidu.com/link?url=twQNJnSn0DyXf-mrZwRflq5U9VuYy6HlxW_oL1Q5ymscv-ygQ65QlFaU5VZL8HPpQLqNn166_XwEsqAGwMLzda [2016-9-13].

power to manage the critical infrastructure (root servers) and the power to assign important resources (IP addresses and domain names) of the internet are in fact controlled for a long period by such a single sovereign state as the US.

One can find that domain name management and address resource management determine the domain name operation system of the international internet, which system can even decide which countries' networks can be addressed and which countries' addressing requests may be rejected.[32] In October 1999, the ICANN adopted the *Uniform Domain Name Dispute Resolution Policy*[33] and the *Rules for Uniform Domain Name Dispute Resolution Policy*,[34] aiming to solve the administrative procedural issues of domain name disputes. It is stipulated that to the extent that the Supplemental Rules of any Provider conflict with these Rules, these Rules supersede. Therefore, the Internet as an international internet has long been subject to the US government's jurisdiction, and the other countries do not actually have the right of equality and the right of independence over the internet.[35]

At a preparatory meeting of the World Summit on the Information Society in July 1, 2002, developing countries such as China, South Africa, Brazil and India advocated breaking the existing organization, and hoped that the UN could abolish the ICANN's right to manage internet top-level domains, and integrate global internet governance into the UN system, neutral regulators or intergovernmental organizations. However, the proposal met with opposition from the US and other Western countries, and thus was not adopted.[36]

In February 2003, the US issued the *National Strategy for the Physical Protection of Critical Infrastructures and Key Assets*,[37] emphasizing the protection of relevant infrastructure. The *National Strategy to Secure Cyberspace*,[38] which was published at the same time, offers the following points of view: the target of enemies' attack on the US would be the infrastructure; cooperation between the government and enterprises should be emphasized; for example, industry managing departments send liaison officers, the enterprises responsible for operation of critical infrastructure information network send coordinators, the two sides cooperate to

[32]The CNNIC proposes early joining the ICANN to speak more for China. 2000. http://www.cnnic.cn/gywm/xwzx/rdxw/2000nrd/201207/t20120710_31258.htm [2016-8-27].

[33]The Uniform Domain Name Dispute Resolution Policy. https://www.icann.org/resources/pages/policy-2012-02-25-zh [2016-9-13].

[34]The Rules for Uniform Domain Name Dispute Resolution Policy (the "Rules"). https://www.icann.org/resources/pages/udrp-rules-2015-03-12-zh [2016-9-13].

[35]Uniform Domain Name Dispute Resolution Policy. https://www.icann.org/resources/pages/policy-2012-02-25-zh [2016-8-27].

[36]Xinhuanet. Multilateral Game and Unilateral Challenge of Global Internet Governance: Exploration of the US's Motivations for Hyping Internet Security Issues. 2013-3. http://news.xinhuanet.com/world/2013-03/04/c_114882943.htm [2016-8-27].

[37]Bush GW (2003) The national strategy for the physical protection of critical infrastructures and key assets. Executive office of the president Washington DC. http://www.globalsecurity.org/security/library/policy/national/physical_strategy2003.pdf [2016-9-27].

[38]The U.S. Department of Defense. Strategy for Operating in Cyberspace (Full Text). http://3y.uu456.com/bp_7ww9a4uavc565jb3uu38_1.html [2016-9-27].

secure network infrastructure and so on. The strategy emphasizes the strategic position of the critical infrastructure of network, it requires acceleration of the construction of cyberspace security strategic system and vigorous strengthening of network combat power construction, thereby achieving a hegemonic position to control cyberspace. Therein, the internet domain name system is naturally part of the critical infrastructure of the US, and the system is incorporated into the US's strategic protection system.[39]

At the World Summit on the Information Society in December, 2003, the US stated that the internet should be space free from jurisdiction and restraint. Given that the US has a monopolistic power to operate and manage the global internet, the International Telecommunication Union (ITU) has proposed sharing part of the internet jurisdiction, but it did not work.[40]

At the World Summit on the Information Society held in 2003 and 2005, there were controversies mainly over the following two internet governance issues: ① should the internet governance (extending to the information society construction) be dominated by governments or the market? ② Should the internet top-level domain names continue being managed by the ICANN which was under the US Department of Commerce then? There are great differences between the developing countries led by China, Brazil, India, and South Africa and the US. When the first preparatory meeting of the Summit was held in 2002, these developing countries wanted to abolish the ICANN's management right and to integrate the global internet governance into the UN system, and they supported the government's leading role in internet governance and information society construction.[41]

In June 2005, the US Department of Commerce said that the US would indefinitely maintain the supervision of the internet servers, which means that the US prepared to monopolize the final control of the global cyberspace for a long period. Although the 13 root servers of the internet are managed by the private organization ICANN, and the members of the ICANN's board come from multiple countries around the world, according to the contract signed by the US Department of Commerce and the ICANN, the US government has the final right of veto over the ICANN's decisions. Of course, the contract expired on September 30, 2016.

In November 2006, the UN established the Internet Governance Forum (IGF), and IGF began to discuss the internet regulatory issues on a regular basis. It seems that the IGF's establishment indicates that the US made a concession and was willing to join the discussion to explore the network management model together with the other countries. However, in fact, the organization does not have any

---

[39]Cai CH (2010) The evolution and evaluation of the US's national strategy of information security. Information Network Security 1:71–73.

[40]Newsgd. The power to manage the global internet falls in the hands of the US, and the ITU's fight ends in nothing. 2005-11. http://www.southcncom/it/itgdxw/200511250430.htm. [2016-8-27].

[41]Chinadaily. Multilateral Game and Unilateral Challenge of Global Internet Governance: Exploration of the US's Motivations for Hyping Internet Security Issues. 2013-3. http://www.chinadaily.com.cn/hqzx/2013-03/04/content_16274913.htm [2016-8-27].

decision-making power, and only have the right to make suggestions, so it is difficult for the organization to perform any practical management functions.[42] In November 2007, Brazil publicly stated at the Internet Governance Forum that the right of assigning the internet domain names should not be controlled by the US.[43]

By 2009, the US National Telecommunications and Information Administration (NTIA) considered that the ICANN's accountability and transparency had been in place. And the NTIA expressed satisfaction and believed that the future transition could be considered.[44] The NTIA also signed the *Affirmation of Commitments*[45] with the ICANN to establish a permanent, multilateral, private sector-leading internet governance model. The accountability and transparency review team widely consist of members from industry, civil societies, internet technology community and other government international stakeholders, together with the NTIA. The review team set accountability standards to evaluate the ICANN's progress and offered suggestions for improvements that had already been carried out.

On June 24, 2010, the National Security and Government Affairs Committee under the US Senate adopted the amendment to the *Homeland Security Act* (2002), that is, the *Protecting Cyberspace as a National Asset Act of 2010*.[46] The amendment provides that in an emergency, the federal government has the absolute power to close the internet, which once again expands the federal government's power in an emergency. This is merely the first step that the US government exerts control of the international internet beyond sovereignty, and the second step is that website operation shall obtain the US government's permission and pass personal authentication. Google, Microsoft, etc. have also admitted that storage data information and the like of cloud services provided in foreign regions should be submitted to the US government for review according to law.[47]

During the Iraq war, the resolution of the Iraqi national top-level domain ".iq" was halted[48]; in April 2004, the Libyan top-level domain ".ly" also disappeared for three days, causing Libya to disappear for three days in the international

[42]Internet Governance Forum To Hold Inaugural Session In Athens. http://www.un.org/press/en/2006/pi1747.doc.htm [2016-10-3].

[43]NetEase Tech. Brazil: the right of assigning the internet domain names should not be controlled by the US alone. http://tech.163.com/07/1114/00/3T7HJ6GC000915BF.html [2016-9- 22].

[44]NTIA-ICANN. http://www.ntia.doc.gov/category/icann [2016-10-3].

[45]Affirmation of Commitments by the United States Department of Commerce and the Internet Corporation for Assigned names and Numbers. https://www.icann.org/en/system/files/files/affirmation-of-commitments-30sep09-en.pdf [2016-9-13].

[46]H.R. 5548 (111th): Protecting Cyberspace as a National Asset Act of 2010. https://www.govtrack.us/congress/bills/111/hr5548/text [2016-9-13].

[47]Full text: Human Rights Record of the United States in 2010. 2011-4. http://www.scio.gov.cn/ztk/dtzt/2014/2013nmgdrqjl/2013nmgdrqjl1/Document/1365460/1365460_1.htm [2016-8-27].

[48]The story behind the deletion of the Iraqi domain name IQ. http://www.edu.cn/xxh/fei/zxz/201410/t20141016_1190504.shtml [2016-9-13].

cyberspace.[49] For whatever reason, it is an objective fact that the ICANN dominates the survival of national top-level domains. The ICANN controls the power to resolute national top-level domains, which is sufficient to demonstrate its authority to control the cyberspace.

Objectively, the US shows the characteristic that technology serves politics, and it is quite easy that the US can technically stop the resolution of a country's international domain name to cause websites to be inaccessible. In May 2009, under orders from the US government, Microsoft closed the MSN service in Cuba, Iran, Syria, Sudan and North Korea.[50] In June 2009, in the unrest situation in Iran, the US government requested Twitter to postpone network maintenance to help the rebels spread information.[51] In January 2010, the US placed three television stations in the Middle East on the blacklist to resist the so-called anti-American sentiment.[52] On December 19, 2014, the US issued the presidential document, the *Executive Order—Blocking Property of Certain Persons and Prohibiting Certain Transactions with Respect to the Crimea Region of Ukraine,*[53] and also restricted the US companies to directly providing services for the netizens in the Crimea region, which caused internet companies including Alibaba (US) to end internet services from the US to the Crimea region. From this point of view, as the degree of US' sanctions against Russia gets higher, Russia has reason to worry that the US will eventually play the trump card–the internet, that is, exercise the privilege of managing the ICANN and issue an executive order to erase the record of the Russian top-level domain name ".ru" from the original root servers, thereby making the Russian internet disappear in the global cyberspace like Iraq and Libya. Various examples reflect that the US takes advantage of its jurisdiction over cyberspace and mixes political factors with the operation and management of the internet.

With the awakening of the international community, the voice from the international community which opposes the US' sole control of the internet gets louder and louder, and the international community opposes letting the US continue enjoying exclusive powers to supervise the DNS and the functions of the IANA. Especially after the Edward Snowden incident, the international community showed serious concern for the US' deep involvement in the internet, and some countries have begun to use the excuse that the US seizes all the powers of the ICANN to

---

[49]The whole story of the suspension of Libyan national top-level domain service. http://www.inforsec.org/wp/?p=86 [2016-9-13].

[50]Microsoft cut off the MSN service in Cuba, Iran, Syria, Sudan and North Korea. http://m.zol.com.cn/article/1352025.html [2016-10-3].

[51]The United States' "Twitter" cannot make waves in Iran. http://news.cntv.cn/20110223/105486.shtml [2016-10-3].

[52]Hegemonism is everywhere: the US double standard of internet management. http://news.xinhuanet.com/politics/2014-01/24/c_126055482.htm [2016-9-13].

[53]The White House Office of the Press Secretary, Executive Order–Blocking Property Of Certain Persons And Prohibiting Certain Transactions With Respect To The Crimea Region Of Ukraine. https://www.whitehouse.gov/the-press-office/2014/12/19/executive-order-blocking-property-certain-persons-and-prohibiting-certai [2016-12-2].

advocate promotion of more control from governments on sovereignty and multilateral bases. As a result, the NTIA announced in 2013 that its latest contract with the ICANN would expire in September 2015, after which the NTIA would transfer all responsibilities to a global multi-stakeholder group that would directly cooperate with the ICANN.[54]

The NTIA pointed out that the role of the US government in the management of the internet domain name system "has long been a source of dissatisfaction to foreign governments". Some countries therefore appealed to the UN, the International Telecommunication Union, or another intergovernmental organization to be established to take over the power to manage the domain name system. If the US government does not complete this transfer of power, the voice from other countries that requires replacing the multi-stakeholder model with a multilateral governmental operation pattern will grow higher and higher.

The NTIA announced in March 2014 that it did not intend to renew its contract with the ICANN, but the NTIA also said that as a prerequisite for withdrawal, the NTIA needed an acceptable transition plan made by the ICANN. Lawrence Strickling, the assistant secretary of the NTIA, said in a statement that he was confident that the ICANN "will convene global internet groups to draft a proper transition plan". He also provides four principles for the ICANN's transition plan: ① to support and enhance the multi-stakeholder model; ② to maintain the security, stability, and resiliency of the internet DNS; ③ to meet the needs and expectations of the global customers and partners of the IANA services; and ④ to maintain the openness of the internet.[55]

The contract between the NTIA and the ICANN was due to expire at the end of September 2015, but it has been postponed because of ICANN's multi-stakeholder transition plan, which had been expected to be made was not yet determined. The plan was expected to end in October 2015, which would allow the transition to be implemented in the summer of 2016. If the transition plan does not fully meet the previously stated requirements of the US, the contract would be further extended to 2017. In June 2016, the NTIA introduced the *IANA Stewardship Transition Proposal Assessment Report*,[56] which preliminarily approved the transfer proposal submitted by the ICANN. The NTIA stated in the issued statement that the submitted proposal met the requirements imposed by the US government two years ago of transferring the domain name control power to a "global internet

[54]The US government announced that it would transfer the power to manage domain names—who dominates the voice in the internet? http://www.scio.gov.cn/zhzc/9/6/Document/1369631/1369631.htm [2016-10-3].

[55]Remarks by Assistant Secretary Strickling at the State of the Net Conference 1/27/2015. http://www.ntia.doc.gov/speechtestimony/2015/remarks-assistant-secretary-strickling-state-net-conference-1272015 [2016-10-3].

[56]IANA Stewardship Transition Proposal Assessment Report. https://www.ntia.doc.gov/files/ntia/publications/iana_stewardship_transition_assessment_report.pdf [2016-10-3].

multi-stakeholder community".[57] Subsequently, the ICANN submitted a further implementation plan status report as required. After assessment of the report, the NITA officially decided on August 16 that it would give up the control of the internet domain names by October 1, which puts an end to the privatization process continuing for nearly 20 years of the core resources of the internet. Thus, from October 1, 2016, the US government, in principle, does not have the power to directly interfere in the operation of the ICANN.[58]

2. Dissatisfaction and Struggle of the International Community with One State's Control of the Internet

In February 2010, the International Telecommunication Union (ITU) appealed to the international community to promote the development of an international convention on cyberspace, several Arab countries including the host country, supported the requests of China and Russia for sharing the responsibility for managing the internet and having the management right of the corresponding technical specifications. In July of the same year, the UN developed a draft treaty to reduce the threat of attacks on computer networks, and 15 state members including the US, China and Russia signed the agreement.[59] The agreement proposes that the UN creates norms of accepted behavior in cyberspace, exchanges information on national legislation and cyber security strategies between the member states, strengthens the capacity of less-developed countries to protect their computer systems. Russia hoped to prevent a new round of arms race by international treaties, and restrict and supervise cyberspace attacks, as a source of attacks, just like weapons of mass destruction. However, the US took a quite different position. The US opposed the establishment of an independent organization to constrain cyberwarfare. And the US believed that the conclusion of a special international treaty is meaningless. As a great power dominating the cyberspace, the US considers more about not restricting its own network technology advantages, rather than how to avoid network attacks. In contrast, the EU is rather active in promoting global negotiations on cyberspace governance.[60]

[57]Transfer progress of the IANA's power of management: the NTIA announces that the IANA transition proposal meets the four principles in the US government's statement. http://mp.weixinqq.com/s?__biz=MjM5MTgzNDk4Mw==&mid=2652355164&idx=4&sn=e8de2327a2da739c14f49808dd8c7f6b. [2016-10-3].

[58]The United States officially abandons the power to manage internet resources and ends the nearly 20-year-control. http://view.inews.qq.com/a/20161001A0173J00 [2016-10-3].

[59]15 nations agree to start working together to reduce cyberwarfare threat. http://www.washingtonpost.com/wp-dyn/content/article/2010/07/16/AR2010071605882.html [2016-9-13].

[60]Lang P. Cyberspace security: A new global agenda. 2013-10. http://theory.rmlt.com.cn/2013/1022/168334_6.shtml [2016-8-27].

In June, 2010, the Chinese government issued the *Internet in China* (White Paper),[61] which points out that the internet is important national infrastructure; that the internet within the territory of the People's Republic of China is under the jurisdiction of Chinese sovereignty; and that the Chinese internet sovereignty should be respected and maintained. The major component of the Chinese cyberspace sovereignty is the jurisdiction over the "internet within the territory of the People's Republic of China", and the Chinese cyberspace sovereignty further includes that the Chinese internet domain name and relevant public services shall not be invaded.

The *China's National Defense in 2010*[62] released by China in March 2011 mentions cyberspace and states that the maintenance of national security interests in cyberspace is the goal and task of China's national defense in the new era.

The London Conference on Cyberspace,[63] held in November, 2011, aimed to discuss the issue of international behavior rules in cyberspace and to promote and develop norms of cyberspace behavior. The consensus reached at the conference is that cyberspace needs "traffic rules", which is considered by many countries as a first step in the development of international rules on cyberspace. At the conference, Russia stressed that cyberspace should also have state sovereignty, and that cyberspace rights and freedom should be based on respect for the relevant domestic laws and regulations.

At the Conference on Cyberspace in Budapest, Hungary, in October, 2012, despite the theme of the conference, which was emphasizing on the importance of openness and transparency, Russia constantly emphasized the respect for state sovereignty in cyberspace and the necessity for implementation of regulations. At the same time, the representative from China proposed that each country should follow the five principles of cyber sovereignty, peaceful use, fair development, balance and international cooperation in cyberspace.[64]

In December, 2012, at the Meeting of the International Telecommunication Union in Dubai, China, Russia and other developing countries proposed, through different proposals, the inclusion of the internet in the revised *International Telecommunication Regulations*, for the purposes of placing the internet under the jurisdiction of the International Telecommunication Union (and the UN) led by sovereign states, and allowing states to manage the operation of the internet and supervise the internet; and suggested that the International Telecommunication Union can have the right to assign at least part of the internet addresses. However, the above actions met with strong opposition from the US and European countries,

---

[61]Information Office of the State Council of the People's Republic of China, the Internet in China (White Paper). 2010-6. http://www.scio.gov.cn/zxbd/tt/Document/1011194/1011194.htm [2016-8-27].

[62]The China's National Defence in 2010. http://www.scio.gov.cn/zfbps/ndhf/2011/Document/883535/883535.htm [2016-8-30].

[63]International Information. London Conference on Cyberspace. 2011-11. http://www.cicir.ac.cn/chinese/Article_3596.html [2016-8-27].

[64]The Xinhua News Agency. The Budapest "Conference on Cyberspace" opens. 2012-10. http://news.xinhuanet.com/2012-10/05/c_113280038.htm [2016-12-31].

who believed that these proposals would change the "borderless" nature of internet governance and give governments the power to interfere in cyberspace. Even though great compromise was made in the final *Regulations*, the US, the UK and other countries still refused to sign the agreement. In that case, the International Telecommunication Union broke the traditional principle of unanimous vote, and passed the new resolution by majority voting, thereby extending the scope of jurisdiction to cyberspace. Although the delegations of the US, Sweden, the UK and many other Western countries successively made speeches and statements to express their regrets about the refusal of the way of forced adoption of the resolution, and disapproval of talking about the issue of the internet in the *International Telecommunication Regulations*, the Arab countries and the African countries including the United Arab Emirates, Saudi Arabia, South Africa and so on still emphasized the importance of the internet for developing countries.[65]

In 2013, the NATO Cooperative Cyber Defence Centre of Excellence publicly published the so called "Tallinn Manual", i.e., the *Tallinn Manual on the International Law Applicable to Cyber Warfare*,[66] which establishes the principles of cyberspace sovereignty. The manual makes explanation of the applicable international law for cyber warfare based on the principle that "cyberspace does not need new rules and the existing international law is applicable to cyberspace". The manual's emphasis is on "cyber-to-cyber operations". The manual affirms that cyberspace is not a "lawless" vacuum zone that anyone can commit hostile acts without restrictions. The manual specifies that cyber operations can be launched as force.[67]

On October 22, 2015, the US Senate adopted the amendment of the *Cyber security Information Sharing Act* (CISA),[68] whose major goal was to lower the threshold for prosecuting cybercriminal suspects of other countries, but how to exercise discretion over network attacks from other countries' citizens still causes great controversy and inevitably involves interference in cyberspace sovereignty of other countries. The current situation is that cyberspace sovereignty still arouses big controversy in the international community, and often become a central issue in the debate between great powers.[69]

---

[65]Guanchazhe. The US refuses to sign the new International Telecommunication Regulations, and insists on holding the power to manage the internet. 2012-12. http://m.guancha.cn/america/2012_12_15_114361?XGYD [2016-8-27].

[66]The NATO Cooperative Cyber Defence Centre of Excellence, Tallinn Manual on the International Law Applicable to Cyber Warfare, 2013. http://www.jku.at/intlaw/content/e275831/e275836/e276629/Tallinn_Manual_CW.pdf [2016-9-8].

[67]People's Liberation Army Daily. The NATO's Manual on Cyber Warfare: Find the Legal Basis for Manipulating Cyberspace. 2014-10. http://www.chinanews.com/mil/2014/10-24/6712323.shtml [2016-8-27].

[68]S.754—Cybersecurity Information Sharing Act of 2015. https://www.congress.gov/bill/114th-congress/senate-bill/754 [2016-10-3].

[69]Science and Technology Daily. Maintenance of Cybersecurity Requires Settlement of Disputes over Cyberspace Sovereignty. 2015-11. http://scitech.people.com.cn/n/2015/1117/c1057-27822151.html [2016-8-27].

Chapter 4
Necessities for Advocating Cyberspace Sovereignty

Abstract It is a realistic need to advocate cyberspace sovereignty. With the continuous extension of cyberspace, and the widespread popularization of various cyber technologies and their applications, all the behaviors in the physical society are naturally mapped into the cyberspace. For this reason, the management model of the physical society will naturally migrate to the cyberspace, only which is only different in the management method, but remains the same in its management goals. Therefore, it is inevitable in the future that the state sovereignty will be extended to cyberspace that people increasingly rely on.

Keywords Conflicts on jurisdiction in cyberspace · Shared interests in the same cyberspace · New order in the cyberspace · Co-governance of cyberspace

Prior to the birth of modern sovereign nations, the size of territory was an important symbol of national strength, and the territory was one of the most basic elements of sovereign nations, so territory sovereignty became the core content of national sovereignty. However, due to the science and technology revolution, economic globalization, information revolution, new military revolution and many other reasons, element structure of geopolitics has been profoundly changed, and a three-dimensional national sovereignty concept, with politics, military, economy and culture as its core, has been formed. Particularly, the rapid development of the network enlarges the exercising space of state sovereignty. Territory is important to national sovereignty; however, due to the impact of network on geopolitics, the maintenance of political, military, economic and cultural sovereignty within the state has greatly crossed territorial boundaries, and the exercising space of state sovereignty has expanded from the traditional territorial boundaries to emerging "network boundaries", so the sovereignty maintenance in the network field has become the high ground of sovereign maintenance. The control of network information, and the exploitation and utilization of network resources will become the main source of national strength and the key of national interest. As stated by the American futurist Alvin Toffler, "The whole world belongs to the one who masters information and controls network".

B. Fang, *Cyberspace Sovereignty*,
https://doi.org/10.1007/978-981-13-0320-3_4

The characteristic of the global information environment is that the states autonomously control the affairs within their sovereignty scopes, and this is decided by the competition logic of world politics; besides, no country wants to be defeated in the new map of geopolitical information distribution. Any new technology, at the beginning of its emergence, won't cause intervention of state sovereignty before it is influential enough to be a threat; once the technology is gradually mature, or when it begins to be important in political field, or when the government begins to have the coping capacity, it will naturally be incorporated into conventional sovereign control. Apparently, the proposal of cyberspace sovereignty conforms to the development law of national sovereignty theory and the logic of information technology development.

If there is no international interconnection of network and no international conflicts caused thereof, cyberspace sovereignty will naturally be not controversial, and no one would think it is worth being discussed, in that it naturally belongs to the state sovereignty. International interconnection exists in the telephone network, but the telephone network has always been recognized by the international community as within the jurisdiction of a sovereign state even since hundreds of years ago, so there is no dispute. However, the situation of the Internet is relatively complex. Since, America began to dominate the construction of the Internet from the very beginning. When the international community generally accepts and uses the Internet, whether the United States is willing to release its control over the Internet becomes very tangled. The ambivalence of America was shown in the power transition of Internet Corporation for Assigned Names and Numbers (ICANN): America does not want the international community to think that the Internet is controlled by the US, but America worries that the Internet may develop in an undesired direction after the relinquishment. As a result, the conflict of cyberspace sovereignty is most obvious in the Internet field, and the focus lies in the selection of an Internet governance mode.

Due to various conflicts and disputes on the Internet, the discussion about cyberspace sovereignty in Internet field is inevitable. Therefore, the discussion in this chapter is about cyberspace sovereignty only in Internet, and the issues to be discussed can also be regarded as Internet sovereignty problems.

4.1 Conflicts Caused by Absence of Cyberspace Sovereignty

In the current international community, there are various conflicts among the Internet, which are awkwardly insolvable due to the lack of Internet sovereignty. When resolving these conflicts, people will inevitably turn to the magic weapon of state sovereignty, so as to solve problems by using national jurisdiction.

4.1.1 *Jurisdiction of Domain Name and Other Internet Resources*

According to the ICANN policies, in case of domain name disputes, the global ruling on the international domain name disputes will be made by the four agencies entrusted by ICANN.[1] The four agencies are respectively: The World Intellectual Property Organization (WIPO) located in Geneva, Switzerland; the National Arbitration Forum (NAF) located in Minnesota, US; CPR[2] located in New York, US; the eResolution.com organization located in Montreal, Canada.

On December 8, 1999, Jinzhita Corporation registered two international domain names "gameicq.com" and "gameicq.net" for its game named "Men of Means" in the registration center of Network Solutions Inc (NSI) of America. The aim of "gameicq" is to reflect the purpose of its online game, i.e. "In Game, I Seek You". However, at the beginning of July 2000, American Online (AOL) sent an official letter to Jinzhita Company, alleging that "ICQ" (network communication software) is a patent of the company, and that the domain name "gameicq.com" containing "ICQ" infringes its intellectual property, so AOL required that Jinzhita Corporation transfer the domain name "gameicq.com" for free. On August 13, AOL sent Jinzhita Company an international letter having as many as hundreds of pages, asking Jinzhita Company to submit a domain name dispute reply to WIPO on August 17. On October 11, 2000, the WIPO arbitration center for domain name disputes made the judgment for domain names "gameicq.com" and "gameicq.net", wherein Ian Barker, an arbitrator from New Zealand, ruled that Shenzhen Jinzhita Computer Software Company had maliciously registered and used the domain names "gameicq.com" and "gameicq.net", and should give these two domain names back to AOL.[3]

In November 1999, 10 months after OICQ was launched by Tencent and had gained more than 1 million registered users, Ma Huateng and his Tencent received two lawyer's letters. In just a few days from August to September in 1999, AOL, who had bought ICQ software and the domain name "icq.com", sent two successive sternly worded complaint letters to Tencent, alleging that "oicq.net" and "oicq.com", which were respectively registered on November 7, 1998 and January 26, 1999, infringe the intellectual property rights of AOL, and asking Tencent to transfer the two domain names to them for free.[4] National Arbitration Forum (NAF) accepted this dispute. On March 21, 2000, according to the NAF's

---

[1]Domain Name Registration System of China. http://www.doc88.com/p-907996106325.html [2016-12-31].

[2]CPR: formed by lead counsels from 500 major companies, major law firms and famous legal research institutions.

[3]Summary: Jinzhita Company fought with AOL for domain name. 2000-10. http://tech.sina.com.cn/internet/china/2000-10-11/38660.shtml [2016-8-27].

[4]Tencent repurchased overseas domain name at a good price, aiming to secretly recast QQ brand strategy. http://www.people.com.cn/GB/it/49/151/20030325/953460.html [2016-9-15].

arbitration award, Tencent lost without suspense, but the ICQ brand did help Ma Huateng to get their localized instant communication tool OICQ quickly known by the public. James Carmody, the arbitrator, decided that Tencent should return the domain names oicq.net and oicq.com to AOL.[5]

Now that the sovereignty is not accepted in cyberspace, ICANN will certainly entrust the designated arbitration organizations to deal with the domain name conflicts, so as to indicate that the cyberspace follows the game rules of its own.

Having a prominent domain name "cnnews.com" and working on network news and other business, Shanghai Meiya Online Company received a lawyer's letter from Cable News Network (CNN) in October 2000. CNN asserted that this domain name was like that of CNN and thus constituted network infringement. CNN required Shanghai Meiya Online to stop using this domain name immediately and transfer the domain name to it. This incident caused a stir in domestic media and industry at once. Rejected by Shanghai Meiya, CNN submitted an "action in rem" over "cnnews.com" to the Eastern Court of Virginia, US.[6] In January 2002, this court issued the judgment, announcing that the domain name infringement by Shanghai Meiya online was true, ordering that Shanghai Meiya Online immediately stop using the domain name. Since the registrar of the domain name "cnnews.com" is NSI of America, the US Court also ordered NSI to stop the registration service for the domain name "cnnews.com".[7] The domain name, which belonged to the Chinese and was extremely engaging, was abandoned.[8]

However, it is somehow weird to see local courts get involved into domain name conflicts, which is not consistent with the conclusion that there is no sovereignty on the Internet.

The occurrence and the judgment of this case reflect a problem: why did the court get involved in the domain name dispute if there is no sovereignty in cyberspace? From the viewpoint of sovereignty, who has the jurisdiction over domain name conflicts? Whether the jurisdiction over Internet resources is subject to the jurisdiction over the department controlling the resources? If these problems are not made clear, and a consensus of jurisdiction scope mode cannot be formed, the cyberspace will naturally be reduced to the jungle based on jungle law.

[5]Stories of Tencent's QQ domain name. 2010-8. http://www.williamlong.info/archives/2305.html [2016-8-27].

[6]CNN Claims Infringement and Dilution by cnnews.com. http://www.inta.org/INTABulletin/Pages/CNNClaims-InfringementandDilutionbycnnewscom.aspx [2016-9-9].

[7]Transnational domain name disputes require law integration. http://ip.people.com.cn/n/2014/0324/c136655-24720867.html [2016-9-27].

[8]Shen L (2003) Domain name users need to safeguard their rights, .COM is not synonymous with Internet. 5. http://tech.sina.com.cn/i/c/2003-05-07/0731183785.shtml [2016-8-27].

4.1.2 The Ownership of Data Rights

Cyberspace is a digital space with some entirely different properties from those of the physical space. For instance, physical space conforms to the law of conservation of matter, and any copy behavior requires not only cost but also skills; however, data in digital space can either be copied limitlessly at an almost zero marginal cost[9] or be deleted without a trace. There are clear rules for the ownership and transfer of property rights in physical space, but there is no definite rule for data rights in digital space. Once a set of data is submitted, it is almost impossible to retract and destroy them, but this set of data can be limitlessly copied and utilized by others and become a profit point. As a result, it is a problem to identify the ownership of the data. Since there is no authorized administrator in cyberspace, the measures and basis for protecting the interests of data are also uncertain.

In cyberspace, once the data owners lose control of their personal privacy data, it would be impossible to specify the spread range of their personal privacy data all over the world. As you can imagine, the personal private data that are popular in the cyberspace but beyond the control of the data owner may become the exhorted objects of merchants and targets coveted by hackers when the data owners are totally unaware of the situation, or even become the blackmailing chips of people having ulterior motives. Docusearch.com, an American website, had once provided its uses' personal privacy data including telephone numbers, social security numbers and so on to others, which caused one of its users to be murdered, so it was sued by the victim's parents.[10]

In 2014, the People's Court of Putuo District of Shanghai has accepted a case of private prosecution for publishing personal privacy data of others on the Internet. Rejected by the young woman he was pursuing, the defendant of this case published on the Internet the young woman's name, address and telephone number, and corrupted her reputation. As a result, the unwitting young woman received constant unwanted calls, which had seriously affected her normal life. The court ordered the defendant to pay a compensation of 100,000 Yuan to the victim.[11]

These two cases have brought profound enlightenment, i.e. the personal data protection in cyberspace is significant to the owners. Nowadays, it is common for people participating online surveys to easily input personal e-mail addresses. Most people think that the only consequence is commercial advertisements and other E-mail spam, which seem to be insufficient to make a big difference to people's

---

[9]Marginal cost refers to, at each level of production, any additional variable costs, including worker's wages, raw material, fuel and so on, required to produce the next unit of production. Theoretically, marginal cost is the change in the total cost that arises when the output has an increment by unit.

[10]See privacy protection from a "Cyber Manhunt" incident. http://www.shanghailaw.gov.cn/yjsChinese/page/mediafocuscase/media_info2495.htm [2016-9-15].

[11]Tang Q (2014) Personal data in cyberspace and the legal protection. 5. http://bbs.szhome.com/30-57200-detail-2841214-0-0-1.html [2016-12-31].

normal life. However, potential risks of casually providing personal privacy data are far more than that. Internet defamation, Internet fraud and other acts infringing data owner's personal right and property right may happen at any time; besides, the infringements may spread from the Internet to real society, it will go far beyond the expectation and control of data owners. The occurrence time and ways of data leakage and infringements are uncertain and thus get personal privacy data out of control. Once the data leakage and infringement happen, ineradicable and permanent threats will be instantly produced. Victims may even know little about where the infringement comes from, and they could not effectively implement self-protection or seek for judicial remedies.

The key point is that the data privacy leakage may be in a cross-border state, while a specific jurisdiction scope for this phenomenon is missing in the judicial system, i.e. users and websites are in different jurisdiction scopes. The judging principle of the data privacy protection laws established by the EU is that the service objects are EU residents, so websites are also subject to this law even they are beyond EU territory. Therefore, a clear and definite cyberspace sovereignty scope is necessary for determining the ultimate judgement standards of the jurisdiction scope of data privacy protection, so as to map the right disputes on the Internet to such a clear jurisdiction scope as in the physical world, thereby solving problems according to the judging principles of the scope.

4.1.3 Problems Brought by Big Data

In August 2005, for the reason of striking online pornography crimes, the US Department of Justice required the big four US network companies having search engines, i.e. Google, Microsoft, Yahoo and AOL, to provide data information about network search, including randomly selected websites and data of users' search results, so as to assist in the investigation. However, this requirement of the government was firmly rejected by Google for the reason as follows: "this was an invasion of users' privacy and damage to the trust between Google and users, and trade secrets of Google search service may be revealed."[12]

Due to Google's refusal to cooperate, the US Department of Justice took Google to court[13] in January 2006, requiring that Google submit 1 million websites linked to the search engine and all the search requests within a week. On March 15, 2006, the district court in northern district of California, US made the following decision: "To assist the government in reformulating laws against online child pornography, Google is required to submit 50,000 randomly selected websites to the US Justice

[12]Secret eavesdropping: "Black World" of America is staring at Internet. http://www.chinadaily.com.cn/hqjs/2006-07/19/content_644185.htm [2016-10-3].

[13]Wenhui News. Google's lawsuit causes concerns about citizens' privacy. 2006-3. http://www.sachina.edu.cn/Htmldata/news/2006/03/1092.html [2016-8-27].

Department, but it is not required to submit information related to users' search requests."

This case reflects that the government has exercised jurisdiction over domestic enterprises. However, since Google is a multinational enterprise serving global users, does the US government have the right to require Google to provide websites outside of America? Clearly, the jurisdiction of US government conflicts with the data privacy protection laws of EU. The regulated objects of the US are enterprises, and the protected objects of the EU are users. The difference between their protection scopes may result in overlapping of legal jurisdictions, so cyberspace sovereignty is needed for decomposing the overlapped legal jurisdictions.

4.1.4 Problems Brought by Different Judging Principles of Legality

Before the age of Internet, information dissemination was regional, the dissemination scope of information was the same as the control scope of regime, and the information dissemination was carried out strictly according to the legal norms of the physical world. However, in the Internet era, information dissemination can easily cross state boundaries and the jurisdiction scopes of regimes, wherein malicious information communicators may deliberately spread, by using different standards for information legality identification of different regimes, specific information from an area where the information is identified as legal to another area where the information is identified as illegal. Similarly, different goods in e-commerce also have different legal attributes in different regions. For example, due to the influence of culture differences, the legal attributes of the same commodity in Muslim communities may be different from those in Christian communities. As a result, on the Internet, merchants may sell the object to the area where the object is deemed as illegal by using the area where the object is deemed as legal. In many cases, the law only cracks down on the spreaders or the sellers rather than the buyers. Apparently, traditional laws show their weaknesses in this case of cross-regional online sale. The countries can solve this problem by using the sovereignty principles in their own ways.

Following are some cross-regional judicial cases, and, with no exception, the courts used the "long-arm jurisdiction" to make judgement for the subjects beyond the jurisdiction. The question is whether the enforcement of the judgment is feasible. It is reported that US courts have applied the theory of "long-arm jurisdiction" to network cases, and a lot in many cases have tried to perfect the application principles.[14]

---

[14]Beware the long arm of the U.S. courts. http://www.canadianlawyermag.com/5382/Beware-the-long-arm-of-the-U.S.-courts.html [2016-9-15].

1. Conflicts of laws in Yahoo's auctions of neo-Nazi items

One typical example of legality judgement conflicts is the case where Yahoo was suspected of auctioning neo-Nazi items.[15] In April 2000, as the plaintiffs, the Union of Jewish Students of France (L'Uejf) and the International League Against Racism and Anti-Semitism (La Licra) filed a law suit against Yahoo! Inc. and Yahoo France (Yahoo.fr) to the Tribunal de Grande Instance of Paris, France for the reason as follows: the auction website of Yahoo! launched a series of neo-Nazi auctions, and Yahoo.fr provided related links to French users. Therefore, the plaintiffs petitioned the court to order the first defendant, Yahoo! Inc., to stop the auctions of neo-Nazi goods that could affect French users; the second defendant, Yahoo France, should take immediate steps to stop linking to the sites involved; the two defendants should pay a compensation of one Franc each to the plaintiffs; the defendant shall pay the litigation expenses.

The defendant Yahoo made the following comments during the defense: firstly, it believes that the business activities of Yahoo.com are mainly in English and should be under the jurisdiction of the US courts, and, according to the U.S. constitution's terms on free speech, the auctions of neo-Nazi items on websites should not be banned; secondly, as the portal of Yahoo! Inc. in France, Yahoo.fr is not the sponsor of the auction, and it merely provides a link service that allows French users to have straight access to the services in other language so as to reach the auction website; thirdly, according to existing technical measures, it is impossible to absolutely forbid French users from participating in the neo-Nazi auction, because identifications and residents of all of the participants cannot be identified by the prior arts; finally, it argues that whether the French court's decision will be executed should be decided by the US courts; however, according to the U.S. constitution, the U.S. courts will not enforce the ruling made by the French court.

As the second defendant, Yahoo! fr put forward three reasons in the course of the trial: firstly, Yahoo! fr merely established a link with Yahoo! Inc., rather than directly getting involved in auctions of neo-Nazi items; secondly, Yahoo! fr has always been cautious in the website business activities, for instance, users are required to accept relevant terms and declarations predetermined by the website before using the services provided by Yahoo! fr; finally, Yahoo! fr has never suggested the public enter into the auction site involved in this case.

On November 20, 2000, the Tribunal de Grande Instance of Paris, France issued the final judgement of the Yahoo case[16]: Yahoo! Inc. should take all possible technical measures to prevent French users from accessing their neo-Nazi auction websites, otherwise, a fine of 100, 000 Francs per day will be imposed; Yahoo! fr should inform the users (even before the users search on Yahoo.com through

[15]France bans internet Nazi auctions. http://news.bbc.co.uk/2/hi/europe/760782.stm [2016-9-15].

[16]Brief comment on the case that Yahoo was suspected of auctioning neo-Nazi goods. http://www.doc88.com/p-3167536009611.html [2016-12-31].

Yahoo. fr): "The visit will be immediately terminated at the retrieval of the web pages or websites that violate the French laws, including those auction websites for neo-Nazi items, otherwise, it would be a violation of French law and face the risk of being accused"; other claims and grounds of pleading are rejected; the court expenses should be paid by the defendants.[17]

2. Conflicts of laws caused by iCrave TV live broadcast

iCrave TV is a small company of Canada, which enables Internet users to watch live TV shows through the Internet. iCrave TV's behavior is legal in Canada, but illegal in America.[18] Superficially, iCrave TV restricts its issue range via conditional access to the website so as not to serve the Americans. Through triple verification and the click wrap agreement, it ensures that the service is available only to the people in Canada. One step is to ask the potential consumers to enter their local area code. The user will be rejected if the area code does not belong to Canada. It seems that the merchant has taken measures to cut off the link between the website and the countries outside Canada, but the problem is that anyone can enter the website only by inputting the area code of Toronto. At last, the US courts exercised jurisdiction over this case and solved the disputes between users.[19] The basis of jurisdiction is that the connection with America is not objectively cut off although measures have been taken by iCrave TV; in fact, iCrave TV owns an amazing number of users in the United States, and has a great influence in the United States; besides, it is not testified that iCrave TV is capable of identifying which country the user is from.[20]

3. The trademark conflict and legal disputes of Marits Company

Marits Company is in California which has its website in this state. It offered online advertisements for a new service, hoping that web users will become its potential customers. Later, this website was visited by 311 users in Missouri, most of whom were employees of a Marits Company in Missouri. The Marits Company in Missouri filed a lawsuit with the court in April 1996, suing the Marits Company in California for infringement of its trademark rights and unfair competition. The

[17]France bans internet Nazi auctions. http://news.bbc.co.uk/2/hi/europe/760782.stm [2016-8-27].

[18]Copyrighted Broadcast Programming on the Internet. http://www.copyright.gov/docs/regstat61500.html [2016-9-15].

[19]Broadcasters pull the plug on iCraveTV. http://library.law.columbia.edu/urlmirror/CVLAJLA/24CVLAJLA1/0-1004-200-1559907.html [2016-9-15].

[20]Researches on jurisdiction issues of e-commerce cases. 2010-7. http://china.findlaw.cn/falvchangshi/dianzishangwu/dzjf/jfgx/22495_34.html [2016-8-27].

Marits Company in California insisted that the jurisdiction of the court of Missouri lacked sufficient grounds, the company asked the court to refuse to accept this case. The court in the eastern district of Missouri made the ultimate judgement, according to which the connection (if there are trading behaviors in this state) between the defendant and Missouri satisfied the long-arm acts of Missouri, and exercised jurisdiction over this case for the reason of "minimum contact".[21]

4.1.5 Problems in the Tracing of Stepping Attacks

On December 23, 2015, the Ukrainian power sector suffered malware attacks. Ukrainian news media (TSN) reported on the 24th: "At least three power regions were attacked, leading to hours of blackouts at around 15:00 local time"; "Attackers invaded the monitoring and management system. More than half of the region and part of the Ivan-Frankovsk region suffered hours of outages. Based on overall event tracking, electricity system analysis and associated sample analysis, the joint analysis team concluded the attack: took the power infrastructure as the goal; Black Energy and other related malware as the main tools; conducted preliminary data acquisition system and environmental presets via BOTNET; sent malware payload via emails; sent power off commands via remote control (Supervisory Control and Data Acquisition) SCADA nodes; destroyed the SCADA system to slow system recovery; used DDoS service calls as interference; finally completed an information warfare level cyber attack."[22]

Different from the internationally interconnected network of telecommunication, many network forms in cyberspace are not necessarily internationally interconnected. The international interconnection method adopted by the telecommunication network is the direct connection mode of circuit connection, in which effective responsibility investigation can be performed in case of any problem. However, since springboards exists in the Internet, it is impossible to get the exact position of the initiator based on only one attack. Country A can see that the direct source of the attack is country B, but the A can't see who is attacking by using the nodes of country B, let alone the real source of the attack, because it is very likely that the nodes of country C attack country A by using the nodes of country B as a springboard. In this case, if country B itself is not the victim, what will urge country B to assist country A to trace the root? What makes country B trace back to country C? How to finish the tracing from country B to country C? In the international community, many countries have the Computer Emergency Response Team (CERT) and many transnational attacks are coordinated and processed by these

[21]Discussion on jurisdiction confirmation in Internet infringement. 2009-2. http://www.110.com/ziliao/article-61945.html [2016-8-27].

[22]Comprehensive Analysis Report on Ukraine Power System Attacks. http://www.antiy.com/response/A_Comprehensive_Analysis_Report_on_Ukraine_Power_Grid_Outage/A_Comprehensive_Analysis_Report_on_Ukraine_Power_Grid_Outage.html [2016-9-27].

CERT organizations. But since permissions can be granted by the government only, it is extremely difficult for non-government organizations to deal with issues beyond national permissions. Therefore, the tracing in country B can be performed by regime only; moreover, only forces of governments have the right, capacity and responsibility for the tracing in foreign countries. Obviously, country B will take the responsibility of tracing only when it affirms that it has the responsibility and obligation attached to sovereignty and it is the obligation of the government to take sovereignty measures, namely, the Internet sovereign. For instance, when country C attacks country A by using a building, then country B has to solve this problem if the building belongs to country B; if this building is ownerless, then country A has to destroy it or otherwise be attacked. Clearly, this situation is the last thing that country A wants to see, so country A would prefer that country B has sovereignty so that it can take its responsibilities and obligations.

4.1.6 Trans-Boundary Issues of Phishing Websites

In March 2011, Epsilon, which is one of the world's largest E-mail marketing companies, suffered a phishing network attack, wherein the hacker tracked confidential information, such as codes and financial details of users by using fake customized emails. In this case, about 60,000,000 mails of more than 100 business clients of Epsilon were leaked.[23]

Since the end of November 2014, ICANN had successively suffered a series of serious phishing attacks from unknown hackers, wherein employees were deceived by the received emails with simulated internal domain names. As a result, the email identification information of many ICANN employees was stolen, and the data were leaked. At the beginning of December, ICANN discovered that this influenced email identification information was used again in the visit to other ICANN systems other than email systems and information in the internal "central area data system" of ICANN about users' names and addresses were also revealed. The affected information also included the official blog system of ICANN, and Who is information portal for querying domain name records and so on.[24]

One phishing website usually involves three roles, namely, the hacker, the attacked website, and the phishing website. In general, it would be hard to strike these three roles if they are in different countries. If the phishing website and the attacked website are in different countries, it will be difficult for the attacked enterprise to cross the border so as to shut the phishing website down even if the phishing website is discovered; when the phishing website and the hacker are not in

---

[23]9 most miserable hacker attacks: Google was on the list. 2012-6. http://people.pedaily.cn/201206/20120614328577_all.shtml [2016-9-9].

[24]ICANN suffered phishing attack from hackers, employees' account information was revealed. 2014-12. http://tech.sina.com.cn/i/2014-12-18/doc-iawzunex6994918.shtml [2016-9-9].

the same country, the hacker can hardly be found even if the phishing website is discovered; if the hacker and the attacked enterprise are in different countries, the attacked enterprise can hardly bring the hacker to justice no matter how high the costs are. However, if Internet sovereignty is unequivocal, then all of the things will involve the responsibilities and obligations attached to the sovereignty, then it is not that easy for the cross-border crimes of hackers to succeed and go unpunished.

4.2 Evolution of Internet into Benefit Space of Countries

So far, many countries have imposed sovereignty over the Internet and the more reason that cyberspace sovereignty is concemed is because international contradictions are frequently reflected here. Instead of seeing it as a global commons, many countries, which have claimed to disapprove cyberspace sovereignty, have imposed state sovereignty in cyberspace.

4.2.1 Sovereignty Interest at Political Level

According to territory sovereignty in traditional international laws, the state shall have the supreme dominance over all persons, things, affairs and behaviors within its territory, and the jurisdiction over information flow is certainly included. If the state sovereignty cannot be applied to the Internet, no action can be taken for the information on the Internet. However, the government of a country will allow no forms of challenge to its laws. It is always said that there should be no vacuum in laws. For instance, it is not true that murdering in the public place is a crime while murdering in a private place is not. Similarly, publications banned by law cannot exist in either real space or cyberspace. Therefore, whether cyberspace sovereignty is openly admitted or not, the same "offline/online" acting norms will be adopted by most countries. For example, due to the disputes between Koreas, South Korea believes that all of the propaganda from North Korea is malicious, and South Korea does not allow official information of North Korea to be spread in South Korea. In the cyberspace, South Korea takes the same measures so as to stop the official website of North Korea, i.e. "Uriminzokkiri", from entering into South Korea. America shouts for free transmission of information, because there is little propaganda in the international community that can challenge the US government. Therefore, the US also allows free flow of paper medium information in the physical space. However, although the radio & television satellite network also belongs to the cyberspace, the landing of CCTV-1 in America is restricted, which is a typical case of restrictive measures taken by America in cyberspace for exercising sovereignty, although America regards the Internet as an exception space.

In a word, no country will allow the current regime to be overturned by any unconventional means, and national laws protect only the regime that is legally produced. Therefore, abnormal malicious activities for overturning the regime by using the Internet will surely be punished by law. About this issue, governments of nations will certainly impose laws over the cyberspace, so the cyberspace sovereignty has become an undeniable fact at political level.

4.2.2 Sovereignty Interest at Military Level

Network warfare forces has been set in many countries including America, and the forces is different from traditional electronic warfare forces. Traditional electronic warfare forces has the property of strategic support, and play the role of assisting the warfare in physical space; however, the current network warfare forces of America takes Internet as the battleground so as to hit the enemy information system through the detection of dynamic enemy information, as a result of which cyberspace is treated as a battle domain. Forces are the main body for defending the national sovereignty, so the battles in cyberspace are substantively the recognition of cyberspace sovereignty, for instance, when the information systems of other countries are attacked within the United States, will America show up and fight back? Sony Corporation was suspected to have been attacked by North Korea, what is the reason for the US government's high-profile declaration of fighting back? The reason is that the Internet is dominated by America, and that the attacks on the Internet dominated by America are taken as challenges to the sovereignty of America. Apparently, these are all specific reflection of sovereignty.

If a country has cyber warfare forces and can explicitly conduct military operations against cyberspace for state actions, it itself shows that the state sovereignty is imposed over the cyberspace, which also shows that cyberspace sovereignty is admitted. In turn, cyberspace sovereignty also provides legal basis for the military presence in cyberspace.

4.2.3 Sovereignty Interest at Economic Level

E-commerce based on Internet has the properties of crossing sovereign countries. As a result, since the network exists across the borders, obstacles exist in the exertion of national economic jurisdiction over the processing of the economic problems in the cyberspace, such as tax collection and administration, protection of the rights and interests of consumers, e-commerce, debtor-creditor relationships or the like, and over the management of information itself as a resource having economic values. From this aspect, it is difficult for the countries to use traditional economy management models in the cyberspace to adapt to the economic activities of the Internet age. For information itself as a resource having economic values, e.g. multi-media electronic publications, there is no way to influence its trading in physical space. If free trade of information is not expected, and a tax system is to be implemented according to the modes in physical space, it is necessary to establish the management mechanism of network economy, thereby forming a projection of cyberspace sovereignty in the circulation of Internet commodities. Furthermore, although tax collection can be performed through logistics of the cross-border Internet commodities, taxation modes in different countries may provide loop-holes for the dealers. For instance, China adopts the taxation system of products production, which means that taxes are required as long as the product is produced and is supplied to the distributor, no matter whether it is sold or not; however, America adopts the taxation system of product consumers, which means that tax needs to be paid after the retail of the commodity. Therefore, the traders can buy American products in China by means of cross-border electronic shopping, so as to avoid the retail taxes in America and the production taxes in China. In the process of logistics, a barrier can be set up through cross-border tariff collection, but, since import taxes are collected only for bulk commodities or high value-added products, general products can exploit an advantage. As the popularization of C2M (Customer To Manufactory), consumers can purchase directly from the manufacturers, which makes the situation worse.

Countries can only set special management modes for the special form of network economy, for instance, a corresponding management mode including tax regulation, business security, and economic dispute handling and so on can be provided specific to Internet economic behaviors. However, this mode itself reflects cyber sovereignty in Internet economy, proving the inevitable existence of cyberspace sovereignty at economic level.

4.2.4 Sovereignty Performance at Cultural Level

Cultural diversity is true in the big world, but conflicts and incompatibility among different cultures also exist. For instance, the faith in Muslim culture and that in Christian culture bring different ways of life, and the maintenance of believes causes violence; due to the difference between western culture and Confucian culture, different perceptions of pornography result in different coping approaches. In the process of defending traditional culture, government departments are bond to draw a certain insurmountable "Red Line". Moreover, this "Red Line" will be everywhere, namely, the national will must be reflected at every corner covered by the regime, including the cyberspace.

In this sense, sovereignty exists wherever the "Red Line" exists. Therefore, it is a given fact at the cultural level that sovereignty exists in the cyberspace.

4.2.5 Sovereignty Performance at the Level of Social Stability

It is well known that Internet is a double-edged sword. To ensure social stability, the government surely cannot ignore the role played by Internet in damaging social stability. Since gambling causes social instability in the physical space, it will be restricted even as a game; the government will not interfere in football if it brings no social problem; when corruption occurs in football games, there will be an intersection between football and the real world, and related criminal activities are still subject to legal sanctions. Although cyberspace is a virtual place, the governments will neither regard it as a place free from legal restrictions, nor ignore the criminal activities in the cyberspace. Particularly, during the combination of the cyberspace with social security, criminal activities existing in the cyberspace, such as data fraud, infringement of individual privacy or the like, will also be investigated by the judicial systems of countries. For the same reason, any attack on information systems is also regarded as a crime by the nations, because there will be no legal vacuum in the cyberspace. It clearly shows that state sovereignty has been imposed over the social security issue in cyberspace.

4.2.6 Sovereignty Interest at Legal Level

The US stresses that Internet should be led by the "stakeholder", but it also definitely expresses that the established laws are applicable to the cyberspace. Sea, land, sky and outer space are visible or tangible physical spaces, which belong to the first space; relatively, cyberspace is virtual, and belongs to the artificial second space. Therefore, Internet is a projection of physical society, and the power scope of physical society should be reflected on the Internet. Legal systems of states play an important role in the regulation of network behaviors, but also have many limits. Particularly, when the virtual space bears real legal relationships, the characteristics of Internet bring a series of difficulties to the implementation and application of laws, and the feasibility and legality of traditional laws based on territory have been challenged. As a result, it is necessary to establish the concept of cyberspace sovereignty so as to make the legislation of cyberspace necessary and provide supporting theories for the application of established laws to the cyberspace, thereby ensuring feasibility and legality of national laws in the cyberspace.

If a country applies laws in the cyberspace, it shows the definite existence of sovereignty in cyberspace. For example, only a relevant committee has the right to decide how to punish the artistic gymnastics athlete who has taken stimulants and the court will never intervene because no country claims sovereignty in this GAME; besides, the punishments from the committee are also limited to the committee's jurisdiction scope, such as being forbidden to participate in the sports meet under the jurisdiction of the committee, and will never be confinement, or being forbidden to perform in night clubs, because the committee's rights are limited to the Olympic Games only.

4.2.7 Conflicts of National Jurisdiction in Cyberspace

In 1997, the consensus reached on the seminar of The Hague Conference of International Private Laws about "Issues about international private laws on the Internet" is that "Internet is substantively transnational". Since the Internet is boundless, global and non-centralized, the jurisdiction over online behaviors by a single country always results in conflicts and Spillover effects of jurisdiction; to make things worse, the jurisdiction of network cases in the territory of one country may be a violation of the sovereignty of another country. One online behavior usually produces corresponding effects in many countries. Due to the traditional jurisdiction rules—the principle of effect, one case may be under the jurisdiction of many countries. However, since legal systems of the countries are different, it is inevitable that the online actor faces inconsistent jurisdiction basis. Brought up to the nation level, jurisdiction conflicts and collisions will be the conflicts and collisions of have been challenged sovereignty. Take the above Yahoo! case as an example, the judgment of France contradicts with the principle of free speech in the constitution of the US. Therefore, if the judgement of France is executed in America, it will be a violation of American sovereignty.

4.3 Countries Share Interests in the Same Cyberspace

Since countries currently act and share interests in the same cyberspace, it is necessary for the countries to explore a shared regulation mode of the cyberspace. The basic starting point is to discuss shared regulation based on sovereignty, and the problem concerned by cyberspace sovereignty is to ensure the application of state sovereignty in a new space.

4.3.1 Not Every Problem Can Be Solved by the "Stakeholder"

In real social activities of Internet, many problems cannot be handled merely by using the regulation mode of the "Stakeholder".

1. From the perspective of resource distribution rationality

At present, the distribution power of core resources of the Internet, such as the assignment of IP address space, verification of domain names or the like. ICANN is now controlled by "Stakeholders" and its members include Internet giants, celebrities, and relevant international organizations and so on. According to the rules, ICANN members are on the behalf of individuals only, and cannot represent any government; however, ICANN has been controlled by the US government for a long time. Put aside the role played by the US government, merely the mastery of the "Stakeholder" will not take national interest of other countries into consideration, or some irrationalities for some roles beyond enterprises, or even some conflicts.

Take IP address space allocation as an example, since the current principle is "first-to-file", the one who files first will have the priority for getting sufficient resources. In IPv4 era, this mode was extremely unequal. Some countries could get one address of B category, and all that China could get as a network power were multiple addresses of B category; however, the institutions who filed earlier, e.g. University of Illinois, was able to get an address of A category, thereby owning tens of millions of addresses. It seems to be the equality of "first come, first served", but it is fake. Limited by the development of information technology, some countries were late to be aware of the significance of resources, so conditions are required so as to provide necessary resources for these countries. In other words, when resources are limited, it should even more ensure balanced development of sovereign countries. Obviously, only the organization formed by sovereign countries, rather than the Stakeholder, would take the equality of states into consideration. It's like the satellite orbits in outer space, namely, only the satellite management organization formed by sovereign countries will provide an orbit distribution principle that is as fair as possible, rather than the principle of the simple routine of endless occupation for those who filed earlier.

Take the domain name naming as another example, the Stakeholder and sovereign countries focus on different contents as for the aspect of domain name licenses. For instance, if someone applies for ".fangongheike" as its top level domain, the protest from China will obviously make an organization of sovereign countries seriously consider whether the application is rational; however, the organization of stakeholders might not care about the opinions of countries, or that some decision-making persons who are biased against China may be pleased to see a top level domain like this. In fact, the domain name containing "fangongheike.com" has already appeared in ".com". More extremely, if someone applies for ".IS" or ".ISIS" as the top level domain, it will certainly be rejected by the organization formed of sovereign countries. But the registration of domain names which are politically sensitive may be permitted by the organization of stakeholders who may care little about politics.

In a word, the management of stakeholders causes a lack of voice of most sovereign countries in cyberspace affairs, and the equality and fairness of decisions could be hardly ensured, thereby inevitably resulting in numerous potential conflicts and hidden dangers.

2. From the perspective of the Computer Emergency Response Team

Computer Emergency Response Team (CERT) is responsible for handling computer network security incidents, and exists at all levels such as governments, forces, enterprises, and academic institutions and so on. "The Forum for Incident Response and Security Teams (FIRST)" was internationally established so as to promote the cooperation of CERT organizations of all countries, thereby handling transnational computer attack incidents jointly. Generally, these CERT organizations are non-government sectors and belong to "Stakeholders". Just because of being non-government organizations, CERT organizations can merely play the role of assisting victim enterprises, but can hardly be qualified in the work of tracing and verification. If things go on like this, transnational cyber crimes will be normal due to legal and regulatory fade areas. Therefore, the transnational cooperation won't be truly effective without government permission.

In its A/70/174 documentation Report of the Group of Government Experts on Developments in the Field of Information and Telecommunications in the Context of International Security,[25] the UN points out "States should consider additional confidence-building measures that would strengthen cooperation on a bilateral, sub-regional, regional and multilateral basis. These would include voluntary agreements by States to: ① Strength cooperative mechanisms between relevant agencies to address ICT security incidents and develop additional technical, legal and diplomatic mechanisms to address ICT infrastructure-related requests, including the consideration of exchanges of personnel in areas such as incident response and law enforcement, as appropriate, and encouraging exchanges between research and academic institutions; ② Enhance cooperation, including the development of focal points for the exchange of information on malicious ICT use and the provision of assistance in investigations; ③ Establish a national computer emergency response team and/or cyber-security incident response team or officially designate an organization to fulfill this role. States may wish to consider such bodies within their definition of critical infrastructure. States should support and facilitate the functioning of and cooperation among such national response teams and other authorized bodies; ④ Expand and support practices in computer emergency response team and cyber-security incident response team cooperation, as appropriate, such as information exchange about vulnerabilities, attack patterns and best practices for mitigating attacks, including coordinating responses, organizing

[25]Report of the Group of Government Experts on Developments in the Field of Information and Telecommunications in the Context of International Security. http://www.un.org/ga/search/view_doc.asp?symbol=A/70/174&referer=/english/&Lang=C [2016-9-19].

exercises, supporting the handling of ICT-related incidents and enhancing regional and sector-based cooperation; ⑤ Cooperate, in a manner consistent with national and international law, with requests from other States in investigating ICT-related crime or the use of ICTs for terrorist purposes or to mitigate malicious ICT activity emanating from their territory."

This UN documentation shows that only the governments of sovereign countries, rather than enterprises, can jointly handle transnational cyber-security incidents, thereby forming a cyber-security co-governance system.

3. From the perspective of transnational e-commerce

During April 21–22, 2016, the United Nations Commission on International Trade Law (UNCITRAL) held the first "Seminar on Legal Issues of Identity Management and Trusted Service" in Vienna International conference center, Austria. The seminar aimed at seeking consensus and feasible solutions to establish uniform laws and rules for transnational identity management, so as to get prepared for the interconnection of global trade based on Internet identity, and is as significant as establishing the mutual recognition rules of global e-passports. Clearly, the promotion of the United Nations Commission on International Trade Law shows that this problem cannot be solved by merely the stakeholders, or by the powerful promotion (e.g. Apple Pay) of a certain large enterprise followed by immediate recognition of states. Therefore, this problem can be solved only by the co-governance of sovereign countries.

4. From the perspective of the operation mechanism of an international military alliance

It is believed that, within the military alliance of NATO, America transferred the Einstein system to NATO nations so as to establish a network defense system in the NATO nations. It seems to be a simple output, while it is the information sharing, or even inter-operation, of the defense system. Obviously, seen from the angle of military, this belongs to the behavior of sovereign nations, and is equivalent to the construction of a network military alliance on the Internet by sovereign countries. If the networks connection of two nations from two different military alliances needs to pass through the communication facility of a military ally, for instance, the connection between China and Brazil needs to pass through the US communication lines, it means that this military ally can possibly interrupt the interconnection channel of these two countries. If this military ally expands a little by dragging in its partner country or even recipient country, then this huge alliance can suround most nations beyond the alliance, then the alliance could put the nations in the danger of being isolated on Internet. This is the result of imposing military forces over the Internet by jointed sovereign countries.

4.3.2 Necessities of the Co-Governance Mode of Cyberspace Sovereignty

Internet is a great progress of human civilization as well as a new challenge to social governance. Due to the high complexity of cyberspace and the high diversity of stakeholders, unipolar thinking is doomed to be unfeasible. It will be more harmful if the Internet is used by a country acting as the "controller" with hypocritical reasons for damaging interests of other countries. The Internet leads the whole world to "interconnection", and makes states all over the world to be a community of common destiny in cyberspace, so it also should be "shared and governed by all", the requires specifically established rules should be required for that. One important prerequisite for maintaining the cyberspace security is the autonomous cyberspace management of different countries. Public policies from countries for maintaining cyberspace security and order should be respected; and the international rules for cyber behaviors should be negotiated by related countries based on equality. Only in this way can the common security of network be really ensured.

At present, the institutional dilemma of cyberspace governance urgently calls for reform of the existing governance mechanism.[26] Security problems, such as network monitoring, exposed in the "PRISM" event[27] reflects that the systems and mechanisms of cyberspace are still controlled by the US even under the background of rapid development of network technologies, and that the cyberspace governance mechanism is still far from meeting the needs of the international community. In recent years, following the change of international power structure and the rise of emerging countries, emerging countries are engaged more and more in the existing mechanism of cyberspace. On the one hand, emerging countries have relied on the United Nations and its institutions to present their views and standpoints; on the other hand, by establishing a global Internet governance alliance, holding global Internet conferences and so on, emerging countries are working hard on exercising new system models after sufficient international consultation, so as to promote the establishment of cyberspace rules and finally make it move from the unofficial conference systems to the official conference systems of inter-government organizations. The "stakeholder" model appears to have handed over the cyberspace governance to non-profit organizations, but it is still actually constrained by the United States.[28]

---

[26]Wang MG (2015) Institutional dilemma of cyberspace governance and breaking-through routes of emerging countries. World Outlook, 6:98–116. http://www.ccpit.org/Contents/Channel_3432/2015/1118/503464/content_503464.htm [2016-9-27].

[27]NSA slides explain the PRISM data-collection program. http://www.washingtonpost.com/wp-srv/special/politics/prism-collection-documents/ [2016-9-9].

[28]Wang MJ (2015) Future of global cyberspace governance: sovereignty, competition and consensus. People's Tribune·academics, 4:15–23. http://www.rmlt.com.cn/2016/0308/419694.shtml [2016-9-27].

However, the American's proposal of the "stakeholder" was widely opposed by the developing countries. Developing countries are more inclined to government domination, and insist on strengthening cyberspace governance through international organizations such as the United Nations, which is also called "the multilateralism mode". The purpose for powerful Internet nations, particularly the US, to insist on the stakeholder mode is to deny the role of government, so it is necessary to deny the cyberspace sovereignty; however, the government-oriented "multilateralism mode" supported by developing countries is based on cyberspace sovereignty, reflects the overall national demand in the mode of sovereignty, and seeks for compromise of the international community by means of sovereignty.

The cyberspace sovereignty is the inevitability of international political reality. Instead of being the fight for the so-called right of control, the declaration of cyberspace sovereignty is an objective and rational understanding of current international political environments. Some of the contradictions and divergences of cyberspace governance by countries are sort of related to value ideas, but more of them are rooted in the calculation of national interests. The denial of cyberspace sovereignty by powerful Internet countries is not equal to the denial of the cyberspace sovereignty of their own; instead, powerful Internet countries ensure their "control" or "cyberspace governance" over the global network by denying cyberspace sovereignty of other nations. Since the key resources and core technology of the Internet are in the hands of Internet companies and non-profit organizations that abide by laws of these countries, powerful Internet countries can conveniently control these resources. It is believed that "Instead of really noticably caring about cyberspace sovereignty, the US just does not want other countries to block the expansion of its hegemony by using the concept of cyberspace sovereignty."[29]

Following are the necessities for establishing the mode of shared governance on the basis of Internet state sovereignty[30]:

(1) To provide the optimal solution for global cyberspace governance.

The principle of cyberspace sovereignty is to establish a comprehensive governance system in the frame of the UN, with nations as the governance unit and by combining many forces such as Internet enterprise, related social organizations, and citizens or the like, so as to jointly cope with cyber crimes, cyber terrorism and so on. Facing increasingly serious cyber threats, the insistence of cyberspace sovereignty is good for wiping out divergences and unifying understandings so as to establish the co-governance system, which is really needed.

---

[29]Wang MJ (2016) Future of global cyberspace governance: sovereignty, competition and consensus. People's Tribune·academics. http://www.360doc.com/content/16/0622/11/11708174_569755228.shtml [2016-10-3].

[30]An J (2016) The principle of cyber sovereignty is an inevitable choice of global cyberspace governance. Red Flag Manuscript, 4:30–31. http://theory.people.com.cn/n1/2016/0225/c143844-28150601.html [2016-9-27].

(2) The advocacy of cyberspace sovereignty principle is moral and helpful in maintaining fairness and justice of global networks.

The principle of cyberspace sovereignty advocates to give full play to the enthusiasm of nations within the frame of UN so as to share the governance of network resources and jointly build the management mechanism, thereby greatly protecting network rights and interests of developing countries, and the fairness and justice of global networks will be ensured. Therefore, the advocacy of the cyberspace sovereignty principle is moral, and is the common expectation of nations all around the world, especially for those with relatively backward network development.

(3) The promotion of the cyberspace sovereignty principle is a historical necessity, and can help the global network governance to be shared and governed by all.

The society will be interconnected, cooperative and profiting in the future, so the effective methods of handling cyberspace security problems lie in multi-element cooperation and the mode of being "shared and governed by all". The governance of international cyberspace should insist on multilateral cooperation and discussion, and give full play to the roles of subjects including government, international organizations, Internet enterprise, technical communities, non-government institutions, individual citizens and so on, rather than by unilateralism and the negotiation dominated by one or several countries, thereby enabling the governance system of global Internet to be more fair and rational, and be capable of reflecting will and interests of majority countries.

4.3.3 *Cyberspace Calls for a New Order*

One of the major concerns of developing countries is that powerful Internet countries are capable of establishing a price monopoly over cyber weak countries through the establishment of cyber hegemony as well as the monopoly of network resources and core technology, thereby plundering and exploiting economy of cyber weak countries; by denying cyberspace sovereignty and opposing regulation of information content, powerful Internet countries sustain their global hegemony so as to form a situation which makes it easy for them to infringe cultural rights and interests of other nations, to perform ideology infiltration, to interfere in other countries' domestic affairs, or even to implement cyber colonialism, which causes the developing countries to be dependent on powerful Internet countries in politics and economy, and damages their long-term rights and interests. Therefore, the developing countries are longing for a new cyberspace order.[31]

[31]Wang MG (2016) Institutional dilemma of cyberspace governance and breaking-through routes of emerging countries. World Outlook, 6:98–116. http://www.360doc.com/content/15/1120/10/28475443_514507436.shtml [2016-10-3].

After the development of cyberspace in recent decades, a bottom-up non-centralized governance mechanism, with ICANN and Internet Society (ISOC) as the core organizations, has been formed in the field of global cyberspace governance. However, serious institutional dilemma and governance failures exist in global cyberspace, due to which emerging countries' cyberspace expectation is not satisfied, and the formation of a new cyberspace order is blocked.

1. Insufficient legality and representation of the design of a current cyberspace system

As the core governance mechanism of cyberspace, ICANN is responsible for the allocation of Internet key resources and domain name systems. But a legality deficit of ICANN exists in the Internet domain name system, which affects its authority in cyberspace. By technical advantages, western countries have long been dominating in ICANN and other organizations, while numerous developing countries are excluded from being decision-makers of this institution. On such a basis, an American scholar Jonathan Weinberg believes that the legality risk of ICANN is rather high.[32] Roxana Radu and so on from Geneva Institute of International and Development Issues in Switzerland thoroughly discussed related Internet governance mechanisms since the 2012 World Conference on International Telecommunications (WCIT). In their opinion, the core to be concerned in the global governance of cyberspace is the legality, involvement and responsibility existing in the mode of the "multi-stakeholder", which involves the international system issue in a greater scope. As a matter of fact, the legality problem existing in current global cyberspace governance system is an objective reflection of unequal international system structure in cyberspace. Besides, cyberspace can also influence the real international political space. Therefore, it became the key requirement for overcoming the institutional dilemma of cyberspace to reform the "multi-stakeholder" dominated by western countries, to promote its legality and accountability, and to realize "function-globalization" of ICANN and other institutions.[33]

2. Limited ability for mechanism implementation

At present, deep differences about cyber security, cyberspace sovereignty and other issues exist between western countries and emerging countries, as a result, the functions of existing governance mechanisms in solving the problem of public order, and promoting social development and so on are greatly reduced. The validity, observation and performance abilities of almost all of existing governance mechanisms, whether it is ICANN, Meridian, the Forum for Incident Response and Security Teams (FIRST) and Internet Governance Forum (IGF) that are traditional

[32]The Regime Complex for Managing Global Cyber Activities. https://www.cigionline.org/sites/default/files/gcig_paper_no1.pdf [2016-10-3].

[33]The Evolution of Global Internet Governance Principles and Policies in the Making. http://www.springer.com/us/book/9783642452987 [2016-10-3].

and western-dominated, or World Telecommunication Development Conference (WTDC), WCIT and World Summit on Information Society Review Process + 10 (WSIS + 10) which are vigorously promoted by emerging countries and dominated by international government organizations.

3. Confrontations and conflicts between developed countries and emerging countries in the concept of a cyberspace governance system

Western countries stick to the mode of the "multi-stakeholder" of cyberspace and oppose the institutional mode dominated by the UN. Western countries insist that the mode of the "multi-stakeholder" can ensure the openness and vigor of cyberspace. However, following the situation of the "Declining West, Rising East" in world political forces, as well as the rising of emerging countries represented by BRICS, emerging countries urged western countries to reform the existing Internet governance system so as to safeguard their interest in cyberspace and promote their economic development and capacity building; bedsides, they try to make plans for the field lack of governance mechanism, such as cyber security and so on.

As for institutional mode, emerging countries propose the mode of sovereignty co-governance, and question the mode of the "multi-stakeholder" agitated by western countries. Emerging countries regard UN as the appropriate place for discussing cyberspace because it's equal and transparent. At the same time, due to the existing authority and exclusiveness of "state sovereignty", emerging countries approve the cyberspace authority of inter-governmental international organizations. However, in the viewpoint of US and other developed countries, the governance prospect will be uncertain if the topics like Internet governance and cyber security are empowered to inter-governmental international organizations. Chances are remarkably greater that network devices will be combined with terrorism, many countries, including the United States, have strongly called for strengthened cyberspace sovereignty. Even so, in order to oppose the nation-centered governance mode, western countries still stress the "return of states" in cyberspace is not the same as the return of state sovereignty in the system of "Westphalia". For example, Britain clearly showed that sovereignty governance could not be solved by signing multilateral treaties, and that cyberspace security might be improved by behavior rules (laws) or other methods. At least within a short period, the problem of cyber security may not be solved by concluding binding multilateral treaties. In order to better promote the mode of the "multi-stakeholder" so as to get more public opinion support, the Bureau of International Information Program of the US State Department made an online video named "Internet Belongs to Everyone" on August 29, 2014, repeatedly advertised the cooperation mode of the "multi-stakeholder" based on openness and cooperation, and tried its best to reject the legitimate rights of sovereign states to regulate and control the Internet.

Emerging countries, particularly China and Russia, are rather cautious about the actors outside of sovereign countries and intergovernmental international organizations. Non-state actors in the cyberspace governance mainly include international non-government organizations, trans-governmental networks, transnational social activities, public-private partnership, transnational corporations, and individual elites and so on. The non-government organizations in the cyberspace governance field include: IANA, every regional Internet registration agency, domain name registrar and internet registration agencies and ICANN and so on. For a long time, China and Russia believe that the cyberspace sovereignty is the principle of state sovereignty natural extension and reflection in cyberspace. It is the performance of exercising sovereignty for each country to manage, review or shield the Internet infrastructure and data information within its territory. Under the background of rapid development of Internet, the sovereignty principle and jurisdiction should be firmly held and strengthened, rather than being cancelled or weakened.

4.4 China's Main Considerations for Advocating Cyberspace Sovereignty

Being widely used by the international community, Internet dominated by America has objectively developed into an international Internet. Internet has entered into a new development step and become a new space for sharing interests, it has enabled nations all around the world to be a community of common destiny in cyberspace, so the Internet requires international co-governance. Since the 20th century, most countries have regarded Internet merely as an ordinary platform for information acquisition, scientific researches and social communications, and the universality of user groups was insufficient. From 1994, CERNET(China Education and Research Network) and CSTNET(China Science and Tecnology Network) began to contact with the international community by themselves, then accessed to the Internet of America with non-governmental status. Instead of belonging to the affiliated sectors of cyberspace competent departments (e.g. the former Ministry of Electronics, and the following former Ministry of Information Industry), China Network Information Center (CNNIC), which is our domain name operation agency, was responsible for China Academy of Science. All of these reflect that cyberspace was regarded as a general space and was free from government's regulation. With the development of information technology, people are more and more dependent on this space, and corresponding interests of nations are borne into this space, such as network education, E-Commerce, E-Government, network service, remote control, network warfare, and telemedicine and so on. China also bears politics, national defense, economy, culture, society and so on into the cyberspace, thus the government began to exercise the jurisdiction. In 2014, CNNIC was removed from the Chinese Academy of Science, and came to the direct jurisdiction of National Internet Information Office.

At the same time, there began to be interest intersections or even interest conflicts among countries in the cyberspace. For instance, what kind of identity management mode will be adopted to build a transnational e-commerce system? How to distribute Internet resources? Being the same as how to distribute the carbon emission index, there are also sovereignty appeals, and naturally requires mutual negotiation of sovereignty countries. Therefore, it is necessary to impose state sovereignty over the cyberspace and form an international co-governance system.

4.4.1 In Favor of Strengthening International Law Status of Nations and Dominating Co-Governance of Network

According to traditional international law, states are the right subjects of international exchanges and play an important role in international legal relations. The spread of the Internet has broken the government's privilege of participating in international co-governance as a representative of a sovereign state, and which enables the "stakeholder" of internet to possibly become the dominator of Internet development by technical advantages, or even makes sovereign nations totally lose international discourse rights in Internet development. The US stresses the governance of the "stakeholder", and pushes Internet the Engineering Task Force (IETF) and ICANN to be in charge of the Internet. It seems to be paving the way for the governance dominated by non-state groups, but it is objectively "dominated by countries powerful in Internet", because basically all the "stakeholders" having the discourse right are countries powerful in Internet. Furthermore, "stakeholders" became the substitutes of the Internet-powerful countries for controlling the Internet, as a result, the strong are stronger and the weak are weaker, and countries weak in information will gradually lose all chances. It is possible to maximize the Internet's positive role within the whole world only by respecting state sovereignty and balancing the nations' strength in information technology, thereby enabling all the countries to have their voice, to forward appeals and to enjoy the benefits brought by the Internet. Therefore, the concept of cyberspace sovereignty is made clear so as to reflect the rationality and necessity of international co-governance and to prevent the International Law Status of nations to be excessively weakened by such super-national actors as Google, Microsoft, Alibaba and so on in the network era.

4.4.2 In Favor of Legal Regulation of the Internet

It is an inevitability of social development as well as a natural embodiment of state sovereignty in the cyberspace to strengthen the governance over Internet. China began to regulate Internet since 1998. After the government succession at that moment, the Ministry of Electronics and the Ministry of Posts and Telecommunications were combined to be the Ministry of Information Industry consisting of Telecommunications Administration in charge of Internet. However, following the rapid development of the Internet and wide popularity of its application, the chaos of Internet order began to influence politics, economy, culture, society and many other aspects, and the Internet administration of China has been increased, e.g. the implementation of website registration. The reinforced management is bound to affect corresponding interest groups and get questioned. Therefore, the current government underlines "legal regulations of Internet", and the first move is, to formulate corresponding laws specific to Internet administration so as to ensure China's cyberspace security and national development, which is a distinct reflection of cyberspace sovereignty. From this point of view, under the background of information revolution and globalization and during the forming process of information society represented by Internet and global communication network and new information view, cyberspace sovereignty is derived by the politics, economy and culture and is combined with new information view and is a part of modern national sovereignty.

4.4.3 *In Favor of Maintaining Regime Stability*

It is a steadfast choice for all governments to maintain the regime stability in any case. Nations can play their role in the control of traditional information field, such as newspapers and periodicals, books, broadcast, and televisions or the like, but, in the world of Internet, the contradiction between the territoriality of national sovereignty and the super-nationality of network has become the bottleneck in the nations' control of transnational Internet behaviors. Internet has greatly weakened a nation's supervision over the information spreading and individual behaviors within its territory. When the concept of cyberspace sovereignty is intensified, the government can stand on the position of safeguarding the national sovereignty. And from the angles of network behavior, economic behavior and information behavior, the government can defend and control the output and input information relying on the border defence of network. The reinforcement of cyberspace sovereignty concept is helpful for providing legal basis for building a national information fort.

4.4.4 *In Favor of Normalizing Military Presence*

The military presence in cyberspace is built based on the existence of cyberspace sovereignty. There has been a lack of protection from the military specific to the threat posed by oversea cyber attacks to China's network infrastructure and vital information systems. The establishment of Strategic Support Forces including net forces has began in China, but the functions of net forces are limited to reinforcement support forces operating in cyberspace in regular wars, which merely considers how to protect its own network information systems. When the concept of cyberspace sovereignty is strengthened, the military's role in safeguarding key information infrastructure will be clear, which enables the military to take the mission of defending the cyber territory and cyberspace sovereignty of the country and to act as a regular army in the cyber security competition among nations.

4.4.5 In Favor of Protecting the Basic Data Resources of the Nation

National basic data resources have important national strategic significance, and the resources are the target in the international competition among nations. Traditionally, one nation can strategically perform strict access control specific to the utilization of geographic mapping information, scare mineral resources, and important animal and plant sample resources. However, as for the cyberspace locating information, medical information, and DNA sample data that exist on the Internet in the form of electronic data, and as for those data containing crucial basis information like social dynamics, market changes, economic laws, signs of national security threats and so on, if cyberspace sovereignty is not clarified and lacks legislative protection, security of national network infrastructure, security of race and biology, and national security will be significantly threatened. Affected by transnational capital infusion and transnational share control, enterprises holding crucial data of national strategies are faced with larger risk of data leakage. Once drastic changes occur in international politics, the "stakeholder" will seriously threaten China through the control over network, biology, economic operation and so on. The emphasis on the concept of cyberspace sovereignty is of great significance to the implementation of the right to use and manage the network basic data resources and to prevent the outflow of strategic basic data.

4.4.6 In Favor of Establishing the Basis of Cyber Security

The occurrence of the concept of cyberspace sovereignty is helpful in making clear the basic position and starting point for processing issues relevant to cyber security, and helpful in establishing the nation's perspective of overall situation in national interest, and more helpful in promoting formulation and practice of cyber security laws and regulations. All this time, the convenience and ease for using the network lead to the blindness of network usage and the sluggishness of management, as a result, citizens lack necessary cyber security awareness and rational habit of risk analysis, which makes it hard for the policies, rules and regulations relevant to cyber security to be completely executed. There even exists an illusion of "Borderless network, borderless science", which brings disturbance and resistance to the correct handling and decision-making of cyber security affairs. Furthermore, the lack of security awareness also causes overstress of individual rights and freedom and resistance to relevant policies, rules and regulations of national security. The concept of cyberspace sovereignty determines the cardinal standpoint for handling cyber security affairs, which is significant for unifying the citizens' recognition of cyber security, deepening the understanding of cyber security and forming a unified consensus, and laying a foundation for the smooth promotion of cyber security administration and legal system.

4.4.7 In Favor of Enhancing the International Voice of the Internet

To be a responsible international network power, China needs to enhance the international voice of the Internet. As a network power, China has a huge online market; however, since China has not joined into the "stakeholder" alignment which is dominating the Internet, China had no chance to get the voice in international Internet development for quite a long period. But, as a network power, we must take the responsibilities of a great power. When cyberspace sovereignty is made clear, state sovereignty can be better reflected in cyberspace, and legal supports can be provided for the country in network behaviors, thereby enabling sovereign countries to participate in the co-governance of the Internet. If Internet is managed with a mode similar to ITU, China will be able to play a positive role in the international co-governance of the Internet and take more responsibilities for the international community by virtue of its status advantage of being a great power and by using its international voice. Therefore, if cyberspace sovereignty is made clear, state sovereignty can be better reflected in the international governance of cyberspace.

4.5 Exceptions of Internet Sovereignty

It's true that the Internet owns sovereignty. But as for the whole Internet, besides the national cyber territory, there should be some exceptions. "Internet commons" objectively exist in the international cyberspace.

4.5.1 About Network Commons

Network commons refers to the cyberspace over which no country has jurisdiction. On the premise of cyberspace sovereignty, "cyber commons" currently exist in the following forms.

1. The space with a platform free from sovereignty jurisdiction

For instance, if the platform is within an international common, such as the South Pole, high seas or the like, then the sovereignty of no country can be imposed on it.

2. The space whose sovereignty has been given up by qualified countries but is not held by other countries

For instance, GPS is open to everyone, but maybe the U.S. authorities still have the power to intervene at critical moments.

3. Services whose sovereignty has been given up by qualified countries but is not held by other countries

For instance, the US government has declared that it would never intervene with Twitter Space, You Tube space and so on.

4. The space over which no countries has declared its jurisdiction

For instance, no country can master such spaces as Bitcoin space[34] and Darknet space.[35]

5. Processing spaces which have become international common

For instance, the routing space between an Autonomous System (AS).[36]

4.5.2 About International Common

The so-called "international common" belongs to the public space of the international community that is commonly accepted by the nations, and international common should belong to the attributes of "international community" in real human society. Following situations should belong to international common.

---

[34]Bitcoin (Virtual Currency). http://baike.baidu.com/link?url=y8iAW7qmONPXnNv_ZvWWTdsuiutdT2Wf7Otyeits2oKW-8HM7ZBIOnJCC4cgcgjYHbxg-HomCcRAUJswuXJAmPucPhqp8WBATkcDBnCjAysP529U_ZdNbzZVcwtnoOqVP [2016-12-30].

[35]What kind of world is Darknet. http://finance.qq.com/a/20151221/038533.htm [2016-10-3].

[36]AS: Autonomous System refers to a sub-network formed by a set of routers using the same routing protocol or following the same routing management strategies, belonging to the governance of the same network operator, and is called as autonomous domain. Global internet is divided into many AS autonomous domains, and operator, institutions or even companies of each country can apply for AS numbers. On the Internet, if an e-mail is to be sent from one IP address to another IP address, the e-mail must know how to get to the AS number B to which IP address belongs from the AS number A to which IP address belongs, and then arrives at the destination IP address along this road. Routing is needed in this process. http://baike.baidu.com/link?url=1FzUnuiyMvmqA46vWY4_ElaItYxCOYeO8YbFZwk7CZzs2lugBe6ldntTF-5oEzijPzHPgH9_KjqHivI0KQNQEK#1 [2016-10-3].

1. The space whose sovereignty has been given up by qualified countries, the space being admitted to be subject to the management of international management

For instance, as for the analytic space of root domain names, America has renounced the management over it, while no other country has the jurisdiction over root domain names.

2. The space whose sovereignty has been given up by qualified countries, the space being identified as serving the international community

For instance, the US telecom operator Sprint Nextel Company[37] operates the largest Internet Backbone network in the world which is accessible to all countries. According to the United States, this network is independently managed by Sprint Company and belongs to international common. As a matter of fact, America will certainly provide "Upstream" monitoring systems[38] on the backbone network of Sprint to manifest its sovereignty.

4.5.3 About the Space of Sovereignty Transfer

The so-called "space of sovereignty transfer" refers to the space with neutral attributes, and the space cannot be dominated by a single country.

1. International organizations recognized by sovereign countries

At present, the operation of the Internet is dependent on relevant standards in the charge of the Internet Engineering Tasking Force (IETF) affiliated to the Internet Society (ISOC); the evolution of Internet in countries is subject to IETF, such as the evolution of IPv6. Therefore, from the angle of Internet evolution, IETF is a typical "space of sovereignty transfer". Of course, ISOC is actually dominated by stakeholders of non-governmental behaviors, and it is not a one-vote system of "sovereignty equality", so it cannot be regarded as a pure sovereignty transfer.

2. International organizations with sovereign countries as members

ITU-T and ITU-R are typical manifestations of sovereignty transfer on the telecommunications networks and the radio and television networks, which are responsible for the telecommunications technologies as well as the radio and television (wireless) technologies, which makes the satellite networks or the like to be the typical international common of sovereignty transfer in the cyberspace.

---

[37]Sprint Nextel Company of America. http://wiki.mbalib.com/wiki/%E7%BE%8E%E5%9B%BD%E6%96%AF%E6%99%AE%E6%9E%97%E7%89%B9Nextel%E5%85%AC%E5%8F%B8 [2016-10-3].

[38]Brother project of "PRISM" was exposed: America's monitoring of intelligence collecting of undersea optical cable. http://www.chinadaily.com.cn/hqzx/2013-07/12/content_16764539.htm [2016-10-3].

3. International organizations in which sovereign countries enjoy equal vote

Following internationalization of ICANN, if the governments of nations could be given the same equal vote as they have in the UN, ICANN would become an international organization accepting "sovereignty transfer", and thus would be able to allocate resources on behalf of the international community. However, such a good wish was firmly stopped by the US government, because America is seeking for "ICANN privatization", rather than "ICANN globalization". In other words, the precondition for America to hand over the power of administration is that no other governments can get their hands into the government of ICANN, and that ICANN can only be controlled by civil power. Apparently, these decisions were made on the basis of America's confidence in the private institutions' management of ICANN, because almost all of the influential enterprises are in charge of America.

Chapter 5
The Relationship Between Cyberspace Sovereignty and Internet Stakeholders

Abstract Cyberspace sovereignty is the extension of state sovereignty in cyberspace. However, as far as the Internet is concerned, there is a more common opinion in the international community that Internet has no border. Since the promotion of the Internet comes from private sectors, the Internet belongs to all stakeholders closely related to it. For this reason, the Internet sovereignty, as a manifestation of the cyberspace sovereignty in the Internet, is not compatible with a fact shared by people for a long time that the Internet is controlled by minority groups.

Keywords Multi-stakeholder · The internet sovereignty · Internet hegemony Coexistence model

At present, the principal contradiction over the issue of cyberspace sovereignty is manifested in the model conflict between a party with governments as the main body which advocates cyberspace sovereignty and a party which emphasizes the non-government attribute of the internet and advocates "multi-stakeholder" domination.

5.1 The Origin of the "Multi-stakeholder" Model

The evolution of the internet is apparently different from that of telecommunications networks. Telecommunications networks were first built by respective countries within their territories. Then because those countries had demand for interconnection, those countries were required to sit together to negotiate the standards of interconnection, and the interests of each country were compromised in an international co-governance environment. In contrast, the Internet originates from the Internet which was first operated in the US, and then the other countries were invited to access the Internet, but the countries accessing the Internet had to comply with the standards developed by the inventor. At the very start, the US avoided the path of dealing with governments of the other countries and transferred the Internet from the US military to the US National Science Foundation, which then commissioned

B. Fang, *Cyberspace Sovereignty*,
https://doi.org/10.1007/978-981-13-0320-3_5

scientific research departments and enterprises to take the responsibility for construction and operation of the Internet. At the same time, the US non-governmental organizations invited countries of the world to access the Internet in non-governmental capacities. Thus, from beginning to end, the US government has not been making any gesture of interference in the development of the internet, and ISOC everything has been being dominated by non-government organizations, but the right to speak has been being retained by the "stakeholder" which made the greatest contribution to the development of the internet. However, as the initiator of the internet, the US in fact established objective leadership of the internet.

Essentially, the "stakeholder" management model in fact built, in the internet space, a "jungle law" model: the strong makes rules, and the weak can only follow those rules; "stakeholders" are the strong, and the weak almost have no right to speak, let alone decision-making power. Since the stakeholders are mainly US-led enterprises, the US indirectly dominates the internet. Therefore, the US certainly has to protect its advantages, and thus would more highly praise this model of civil autonomous management. In that case, it is an understandable strategic gesture that the US abandoned the administration of the Internet Corporation for Assigned Names and Numbers (ICANN) and handed it over to the "stakeholders" in the international community. The US government's control of the ICANN would be criticized by the international community, but handing the control over to the international community, which works based on the "jungle law", on the contrary, maximizes the interests of the US because the US's enterprises are "the pride" in "the upstream of the food chain" in the jungle. In that case, the other countries' coping style can only be trying to make their own enterprises become a member of the pride.

In 2001 the UN General Assembly approved the proposal from the International Telecommunication Union, and agreed to convene the World Summit on Information Society (WSIS) under the leadership of the International Telecommunication Union. The first summit, which began in 2002 and ended in November 2005, was divided into two phases, which are respectively called the "Geneva Summit" and the "Tunis Summit". At the Geneva conference, all parties involved in the negotiation requested Annam, the UN Secretary-General then, to establish a Working Group on Internet Governance (WGIG). And during the Tunis Summit, the Working Group on Internet Governance gave a clear definition of internet governance, that is, "a working definition of Internet governance is the development and application by governments, the private sector and civil society, in their respective roles, of shared principles, norms, rules, decision-making procedures, and programmes that shape the evolution and use of the Internet",[1] and at the same time, put forward the three major stakeholders - governments, the private sector and civil society, and their respective roles and responsibilities.[2] This is the

[1]See paragraph 34 of the TUNIS AGENDA. http://www.un.org/chinese/events/wsis/agenda.htm [2016-9-9].

[2]See paragraph 35 of the TUNIS AGENDA. http://www.un.org/chinese/events/wsis/agenda.htm [2016-9-9].

essence of "multistakeholderism". The "multi-stakeholder" model is not only considered as the best way of internet governance, but also considered to be a more general innovative model of global governance.[3]

5.2 The Principal Members of the "Multi-stakeholders"

Although the "multi-stakeholders" consist of governments, the private sector and civil society in the specific practice, the will of governments is substantially diluted, and the UN has not been able to play its due role. Thus, the role of governments is substantially replaced by international organizations composed of civil representatives. The roles of the private sector and citizens are played by influential enterprises and well-known figures of the internet community.

5.2.1 Important International Organizations of the "Multi-stakeholders"

The international organizations of the multi-stakeholders include the Internet Corporation for Assigned Names and Numbers (ICANN), the Internet Assigned Numbers Authority (IANA), the Internet Society (ISOC), the Internet Engineering Task Force (IETF), the Internet Research Task Force (IRTF), the Internet Engineering Steering Group (IESG), the Internet Architecture Board (IAB), the Regional Internet Registry (RIR), the Internet Governance Forum (IGF) and so on.

1. The Internet Corporation for Assigned Names and Numbers

Since the internet was born, it has undergone a process from individual management to "network management" with the Internet Corporation for Assigned Names and Numbers (ICANN)[4] at the core, while the US has been the only country that dominates the internet. The so-called "Governing by Network" is networking of the governance organizations,[5] which includes the relative loose alliance between organizations and individuals, and which achieves the goal of cooperation based on regular interaction.[6] The ICANN, as a networked organization, was established in

[3]Bertrand de la Chapelle (2009) Internet Governance: Infrastructure and Institutions. Oxford University Press, Oxford, pp 256–270. http://www.oxfordscholarship.com/view/, https://doi.org/10.1093/acprof:oso/9780199561131.001.0001/acprof-9780199561131 [2016-9-28].

[4]ICANN. https://www.icann.org/en [2016-9-9].

[5]Goldsmith S, Eggers WD (2005) Governing by network: The new shape of the public sector. Brookings Institution Press, Washington, DC. https://books.google.com/books/about/Governing_by_Network.html?id=hXb-OCvyEpcC [2016-9-28].

[6]Mueller ML (2015) Networks and states: The global politics of internet governance (trans: Zhou C et al). Shanghai Jiao Tong University Press, Shanghai, pp 7, 72–73 and 75. http://www.doc88.com/p-9156960393372.html [2016-9-27].

1998. It is a "union of internet technology, business, political factions and academic communities, with a wide range of actors, including regional internet address registries, technical liaison groups, scientific researchers, representatives of interest groups, etc.", and is a "global, non-profit, seeking consensus" organization.[7] Since the establishment of the ICANN in place of individual technology experts' management of the internet, the internet governance model with the ICANN at the core has not changed so far. Milton Mueller, a professor at School of Information Studies, Syracuse University (US), who has long been focusing on the global internet governance, points out that the ICANN is one of the most significant and important manifestations of changes made by the internet in the relationship between the public and governments. Formally it is the implementation of international cyberspace governance, and represents the privatization of global governance functions. The Clinton administration then decided to allow non-state members to formulate internet policies and exclude organizations of international agreements or intergovernmental organizations. Although the US declared that it prevented any government from participating in the management of the internet, since establishment of the ICANN, the ICANN has been supervised by and reported to a single state, the US. Therefore, the ICANN, as a global organization, is substantively "a private corporation which is directly and formally unrestrictedly controlled by a government; and meanwhile, a private company to which a right to formulate policies that has impacts on the core of the global internet identifier system has been granted."

2. The Internet Assigned Numbers Authority

The US government authorized, by means of contract via the Internet Assigned Numbers Authority (IANA),[8] the ICANN to perform the IANA's technical functions. The US Department of Commerce had entered into a Memorandum of Understanding with the ICANN and provided a list of policy missions that the ICANN was expected to implement, wherein the specific priorities and the periodical targets explicitly reflected the interests of the US government. From this point of view, the IANA is the key department that determines the ICANN's behavior, and even internet policies.[9]

3. The Internet Society

In 1992, due to the rapid increase of the internet users and the continuous expansion of application scope, the Internet Society (ISOC)[10] aiming to setting internet-related standards and promoting the applications came into being. The ISOC marks the beginning of true transition of the internet to

[7]Mathiason J (2009) Internet Governance: The New Frontier of Global Institute. Routledge, London, pp 70–96. http://www.doc88.com/p-2933123950519.html [2016-9-28].

[8]The Internet Assigned Numbers Authority (IANA). http://www.iana.org/ [2016-9-9].

[9]An Introduction to the Internet Assigned Numbers Authority (IANA) Functions. http://www.iana.org/about/informational-booklet.pdf [2016-9-9].

[10]The Internet Society (ISOC). http://www.internetsociety.org/ [2016-9-9].

commercialization. In June 1991, the idea of establishing the ISOC was presented at the International Internet Conference in Copenhagen, the capital of Denmark. The founders hoped to set up a global internet organization to fulfill important functions in promoting the globalization of the internet, speeding up the development of network interconnection technology and application software, improving internet penetration and so on. The ISOC is a non-governmental, non-profit industry organization whose goal is to ensure the open development of the internet for the benefit of all people throughout the world.

The ISOC is responsible for taking a leadership role in solving problems that trouble the future development of the internet, and ISOC is also a parent organization in charge of part of the organizations of the internet structure standards. Its subordinate bodies include the Internet Engineering Task Force (IETF) and the Internet Architecture Board (IAB). The ISOC not only is an organization for international internet information and education exchange, but also facilitates and coordinates internet-related acts. The ISOC has hosted the international internet education program in developing countries for more than 20 years, which has greatly promoted application of the internet in countries all over the world. The ISOC has more than 80 organization members and more than 30,000 individual members in more than 80 countries and regions in the world. Thus, the ISOC established several regional branches respectively located in Buenos Aires of Argentina (Latin America and the Caribbean branch), Addis Ababa of Ethiopia (Africa branch), and Suva of Fiji (South Asia and Southeast Asia branch). The goal of the ISOC is to enhance the availability and practicality of the internet in the widest possible scope.

The purpose of establishing the ISOC is to create advantageous and open conditions for the development of the Internet, developing standards, publishing information, giving training, etc. in respect of internet technology. In addition, the ISOC is also actively engaged in political, economic, social, moral, legislative and other works that can influence the direction of the internet. Its main functions include the following:

(1) To promote the legal protection of the word "internet"

The ISOC believes that "internet" is an ordinary, unrestricted word, and protect the term, the ISOC provides that no organization or individual should register "internet" as a trademark, otherwise they will take legal actions.

(2) To promote the self-discipline of internet companies

The ISOC actively participates in the development of various technical fields, such as global e-commerce, encryption technology, review system, privacy and so on.

(3) To promote the development of internet standards

To support the work of internet standards and protocol organizations is an important part of the work of the ISOC. The ISOC, as a support organization for internet standards development and research institutions such as the Internet Engineering Task Force (IETF), the Internet Architecture Board (IAB), the Internet Engineering Steering Group (IESG), the Internet Research Task Force (IRTF), and so on, widely engages in activities in this field.

(4) To promote the public policy research

The board of trustees of the ISOC is responsible for determining key research issues in the field of public policy. Taking the wide differences between various regions and countries into account, the ISOC should determine its opinions on formation and development of each issue after detailed analysis and discussion.

(5) To hold meetings

The ISOC holds global annual meetings twice per year: the INET conference focuses on how to develop and implement internet technologies, applications, and relevant policies on a global scale; the Network and Distributed System Security (NDSS) conference aims to promote communication in the field of the global information technology security development.

(6) For the education and training programs

At the INET conference in 1993, an annual meeting of the ISOC held in Los Angeles, the ISOC decided to set up a series of training courses to help all the countries around the world, especially the developing countries, to strengthen internet access and to promote development of the internet in these countries. The ISOC organized various forms of network training courses to train professionals from all over the world in design, operation, maintenance and management of network interconnection technology and so on.

4. The Internet Engineering Task Force

The Internet Engineering Task Force (IETF)[11] is the world's most authoritative internet technology standardization organization. It is a large and open international group which consists of network designers in the industry. The IETF's main task is to develop and formulate internet-related technical specifications. The clear majority of current international internet technical standards are from the IETF. The IETF produces two kinds of documents, one being the Internet Draft,[12] and the other being the Request for Comments (RFC).[13]

All participants of the IETF are volunteers who participate in the IETF three times per year and complete the organization's following goals: to identify the internet's operational and technical issues, and propose solutions; to explain development or usage of internet protocol in detail, and solve relevant problems; to offer the Internet Engineering Steering Group (IESG) suggestions for internet

[11]The Internet Engineering Task Force (IETF). https://www.ietf.org/ [2016-9-9].

[12]The Internet Engineering Task Force. http://www.ietf.org/id-info/ [2016-9-9].

[13]Request for Comments (RFC). http://www.ietf.org/rfc.html [2016-9-9].

protocol standards and usage thereof; to promote technical research results of the Internet Research Task Force (IRTF) to the internet community; and to provide an information exchange forum for internet users, researchers, marketers, contractors and managers, etc.

The actual technical work of the IETF is mostly done in its working groups, which are divided according to topic into several areas (e.g., routing, transport, network security, etc.). Each area is overseen by one or two area directors and all the area directors constitute the Internet Engineering Steering Group (IESG).

At present, the IETF includes 8 research areas and 133 active working groups.[14]

(1) Applications Area (APP), with 20 working groups;
(2) General Area (GEN), with 5 working groups;
(3) Internet Area (INT), with 21 working groups;
(4) Operations and Management Area (OPS), with 24 working groups;
(5) Routing Area (RTG), with 14 working groups;
(6) Security Area (SEC), with 21 working groups;
(7) Transport Area (TSV), with 1 working group;
(8) Sub-IP Area (SUB), with 27 working groups.

From this point, the IETF has played a very important role in the Internet's technology evolution.

5. The Internet Research Task Force

The Internet Research Task Force (IRTF)[15] focuses on long-term research issues relating to the internet, while the IETF focuses on short-term issues of engineering and standards making. The IRTF is composed of several research groups focusing on future technology research. The research fields of these groups involve internet protocol, applications, architecture and technology. The research groups have long-term stable researchers to promote team collaboration in exploring and researching issues. The participants are individuals, rather than representatives of organizations.

6. The Internet Engineering Steering Group

The Internet Engineering Steering Group (IESG)[16] receives special permission from the ISOC, and the IESG is responsible for technical management of various affairs of the IETF and provision of all kinds of internet standards procedures. The IESG is responsible for technical management of the IETF's activities and standards formulation procedures, examining and approving or correcting research results of respective working groups in the IETF, dismissing working groups (it has the right), and ensuring accuracy of drafts when they become RFCs. The IESG administers the working groups of the IETF and is directly responsible for any

---

[14]Internet Engineering Task Force (IETF). http://www.ietf.org/wg/ [2016-9-9].

[15]Internet Research Task Force (IRTF). https://irtf.org/ [2016-12-2].

[16]The Internet Engineering Steering Group (IESG). https://www.ietf.org/iesg/ [2016-9-9].

relevant activities involved in the process of forming a certain internet specification into internet standards, including registration, processing according to "standard procedures", final approval, and is responsible for management of standards formulation process according to the provisions and procedures approved by the board of trustees of the ISOC. Therefore, the IESG has a direct impact on the development of internet technology.

7. The Internet Architecture Board

The Internet Architecture Board (IAB)[17] is a technical advisory body of the ISOC. Its responsibilities include appointment of staff in various internet-related organizations, such as the IETF chair and the IESG candidates; and management of editing and publishing of various contents (such as RFC). The IAB is appointed by the trustees of the ISOC.

8. The Regional Internet Registry

Now there are 5 Regional Internet Registries (RIRs)[18] in the world, which are non-profit member organizations responsible for assigning IP (IPv4 and IPv6) addresses and autonomous systems (AS) to regional economies and providing reverse DNS authorized service. Its members include internet service providers, national (or regional) internet registries (NIRs) and other internet organizations.

According to the provisions of the ICANN, the ICANN assigns part of the IP addresses to the regional-level RIRs, and then those RIRs are responsible for the register service in respective regions. At present, the 5 RIRs all around the world include the American Registry for Internet Numbers (ARIN),[19] the Réseaux IP Européens (RIPE),[20] the Asia-Pacific Network Information Centre (APNIC),[21] the Latin America and Caribbean Network Information Centre (LACNIC),[22] and the African Network Information Center (AfriNIC).[23] There are several registries under RIRs, such as national registries (NIRs), local internet registries (LIRs) and so on.

9. The Internet Governance Forum

At the Tunis phase of the WSIS, the countries called on the UN Secretary-General to convene "a new forum for multi-stakeholder policy dialogue", which is now known as the Internet Governance Forum (IGF).[24] The main mission of the IGF is to further discuss the issue of major internet governance-related public

[17]The Internet Architecture Board (IAB). https://www.iab.org/ [2016-9-9].

[18]Regional Internet Registry. https://en.wikipedia.org/wiki/Regional_Internet_registry [2016-10-6].

[19]ARIN. https://www.arin.net/ [2016-10-6].

[20]Ripe. https://www.ripe.net/ [2016-10-6].

[21]APNIC. https://www.apnic.net/ [2016-10-6].

[22]LACNIC. http://www.lacnic.net/ [2016-10-6].

[23]AFRNIC. http://www.afrinic.net/ [2016-10-6].

[24]The Internet Governance Forum (IGF). http://www.intgovforum.org/cms/ [2016-9-9].

policies, so as to promote the sustainable, safe and stable development of the internet.[25] From 2006 to 2016, the IGF has held 11 meetings.

The IGF is a gamble for the internet resources and governance that the developing countries play with the developed countries. As the disparity of the interests between the two parties is too large, the previous meetings have not made any substantial progress. Nevertheless, some results were achieved in areas of some common interests. For example, the results of the first IGF meeting were mainly manifested in anti-spam. On the issue of anti-spam, the parties reached an agreement, and announced the establishment of a new website dedicated to facilitating anti-spam efforts at www.StopSpamAlliance.org; released the "Anti-Spam Toolbox" program; and decided to describe and analyze the status of the global malware, so as to provide information for policymakers.[26] From the topics for discussion in the past years, we can see that the contents on which the IGF focuses change from theoretical ones to applicable ones. The IGF is a platform for dialogue between the developing countries and the developed countries, and it is a good thing to concretize issues in the absence of substantial progress for several years.

5.2.2 Key Enterprises in the "Multi-stakeholders"

The key enterprises in the "multi-stakeholders" are mainly those heavyweights who have the right to speak in internet governance, and whose representatives are involved in internet organizations and have the right to speak, such as Amazon, Apple, AT&T, Cisco, Dell, EMC, Ericsson, Facebook, Google, Huawei, IBM, Isode, Juniper, LG, Microsoft, Oracle, Red Hat, Samsung Electronics, VeriSign and so on.

1. Amazon (Amazon.com)

Amazon[27] is an American electronic commerce and cloud computing company that was founded in July 1994, by Jeff Bezos based in Seattle, Washington. It is one of the Internet-based retailers that have the largest total sales and market value in the world, and is the world's largest provider of cloud infrastructure services (Infrastructure as a Service, IaaS). Leading areas: e-commerce, web services, AWS cloud computing, and robots. Amazon participates in the Internet Governance Forum (IGF).

---

[25]Internet_Governance_Forum. https://en.wikipedia.org/wiki/Internet_Governance_Forum [2016-9-27].

[26]New Progress in International Internet Governance from the Perspective of the IGF Conference. http://www.educity.cn/tx/950154.html [2016-9-27].

[27]Amazon. https://www.amazon.com/p/feature/rzekmvyjojcp6uc?ref_=aa_nav_footer [2016-9-15].

2. Apple Inc.

Apple Inc.[28] is an American multinational technology company headquartered in Cupertino, California. It is founded by Steve Jobs, Stephen Wozniak, and Ronald Wayne on April 1, 1976. Apple Inc. is dedicated to design, development, selling of consumer electronics, computer software, and online services. The most famous hardware products include Mac personal computers, iPod portable media players, iPhone smartphones, and iPad tablet computers; online services include iCloud, iTunes Store and App Store; consumer software includes the OS X and iOS operating systems, the iTunes multimedia vedio, the Safari web browser, and the iLife and iWork creativity and productivity suites. Apple Inc. is a member of the Telecommunications Industry Association (TIA) and participates in the Internet Governance Forum (IGF).

3. AT&T (American Telephone & Telegraph) Corporation

AT&T (American Telephone & Telegraph) Corporation[29] was founded on March 3, 1885, and is headquartered in Beidminster, New Jersey. AT&T Corporation provides professional services of voice, video, data, the internet, etc. for individuals, businesses and government agencies. In the long history, AT&T Corporation was the world's largest telephone and cable operator. In terms of internet governance, AT&T Corporation has always viewed the internet as a necessary medium for communications, and development of economy and social welfare. In order to promote further healthy development of the internet, AT&T Corporation believes that it is necessary to maintain the existing multi-party Internet regulatory system, and hopes that committees, parliaments and administrative departments of respective countries work together to maintain and promote the openness of the internet. Persons in AT&T Corporation who participate in internet governance organizations include: Ed Cholerton (senior vice president of public relations at AT&T Corporation, director of TIA) and Deborah Brungard (who leads the technical staff at AT&T Corporation to perform network architecture and service planning; director of the Routing Area in the IESG).

4. Cisco

Cisco[30] was founded in 1984 by a teacher couple of Stanford University, Leonard Bosack and Sandy Lerner. It is an American multinational technology company headquartered in San Jose, California. Cisco's products are mainly used to connect computer network systems, including broadband cable products, boards and modules, IOS software, content networks, network management, fiber platforms, routers, network security products and VPN devices, network storage products, switches, video systems, IP communications systems, and wireless products. In terms of internet governance, Cisco claims to work with partners to

[28]Apple Info. http://www.apple.com/about/ [2016-9-15].

[29]About AT&T. http://about.att.com/category/all_news.html [2016-9-15].

[30]About CISCO. http://www.cisco.com/c/en/us/about.html [2016-9-15].

build an open and innovative, transparently supervised, market-based, and distributed governance Internet environment. It also advocates that the internet belongs to everyone, and the policy must be consistent with the principle of transparency to ensure that all stakeholders can participate in policy discussions in a meaningful way. In addition, Cisco claims to achieve the goals of "maintaining access diversity", "protecting user privacy" and "safeguarding the interests of consumers in the online world" by promoting rapid development of technologies such as LISP (List Processor, list processing language), DNSSEC (Domain Name System Security Extension), BGPSEC (Border Gateway Protocol Security), Lawful Interception and so on. Persons in Cisco who participate in internet governance organizations include: Jeff Campbell (vice president of the Americas of Global Government Affairs for Cisco Systems, director of TIA), Alissa Cooper (outstanding engineer at Cisco, responsible for privacy and strategic policy, and director of the Applications and Real Time Area in the IESG), Benoit Claise (outstanding engineer at Cisco, architect of embedded management and device instrumentation).

5. DELL

Dell[31] was founded in 1984 by Michael Dell. Dell and is an American multinational information technology company headquartered in Citrus, Texas. Dell sells electronic devices such as personal computers, servers, data storage devices, network switches, software, computer peripherals, high-definition televisions, cameras, printers, MP3 players and so on. In 2009, Dell acquired the Perot system to enter the IT services market. Dell is a TIA member and participates in the IGF. The participant is Joyce Mullen (vice president and general manager of Dell's OEM Solutions Division, second vice chairman of TIA).

6. EMC

EMC[32] was founded in 1979 and which is an American multinational IT company headquartered in Massachusetts. It provides products and services for storing, managing, protecting and analyzing large amounts of data, such as data storage, information security, virtualization, cloud computing and so on. EMC has more than 70,000 employees and is a data storage system provider taking the largest share of the market. In terms of internet governance, EMC believes that there is a need to improve and strengthen the existing multi-stakeholder internet regulatory ecosystem, wherein the focus is the capacity building of the participants themselves; and that the existing internet regulatory mechanism does not address many issues appropriately, so as one of the institutions dealing with such issues, the IGF needs to improve itself. The person in EMC who participates in internet governance organizations is Kathleen Moriarty, (EMC's Technology Strategy and Chief

[31]About DELL. http://www.dell.com/learn/cn/zh/cncorp1/about-dell?~ck=mn [2016-9-15].

[32]Overview of EMC Corporation. http://china.emc.com/corporate/emc-at-glance/corporate-profile/index.htm [2016-9-15].

Technology Officer, architect responsible for global security, director of the Security Area in the IESG).

7. Ericsson

Ericsson[33] was founded in 1876 by Lars Magnus Ericsson, headquartered in Stockholm, Sweden. It is a multinational network and telecommunications equipment and services company. Ericsson mainly offers services such as software and infrastructure, information and communication technology, traditional telecommunications and IP (Internet Protocol) network equipments, mobile and fixed broadband, operations and business support services, cable television, IPTV (Internet Protocol Television) and video system. Ericsson's 2G, 3G and 4G wireless communications networks are widely used and deployed by major operators around the world. Ericsson is also one of the global leaders in mobile communications standardization. In terms of internet governance, Ericsson believes that the original business model is not conducive to the healthy development of the network environment, and that government, individual organizations and academia should work together. As a member of the Internet Society (ISOC), Ericsson actively organizes relevant meetings and forums, and supports open Internet policies designed to promote the healthy development of the network environment. Here are the persons in Ericsson who participate in internet governance organizations: Jari Arkko (expert in network architecture at the Ericsson Research Center, director of the General Area and chairman of the IETF&IESG), Glenn Laxdal (CTO&North American Strategy Officer, secretary general of the TIA's board of directors), Suresh Krishnan (outstanding engineer at Ericsson, director of the Internet Area in the IESG).

8. Facebook

Facebook[34] was founded by Mark Zuckerberg and his roommates at Harvard University, Eduardo Savelin, Andrew McCollum, Dustin Moskovitz and Chris Hughes on February 4, 2004. It is an online social media and a for-profit company based on social networking services, and headquartered in Menlo Park, California. Facebook is committed to providing people with a platform to share and to make the world more open and connected. Through Facebook, people keep in touch with friends and family, get the latest information, and share life stories. Facebook is rated as the world's most popular social networking site. Facebook participates in the IGF.

9. Google

Google[35] was founded on September 4, 1998 and is a multinational technology company. Its purpose is to design and manage the Internet search engine "Google search". Google's headquarters is in Mountain View, Santa Clara County,

[33]ERICSSON. https://www.ericsson.com/about-us [2016-9-15].

[34]Facebook. https://www.facebook.com/facebook [2016-9-15].

[35]Google Corporation. https://www.google.com/intl/zh-CN/about/company/ [2016-9-15].

California, which is known as "Googleplex". Google's current business scope covers Internet search, cloud computing, advertising technology and other fields, as well as developing and providing many Internet-based products and services.[36] Its main profits come from AdWords and other advertising services. In terms of internet governance, Google receives requests from courts and government agencies around the world about the removal of information from Google products; in addition, Google also supports deletion requests from individuals. Google would scrutinize these requests, and determine whether the contents should be deleted, whether the contents violate the law or Google's product strategy, whether they have legitimacy and integrity, and if necessary, Google would ask for explanation about which contents are illegal. Google believes that the power to control the internet should belong to the international community. According to Reuters, Google, together with many well-known technology companies, has recently signed a strongly-worded open letter to call on the US to hand over the power to control the internet. The person at Google who participates in internet governance organizations is Johanna Shelton (senior policy advisor of the Software and Information Industry Association [SIIA]).

10. Huawei

Huawei[37] is a Chinese provider of information and communication technology solutions, headquartered in Shenzhen, Guangdong. Huawei was incorporated in 1987 with its business scope covering telecommunications networks, enterprise networks, consumer electronics and cloud computing. Its telecommunications network products mainly include switched networks, transmission networks, wireless and wired fixed access networks, data communication networks, and wireless terminal products. Since 2012, Huawei has become the world's largest telecommunications equipment manufacturer. At present, Huawei has increased the importance of network security, built a security capability center in the company and strictly guaranteed security of Huawei's products and solutions themselves; increased investment in studies on new threat technology and defense solutions, construction of threat intelligence, and security emergency response, so as to better serve users and protect the customers' network security. The person at Huawei who participates in internet governance organizations is Spencer Dawkins (senior standards manager at Huawei America, director of the Transmission Area in the IESG).

11. IBM (International Business Machine)

IBM (International Business Machine)[38] was founded in 1911 and is an American multinational technology company and consulting company headquartered in Armonk, New York. IBM manufactures and sells computer hardware,

---

[36]Google Search. http://research.google.com/ [2016-9-9].

[37]Introduction to Huawei. http://www.huawei.com/cn/about-huawei [2016-9-15].

[38]About IBM. http://www.ibm.com/ibm/us/en/?lnk=fab [2016-9-15].

middleware and software, as well as providing consulting services for system architecture and web hosting. Products invented by IBM include: hard disk, ATM, Universal Product Code, SQL (Structured Query Language), relational database management system, DRAM (Dynamic Random-Access Memory) and Watson. In terms of internet governance, IBM wants to ensure that online information is free, and anyone can contribute contents, and governments should not interfere by policies and legislation (such as content taxation, content removal, etc.).

12. Isode

Isode[39] is a UK software product company, and which has been committed to the development and support of security information and directory system of the COTS (Commercial off the shelf) server software since 2002. Isode's employees have played an active leading role in the Internet Engineering Task Force (IETF) and the XSF (XMPP Standards Foundation). Isode was originally established in 1992 as the "ISODE Consortium". In 1999, it became MessagingDirect and was sold to ACI Worldwide in 2001. Isode was re-established as an independent UK company in 2002 to re-focus on supporting existing products and new product development. In terms of Internet governance, Isode's employees have played an active role in the IETF. Isode participates in the Internet Governance Forum and the participant is Alexey Melnikov (director of Applications and Real-time Leadership Area in the IESG, head of the Isode Internet Information Research Team).

13. Juniper Networks

Juniper Networks,[40] an American multinational IT corporation headquartered in Sunnyvale, California, was founded in February 1996. Its products include routers, switches, network management software, network security products and so on. Juniper Networks originally focused on core routers, which are used by internet service providers (ISPs) to perform IP address lookups and to direct detect the internet traffic. After buying Unisphere in 2002, Juniper Networks entered the market of edge routers. Juniper Networks entered the IT security market with its own security tool in 2003 JProtect. In terms of internet governance, Juniper Networks believes that the internet does not need central managers, otherwise innovation, democracy and freedom of the internet would be hindered; and Juniper Networks believes that the diversity of internet participants determines that the regulatory process of the internet also requires multi-participation; given that the detection process of network attacks may violate users' privacy, Juniper Networks believes that it is necessary to balance the responsibilities of the participants in the process. The person at Juniper Networks who participates in internet governance organizations is Alia Atlas who is engaged in network routing architecture and technology.

[39]Isode: About us. http://www.isode.com/company/index.html [2016-9-15].

[40]About Juniper Networks. http://www.juniper.net/cn/zh/company/ [2016-9-15].

14. LG

LG Group[41] was established in 1947 in Seoul, South Korea and is a South Korean multinational corporation. LG Group is a large Korean group which produces electronic products, mobile phones, petrochemical products and so on. It has more than 220,000 employees serving at the 112 operating bases all over the world (including 81 subsidiaries). LG Group has five major businesses: home entertainment, mobile communications, home appliances, air conditioning and enterprise solutions. LG Group is a member of the TIA and participates in the IGF. The participant is Dr. Nandou Gumar (president of LG America Technology Center, member of the TIA's board of directors).

15. Microsoft

Microsoft[42] was founded by Bill Gates and Paul Allen in 1975. Microsoft is an American multinational computer technology company headquartered in Redmond, Washington. It develops, manufactures, licenses, supports and sells computer software, consumer electronics, personal computers, and services. Its best-known software products are Windows operating systems, Microsoft Office suite, and the Internet Explorer. Its flagship hardware products are the Xbox video game consoles and the Microsoft Surface tablet lineup. In terms of internet governance, Microsoft's Telecommunications and Internet Governance Group is committed to addressing global internet governance policy-related issues and to developing related measures with global partners, including privacy, security, big data, internet of things, intelligent systems and their impact on economy, society and policy frameworks, as well as taking a holistic approach to policy through collaboration with multidisciplinary researchers and experts in other fields (including the Digital Enlightenment Forum, the World Economic Forum and the Microsoft Research Institute). Microsoft is a member of the TIA and a member corporation of the International Chamber of Commerce.[43] Microsoft's research department is widely involved in internet governance organizations and activities. The person at Microsoft who participates in internet governance organizations is Amy Marasco (general manager of Standard Strategy, director in the TIA).

---

[41]About LG. http://www.lg.com/cn/about-lg [2016-9-15].

[42]About Microsoft. http://news.microsoft.com/zh-cn/#sm.00002gg2yzz8ncp5qp42qjycrt0ot [2016-9-15].

[43]The five company representatives of the International Chamber of Commerce's Business Allied to Support the Information Society (ICC BASIS) all come from the US, including Facebook, Google, Microsoft, 21th Century Fox, and an ICANN advisor. Milton Mueller and Ben Wagner (2014), Finding a Formula for Brazil: Representation and Legitimacy in Internet Governance. http://www.internetgovernance.org/wordpress/wp-content/uploads/MiltonBenWPdraft_Final_clean2.pdf [2016-9-9].

16. Oracle

Oracle[44] was co-founded by Lawrence Joseph Ellison, Bob Miner and Ed Oates in 1977 at Santa Clara, California. It is an American multinational computer technology corporation, headquartered in Redwood Shores, California. The company mainly focuses on developing and selling database software and technology, cloud engineer systems and enterprise software products, and particularly its own brands of database management systems. By 2013, Oracle was the second-largest software corporation in revenue, after Microsoft. Oracle is a member corporation of the International Chamber of Commerce's Business Allied to Support the Information Society, also participating in the IGF. The participants include Ben Campbell (chief engineer of Oracle, director of the Applications and Real-time area in the IESG, chairman of the DART,[45] XMPP [Extensible Messageing and Presence Protocol], SIMPLE[46] Working Group), and Jason Mahler (senior executive of the Software and Information Industry Association [SIIA]'s board of directors, head of government affairs).

17. Red Hat

Red Hat[47] was founded in 1993. It is an American multinational software company headquartered in Raleigh, North Carolina and is an enterprise community providing open-source software products. Red Hat provides many important IT technologies such as software and services for operating systems, storage, middleware, virtualization and cloud computing platforms. Red Hat's open source model provides enterprise transaction solutions across physical, virtual and cloud environments to help enterprises reduce costs and improve performance, stability and security. Red Hat also provides technical support, training and consulting services to customers worldwide. Red Hat is a TIA member and participates in the IGF. The participant is Mark Bohannon (responsible for Red Hat's cooperative transactions and global public policy, vice president of the SIIA's board of directors).

18. Samsung Electronics

Samsung Electronics[48] is a South Korean multinational electronics company headquartered in Suwon, Gyeonggi-do. Through extremely complicated ownership structure with some circular ownership, it is part of the Samsung Group. Samsung Electronics mainly manufactures ion batteries, semiconductors, chips, flash memory and hard drive devices for clients such as Apple, Sony, HTC and Nokia. Samsung Electronics is also the Korea's largest electronics goods and electronics component

---

[44]About Oracle. https://www.oracle.com/corporate/index.html [2016-9-15].

[45]DART is an application programming language that's easy to learn, easy to scale, and deployable everywhere. Google depends on Dart to make very large apps.

[46]SIMPLE is instant messaging protocol.

[47]Introduction to Red Hat. https://www.redhat.com/zh/about/company [2016-9-15].

[48]Samsung Electronics. http://www.samsung.com/cn/aboutsamsung/ [2016-9-15].

manufacturer, the world's largest smartphone and feature handset manufacturer, and the world's largest information technology company. In 2011, Samsung Electronics, in place of Apple, became the world's largest technology company and is a major part of the South Korean economy. Samsung Electronics is a member of the TIA and participates in the IGF.

19. VeriSign

Verisign,[49] the global leader of internet infrastructure and security, was founded at June 2, 1995, by James Bidzos. It is a listed American company based in Reston, Virginia that focuses on a diverse array of network infrastructure services. The major business of Verisign includes management of 2 (Root A and Root J) of 13 root serves over the world; registry for the generic top-level domains (.com, .net, and .name) and the country-code top-level domains (.cc and.tv); and operation of back-end systems for the top-level domains (.jobs, .gov, .edu). Besides, Verisign also offers a range of security services, including managed DNS, distributed denial-of-service (DDoS) attack mitigation and cyber-threat reporting. In terms of internet governance, what concerns VeriSign most is security and stability of the internet. From the perspective of public policy and government relations, VeriSign advocates policies to strengthen security and improve the Internet infrastructure, so as to promote a sound and stable governance environment. VeriSign closely focuses on data protection, cyber security, cybercrime and a variety of emerging threats. VeriSign also participates extensively in cooperation with industry and non-governmental organizations to foster strong security policies. VeriSign also participates in the ICANN's work.

5.2.3 Generally-Acknowledged Influential Individuals in the Internet Field

On April 23, 2012, the ISOC released the first inductees in the list of "Internet Hall of Fame"[50] to celebrate founders at the early age of the internet, innovators and individuals from all walks of life who had funded the internet, internet spirit evangelists, and individuals who turned the global internet into enormous economic benefits. Following that, ISOC released the second inductees.[51]

[49]About VeriSign. http://www.verisign.com/zh_CN/company-information/index.xhtml [2016-9-15].

[50]The first inductees in the list of "Internet Hall of Fame" (2012) http://www.isc.org.cn/ihf/info.php?cid=213 [2016-9-9].

[51]The second inductees in the list of "Internet Hall of Fame" (2013) http://www.isc.org.cn/ihf/info.php?cid=214 [2016-9-24].

1. The Internet founders/pioneers

The Internet founders/pioneers recognized by the Internet Society are the individuals who were instrumental in the early design and development of the internet with exceptional achievements. The two groups are released as follows.

Vinton Cerf[52]: American; known as one of the “fathers of the Internet”; a co-designer of the TCP/IP protocols and the architecture of the internet; the vice president and chief internet promoter of Google since 2005.

Danny Cohen[53]: American; Cohen developed the first real-time visual flight simulator and the first real-time radar simulator on a general-purpose computer in 1967; he applied the packet switching technology to real-time applications for the first time; he is a member of the American National Academy of Engineering.

Steve Crocker[54]: American; a developer of the early internet standards; the chief executive officer of Shinkuro, which focuses on cross-network dynamic information sharing and security protocol deployment; Crocker has been the chair of the board of the Internet Corporation for Assigned Names and Numbers (ICANN).

Donald W. Davies[55]: British; one of the inventors of the packet-switched computer network; he created the term “data packet” and explored the packet switching technology; Davis designed the early electronic storage program digital computer which was one of 4 or 5 similar devices around the world at that time; Davies won the 1974 British Computer Association Award.

Elizabeth Feinler[56]: American; Feinler started the ARPANET, which eventually evolved into the Internet, and the Defense Data Network and was responsible for the management of network information center; Feinler developed the first Internet “yellow page” and “white page” servers, the first query-based network host name and address (domain name) server, as well as developing the top-level domain naming scheme; Feinler is a member of the Association for Computing Machinery (ACM), the Institute of Electrical and Electronic Engineers (IEEE) and a representative of the White House Information Center Meeting.

Charles Herzfeld[57]: Austrian; he promoted the importance of computers and oversaw and created the ARPANET; Hertzfeld is the vice president of research and technology at AT&T, the director of defense research and engineering, and a science senior advisor of the president.

Robert Kahn[58]: American; known as one of the “fathers of the Internet”; he put forward the importance of packet switching technology, along with the concept of national information infrastructure (later known as the information highway) based on open network structure; Kahn won the National Medal of Technology, Turing

[52]Vint Cerf. http://www.internethalloffame.org/inductees/vint-cerf [2016-9-15].

[53]Danny Cohen. http://www.internethalloffame.org/inductees/danny-cohen [2016-9-15].

[54]Steve Crocker. http://www.internethalloffame.org/inductees/steve-crocker [2016-9-15].

[55]Donald Davies. http://www.internethalloffame.org/inductees/donald-davies [2016-9-15].

[56]Elizabeth Feinler. http://www.internethalloffame.org/inductees/elizabeth-feinler [2016-9-15].

[57]Charles Herzfeld. http://www.internethalloffame.org/inductees/charles-herzfeld [2016-9-15].

[58]Robert Kahn. http://www.internethalloffame.org/inductees/robert-kahn [2016-9-15].

Award and Medal of Freedom, and is the director of the National Information Processing Technology Office.

Peter Kirstein[59]: British; Vint Cerf's colleague; the first person who carried out IP network collaboration research in Europe and both sides of the Atlantic; Kirstein is a member of the Royal Academy of Engineering and a senior member of the IEEE.

Leonard Kleinrock[60]: American; honored as one of the "fathers of the Internet" because of outstanding contributions to the field of the packet network theory, which is the fundamental field of the internet; Kleinrock won a number of awards including the 2007 National Medal of Science; Kleinrock is also one of the developers of the ARPANET; Kleinrock is an honorary professor at the University of California, Los Angeles (UCLA), a member of the American National Academy of Engineering, a member of the American Academy of Arts and Sciences, as well as a member of the ACM, the IEEE, the Institute for Operations Research and the Management Sciences (INFORMS), the International Electrotechnical Commission (IEC) and so on.

John Klensin[61]: American; Klensin participated in the early management of domain name system and procedural and definitional work for top-level domain definitions, and contributed to the transition from the early domain name management by University of Southern California-Information Sciences Institute, USC-ISI[62] to the domain name management by the ICANN; in 1992, he and Randy Bush created the Network Startup Resource Center (NSRC), which helped many countries to access the internet; in 2003, Klensin received a Merit Award from the International Committee for Information Technology Standards; he is a member of the ACM.

Jon Postel[63]: American; known as the protocol master inventor; a joint developer of protocols such as TCP/IP, SMTP, DNS, etc.; he also participated in the formulation of RFC document standards; Postel's greatest contribution was creating the Internet Assigned Numbers Authority (IANA); Postel was one of the founders and the first individual member of the Internet Society; Postel passed away on October 16, 1998.

Louis Pouzin[64]: French; he devoted himself to the design and implementation of computer systems, such as the CTSS (the first large compatible time sharing system) and the CYCLADES (datagram switching system); his most significant contribution is invention of datagram switching technology from which the TCP/IP was derived; in addition, he participated in early network standardization activities within the International Federation for Information Processing (IFIP), the

[59]Peter Kirstein. http://www.internethalloffame.org/inductees/Peter-Kirstein [2016-9-15].

[60]Leonard Kleinrock. http://www.internethalloffame.org/inductees/leonard-kleinrock [2016-9-15].

[61]John Klensin. http://www.internethalloffame.org/inductees/john-klensin [2016-9-15].

[62]USC-ISI, responsible for one of the 13 root servers around the world (root B).

[63]Jon Postel. http://www.internethalloffame.org/inductees/jon-postel [2016-9-16].

[64]Louis Pouzin. http://www.internethalloffame.org/inductees/louis-pouzin [2016-9-16].

International Organization for Standardization (ISO), the International Telegraph and Telephone Consultative Committee (CCITT) and other organizations; Pouzin is a project leader of the EUROLINC organization (an organization that aims to promote the use of the internet's underlying language).

Lawrence Roberts[65]: American; Roberts participated in the design of the ARPANET; the chief scientist of the Defense Advanced Research Projects Agency (DARPA), taking on the task of designing and managing new data exchange networks; Roberts has received numerous awards, including the Draper Prize from the American National Academy of Engineering; Roberts has founded 5 startups and is the CEO of Netmax.

Paul Baran[66]: Born in Poland and then immigrated to the US where he invented the packet switching technology that plays a crucial role in the development of the internet; in RAND Corporation, Baran participated in developing a communications system that could survive the damage of a nuclear weapon, as well as inventing a metal detector; Baran received many awards including the IEEE Alexander Graham Bell Medal, and the National Medal of Technology and Innovation; Baran passed away on March 26, 2011.

Joseph C. R. Licklider[67]: American; known for his vision of the development of the internet; it was Licklider's work that ultimately led to the creation of the ARPANET; he predicted many of the features of current development of the internet and he put forward the ideas of "man-computer symbiosis" and "global computer network"; he was a director at the DARPA; Licklider passed away on June 26, 1990.

David Clark[68]: American; Clark began to engage in internet-related research since the 1970s, served as chief architect of the internet protocol, and studied the internet quality of service (QoS) mechanism and the internet performance and security issues; Clark's subsequent research was focused on designing the infrastructures of the next generation of the internet, while helping the National Science Foundation to advance its future internet infrastructure plan; Clark is a researcher at the MIT Computer Science and Artificial Intelligence Laboratory, a member of the American National Academy of Engineering, and a member of the American Academy of Arts and Sciences.

Robert Raylor[69]: American; Raylor funded most of the US computer system research projects; he initiated and was responsible for the ARPANET project, which laid the foundation of today's internet; Taylor founded and managed the system research center of a digital equipment corporation until retired; Taylor received the National Medal of Technology and the Draper Prize.

---

[65]Lawrence Roberts. http://www.internethalloffame.org/inductees/lawrence-roberts [2016-9-16].

[66]Paul Baran. http://www.internethalloffame.org/inductees/paul-baran [2016-9-16].

[67]J. C. R. Licklider. http://www.internethalloffame.org/inductees/jcr-licklider [2016-9-16].

[68]David Clark. http://www.internethalloffame.org/inductees/david-clark [2016-9-16].

[69]Robert Taylor. http://www.internethalloffame.org/inductees/robert-taylor [2016-9-16].

Stephen Wolff[70]: American; he set up computer network research and higher education for the first time in the US, and the research results eventually became a major constituting part of the internet backbone to promote the internet to be transformed from a government project to a global commercial project; Wolff has served as an interim vice president and chief technology officer of Internet2,[71] which offers services for more than 60,000 educational and research institutions; Wolff is the director of the network department of the National Science Foundation (NSF).

Bob Metcalf[72]: American; he invented the Ethernet, standardized and commercialized it; he pioneered the internet by building a packet switching between high-speed network interfaces and protocol software; Metcalfe received the National Medal of Technology in 2005; he is a professor of innovation in the Cockrell School of Engineering at the University of Texas at Austin, and also a member of the National Academy of Engineering.

Kees Neggers[73]: Dutch; Neggers promoted the construction of the Dutch National Computer Network (SURFNET), led and coordinated the development of the Dutch internet; based on the concept of Open Exchanges, Neggers created the first European Internet Provider (IP) backbone which paved the way for the commercialization of the internet in Europe; Neggers is the director of the European Center for Academic Research Network.

Dave Farber[74]: American; Farber created the world's first distributed computer system; Farber helped build the computer network organized by the National Science Foundation and spread computer network technology in the global academia and industry; Farber received the Medal of the Special Interest Group on Data Communication (SIGCOMM) of the International Computer Association in the field of computer communication, as well as the Philadelphia John Scott Medal in the field of humanity; Farber is a professor at the School of Computer Science and Public Policy of Carnegie-Chimelon University.

Nii Narku Quaynor[75]: Ghanaian; known as "the father of African Internet"; Quaynor pioneered internet development and expansion throughout Africa for nearly two decades by establishing the African first internet operator group and improving the African internet numbers registration; Quaynor is a member of the United Nations Secretary General Advisory Group, chair of the OAU Internet Task Force and president of the Internet Society of Ghana.

---

[70]Stephen Wolff. http://www.internethalloffame.org/inductees/stephen-wolff [2016-9-16].

[71]Internet2 refers to a network constructed by co-efforts of more than 120 colleges and universities, associations, companies and government institutes, aiming to satisfy the needs of higher education and scientific research, and developing the next generation of internet advanced network application projects; however, to some extent, Internet 2 has become a synonym of the world's next generation of Internet construction.

[72]Bob Metcalfe. http://www.internethalloffame.org/inductees/bob-metcalfe [2016-9-16].

[73]Kees Neggers. http://www.internethalloffame.org/inductees/kees-neggers [2016-9-16].

[74]Dave Farber. http://www.internethalloffame.org/inductees/dave-farber [2016-9-16].

[75]Nii Quaynor. http://www.internethalloffame.org/inductees/nii-quaynor [2016-9-16].

Howard Frank[76]: American; he conducted the original topological analysis for the ARPANET, evaluated the network's performance and reliability, and founded Network Analysis Corp. (NAC) to analyze and design commercial and government networks research strategies and how to apply technology to the larger fields; in addition, Frank developed a technique to design offshore natural gas pipeline systems; Frank worked in Defense Information Systems Agency.

Glenn Ricart[77]: American; in 1988, Ricart set up the world's first Internet Exchange point, which connected the original federal TCP/IP networks and the American first commercial and non-commercial internet; Ricart is the founder and CTO of US Ignite.

Kanchana Kanchanasut[78]: Thai; a pioneer that introduced the internet to Thailand; Kanchanasut's efforts led to the construction of the first leased line connecting Thailand to the global networks via TCP/IP; Kanchana has served as the executive director of AVIST (a Czech South East Asian Nations' Virtual Institute of Science and Technology); later, her research focused on competitive networks and emergency networks, digital media communication and tele-education.

Werner Zorn[79]: German; called the "Father of the German Internet"; the first email sent from China to the world was written by him; Zorn founded Xlink, one of the founding members of Réseaux IP Européens (an organization dedicated to ensuring the maintenance and development of the administrative and technical coordination needed by the Internet); Zorn was appointed to a professor of communication systems at Hasso-Plattner-Institut located in Potsdam since 2001.

Jun Murai[80]: Japanese; called the "Father of the Japanese Internet"; in 1984, Jun Murai developed, with Nihon University, the UNIX Network (JUNET), which is the first university network ever in that Japan; in 1988, he founded the Widely Integrated Distributed Environment Project and a Japanese internet research consortium; in 2005, He won the Internet Society's Jonathan B. Postel Service Award; he is a professor and dean of the Faculty of Environment and Information Studies at Keio University.

2. The Internet innovators

The Internet innovators recognized by the Internet Society are the individuals who have made outstanding contributions to internet technological, commercial and regulatory or policy advances, and have helped to expand the internet. The two groups are released as follows.

---

[76]Howard Frank. http://www.internethalloffame.org/inductees/howard-frank [2016-9-16].

[77]Glenn Ricart. http://www.internethalloffame.org/inductees/glenn-ricart [2016-9-16].

[78]Kanchana Kanchanasut. http://www.internethalloffame.org/inductees/kanchana-kanchanasut [2016-9-16].

[79]Werner Zorn. http://www.internethalloffame.org/inductees/werner-zorn [2016-9-16].

[80]Jun Murai. http://www.internethalloffame.org/inductees/jun-murai [2016-9-16].

Mitchell Baker[81]: American; in 2005, Time magazine included her in its annual list of the 100 most influential people in the world; Baker helped legitimize open source internet applications; Baker is the Executive Chair of the Mozilla Foundation and of Mozilla Corporation.

Tim Berners-Lee[82]: British; known as the "Inventor of the World Wide Web"; he invented web server, web browser, HTTP and HTML; on December 25, 1990, Berners-Lee and Robert Cailliau succeeded in the first communication between the World Wide Web and the NeXT server through the internet at the Conseil Europeen Pour la Recherche Nucleaire (CERN); Berners-Lee is the chairman of the World Wide Web Consortium and the founder of the World Wide Web Foundation; in addition, Berners-Lee is also the director of the website science research initiative, and a member of the collective intelligence center advisory committee of Massachusetts Institute of Technology.

Robert Cailliau[83]: Belgian; he co-created the World Wide Web (WWW) with Tim Berners-Lee, a colleague of the Conseil Europeen Pour la Recherche Nucleaire (CERN), and developed the first Web browser for Apple Mac Device; in 1993, in collaboration with the Fraunhofer Gesellschaft Cailliau started the European Commission's first web-based project for information dissemination in Europe (WISE); As a result of his work with CERN's Legal Service, CERN released the web technology into the public domain on April 30, 1993.

Van Jacobson[84]: American; one of the primary contributors to the TCP/IP protocol stack; he proposed the TCP flow control algorithm; Jacobson is renowned for his pioneering achievements in improvement and optimization of network performance; between 1988 and 1989, Jacobson redesigned the TCP/IP's flow control algorithm (Jacobson algorithm), which saved the internet from current collapsing; in August 2006, Jacobson joined the Palo Alto Research Center as a researcher and served as chief scientist at Packet Design.

Larry Landweber[85]: American; a leader in the development of the international internet; in 1979, he proposed the Computer Science Network (CSNET) project which later substituted for the ARPANET; the CSNET is a network connecting all US universities and industrial computer research groups. By 1984, it connected 180 computer systems of universities, corporations and government; his team also developed and implemented one of the first Internet protocols (1981-84, IBM VM systems).

Paul Mockapetris[86]: American; the inventor of the domain name system; Mockapetris had discovered the shortcomings of domain name and IP address translation at a single level based on a single host in the early Internet, including the

[81]Mitchell Baker. http://www.internethalloffame.org/inductees/mitchell-baker [2016-9-16].

[82]Tim Berners-Lee. http://www.internethalloffame.org/inductees/tim-berners-lee [2016-9-16].

[83]Robert Cailliau. http://www.internethalloffame.org/inductees/robert-cailliau [2016-9-16].

[84]Van Jacobson. http://www.internethalloffame.org/inductees/van-jacobson [2016-9-16].

[85]Larry Landweber. http://www.internethalloffame.org/inductees/larry-landweber [2016-9-16].

[86]Paul Mockapetris. http://www.internethalloffame.org/inductees/paul-mockapetris [2016-9-16].

ARPANET, and improved the system into a distributed and dynamic database domain name system; Mockapetris is a chief scientist and chairman of Nominum corporation.

Craig Newmark[87]: American; founder of the Craigslist website; Newmark changed the way people used to sorting and turned it into an Internet-based industry; Newmark served as the CEO of Craigslist.

Raymond Tomlinson[88]: American; a programmer that known as the "Father of E-mail"; he is known for inventing e-mails, which fundamentally changed people's way of communication and brought a radical revolution to the world; in 1971, Tomlinson implemented, on the ARPANET system, the first email program, which was the first system capable of sending mails between users on different hosts connected to the ARPANET; Tomlinson is deceased.

Linus Torvalds[89]: Finn having American citizenship; Torvalds is the earliest creator of the Linux kernel, then launched the open source project, and served as the chief architect and project coordinator of Linux kernel; Torvalds is one of the most famous computer programmers and hackers.

Philip Zimmermann[90]: American; an advocate of privacy and security, and creator of Pretty Good Privacy; Zimmermann is the co-founder and chairman of Silent Circle.

Mark Andreessen[91]: American; the founder of Netscape browser; Andreessen is an American entrepreneur, investor and software engineer and has participated in the development of the famous Mosaic browser, which is the first widely used browser; Andreessen founded the Netscape Communications company, Silicon Valley venture capital firms, i.e., Andreessen Horowitz and Ning; Anderson is a board member of Facebook, eBay (the world's largest e-commerce company), HP and other companies.

Henning Schulzrinne[92]: American; he co-developed the Voice Over Internet Protocol (VoIP) and other multimedia applications; he is one of the main designers of the SIP (Session Initiation Protocol); since December 2011, Schulzrinne has been the Chief Technology Officer for the United States Federal Communications Commission (FCC).

John Perry Barlow[93]: American; one of the founders of the Electronic Frontier Foundation, is a member at Harvard Law School's Berkman Center for Internet&Society; he published the famous "Declaration of Independence of

---

[87]Craig Newmark. http://www.internethalloffame.org/inductees/craig-newmark [2016-9-16].

[88]Raymond Tomlinson. http://www.internethalloffame.org/inductees/raymond-tomlinson [2016-9-16].

[89]Linus Torvalds. http://www.internethalloffame.org/inductees/linus-torvalds [2016-9-16].

[90]Philip Zimmermann. http://www.internethalloffame.org/inductees/philip-zimmermann [2016-9-16].

[91]Mark Andreessen. http://www.internethalloffame.org/inductees/mark-andreessen [2016-9-16].

[92]Henning Schulzrinne. http://www.internethalloffame.org/inductees/henning-schulzrinne [2016-9-16].

[93]John Perry Barlow. http://www.internethalloffame.org/inductees/john-perry-barlow [2016-9-16].

Cyberspace"; Barlow currently serves as the vice-chairman of the Electronic Frontier Foundation (EFF)'s board of directors.

Richard Stallman[94]: American; the spiritual leader of the Free Software Movement, the sponsor of the GNU (an open source free operating system) project, and founder of Common Public License Agreement and Free Software Foundation; Stallman is a famous hacker, and the GNU General Public License he wrote is the world's most widely used free software license, which also opens up a new path for the non-profit copyright (copyleft) concept.

Anne-Marie Eklund Löwinder[95]: Sweden; a pioneer in cyber security in Sweden; since 2014, she has been a board member of the Council of European National Top-Level Domain Registries (CENTR), and she is also a member of the Information Security Council of the Swedish Civil Contingencies Agency.

Aaron Swartz[96]: American; a co-founder of Reddit, a co-author of the web feed format RSS (Really Simple Syndication) version 1.0; Swartz participated in the design of the RSS and the Markdown publishing format (a lightweight markup language), in the creation of the sharing website framework web.py, and in the development of the social news site Reddit; Swartz is deceased.

François Flückiger[97]: French; the leader of the struggle for promoting the Internet in Europe. He was the director of the School of Information Technology and Computing in the European Coordinating Committee for Intercontinental Research Network (CERN); at CERN, Flückiger took over Tim Berners-Lee's job.

Jimmy Wales[98]: American; one of the founders of Wikipedia, a free internet encyclopedia to which anyone can contribute, and the world's largest encyclopedia that helps a trend of collaboration and sharing among users; Wales is the honorary chairman of Wikimedia Foundation.

Stephen Kent[99]: American; a pioneer in the architecture of network security systems; he designed and developed the network layer encryption and access-control systems and standards, transport layer security, secure e-mail technology, Public Key Infrastructure standards and certification authority systems; Kent is the vice president and chief scientist for security technologies at BBN Technologies.

94 Richard Stallman. http://www.internethalloffame.org/inductees/richard-stallman [2016-9-16].

95 Anne-Marie Eklund Löwinder. http://www.internethalloffame.org/inductees/anne-marie-eklund-löwinder [2016-9-16].

96 Aaron Swartz. http://www.internethalloffame.org/inductees/aaron-swartz [2016-9-16].

97 François Flückiger. http://www.internethalloffame.org/inductees/fran%C3%A7ois-fl%C3%BCckiger [2016-9-16].

98 Jimmy Wales. http://www.internethalloffame.org/inductees/jimmy-wales [2016-9-16].

99 Stephen Kent. http://www.internethalloffame.org/inductees/stephen-kent [2016-9-16].

3. The Global Connectors

The global connectors recognized by the Internet Society are the individuals who have made significant contributions to the growth and use of the internet wordwide. The two groups are released as follows.

Randy Bush[100]: American; the founder of the Network Venture Resource Center (NSRC), which supports networking in southern Africa; Bush started Japan's first commercial ISP to develop and maintain internet infrastructure; Bush is a member of the board of trustees in the American Registry of Internet Numbers.

Kilnam Chon[101]: Korean; he promotes the rapid development of the internet in Asia and developed the first internet in Asia (SDN); he is the chairman of the regional network organization, the Asia Pacific Networking Group (APNG), and the Intercontinental Research Network Coordination Committee.

Al Gore[102]: a former US Vice President, Senator and the founder of legislation to protect the internet; he encouraged increased public access to the internet; during his time in Congress, Gore actively supported and funded the development of the internet, and helped to create the "information highway"; he is the first government official who realizes that the impact of the Internet could go beyond academic education and economic growth.

Nancy Hafkin[103]: African; an African representative of United Nations Economic Council; she actively promoted the development of computers and internet in Africa, and he helped build the African ICT framework through partnerships with governmental and nongovernmental institutions; she enabled email connectivity and internet connectivity in more than 10 countries during the early 1990s; she served as team leader and coordinator for UN African Information Society Initiative.

Geoff Huston[104]: Australian; honored as the "Father of the Internet" in Australia; He established a national academic research network which helped the Internet to drive deep into the Australian universities and professional research institutions within one year.

Brewster Kahle[105]: American; the founder of the Internet archives; he invented the Internet's first distributed search system-WAIS (Wide Area Information Server); he founded the Alexa Internet (which offers search and discovery services, and which includes more than 90% of Web browsers); Carl is a member of the American Academy of Arts and Sciences, and is also the director of the Internet Archive.

Daniel Karrenberg[106]: Dutch; he helped build the EUnet and the first pan-European Internet Service Provider (ISP) besides establishing the world's first

[100]Randy Bush. http://www.internethalloffame.org/inductees/randy-bush [2016-9-17].

[101]Kilnam Chon. http://www.internethalloffame.org/inductees/kilnam-chon [2016-9-17].

[102]Al Gore. http://www.internethalloffame.org/inductees/al-gore [2016-9-17].

[103]Nancy Hafkin. http://www.internethalloffame.org/inductees/nancy-hafkin [2016-9-17].

[104]Geoff Huston. http://www.internethalloffame.org/inductees/geoff-huston [2016-9-17].

[105]Brewster Kahle. http://www.internethalloffame.org/inductees/brewster-kahle-0 [2016-9-17].

[106]Daniel Karrenberg. http://www.internethalloffame.org/inductees/daniel-karrenberg [2016-9-17].

regional Internet registry, RIPE (The Réseaux IP Européens, European IP address management and distribution organization); he plays a leading role in Routing Information Service (RIS), Test Traffic Measurement Service (TTM), DNS Monitoring Service (DNSMON); Karrenberg was awarded the "Internet Service Award" and is the director of the Internet Association.

Toru Takahashi[107]: Japanese; he is known as a journalist and evangelist in the development of Japanese Internet, also being instrumental in bringing the Internet to Asia; he helped to establish several key industry groups that continue to influence the internet today; he wrote the first book about the Internet in Japan; he was a member of the Japan UNIX Society and the Internet Association of Japan.

Tan Tin Wee[108]: Singaporean; an internet pioneer in Singapore and a founder of the multilingual Internet domain name system; he is also a founder of Singapore InfoWeb and the forerunner of the present National Web Homepage. Under his leadership, Singapore hosted the first Chinese Website and Tamil Website; he currently serves as an Associate Professor of the Department of Biochemistry of the National University of Singapore.

Hu Qiheng[109]: Chinese; she led the National Computing and Networking Facility of China (NCFC) project team that brought the Internet to China and promoted China's access to the Internet and assisted its development; she founded the China Internet Association and served as the first chair of the board, helping to promote internet application in peripheral and disadvantaged areas of China; she is a member of the Chinese Academy of Engineering and was vice-president of the Chinese Academy of Sciences before retirement.

Steve Goldstein[110]: American; he helped to promote many countries' access to the Internet, as well as playing a key role in evaluating and funding development of internet projects around the world; Goldstein helped to establish the NASA Space Science Network, and he was a former head of the National Science Foundation's International Networking Division.

Karen Banks[111]: British; one of the founders of the Association for Progressive Communications; she advocated empowering women around the world to use information and communication technologies, improved governance and promoted gender equality; Banks led the Association for Progressive Communications (APC)[112] to participate in the information society and internet governance; Banks is the head of the international portal "GnFido" of Green Net (a non-profit Internet service provider in London), as well as the APC's financial manager.

---

[107]Toru Takahashi. http://www.internethalloffame.org/inductees/toru-takahashi [2016-9-17].

[108]Tan Tin Wee. http://www.internethalloffame.org/inductees/tan-tin-wee [2016-9-17].

[109]Qiheng Hu. http://www.internethalloffame.org/inductees/qiheng-hu [2016-9-17].

[110]Steve Goldstein. http://www.internethalloffame.org/inductees/steve-goldstein [2016-9-17].

[111]Karen Banks. http://www.internethalloffame.org/inductees/karen-banks [2016-9-17].

[112]APC, an international network and non-profit organization dedicated to establishment and maintenance of free and open internet.

Anriette Esterhuysen[113]: African; Executive Director of the APC; she promoted development of information and communication and human rights organizations in South Africa and Zimbabwe, helped to establish e-mail and the internet in southern Africa, and advocated improvements to the internet governance; Esterhuysen is a member of the African Technical Advisory Committee and a member of the Internet Governance Forum as one of the multi-stakeholders.

Ida Holz[114]: Uruguayan; she helped Uruguay's access to the internet and promoted the rapid development of the internet in Latin America and played an important role in the construction of the Latin American Network Forum; Holz oversees the development and maintenance of connectivity among the now 64 nodes at academic and research institutions throughout the country; she is a member of the board of directors of the Agency for Development of Electronic Governance and the Information Society, and is a member of the Program Committee of Ceibal Center.

Gihan Dias[115]: Sri Lankan; in addition to being the founder of the Lanka Academic Network, he is also the founder of the Lanka ".lk Domain Registry; he enhanced the opportunities for students to receive information technology education by increasing the accessibility of information technology to the students; he applied a non-profit top-level domain name, .lk, for Sri Lanka; he has also assisted a number of Internet service providers in setting up their own networks.

Barry Leiner[116]: American; he established the Internet Activities Board (later the Internet Engineering Task Force (IETF) were established within the framework); Leiner set up and developed internet communication protocols and is the author of more than 60 internet technology-related publications; Leiner was assistant director of the Research Institute for Advanced Computer Science in the NASA Ames Research Center's; Leiner is deceased.

Teus Hagen[117]: Dutch; he promoted the development of UNIX networks and UNIX Internet in Europe, helped NLNET to become the first Internet service provider in the Netherlands; Hagen is the president of Cacert's board of directors.

Haruhisa Ishida[118]: Japanese; a pioneer who introduced UNIX and internetworking technology to Japan and is one of the founders of ISOC; he promoted the TCP/IP technology aggressively, as well as playing an important role in internet security; he also was a board member of the Japan Network Information Centre; he has passed away.

[113]Anriette Esterhuysen. http://www.internethalloffame.org/inductees/anriette-esterhuysen [2016-9-17].

[114]Ida Holz. http://www.internethalloffame.org/inductees/ida-holz [2016-9-17].

[115]Gihan Dias. http://www.internethalloffame.org/inductees/gihan-dias [2016-9-17].

[116]Barry Leiner. http://www.internethalloffame.org/inductees/barry-leiner [2016-9-17].

[117]Teus Hagen. http://www.internethalloffame.org/inductees/teus-hagen [2016-9-17].

[118]Haruhisa Ishida. http://www.internethalloffame.org/inductees/haruhisa-ishida [2016-9-17].

George Sadowsky[119]: American; he helped more than 50 developing countries to develop and deploy information and communication technologies; he developed the Leland Initiative of the United States Agency for International Development (USAID) and provided internet access for 20 African countries; Sadowsky is a member of the ICANN's board of directors.

5.3 Presentation of Internet Sovereignty Challenges Internet Hegemony

The "stakeholder" governance model is, objectively, a model in which powerful internet states govern the internet. An idea opposite to the "stakeholder" is government-led "internet co-governance", that is, a co-governance model in which one country has one vote. Apparently, a government can better represent a country to reflect and respond to the country's appeals about the internet than a stakeholder. The US, as the origin of the internet, seems to not reserve any space for the other countries to request internet co-governance, but once the concept of cyberspace sovereignty is introduced, the model in which stakeholders govern the internet would be inevitably challenged. More precisely, when countries recognize the existence of sovereignty over the internet, what matters is no longer whether powerful internet states allow the other countries to participate in the governance of international internet, but whether the government of each country participates in the governance and in what form, and how to express its own country's internet sovereignty. Therefore, how to protect a country's own legitimate rights and interests according to the concept of cyberspace sovereignty will become a top priority.

5.3.1 The International Community Starts to Be Alert to the Powerful Internet States' Control of the Internet

As the political, military, economic, cultural and social interests of countries are put into the internet, the internet has become vital infrastructure for all countries. In China, the importance of cyberspace has been elevated to such a high level that "without network security, there is no national security". Therefore, countries that remain extremely vigilant against internet hegemony certainly begin to reflect on the risks of the internet, which is established under the control of powerful internet states and bears enormous interest, and seriously explore how to build a national information infrastructure so that it is not subject to other countries. China, Russia and other countries began to promote the idea of international co-governance of the

[119]George Sadowsky. http://www.internethalloffame.org/inductees/george-sadowsky [2016-9-17].

internet, which, however, is robustly obstructed by the US and other powerful internet states. At the World Congress on International Telecommunications held in December 2012 (WCIT2012), Russia, China, the United Arab Emirates, Saudi Arabia and other countries submitted proposals concerning internet management, equal rights of countries to internet resource allocation, and so on. However, the US Congress passed a special resolution against the involvement of the International Telecommunication Union in internet management; in addition, many Western countries also explicitly opposed the incorporation of internet-related provisions into the new *International Telecommunication Regulations.*[120]

5.3.2 The Consensus Reached in the UN Lays the International Legal Foundation for Cyberspace Sovereignty

In 2013, *in the Report of the Group of Governmental Experts on Developments in the Field of Information and Telecommunications in the Context of International Security*, China put forward the suggestion that "state sovereignty can extend to the State's own cyberspace and the State can exercise jurisdiction over network infrastructure and network behavior within their territory", which was supported by Russia, Brazil, Pakistan, Belarus and other countries. After heated debate, matching, compromise and exchange of conditions, the above opinion was finally incorporated as international consensus into the UN documents. James A. Lewis, an expert at the Center for Strategic and International Studies (CSIS), as a consultant in the expert group secretariat, described this opinion as follows: "State sovereignty and international norms and principles that flow from sovereignty apply to State conduct of ICT-related activities and to their jurisdiction over ICT infrastructure within their territory." And the above description was included in Item 20 of Part III (Recommendations on Norms, Rules and Principles of Responsible Behavior of States) in the third GGE report, which was formed in early June, 2013. The report was published on June 24 2013 at the 68th UN General Assembly with the document No. A/68/98.[121] It is the above result that laid the international legal foundation for the presentation of the idea of cyberspace sovereignty by China.[122]

---

[120]Revision of the International Telecommunication Regulations is complete, and the demands of developing countries are satisfied. http://news.xinhuanet.com/tech/2012-12/14/c_124099013.htm [2016-9-17].

[121]Item 94 of the Provisional Agenda of the Sixty-eighth Session of the General Assembly of the United Nations, Developments in the field of information and telecommunications in the context of international security. http://www.un.org/ga/search/view_doc.asp?symbol=A/68/98&referer=/english/&Lang=C [2016-9-1].

[122]On Autonomous Root Domain Name System Based on Association of Nations from the Perspective of "Cyber Network Sovereignty". http://news.xinhuanet.com/politics/2014-11/27/c_127255092.htm [2016-9-17].

5.3.3 The Demand for Protection of Netizens in Respective Countries Exceeds the Technical and Service Advantages Provided by Stakeholders

Cyberspace construction depends on the technical and service advantages. The US is the information center of the international internet–most of the traffic around the world flows through the backbone networks built by American enterprises such as Sprint Nextel Corporation; the US is the information service center of the international internet–Google, Twitter, Facebook, YouTube and other internet information service providers occupy more than half of the world of information services; the US is the international information technology center–the products of Intel, IBM, Oracle, EMC, Microsoft, Qualcomm and other information technology enterprises take up the majority of the international market. For the above reasons, the US and other powerful internet states actively promote the idea of stakeholders dominating the internet. However, the other countries around the world also have the right to decide whether they accept the stakeholders' occupation of the market. For example, if China, as a huge internet market, restricts the market open to American enterprises for some reasons, then the above advantages of powerful internet states will no longer exist. Of course, such a restriction is based on the following premises: (1) there is a replacement, even a replacement with relatively poor performance; and (2) the market itself has the demand and capacity for human intervention.

At present, there are replacements for most products and technologies. With respect to whether human intervention exists in the market itself, the undeniable fact that the internet is closely related to the interests of netizens in political, economic, cultural, social stability and other aspects, as well as the advantage of number of netizens is more decisive than technical and service advantages. Besides, the Rules of World Trade Organization (WTO) also recognize intervention in the market for security reasons. In terms of intervention capacity, a government's own market and security review mechanism, market access mechanism and so on all can become means of market regulation. In such circumstances, the stakeholders must act prudently and cannot infringe the interests of netizens of the other countries. Obviously, making use of stakeholders' technical and service interests to harm the interests of netizens of the other countries is unacceptable to any sovereign state.

5.3.4 Cyberspace Sovereignty Has Challenged Cyber Hegemony

In 2014, President Xi Jinping, at the Wuzhen World Internet Conference appealed for "respect for cyber sovereignty", and put forward, as a head of a state, a proposal to "respect cyber (cyberspace) sovereignty" for the first time in the world. The

National Security Law of the People's Republic of China[123] introduced in 2015 also clearly put forward the legislative intention of "maintaining the sovereignty of the State's cyberspace".[124] When it was suggested that the internet should be co-governed by the international community, most countries did not feel the urgency to participate in internet governance because they were backward in information technology and needed to rely on the technology of powerful internet states. As a result, the appeal for international co-governance of internet did not pose a serious challenge to powerful internet states. However, when countries realize that cyberspace governance belongs to the sovereign act, they are faced with the problem whether to hand over the sovereignty, leaders with national consciousness will be alert and will seriously consider whether a country's cyberspace is sovereign territory which needs self-management, self-protection, independence, pursuit of equal status. If all the countries can be well aware of the importance of cyberspace sovereignty, the countries will positively respond to the proposal of internet co-governance because it involves sovereignty. Such a situation poses an enormous challenge to the jungle rules that "stakeholders" dominate the internet, and it will lead to more violent conflicts.

5.4 The Mode of Co-existence of Internet Sovereignty and Internet Stakeholders

In respect of cyberspace sovereignty, China upholds the principle of actively advocating and insisting on safeguarding cyberspace sovereignty. However, before the international community fully understands cyberspace sovereignty, the mainstream is still that stakeholders dominate the internet. In that case, China needs to accept a coexistence model which adapts to the existing situation, does not easily contradict the trend, and compromises in some ways.

5.4.1 Basic Principles of the Coexistence Model

Objectively, in respect of network commons, global commons, sovereign transferring space and so on, the stakeholder-led model is acceptable; however, in respect of personnel activities and protection of interests, it is necessary to adhere to the sovereignty co-governance model.

---

[123]National Security Law of the People's Republic of China, voted through by the Standing Committee of National People's Congress on July 1, 2015. http://www.gov.cn/xinwen/2015-07/01/content_2888316.htm [2016-9-1].

[124]Chapter II, Article 25 of the National Security Law of the People's Republic of China, 2015. http://news.mod.gov.cn/headlines/2015-07/01/content_4592594_2.htm [2016-9-27].

Therefore, the basic principles of the coexistence model include the following:

Adopting the sovereignty co-governance model to deal with internet-related public policy issues (the decision-making power over cyberspace public policy belongs to state sovereignty, as well as the states having the right and responsibility to deal with public policy issues).

Adopting the stakeholder-led model in the technical and economic fields (stakeholders can continue to play an important role in the evolution of internet technology as always, and governments may not intervene).

5.4.2 Basic Strategy for the Coexistence Model

The basic strategy for deciding compromise can be made and shall not be made in the following aspects: compromise can be made when it comes to matters which relate to respective countries' interests and each country's interests are equal, simple market behavior, as well as issues in which a country cannot compete with the existing stakeholders; and compromise shall not be made when it comes to matters which may hurt national interests and issues which relate to national interests that can be safeguarded only depending on sovereignty.

1. Those that cannot be compromised

(1) **It shall be maintained that each state has jurisdiction over its own networks, and no compromise shall be made**. It is unacceptable to sovereign states that powerful internet states intervene, in the name of freedom of internet information, in other states' management of their own internet according to law. For example, the construction of national firewalls and network forts belongs to state sovereignty and should not be interfered with by other states.

(2) **The management of the cyberspace boundary system is developed by the states together and shall not be controlled by the stakeholders and the powerful internet states behind them, and no compromise shall be made**. It is an objective fact in the global commons that Google uses outer space. Google alleges that it builds a satellite free WiFi system, that is, Google public network,[125] and affirms that it is corporate behavior. However, that public network can be closely connected with cyberspace within each state's territory, and its intention implied breaking cyberspace boundaries of states and striking management of cyberspace boundary system. Such behavior and the consequences of the behavior should not be ignored.

[125] Is Global Free WiFi Coverage Possible? http://news.xinhuanet.com/info/2016-06/14/c_135434500.htm [2016-9-17].

(3) **The jurisdiction over territorial cyberspace should be retained, and no compromise shall be made**. At present, the ownership of cyberspace data can be interpreted in two ways: the interpretation in the stakeholder model is that data should be managed by one who owns the system where the data is stored; whereas the interpretation in sovereignty co-governance model is that a government, which has jurisdiction over its territory where a system bearing data is located, has jurisdiction over the data, namely, the government has "jurisdiction over territorial cyberspace" (for example, the government can delete malicious remarks and information that exist in the system within its territory). From the perspective of state administration, each state should retain jurisdiction over territorial cyberspace.

(4) **It shall be maintained that issues involving public affairs, including the ICANN's top-level domain open policy, are issues about cyberspace sovereignty, and no compromise shall be made**. At present, the ICANN's top-level domain management seems to involve only technology and services, but not involve public affairs, and it is controlled by stakeholders. However, if someone applies for the domain name ".falungong", the act is essentially a public malicious challenge to the Chinese government, which is no longer a matter of technology and business, but a public policy issue, and no compromise shall be made in this respect.

2. Those that can be compromised

(1) **Promotion of the internationalization progress of the ICANN**. The root domain system is a centralized management system that has been in use for decades. Although IPv6 is the next generation of internet protocols, the original system framework will still be used, and the centralized management system cannot be changed. Unless a new network is constructed all over the world and the centralized management system is replaced with a distributed shared addressing approach like "block chain", it is impossible to abolish centralized management system within the system of the existing framework. However, people can still improve the centralized management approach of the ICANN from the aspect of who has the power to manage the system. Therefore, managing the ICANN in an international co-governance model or establishing an alliance-based root domain name resolution system can serve as a compromise.

(2) **The stakeholders still control and are responsible for assigning the internet address resources (such as IPv6 address resources)**. It is noteworthy that the IPv4 addresses are substantially exhausted, and there is no such a problem as re-distribution. In respect of application for IPv6 address resources, in view of the experience and lessons that each state learned from the use of IPv4 address space, enterprises of each state should actively apply for IPv6 address space and avoid disputes from the viewpoint of their own interests. As a result, the stakeholders still controlling and being responsible for assigning the internet address resources can serve as a compromise.

(3) **The internet technical standards are still mainly contributed by the stakeholders**. It is an objective fact that the stakeholders contribute a lot of internet technology standards. As to the internet technology standards raised and used by the stakeholders, sovereign states often decide whether to refer to or use them according to their own circumstances. The internet technical standards are not interference in space by power, so they can maintain the status quo. In regard to the internet technical standards, each state should try to make their own enterprises actively participate in the establishment of standards.

Chapter 6
China's Declaration of Cyberspace Sovereignty

Abstract President Xi Jinping is the first national leader to put forward the concept of cyber sovereignty in the world. China has voiced a lot in cyberspace sovereignty, including the leaders' speech, laws and regulations, documents, international bilateral agreements and so on, which clearly put forward the view of cyberspace sovereignty.

Keywords Xi Jinping's speeches · Liu Yunshan's speech · Speech from the director of the office of the central leading group for cyberspace affairs Cybersecurity law · Bilateral agreement

China has systematically given the "China voice" in terms of the problem about cyberspace security and sovereignty. Both state leaders and relevant government departments have successively delivered a series of important speeches, including putting forward a series of standpoints and ideas of jointly governing cyberspace from the perspective of jointly building a community of common future in cyberspace by nations around the world, and putting forward a series of significant thoughts and measures from perspectives of building cyber power in China and ensuring the cyberspace security and cyberspace sovereignty.

6.1 President Xi Jinping's Speeches

In view of cyber sovereignty, President Xi Jinping has proposed related assertions in many international occasions since 2014 and clarified China's attitude towards cyberspace sovereignty.

B. Fang, *Cyberspace Sovereignty*,
https://doi.org/10.1007/978-981-13-0320-3_6

6.1.1 Speech at the Third World Internet Conference (November 2016)

In the speech released via video at the opening ceremony of the third World Internet Conference[1] on November 16, 2016, President Xi Jinping said: "The Internet is the most vibrant sector in our times. Its rapid development has brought profound changes to our life and work as well as new opportunities and challenges to human society. The development of the Internet knows no national or sectoral boundaries. The sound use, development and governance of the Internet thus call for closer international cooperation and joint efforts to build a community of common future in cyberspace. As a Chinese saying goes, 'A gentleman puts basic principles first, which will illuminate the way forward.' At last year's WIC, I put forward four principles and five proposals on global development and governance of the Internet. They have been well received in the world. China will work together with the international community to ensure the common well-being of humanity, uphold cyber sovereignty, promote more fair and equitable global Internet governance and bring about an open, inclusive and secure cyberspace that features equality, mutual respect, innovation and orderly development."

6.1.2 Speech at a Symposium on Cyber Security and IT Application (April 2016)

At a symposium on cyber security and IT application[2] held on April 19, 2016, President Xi Jinping made the following remarks: "The cyber security game of great powers is now not only a technical game, but a game of idea and a game of discourse right. We put forward four principles and five proposals on global development and governance of the Internet, and particularly we advocated respect for cyber sovereignty and building of a community of common future in cyberspace, which won approval of most countries in the world."

[1]Xi Jinping: Video speech at the opening ceremony of the third World Internet Conference (full text). http://news.cctv.com/2016/11/16/ARTI8yGw6u37r9eT21580zHS161116.shtml [2016-11-17].

[2]Xi Jinping's speech at a symposium on cybersecurity and IT application (release of full text). http://news.cctv.com/2016/04/25/ARTIa8uTHXqX8JF25uz6S7Yh160425.shtml [2016-8-27].

6.1.3 *Speech at the Second World Internet Conference (December 2015)*

In the speech delivered at the opening ceremony of the second World Internet Conference[3] on December 16, 2015, President Xi Jinping put forwards four principles and five proposals. The first of the four principles is "respect for cyber sovereignty", and President Xi Jinping stated that "The principle of sovereign equality enshrined in the *Charter of the United Nations* is one of the basic norms in contemporary international relations. It covers all aspects of state-to-state relations, which also includes cyberspace. We should respect the right of individual countries to independently choose their own path of cyber development, model of cyber regulation and Internet public policies, and participate in international cyberspace governance on an equal footing. No country should pursue cyber hegemony, interfere in other countries' internal affairs or engage in, connive at or support cyber activities that undermine other countries' national security."

6.1.4 *Message of Congratulations to the First World Internet Conference (November 2014)*

On November 19, 2014, Xi Jinping conveyed a message of congratulations to the first World Internet Conference[4] as below: "Amid a new round of scientific and technological revolution with information technology at its core, the Internet is increasingly becoming a pacesetter of innovation-driven development, profoundly changing people's way of production and life and powering social development. It has turned the world into a global village and made the international community a highly interdependent community of common destiny. Meanwhile, the development of the Internet has posed new challenges to national sovereignty, security and development interests, which requires the international community to meet urgently and seriously to pursue common governance and conclude a win-win outcome. China is actively advancing the development of the Internet and extending its benefit to the 1.3 billion Chinese people. Following the principle of mutual respect and mutual trust, China is ready to work with other countries to deepen international cooperation, respect sovereignty on the Internet, uphold cyber security, and jointly build a cyberspace of peace, security, openness and cooperation and an International Internet governance system of multilateralism, democracy and transparency."

---

[3]Xi Jinping's speech at the opening ceremony of the second World Internet Conference (full text). http://news.xinhuanet.com/fortune/2015-12/16/c_1117481089.htm [2016-10-2].

[4]Message of Congratulations from Chinese President Xi Jinping to the First World Internet Conference (full text). http://news.xinhuanet.com/live/2014-11/19/c_127228771.htm [2016-11-21].

6.1.5 Speech at the National Congress of Brazil (July 2014)

On July 16, 2014, President Xi Jinping delivered a speech at the National Congress of Brazil entitled "Carry Forward Traditional Friendship and Jointly Open up a New Chapter of Cooperation",[5] "In today's world, the Internet's development poses new challenges to the sovereignty, security and interests of a country and should be handled seriously. Although the Internet is highly globalized, the sovereignty of the information sector of every country should not be violated and no matter how developed a country's Internet technology is, it just cannot violate the information sovereignty of other countries. There are no double standards in the information sector, and all countries have the right to safeguard their information security. We cannot just have the security of one or some countries while leaving the rest insecure, still less should one seek the so-called absolute security of itself at the expense of the security of others. Following the principle of mutual respect and mutual trust, the international community requires active and effective international cooperation to uphold cyber security, and jointly build a cyberspace of peace, security, openness and cooperation and an International Internet governance system of multilateralism, democracy and transparency."

6.2 Chinese Leader Liu Yunshan's Speech at the Opening Ceremony of the Third World Internet Conference (November 2016)

On November 16, 2016, Liu Yunshan proposed the following five proposals in his speech at the opening ceremony of the third World Internet Conference[6]:

"First, we should deepen cooperation in improvement over governance rules and promotion of the transformation of Internet governance system. Cyberspace is a common space for human beings, so promotion of the international cyberspace governance requires collecting the wisdom of the world and gathering the power of all countries. At present, the global development and governance of the Internet are at a critical crossroad, and particularly require all countries to adopt a long-term perspective, adhere to treatment on an equal footing, promote equality and justice, and promote a global Internet governance system of multilateralism, democracy and transparency. We should regard the "respect of cyber sovereignty" as a basic principle, and safeguard countries' equal rights and power in cyberspace in terms of development, participation and governance arrangements. We should increase the representation and voices of emerging markets and developing countries. We

[5]Xi Jinping's speech at National Congress of Brazil. http://news.xinhuanet.com/world/2014-07/17/c_1111665403.htm [2016-11-21].

[6]Opening ceremony of the third World Internet Conference, Liu Yunshan's speech (full text). https://www.easyaq.org/info/infoLink/979062845.shtml [2016-11-20].

should not be engaged in cyber hegemony and avoid making unilateral decisions or making decisions only by very few parties. We should fully leverage the role of various players, including governments, international organizations, Internet companies, technology communities, non-government institutions and individual citizens to speed up the course of internationalization of managing basic resources of the Internet and form a pattern of governance featured in a multilateral approach with multi-party participation. China stands ready to work with the international community to jointly push for the formulation of international rules and standards in the sectors of digital economy, information technology, cyber security and so on so as to reflect in a more balanced way the interests and concerns of all parties."

"Second, we should deepen cooperation in promotion of Internet innovation and creation and fulfillment of common development. The Internet plays a leading role in promoting innovation-driven development and provides an important support for economic structural optimization. We encourage and support various Internet-based innovation and creation to accelerate the development of a new generation of information technology such as cloud computing, big data, Internet of Things and artificial intelligence, speed up the cultivation of new technologies, new applications and new formats of the Internet, accelerate deep integration of the Internet and the real economy, and promote transformation of digitalization, networking and intelligence of traditional industries. Following the principle of openness and cooperation as well as mutual benefit and win-win outcomes, all countries should deepen cooperation in the sectors of technology research and development, cross-border e-commerce, SME innovation, etc. and create more converging points and new highlights for cooperation. In the past, China's Internet development benefited from the reform and opening policy, and its future development is still inseparable from this policy. We invite all countries to ride on the fast train of the China's Internet development and share the opportunities and benefits of Internet development."

"Third, we should deepen cooperation in accelerating the popularization of the Internet and better benefiting people across the world. With the acceleration of information technology, the Internet has become a main artery of economic and social development, and an indispensable new infrastructure in the modern society. The international community has a responsibility to promote the prevalent development of information technology on a global scale, to provide necessary financial, technical and talent support for acceleration of cyber construction in developing countries and underdeveloped countries, to enhance those countries' own Internet development abilities, and to create conditions for eliminating poverty and promoting common development. We should strengthen the international exchange and cooperation in the sectors of telemedicine, online education, e-government and intelligent cities and other sectors, and jointly explore new approaches and ways of making life convenient and better for our people through Internet. China is willing to take the opportunity of 'the Belt and Road' to accelerate the construction of online Silk Road and strengthen the strategic connectivity, so that people across the world can all enjoy the benefits of Internet development."

"Fourth, we should deepen cooperation in expansion of cyber exchange and promotion of civilization through mutual learning. The Internet has a unique advantage in spreading of ideologies and cultures, and it is an important carrier to facilitate exchange and mutual learning of civilization. We should work together to build an online platform for cultural exchange, fully show the diversity of human civilization, and learn from each other and achieve common development through interaction and mutual learning. All countries should give active play to the role of the Internet in spreading civilization to urge digital production and networking communication of fine spiritual and cultural products and to promote positive energy of justice, goodness, brightness and happiness. Greater efforts should be made to strengthen ethical standards in cyber, operate and use the cyberspace in a civilized manner, and enhance the Internet protection of juveniles. China is willing to deepen communication with all countries in cyber cultures at different levels and different sectors to promote mutual understanding between people, so that different flowers of civilization bloom and vary."

"Fifth, we should deepen cooperation in responding to challenges of cyber security and maintaining good order. Cyber security is a global issue and no country can immune from it; we must work together to deal with it. The importance of maintaining cyber security is to establish a common, mutual trust, cooperative and sustainable cyber security concept. We cannot just have the security of one or some countries while leaving the rest insecure, still less should one seek the so-called absolute security of itself at the expense of the security of others. We should set up communication and consultation in the sector of cyber security, continuously enhance the strategic mutual trust in the sector of cyber security, establish a normal emergency response mechanism, and effectively manage differences and avoid misjudgment. Meanwhile, we should also deepen exchanges and cooperation in the technical research and development, rule-making, information sharing, talent training and other aspects, strengthen security of key information infrastructures, and enhance cyber security safeguarding abilities. China will work with the international community, to resolutely crack down on any kind of cyber attack, cyber terrorism activities and all kinds of illegal activities on the cyberspace. China will protect the intellectual property, safeguard individuals' privacy and safeguard the national security, public interests and citizens' legal rights, and jointly build a peaceful and secure cyber."

6.3 Vice-Premier Ma Kai's Speech at the First World Internet Conference (November 2014)

On November 19, 2014, vice-premier Ma Kai put forward the following four suggestions in his speech at the first World Internet Conference[7]:

[7]Speech from Ma Kai, Vice-premier of State Council, at the first World Internet Conference. http://news.xinhuanet.com/2014-11/19/c_127228952.htm [2016-11-21].

"First, to promote interconnected Internet facilities. Cyber infrastructure is a cornerstone of development of the Internet. To enhance exchanges and cooperation in the Internet field, we must promote interconnected infrastructures. China is ready to work with all other countries to deepen cooperation, speed up the building of cyber facilities and communication facilities, vigorously upgrade broadband, promote the research and development and popularization of a new generation of mobile communication technology, and set up an information superhighway access to the world. The Asian Infrastructure Investment Bank and Silk Road Fund are now actively preparing, and the building of cyber infrastructures will also become a key investment area."

"Second, to promote the prosperity and development of the Internet economy. At present, the network economy has become one of the world's fastest-growing, most potential and most cooperative areas. China will work with the international community to formulate complete cyberspace commerce rules, strengthen the effective connection with legal policies, carry out cross-border e-commerce cooperation, facilitate customs clearance, logistics and other conveniences, oppose trade protectionism, form the world Internet market, and push the prosperity and development of the global Internet economy."

"Third, to enhance shared technical cooperation in the Internet. Technological innovation is the fundamental force of cyber development, and international cooperation is a major basis for technological innovation. We hope that all countries firmly seize a historic opportunity of a new round of scientific and technological revolution, strengthen the technical cooperation in the fields of cyber communication, mobile Internet, cloud computing, Internet of things, big data and so on, jointly solve the problems about the Internet technology development and jointly promote development of new industries and new formats. Breakthrough in the Internet technology depends mainly on talents. We are willing to carry out a wide range of talent exchanges with all other countries to jointly cultivate top-notch innovative cyber talents. China will actively create a good environment of innovation and entrepreneurship for foreign talents, and warmly invite foreign cyber experts and talents to come to China for exchange and cooperation as well as entrepreneurship and development."

"Fourth, to achieve powerful Internet security. The Internet is a double-edged sword. If it is properly used, it is a treasury of Alibaba; if badly used, it is a Pandora's Box. Cyber security is a common challenge faced by human society, and it is a common responsibility of governments of all countries to effectively cope with it. All countries should strengthen cooperation, fully respect different concerns of the Internet security, crack down on cyber-crimes in accordance with law, resolutely defeat cyber terrorisms, jointly crack down on cyber-attacks and invasion of privacy, and jointly maintain cyber sovereignty security, data security, technical security and application security, so that the Internet becomes secure and sound."

6.4 Speech from Deputy Chief of General Staff of PLA (May 28, 2012)

On May 28, 2012, Ma Xiaotian who is Deputy Chief of General Staff of PLA at the time, gave a speech titled "Pay Attention to Cyberspace security and Build a Harmonious Cyber World" at the opening ceremony of the "Cyberspace Security: China and the world" international symposium.[8] He pointed out that: "network information resource, as a very important factor of production, provides a strong impetus for global economic and social development. Effective maintenance of cyberspace security has become our common issue and responsibility. The international community should respect the sovereignty of the states in cyberspace, make peaceful use of cyberspace, maintain the order in cyberspace under laws and regulations, and actively carry out international exchange and cooperation. We should be more open and broad-minded and with a more active and constructive attitude in cooperation to develop cyberspace rules, deepen international cooperation against cybercrime, speed up research and development for network protection technologies and improve network security dialogue mechanism, thereby contributing to the construction of harmonious cyber and real world."

6.5 Speech from XU Lin, the Director of the Office of the Central Leading Group for Cyberspace Affairs

The Central Leading Group for Cyberspace Affairs is the highest leading organ in the field of cyberspace in China. The Office of the Central Leading Group for Cyberspace Affairs (hereinafter referred to as "Cyberspace Administration of China") specifically implement all decisions in cyberspace made by the highest leading organ. The speech from the director of the Cyberspace Administration of China clearly reflects the stance and attitude of the Chinese government.

Xu Lin, director from the Cyberspace Administration of China, delivered a speech at the closing ceremony of the third World Internet Conference on 18 November 2016,[9] and proposed four deep recognitions:

"We deeply realize that the future of cyberspace should be in the hands of all countries. The global Internet governance system will surely be more fair and equitable as long as we adhere to a multilateral approach with multi-party participation on the basis of respect for state sovereignty in cyberspace, further accelerate the globalization of managing basic Internet resources, promote the formulation of

[8] "Cyberspace Security: China and the world" International Symposium Launches. http://news.xinhuanet.com/politics/2012-05/29/c_123203122.htm [2016-9-17].

[9] Xu Lin: four fruitful achievements made in the third World Internet Conference. http://news.china.com.cn/2016-11/18/content_39733611.htm [2016-11-23].

generally accepted global Internet governance rules and norms and promote equality and respect in cyberspace."

"We deeply realize that with innovation in its genes, the Internet is increasingly becoming an important driver for economic and social development. The leading role of the Internet in driving and leading the economic and social development will certainly be more prominent as long as we continuously speed up innovation in the network information technology, create a universal, mobile, intelligent and secure network infrastructure, cultivate the new technologies, new applications and new formats of the Internet, accelerate deep integration of the Internet and the real economy, make digital economy bigger and stronger and promote innovation and development in cyberspace."

"We deeply realize that the promotion of an interconnected world shared and governed by all in cyberspace is a common aspiration of people around the world. People across the world will surely more benefit from opportunities and outcomes of the Internet development as long as we ensure the common well-being of humanity, actively build an online platform for exchange in the economic, technological, cultural sectors and the like, formulate perfect trade rules favorable for development of the global digital economy, strive to eliminate trade barriers to create more converging points and new highlights for cooperation in cyberspace, and push for open and shared cyberspace."

"We deeply realize that the Internet knows no national or sectoral boundaries and all countries are interlinked in cyber security so maintenance of cybersecurity is a common responsibility of the international community. Cyberspace as a common spiritual homeland for the humankind will certainly be more secure, stable and prosperous as long as we promote close cooperation, strengthen the protection of key information infrastructure, defeat cyber-attacks, cyber terrorisms and various kinds of cyber-crimes in accordance with law, protect individual privacy and intellectual property rights, ensure the legitimate rights and interests of hundreds of millions of Internet users, enhance the cyber ethics and cyber civilization, and promote a secure and orderly cyberspace."

6.6 Relevant Documents of China

6.6.1 International Cooperation Strategy on Cyberspace (March 1, 2017)

On March 1, 2017, the Ministry of Foreign Affairs introduced the International Cooperation Strategy on Cyberspace (hereinafter referred to as "the Strategy"). The Strategy fully announces China's policy position on cyberspace-related international issues, systematically interprets the basic principles, strategic objectives and operational points in China's foreign works in the field of cyber, and aims to guide

China's participation in cyberspace international exchange and cooperation in the coming period, promote the international community to work together, so as to strengthen dialogue and cooperation, jointly build a peaceful, safe, open, cooperative and orderly cyberspace and establish a multilateral, democratic and transparent global Internet governance system.

The Strategy points out in the section of Opportunities and Challenges that "cyberspace brings great opportunities to mankind, meanwhile brings a number of new issues and challenges, cyberspace security and stability become a global concern in terms of state sovereignty, security and development interests of the states."

The Strategy clarifies in the section of Basic Principles that "China's international cooperation strategy on cyberspace is themed with peaceful development, with win-win cooperation as the core, advocates peace, sovereignty, co-governance, and common benefits as the basic principles for international exchanges and cooperation in cyberspace." In the Strategy, explicit interpretation of the following principles of sovereignty is provided.

"The principle of sovereign equality, which is established by the Charter of the United Nations, is the basic criterion of contemporary international relations, covering all areas of inter-nation communications, and should also apply to cyberspace. The states shall give mutual respect for the right to independent choice of cyber developmental path, cyber management mode, Internet public policy and equal participation in international cyberspace governance, and shall not engage in cyber hegemony, shall not interfere in the internal affairs of other countries, shall engage in, condone or support cyber activities endangering the national security of other countries.

"Clarifying the sovereignty in cyberspace not only reflects the responsibility and rights of the governments of the states in cyberspace governance under the laws and regulations, but also helps to promote the states to develop a sound interaction platform for governments, enterprises and social groups, so as to create a healthy ecological environment for the development of information technology and international exchanges and cooperation."

"Governments of the states have the authority to govern the network under the laws and regulations, they are entitled to jurisdiction of information and communication infrastructure and resources and information and communication activities in their territories, and they have the right to protect their information systems and information resources from threats, disturbances, attacks and sabotage, and to protect the legal interests of the citizens in cyberspace. The governments of the states have the right to formulate their own Internet public policies and laws and regulations, without incurring any external intervention. While the states exercise their rights in accordance with the principle of sovereign equality, they shall also fulfill their corresponding obligations. The states shall not use information and communication technology to interfere with domestic affairs of other countries, shall not take its own advantages to damage the security of information and communication technology products and service supply chain of other countries.

The Strategy points out in the section of Strategic Objectives that "the strategic objectives of China's participation in cyberspace international cooperation include: to firmly safeguard China's cyber-sovereignty, cyber security and cyber developmental interests, to ensure the orderly flow of Internet information, to improve international interconnection, to maintain peace, security and stability in cyberspace, to promote international rule of law in cyberspace, to promote global digital economic development, to deepen cyber culture exchange and learning, so that the fruit of Internet development benefits the globe and better benefits the people of all countries.

The Strategy points in the section of Maintenance of Sovereignty and Security state that "China is committed to maintaining peace and security of cyberspace and building a just and rational order of international cyberspace based on state sovereignty and actively promoting and consolidating international consensus in this regard. China resolutely opposes any state's interference in the internal affairs of other countries. China advocates that the states have the right and responsibility to safeguard their own cyber security and protect the legitimate rights and interests of all parties in cyberspace through national laws and policies. The trend in cyberspace to strengthen armaments and to enhance deterrence is not conducive to international security and strategic mutual trust. China is committed to promoting the parties to be abode by the basic principles of international relations, including peaceful settlement of disputes and non-use or threat of use of force, establishing a consultation and mediation mechanism, so as to prevent and avoid conflicts and to prevent the cyberspace from becoming a new battlefield."

"National defense force establishment in cyberspace is an important part of China's military defense and military modernization, which follows the consistent active defense military strategic policy. China will take advantage of the significant role of military force in the maintenance of national cyberspace sovereignty, security and development interests to accelerate the establishment of cyberspace forces and to improve the capability of cyberspace situational awareness, cyber defense, and the capability of supporting national cyberspace operations and participating in international cooperation, curbing major crisis in cyberspace, safeguarding national cyber security, and maintaining national security and social stability."

The Strategy clarifies in the section of Action Plan that "China will actively participate in relevant international processes involving the cyber, strengthen bilateral, regional and international dialogue and cooperation, enhance international mutual trust, seek common development and join hands to tackle cope with threats, with a view to achieving a general accepted international rules of cyberspace, so as to build a just and rational global cyberspace governance system." Meanwhile, the Strategy proposes nine action plans, including "to advocate and promote cyberspace peace and stability", "to promote the construction of rules-based cyberspace order", "to continuously expand cyberspace partnership", "to actively promote reform in the global Internet governance system", "to deepen international cooperation against cyber terrorism and cybercrime", "to advocate the protection of privacy and other civil rights and interests", "to promote the digital economic development and digital dividend common benefits sharing", "to strengthen the global information infrastructure construction and protection", "to promote cyber culture exchange and learning".

6.6.2 National Cyberspace Security Strategy (December 27, 2016)

On December 27, 2016, the Office of the Central Leading Group for Cyberspace Affairs issued *National Cyberspace Security Strategy.*[10] The *Strategy* describes the following contents in Part I. "Opportunities and Challenges": "Cyberspace has become a new area for important human activity of equal importance to land, sea, air and space, state sovereignty has extended and stretched into cyberspace, sovereignty in cyberspace has become an important component part of state sovereignty. Respect for sovereignty in cyberspace, safeguarding cyber security seeking common governance, and realizing win-win, are becoming the consensus in international society." The *Strategy* mentions the following contents in Part III. "Principles": "(1) respecting and protecting sovereignty in cyberspace. No infringement of sovereignty in cyberspace will be tolerated; the rights of all countries to independently choose their development path, network management method and Internet public policy, as well as to equally participate in international cyberspace governance will be respected. The peoples of all countries are to decide on cyber affairs within the scope of sovereignty of all countries, all countries have the right to formulate laws and regulations concerning cyberspace on the basis of their national circumstances and learning from international experience, to adopt necessary measures according to the law, to manage their national information systems and online affairs within their national territories; to protect all countries' information systems and information resources from intrusion, interference, attack and destruction, and guarantee the lawful rights and interests in cyberspace of their citizens; to prevent, curb and punish the online dissemination of harmful information endangering national security and interests, and to safeguard order in cyberspace. No country should engage in cyber hegemonies, uphold double standards, use the network to interfere in the domestic affairs of other countries, or engage in, connive in or support online activities endangering other countries' national security." The *Strategy* mentions the following contents in Part IV. "Strategic Tasks": (1) "resolutely defending sovereignty in cyberspace. Manage online activities within the scope of our country's sovereignty according to the Constitution, laws and regulations, protect the security of our country's information infrastructure and information resources, adopt all measures, including economic, administrative, scientific, technological, legal, diplomatic and military measures, to

[10]National Cyberspace Security Strategy (full text). http://www.cac.gov.cn/2016-12/27/c_1120195926.htm [2016-12-28].

unwaveringly uphold our country's sovereignty in cyberspace. Resolutely oppose all actions to subvert our country's national regime or destroy our country's sovereignty through the network."

6.6.3 Cyber Security Law of the People's Republic of China *(November 7, 2016)*

The *Cyber Security Law of the People's Republic of China*[11] was adopted by the Standing Committee of the Twelfth National People's Congress at its Twenty-Fourth Session on November 7, 2016. Article 1 of the *Cyber Security Law* prescribes that "This Law is formulated so as to ensure cyber security, to safeguard the cyber space sovereignty, national security and the societal public interests, to protect the lawful legal rights and interests of citizens, legal persons and other organizations, and to promote the healthy development of economic and social informatization."

6.6.4 Outline of National Informatization Development Strategy *(July 27, 2016)*

On July 27, 2016, the General Office of CPC central committee and the General Office of the State Council released an *Outline of National Informatization Development Strategy*, and issued a notice requiring all regions and departments to implement the *Outline* practically and earnestly.

The portion of "Forcefully strengthening informatization development capacities" in the *Outline* describes the following contents: "Jointly build a new order on international networks. Persist in the principles of respecting for cyber sovereignty, maintaining peace and security, stimulating openness and collaboration, and building a desirable order, promote the establishment of a multilateral, democratic and transparent international Internet governance system. Vigorously participate in moving forward the internationalization and reform of the Internet Corporation for Assigned Names and Numbers (ICANN). Strengthen international law enforcement cooperation in cyberspace, promote the formulation of international anti-terrorism pacts in cyberspace. Complete mechanisms for judicial assistance in attacking online crime, and jointly ensure peace and security in cyberspace."

---

[11]Cyber Security Law of the People's Republic of China. http://www.npc.gov.cn/npc/xinwen/2016-11/07/content_2001605.htm [2016-11-23].

The portion of "Incessantly optimizing the informatization development environment" in the *Outline* describes the following contents: "Establish correct cyber security views, persist in vigorous defense and effective response, strengthen cyber security defense capabilities, and realistically safeguard national sovereignty, security and development interests in cyberspace. Safeguard cyber sovereignty and national security. Manage online activities within the range of our country's sovereignty according to the law, persist in defending our country's cyber sovereignty. Persist in preventing and attacking acts to divide the country, incite rebellion, overthrow the regime, destroy unity, steal secrets, etc., through the network."

6.6.5 National Security Law of the People's Republic of China *(July 1, 2015)*

A new *National Security Law of the People's Republic of China* was adopted at the 15th Meeting of the Standing Committee of the Twelfth National People's Congress[12] on July 1, 2015. Article 25 of the *National Security Law* prescribes "the state shall establish an Internet and information security system, strengthen its capability to protect cyber and information security, enhance Internet and IT innovation research, development and application, and make Internet and information core technology, key infrastructures, information systems and data in key sectors secure and controllable; strengthen cyberspace governance, prevent, stop and punish cyber-criminal actions such as cyber-attacks, cyber intrusion, cyber thefts and spreading of illegal and harmful information, and safeguard the national cyberspace sovereignty, security and development interests." The Law specifies the concept of "cyberspace sovereignty" at the legal level for the first time, and the cyberspace sovereignty can be interpreted as the embodiment, extension and reflection of state sovereignty.

6.6.6 The Internet in China *(White Paper) (June 8, 2010)*

On June 8, 2010, the Information Office of the State Council of the People's Republic of China published *The Internet in China* (White Paper).[13] The White Paper indicates the following contents: "The Internet is an important infrastructure facility for the nation. Within Chinese territory the Internet is under the jurisdiction of Chinese sovereignty. The Internet sovereignty of China should be respected and

[12]National security law of the People's Republic of China. http://www.npc.gov.cn/npc/xinwen/2015-07/07/content_1941161.htm [2016-9-17].

[13]The Internet in China (White Paper) (full text). http://www.scio.gov.cn/zxbd/tt/Document/1011194/1011194.htm [2016-8-30].

protected. Citizens of the People's Republic of China and foreign citizens, legal persons and other organizations within Chinese territory have the right and freedom to use the Internet; at the same time, they must obey the laws and regulations of China and conscientiously protect Internet security. No organization or individual may produce, duplicate, announce or disseminate information having the following contents: being against the cardinal principles set forth in the Constitution; endangering state security, divulging state secrets, subverting state power and jeopardizing national unification; damaging state honor and interests; instigating ethnic hatred or discrimination and jeopardizing ethnic unity; jeopardizing state religious policy, propagating heretical or superstitious ideas; spreading rumors, disrupting social order and stability; disseminating obscenity, pornography, gambling, violence, brutality and terror or abetting crime; humiliating or slandering others, trespassing on the lawful rights and interests of others; and other contents forbidden by laws and administrative regulations. These regulations are the legal basis for the protection of Internet information security within the territory of the People's Republic of China. All Chinese citizens, foreign citizens, legal persons and other organizations within the territory of China must obey these provisions."

6.7 Documents Drafted by China and International Organizations

6.7.1 Initiative Proposed at the Second World Internet Conference (December 18, 2015)

Wuzhen Initiative[14] was released at the Second World Internet Conference on December 18, 2015:

"Ensuring peace and security in cyberspace; we underscore the importance of respect for nations' sovereignty in cyberspace, and protection the cyberspace and critical information infrastructure from threats, interference, attacks and destructions, safeguarding individual privacy and intellectual property rights, and undertaking collective efforts to combat cyber-crime and cyber-terrorism."

"Improving the global Internet governance; we call for the international community to cooperate in good faith, basing on mutual trust and in pursuit of common values and interest, in developing a joint approach to and common understanding of cyber-related international norms and rules in cyberspace, protecting and respecting basic rights and fundamental interests on the Internet, to foster and encourage innovation, and to bring the rule of law into cyberspace to jointly establish a peaceful, secure, open and cooperative cyberspace, and feature a multilateral, democratic and transparent global Internet governance system, with more valuable

[14]Wuzhen Initiative released at the Second World Internet Conference. http://news.xinhuanet.com/world/2015-12/18/c_128546176.htm [2016-9-17].

and inclusive involvement of governments, private sector, civil society, technical and academic community, international organizations and all other relevant stakeholders in accordance with their respective roles and responsibilities to contribute in a meaningful manner, helping to forge a genuine community of common destiny in cyberspace."

6.7.2 United Nations Documents (July 22, 2015)

The United Nations Report by *the Group of Governmental Experts on Developments in the Field of Information and Telecommunications in the Context of International Security,*[15] in which the Chinese government was involved, was publicly released on July 2015, including:

"The 2013 report stated that international law, especially the Charter of the United Nations, is applicable and is essential to maintaining peace and stability and promoting an open, secure, stable, accessible and peaceful ICT environment. Pursuant to its mandate, the present Group considered how international law applies to the use of ICTs by States."

"The adherence by States to international law, especially their Charter obligations, is an essential framework for their actions in their use of ICTs and to promote an open, secure, stable, accessible and peaceful ICT environment. These obligations are central to the examination of the application of international law to the use of ICTs by States."

"In considering the application of international law to State use of ICTs, the Group identified as of central importance the commitments of States to the following principles of the Charter and other international law: sovereign equality; the settlement of international disputes by peaceful means in such a manner that international peace and security and justice are not endangered; refraining in their international relations from the threat or use of force against the territorial integrity or political independence of any State, or in any other manner inconsistent with the purposes of the United Nations; respect for human rights and fundamental freedoms; and non-intervention in the internal affairs of other States."

"State sovereignty and international norms and principles that flow from sovereignty apply to the conduct by States of ICT-related activities and to their jurisdiction over ICT infrastructure within their territory."

"Building on the work of the previous Groups, and guided by the Charter and the mandate contained in General Assembly resolution 68/243, the present Group offers the following non-exhaustive views on how international law applies to the use of ICTs by States: (a) States have jurisdiction over the ICT infrastructure located

[15]Report by the Group of Governmental Experts on Developments in the Field of Information and Telecommunications in the Context of International Security. http://www.un.org/ga/search/view_doc.asp?symbol=A/70/174&referer=/english/&Lang=C [2016-9-19].

within their territory; (b) In their use of ICTs, States must observe, among other principles of international law, State sovereignty, sovereign equality, the settlement of disputes by peaceful means and non-intervention in the internal affairs of other States. Existing obligations under international law are applicable to State use of ICTs. States must comply with their obligations under international law to respect and protect human rights and fundamental freedoms; (c) Underscoring the aspirations of the international community to the peaceful use of ICTs for the common good of mankind, and recalling that the Charter applies in its entirety, the Group noted the inherent right of States to take measures consistent with international law and as recognized in the Charter. The Group recognized the need for further study on this matter; (d) The Group notes the established international legal principles, including, where applicable, the principles of humanity, necessity, proportionality and distinction; (e) States must not use proxies to commit internationally wrongful acts using ICTs, and should seek to ensure that their territory is not used by non-State actors to commit such acts; (f) States must meet their international obligations regarding internationally wrongful acts attributable to them under international law. However, the indication that an ICT activity was launched or otherwise originates from the territory or the ICT infrastructure of a State may be insufficient in itself to attribute the activity to that State. The Group noted that the accusations of organizing and implementing wrongful acts brought against States should be substantiated."

"The Group noted that common understandings on how international law applies to State use of ICTs are important for promoting an open, secure, stable, accessible and peaceful ICT environment."

6.7.3 International Code of Conduct for Information Security (January 9, 2015)

On 12 September 2011, the permanent representatives of SCO member states China, the Russian Federation, Tajikistan and Uzbekistan to the United Nations submitted a letter jointly to the United Nations Secretary-General Ban Ki-moon,[16] asking him to circulate the International Code of Conduct for Information Security as a formal document of the sixty-sixth session of the General Assembly (A/66/359).[17] The International Code of Conduct for Information Security raises a series of basic principles of maintaining information and network security, which covers political, military, economic, cultural, social, technical and other aspects, including:

---

[16]"International Code of Conduct for Information Security" submitted by China, Russia and other countries to the United States. http://wwwgov.cn/jrzg/2011-09/13/content_1945825.htm [2016-8-30].

[17]Letter dated 12 September 2011 from the Permanent Representatives of China, the Russian Federation, Tajikistan and Uzbekistan to the United Nations addressed to the Secretary-General. http://www.un.org/zh/documents/view_doc.asp?symbol=A/66/359 [2016-8-30].

not using ICTs including networks to carry out hostile activities or acts of aggression and pose threats to international peace and security; reaffirming all States' rights and responsibilities to protect, in accordance with relevant laws and regulations, their information space and network space as well as critical information and network infrastructures from threats, disturbance, attack and sabotage; establishment of a multilateral, transparent and democratic international management of the Internet; fully respecting the rights and freedom in information and network space on the premise of complying with relevant national laws and regulations; assisting developing countries in developing information and network technologies; cooperating in combating network criminal activities, etc.

On 9 January 2015, the Permanent Representatives of SCO member states, including China, Kazakhstan, Kyrgyzstan, Russian Federation, Tajikistan and Uzbekistan, addressed to the Secretary-General Ban Ki-moon and requested him to circulate an updated draft of the International Code of Conduct for Information Security as a document of the provisional agenda of the sixty-ninth session of the General Assembly.[18] The International Code of Conduct for Information Security[19] reads as follows:

Each State voluntarily subscribing to this Code pledges:

(1) To comply with the UN Charter and universally recognized norms governing international relations, which enshrine, inter alia, respect for the sovereignty, territorial integrity and political independence of all states, respect for human rights and fundamental freedoms, as well as respect for diversity of history, culture and social systems of all countries.
(2) Not to use information and communications technologies and information and communications networks to carry out activities which run counter to the task of maintaining international peace and security.
(3) Not to use information and communications technologies and information and communications networks to interfere in the internal affairs of other States or with the aim of undermining their political, economic and social stability.
(4) To cooperate in combating criminal and terrorist activities that use information and communications technologies and information and communications networks, and in curbing the dissemination of information that incites terrorism, separatism or extremism or that inflames hatred on ethnic, racial or religious grounds.
(5) To endeavor to ensure the supply chain security of information and communications technology goods and services, in order to prevent other States from exploiting their dominant position in information and communications technologies, including dominance in resources, critical infrastructures, core

[18]Updated draft of the "International Code of Conduct for Information Security" submitted by China and Russia to Ban Ki-moon. http://world.people.com.cn/n/2015/0110/c157278-26361324.html [2016-6-6].

[19]International Code of Conduct for Information Security. http://www.un.org/zh/documents/view_doc.asp?symbol=A/69/723 [2016-10-6].

technologies, information and communications technology goods and services and information and communications networks to undermine States' right to independent control of information and communications technology goods and services, or to threaten their political, economic and social security.

(6) To reaffirm the rights and responsibilities of all States, in accordance with the relevant norms and rules, regarding legal protection of their information space and critical information infrastructure against damage resulting from threats, interference, attack and sabotage.

(7) To recognize that the rights of an individual in the offline environment must also be protected in the online environment; to fully respect rights and freedoms in the information space, including the right and freedom to seek, receive and impart information, considering the fact that the International Covenant on Civil and Political Rights (article 19) attaches to that right special duties and responsibilities. It may therefore be subject to certain restrictions, but these shall only be such as are provided by law and are necessary: (a) for respect of the rights or reputations of others; (b) for the protection of national security or of public order (order public), or of public health or morals.

(8) All States must play the same role in, and carry equal responsibility for, international governance of the Internet, its security, continuity and stability of operation, and its development in a way which promotes the establishment of multilateral, transparent and democratic international Internet governance mechanisms which ensure an equitable distribution of resources, facilitate access for all and ensure the stable and secure functioning of the Internet.

(9) All States must cooperate fully with other interested parties in encouraging a deeper understanding by all elements in society, including the private sector and civil-society institutions, of their responsibility to ensure information security, by means including the creation of a culture of information security and the provision of support for efforts to protect critical information infrastructure.

(10) To develop confidence-building measures aimed at increasing predictability and reducing the likelihood of misunderstanding and the risk of conflict. Such measures will include, inter alia, voluntary exchange of information regarding national strategies and organizational structures for ensuring a State's information security, the publication of white papers and exchanges of best practice, wherever practical and advisable.

(11) To provide financial and technical assistance in developing countries in their efforts to enhance capacity-building on information security and to close the digital divide and fully implement "Millennium Development Goals".

(12) To bolster bilateral, regional and international cooperation, promote a prominent role for the United Nations in areas such as encouraging the development of international legal norms for information security, peaceful settlement of international disputes, qualitative improvements in international cooperation in the field of information security; and to enhance coordination among relevant international organizations.

(13) To settle any dispute resulting from the application of this code of conduct through peaceful means, and to refrain from the threat or use of force.

6.7.4 Tunis Agenda for the Information Society (November 18, 2005)

On November 18, 2015, the Tunis Agenda for the Information Society passed at the second phase of the World Summit on the Information Society defined "Internet governance" as follows: "Internet governance is the development and application by governments, the private sector and civil society, in their respective roles, of shared principles, norms, rules, decision-making procedures, and programs that shape the evolution and use of the Internet", which was unanimously confirmed by 174 countries.[20]

The document indicates the following:

"We reaffirm the principles enunciated in the Geneva phase of the WSIS, in December 2003, that the Internet has evolved into a global facility available to the public and its governance should constitute a core issue of the Information Society agenda. The international management of the Internet should be multilateral, transparent and democratic, with the full involvement of governments, the private sector, and civil society and international organizations. It should ensure an equitable distribution of resources, facilitate access for all and ensure a stable and secure functioning of the Internet, taking into account multilingualism."

"We reaffirm that the management of the Internet encompasses both technical and public policy issues and should involve all stakeholders and relevant intergovernmental and international organizations. In this respect it is recognized that: (a) Policy authority for Internet-related public policy issues is the sovereign right of States. They have rights and responsibilities for international Internet-related public policy issues. (b) The private sector has had, and should continue to have, an important role in the development of the Internet, both in the technical and economic fields. (c) Civil society has also played an important role on Internet matters, especially at community level, and should continue to play such a role. (d) Intergovernmental organizations have had, and should continue to have, a facilitating role in the coordination of Internet-related public policy issues. (e) International organizations have also had and should continue to have an important role in the development of Internet-related technical standards and relevant policies."

[20]World Summit on the Information Society. http://www.un.org/ga/search/view_doc.asp?symbol=A/60/687&referer=/english/&Lang=C [2016-12-31].

Under the guidance of this definition, the third portion of Report of the World Summit on the Information Society further divided the issues that are relevant to Internet governance into four large sections and specified extension of the Internet governance. The four sections include:

(1) "Issues relating to infrastructure and the management of critical Internet resources", including distribution and administration of IP addresses and the domain name, and issues regarding elementary position of the domain name root server system and the like;
(2) "Issues relating to the use of the Internet", mainly involving network security, cybercrime and Internet abuse;
(3) "Issues that are relevant to the Internet but have an impact much wider than the Internet and for which existing organizations are responsible", such as online international trade and intellectual property rights;
(4) "Issues relating to the developmental aspects of Internet governance", mainly including public policy decision-making issues that are relevant to Internet affairs.

The document states:

"In order to ensure effective participation in global Internet governance, we urge international organizations, including intergovernmental organizations, where relevant, to ensure that all stakeholders, particularly from developing countries, have the opportunity to participate in policy decision-making relating to Internet governance, and to promote and facilitate such participation."

"Countries should not be involved in decisions regarding another country's country-code Top-Level Domain (ccTLD). Their legitimate interests, as expressed and defined by each country, in diverse ways, regarding decisions affecting their ccTLDs, need to be respected, upheld and addressed via a flexible and improved framework and mechanisms."

"We recognize that all governments should have an equal role and responsibility for international Internet governance and for ensuring the stability, security and continuity of the Internet. We also recognize the need for development of public policy by governments in consultation with all stakeholders."

"We further recognize the need for enhanced cooperation in the future, to enable governments, on an equal footing, to carry out their roles and responsibilities, in international public policy issues pertaining to the Internet, but not in the day-to-day technical and operational matters, that do not impact on international public policy issues."

The report draws the outline of the existing Internet governance mechanisms. Internet is built from the bottom up, that is, the progressive interconnection of the domestic networks constitutes a pyramid tower, and the top of the pyramid is the interconnection at an international level, which connects the backbone networks of respective countries one by one into a whole. At a domestic level, all countries generally have a designated one government department or quasi-government organization (such as the Federal Communications Commission of the United States, the British Internet Watch Foundation, and the Media Development Authority of Singapore) to jointly develop governance with private, civil institutions of their countries. The degree of government participation varies considerably from country to country due to its policy, and it either plays a leading role, or acts as a coordinator, or only regulates without participating in any decision. At the international level, the existing mechanisms have adopted a model of governance by non-governmental international organizations and commercial organizations. For example, the distribution and management of the most watched IP addresses and domain names are currently under the control of the "Internet Corporation for Assigned Names and Numbers (ICANN)".

6.8 Bilateral Agreement Involved in China

6.8.1 Joint Statement Between President Xi Jinping and President Putin (June 2016)

On June 25, 2016, China and Russia released the Joint Statement between the Presidents of the People's Republic of China and the Russian Federation on Cooperation in Information Space Development[21]:

"Uphold as always, the principle of respecting state sovereignty in information space; support each nation's reasonable demands of maintaining its own security and development; advocate for building of a peaceful, secure, open and cooperative information space; and explore the possibilities of developing universal rules of responsible behavior in information space within the UN framework."

"Advocate for equal rights of all country to participate in Internet governance and acknowledge the right to ensure national security in information space based on its own laws and state system. Support the initiative of building a multilateral, democratic and transparent global Internet governance system and maintain UN's important role in setting up global Internet governance mechanisms."

"Jointly advocate respect to and oppose infringements on every country's sovereignty in information space."

"Jointly promote respect to every country's cultural traditions and social customs; resist the interference via information space in other countries' internal affairs, disruption of social order, incitement of inter-ethnic, inter-racial and inter-religious antagonism, and undermining national governance."

"Make more efforts in preventing and combating the use of Internet for terrorist and criminal purposes; promote an initiative of setting up a coordinated response

[21]Joint Statement between the Presidents of the People's Republic of China and the Russian Federation on Cooperation in Information Space Development. http://news.xinhuanet.com/politics/2016-06/26/c_1119111901.htm [2016-9-17].

and cooperation mechanism within the UN framework, including on the issues of exploring the possibilities of new global legal instruments."

6.8.2 Cooperative Agreement Between China and Russia (May 2015)

On 8 May 2015, China and Russia released a *Russian-Chinese Intergovernmental Agreement on Cooperation in Ensuring International Information Security*[22]: "Information and communication technology should be applied to promotion of social and economic development, as well as human well-being, and promotion of international peace, security and stability; state sovereignty is applicable to information space. China and Russia shall be committed to building a peaceful, secure, open and cooperative international information environment, establishing a multilateral, democratic and transparent global Internet governance system, and safeguarding equal rights of all countries to participate in global Internet governance. Actions, through information and communication technology, including infringement of other nations' sovereignty and security, destruction of information infrastructure, terrorisms and illegal and criminal activities, interference in other nations' internal affairs, inflaming of hatred on ethnic, racial or religious sects and so on are main threats to the field of international information security."

6.8.3 Joint Statement Between China and Brazil (July 2014)

On 17, July 2014, the Joint Statement between the People's Republic of China and the Federal Republic of Brazil on Further Deepening Sino-Brazil Comprehensive Strategic Partnership[23] states "Both parties express concern about behaviors of invading individual privacy and violating the current purpose of maintaining international stability and security by the information and communication technology. Both parties think that the international community should cooperate based on mutual respect, equality and mutual benefit, and jointly cope with threats to cyber security. Both parties support their sovereignty over governing their own Internet and safeguarding its security, call for the international community to formulate a universally acceptable code of conduct, continue to adhere to the principle of multilateralism, democracy, transparency and full participation of all

---

[22]Agreement on Cooperation in Ensuring International Information Security signed by China and Russia. http://news.xinhuanet.com/world/2015-05/12/c_127791418.htm [2016-9-17].

[23]Joint Statement between the People's Republic of China and the Federal Republic of Brazil on Further Deepening Sino-Brazil Comprehensive Strategic Partnership. http://news.xinhuanet.com/politics/2014-07/18/c_1111685756.htm [2016-9-17].

stakeholders, improve the Internet multidisciplinary governance system, and devote joint efforts to achieve common management and equitable distribution of basic Internet resources. Both parties are now committed to promoting globalization of the 'Internet Corporation for Assigned Names and Numbers', accepting the joint supervision of the international community and enhancing the role of the 'United Nations Internet Governance Forum' in the Internet governance system."

6.9 China's Position at the Fifth Session of the United Sates GGE (Years 2016–2017)

Chinese representatives expressed the following views at the 2016—2017 Fifth Session of the Group of Governmental Experts on Developments in the Field of Information and Telecommunications in the Context of International Security (GGE):

In cyberspace, the international community should be committed to building a generally acceptable system of international laws and regulations. We cannot underestimate the importance of norms and standards, but do not rule out binding legal norms evolved from practices and development of all countries from the long run.

Whether or not the prudential obligation, "it is not allowed to knowingly take actions in one's own state territory that cause serious destructions or damage to the interests of other states", constitutes a general principle of the international law is not currently universally recognized by the international community. Whether the prudential obligation is applicable and how to apply it in cyberspace is still faced with a lot of technical and legal issues, especially there is no uniform agreement on the international delinquency in cyberspace and definitions such as illegal cyber actions and cyber attacks are far from conclusive.

In cyberspace, there are a lot of legal and technical problems about affirmation of an international illegal action, traceability to cyberattacks and ascertainment of national behavior. The network traceability technology is now far from immature and the network technology capabilities of countries are obviously varied. Upon encountering such problems, the first concern is peaceful settlement of disputes. Once cyberattacks occur, only through constructive coordination and cooperation among countries, we can accurately and effectively investigate the responsibility of cyber attacjers and promote cyber security. Overemphasis on international legal resolutions is not conducive to or not helpful in creating a harmonious and constructive atmosphere of cooperation in cyberspace, which, however, do not prevent the international community from formulating some international cooperation measures and some Confidence Building Mechanisms (CBM) to jointly handle cyber security incidents.

We should ensure the peace of cyberspace without introducing war, conflicts or military confrontation into cyberspace, and we should try our best to avoid the armament race. Even if we cannot prohibit the development of cyber weapons at present, all countries should at least exercise restraint to the greatest degree. Some countries have already published their so-called network military theory strategies, and of course, this is their decision and choice, but it will convey a message of whether to encourage the development of military offensive capability or restrict its development, as it is contradictory to what we want to achieve.

We believe that the international community must be extremely cautious and responsible for issues such as the application of the Law of Armed Conflict, state responsibility and countermeasures, and make rational expectations for unstable rise of cyberspace caused by possible friction or misjudgment or confrontation adopted to deal with these issues. This involves the application of the concept of countermeasures in cyberspace, especially complex problems such as traceability and identity recognition. Before these problems are better settled, we should not rush to confirm the issue of countermeasures or clarify the use of countermeasures in cyberspace. Overemphasis on the so-called counter-unilateral action is not constructive.

Sovereignty means not only power, but also responsibility, both of which are inseparable. Sovereignty should be further enriched and deepened based on the principle of state sovereignty in cyberspace, which not only reflects the responsibility and rights of all countries in cyberspace, but also enables countries to build platforms for sound interactions among governments, businesses and social groups. The principle of sovereignty should be further enriched and deepened from the following aspects: firstly, all countries exercise jurisdiction over ICT infrastructure, resources and activities within their territories; secondly, all countries are entitled to enact Internet public policies in line with their national circumstances and manage their own Internet affairs, and no country should use ICT to interfere in other countries' internal affairs or undermine other countries' political, economic and social stability; thirdly, countries are entitled to equal participation in management and distribution of Internet resources and protection of the security of their countries' information technology product and service supply chain, and no country should leverage its resources, key facilities, core technologies and other advantages to undermine other countries' autonomy of information technology products or threaten other countries' political, economic and social security; fourthly, countries are entitled to protect their critical information infrastructures from threat, disruption, attack and destruction, and to protect major data about national security, critical infrastructure security and citizen privacy.

Safeguarding the sovereignty of a country and exercising its sovereignty are an important aspect of safeguarding the human rights of the country. If the sovereignty of a country does not exist, where and how should the human rights of the country be protected? The principle of state sovereignty and other principles in *International Law* are not mutually restrictive or exclusive but are mutually promotional and complementary.

We are now in a rule formulation stage. On the premise of respect for sovereignty, we can promote mutual trust and cooperation by capacity building, setting up contact points, sharing practice and experience, and enhancing technical assistance.

Terrorism is a common challenge to the international community. The real threat, cyber terrorist activities, is increasing, and propaganda of terrorism as well as financing and recruiting, inciting and planning terrorist activities by combining terrorism with the Internet are currently violent terrorist activities, which seriously threaten the international security and stability. The United Nations has expressed serious concern about the dangers of cyber terrorism by passing several resolutions, which reflects a high degree of consensus of the international community on this issue. We should promote the following concrete cooperative measures based on this consensus: one is to prohibit terrorist organizations identified by the United Nations utilizing their Internet resources to start sites, forums, blogs and other information services for terrorist activities, including the production, release, storage or dissemination of terrorist audios and videos, the propagation of violent terrorist speeches and thoughts, raising capital, recruiting members or inciting implementation of terrorist activities; second is that countries exchange intelligence clues about fighting against cyber terrorisms and develop law enforcement cooperation; third is to encourage international organizations, governments, companies and citizens to jointly participate and enhance cooperation.

The security of critical infrastructure is related to the economic lifeblood, social stability and public interests of countries, and even national security, and involves common concerns of all countries. Its relevant norms can be refined from the following aspects: First is to drive countries to promise not to attack other countries' critical infrastructures. Given that standards for defining critical infrastructure by countries are varied, we can start from an area of common concern of countries and start with the most severely affected facilities upon destruction, such as finance, energy and civil aviation, progressively. We should increase mutual trust among countries, enable governments and companies of all countries to exchange standards for protection of critical infrastructure and best practices, learn from each other, improve cyber security protection capabilities of all countries and explore mechanisms for establishing cyber risk early warning and intelligence sharing for critical infrastructure. We should promise not to leverage our technical and policy advantages to undermine the integrity and security of other countries' infrastructures. We should respect the objective differences in critical infrastructure and cyber security capabilities of countries, strengthen technical assistance to developing countries and enhance the overall level of global cyber security.

As for Internet governance, the representativeness of the governance of developing countries is seriously inadequate in the current governance model, and the role of government is also marginalized. The decision-making process and operation of Internet governance are not transparent and democratic enough, which relates to the security of the entire Internet, the mutual trust among countries and the stability of the entire Internet. Discussion of cyber security issue and international security-related network issue cannot get rid of the Internet governance. Internet governance also involves capacity building, and how to enable developing countries to have the enough capacities to participate in the decision-making process of

Internet governance on equal footing is highly relevant to capacity-building. An important factor that restricts capacity-building in many developing countries today is the issue concerning the current management and contribution of critical Internet resources and the allocation of Internet resource operations, which fails to embody such a principle as equal participation, co-determination and co-management. If such an issue is not well settled, it is difficult to fundamentally solve the problem about capacity.

The capacity-building issue is so vital that we can never put too much emphasis on its importance. No matter whether providing technical assistance to developing countries is applicable to international law, voluntary norms or CBM, and if without necessary capacity, everything is out of the question, so we need to strengthen technical assistance to developing countries, including the ability to help build computer emergency response and enhance the emergency response capability of security incidents. Countries and businesses with capability of detecting vulnerabilities and threats should publish them timely to improve the overall level of global cyber security.

Focusing on the future, we need to consider building a cooperative framework mechanism or institution within the framework of the United Nations to not only study issues, new development of the situations and new threats and challenges in change, but also promote information exchange and cooperation among member states.

Chapter 7
Objective Existence of Cyberspace Sovereignty in Countries' Affairs

Abstract One of the fundamental rights of cyberspace sovereignty is jurisdiction. In fact, each country's jurisdiction over the Internet has long been an indisputable fact. These forms of administration are reflected in judicial precedents, website supervision, illegal information blocking, as well as combating on illegal cyber speech, infringement of cyber privacy, cyber hackers, internet bank crimes, cyber fraud, online pornography, cyber piracy, online gambling, etc., these are enough to reflect the objective existence of cyberspace sovereignty.

Keywords Jurisdiction · Combating cybercrime · Illegal information blocking Website supervision

Many countries insist on "stakeholders" dominating the international Internet and therefore do not admit the existence of cyberspace sovereignty, but almost all countries objectively exercise their sovereignty in cyberspace because no countries will let their own cyberspace out of order. Once conflicts occur in cyberspace, only the government can effectively settle them, which requires the government to have the authority to resolve the conflicts in cyberspace, and this authorization is a manifestation of cyberspace sovereignty. There may be a variety of criminal acts in cyberspace, and if some criminal activities in the physical society interact with those in cyberspace, criminal acts in the physical society must be combatted together with cyberspace crimes, which also requires the government to have law enforcement power to combat cyberspace crimes, and this further shows the necessity of admitting the existence of sovereignty in cyberspace.

No matter how the international community evaluates the existence of cyberspace sovereignty, the various events that have occurred in cyberspace have objectively reflected the concrete existence of sovereignty in cyberspace. For example, some cases reflect the objective existence of cyberspace sovereignty, including the design and operation of the domain name system, the governments' judicial precedents of the Internet domain name, military protection of the cyberspace, protection of network data, supervision over websites, cease of supply of network services to the specific targets, prevention of dissemination of harmful

B. Fang, *Cyberspace Sovereignty*,
https://doi.org/10.1007/978-981-13-0320-3_7

information via the Internet, elimination of cyber terrorist information, and fighting against cyber threats and inflammatory views, spreading of online rumors, personal attacks, invasion of cyber privacy, cyber prejudices and racial discrimination, cyber hacker attacks, network bank crimes, fake e-commerce, network identity thefts, cyber frauds, cyber piracy, cybersex, online gambling and propagation of spam mails.

7.1 Design and Operation of the Domain Name System

The Internet domain name is a key factor in the operation of the Internet and is always under the control of the Internet Corporation for Assigned Names and Numbers (ICANN) as a "stakeholder". ICANN is a non-profit international organization, which gathers commercial, technical and academic experts in the network area all around the world and is responsible for coordination of the global Internet's unique identifier systems and their secure and stable operations. Such an important and influential global organization has been subject to the supervision of the United States Department of Commerce in a long period.

The domain name system is designed in a centralized operation mode. All Internet accesses via the domain name need to proceed with an analysis by the root name so as to give ICANN an opportunity to control the foundation of the Internet operation. Even so, the operation of the domain name system still shows the equal status and rights of independence in all countries, and that reflects respect for the equality and independence of cyberspace in each country. This "unity of democracy and concentration" mode reveals an entangled contradictory state that it not only possesses a confidence in unified control, but also relies on the management power of each country.

7.1.1 Design for a Top Level Domain

The domain name system of the Internet is a hierarchical analysis system, that is, first is a root name, where all analytical behaviors will firstly direct at 13 root name servers; and then the root name servers direct at Top Level Domain (TLD) servers. Top-Level Domain is divided into the following two categories: one is a country code Top-Level Domain (ccTLD) and the other is a generic Top-Level Domain (gTLD), wherein the ccTLD has been substantially governed and operated by the authorities of the respective countries, unless a country is assigned a ccTLD, but it is not accepted, and the TLD of this country may be entrusted to a department to operate and maintain. Since each country and region have equitably obtained a corresponding ccTLD and it uniquely represents the geographical area of its own country/region, which shows the existence of right of equality in the Internet world.

7.1.2 ICANN Governed by Government

Among operations of the domain name systems managed by ICANN, the TLD is required to be entrusted to an operation department for operation and maintenance, wherein the gTLDs are operated by the corresponding Internet companies; for example, .com, .net, .cc, .tv, and.name are run by the VeriSign, and the ccTLDs are operated by administrative departments approved by the governments of the countries and regions concerned, unless the country or region is not yet concerned about the existence of the Internet at its government level; for example, the early Libyan TLD.ly is not in the hand of Libya. The TLDs of all countries are entrusted by ICANN to the authorization departments of the countries concerned for management and the ICANN and all operation departments hereby sign an operational agreement that is called "ICANN ccTLD Sponsorship Agreement". The Agreement explicitly describes that "Other topics, in the circumstance that the registration policies for the Delegated ccTLD encourage or promote registrations from entities or individuals resident outside the territory of the Governmental Authority, to the extent those policies are applicable to the Delegated ccTLD, except where (a) the Sponsoring Entity is prohibited by law from implementing such another ICANN policy or (b) the Governmental Authority instructs the Sponsoring Entity in writing to refrain from implementing such another ICANN policy, with three months written notice to ICANN and the ICANN Governmental Advisory Committee."[1] The Agreement further describes that "After ICANN is notified by the Governmental Authority that the Sponsoring Entity has contravened the terms of the Governmental Communication, or the term of the Governmental Authority's designation of the Sponsoring Entity as manager of the Delegated ccTLD has expired, ICANN gives notice of its intent to terminate to the Sponsoring Entity."[2]

It can be shown that such an influential ICANN also need to face up to the existence of state sovereignty in cyberspace meanwhile, this is also a manifestation of respect for right of independence of all countries in cyberspace.

7.2 Judicial Precedents of Internet Domain Names

Due to uniqueness and absolute exclusiveness of domain names in the network world, domain names contain huge commercial opportunities, which are known as "online trademark" and usually valuable. For example, it is said that the network worth of mi.com is $3.6 million,[3] and thus there are often some irreconcilable contradictions and conflicts.

---

[1]Model ccTLD Sponsorship Agreement-Triangular Situation. https://archive.icann.org/en/cctlds/model-tscsa-16dec01.htm [2016-9-10].

[2]ccTLD Sponsorship Agreement (.tw ccTLD). https://www.icann.org/resources/unthemed-pages/sponsorship-agmt-2003-03-26-en [2016-9-10].

[3]Exposure of price of new domain name mi.com for XIAOMI: $3.6 million! http://news.ename.cn/yumingjiaoyi_20140422_54842_1.html [2016-12-31].

In order to settle conflicts over domain names, ICANN designs corresponding conflict processing mechanisms. ICANN trusts disputes over domain names to four worldwide organizations that have the power to adjudicate international disputes over domain names, namely, the World Intellectual Property Organization (WIPO) in Geneva, Switzerland; the National Arbitration Forum (NAF) in Minnesota, USA; the International Institute for Conflict Prevention and Resolution (CPR) in New York, USA; and the eResolution.com organization in Montreal, Canada. However, not all conflicts over domain names are resolved in accordance with ICANN's ideas, but some cases of conflicts over domain names are handled directly by the courts. Government intervention in cyberspace to deal with domain name-related affairs indicates the objective existence of cyberspace sovereignty.

7.2.1 Judicial Precedents of Conflicts Over Domain Names

On October 6, 2000, Shanghai Maya Online (cnnews.com) received a lawyer's letter[4] from the international media magnate CNN (Cable News Network), in which the core requirements and opinions are as follows: CNN enjoys numerous trademark rights containing "CNN" logos; in addition to its broadcast networks, CNN operates a number of web sites, including "cnn.com", which is a world leader in online news and information delivery; the Shanghai Maya Online has registered "cnnews.com", and is posting competitive, Chinese-language news content on the web site associated with that domain name; the acts of the Shanghai Maya Online infringe and dilute the CNN trademark rights in violation of the provisions specified by the United States "*Federal Trademark Dilution Act*[5]", and constitute cyberpiracy; CNN demands that the Shanghai Maya Online immediately ceases and desists all further use of the cnnews.com domain name, transfers the domain name to CNN, and agrees not to register or use in the future any marks that consist, in whole or in part, of the CNN's famous mark. The Shanghai Maya Online must fully agree to these requirements within ten days, or CNN will appeal to law in accordance with the US "*Anticybersquatting Consumer Protection Act (ACPA)*[6]".

The Shanghai Maya Online thereby issued a written statement that CNN's requirements and opinions seriously violate the conditions[7] for initiating a domain name dispute as approved by ICANN. Pursuant to Item b(ix) of Section 3 of the

[4]CNN Claims Infringement and Dilution by cnnews.com. http://www.inta.org/INTABulletin/Pages/CNNClaims-InfringementandDilutionbycnnewscom.aspx [2016-9-10].

[5]FEDERAL TRADEMARK DILUTION ACT. http://commdocs.house.gov/committees/judiciary/hju77698.000/hju77698_0f.htm [2016-9-20].

[6]United States Anticybersquatting Consumer Protection Act (translation text). http://www.cnnic.net.cn/ggfw/fwzxxgzcfg/2012/201207/t20120731_32906.htm [2016-9-20].

[7]Statement issued by Maya Online in terms of CNN's domain-name requirements. http://tech.sina.com.cn/internet/china/2000-10-19/39401.shtml?from=wap [2016-9-10].

Rules for Uniform Domain Name Dispute Resolution Policy[8] released by ICANN, the initiation of a domain name dispute shall satisfy the following three conditions: ① the manner in which the domain name(s) is/are identical or confusingly similar to a trademark or service mark in which the Complainant has rights; and ② the Respondent (domain-name holder) should be considered as having no rights or legitimate interests in respect of the domain name(s) that is/are the subject of the complaint; and ③ the domain name(s) should be considered as having been registered and being used in bad faith. "Confusing similarity" means that both the domain name and service content are similar, but cnnews has three more letters than CNN in spelling, and regardless of the interpretation of "CN (cn refers to China in the Internet domain name) NEWS", or interpretation of "China Network News", the meaning of cnnews greatly differs from that ("Cable News Network") of CNN. What's more, the main contents of cnnews.com are the Chinese news and the service target mainly includes Chinese and foreigners knowing Chinese, but CNN's main contents and service target are very different from those of cnnews.com. Hence, there is no "confusing similarity" at all.

Afterwards, CNN instituted an "*in rem* suit" against the "cnnews.com" domain name to the United States District Court for the Eastern District of Virginia to seek the judicial transfer of this domain name. On December 21, 2001, the Eastern District Court finally made a judgment and announced the Shanghai Maya Online lost and ordered Shanghai Maya Online to cease use of the "cnnews.com" domain name.[9]

From the spectator's point of view, this judgment does not make sense. Obviously, cnnews = cn + news, which means "Chinese news", while cnn + ews apparently does not make sense, so cnnews has nothing to do with cnn. If it is only because of a cnn* mode (all names starting with cnn) that is called an infringement of cnn, the cnnic.org.cn domain name of the famous China Internet Network Information Center (CNNIC) will not be protected, which is apparently absurd. However, the NSI (Network Solutions Inc.) has terminated its registration and resolution services for "cnnews.com" because the agency responsible for registering the cnnews.com domain name is the US domain name registrar NSI, which is governed by the US government, and thus Shanghai Maya Online lost the domain name helplessly and angrily.

The dispute was not settled by an arbitration institution entrusted by ICANN, but was taken by the United States District Court for the Eastern District of Virginia, with the prima facie ground that "cnnews.com" was registered by the United States NSI, which is an incorporation responsible for registering Second-Level Domains under the Top-Level Domain COM, ORG, GOV, EDU and NET and is located within the precinct of the United States District Court for the Eastern

[8]Rules for Uniform Domain Name Dispute Resolution Policy (the "Rules"). https://www.icann.org/resources/pages/udrp-rules-2015-03-12-zh [2016-9-13].

[9]In the United States District Court for the Eastern District of Virginia. http://pub.bna.com/ptcj/002022.htm [2016-9-10].

District of Virginia, so it is affirmed that the court has a right of jurisdiction over this conflict.[10] However, the actual reason behind this is that ICANN's conditions for initiating a domain name dispute cannot support CNN's complaint, but the US law is in favor of CNN's litigation. The United States District Court for the Eastern District of Virginia accepted the dispute, and this indicated that the United States identifies that the generic Top-Level Domains registered by NSI are within the United States jurisdiction, which objectively shows the United States possesses and exercises its cyberspace sovereignty in the Internet.

In July 2004, AOL (America Online) complained that the "icq.com.cn" domain name "hoarded" by www.net.cn was registered in bad faith on the grounds that "ICQ (instant messaging service) is its world famous trademark, but the domestic domain name registered by www.net.cn was identical with AOL's registered trademark and unique name, which are confusing enough, so it is a bad faith cybersquatting", and required www.net.cn to return the "icq.com.cn" domain name. However, because the United States courts could not succeed in protecting the interests of US companies in China in accordance with the principle of territorial management, AOL complained to the Domain Name Dispute Settling Center of the China International Economic and Trade Arbitration Commission.[11]

In response to the suit, www.net.cn expressed that ICQ was not a Chinese famous trademark and it was not a famous brand when registered in China (September 23, 1998), so it was not well known in China; in particular, "com.cn" is a country code assigned to the Chinese domain names and thus "icq.com.cn" is a Chinese domestic domain name, so the complainant AOL as a US corporation does not enjoy any main body or legitimate business behavior in China, and its holding of China's domestic domain name will directly cause a loss of Chinese legal domain name resources.

In this regard, the Panel from the Domain Name Dispute Settling Center of the China International Economic and Trade Arbitration Commission decided that the complainant AOL could not provide sufficient evidence to prove that it had civil rights in China over the "icq" mark, thereby rejecting its lawsuit over transfer of a disputed domain name "icq.com.cn".

It superficially seemed to be absolute nonsense that CNN claimed "cnnews.-com", but its claim succeeded; however, as an owner of the ICQ brand, AOL lost even though its claim for "icq.com.cn" was evidence-based from the spectator's point of view and especially www.net.cn as a domain name "hoarder" was "in bad faith" to some extent. This essentially reflects the objective existence of cyberspace sovereignty because different domain registrars are governed by the host country and are naturally restrained by the legal system of the host country. The United States has a *Federal Trademark Anti-Dilution Act* for the protection of registered

[10]".com" Domain Names can Lead to U.S.Jurisdiction. http://www.pkulaw.cn/fulltext_form.aspx?Db=qikan&gid=1510031222 [2016-12-31].

[11]America Online Loses ICQ Domain Name In China. http://www.techsecuritychina.com/2004/08/17/1726-america-online-loses-icq-domain-name-in-china/ [2016-9-12].

trademarks; CNN won the lawsuit just under the protection of this Act, because the US court affirmed that the use of "cnnews.com" constituted a dilution risk to CNN trademark, and that there was a potential infringement against the corresponding rights of CNN and it was liable to cause CNN users to be confused. However, the claim for "icq.com.cn" was judged according to Chinese law; although the ICQ was already a world-famous trademark at that time, it should also be protected by corresponding laws of Chinese famous trademarks according to international conventions involving China. Nonetheless, China has no corresponding *Trademark Anti-Dilution Act*, so this protection can only work when a trademark is identified as a famous one. Although China's *Trademark Law*[12] and *Implementing Regulations of the Trademark Law*[13] provide special protection for the well-known trademarks, the standard in legal protection depends on whether they will be confused, whether they will cause consumers to make mistakes; only where a trademark implies that goods or services are associated with the registrant of a famous trademark, so that the rights and interests of the registrant of a famous trademark may be damaged, can it constitute an infringement against the famous trademark. Therefore, it is rather difficult for AOL to present proof to protect the ICQ trademark.

The above cases show that cyberspace sovereignty has been imposed to domain name disputes according to the regional attributes, and different sovereign acts will naturally result in different legal consequences.

7.2.2 US Combat Against Piracy by Seizing Domain Names

In June 2010, the US National Intellectual Property Rights Coordination Center launched "Operation in Our Sites" action[14] to inspect and dispose of infringement against intellectual property rights over the Internet. One of the significant measures of the action is to seize website domain names posting infringement information. If the website domain name is registered in the United States, the prosecution will offer a seizure warrant.[15] Once a domain name is seized, the government will issue a written notice to the site owner, but if the site owner does not file a review within a certain time limit, the domain name will be officially owned by the government

[12]Trademark Law of the People's Republic of China. http://www.gov.cn/jrzg/2013-08/30/content_2478110.htm [2016-9-20].

[13]Implementing Regulations of the Trademark Law of the People's Republic of China (State Council Decree No. 651). http://www.gov.cn/zhengce/2014-04/30/content_2670953.htm [2016-9-20].

[14]Operation In Our Sites. https://www.ice.gov/factsheets/ipr-in-our-sites [2016-9-18].

[15]Rob Fischer. A Ninja in Our Sites. The American Prospect. 2011-12-15. http://prospect.org/article/ninja-our-sites [2016-9-10].

upon expiration.[16] Subsequently, the government will update the corresponding IP address of the domain name, and the user who visits the site again will see the government's ban or related warning message. The government had seized a total of 2713 domain names[17] from June 2010 to January 2014. The government's seizure banner had received more than 122 million individual views till December 2013.[18]

The United States combat against piracy by seizing domain names specifies that the United States has a right of jurisdiction over its cyberspace.

7.3 Military Protection for Cyberspace

In May 2011, former U.S. Secretary of State Hillary announced *International Strategy for Cyberspace: Prosperity, Security, and Openness in a Networked World*[19] to the world. The *Strategy* describes the following contents: "When warranted, the United States will respond to hostile acts in cyberspace as we would to any other threat to our country. All states possess an inherent right to self-defense, and we recognize that certain hostile acts conducted through cyberspace could compel actions under the commitments we have with our military treaty partners. We reserve the right to use all necessary means-diplomatic, informational, military, and economic-as appropriate and consistent with applicable international law, defend our Nation, our allies, our partners, and our interests. In so doing, we will exhaust all options before military force whenever we can; will carefully weigh the costs and risks of action against the costs of inaction; and will act in a way that reflects our values and strengthens our legitimacy, seeking broad international support whenever possible."

This statement is essential to informing the international community that once the US cyberspace is attacked, the United States is likely to employ military force to fight back according to the right of self-defense. From this point of view, the United States substantially establishes its self-defense status in cyberspace.

---

[16]Breaking News: Feds Falsely Censor Popular Blog For Over A Year, Deny All Due Process, Hide All Details. TechDirt. 2011-12-8. http://www.techdirt.com/articles/20111208/08225217010/breaking-news-feds-falsely-censor-popular-blog-over-year-deny-all-due-process-hide-all-details.shtml [2016-9-10].

[17]Federal agencies seize more than $21.6 million in fake NFL merchandise during 'Operation Team Player'. U.S. Immigration and Customs Enforcement. 2014-01-30. http://www.ice.gov/news/releases/1401/140130newyork.htm [2016-9-10].

[18]ICE, International Law Enforcement Agencies Seize 706 Domain Names Selling Counterfeit Merchandise. U.S. Immigration and Customs Enforcement. 2014-01-30. http://www.ice.gov/news/releases/1312/131202washingtondc.htm [2016-9-10].

[19]United States. White House Office, Obama B. International Strategy for Cyberspace: Prosperity, Security, and Openness in a Networked World. White House. 2011. Chinese translation of the full text of the International Strategy for Cyberspace from the Obama administration. https://www.douban.com/note/263597739/ [2016-9-24].

7.4 Protection of Network Data

On July 4, 2014, the Russian parliament passed legislation to prescribe that servers storing Russian citizens' personal data must be located inside Russia since September 1, 2016.[20] The authors of the legislation believed that it gave both foreign and domestic internet companies enough time to create data-storage facilities in Russia.[21] The bill was proposed after some Russian MPs deemed it unwise that the bulk of Russians' online personal data was held on foreign servers, mostly in the US.

Some media reported that in accordance with this Russian law, Google, Facebook, Twitter, Apple and other Internet giants could only store users' personal data information locally inside of Russia, rather than their headquarters in the United States. The Russian Congress said that all technology companies that opened Internet services in Russia were obliged to set up physical offices in Russia.

Russian MPs believed the new law was in tune with the current European policy of trying to legally protect online personal data. Deputy Chairman of the Duma's committee on information policy, Leonid Levin, said the Russian law served goals similar to those of the recent decision by the European Court of Justice, which endorsed the so-called "*right to be forgotten*", obliging Google to remove upon request links to personal data. Of course, some were afraid two years could be not enough for certain companies to have their online data storage organized in Russia, the concerns had been voiced in relation to online travel and airline booking services. Leading Russian airlines Aeroflot and Transaero, for example, used the same GDS system (Global Distribution System) for online ticket sales as most of the other airlines in the world. Developing the Russian system might take longer than the law allows. The Russian Association for Electronic Communications (RAEC) had warned of the potential economic losses the law might entail. "The law puts under question cross-border transmission of personal data", RAEC said in a statement. "Passing similar laws on the localization of personal data in other countries has led to withdrawal of global services and substantial economic losses."[22]

By creation of the law, the Russian government requires its citizens' personal data to be necessarily stored on servers inside of Russia, which reflects Russia's attention to its cyberspace sovereignty.

---

[20]New Russian law: banning citizens' data being held on foreign servers. http://tech.sina.com.cn/i/2014-07-06/08309478459.shtml [2016-9-17].

[21]New Russian law bans citizens' personal data being held on foreign servers. https://alethonews.wordpress.com/2014/07/05/ [2016-9-10].

[22]Russia passes a new Internet law; citizens' personal data must be stored on domestic servicers. http://www1.guancha.cn/indexnews/2014_07_07_244460.shtml [2016-6-6].

7.5 Monitoring of Websites

To maintain national security, the Indian government has requested to monitor communication software such as BlackBerry e-mails and instant messaging services as well as social networking platforms such as "Facebook" and "Twitter" since September 2010, and the above network operators has be repeatedly asked to assist the government in deleting suspected illegal network items.[23]

It was reported that Milind Deora, a minister of Indian Department of Telecommunications, told the Parliament that due to fear of Twitter, Facebook and other social networking sites being used by terrorists to plan to launch attacks, India Telecom service providers would provide eavesdropping and monitoring tools for the government according to the agreement signed at the time of issuing the license. India's Ministry of State Security has, under this agreement, requested the Department of Communications to monitor communications including such sites. Deora said some of the communications had been encrypted. However, the Indian government did not disclose in detail which encrypted communications data are expected to be monitored.[24]

According to Indian law, even without a court order, the website and service providers have to provide the government security department with account details, including passwords.

Although the Indian government's behavior has incurred criticism of "restriction on freedom of information and speech", it shows that India has exercised the right of jurisdiction over cyberspace.

7.6 Cease of Network Services for Specific Targets

On May 29, 2009, all MSN (Microsoft Service Network, Instant Messenger services) accounts in Cuba were off-line because Microsoft had shut off the MSN network service port linked to Cuba. Syria, Iran, Sudan and North Korea suffered from the same. When citizens of these five countries logged into MSN, they would be left with the error message: "Error 810003c1".[25]

---

[23]India in talks on BlackBerry e-mail access: source. http://www.theglobeandmail.com/technology/india-in-talks-on-blackberry-e-mail-access-source/article4327182/ [2016-12-31].

[24]India demands monitoring of social networks "Facebook, Twitter". http://roll.sohu.com/20110809/n315816024.shtml [2016-10-6].

[25]Microsoft Shuts Off Windows Live Messenger IM For Users In Countries Embargoed By The US. http://www.liveside.net/2009/05/21/microsoft-shuts-off-windows-live-messenger-im-for-users-in-countries-embargoed-by-the-us-error-810003c1/ [2016-9-11].

The www.microsoft.com posted a piece of news that Microsoft had shut off MSN services in Cuba, North Korea, Syria, Iran and Sudan.[26] Microsoft announced in a statement that it was disabling the program's availability in Cuba, Syria, Iran, Sudan and North Korea to come into compliance with a U.S. ban on transfer of licensed software to embargoed countries. Cuba, Syria, Iran, Sudan and North Korea cannot continue to use Microsoft's free MSN services at that moment. For a long time, the US government has listed Cuba, Iran, Syria, Sudan and North Korea in a "blacklist" that supports terrorist countries, and has imposed sanctions on politics, economy and turnover of the above countries in accordance with domestic laws of the United States. Microsoft said it would not have business dealing with the countries on the sanctions list until the government ban was lifted.

Thus, the United States cyberspace sovereignty clearly covers network services, so that the network services inside the United States are subjected to the United States' right of jurisdiction over cyberspace.

7.7 Prevention of Dissemination Diffusion Harmful Information on the Internet

At present, the major countries across the world have all established regulators and have developed and improved various targeted regulatory measures to prevent the dissemination of harmful information. These cases can also support practical existence of the cyberspace sovereignty in the countries that have taken these measures.

7.7.1 Russia's Blockage of Access to Specific Webpages

In 2014, the Federal Service for Supervision of Communications, Information Technology and Mass Media blocked Internet users within Russian territory from accessing a page on Facebook on grounds of calling for an "unauthorized mass event". The Facebook account owner of this page was a prominent dissident who intended to launch a protest through Facebook. The Federal Service for Supervision of Communications, Information Technology and Mass Media said that the protest would "infringe the public order" and it was empowered to prevent appeal for similar protests via Internet. Facebook blocked the page at Russia's request, which

[26]Cuba Criticized Microsoft Blocking Messenger. http://www.nbcnews.com/id/31005365/#. Vw9nm_6heUl [2016-9-11].

arouse controversy, and Facebook was criticized for surrendering to the Russian government.[27]

Russia said that it was empowered to shut off any sites if necessary in terms of the Internet governance.[28] Russia exercises its cyberspace sovereignty by blocking access to specific webpages, blocking pages and other methods to prevent the dissemination of harmful information.

7.7.2 *Australia's Demand for Installation of Filters*

In May 2008, the Australian government introduced a policy of forcing the installation of filters. Such mandatory filters supplied to Internet service providers (ISPs) could prevent users from downloading harmful information about terrorist content and the like. The policy is an item of the 82 million Australian dollars "cyber-safety plan" implemented by the Australian government.[29] According to the survey, 85% of Australian ISPs are welcome to the filters. In 2011, Australia's two major ISPs (Telstea and Optus) confirmed that installation of filters blocked more than 500 website URLs related to child abuse provided by the Communications and Media Authority.[30]

On July 9, 2010, Stephen Conroy, a minister for Australian communications, said that the three largest ISPs (Telstra, Optus and Primus) agreed to voluntarily block access to child porn sites before the government launched mandatory filters. They would block the relevant sites according to the URLs compiled by the Australian Communications and Media Authority.[31]

Australian laws stipulate that the Australian Communications and Media Authority is empowered to censor and control the website content on the servers located in Australia. Upon receipt of complaints about some website contents from the public, the Authority will censor these website contents. Once they are considered as "prohibited contents", the site will receive a notice to delete the relevant contents. If they are not deleted upon expiration, the site will be fined 11,000 Australian dollars per day. When the illegal contents are from foreign servers, the

[27]Facebook blocks the page at the Russia's request; Facebook is criticized for surrendering to the Russian government. http://world.huanqiu.com/exclusive/2014-12/5290338.html [2016-9-11].

[28]Federal Service for Supervision of Communications, Information Technology and Mass Media says it was empowered to shut off any sites if necessary. http://world.people.com.cn/n/2015/0831/c1002-27535196.html [2016-9-11].

[29]Consultative Working Group on Cyber-safety. http://www.amta.org.au/pages/Consultative.Working.Group.on.Cyber-safety [2016-9-11].

[30]Australia: full governance and filtering of illegal and harmful information. http://news.sina.com.cn/o/2012-06-11/073924571192.shtml [2016-12-31].

[31]Three largest Australian ISPs voluntarily block child porn sites. http://tech.sina.com.cn/i/2010-07-09/14054408039.shtml [2016-9-11].

site will be listed in the "blacklist", and the network operators in Australia are informed of blocking it.[32]

It is clear that Australia censors the network contents to show that the government is exercising its cyberspace sovereignty.

7.7.3 German Filtering Requirements for Dissemination of Illegal Information on Internet

When searching for "hitler" through www.google.de, one can see some search results have been filtered, and when the search results are browsed, they show that "Ihre Suche hätte in den Suchergebnissen einen Treffer generiert, den wir Ihnen nicht anzeigen, da uns von einer zuständigen Stelle in Deutschland mitgeteilt wurde, dass die entsprechende URL unrechtmäßig ist."[33] (*I.e. A URL that otherwise would have appeared in response to your search, was not displayed because that URL was reported as illegal by a German regulatory body.*) However, the same information searched by the Google search engines of other countries will not show such results, which indicates that Google is subject to the decrees of the German government sectors when providing services inside of Germany.[34]

Germany prevents the dissemination of harmful information by enacting laws, installing network filters and network protection nets and other measures, and limiting the search results from the Google search engine, which indicates that Germany is also exercising its cyberspace sovereignty.

7.7.4 Japan's Blockage of Child-Porn Websites

On March 3, 2011, the Internet Content Security Association (ICSA) announced a mandatory blockage of access to child pornography and forcibly cutting off web links involving child porn from the perspective of Internet service providers (ISP).[35] The ISPs, who participate in the action of cutting off links, will block these illegal websites according to the illegal website information provided by the ICSA. To acquire a list of child-porn websites to be isolated, ICSA cooperates with all organizations within the association, including four organizations in the

[32]Descending heavy hand on Internet censorship, resolutely blocking illegal sites. http://world.huanqiu.com/roll/2010-07/962856.html [2016-9-12].

[33]German regulatory body reported illegal material. https://www.lumendatabase.org/notices/9415 [2016-9-18].

[34]German combats unlawful network acts in accordance with law. http://news.xinhuanet.com/zgjx/2011-04/20/c_13837830.htm [2016-9-18].

[35]児童ポルノのブロッキング、日本でも4月スタート、業界団体が発足. 2011-3-3. http://internet.watch.impress.co.jp/docs/news/20110303_430786.html [2016-9-11].

communication industry, large ISP companies, search engines such as Yahoo! and Google. Nine large network communications service providers, including NTT Communications and NEC BIGLOBE, participate in this action, and the nine ISPs have a total of about 20 million customers with the market share of about 60%.

It is a manifestation of exercise of cyberspace sovereignty that the Japanese government blocks child-porn websites at the network communications service provider level and filters child pornographic contents on the search result pages.

7.7.5 U.K. Blockage of Copyright-Infringement Sites

In 2012, British Phonographic Industry (BPI) appealed to the High Court to claim direct blockage of copyright-infringement site "The Pirate Bay".[36] The Pirate Bay is a site specialized in storing, classifying and searching for BT,[37] and its concurrent users broke through 10 million in January 2008 and it became the largest BT site in the world. Data from the research company comScore shows that The Pirate Bay boasts 3.7 million users in the U.K.

In this case, major record companies, including Sony, Electric and Musical Industries Ltd. (EMI) and UMG, expected the court to force British ISPs to block the Pirate Bay site. The judge said that "The Pirate Bay has not taken steps to stop infringement; even though it has the ability to do so, it still encourages infringement." In June 2012, the London High Court stated in the award on Monday: "both The Pirate Bay and its users have infringed the copyright".[38] A ban of the ruling on The Pirate Bay means to give a green light to the copyright owner requiring the ISP to restrict their users from accessing file sharing sites. After the ban comes into effect, users in the U.K. will not able to easily access these pirated sites any longer.

In 2014, the British High Court ordered another six British ISPs (BT, EE, TalkTalk, O2, Sky and Virgin Media) to block piracy websites, so that the blocked websites rose from 40 to 93.[39] What was worth mentioning was that the blocked websites included 32 individual piracy websites, which were blocked for the first time in Britain. New members in the blocked piracy site list included Demonoid,

---

[36]U.K. High Court orders ISPs to block the Pirate Bay. http://www.pcmag.com/article2/0,2817,2403749,00.asp [2016-9-18].

[37]BT network: a centerless and content-based addressing file transfer network. Users query files according to the contents, and the file recipients cannot perceive where the files are stored, but they search and download the appropriate files only by the "BT seed". A file may exist anywhere on the network and may have multiple copies, and even a file can be divided into multiple parts and stored in different locations and then they are automatically integrated by the BT network and pushed to users who are conducting search.

[38]British High Court rules The Pirate Bay infringes copyright. http://tech.sina.com.cn/i/2012-02-20/23526746542.shtml [2016-10-6].

[39]Blocked piracy site list more than doubles after ruling. http://www.bbc.co.uk/news/technology-30234790 [2016-9-18].

Watchseries, IPTorrents, TorrentDay and so on, whose daily website visits were all more than one million. After the ban went into formal effect, when proceeding access to these sites, users would see a prompt of inaccessibility.

The U.K. establishes regulators for regulating harmful information on the Internet and prevents dissemination of harmful information by blocking copyright-infringement sites, which reflects that the U.K. is exercising its cyberspace sovereignty.

7.7.6 France's Blockage of Terrorism Websites

In 2014, the French parliament approved an anti-terrorism measure, wherein the French government was empowered to block websites without going through a court with due diligence and the power was applicable to those sites accused of promoting or proposing terrorism or publishing child pornography. Visitors to the blocked sites are now redirected to a page from the French Interior Ministry, containing a warning graphic of a big red palm, to show access forbidden. In March 2015, French authorities used new powers to directly block five websites accused of scheming terrorism without seeking a court order and required ISPs to comply within 24 h and implement relevant plans for a blockage.[40]

In March 2015, the new decree issued by the French government stipulates that the ISPs must block all websites containing terrorism and child pornography within 24 h of receiving a government order.[41]

Because of terrorist attacks, France has introduced some more powerful measures in the governance over Internet terrorism information and carries out anti-terrorism activities by exercising its cyberspace sovereignty.

7.7.7 Indian Government's Blockage of Illegal Websites

In July 2012, ethnic clashes struck the northern region of India and meanwhile social networking sites posted rumors that people in the northeast of India were about to suffer from racial attacks, so the Indian government temporarily closed more than 200 websites suspected of disseminating misinformation to block spreading of harmful information.[42]

[40]France exercises anti-terrorism powers to block five websites suspected of condoning terrorism. http://news.xinhuanet.com/world/2015-03/18/c_1114680592.htm [2016-9-11].

[41]France blocks all websites containing child pornography and terrorism. http://www.weilairibao.com/show-10-31766-1.html [2016-9-11].

[42]Indian cyber silence: Journalists muted after race riots. https://www.rt.com/news/india-twitter-crackdown-riots-348/ [2016-9-11].

On August 17, 2012, Sushil Kumar Shinde, a minister of Home Affairs in India, declared forbidding batch sending of text messages and multimedia messages using mobile phones across India within 15 days. At the same time, the Indian government further required relevant organizations to check all social media platforms to seek inflammatory and aggressive content. Up to August 20, 2012, the Indian government had temporarily closed 245 websites disseminating inflammatory speeches, including well-known social sites such as Facebook and Twitter.[43]

On June 13, 2013, the Department of Telecommunications (DoT) of the Indian government ordered Internet Service Providers (ISPs) to block 39 websites,[44] most of which were web forums mainly for sharing and downloading pornographic files, but some of them were mostly used to host images and files that were not pornographic. While watching or distributing child pornography is illegal in India, watching adult pornography is not. The DoT did not specify a reason or law under which the websites were blocked, but DoT required the ISPs to "immediately block the access to the following URLs" in the order. A DoT official, who pleaded anonymity, said the department was just following the orders issued by the cyber security coordination committee and hence could not talk about the specific reasons behind the block.

On December 19, 2014, the Indian government blocked more than 60 sites and URLs, including the two largest open source project hosting platforms Github and Sourceforge, on the grounds of anti-terror. These sites were suspected of hosting content related to terrorist organizations in the "Islamic State" (ISIS) and refused to cooperate with the Indian government in investigation.[45]

On December 2014, DoT required all Indian ISPs to block 32 URLs, including Vimeo (HD video blog site), archive.org (video sharing and domain name query site), Github.com (software code base) and so on.[46] The circular told that the above 32 URLs were blocked in accordance with Section 69A of the *Information Technology Act*, 2000.[47] Section 69A of the *Information Technology Act* specifies that the Central Government or a State Government is empowered to issue directions for intercepting or monitoring digital information if necessary. Arvind Gupta, a senior IT executive of Bharatiya Jana Party (BJP), said this was an anti-terrorism

---

[43]India's ethnic clashes have evolved into a national crisis and cast a shadow over politics. http://www.360doc.cn/article/10301333_232196672.html [2016-8-30].

[44]India blocks 39 websites without specifying a reason. http://tech.ifeng.com/internet/detail_2013_06/28/26909855_0.shtml [2016-9-11].

[45]India blocks Github and Sourceforge for anti-terror. http://www.zmke.com/i/12191.html [2016-9-11].

[46]DoT Orders ISPs To Block Vimeo, Github, Archive.org, Pastebin. http://www.huffingtonpost.in/2014/12/31/ dot-blocks-vimeo_n_6399550.html [2016-9-11].

[47]India's Information Technology Act, 2000, and amendments 2006, 2008 and 2011 thereof. http://www.infseclaw.net/news/html/1032.html [2016-10-6].

measure and the URLs were blocked because they were utilized by ISIS (extremist terrorist group) and posted anti-India content.[48]

India's blockage of harmful sites shows that the Indian government implements strong supervision over the sites and indicates the existence of cyberspace sovereignty in India.

7.8 Removal of Cyber Terrorism Information

In 2010, the British government began to launch a special action of removal of Internet terrorism information, which was specifically charged by the Counter Terrorism Internet Referral Unit (CTIRU), so as to remove the content that incites or glorifies terrorist acts from the Internet[49] in accordance with the provisions of the *Terrorism Act 2006*[50] issued by the United Kingdom.

CTIRU is a subsidiary body of the Association of Chief Police Officers (ACPO). In this action, CTIRU compiled a blacklist of terrorism-related sites outside the UK and cooperated with the Internet service provider (ISP) in integrating the blacklist of the sites into the ISP's filtering system. In addition, CTIRU also encouraged the British people to report anonymously via the internet terrorism information report website that was dedicated to the government,[51] and was responsible for answering citizens' questions as to removal of Internet terrorism information and blockage of relevant sites on the governmental information service website of the British government.[52]

In November 2014, Home Secretary Theresa May delivered a speech on counter-terrorism in the Royal United Services Institute and stated[53] CTIRU has secured the removal of a total of 65,000 items related to acts of terrorism from the Internet since February 2010, 70% of which are relevant to ISIL (Islamic State of Iraq and the Levant), Syria and Iraq. The total number of removed data items

---

[48]India blocks 32URLs to prevent ISIS disseminating anti-India content. http://tech.sina.com.cn/i/2014-12-31/doc-icczmvun4573219.shtml [2016-9-11].

[49]Counter Terrorism Internet Referral Unit. Open Rights Group Wiki. 2015. https://wiki.openrightsgroup.org/wiki/Counter_Terrorism_Internet_Referral_Unit [2016-9-11].

[50]The Terrorism Act 2006. https://www.gov.uk/government/publications/the-terrorism-act-2006 [2016-9-18].

[51]Report online terrorist material. https://www.gov.uk/report-terrorism [2016-9-11].

[52]What is the CTIRU? http://www.borderscollege.ac.uk/resources/counter-terrorism/[2016-10-6]. https://www.whatdotheyknow.com/request/number_of_websites_taken_down_by#incoming-103269 [2016-9-11].

[53]Speech: Home Secretary Theresa May on Counter-Terrorism. Home Office and The Rt Hon Theresa May. 2014-11-24. https://www.gov.uk/government/speeches/home-secretary-theresa-may-on-counter-terrorism [2016-9-11].

reached 75,000 till March 2015,[54] including some typical social sites such as Facebook and Twitter. CTIRU would inform corresponding companies of removing the information once the information was believed to be terrorism-related.[55]

In October 2014, the British government summoned internet companies such as Google, Facebook, Twitter and Microsoft to a meeting where they discussed how to further track down network extremist information.[56] This meeting was held under the background where the extremism-related information was increasingly proliferated on the Internet and extremist organizations including the Islamic State was devoting greater efforts for recruitment in Britain by posting various extremism information. At present, Facebook, Twitter and Google possessing YouTube usually remove the extremist content that clearly violates the British law on the sites within their jurisdiction, but they will not submit the relevant content and the information of publishers who post the extremist content to the police. If the authorities intend to launch an investigation, the police must file a request for some specific information to the Internet companies so as to acquire the corresponding investigation. To this end, at the meeting, Boris Johnson on behalf of the British government requested the Internet companies to automatically hand over every relevant information helpful for the police to track the extremists, while further rising up the scale of removing the extremism information, that is, deleting "all" videos and messages containing the extremism content, instead of only deleting obvious illegal information such as bomb-making videos or religious provocative remarks at the present stage. Under the auspices of this meeting, efforts to combat illegal web content have made considerable progress, and the government hopes to continue working with search engines and Internet service providers to explore ways to quickly remove extremist and terrorist content on the Internet.[57] Under the impetus of this meeting, a great deal of progress has been made to take down illegal material online and the government wants to work collaboratively with search engines and ISPs to look at what more can be done to swiftly remove extremist and terrorist material.[58]

In November 2014, the British operators and the British government came to an agreement of doing more to tackle the problem about dissemination of extremism

---

[54]Counter-terrorism.TheyWorkForYou. 2015-02-26. http://www.theyworkforyou.com/wrans/?id=2015-02-26.225636.h [2016-9-11].

[55]Prevention and Suppression of Terrorism. They Work For You. 2014-04-02. http://www.theyworkforyou.com/debate/?id=2014-04-02a.957.0 [2016-9-11].

[56]British govt to request information from web giants on extremists. AL Arabiya News. 2014-10-19. http://english.alarabiya.net/en/media/digital/2014/10/19/British-government-to-request-access-to-details-of-extremist-users.html [2016-9-11].

[57]British government intends to enhance network monitoring and beat network extremism, Xinhuanet. 2014-10-20. http://news.xinhuanet.com/world/2014-10/20/c_127114378.htm [2016-9-11].

[58]Fackbook. Twitter and YouTube told to 'automatically' hand over Isis terrorists' data. The Independent. 2014-10-20. http://www.independent.co.uk/life-style/gadgets-and-tech/uk-government-will-ask-twitter-and-youtube-to-automatically-hand-over-isis-extremists-data-9805710.html [2016-9-11].

information on the Internet with the help of governmental coordination.[59] The main measures comprise filtering network requests for access to sites suspected of containing terrorist information and establishing an online reporting mechanism for extremist information. In addition, operators agree to ensure to block terrorist and extremist information by using their network filters to prevent children and adolescents from accessing such radical information.

It is observed that, from the removal of online terrorism information in Britain, Britain has devoted great efforts in cyber anti-terrorism and this fully reflects how Britain highlights their cyberspace sovereignty.

7.9 Taking Down Network Threats and Inflammatory Speech

With the rise of emerging social tools such as blogs, social networking sites (Facebook) and microblogs (Twitter), the network is gradually becoming a breeding ground for threats and inflammatory speech. In recent years, all countries have increasingly monitored and combated the network threats and inflammatory speech, which reflects the existence of cyberspace sovereignty.

7.9.1 US Striking Dissemination of Online Threats

On May 1, 2013, the US police arrested an 18-year-old High School student Cameron B. Dambrosio, who made threats on his Facebook page and threatened to outdo the Boston Marathon bombings.[60] Dambrosio wrote on his Facebook page "(expletive) the Boston bombing, wait till you see what I do. I'm going to be famous." This arouse the police's attention, and the police chief Joseph Solomon said that, "he's telling people to shut up and in order to get some props he'll have to go kill somebody." Solomon said that, "the guard attached importance to such a statement, and that although the high school student did not directly specify a person and facility, he was still accused of dissemination of terrorist threats and speech." The police have turned over Dambrosio's relevant information to the FBI.[61]

---

[59]Patrick Wintour. UK ISPs to introduce jihadi and terror content reporting button. The Guardian. 2014-11-14. http://www.theguardian.com/technology/2014/nov/14/uk-isps-to-introduce-jihadi-and-terror-content-reporting-button [2016-9-11].

[60]Methuen High student accused of making terrorist threats on Facebook. http://www.myfoxboston.com/news/methuen-high-student-accused-of-making-terrorist-threats-on-facebook-2/140144147 [2016-9-11].

[61]US High schooler threatens to outdo the Boston Marathon bombings or faces up to 20 years in prison. http://www.chinanews.com/gj/2013/05-03/4785317.shtml [2016-9-11].

On June 1, 2013, Joshua Phillip Klimas, 32-year-old man from Coventry, Connecticut, U.S., made threats toward Obama and his family on the whitehouse.gov site and wrote "If you do not resign by the end of the year I will kill you!" He was thus arrested by the police at home on November 20. Judge Donna F. Martinez ordered Klimas to be admitted to a local hospital for a psychiatric evaluation. The situation was investigated by the U.S. Secret Service with the assistance of the UConn Police Department and the Coventry Police Department.[62]

Hence, despite of boasting freedom of speech, the United States still severely cracks down on those who make online threats, and this indicates the exercise of cyberspace sovereignty in the United States.

7.9.2 German Striking Dissemination of Online Threats

A media reported[63] that in a secondary school in a city of the western region in Germany, a grade eight student was often ridiculed and bullied, so he wrote angrily on his blog, "I cannot bear the bullying of you guys, I decide to risk my life with you." His threatening remarks caused his schoolmates to panic, so the school leaders had to call the police. The local court accepted the case and held that his threatening remarks on the blog could be regarded as a behavior of disturbing the public order. Although the student was still underage, he has a disposing capability, so he was sentenced to 20-h unpaid social work.

The media also reported that in March 2012, when the German police was investigating a rape and murder case, an 18-year-old citizen called on the Internet, "We all take action, smash the police office, kill the rapist", which caused more than 50 people to besiege the local police office. The Berlin court sentenced this citizen for two-week imprisonment on the grounds of inciting and calling on cyber citizens to besiege the police office. Pursuant to Section 111 of the German Criminal Code, whosoever publicly incites the commission of a criminal offense shall be condemned to a fine and imprisonment not exceeding five years if the incitement had been successful. German laws and regulations even stipulate that whosoever disseminates information inconsistent with the fact will also be subject to civil or criminal prosecution.

The German Constitution stipulates that citizens enjoy a high degree of freedom of speech, and people can "speak out freely" except for deliberately making lies. On the other hand, the German Basic Law also requires legislators to protect individual honor and adolescents from being hurt by others' remarks. In other words, it is precisely ensure an orderly environment, that is not only free, but has not caused

[62]American Man Arrested For Threatening To Kill Obama. http://www.chinadaily.com.cn/hqzx/2013-11/23/content_17126289.htm [2016-9-11].

[63]German: Internet is not free field. http://news.xinhuanet.com/world/2012-06/13/c_123274877.htm?prolongation=1 [2016-9-18].

harm to others, and that the government must strengthen the restrictions on the use of the Internet. This shows that Germany needs to guarantee the authority of the German Constitution in cyberspace so as to exercise its cyberspace sovereignty.

7.9.3 Britain Taking Down Dissemination of Illegal Speech

26-Year-old British passenger Paul Chambers was scheduled to leave for Ireland from Doncaster Robin Hood airport in South Yorkshire, England on January 15, 2010. Robin Hood airport was closed because of heavy snow, so the flight that Chambers planned to take might be delayed. Chambers sent a message in frustration on his "Twitter" main page of his blog on January 7, and he tweeted that "Crap! Robin Hood airport is closed. You've got a week and a bit to get your shit together; otherwise I'm blowing the airport sky high!!" After receiving a report, the police in South Yorkshire arrested Chambers at his office for posting menacing remarks on January 13, and then interrogated him for 7 h and took away his computer and mobile phone. Chambers was then released, but he has been granted a lifetime ban by the police from entering Robin Hood airport.[64]

Large-scale riots occurred in London, England in August 2011 and spread to seven cities across England. Two men have been jailed for four years each for using Facebook to spread rumors and incite disorder during riots, BBC (British Broadcasting Corporation) reported it.[65] It was reported that 22-year-old Perry Sutcliffe-Keenan who lived in Warrington and 21-year-old Jordan Blackshaw who lived in Marston, had created a Facebook event called "Smash d[o]wn in Northwich Town". The page went on to specify a meeting time and place of 9 August, between 13:00 and 16:00 BST, "behind maccies"—thought to be the McDonald's restaurant in Northwich town centre. The page invited people to "riot" on 10 August between 19:00 BST and 22:00 BST. Afterwards, both Blackshaw and Sutcliffe-Keenan were jailed at Chester Crown Court. It was reported that this was the most severe sentencing for troublemakers made by the judge after riots and shop-robbing events occurred that week in London and other cities in England. Both men pleaded guilty under Sections 44 and 46 of the Serious Crime Act to intentionally encouraging another to assist the commission of an indictable offence.

35-Year-old Runa Khan was a mother-of-six from Bedfordshire, Luton, England. She was found to transmit and incite extremism "jihad" using Facebook in 2014 and was jailed for five years and three months by the British court. According to the adjudication of a district criminal court in England, investigators found on

[64]British man jokes about bombing airport on the Internet, the police arrests him at once. http://news.xinhuanet.com/world/2010-01/20/content_12840412.htm [2016-9-11].

[65]England riots: Two jailed for using Facebook to incite disorder. http://www.bbc.com/news/uk-england-manchester-14551582 [2016-12-2].

some sites she had accessed that she had posted a picture of a suicide vest and photos of her underage children holding guns and swords and that she hoped her 8-year-old son to participate in "jihad" when he grew up. In addition, she expressed her wish of going to Syria for many times via mobile social software.[66]

The British government monitors the public speech through the Internet and is followed up by the British police. In addition, the British government has said it will study whether to close social networking sites and prohibit sending SMS messages when riots occur.[67] All this shows that the United Kingdom effectively imposes sovereignty in cyberspace.

7.10 Combating Distribution of Online Rumors

In October 2008, South Korean star Choi Jin-sil was found to be hanged at her home in Seoul. The cause of the incident was a rumor about Choi Jin-sil being plagued by a "KRW 2.5 billion private debt". She was investigated by the South Korean police on September 29 due to this rumor.[68]

Police examining the case concluded that Choi Jin-sil was primarily driven to suicide as a result of the rumors distributed by two members of staff from some security company in South Korea, which imposed heavy pressure upon Choi Jin-sil. In June 2009, for accusations such as damaging individual reputation, the South Korean court condemned them for 10-month imprisonment, two years suspension, and engagement in social services for 120 h, respectively.

South Korean experts said that various online rumors had surpassed the "warning line", which would increase mutual distrust and anxiety of the whole society, so the government should adopt a more effective solution of not only ensuring the freedom of speech but effectively preventing the spreading of rumors to return a pure land to the Internet.[69]

The administrative means adopted by the South Korean government to govern online rumors usually include abundant reviews and identifying means and an increase in the intensity of punishment, which also reflects the exercise of its national cyberspace sovereignty.

---

[66]England woman is jailed for five years for promoting extremism on Facebook. http://news.xinhuanet.com/2014-12/12/c_1113620023.htm [2016-9-11].

[67]Two British teenagers were jailed for four years for organizing and inciting riots online. http://www.chinanews.com/gj/2011/08-17/3264275.shtml [2016-9-11].

[68]Choi Jin-sil is committed suicide before dawn at home; it is said to be related to Ahn Jae-hwan's death. http://ent.qq.com/a/20081002/000083.htm [2016-9-18].

[69]South Korea: rumors become more furious if without heavy penalty. http://news.xinhuanet.com/world/2013-08/29/c_117150197.htm [2016-10-6].

7.11 Fighting Cyber Personal Attacks

Countries all over the world are making efforts to fight cyber personal attacks to guarantee a healthy development of the Internet. The usual practice of the countries is to establish specialized regulators to effectively supervise and fight cyber personal attacks and to perform cyberspace jurisdiction.

7.11.1 The United States Punishes People, Who Commit Personal Attacks, with Laws

In 2006, an American female netizen kept insulting another woman on the Internet using words such as "liar" for up to 10 months. The victim filed a lawsuit against the calumniator for libel, and the federal court convicted the calumniator of libel in accordance with the *Federal Law Prohibiting Use of Computers for Committing Crimes* and ruled that the defendant pay compensation of 11.3 million dollars to the plaintiff, which set the highest record of compensation for cyber calumniation.[70]

The above case shows that although in the United States the Constitution endows citizens with the right to free speech, this does not mean that its citizens are free of restriction on what they say. Once a person's calumniation affects others' normal life, the calumniator and those who spread the rumor shall be severely punished by laws. For decades, the United States continues to enhance control on cyber rumors to let the cyber rumormongers pay a large fine. Some brought ruin and shame upon themselves, some became bankrupt and some ended up in jail.[71] This shows that the United States also exercises its jurisdiction in cyberspace.

7.11.2 The German Court Ruled that Part of the Function of the Google Search Engine Was Illegal

In May 2013, the German Federal Court announced a ruling that the auto-complete function of Google search was illegal and ordered Google to remove the auto-complete entry that was unfavorable to the victim. According to the ruling of the German Federal Court, the "auto-complete" function of the search engine had no problem in principle, but it was the responsibility of the search engine operator to remove the infringing speeches and to compensate for further infringement if

[70]Many countries around the world crack down on cyber rumors. http://news.xinhuanet.com/newmedia/2013-08/28/c_125263548.htm [2016-9-11].

[71]What moves does the United States take to fight cyber rumors? http://news.xinhuanet.com/tech/2015-08/24/c_128158456.htm [2016-9-11].

someone pointed out that a search tip had infringed his/her rights or damaged his/her reputation.[72]

After the above ruling was made, Google's spokesman in Germany, Kay Oberbeck, argued that he "could not understand" the courts view that Google should be responsible for the defamatory contents showing up in the search textbox. The spokesman said that "it is a prediction made by algorithms based on the search frequency and is not made by Google"; at the same time, he expressed "relief" since the German Federal Court did not forbid Google of providing the "auto-complete" function in Germany. The public opinion in Germany thought that the ruling was a milestone.[73]

This ruling should warn the enterprises and individuals to prevent defamatory contents from showing up in the auto-complete text in the future. The method for doing so is to request the search engine operators to perform an "informing-removing" procedure,[74] which means that the search engine should be responsible for the accused infringement of the right of personality if the search engine fails to stop the further infringement after receiving the notice of infringement. This ruling fully demonstrates the jurisdiction performed by Germany in cyberspace and the effective functioning of the German cyberspace sovereignty.

7.12 Fighting Invasion of Internet Privacy

Civil rights are one of the most valued rights of all countries, and the protection of civil rights from being invaded is a concrete manifestation of the implementation of human rights by the governments. Invasion of citizen privacy is one of the most common invasions of civil rights and one of the reasons why governments take measures to protect privacy.

7.12.1 The US Police Protected "the Man Abusing a Dog" Who Suffered from Human-Powered Search on the Internet

In May 2008, a video showing a US navy soldier throw a puppy off a cliff was posted on YouTube, which sparked public outrage. The video showed that the

[72]Germany tells Google to tidy up auto-complete. http://www.bbc.com/news/technology-22529357 [2016-9-11].

[73]German enterprisers won the case against Google for infringement. http://www.bjnews.com.cn/world/2013/06/03/266789.html [2016-9-11].

[74]Germany: Two Interesting German Decisions On Internet Law. http://www.mondaq.com/x/246822/Licensing+Syndication/Two+Interesting+German+Decisions+On+Internet+Law%EF%BC%89 [2016-9-11].

soldier cruelly threw the puppy off the cliff as he praised the cuteness of the puppy. In less than two days, about 150,000 people watched the video and published more than 4000 pieces of comments. YouTube was pressured into removing this video.[75] On March 4, 2008, Kurt Nimmo published on the website "blogspot" the personal information of the abuser including his name, identity, place of service and social network account. The results of the "human-powered search" spread rapidly on the Internet.[76] Various reports and discussion directly aimed at David Motari, the man in the video, emerged in an endless stream and brought serious troubles to the personal life of David Motari. Some news reported that even the family of David Motari was threatened, and the police had to regularly patrol the area around the house of David Motari to prevent occurrence of violence.

7.12.2 South Korea Fights Human-Powered Search on the Internet

On June 5, 2005, a South Korean girl's pet dog defecated in a carriage of Seoul Metro line 2. An old man sitting next to the girl asked her to clean the excrement of the dog, but the girl refused and hurled insults at the old man. This incident was recorded by someone with a cell phone and posted on the Internet and aroused deep public anger. After days of human-powered search on the Internet by the netizens, the girl's personal information including her real name, phone number, address, and school was made public. The offensive nickname "dogshit girl" soon overwhelmed her, and "further-processed stories" that insulted and ridiculed her flooded the Internet. The girl's parents received many anonymous phone calls which accused them of failed upbringing.[77] The girl was pressured into making a public apology and at last dropping out of school. Later, she contracted mental illness, her sisters had to change jobs, and her parents were forced to move and conceal their real names.[78]

[75] 2 Marines disciplined over puppy-tossing video. http://edition.cnn.com/2008/US/06/11/marine.puppy/ [2016-9-11].

[76] David Motari, Alleged Puppy Killer, Tracked Down. http://www.infowars.com/david-motari-alleged-puppy-killer-tracked-down/ [2016-9-11].

[77] Talk:Dog poop girl. https://en.wikipedia.org/wiki/Talk:Dog_poop_girl#Edited_Picture [2016-9-11].

[78] Subway Fracas Escalates Into Test Of the Internet's Power to Shame. http://www.washingtonpost.com/wp-dyn/content/article/2005/07/06/AR2005070601953.html [2016-9-11].

In September 2005, three months after the event of the “dogshit girl”, the Korea Ministry of Information and Communication held a hearing, requiring that when users posted replies on the message boards of the websites, they had an obligation to use their real names. The Korea Ministry of Information and Communication required the major portal sites to carry out the Limited Real Name System which was also called the “Identity Authentification System”. The implementation of the system employs the principle of “backstage real name”: when a user registers an account or logs into his/her account on a website, he or she must use his or her real name and ID number, but an assumed name can be used when posting information at the foreground.[79] In the year 2006, when the South Korean government set out to make amendments to the *Act on Promotion of Information and Communications Network Utilization and Information Protection*, it had decided to expand the scope of the websites involved.[80] The CHOSUNILBO of South Korea quoted that this act was intended to “purify cyber culture” and “energetically control vicious comments and invasion of personal privacy by using the Internet which have recently become a social problem in South Korea”. Once there is any legal dispute, the police can rapidly confirm the real identity of the user.

On July 3, 2008, after the street demonstrations in South Korea opposing import of American beef,[81] the name of a policeman surnamed Li in the fourth mobile team of the Seoul Local Police Agency, photos titled “the police assaulted demonstrators” and the personal home page address of the policeman surnamed Li on Cyworld were posted on the forum of the South Korean portal website Daum, Agora Message Board. After some netizens accused the policeman of beating citizens’ hindbrains with a bladed glove worn on his hand, many netizens made vicious comments on the personal home page of the policeman, such as “never go back to school”, “live a sneaky life”, etc. However, the police said that the bladed glove in the photos was very rare in South Korea, and it could not be worn outside the glove of a policeman.

---

[79]The spectacular “dogshit girl” event makes South Korean people reflect on cyber violence and government decide to establish a law to promote network real name system. http://play.163.com/special/jianzheng_44/ [2016-9-11].

[80]Amendment to Enforcement Decree of Information and Communications Network Law. http://baike.baidu.com/link?url=JnLI5lgOox00-zgkyQeCAYm189ZipjISuLsNLTQw8aB2s4_OonlODSS1Z2ILJVDYUNl8WYdABT9o8YHSAhipfgWtV9m16AasTjEfLpeqsLtA3Lf6kb93GYTCULMEjgbeD_FclQkAd7jHAOP32NF7DdaNoVbgObroCmzbtR1G3f9ZOuNKisxuC1x5Sku4mTA4lS2U2iniHSRG3zTkJnLtCVfcN-o8hOKqzLZD4Hp3pFIG [2016-9-11].

[81]Korea-US “Beef Disturbance” is becoming increasingly fierce. http://news.sohu.com/20080610/n257386054.shtml [2016-9-11].

Some netizens alleged on the message board that “a policeman surnamed Kim in the Gunpo Police Station beat a patriotic girl with a metal shield” and published Kim’s university, student number and the address of his personal home page on Cyworld. On July 3, the number of visitors to the personal home page of Kim was more than 8000, and they left invectives which were almost “curses”. However, the netizens did not stop, and they also “visited” the home pages of Kim’s relatives and friends of which the links were shown on the home page of Kim and hurled insults and threats on their home pages.

On the Agora Message Board of Daum, there existed a section titled “Personal Information of Violent Policemen” which revealed the personal information of more than 10 policemen including Li and Kim.[82]

In South Korea, the behavior of spreading personal information on the Internet is determined as violating the *Act on Promotion of Information and Communications Network Utilization and Information Protection*[83] and committing the crime of defamation, which shows that South Korea fights human-powered search and exercises the cyberspace sovereignty by using legal means.

7.12.3 The United States Ruled that Schools' Monitoring Invaded Students' Personal Privacy

In the year 2010, two high schools in Philadelphia, USA provided all of their 2300 students with Apple laptops and used these laptops to take pictures and screenshots. One of the plaintiffs, Blake Robbins, said that he was secretly photographed for more than 400 times within two weeks, part of which took place when he was sleeping in the bedroom. The school side explained that the purpose of the school technicians using the remote tracking program was for seeking missing laptops, but they could not explain what legal use the at least 50.6 thousand “candid photographs” had. In October 2010, the US Justice Department judged that the school violated the *Computer Fraud and Abuse Act*[84] and should pay compensation of 610, 000 dollars in addition to stopping the “candid photographing” of the students by using the remote tracking program.[85]

The US attaches great importance to the protection of the right of privacy in the Internet Age and makes specialized information data protection acts to protect

[82]South Korean Policeman suppressing beef-related demonstrations was hunted on the Internet. https://www.douban.com/group/topic/3369678/ [2016-12-31].

[83]Act on Promotion of Information and Communications Network Utilization and Information Protection. https://www.aliyun.com/zixun/content/2_6_97320.html [2016-9-19].

[84]Computer Fraud and Abuse Act in the US. http://www.infseclaw.net/news/html/?937.html [2016-9-25].

[85]Lower Merion School District Settles Webcam Spying Lawsuits For $610,000. http://www.huffingtonpost.com/2010/10/11/lower-merion-school-distr_n_758882.html [2016-9-19].

personal information, which proves the existence of the cyberspace sovereignty in the US.

7.12.4 The Rule of "Right to Be Forgotten" in the European Union

The rule of "Right to Be Forgotten" in the EU started from a case ruled by a European court in May 2014. The plaintiff Mario Costeja González was a Spanish citizen whose estate was confiscated in the year 1988 due to tax debt. The announcement of his house sale was officially printed in the local newspaper. Ten years later, when Mario Costeja González googled his own name, he found that the announcement of his house sale was still listed in the results. Mario Costeja González filed a lawsuit against Google according to the EU Privacy Act and forced Google to screen the announcement in the future search results.[86]

The ruling of the EU High Court was favorable to Mario Costeja González and created a rule called "Right to Be Forgotten". When users search certain information, the EU High Court requires Google and other search engines to stop providing links of personal information that is "insufficient, irrelevant, no longer relevant, or excessive". This decision does not affect the search of basic information, and media websites still can keep such information on the Internet. The only thing that the search engines are forbidden to do is providing any information that needs "to be forgotten" for search requests using people's names.[87]

In November 2014, the EU "working team" made a further guideline for the above issue, listing 13 factors to determine whether a link should be removed or not. The 13 factors included whether the published information was accurate or not? Whether the object was a public character or not? Whether the information involved a crime or not? Whether the information was an opinion or a fact? However, none of these factors were decisive, and problems should be dealt with on a case by case basis.

This decision triggered a slight tsunami of requesting to forget the past. It was reported that within six months since the implementation of the above stipulation, Google had received altogether 348,000 requests for cancelling links, involving more than 1.23 million websites among which about 520,000 websites were finally removed. Removal of those websites meant that they would never appear in the search requests, so the information on those websites was effectively concealed.[88]

---

[86]Google should be examined. http://www.tuicool.com/articles/3qeqIz [2016-10-6].

[87]Stories of Britain: You have "The Right to Be Forgotten". http://www.bbc.com/zhongwen/simp/britain_focus/2014/06/140606_britain_focus_forget_right [2016-9-12].

[88]Google Issues A Transparency Report on "Right to Be Forgotten": 42% has been cancelled. http://tech.sina.com.cn/i/2015-11-27/doc-ifxmaznc5683204.shtml [2016-10-6].

The supporters of the EU new rule deemed that the rule was an important safeguard of the right of privacy. They asserted that a person should not suffer from long-term obsession and damage of reputation or loss of business because of the rash behaviors conducted when he or she was young.

The concept of the "Right to Be Forgotten" is now spreading to other countries. Russia just enacted a similar act, which undoubtedly implied that Russia had realized the potential of the "Right to Be Forgotten" being used as a political censoring tool. In June 2015, the Supreme Court of British Columbia in Canada, when hearing a case involving business secrets, ordered Google to globally block certain websites from Google.com.[89]

7.12.5 France's Ruling for Google.Fr

In a ruling in June 2015, the Commission nationale de l'informatique et des libertés (CNIL) ordered Google.fr (the French version of Google) to globally obey the rule of the EU—the "Right to Be Forgotten", but Google refused. Later, CNIL decided to expand the law enforcement of the rule. CNIL found that it was not enough for the search engines to delete the search results on the websites of certain countries, because people in Europe still could see the unscreened search results on Google.com. Therefore, CNIL commanded that the search results should also be applied to "all the extensions" of the search engines, which also included Google.com. In addition, the French authorities said that they wanted the search results screening to be conducted beyond the borders of France. The chief of CNIL, Isabelle Falque-Pierrotin said that "If people have the right to remove self-related information from the search results, then the whole world should exercise this right." This is a difficult task and means that CNIL wants to force the search engines to globally screen all the search results and means that any netizen can no longer see the information "to be forgotten" no matter where he or she conducts the search. This also means that when Americans use American search engines in the US, their search results will be subject to review of France.[90]

[89]The Supreme Court of British Columbia ordered Google to delete all domain names. http://www.ipr.gov.cn/article/gjxw/gjbh/201406/1825949_1.html [2016-10-6].

[90]Google to defy France's ruling on 'right to be forgotten'. http://www.panarmenian.net/eng/news/195456/ [2016-9-12].

7.13 Fighting Cyber Prejudice and Racial Discrimination

Events involving racial discrimination and extremism on the Internet usually have numerous participants and have a great impact and potential destructiveness. Therefore, various countries and regions usually consider the control of this kind of undesirable information as an important part of the control of bad information on the Internet.

7.13.1 France Fights Cyber Racial Discrimination

An online auction website of Yahoo once included the address of a website which auctioned Nazi souvenirs, and auctioned items in memory of Nazi. Several French non-governmental organizations protested against the behavior of the online auction website of Yahoo many times and filed a complaint with the court in France. An organization named "Anti-Racism and Support for Inter-Ethnic Friendship Movement" criticized that it was "a crime that cannot be tolerated at all" for this Internet company which mainly offered search engines to provide the link of the website advocating Nazism in order to attract advertisement to gain profits. This organization further called on a boycott of Yahoo around the world.[91]

This incident developed into an important event of international concern after it was heard by the French court.[92] The French court deemed that if Yahoo did not prevent the French netizens from browsing the advertisement of auctioning Nazi-related articles, Yahoo would violate the French law of prohibition of inciting racism. In May 2000, the French court ruled that the behavior of the online auction website of Yahoo, i.e., assisting users in logging on the website selling Nazi souvenirs, was illegal according to the provisions relating to "prohibition of inciting racism". Since the French laws forbade sale or display of any item that might incite racial sentiments, the judge then ordered Yahoo to try to prevent users from logging on the website selling Nazi-related items via French websites.

Although Yahoo withdrew the relevant content, Yahoo defended itself both legally and technically by noting that "the French courts have no jurisdiction over a website registered and headquartered in the United States." Yahoo also argued that the cyberspace had no boundary, so the ruling of the French court was impossible to fulfill technically, and Yahoo could not forbid users to input the word "NAZI" when they were conducting searches, and not all the websites including the word "NAZI" advocated Nazism.

---

[91]Yahoo bans sale of Nazi memorabilia from its Internet auctions. https://www.wsws.org/en/articles/2001/01/yaho-j05.html [2016-9-11].

[92]France filed a lawsuit against Yahoo for auctioning Nazi-related items on the Internet. http://www.gmw.cn/01gmrb/2000-10/07/GB/10^18566^0^GMA3-012.htm [2016-9-11].

In the end of July 2000, the court announced that in order to verify the court's judgment that its ruling was technically feasible, the judge appointed an expert team made up by three technical experts to jointly study whether there was any method to stop French users from entering the Yahoo website.

On November 20, 2000, the Paris court ruled that Yahoo should take effective screening measures within three months to prohibit French netizens from entering relevant web pages; and if Yahoo failed to do so within the time limit, it would be fined 100,000 francs.[93]

The above ruling of France fully demonstrated that France exercised cyberspace sovereignty.

7.13.2 *Germany Penalized the Person Running a Website in Favor of Massacre*

On December 12, 2000, the Supreme Court of Germany made an unprecedented judgement that where the content on a website of another country involved denial of the atrocities committed by the Nazis to the Jews during the Second World War or the website was set up by non-Germans, the German prosecutor had the right (to try) to arrest and punish the person in charge of the website as long as the German network users were able to visit the website.[94] This was a precedent set based on the principle that the victim was in the native cyberspace, which expanded the application of the laws originally enforced in Germany to other countries and regions and foreigners.

In December 2000, the Supreme Court of Germany ordered that since German citizens could log on to Yahoo's website, Yahoo should comply with German laws. The court in the Bavarian region of Germany was also investigating Yahoo's auction of Hitler's book *my struggle*.[95]

7.13.3 *Singapore Fights Behavior of Spreading Hate Speeches on the Internet*

Huaixu Yan was a 17-year-old middle school student in Singapore. In life, he was incommunicative and unsociable. In April 2005, Yan had his first blog which

---

[93]The Paris court ruled that Yahoo must prevent French netizens from visiting Nazi-related webistes. http://www.chinanews.com/2000-11-21/26/57081.html [2016-10-6].

[94]Bundesgerichtshof: Volksverhetzung per Internet strafbar. http://www.golem.de/0012/11306.html [2016-9-11].

[95]Jewish organizations in Germany are ready to "strike out" Nazi websites. http://tech.sina.com.cn/i/w/54284.shtml [2016-10-6].

gradually became a place for him to express his private emotions. In the blog named "The Second Massacre", Yan was a self-styled "ultra racist", and while expressing a hatred for Malays and Muslims, he clamored to "use a sniper rifle to assassinate some political figures".

On November 23, the Singapore court, in accordance with the *Sedition Act,*[96] sentenced Huaixu Yan to a probationary surveillance for two years and 180 h of community service.[97] In fact, before Yan, two young bloggers had already been convicted in accordance with the *Sedition Act,* which set a precedent of being sentenced for opinions on blogs. The 28-year-old Songfa Xu was sentenced to 2 months in jail and the 25-year-old You Lin was sentenced to 1 day in jail and fined 5000 Yuan.[98]

The Singapore government combats netizens who spread hate speeches on the Internet by monitoring the speeches on blogs, demonstrating the Singapore government's insistence on cyberspace sovereignty.

7.14 Fighting Attacks from Hackers

In the era of globalization of the computer network, e-commerce is increasingly popular. The value of hardware and software, digital property and information data is increasing. Hackers not only invade other people's computer systems, but also are used by lawless people to seek illegal benefits. Hacker's attacks are becoming more profit-orientated, and even a hacker industry chain has been formed, which leads to the spread of cybercrime. The nature of cybercrimes has been expanded from the original simple computer crimes to unsimple computer crimes such as extortion. Hence, governments around the world are in high agreement with each other in their attitudes toward the crackdown on and the sanction of hackers.

7.14.1 The US's "Operation Clean Slate" Plan for Fighting Botnets

In April 2013, the FBI, with the assistance of more than 80 national government departments around the world, identified the Citadel botnet as the highest-level

[96]Sedition Act. http://statutes.agc.gov.sg/aol/search/display/view.w3p;page=0;query=DocId: "1f6d9e4b-1cf1-4575-9480-da4bdeff9ef4"Status:publishedDepth:0;rec=0 [2016-10-6].

[97]Third racist blogger sentenced to 24 months supervised probation. http://forums.vr-zone.com/chit-chatting/44764-third-racist-blogger-sentenced-24-months-supervised-probation.html [2016-9-11].

[98]The "cross-the-line" blog in Singapore was sentenced. http://news.sina.com.cn/o/2005-11-30/00007575560s.shtml[2016-9-11].

botnet threat and launched an "Operation Clean Slate" plan to combat botnets.[99] The Citadel botnet is malicious software which is a kind of bank Trojan horse program and is used to steal online banking certificates, credit card information, and other identifiable information. While governments around the world still don't know who the leader of the Citadel criminal organization is, the international cooperation has already given a heavy blow to the criminal organization. In this action, the FBI and its global partners acted jointly to oppose Citadel.[100] Through authorization of the courts and industrial partnership, more than 1400 control servers for botnets were removed and consequently the operation of these botnets was basically halted. It was estimated that the "Operation Clean Slate" protected more than 21 million computers from invasion of malware.

The US's fight against botnets through the "Operation Clean Slate" plan and the authorization of the courts demonstrate the existence of cyberspace sovereignty.

7.14.2 International "Operation Tovar" for Fighting Botnets

In June 2014, law enforcement agencies such as the United States Department of Justice, the European Criminal Police Organization, FBI, the British National Crime Bureau and South Africa police service and other relevant law enforcement agencies of Australia, the Netherlands, the European Union, Germany, France, Italy and Japan jointly launched the "Operation Tovar" which was an international law enforcement action for fighting a botnet called "Gameover Zenus". The "Operation Tovar" involved Dell Secure Works, Deloitte Cyber Risk Services, Microsoft, F-Secure,[101] McAfee, Symantec, Trend Micro, Carnegie Mellon University, Georgia Tech and other cooperative institutions. After investigation, Gameover Zenus was mainly used for bank fraud and blackmailing Internet users through invasion of computers. After the botnet infected the user's computer, the user's data file was encrypted by means of blackmail software called "Crypto Locker" and the user was required to pay Bitcoins to decrypt the file. The "Operation Tovar" successfully cut off the communication between the Gameover Zenus zombie computer and its control server.[102] In the action, the law enforcement department intercepted the botnet database that the criminals attempted to transfer, and which contained

[99]The FBI's Role in Cyber Security. https://www.fbi.gov/news/testimony/the-fbis-role-in-cyber-security [2016-9-11].

[100]Microsoft joins FBI to crack down on the botnet Citadel. http://tech.sina.com.cn/i/2013-06-06/22288419405.shtml [2016-9-11].

[101]Original name: Data Fellows, established in 1988 and headquartered in Helsinki of Finland, a famous computer and network security provider in Europe and even in the world.

[102]U.S. leads multi-national action against "Gameover Zeus" botnet and "Cryptolocker" ransomware, charges botnet administrator. U.S. Department of Justice. 2014-6-2. http://www.justice.gov/opa/pr/2014/June/14-crm-584.html [2016-9-11].

information about the botnet attacks, and identified a Russian hacker as the wire-puller of the botnet and filed a lawsuit against him.

According to the information released by the US Department of Justice, Gameover Zenus controlled 0.5–1 million computers running Windows around the world, 25% of which were in the United States. 1.3% of the infected users paid the hackers ransom, and many users avoided loss by backing up their data, while some users lost a lot of data. The total sum of money extorted by Gameover Zenus was estimated to be 3 million dollars.[103]

In August 2014, the security companies Fox-IT and FireEye, which participated in the above operation, established a website called "Decrypt CryptoLocker" to help users decrypt some of the files that were encrypted by the virus, by using the hacker database intercepted in the operation.

The "Operation Tovar", carried out by transnational organizations led by the US Department of Justice, showed the existence of cyberspace sovereignty in various countries and the joint efforts made by the sovereign states to attack hackers to safeguard their own interests.

7.15 Fighting Cyber Bank Crimes

Bank crime has always been the object of attack by governments. With the emergence of online finance, bank crime also turned to cyberspace. Criminals steal users' funds and commit credit card skimming through the cyberspace. Governments have also taken various measures to combat this crime.

7.15.1 Australia Cracked Down on Cyber Credit Card Skimming

On 29 November 2012, the Australian police arrested seven criminals in Romania through a joint investigation of the international criminal police, uncovering the biggest-ever credit card ID theft case in the history of Australia. The criminal gang used the hacker technology to steal account information to conduct Card Not Present (CNP) transactions or make fake credit cards, and then made thousands of false transactions across Asia, Europe, the United States and the world.[104]

---

[103]Wham bam: global Operation Tovar whacks CryptoLocker ransomware and Gameover Zeus botnet. Computer World. 2014-6-2. http://blogs.computerworld.com/cybercrime-and-hacking/23980/wham-bam-global-operation-tovar-whacks-cryptolocker-ransomware-gameover-zeus-botnet [2016-9-11].

[104]Romanian gang arrested in Australia's biggest-ever credit card ID theft. http://edition.cnn.com/2012/11/29/business/australia-credit-card-fraud/ [2016-9-11].

Brad Marden, a superintendent of the High-Tech Crime Investigation Unit of the Australian Federal Police, said that the gang had hacked into the computer systems of about 100 small retailers such as gas stations and grocery stores in Australia by using the hacker technology, obtaining nearly 500,000 Australian citizens' credit card information. The stolen credit card information was mostly used for overseas transfers, and the countries where the crimes took place included Hong Kong of China, the US, South Korea and some countries in Europe. As of the time when the case was broken, about 30,000 people's credit cards had been used for such illegal transfers, and the amount of money involved had been up to 30 million Australian dollars. In addition, the Romanian police confirmed that this criminal gang had sold the detailed information of about 68,000 credit cards to other criminals from around the world.[105]

"Without the cooperation of the other 13 countries and the assistance of the Australian banks and financial institutions," said Glen McEwen, head of the Digital Crime Action Group of the Australian Police, "it would be impossible to track these illegal transactions and capture the criminal gang in Romania."[106]

That Australia made international exchanges and cooperation with other countries to crack down on cyber credit card thefts in Australia showed that Australia exercised its cyberspace sovereignty.

7.15.2 The US Combated Thefts of Bank Users' Funds

On June 13, 2013, the New Jersey federal prosecutor launched a criminal charge against eight hackers, saying that they had tried to steal at least 15 million dollars in an international cybercrime from American clients targeting 15 financial institutions and government departments.[107] Federal prosecutor Paul Fishman said that the eight hackers conspired to hack into the computer systems, transferring customers' funds to bank accounts and prepaid debit cards and using ATMs to extract cash and conducting fraudulent purchasing activities in Georgia, New York and other places.[108]

An agent of the US Secret Service described this international cybercrime in the court documents. The federal prosecutor filed three charges of telecommunications fraud, money laundering and identity theft against the eight defendants. If the first

[105]Keep a close eye on your credit card bills. http://www.chinadaily.com.cn/hqgj/jryw/2012-11-30/content_7638492.html [2016-10-6].

[106]Australia broke a credit card information theft case involving 30 million Australian dollars. http://world.people.com.cn/n/2012/1130/c57507-19747578.html [2016-9-11].

[107]Eight Charged With Fraud, ID Theft, Money Laundering In Multimillion-Dollar International Cybercrime Scheme. https://www.justice.gov/usao-nj/pr/eight-charged-fraud-id-theft-money-laundering-multimillion-dollar-international [2016-9-11].

[108]Eight hackers attacked Citibank and other banks to steal tens of millions of dollars. http://news.xinhuanet.com/info/2013-06/13/c_132450744.htm [2016-10-6].

two charges were established, each defendant would face a term of imprisonment of up to 20 years; and if the third charge was established, they would face a maximum term of imprisonment of 15 years. Fishman said in a statement that “Cybercriminals have infiltrated some of our most trusted financial institutions.”[109]

That the United States arrested the hackers who attacked banks through ID theft and combated illegal cyber ID thefts showed that the United States exercised cyberspace sovereignty.

7.16 Cracking Down on E-Commerce Websites Which Sell Fake Products

In June 2014, the British intellectual property crime supervision department, in cooperation with the European Interpol, the US Immigration and Customs Enforcement Agency, investigated and shut down 188 transnational websites which sold fake products including mobile phones, sportswear, luxury goods, etc. Since the beginning of the cooperation program in 2012, the three parties have investigated and punished altogether 1349 websites selling counterfeit goods.[110]

October 17, 2014, the British High Court ruled that the five major network service providers including the British Telecom and Virgin Group must block six websites selling products which were fakes of the products of the Swiss Richemont, which provided a criterion for the businesses to request the network service providers to block the fake links.[111]

In 2014, the British intellectual property regulators investigated and closed 2500 fake-selling websites in eight months. The law enforcement agencies imposed criminal punishment on individuals who used the Internet to commit fraud and the circumstances of the crime were serious. In 2015, a man in Kent of England was sentenced to 16 months' imprisonment for selling counterfeit cosmetics and pirated audio and video products on the Internet.[112]

That the British administrative department cooperated with the law enforcement agencies to impose administrative penalties or criminal penalties on cyber-fraud and sale of fake goods demonstrated the existence of cyberspace sovereignty.

---

[109]Eight hackers attacked Citibank and other banks to steal tens of millions of dollars. http://news.xinhuanet.com/info/2013-06/13/c_132450744.htm [2016-9-11].

[110]188 Internet Domain Names Seized Selling Counterfeit Products. https://www.europol.europa.eu/content/188-Internet-domain-names-seized-selling-counterfeit-products [2016-9-11].

[111]Judgment. http://s.conjur.com.br/dl/uk-provedor-site-falsificado.pdf [2016-9-11].

[112]Britain did a good job in cracking down on online sale of counterfeits. http://world.people.com.cn/n/2015/0209/c1002-26528606.html [2016-10-6].

7.17 Fighting Cyber ID Theft

On December 23, 2015, the Australian Federal Police and the New South Wales Police recently arrested four members of a criminal group suspected of identity fraud in a joint search operation in the various regions of Sydney, seizing a large number of fake Medicare Cards, fake driver's licenses and fake credit cards. Authorities also seized fake documents and 60,000 dollars in cash as well as printers, computers, laminating machines and other tools for making fake identity documents.[113] Breaking this case showed that the means employed in Australia's most common types of fraud crimes—theft and identity documents forgery was becoming more and more advanced. With the assistance of the Federal Immigration and Border Protection Department, the Identity Security Strike Team (ISST) made up by the Federal Police and the New South Wales Police launched an "Operation Drax" in which four males with the ages of 33, 37, 44 and 50 were arrested and accused of being suspected of theft of identity documents.[114]

David Nockels, Assistant Director of the Australian Border Forces, pointed out that identity theft was the most common fraud crime in Australia, and the above latest case was just the tip of the iceberg. Peter Crozier, head of the division of anti property crimes, anti-fraud and anti-corruption at the Federal Police, said that the young people were most likely to be the victims of identity theft because they often hastily revealed their personal identity information on the social media; and small enterprises and government departments were also vulnerable to frauds using fake identity documents.[115]

The Australian government's efforts made in cyber identity management fully reflected its emphasis on cyberspace sovereignty.

7.18 Fighting Cyber Fraud

On December 26, 2012, a South Korean pair in their twenties claimed on the Internet that they sold infant milk powder at prices 30% lower than the market prices, but they disappeared after receiving remittance from the buyers, resulting in more than 130 South Korean netizens deceived, and the amount of fraud was up to

[113]Four nabbed in NSW high-quality ID theft. http://www.echo.net.au/2015/12/four-nabbed-in-nsw-high-quality-id-theft/ [2016-9-11].

[114]Four arrested in identity crime investigation–joint agency operation. http://newsroom.border.gov.au/channels/NEWS/releases/four-arrested-in-identity-crime-investigation-joint-agency-operation [2016-10-6].

[115]A gang stealing ID information to make fake IDs was captured, with 4 suspects arrested by police. http://oversea.stnn.cc/Au/2015/1224/271829.shtml [2016-9-11].

20 million won. The young man and young woman were finally arrested by the South Korean police for suspected cyber fraud.[116]

On December 10, 2012, the Korea Fair Trade Commission announced that from the year 2013 a "temporary termination system" of online trading would be implemented; that is, once it was found in the cyber transactions that a website cheated consumers or might bring great loss to consumers, the Korea Fair Trade Commission would suspend the website's online transactions, or temporarily close the website until the problem was resolved.[117]

The Korean law provides that where Internet users use the Internet to spread, sell or rent obscene pornographic videos and pictures, and use the Internet to publish news, videos, pictures and other information to a specific group of people to cause fear, anxiety and other unrest feelings in these people, the Internet users shall be sentenced to less than one year's imprisonment or a fine of not more than 10 million won.

That the South Korean government cracked down on cyber swindlers by means of criminal penalties demonstrated its exercise of cyberspace sovereignty.

7.19 Fighting Cyber Piracy

The international community has reached a consensus that once the piracy information is disseminated without control, the enthusiasm of innovation of the whole society and even the whole country will be frustrated in the long run, and the development of the cultural industry, the information technology industry and the like will be hindered. Thus, the countries in the world exercise cyberspace sovereignty to combat cyber piracy.

7.19.1 International "Operation Site Down" for Combating Cyber Privacy

In June 2005, an international joint action "Operation Site Down" led by the Federal Bureau of Investigation (FBI) and participated in by the law enforcement agencies from 10 other countries was launched to crack down on cyber privacy.[118] This operation was known as several enforcement actions for cracking down on piracy that infringed the intellectual property on the Internet, which included a

[116]South Korea keeps strengthening Internet management. http://legal.people.com.cn/n/2012/1226/c42510-20018994.html [2016-9-11].

[117]South Korea keeps strengthening Internet management (Supervision according to law in various countries Aspects of the Internet). http://www.chinalaw.gov.cn/article/xwzx/fzxw/201212/20121200379437.shtml [2016-10-6].

[118]Operation Site Down.Wikipedia. 2014-9-10. http://en.wikipedia.org/wiki/Operation_Site_Down [2016-9-11].

number of separate investigations in the United States, namely the "Operation Jolly Roger" in Chicago and the "Operation Copycat" in Charlotte and San Jose.

The above investigation operations were carried out in the United States for about 70 times and about 20 times in other countries, banning many major piracy organizations that published and traded pirated software, movies, music, games and the like on the Internet.[119]

In February 2006, the United States filed a lawsuit against 19 members of an organization called Risciso which engaged in pirated software and films.[120] As of May 2008, suspects of a total of 40 cases were convicted in this series of actions, with a total of 25 piracy websites and 11 piracy organizations being investigated in the actions. In the actions, the FBI also obtained the IP addresses of some providers of the top-level pirated products through the websites set up by undercover agents.[121]

As part of the defense work, most of the defendants agreed to surrender the electronic equipments seized by the police, including 118 computers, 13 laptops, 4567 pirated discs, 413 video tapes, 28 keyboards and monitors, 5 digital cameras, 28 game players, some telephones and microphones and the like.

The United States and other countries' crackdown on cyber piracy also reflect the existence of cyberspace sovereignty.

7.19.2 Sweden Cracked Down on Film Piracy

On September 8, 2010, the Swedish government announced that police from 14 European countries had launched a series of actions to jointly combat the pirated movie download websites. The main goal of the action was a large site called "The Scene" which specialized in providing pirated movies for users to download. This joint action successively destroyed 48 dens of "The Scene" all over Europe.[122] The Pirate Bay was forced to be offline for hours because of this sudden attack. The police arrested people suspected of infringing the copyright of others and detained a number of servers.

The above underground network was deemed to provide high-quality private content, resulting in a large number of popular movies published on the Internet before the release of DVD and blu-ray. The Swedish police raided a number of network addresses, one of which was in the suburbs of the capital city Stockholm

[119]FBI cracks down on 'warez' piracy sites. http://www.computerworld.com/s/article/102925/FBI_cracks_down_on_warez_piracy_sites [2016-9-11].

[120]19 Indicted In Software Piracy Plot. http://www.cbsnews.com/stories/2006/02/01/tech/main1270188.shtml [2016-9-11].

[121]Louis M. Reigel Assistant Director, Cyber Division Federal Bureau of Investigation. https://www.fbi.gov/news/speeches/operation-site-down [2016-9-11].

[122]Swedish police raid file sharing 'scene'. http://www.thelocal.se/20100907/28826 [2016-9-11].

and had been an information center for storing the Pirate Bay and Wikileaks and the other of which was located at Umea University.[123]

That the police from 14 European countries jointly launched a series of actions to combat the pirated movie download sites shows that various countries rely on cyberspace sovereignty to jointly safeguard the legitimate rights and interests of intellectual property owners.

7.20 Combating Cyber Pornography

The special projections to address the online pornographic and violent murder information are the most common special projections for combating cybercrimes. Taking the measures such as shutting down the websites and investigating the relevant people can often get huge disposal results and significant social impact in the short term.

7.20.1 The "Operation Avalanche" of the United States for Cracking Down on Cyber Child Pornography

Landslide Productions was founded in 1997 by an American programmer Thomas Reedy and was an Internet pornographic information service company located in Fort Worth, Texas. The service websites of the company did not directly provide services such as child pornographic images, but the company employed a business model similar to C2C to establish a public service platform for child porn resource owners and demanders to register, browse and pay. The pornographic business on the platform ran by itself, and the company collected about 35% of the users' registration fee as the source of profit. With the continuous expansion of the business, the company once became a very influential child porn service provider, with its business across more than 60 countries in three continents and having registered users of 300,000. However, due to the reason that some malicious users used a large quantity of false credit card information, Landslide Productions was closed in 1999.[124]

In August of the same year, in a joint investigation by about 50 law officials from several law enforcement agencies in the United States, a home computer with child pornographic images and evidence of users' obtaining of child pornographic information through the payment platform operated by Landslide Productions were found in the

[123] Zack Whittaker. Swedish ISP raided over links to PirateBay and Wikileaks. ZDNet. 2010-9-8. http://www.zdnet.com/article/swedish-isp-raided-over-links-to-pirate-bay-and-wikileaks/ [2016-9-11].

[124] Duncan Campbell. Operation Ore flawed by fraud. The Guardian. 2007-4-19. http://technology.guardian.co.uk/weekly/story/0,,2059832,00.html [2016-9-11].

residence of Riddy in Fort Worth. Accordingly, the police seized the assets and business records of Landslide Productions and arrested the Riddy couple. In January 2000, the couple was convicted on the grounds of trafficking in child pornography services, and the principal, Thomas Riddy, was sentenced to 18 years' imprisonment.[125]

In August 2001, after the destruction of Landslide Productions, the US law enforcement agencies cracked the company's database and obtained a lot of users' identity information. Based on the results of the investigation into Landslide Productions, the United States set up a nationwide working network of more than 30 federal government working groups to launch a special action called "Operation Avalanche" to combat child pornography, focusing on the search and collection of evidence of users' use of the access to child pornographic services and the payment system provided by Landslide Productions and making follow-up investigation into the ID of the users buying the pornographic services. In order to achieve this effect better, and as an important part of the operation, the government continued to run the Landslide Productions' website undercover for a period of time to collect information.[126]

The impact of "Operation Avalanche" was tremendous. Of the 144 US suspects, 100 were arrested in this special operation.[127] In addition, the FBI also obtained a large quantity of foreign users' identity information from the database of Landslide Productions, including the names of 7272 British users and the names of 2329 Canadian users. The FBI handed over the foreign users' information to the government agencies of the corresponding countries and carried out cross-border cooperation with the countries concerned, and a series of targeted investigation actions were set off, including "Operation Snowball"[128] in Canada, "Operation Ore"[129] in Britain, "Operation Amethyst"[130] in Ireland and "Operation Genesis"[131] in Switzerland, etc.[132]

In June 2000, Canadian investigators traveled to the United States to get the names of the Canadian users who were seized in the "Operation Avalanche" for alleged use of child pornography.[133] Unlike the countries such as the United States and Britain, because the Canadian police were not yet ready to deal with such a large-scale

[125]Operation Avalanche (child pornography investigation). https://en.wikipedia.org/wiki/Operation_Avalanche_(child_pornography_investigation) [2016-9-27].

[126]Operation Avalanche (child pornography investigation). Wikipedia. 2014-6-22. http://en.wikipedia.org/wiki/Operation_Avalanche_(child_pornography_investigation) [2016-9-11].

[127]Stephen Yagielowicz. Child Pornography: An Unsolvable Problem? XBIZ. 2001-8-10. http://www.xbiz.com/articles/1405 [2016-9-11].

[128]Computer child porn: Operation Snowball is a Witch-hunt. Injustice Busters. http://injusticebusters.org/2003/childporn_witchhunt.htm [2016-9-11].

[129]See Footnote 128.

[130]See Footnote 128.

[131]See Footnote 128.

[132]See Footnote 128.

[133]Sex Crime Sting Operation. Premier Defense Group. http://www.premierdefensegroup.com/sex-crime-sting-operations [2016-9-11].

nationwide investigation and arrest operation, it was then reported that the action was not fruitful and only touched the tip of the iceberg of Internet child pornography crime. The Canadian police arrested 100 suspects in the operation, less than 5% of the total number of suspects. Despite this, the "Operation Snowball" had become Canada's largest national action to combat Internet child pornography crime at that time.[134]

In May 2002, based on the name list provided by the FBI, Britain investigated and prosecuted 7272 British users who used Landslide Productions' website for child pornography. In this operation named "Operation Ore", under the circumstances of clear evidence, the British law enforcement agencies charged the pedophiles with the crime of holding child pornography information. For other users who were in Landslide Productions' user database but in whose houses no child pornographic images and other related information were found were charged with a minor offense of incitement to pornography. During the investigation, due to the huge number of people involved in the list provided by the FBI, the large-scale investigation had made the British law enforcement agencies very busy. However, the British standard processing procedure required that all pedophiles involved must be promptly arrested because their presence posed a great potential threat to some children. For this reason, the police applied to the government for a special fund for promoting this action. It was reported that the "Operation Ore" cost about 7 million pounds[135] and finally arrested 3744 suspects,[136] giving a heavy blow to the pedophiles in Britain.

That the United States and other countries took the measures such as closing suspected websites and investigating relevant suspects to combat cyber child pornography highlights the effective exercise of cyberspace sovereignty.

7.20.2 Germany Combated Cross-Border Child Porn Networks

In September 2003, Germany launched a special investigation campaign against transnational child pornography networks. In this operation, 26,500 suspects from 166 countries were suspected of spreading child pornographic pictures on the Internet. In the course of the investigation, the court asked the Internet service providers to provide the information of the 1000 suspects, and the police therefore obtained a list containing 38,000 e-mails and thousands of illegal pictures, and searched more than 500 shelters all over Germany, confiscating 745 computers, 5800 videotapes, 35,500 CDs and 8300 floppy disks and exposing a total of 38

[134]See Footnote 128.

[135]Operation Avalanche: Tracking child porn. BBC News. 2002-11-11. http://news.bbc.co.uk/2/hi/uk_news/2445065.stm [2016-9-11].

[136]Rebecca Smithers. Staff at public school in child porn inquiry. The Guardian. 2003-9-27. http://www.theguardian.com/uk/2003/jan/25/schools.publicschools [2016-9-11].

Internet groups that exchanged child pornographic pictures. Among the suspects, there were police officers, doctors and teachers, etc.[137]

In September 2009, the German Federal Criminal Investigation Agency launched a nationwide large-scale campaign to combat child pornography crimes on the Internet. Approximately 800 policemen participated in a two-day raid. The police searched altogether 163 office locations and shelters and arrested nine suspects and seized 220 computers and several digital storage devices such as CD-ROM and hard drives. The police suspected that these suspects were members of a German online pedophile community and were suspected of abusing children and spreading child pornographic information. Since January 2009, the German police had investigated a total of 136 child porn suspects. While the German police carried out the above operation, the police in Austria, Bulgaria, Switzerland, Canada and the United States also launched searches for Internet child pornography suspects.[138]

That Germany imposed legal means on the spread of unhealthy information in cyberspace demonstrated Germany's cyberspace sovereignty.

7.21 Combating Online Gambling

In October 2012, Israel launched a one-year secret investigation by the police, tax authorities and money-laundering research institutions, which cracked the country's largest-ever illegal online gambling network. The online gambling network relied on a website called Don-Bet.[139] Israeli law stipulates that only the gambling activities of the Israeli Sports Gaming Commission and the National Gaming Center are lawful while other online gambling activities are illegal.[140] The Don-Bet website appeared to be a legitimate online gambling site that showed links to credit card payment options, but in fact engaged in illegal online gambling. Don-Bet employed specialized brokers to solicit customers and take charge of financial transactions.[141]

The police monitored the suspects' calls and tracked the group's capital operation flow. The site is said to have more than 200 brokers and have more than 3000 fixed customers in Israel. Don-Bet had been in operation for more than five years

[137]Richard Bernstein. Germany Says It Uncovered Huge Child Pornography Ring. The New York Times. 2003-9-27. http://www.nytimes.com/2003/09/27/world/germany-says-it-uncovered-huge-child-pornography-ring.html [2016-9-11].

[138]Nine Internet child porn suspects arrested in Germany. http://news.sina.com.cn/w/2009-10-01/121018766225.shtml [2016-10-6].

[139]Peter Amsel. Israeli police bust 'biggest illegal online gambling network' in country's history. CalvinAyre.com. 2012-10-10. http://calvinayre.com/2012/10/10/business/israeli-police-bust-biggest-don-bet-illegal-online-gambling-network/ [2016-9-11].

[140]Online Casino City: Israel. http://online.casinocity.com/jurisdictions/israel/ [2016-9-11].

[141]Israeli Police Bust 'Biggest Illegal Online Gambling Network' in Country's History. http://calvinayre.com/2012/10/10/business/israeli-police-bust-biggest-don-bet-illegal-online-gambling-network/ [2016-9-11].

and the sum of money involved in the last two and a half years reached 1 billion dollars. In this operation, about 200 police officers raided the homes of 44 suspects and took them away. The cash exchange points in places such as Tel Aviv, Bat Yam, Herzliya, Rishon Lezion in Israel were also raided, and the police confiscated the cash found and the information related to the operation of Don-Bet. A certain proportion of the homepages of the server of Don-Bet in Israel was replaced by the content that "the site is being upgraded; please try again in a few minutes".[142]

Israel's crackdown on cyber gambling shows that the content of web servers is regulated by the government and reflects Israel's exercise of cyberspace sovereignty.

7.22 Fighting the Spread of Spam

In 2009, the Australian Communications and Media Administration filed a lawsuit against a man named Lance Thomas Atkinson who sent many spam messages of advertisements of herbal products, watches and the like. The Brisbane Federal Court of Australia fined the man 210,000 Australian dollars and forbade him to take the initiative to send commercial e-mail in the next seven years.[143]

Atkinson and his brother in New Zealand operated a website that had businesses in the US, Australia, New Zealand, China, India, Russia and Canada. It was estimated that as many as one-third of the world's spam messages were likely to be related to the brothers. In 14 months, there had been 61 days leading the sending of spam. They also hired people to send billions of spam messages every day, selling aphrodisiacs, diet pills and prescription drugs.[144] The man had previously admitted that he had been involved in an international spam network that could send 10 billion spam messages in one day, and the inspecting authorities accused him of being the master of the world's largest known "spam gang".

The Australian Communications and Media Administration filed a lawsuit against Atkinson under the Australian Anti-Spam Act, and the Australian citizens had previously filed more than 100,000 spam complaints. The US court also fined the Atkinson's website 15.5 million dollars.

Regarding the penalty for spam, the civil liability stipulated in Australia is stringent. At the same time, the object of punishment includes not only their native people but also foreigners who send spam to Australia, showed that Australia exercises its cyberspace sovereignty.

---

[142]Police bust multi-billion online gambling ring. http://www.jpost.com/National-News/Police-bust-multi-billion-online-gambling-ring [2016-9-11].

[143]Herbal King Ringleader Fined in Australia. http://news.softpedia.com/news/Herbal-King-Ringleader-Fined-in-Australia-130481.shtml [2016-9-11].

[144]"King of Spam" Fined 186,000 dollars in Australia. http://tech.sina.com.cn/i/2009-12-22/20333700802.shtml [2016-9-11].

Chapter 8
Positions of States Toward Cyberspace and Cyber-Relating Regulations

Abstract In cyberspace, countries hold their own position in accordance with its own interests. Laws and regulations launched by governments are the best manifestation. Governments of all countries have promulgated relevant laws and regulations on defending national security, maintaining social order, guaranteeing cybersecurity and cyberspace order, protecting data security and personal privacy. China has also issued the Cybersecurity Law to establish the principle of cyberspace sovereignty.

Keywords Laws and regulations concerning cyberspace · National positions of the governments toward cyberspace · Cybersecurity law of China

The core proposition of cyberspace governance for various States and regions is to enable cyber communication, industry and security to be intertwined with each other in competition and cooperation, and to be unified in order. This is also a legislative problem confronting all States in the world.

China, based on its own domestic and foreign needs, is forming a rule of law for cyberspace featured with Chinese characteristic, with the National Security Law and the Cyber Security Law as the core, covering "five levels" of overall leadership, decision arrangement and overall planning, coordination, concerted efforts, and local responsibility. The rule of law includes the department of overall leadership for national security (National Security Council), the department of decision arrangement and overall planning for cyberspace security (Central and Provincial Cyber Security and Informatization Leading Group, the State Council, and Municipal Governments of the provinces, autonomous regions and municipalities), the department of coordination for cyberspace security (National Net Info management Department), and various relative national departments of concerted efforts for net message service (Competent authority of the State Council for net-info management, the public security sector and other relating sectors), and local responsible departments (municipal governments above county level and relative local management).

In fact, various sovereign States are in the development of different cyberspace sovereignty rule of law system. The Central Net-Info Management Office of China

B. Fang, *Cyberspace Sovereignty*,
https://doi.org/10.1007/978-981-13-0320-3_8

organized a compilation of over 50 network legislations of the USA, Russia, Germany, the UK, Australia, New Zealand, Japan, Singapore, India, Thailand, Vietnam and other States and the EU, and compiled the "Chinese Regulations and Provisions of the Internet",[1] including five categories of laws, regulations, rules, normative documents and judicial interpretations, to explain the rule of law of cyberspace featured with Chinese characteristics.

In the United States, for example, the National Telecommunications and Information Administration website (NTIA) sets out more than 200 US-based rules of cyberspace sovereignty having been issued since 1901, which indicates that States are building their own cyberspace law system.

8.1 The Current Overall View of Cyberspace of the United Nations

Since the United Nations Conference on Information Society and Development in South Africa in 1996 and the Ministerial Conference on Terrorism held in Paris by the United Nations in 1999 has made the following actions: ① starting to note that "dissemination and use of information and communication technologies relates to the interests of the international community as a whole"; ② Starting to "express concern that information and communication technologies and means may be used for a purpose that in conformity with maintenance of international stability and security and adversely affect the security of each State"; ③ Call upon all member States to submit reports to inform the Secretary-General of their "definition of various basic concepts relating information security", "overall view of information security issues", and their ideas on "whether international principles should be established to enhance the security of global information and telecommunication systems"; ④ Starting to include the topic of "Development of information and telecommunications in the context of international security" in the agenda of the United Nations General Assembly. By far, the United Nation has organized the member States to summarize the 20-year history of refining information and understanding of information cyberspace.

Through 20 years of thinking, communication, mediation and game, the United Nations General Assembly emphasizes the importance of the application of the Charter of the United Nations and the principle of sovereignty in cyberspace. Specifically, ① it is proposed that the Charter of the United Nations and the principle of sovereignty are the foundation for improving safety in the use of information and communication technology; ② in the context of refining an overall view of cyberspace, the United Nations General Assembly proposed "five

[1]Central Cyber Security and Information Leading Group Office. National Internet Information Office Policy and Regulation Bureau. Compilation of Chinese Internet Regulations and Provisions (First Edition, Hardcover) (2015) China Legal Publishing House, Beijing. http://spu.jd.com/1681195069.html [2016-12-4].

principles of international information and communication technology environment", and pointed out that an information and communication technology environment that is "open, safe, stable, free of obstacles, and peaceful"[2] is of great importance to everyone, that such an environment requires solid cooperation of the States to reduce risks confronting international peace and safety.

About the definition of cyberspace, the United Nations has reached basic consensus on two issues.

(1) The "ICT-related activities" consensus and the "ICT-infrastructure within their territory" consensus (hereinafter referred to as the "IC activity consensus" and the "cyber facility consensus"), which bridges state sovereignty and the International laws.
(2) In Document A/68/98 of the UN issued on June 24, 2013 and titled "Group of Governmental Experts on Developments in the Field of Information and Telecommunications in the Context of International Security",[3] the United Nations General Assembly has arrived at the principles for the application of state sovereignty and International laws in information and communication activities and information and communication infrastructures, i.e. "state sovereignty and international norms and principles derived from sovereignty is applicable to national ICT activities and to national jurisdiction over ICT infrastructures in their territories."

In general, the United Nations in the future will, based on the IC activity consensus and the cyber facility consensus, set up on a journey of seeking international co-governance of cyberspace. These two consensus definitions are broadly defined above the "activities" and "facilities" elements, and the "role" and "data" of the network are not clear, indicating that the issue has not yet been further developed at the United Nations level. These two consensuses are broadly defined based on the elements of "activities" and "facilities", and the "role" and "data" of cyber is not clarified, which means that this issue has not yet been further developed in the United Nations.

Certainly, "activity" also contains the factor of the role, and the "facilities" includes the factor carrying data. As the United Nations has not yet discussed the details, cross-border judicial conflicts and other issues are not included in discussion. Although the United Nations has not reached a unified conclusion on the subject and the sovereignty of information in the territories, the consensuses on the "activities" and the "facilities" in cyberspace is rooted in the territorial sovereignty of all States.

---

[2]Report of Group of Governmental Experts on Developments in the Field of Information and Telecommunications in the Context of International Security, article 2 in the introduction. http://www.un.org/ga/search/view_doc.asp?symbol=A/70/174&referer=/english/&Lang=C [2016-12-4].

[3]Tentative schedule Project 94 of the 68th session of United Nations Conference, Developments in the field of information and telecommunications in the context of international security. http://www.un.org/ga/search/view_doc.asp?symbol=A/68/98&referer=/english/&Lang=C [2016-9-1].

8.2 Positions of the Governments of Various States Toward Cyberspace

At the 68th session of the United Nations Conference held in 2013, the Group of Governmental Experts, which is composed of 15 representative States, has reached a consensus on the issue of "Development of Information and Telecommunications from the Perspective of International Security", and recognized in the report of the Group of Governmental Experts the idea of cyberspace sovereignty. Later, the United States subsequently in the tentative project items (Project 93)[4] of the 69th session of the United Nations Conference on June 30, 2014, the tentative schedule (Project 92)[5] of the United Nations Conference on September 18, 2014, the tentative agenda (Project 93)[6] of the 70th session of the United Nations Conference on July 22, 2015, and the tentative schedule (Project 94)[7] of the United Nations Conference on July 19, 2015 issued the report of the Secretary-General titled "Development of Information and Telecommunications from the Perspective of International Security". In the report, there are provided the views and suggestions of the governments regarding the subject of "Development of Information and Telecommunications from the Perspective of International Security". States that submitted their opinions on the above subject to the United Nations include Albania, Australia, Austria, Botswana, Brazil, Canada, Colombia, Cuba, Egypt, EI Salvador, Estonia, Finland, France, Georgia, Germany, India, Indonesia Japan, Jordan, Kazakhstan, Kenya, Lebanon, Mexico, Netherlands, Panama, Peru, Poland, Portugal, Qatar, South Korea, Russia, Senegal, Serbia, Spain, Sweden, Switzerland, Togo, Turkmenistan, the United Kingdom, and United States of America.

8.2.1 Albania

Albania holds the idea that the main priority around information security secrecy and protection is the signing of a safety procedure agreement between Albania and the European Union on the exchange and protection of confidential information. In

---

[4]Report of the Secretary-General on Development of Information and Telecommunications from the Perspective of International Security. http://www.un.org/ga/search/view_doc.asp?symbol=A/69/112&referer=/english/&Lang=C [2016-9-12].

[5]Report of the Secretary-General on Development of Information and Telecommunications from the Perspective of International Security (addition). http://www.un.org/ga/search/view_doc.asp?symbol=A/69/112/ADD.1&referer=/english/&Lang=C [2016-9-20].

[6]Report of the Secretary-General on Development of Information and Telecommunications from the Perspective of International Security. http://www.un.org/ga/search/view_doc.asp?symbol=A/70/172&referer=/english/&Lang=C [2016-9-12].

[7]Report of the Secretary-General on Development of Information and Telecommunications from the Perspective of International Security. http://www.un.org/ga/search/view_doc.asp?symbol=A/71/172&referer=/english/&Lang=C [2016-9-19].

order to take measures, Albania has amended the relevant laws and regulations so as to strengthen information security and to promote relevant international cooperation.

On March 4, 2015, it was stated in the Albanian Council of Ministers Decision No. 189 "to ensure that confidential information [is] marked as 'national secrets' and physical security of NATO information". On October 22, 2014, Ministerial Conference Decision No. 701 stated the "approval of the rules for ensuring confidentiality of information security in the industrial sector". Albania has more comprehensive laws and regulations on physical protection of confidential information. Considering the different levels of confidential information, Albania redefines and locates the "security realm".

Albania believes that, following the adoption of new decisions on the safety of staff, inter-agency cooperation, oversight and national institutional inspections are increased. The national structures start to revise the list of staff responsibilities and issue relevant safety certificates in accordance with the area of responsibility.

About industrial safety, Albania reviewed with special attention to information security policies. Another important step highlighted by Albania is the elaboration of a new law dealing with confidential information, which will remain efficient, modern and consistent with the high standards of Europe.

As shown above, the focus of Albania in cyberspace security lies in the field of information secrecy. But Albania regulates confidentiality in cyberspace through legislation.

8.2.2 Australia

Australia holds the idea that the existing International laws provide, where applicable, a framework for the State's response to acts in cyberspace and illegal activities on the Internet, including the International Humanitarian Law, laws on the use of force, international human rights law and International laws on State responsibility. When any new or additional national cyberspace norm is established, the International laws shall be obeyed.

The consensus report "Group of Governmental Experts on Developments in the Field of Information and Telecommunications in the Context of International Security" is of great guiding significance to the States. The report States that International laws, especially the Charter of the United Nations, is applicable to the use of cyberspace by the States and is indispensable for the maintenance of peace and stability. Australia considers this conclusion to be fundamental. Australia believes that the States should individually and collectively publicly reaffirm their understanding that International law is applicable to the acts of the States in cyberspace and undertakes to act in cyberspace in accordance with its understanding of the International laws.

Australia believes that, given the common interest in protecting the global dimension of the Internet, it is necessary to make further efforts to clarify how key concepts such as sovereignty and jurisdiction can be applied to cyberspace. The report of the Group of Governmental Experts 2015 sets out voluntary guidelines on key infrastructure protection, computer emergency response organizations, national responsibility for assistance, cooperation against cybercrime, prevention of diffusion of malicious network tools and technology. The above guidelines may have further development. It is important to shift confidence-building measures from promoting transparency to implementing cooperative measures.

Australia believes that, while recognizing the complexity of the issues involved, it is a priority for the international community to clarify how International laws apply to acts of cyberspace in conflict and non-conflict situations. Australia recognizes that it is a long-term task to clarify the application of International laws to the use of cyberspace by the State. In the short term, it is necessary to take practical measures to address and prevent problems that may arise from misinterpretation between States and may lead to conflict due to miscarriage of justice and escalation. Regional security organizations are particularly well suited to consider, develop and implement network confidence-building measures. Australia is taking the lead in working with the Association of South-East Asian Nations (ASEAN) Regional Forum to advance this important agenda; given the differences in capability of the Member States, the agenda should include capability-building objectives.

Australia believes that cyber security is intrinsically linked to innovation and national security. Network security is the foundation of innovation, growth and prosperity, and is also a global opportunity for governments, the private sector and communities to invest and at the same benefit from it. Global society needs to accurately understand the network security. Each role, including government, enterprise and individual, should work together to create a trustworthy cyber environment. This is not only for the protection of key information, but also for providing an innovative and thriving environment, so that the technical industries can flourish. There is a need to take advantage of growing global demand to deliver better cyber security solutions, equipment and technicians.

Australia recognizes that strong cyber security is an essential element of global economic growth and prosperity. In 2015, Australia reviewed its approach to cyber security and launched a new cyber security strategy on 21 April 2016.

Australia believes that the States, when implementing prevention of the spread of malicious ICT tools, should give due consideration to the legitimate interests of cyber, enterprises and the research community.

The purpose of the establishment of Confidence Building Measures (CBM) is to solve the problems of accidents involving national security. However, priorities should be sorted out; merely those cyber accidents having significant impacts have the need of engaging the policy-level contact points.

Australia considers capability building as an important aspect of national cyber security strategy, and the government works closely with private cyber research institutions in this regard.

From the above point of view, Australia mainly focuses on the following six aspects of cyberspace security: first, the application of International laws in cyberspace; second, existence of sovereignty and jurisdiction in cyberspace; third, support of a credible cyber environment to an innovative environment; fourth, the role of cyber security in economic growth; fifth, the control of ICT tools should not affect the legitimate use; sixth, strengthening cooperation with the private sector to improve capability building, and to build national emergency response contacts.

8.2.3 Austria

Austria believes that the "Austrian Strategy for Cyber Security"[8] (Österreichische Strategie für Cyber Sicherheit), which is approved in March 2013, provides a comprehensive and positive approach to protecting people in cyberspace while ensuring human rights. It enhances safety and viability of Austrian cyberspace infrastructure and services. Most importantly, it contributes to the establishment of Austrian social awareness and confidence. In the "Austrian Strategy for Cyber Security", global liaison and international cooperation are of paramount importance.

Austria believes that cyberspace security is guaranteed through policy coordination at both national and international levels. Austria will actively participate in "Cyber Diplomacy" within the framework of the European Union, the United Nations, the Organization for Security and Cooperation in Europe, the Council of Europe, the Organization for Economic Cooperation and Development and the North Atlantic Treaty Organization, with a coordinated and targeted approach.

Austria will vigorously promote the implementation of the European Union Network Security Strategy and participate fully in the strategic and operational work of the European Union. The competent authorities will take necessary measures to implement and make full use of the European Treaty Series—No. 185, Cyber-crime Convention.[9] Austria advocates free Internet at the international level, emphasizes the need to guarantee free exercise of all human rights in cyberspace. The right of expression and information freedom on the Internet shall not be inappropriately restricted. Austria will continue to carry out bilateral cooperation within the framework of NATO partnership and actively support the preparation of a list of specific OSCE confidence-building and security measures. Austria is actively involved in the planning and implementation of transnational cyber exercises, with the experience gained directly integrated into the planning and for further development of business cooperation. The Ministry of Foreign Affairs coordinates diplomatic measures concerning cyber security and, as appropriate, considers bilateral or international agreements.

[8]Österreichische Strategie für Cyber Sicherheit. https://www.bka.gv.at/DocView.axd?CobId=50748 [2016-10-6].

[9]Cyber-crime Convention. http://www.europarl.europa.eu/meetdocs/2014_2019/documents/libe/dv/7_conv_budapest_/7_conv_budapest_en.pdf [2016-10-6].

In Austria, a steering group is developing an implementation plan for the "Austrian Strategy for Cyber Security". Under the coordination of the steering group, the competent bodies are responsible for the implementation of these measures within their respective mandates. The competent bodies will develop sub-strategies in the areas of their respective responsibilities under the "Austrian Strategy for Cyber Security". One of the tasks undertaken by the ministries participating in the Steering Group is to submit two implementation plans to the federal government each year. The "Austrian Strategy for Cyber Security" will be reviewed when the plans are drafted, and the strategy would be revised and updated where necessary.

As shown above, Austria believes that cyber security requires cooperation between domestic and international level and then focus on cyber space security is mainly in two aspects: the implementation of the Austrian Strategy for Cyber Security and the landing of the European Union cyber security strategy.

8.2.4 Botswana

Botswana hopes that the international community may help solve the problem of product safety inspection so as to prevent multinational companies from causing any harm to the citizens with the ICT technology they export.

Botswana believes that, when a network service provider supervises cyber activity and website information, it should ensure that human rights, privacy right, and the like are not violated; if the international community requests terrorist websites to be shut down, it is necessary to determine that the request is also in conformity with the national law.

The personal information obtained in our State should be retained within our territory. However, as Botswana lacks the power to influence transnational corporations, it cannot yet propose such a legal requirement to protect the data stored on the cloud.

In general, Botswana has mainly stressed the need to protect its national cyber security. However, due to the small size of the State, Botswana may be powerless in some areas and need support from the international community. Botswana recognizes sovereign action in cyberspace.

8.2.5 Brazil

On 24 September 2013, Mrs. Dilma Rousseff, President of Brazil, spoke in her general debate at the 68th session of the United Nations General Assembly that the act of the United States of monitoring of e-mails and phone calls of Brazilian citizens and government agencies violated the International laws, the guiding principles of relations between States, as well as the principle of good neighborliness, which is a serious violation of the privacy rights, freedom of expression and civil liberty of Brazilian citizens, and constitutes a violation against the sovereignty of Brazil. Brazil emphasized that sovereignty cannot be maintained by violating the sovereignty of another State, and the security of citizens cannot be defended by destroying the fundamental rights of citizens of another State.[10]

On September 17, 2013, Bradley Brooks and Frank Bajak published an article on Brazilian cyber sovereignty on the Yahoo website of the United States. The tile of the article was Brazil looks to break from US-centric Internet.[11] The article pointed out the following contents: in December, countries advocating greater "cyber-sovereignty" pushed for such control at an International Telecommunications Union meeting in Dubai, with Western democracies led by the United States and the European Union in opposition. The article also described some important initiatives of Brazil to break from the US-centric Internet: ① urging the Brazilian parliament to force Facebook, Google and other enterprises to accept the requests for the data stored in Brazil to be retained within Brazil; ② planning to build more Internet nodes and a bunch of data transmission hubs, so as to ensure that the flow passing through Brazil keeps away from potential interception; ③ intending to increase cyber connection with other States; ④ planning to create an encrypted e-mail service next year to replace Google, Gmail and Yahoo e-mail service.

Brazil believes that, there should be a corresponding legal framework for international conflicts regarding cyberspace, so as to resolve disputes peacefully; that prohibitions shall be clearly enumerated; a survey platform should be established to avoid determining a State as an agent of cyber-attack without consent of the concerned State. When international rules, norms and principles are being set to manage cyberspace acts of States, developing countries should be directly involved in the process; In terms of cyberspace governance the works shall be carried out through the United Nations. The principle of countervailing leaves a risk that may lead to instability of the new technological environment, exacerbating the seriousness of the matter and causing an escalation of the conflict. The provisions of Article 51 of the Charter of the United Nations are not applicable to cyber-attacks, because in many cases, it is difficult to determine the cyber attacker. ICT should be used for peaceful purposes, and military use of ICT should be banned. At least, it should be forbidden to use ICT to implement an attack.

As shown above, there are four major aspects of focus in cyberspace security of Brazil: the first is to emphasize cyber sovereignty and guarantee data security; the second is to prevent data from being intercepted by other States; the third is to avoid militarization of information technology; the fourth is that the Laws of Armed Conflict of the United Nations is not applicable for cyberspace.

---

[10]President Roosevelt Protesting at UN, Communication in Brazil being monitored. http://www.un.org/chinese/News/story.asp?newsID=20568 [2016-9-9].

[11]Bradley Brooks, Frank Bajak. Brazil looks to break from US-centric Internet. 2013-09-17. http://news.yahoo.com/brazil-looks-break-us-centric-internet-040702309.html [2016-9-21].

8.2.6 Canada

Canada believes that cyberspace, which is a driving force for economic growth, innovation and social development, improves social interaction and changes the industry and governance. At the same time, cyberspace has brought new threats and challenges to the society (e.g., cyber bullying, cybercrime and the use of the Internet for horrific purposes). The report of the Group of Governmental Experts of Canada in 2013 says: it was a great pleasure to see various States clearly affirm that the International law is applicable to cyberspace and to national use of ICTs as the cornerstone of codes of conduct and principles for the responsible nations. Canada will continue to contribute to the establishment of a code of conduct of States in cyberspace in a peaceful era. We will promote the results of the United Nations Group of Governmental Experts in the year 2012–2013 and the year 2014–2015. This will help to maintain an environment, in which national actions are guided by a responsible code of conduct, and stability of cyberspace is supported; confidence-building measures have been proved to be able to mitigate tensions and reduce the risk of armed conflict.[12]

Canada believes that a free, open and secure cyberspace is essential to global security, economic prosperity and the promotion of human rights, democracy and inclusion; that any approach to cope with cybercrime must respect human rights and fundamental freedom at the same time.

Canada believes that cyber security is not only for the economic prosperity of Canada, but also to support Canadian values and interests and to protect the safety of Canadian citizens. Canada has a strong interest in maintaining a free, open and secure Internet.[13]

(1) At the national level, the Canadian government has been working to help ensure the security of the Canadian cyber system since the introduction of the cyber security strategy in 2010, providing protection for the Canadian people's access to the Internet, and guaranteeing cyber security of Canada through active collaboration with major infrastructure sectors (e.g., finance, transportation and energy).
(2) Canada has established a cyber-incident management framework to coordinate at the national level the management and coordination of cyber threats or cyber incidents that may or will emerge. Canada also launched a public awareness campaign to "ensure cyber security". The government has also recently undertaken to review the existing measures to protect the Canadian people and key infrastructure from cyber threats. Canada is working closely

[12]Developments in the Field of Information and Telecommunications in the Context of International Security. https://unoda-web.s3-accelerate.amazonaws.com/wp-content/uploads/2014/10/Canada.pdf [2016-9-19].

[13]Developments in the Field of Information and Telecommunications in the Context of International Security. https://unoda-web.s3-accelerate.amazonaws.com/wp-content/uploads/2015/08/CanadaISinfull.pdf [2016-9-19].

with multilateral partners and private sector partners to enhance cyber security on which economic prosperity and security rely.

(3) Canada's new anti-spam legislation helps clarify legal rights and obligations, clarifies the respective responsibilities of government agencies, and strengthens law enforcement and international cooperation.
(4) At the international level, Canada supports cyber security capability-building projects, mainly in the Americas and South-East Asian States, including the establishment of computer emergency response organizations.
(5) Canada supports the efforts of the North Atlantic Treaty Organization and its allies for strengthening the cyber security alliance. Canada ratified the Budapest Convention in July 2015 and encouraged various States to become parties to the Convention or to take the Convention as a model for the implementation of national laws on cybercrime.
(6) Canada and the Association of South-East Asian Nations (ASEAN) Regional Forum cooperate to carry out capability-building activities, highlighting the significance of confidence-building measures and transparency measures in terms of achieving cyberspace security.
(7) Canada and the United States, through the Canadian and the United States' network security action plan, cooperate to strengthen their own network infrastructure and defense capabilities, enhance interaction, collaboration and information sharing at business and strategic level.
(8) Canada is also involved in the actions of the Group of Seven, the United Nations Office on Drugs and Crime, the Organization of American States and ASEAN in combatting cybercrime. Canada is also a member of the Global Coalition against Child Sexual Abuse.
(9) Canada is a founding partner of the Global Network Expert Forum. Canada recommends that all member States interested in strengthening cyber security and preventing cybercrime refer to the European Commission's Cybercrime Convention.

Canada holds the following opinions: accountability of source of international attacks should be prudently dealt with; legal accountability is governed by law of State responsibility; the international standard of accountability shall not be set as such international standards of accountability, otherwise the sovereignty of States will be violated, and sovereignty of the injured State will be violated.

Counter-measures are an integral part of state sovereignty which shall be respected by the International laws.

The principles including sovereignty equality are a part of the International laws. When supporting state sovereignty, other obligations shall be supported as well, including the general obligations prescribed by the International laws, the International Humanitarian Law, the International Human Rights Law and the Customary International laws.

Some ICTs are legally even used in military actions. When the Council authorizes military operations, military use of ICT cannot be ruled out.

As shown above, Canada mainly focuses on the following six aspects of cyberspace security: the first is the application of the International laws in cyberspace, especially to encourage the international community to establish a code of conduct in cyberspace; the second is to approve cyberspace sovereignty, and recognize that countervailing measures and accountability are within the scope of national sovereignty and shall not be applied an international standard; the third is to emphasize human rights and freedom in cyberspace; the fourth is to implement their national cyberspace security strategy, and take measures to deal with the threat from cyberspace; the fifth is to strengthen international cooperation in order to cope with the problems in cyberspace with various methods; the sixth is to be prudent in controlling ICT tools, because there is a demand for legal proliferation.

8.2.7 Colombia

Colombia believes that[14] significant progress has been made in the development and application of information and communication technologies in recent years, bringing changes and benefits that have played a significant role in the development of many States, and at meantime promoting international cooperation in the dissemination of information. However, there is a concern that these advances may be used to undermine international stability and security and adversely affect the integrity of national infrastructure, thereby weakening national civil and military security. As a result, Colombia is extremely concerned about computer threats formed by the use of new technologies and the threat of cybercrime, and Colombia considers these issues of great importance to the State. Therefore, Colombia must define policies and strategies to prevent the use of information technology for terrorist or criminal purposes.

Colombia introduced the ISO 27001 standard in 2005 as a quality standard for national entities using information security management systems to maintain confidentiality, integrity and availability of information. In 2009, the Congress of the Republic of Colombia issued Decree No. 1273 of the Penal Code, i.e., the "Information and Data Protection". The amendment sets the national legal framework for the prosecution and trial of information technology-related offenses by relevant authorities. In this framework, Colombia criminalizes the following acts: illegal entry, illegal interception, attack on integrity of data, attack system integrity, abuse of information technology devices, computer forgery, computer fraud, child pornography and crime of infringement of intellectual property rights and related rights. Colombia enacted a legal framework for the protection of personal data through Act No. 1581 of 2012 and Decree No. 1377 of 2013, which partially

---

[14]Avances en la esfera de la información y las telecomunicaciones en el contexto de la seguridad internacional. https://unoda-web.s3-accelerate.amazonaws.com/wp-content/uploads/2014/07/Colombia.pdf [2016-9-19].

governs the decree of the Act. In addition, a Personal Data Protection Division was established under the Industrial and Trade Inspectorate. The Ministry of Information Technology and Communications has also developed and implemented a government online strategy that requires the use of information security management system for information entities.

Colombia has recently launched a new national digital security strategy to ensure that the Colombian Government, public and private organizations, law enforcement officers, the academics and individuals are able to have maximal access to economic and social benefits in a reliable and secure digital environment, meanwhile significantly increasing the competitiveness and productivity of all sectors of the economy. The policy was set by several stakeholders, as contained in Document CONPES 3854 issued in 2016. Colombia became, thanks to this policy, one of the first States in the world to include in national strategy the digital security risk management recommendations issued by the Organization for Economic Cooperation and Development in September 2015, and Colombia is also the first State in the region to do so. Colombia's national digital security strategy includes the following aspects.

(1) To develop a clear framework for digital security systems. For this purpose, coordination and advisory bodies will be established at the highest level of government; and cross-sectorial liaison offices will be established in all units of national administration.
(2) To create appropriate conditions that enable a wide range of stakeholders to manage digital security risks in socio-economic activities; and to build confidence during the use of the digital environment, including the establishment of mechanisms for active and sustained participation to ensure the development of appropriate laws and regulatory frameworks, as well as providing training for responsible acts in the digital environment.
(3) Risk management practices will be adopted to strengthen national defense and security in the digital environment at the national and transnational levels. Finally, it is equally important to establish a standing mechanism with strategic priorities to promote cooperation, collaboration and assistance in the field of digital security at the national and international levels.

In 2011, Colombia introduced the National Network Defense and Network Security Policy[15] through Document CONPES 3701, which is based on three basic pillars:

(1) To adopt appropriate inter-agency frameworks for prevention, coordination and monitoring purposes and to provide suggestions for addressing any threat and risk that may arise;
(2) To draft a professional training program on information security;

[15]Lineamientos de política para ciberseguridad y ciberdefensa. http://www.mintic.gov.co/portal/604/articles-3510_documento.pdf [2016-10-6].

(3) To strengthen legislative and international cooperation on these matters and to accelerate the process of accession by Colombia to various international instruments within the framework, including the Budapest Convention.

To achieve the above-mentioned strategic approach, Colombia has developed and established four divisions:

(1) The Intersectional committee, which is responsible for advising on the strategic prospects for information management and the development of policy guidelines for the management of public information technology infrastructure, cyber security and cyber defense;
(2) The Colombian Computer Emergency Response Organization, a national coordinating body for cyber security and cyber defense services;
(3) The Joint Force Command of the Armed Forces, whose mission is to prevent and combat any cyber threats or attacks that affect the value and interests of the State;
(4) The network police center, responsible for the network security in Colombia, to provide information to support and prevent cybercrime.

Around international cooperation, Colombia formally applied in 2013 for participation in the European Convention for the Prevention of Cybercrime, which established the International Network Security Agreement and the penalty principles for corresponding crimes, with the primary objective of appropriate legislation and international cooperation to protect the society from destruction caused by cybercrime. In addition, Colombia joined a multilateral agreement of the World Economic Forum in 2012, known as the "Partnership for Promoting Network Survivability", with the aim of identifying and addressing global systemic risks brought by the increasing connectivity between people, procedures and objects. At the same time, the secretariat of the Inter-American Commission on Counter-Terrorism of the Organization of American States has developed a comprehensive approach for the member States to capability-building around cyber security. In this framework, Colombia has established, in cooperation with the Inter-American Committee against Terrorism, a national "alert, watch and warn" organization (also known as the "Computer Emergency Response Organization") that is responsible for and capable of responding to crises, incidents and threats to cyber security, which contributes to the development of national cyber security strategies. Colombia also participates in workshops, training courses and conferences on the handling of incidents involving cyber security, information security and cybercrime.

Colombia believes that the international cyber security measures taken to strengthen information security are not entirely government issues and cannot be resolved solely by the government; support from other actors, i.e., academia, industry and civil society, is necessary to effectively address the risk associated with the increasing use of information and communication technologies by various departments. In order to strengthen international information security at the global level, the international community must: ① design appropriate mechanisms to enable societies, elected officials and entities in each State to recognize the need to create an information security culture and the significance of international cooperation in combating cybercrime; ② facilitate the development of strategies of each State to improve national capabilities in cyber security and cyber defense; ③ urge the States to verify essential infrastructure and develop a special program for enhancing security and resilience; ④ encourage the consistency of domestic legal frameworks with existing international instruments in the field of cyber security; improve coordination mechanism among different States to make it easier for States to establish cooperation channels for the prevention, investigation and prosecution of cybercrime; The international coordination mechanism should help identify technology-related offenses and help establish clear rules of jurisdiction and prosecution rights; ⑤ promote the establishment of the obligation that national public and private State entities preserve computer records for subsequent investigation and trial purposes; ⑥ prepare a computer glossary concerned with cybercrime including terms that officials in criminal justice system are generally not quite familiar with, so as to ensure the confidentiality and integrity of system, network and computer data; ⑦ promote exchange of experience and best practices in the field of cyber defense and cyber security, as well as the establishment of a special training network; ⑧ urge States to join the network security incident pre-warning system.

As shown above, there are four main aspects of focus of Colombia in cyberspace security: the first is crimes in cyberspace; the second is to build the system of law, strategy, mechanism and institution in cyberspace for strengthening domestic safety capability, thereby facing up to the existence of cyberspace sovereignty; the third is to be concerned with international cooperation in cyberspace security; the fourth is the construction of cyber warfare forces to practice right of self-defense in cyberspace.

8.2.8 Cuba

In view of the fact that information technology and telecommunications could be used for the purpose of influencing international stability and security, endangering national integrity and undermining the security of national civil and military fields, Cuba fully agrees with the need to worry about the above issues. Cuba expresses deep concern with the theft of individual, organization and State secrets and the illicit use of computer systems of another State to attack a third State, which may trigger international conflicts, as some governments even say that conventional weapons can be used to cope with such attacks. The only way to prevent and resolve these new types of threats and to avoid cyberspace from turning to a military operational area is common cooperation among all States.

Cuba believes that using telecommunication means to maliciously, openly/secretly destroy legal and political order of another States which violates the recognized international norms in the area, resulting in tensions without compromising international peace and security. Accordingly, Cuba repeats to condemn the Government of the United States of America to violate the current in-force International laws and regulations concerning radioactive International laws in the field of Cuba, which, in the course of the implementation of this aggression, do not materially cause damage to international peace and security due to the creation of dangerous situations. Illegal radio and television broadcasting in Cuba is aimed at promoting illegal migration, encouraging and inciting violence, defying constitutional order and committing acts of terrorism, which violates the purposes and principles of the Charter of the United Nations and violates the various aspects of the International Telecommunication Union Regulations. And these broadcasts violated Cuban sovereignty. Accordingly, Cuba once again condemns the Government of the United States of America for starting a radio and TV war against Cuba, which violates the existing International laws and regulations in the field of radio. During this aggression, they neglected possible damage to international peace and security caused by creating dangerous situations. Illegal radio and television broadcasting against Cuba is aimed at promoting illegal migration, encouraging and inciting violence, defying constitutional order and committing acts of terrorism, which violates the purposes and principles of the Charter of the United Nations and various regulations and provisions of the International Telecommunication Union. Moreover, these radios violate the sovereignty of Cuba. Further, in this year, the case of ZunZuneo (an online social blog platform of Cuba) is revealed. It is a sophisticated conspiracy of the American government to support with millions of dollars and use SMS service on social networks to promote subversion in Cuba. Just like other subversive activities, ZunZuneo violated Cuban and American law, such as the "Controlling the Assault of Non-Solicited Pornography and Marketing Act of 2003 [CAN-SPAM]" (Public Law No. 108–187)[16] passed by the US Congress in December 2003, which prohibits the sending of commercial or any other type of text message without the express consent of the addressee. The harmful use of e-mails (spam) has been the target of the Telecommunication Standardization Bureau in over 10 suggested items. ZunZuneo also violated Article 37 of the Declaration of Principles of the World Summit on the Information Society, held in Geneva in 2003.

Cuba reaffirms that the use of information as a means of political, which violates state sovereignty to subvert their internal order and to cause their instability, and which intervenes and interferes in the internal affairs of other States, is an illegal act and must be stopped. Cuba reaffirms that Cuba is strongly against the use of information and communication technology in a manner contrary to International laws, and Cuba is against all such acts. Cuba stresses the need to ensure that the use of these technologies is in full conformity with the purposes and principles of the Charter of the United Nations and International laws, especially the principles of

[16]Controlling the Assault of Non-Solicited Pornography and Marketing Act of 2003 (CAN-SPAM). http://www.internetlibrary.com/statuteitem.cfm?Num=8 [2016-10-6].

sovereignty, non-interference in internal affairs and the internationally recognized standards of peaceful coexistence among States.

Cuba reaffirms that international cooperation is essential to the elimination of the dangers posed by the misuse of information and communication technologies. Cuba also stressed the important role of the International Telecommunication Union in the intergovernmental debate on cyber security. Cuba hopes that the new posture of bilateral relations between Cuba and the United States (including the decision to restore diplomatic relations between the two States) that will be announced on 17 December 2014 will lead to a process of normalizing relations, putting an end to these radical policies and removing economic, commercial and financial blockade causing serious damage to the Cuban people. The embargo has had a detrimental effect on the field of information and the other aspects of the daily lives of the Cuban people.

Cuba established a Computer and Network Security Council, which is guided by the highest authorities of the State, i.e., the Government and the Cuban Communist Party. The mandate of the Council is to advise, coordinate and oversee overall policies and strategies for this process. The establishment of the Cuban Computer Users Union has also been carried out.

Cuba believes that the information technological capability of developing countries shall be improved, so that they can understand the situation and know how the national network is affected and how international security is affected. Developing countries mainly rely on developed countries to deal with international security issues concerning information. Therefore, the exchange of experience in this regard is very important to developing countries. Counter-measures are more applied by developed countries. These measures can only be applied to extreme situations, because the use of such measures is intentional, and will be destabilizing. The counter-measures involved are unimaginable without capability. If cyber-attacks are regarded as armed attacks, the problem will be very complicated, because there is currently the lack of a standard definition of cyber weapons. Non-intervention should be a principle. Non-intervention with the affairs of another State is essential, especially regarding the issue of colleague examination that may result in interference with the affairs of other States. In developing countries, all the data of online activities of the citizens is on a platform outside the territory. Multinationals record data of our citizens and then store them in other States, which can lead to some kind of conflict. Therefore, sovereignty should be respected. Any State can provide systems or technologies for developing countries to increase their capability. However, experience has shown that sovereignty may be affected and compromised during the establishment of capability. Thus, the impact on sovereignty in the process of building capability should be considered.

As shown above, Cuba is mainly concerned with the following three aspects of cyberspace security: the first is to emphasize the existence of sovereignty in cyberspace, to respect cyberspace sovereignty, sovereignty shall not be violated and interfered; the second is to carry out international cooperation to help developing countries to improve their response capability, so as to cope with cross-border cyber-attacks; the third is to strongly condemn the United States for carrying out the persistent cyberspace ideological attack against Cuba.

8.2.9 Egypt

Egypt believes that, attention should be given to the threat of attacks on key international infrastructure and critical organizations, based on whether it is a threat to international peace and security.

Egypt believes that it is suffering from cyber terrorism, and often experiences various terrorist incidents. To prevent terrorism from acquiring information technology, effective means should be taken. Egypt believes that the human rights issue shall not become an obstacle to the fight against terrorism.

Egypt is primarily concerned with the international community's joint effort in fighting against cyber terrorist incidents and hopes that the United Nations will play a greater role.

8.2.10 El Salvador

To strengthen the security of information and telecommunications, the Armed Forces of El Salvador has unified management of independent audio, video and data communications on the public network, and has established and set up a "Boundary Information Security Working Group" and upgraded the border security computer equipment. In addition, El Salvador uses an encryption system to deal with official information to protect all information and to prevent any external personnel attempt to penetrate the system to attack, so as to prevent cyber-attacks. The Armed Forces of El Salvador have also implemented security policies for computer cyber resources, including regular replacement of user passwords, restrictions on the use of USB interfaces and DVD and CD readers, and the prohibition of the use of Class C equipment.

As shown above, El Salvador stresses in cyberspace security that information system is protected by military force, especially to prevent information disclosure.

8.2.11 Estonia

Estonia believes that one aspect of sovereignty is the exercise of responsibility to manage cyberspace, and the obligation to ensure that the territory is not used by a third party for misconduct. Meanwhile, States should settle the conflict between jurisdictions in a peaceful manner, solving disputes peacefully.

The international community should work together to build a global Internet governance system that is multilateral, democratic, transparent and multi-stakeholder.

Estonia focuses on three issues: the first is the responsibilities and obligations indicating cyberspace sovereignty; the second is that the international community should resolve disputes in cyberspace in a peaceful manner; and the third is to build a global Internet governance system guided by multi-stakeholders.

8.2.12 Finland

At the national level, Finland has made the following efforts.

(1) The Finnish National Cyber Security Strategy (2013) and its Implementation Program (2014) identified key criteria and actions to strengthen cyber security and resilience. The implementation program is currently being updated through a multi-stakeholder consultation process, which is to be completed in 2016.
(2) Since the adoption of the National Cyber Security Strategy in February 2016, Finland has established the National Cyber Security Center and the Center for Cybercrime Prevention and has appointed a cyber-ambassador.
(3) As a part of Finland's development cooperation, Finland supports a variety of projects that promotes development and cyber capability-building by information and communication technologies. Finland is a founding partner of the Global Network Expert Forum and has joined the US-led Global Connectivity Initiative for 1.5 billion people to have access to the Internet by 2020. Finland intends to join the newly established Development Partnership Fund of the World Bank Digital Partnership, and Finland supports Internet governance in a multi-stakeholder model.
(4) In multilateral and regional forums and in bilateral contacts, Finland has actively engaged in international dialogue on cyber issues. Within the framework of the Organization for Security and Cooperation in Europe (OSCE), Finland is committed to strengthening the confidence, security and stability of cyberspace and implements the agreed measures for cyber confidence-building and security.
(5) Finland endorsed the report of the United Nations Group of Governmental Experts in 2015 on information and telecommunication technology in the context of international security. Finland is actively involved in the discussion of cyberspace International laws, including the consultations on Tallinn Handbook 2.0 and participation in the United Nations Institute for Disarmament Research. Finland joined the "Free Online Alliance" in 2012 and contributed to the "Digital Guards Partnership".

(6) Finland became a party to the Budapest Convention in 2007 and launched a new strategic policy plan in 2015 to use resources for the prevention of computer crime and the development of cyber security.

In addition, Finland has developed a comprehensive cybercrime prevention program, determining priority areas for further work in the international community: ① Finland attaches great importance to the work of the newly established Group of Governmental Experts and is prepared to contribute to its success, including promoting the determination of a code of conduct for responsible States in cyberspace, with particular emphasis on peacetime activities; ② regional confidence-building measures is further developed and implemented within the framework of the OSCE; ③ Finland will continue to support cyber capability-building with a vision to enhance the viability and security of cyberspace; ④ Finland will continue to support and encourage the multi-stakeholder dialogue and give priority to improvement of national and international partnerships.

Finland believes that as for State obligations, the territory of the State should not be allowed to be used in an informed manner for actions that would cause serious damage to another State or violate the rights of another State; the States may take the steps recommended by the international guidelines to ensure that their territory is not used as a detrimental action causing great damage to other States. An appropriate legal framework and legal system should be established to deal with cyber-attacks; when cyberspace problems arise, precautionary measures should be taken to avoid harm to a third State or to harm the people of the injured State. Countering action should be an orderly process that is not mandatory and should not use force; to take counteraction is to take a certain risk; the State invoking the counteraction should ensure that there is evidence or proof. Moreover, it is likely that the countering State itself has committed an international misconduct, for which the countering State should be responsible. There should be a distinction between policy and technical aspects of Confidence Building Measures (CBM). States with cyber strategies should share with other States as much as possible.

As shown above, Finland mainly concerns cyberspace security in the following four aspects: the first is the implementation of the domestic cyberspace security strategy; the second is to start international cooperation, and the establishment of international trust measures and security system; the third is to support a multi-stakeholder cyberspace governance model; the fourth is to be in accordance with International laws in coping with international cyber-attacks, with careful use of counter-measures.

8.2.13 France

France believes that,[17] as a State that actively advocates freedom of expression on the Internet, information is not such a potential weakness that it needs to be protected in an appropriate and transparent manner in accordance with article 19 of the International Covenant on Civil and Political Rights,[18] unless there is a more stringent legal requirement.

France believes that the operation of society today is increasingly dependent on information systems and the cyberspace, including the Internet. Therefore, the action of attacking important information systems, once successful, can have serious consequences for people and the economy. To this end, France in 2011 developed information systems defense and security strategies, so that cyber security truly becomes national priority. The 2013 White Paper on Defense and National Security points out the State's two major dangers, namely cyber espionage and cyber damage against key infrastructures. The white paper further clarifies the State's perception of the threat. In response to these challenges, France established the French network and information security institutions in 2009 and, since then, has continuously strengthened the agency's resources and strength. Today, the institution is responsible for all cyber security-related prevention and response for key infrastructure, including government infrastructure. The Department of Defense, which is responsible for cyberspace, has also strengthened itself in this regard, as evidenced by an ambitious strategic document network defense agreement issued by the Department of Defense in February 2014.

At the same time, France is actively involved in strengthening international cyber security cooperation. Without this cooperation, efforts at the national level would be limited. Since the G8 held its meeting in Deauville in 2011, France has been very interested in strengthening international regulation of cyberspace. To that end, France actively participates in the work of the United Nations Group of Governmental Experts and the Organization for Security and Cooperation in Europe to develop an international normative framework in accordance with existing International laws and to develop confidence-building measures and specific codes of conduct in cyberspace.

Finally, France is working to achieve the objectives of international cyber security capability building through bilateral and multilateral concrete programs (with the European Union and the North Atlantic Treaty Organization).

France believes that, in some cases, a State acts as an agent against key infrastructure of another State, thus, the agency is obliged to accept investigations conducted by the target State; the retrospective attribution involves sovereignty

---

[17]Réponse de la France à la résolution 68/243 relative aux "Développements dans le domaine de l'information et des télécommunications dans le contexte de la sécurité internationale". https://unoda-web.s3-accelerate.amazonaws.com/wp-content/uploads/2014/10/France.pdf [2016-9-19].

[18]International Covenant on Civil and Political Rights. http://www.un.org/chinese/hr/issue/ccpr.htm [2016-10-6].

issues requiring a lot of information material and materials from all parties; the retrospective attribution of a cyber-attack depends on the sovereignty, and should be a policy-based judgement; the attribution of a cyber-attack does not belong to the same judicial scope as a judicial investigation, and has a different urgency degree. Traceability should be reasonably deterministic; and the quality of the evidence should be proportional to the number of coping; A State, within its jurisdiction, shall limit the use of cyber technology by a non-State actor to adversely affect a third party. the basic criterion of the International laws is that it is not allowed to cause the territory of the State to be destroyed by the use of other States knowingly; individuals or organizations should be encouraged to spend time to find vulnerabilities in the ICT system and inform the system owner where the vulnerability lies; a mechanism should be established, which can regularly monitor the implementation of CBM monitoring specifications, the mechanism could be implemented by intergovernmental working groups that may be linked to the United Nations and may remain open to all Member States that are willing to participate.

As shown above, France mainly emphasizes six aspects in cyberspace security: first, there should not be any restrictions on information itself; freedom of speech should be supported; second, security of cyber infrastructure should be protected; third, international cooperation should be adopted to cope with the issue of cyber security; fourth, sovereignty is recognized in cyberspace; however, the States should undertake the obligations brought by sovereignty and restrict cyber-attacks happening in their territory; fifth, discovery of the vulnerability of information systems should be encouraged, and should not be regarded as illegal behavior; sixth, an international mechanism should be established for the responsibility and obligations of review.

8.2.14 Georgia

Georgia believes that[19] widely publicized cyber-attacks in 2008 put the protection of the critical infrastructure high on agenda of the Government of Georgia. Rapidly growing dependence of the critical infrastructure and government services on the IT increases vulnerability to cybercrime-related incidents. Accordingly, Adequate Protection of critical Infrastructure from Cyber threats is one of the priorities of the Government of Georgia. Therefore, full protection of critical infrastructure from cyber threats is one of the priorities of the Government of Georgia. The first goal of the 2008 cyber-attack was government websites and news media websites. Later, the scope of the attack expanded to include more government websites, Georgian financial institutions, business associations, educational institutions, more news media sites and a Georgian hacking forum. The purpose of these attacks is to

[19]GEORGIA General appreciation of the issues of information security. https://unoda-web.s3-accelerate.amazonaws.com/wp-content/uploads/2014/07/Georgia.pdf [2016-9-19].

disrupt normal business activities. In addition to the two major banks, business-related objectives are mainly those organizations capable of communicating and coordinating responses among different enterprises. The above experience shows that cyber-attacks by State and individual actors on the critical infrastructure of Georgia can cause serious physical damage and huge financial losses to the public sector and the private sector. The Government of Georgia therefore considers that cyber security is an integral part of overall national security policy, particularly as the Government increasingly uses information technology as a tool for the provision of government services.

The Georgian National Security Council and a special working group of government agencies have developed the Cyber Security Strategy of Georgia[20] in 2011, which is a part of the national security review process. The Cyber Security Strategy of Georgia and its implementation plan were submitted to the public for discussion in March 2012 and were finally adopted in January 2013. Another step is the establishment in 2010 of the Georgian Ministry of Justice Data Exchange as an entity for the central government to formulate and implement e-government policies and solutions. An important task of the Office is to maintain information security in the public and private sectors, including the adoption and implementation of information security policies and standards in the public sector and critical infrastructure, the provision of advisory services in the field of information security and the implementation of information security audits, awareness activities being carried out on information security in the private sector, and performance of cyber security tasks through the National Computer Emergency Response Organization.

The Georgian Information Security Legal and Regulatory Framework include the Information Security Act promulgated in 2011 and 2012 and the sub-normative law supplementing the Act. The main concepts used in the Georgian legislation detail the information security policy based on the International Organization for Standardization 27,000 standard series. The law highlights some of the rights and obligations concerning core infrastructure in the implementation of the international information security policy and establishes a mechanism for cooperation with the National Government Computer Emergency Response Organization.

Georgia has taken important steps to enhance international cooperation and share accumulated knowledge with partners. One of the noteworthy examples is that the Data Exchange has signed bilateral cooperation agreements and memoranda of understanding with the European Union Military Staff Committee (from Austria, Estonia, Poland and other States) and neighboring States (Azerbaijan, Armenia, Republic of Moldova, Turkey and other States). Georgia recognizes that regional and international cooperation mechanisms are becoming increasingly important in response to information security challenges. To that end, efforts should be made to increase the number of international activities devoted to such important issues, to

[20]Cyber Security Strategy of Georgia. https://www.itu.int/en/ITU-D/Cybersecurity/Documents/National_Strategies_Repository/Georgia_2012_NationalCyberSecurityStrategyofGeorgia_ENG.pdf [2016-10-6].

enhance trust with key stakeholders and to continue to work with the international community to define strategic principles and legal concepts.

As shown above, Georgia mainly focuses on cyberspace security in the following three aspects: first, because of the cyber warfare attacks, domestic cyber security has become a top priority; second, through implementation of cyberspace security policy at the strategic, legal and other levels, cyberspace jurisdiction is improved; third, international cooperation is strengthened so as to jointly cope with the challenges of cyberspace security.

8.2.15 Germany

Germany believes that[21] information and communication technologies offer unprecedented opportunities for industrialized and developing countries, as well as vulnerability and systemic weaknesses. The current malicious activities have a trend continuing towards hard-to-detect, sophisticated malicious activities using information and communication technologies and targeting high-value objectives, which may have serious consequences. At present, malware activity targeting eye-catching goals such as media platforms is increasing. Especially attacks against core infrastructure can have serious consequences. Cyber-attacks on critical infrastructures can cause more damage than isolated violent attacks and sometimes have unpredictable consequences for other networking entities. Despite these risks, it seems unlikely that a full "cyber warfare" will occur for the time being. The attacks may be limited use of cyber capabilities to support larger combat operations. However, there is a risk in the real society that cyber accidents may be upgraded to "real" conflicts. Under such circumstances, Germany advocates a three-pronged approach: one is to reach consensus on the principle of responsible behavior in cyberspace; second is to participate in confidence-building measures; and third is to strengthen cyber defense capabilities.

The United Nations is the core platform for establishing rules of responsible behavior in cyberspace. In the period from 2012 to 2013, the Group of Governmental Experts has reached a consensus on the Development of Information and Telecommunications from the Perspective of International Security, which is that international laws, especially the Charter of the United Nations, is applicable to cyberspace. This is an important starting point. The Group also believes that national sovereignty and international norms and principles originated from sovereignty can be applied to national ICT activities and to the jurisdiction of States in their territories for ICT infrastructure. From 2014 to 2015, the Group of Governmental Experts continued its work on this basis, where Germany again

[21]Germany: "Report on Developments in the Field of Information and Telecommunications in the Context of International Security". https://unoda-web.s3-accelerate.amazonaws.com/wp-content/uploads/2015/08/GermanyISinfull.pdf [2016-9-19].

actively participated in the work of the Group of Experts. Consistent understanding of the rules, norms and principles of responsible national conduct in cyberspace can enhance international transparency and predictability and thus promote peace and stability. This, for example, contributes to a further consensus on how the armed conflict law applies to the use of military cyberspace capabilities, and an increasing number of States are developing that capability.

Regarding confidence-building measures, the OSCE has made significant progress: a first bunch of steps are taken to improve cooperation, transparency, predictability and stability among States with a view to reducing the risk of misinterpretation, escalation and conflict arising from the use of information and communication technologies. The above agreement of OSCE could serve as a model for other regional organizations to follow. The cyber security strategy of Germany (2011) is established based on the recognition that cyberspace security, the integrity, authenticity and confidentiality of cyberspace data have become extremely important. Ensuring cyber security has become a central challenge for States, businesses and societies. All parties need to act together, including at the national level, as well as cooperate with international partners.

Germany is preparing information technology security law to strengthen cyber defense at the national level. The draft law defines the minimum requirements for information technology security at the core infrastructure. The draft sets out the obligation to report major events to improve the overall security system and to better protect the public. Germany also supports other States to strengthen their ability to manage cyber security risks.

The Cyber Security Strategy sets out the following objectives and measures[22]: ① Protecting critical information infrastructures, ② Securing IT systems in Germany, ③ Strengthening IT security in public administration, ④ Running a national cyber response center,⑤ Establishing a national cyber Security council, ⑥ Effective crime control in cyberspace, ⑦ Effective coordinated action ensuring cyber security in Europe and worldwide, ⑧ Using reliable and trustworthy information technology, ⑨ Personnel development in federal authorities, and ⑩ Tools to respond to cyber-attacks.

After the German election in September 2013, in accordance with the joint agreement, cyber security has placed an important position on the agenda of the government. Data privacy standards will be improved. The current primary themes include how to better protect consumers, revising criminal law to better protect individuals, passing an information technology security law to impose mandatory minimum information technology safety standards for critical infrastructure, and all federal authorities having an obligation to use 10% of its IT budget for the improvement of the security of its systems. The German government strongly encourages information technology service providers to encrypt telecommunication

---

[22]Germany: "Report on Developments in the Field of Information and Telecommunications in the Context of International Security". https://unoda-web.s3-accelerate.amazonaws.com/wp-content/uploads/2014/07/Germany.pdf [2016-9-19].

data and not to transfer telecommunication data to foreign intelligence agencies, so as to prevent illegal or arbitrary monitoring/interrogation of communications and unauthorized or arbitrary collection of personal data by a third party.

Germany believes that confidence building measures and transparency should be established; Obligations assigned to States by the International laws should be fulfilled; internationally wrongful acts of combatting other States using ICTs from our territory must be prevented; the international business of the State has certain restrictions on sovereignty, such as international human rights obligations; the issues of data ownership and jurisdiction are very complicated; thus, the States should strive to establish principles for protecting data integrity and data usage; There are three ways to deal with international cyber conflicts. The first is to peacefully settle the disputes. The second is to use corresponding rules to guide non-force counterattack. The third is violent counterattack. It is necessary to act within the scope of existing international laws to track the source of an attack and to respond to international wrongful acts. It is necessary to find a peaceful way to resolve conflicts and to resolve conflicts in ICTs through dialogue.

As shown above, Germany has four aspects of focus on cyberspace. First, to strengthen international cooperation, to reach consensus on the principle of responsible behavior in cyberspace, especially Germany stressed to recognize that "national sovereignty and international norms and principles of sovereignty are applicable to national ICT activities and jurisdiction of the State in its territory over the ICT infrastructure". Second, to participate in confidence-building measures and to enhance mutual trust. Third, from the perspective of law, strategy and measures, to strengthen the State's cyberspace security and defense capabilities. Fourth, there are three ways to recognize international cyber conflict: peaceful settlement of disputes, non-military counterattack, and violent counterattack, but it is advocated to act according to the international laws, and preferably resolve ICT conflict through dialogue.

8.2.16 India

India believes that information technology contributes to economic growth and social connectivity, but there are also serious challenges that need to be addressed. While the ICT sector is growing, cybercrime increases, including cyber-attacks, cybercrime, cyber terrorism, espionage and money laundering. There is evidence that terrorist groups (e.g., the Islamic State) use the Internet and social media platforms to carry out evil activities, including recruiting, fund raising, promoting and advocating radicalism. Abuse of social media is a major concern. While social media brings great connectivity, it may also be abused to exacerbate ethnic and social divisions.

India believes that, for the international community, it is important to have a common understanding of cyberspace national behavior and to take actions for confidence-building measures and capability-building, as recommended by the

United Nations Group of Governmental Experts in its report for 2015. The discussion of Internet governance cannot be stalled because of semantic differences. While different stakeholders play different roles in their respective fields, governments have a primary role to play in cyber security involving national security. For cyber threats, cybercrime and cyber-terrorism, an appropriate information-sharing mechanism should be established. There should also be pragmatic cooperation between government institutions to deal with cybercrime.

India believes that cyber warfare and cyber theory and its impact on international security should also be discussed in all international forums. While the principle of responsible cyberspace is still to be agreed upon, the common understanding of confidence-building measures set out in the United Nations GAO report of 2015 can be used to take appropriate capability-building measures around cyber security. In this regard, the framework developed by the Global Network Expert Forum provides useful guidance.

India is an important stakeholder for information and communication technology. It supports implementation of the multi-stakeholder approach in Internet governance and have taken the initiative to participate in a comprehensive review of the implementation of various international forums, including the Group of Governmental Experts and the World Summit on the Information Society Public consultation process, and the Internet name and digital address distribution agency. India, in consultation with all stakeholders, has adopted an integrated approach to address cybersecurity issues through a range of policy, legal, technical and administrative steps and improves international cooperation in this area. India's legal framework has been consistent with other legal frameworks in the world. The National Network Security Policy, launched in 2013, aims to build secure cyberspace for citizens, businesses and governments, emphasizing capability building, skills development and public-private partnerships around cybersecurity.

As shown above, India is mainly concerned with the three aspects of cyberspace security: first, social media is an important factor that threatens cyberspace security; second, the government should play a leading role in the multi-stakeholder international cyberspace governance; third, the issue of cyberspace security should be strengthened at the international level.

8.2.17 Indonesia

Indonesia believes that, the domain name system should be managed under the United Nations framework, so as to prevent the cyberspace from being controlled by one or several States. The United Nations should set up an exchange center for the sharing of information on cyberspace security. Information sharing means, and cooperative measures should be established, so as to address risks of cross-border cyber-attacks. Multiple parties should be encouraged to participate in global Internet governance. Cyber security incident accountability should be established at a national level, where the State should fulfill its sovereign responsibilities and obligations. Affairs of States in cyberspace should not be interfered. There should be set norms for the naming of domain names, so that through the domain name, it can be determined whether the attack system is a military target, thereby determining whether the attack is a military action.

The awareness of citizens on cyber security risks should be enhanced, so that citizens will resist the occurrence of cyber security incidents. Personal data should be protected from infringement.

Indonesia has mainly emphasized two aspects of cyberspace security. One is to rely on the United Nations to govern the global Internet, and to recognize the sovereignty of cyberspace. And the other is that the State should take measures to improve awareness of citizens on cyber security risks, and to protect personal data from Infringement.

8.2.18 Japan

Japan believes that cyberspace should be a space that guarantees freedom, without unnecessary restrictions, without unreasonable rejection or exclusion of all desired visitors. Japan emphasizes the five principles of "free flow of information, rule of law, openness, autonomy and multi-stakeholder". Japan is committed to strengthening information security, and in September 2015 developed a network security strategy.

In terms of promoting international cooperation, Japan's efforts are divided into the following three parts: ① rule of law in cyberspace: promoting common understanding of the existing international laws in cyberspace being applied to cyberspace, and developing non-binding voluntary norms of responsible national conduct; ② confidence-building measures: actively promoting confidence-building mechanism through bilateral frameworks and multilateral frameworks such as the Association of Southeast Asian Nations (ASEAN) regional forums; ③ capability-building: active participation in human resources development assistance and technical cooperation with the focus of the ASEAN region.

Japan believes that the recognition of the applicability of international laws and the development of a non-binding voluntary code of conduct for responsible cyberspace are bases for ensuring the stability and predictability of the international community. Japan considers it necessary to elaborate further on the rules of international laws of peace, the law relating to the right of self-defense and the consideration of IHL, and to develop voluntary guidelines in the next group of governmental experts. The key for the establishment of confidence-building measures and capability-building is to promote the implementation of the recommendations of the report of the Group of Governmental Experts in each State and region. It is necessary to study a way for carrying out practical cooperation.

Japan believes that, when a State is under cyber-attack, the injured State may require the territorial State that has initiated the attack to take measures and, in effect, produce a preventive effect; if the territorial State does not take appropriate measures, the injured State or the State under attack can take counter-measures against the territorial State of the attack; counter-measures are, in some cases, a response to a wrongful act of another State in the international community, which is permissible according to the international laws; if a cyber-attack cannot be attributed to a particular State, the injured State may request the territorial State that has given the attack to take the necessary measures; cyber activities may constitute use of violence or violent attack; according to the International laws and the International Humanitarian Law, States can exercise their right of self-defense, which is recognized by Article 51 of the Charter, so as to cope with armed attack in cyberspace; control over offensive information and communication tool export is critical for the purpose of preventing those who have malicious intentions from using such tools; transparency has been the key and foundation of all confidence-building measures. It should be encouraged that States and governments disclose relative measures and laws they formulated; on Internet governance, the participation of multiple stakeholders should have special importance attached.

As shown above, Japan is concerned with the following seven aspects of cyberspace security: first, freedom of speech in cyberspace; second, to support a multi-stakeholder governance model; third, to recognize the applicability of international laws without binding; fourth, to admit that sovereignty exists in cyberspace, which at the same time bring obligations, including the duty of care; fifth, to support counter-measures; sixth, to recognize the law of armed conflict being directly applicable to cyberspace; seventh, control of offensive ICT Tools, without affecting normal needs.

8.2.19 Jordan

Jordan believes that information and communication technology has become an integral part of people's daily life, promoting social, cultural and economic growth and local community development while facilitating interaction with individuals and local communities and the wider world. The rapid development of ICTs is also a subject to risks and challenges and must be coped with through technical and legal means so as to find effective ways to reduce risk and to prevent possible catastrophic consequences.

The Jordanian army, through technology development, ensures the security of information and wired and wireless communication, and has played a positive role in promoting security and peace at national, regional and global levels. The action of the Jordanian army includes: ① updating the communication and information system, for which cryptographic IP technology is used, protected networks are installed throughout Jordan including the border zones, so as to enhance national and regional security; ② participating in security cooperation with the international community for the purpose of a communications system that is compatible with the North Atlantic Treaty Organization and the US Army and does conform with the Class 1 international encryption standard; ③ increasing technical capability by providing an infrastructure-independent communication system for maintaining national security of conflict zones, refugee camps and remote areas, and this technology is also used to support peacekeeping operations in conflict areas around the world; ④ training all users and operation and maintenance personnel of communication system to ensure the highest level of reliability and dependability at any time; ⑤ applying the highest command and control standards to all systems used by the military to improve the level of national and regional security coordination and cooperation; ⑥ actively participating in international conferences and understanding the outcome of the conferences so as to enhance the complementarity between friendly forces and avoid interference in the communication systems used by neighboring States and ensure a coordinated control and monitoring of international borders.

Jordan has taken the following measures to protect the national key information network infrastructure: ① encrypt all voice, data and video communication systems; ② use physical isolated network (internal network); ③ through self-contained peripherals, establish connections with other security institutions; ④ use information and communication security measures and apply the "need to know" principle to perform uninterrupted checks on the access and user identity; ⑤ use virtual networks, and, according to the permission of information access, allow users to access remote servers, the access or connection not being allowed to be carried out by other devices such as flash drives; ⑥ promulgate laws on cyber security, among which the laws on cybercrime and electronic transactions have been issued. The national cyber security and protection strategy have been approved by the cabinet in 2012; the national cyber security and protection policies have been developed.

Jordan suggests that the following measures be taken in a global extent: ① classify communication networks and information according to the significance; ② implement cyber security and protection measures; ③ apply the "need to know" principle; ④ use encryption and frequency hopping and other technical measures; ⑤ check the permission of users and cyber service and conduct classification; ⑥ interconnect the cyberspace through self-contained peripherals; ⑦ use physical isolated internal network in some networks, and try to avoid the use of the World Wide Web; ⑧ strengthen the security of the internal network of United Nations, isolate it form the public network, and to protect it by adopting technical and security measures such as encryption, security and service permission verification; ⑨ promote cooperation between computer emergency response organizations, track irregularities, install protective facilities and make up for deficiencies; ⑩ popularize security measures and deal with irregular procedures.

Jordan believes that ICTs have the potential to promote sustainable development, especially in poor and remote areas: ① ICTs can accelerate the eradication of poverty, for example, through mobile banking services, bringing direct and actual benefit to millions of people who never have banking experiences; ② the impact of famine can be alleviated by providing farmers with key crop farming information with modern technology and new communication media.

As shown above, Jordan mainly stressed the following three aspects of cyberspace security: First, military force is dominant for protecting the cyberspace security, including being involved in international cooperation; second, cyberspace security focus on the prevention of information from being stolen; third, national initiatives on information security are recommended to the international community.

8.2.20 Kazakhstan

Kazakhstan believes that there is a need to advocate the path under international laws, to enhance people's confidence with the international laws, and to ensure equality and show respect for sovereignty; attack on any of the facilities in the territory of the sovereign State is a violation of the sovereignty; it is also a violation of national sovereignty to collect information and intelligence in other States; the States should cooperate to build capability and foster confidence and fight against terrorism, so as to reduce risk and prevent our territory from becoming a birthplace of terrorist attacks; when a State accepts assistance in cyberspace security, sovereignty issue is involved; the donor State should guarantee the independence of cyberspace sovereignty of the receiving State; The States should not develop or support activities that violate international obligations; under the principle of sovereignty, the cyber security activities that take place on the territory of a State is the responsibility of the State; it must be recognized that terrorist acts can cause damage, and restrict the activities encouraging terrorism. We should deprive terrorists of their opportunities, even if doing so is to limit the freedom of expression.

Kazakhstan emphasizes on four aspects in cyberspace security: first, actions in cyberspace should be in accordance with international laws, without bullying the weak; second, national cyberspace sovereignty should be guaranteed; third, cyberspace militarization is opposed; fourth, as compared with freedom of speech, restricting and striking terrorism is given a priority.

8.2.21 Kenya

Kenya believes that the States should not allow its territory to be used for cyber-attacks; if a transnational cyber-attack emerges, the State of the origin of the attack should be informed to ease the tension; the issue of supply chain security is of great importance to developing countries. There is a special need for international principles to be set to constrain the spread of cyber offensive weapons; regional organization is a good model for advancing international cooperation; states with relatively weak capability are encouraged to participate in actions to guarantee international peace and security.

Kenya expressed the will to rely on the international community to protect the security of cyberspace.

8.2.22 Lebanon

Lebanon believes that today, cyber security affects a range of issues in economy, society, politics, military, and humanitarian issues. Cyber terrorism will be one of the most significant threats to both the superpowers and the developing countries in the future. Cyber wars may occur at multiple levels, including recruiting and mobilizing websites, psychological warfare, Internet information exchange and dissemination, cybercriminals attacking web sites, data and information systems, and cyber terrorism, etc. The threat of cyber terrorism has increased in all States. Lebanon is mainly attacked in the banking industry (e.g., the attack of the Gaussian virus) and the communication industry. Most cyber services are frequently attacked.

Lebanon's efforts to promote cyber security and international cooperation include: ① Law No. 140 on Telecommunication Confidentiality and Law No. 75 on Intellectual Property Rights are put in force in 1999, both of which deal with software piracy to some extent; ② in 2006, Criminal Investigation Division of the Internal Security Force Bureau established the Office for Combating Cybercrime and the Protection of Intellectual Property Rights; ③ the Communication Regulatory Authority was established in 2007, which has become an active member of the international partnership against cyber threats; ④ in 2009, the Army Command established the Electronics Forensics Division inside the main Office of Intelligence; ⑤ in 2012, the Cabinet issued a decision on the establishment of the National Security Council to administer governmental websites; ⑥ in 2013, the Cabinet formed a committee responsible for the study of the threat posed by the Israeli enemy communication towers oriented towards Lebanese territory, with the Department of Defense being the chairperson and the members including other associated departments and committees; ⑦ in 2015, the Lebanese Army established a special Cyber Security Division, and the Department of Defense is currently working with national and global authorities to establish a Lebanese computer emergency response organization.

Lebanon believes that the international community can take the following measures to strengthen information security at the global level: compliance with the resolutions adopted by the United Nations and the World Summit on the Information Society, which aims at disseminating information culture, and establish a cooperation framework with relevant international agencies to ensure the sharing of information and optimized practice; national laws and regulations for combating information crime should be consistent with the global rules to prevent the emergence of digital paradise; establish a global information crisis management system, and strengthen national laws to deal with global and international cybercrime ability by strong international legislation.

As shown above, Lebanon mainly focuses on the following two aspects of cyberspace security: first, perform legal construction, institutional construction and so on to strengthen cyberspace security; second, perform international cooperation to jointly deal with cyberspace security problems.

8.2.23 Mexico

Mexico believes that international norms and guidelines should be applied to cyberspace; the international community should make efforts to address the digital divide. When emphasizing cyberspace sovereignty, it should be clarified which powers and obligations are involved, because it concerns with jurisdiction and international responsibility. Disputes between nations should be settled in a peaceful and friendly manner; human rights and the right to free access to information in cyberspace should be guaranteed; there is a need to be cautious about cybercrime and cyber terrorism when it comes to human rights.

Mexico, in the discussion on cyberspace sovereignty, places greater emphasis on responsibilities, human rights, freedom of information and other factors.

8.2.24 The Kingdom of the Netherlands

The Netherlands believes that[23] the international community has a shared interest and responsibility to ensure that cyberspace remains open, free and secure. In the view of the Netherlands, security would be served by the broad acceptance of and adherence to a set of norms of responsible behavior of States. Much work has been done already by the Group of Governmental Experts on Developments in the Field of Information and Telecommunications in the Context of International Security. However, the following areas would benefit from further work and the following concrete measures.

(1) Enhancing States' understanding of how these existing international laws and norms for State conduct apply to cyberspace. especially the international legal framework that can be applied to cyber operations that do not rise to the threshold of an armed attack.
(2) Strengthening legal, diplomatic and policy capability and the exchange of best practices in the field of cyber norm development and confidence building measures in the field of cyberspace international peace and security. The Global

[23]Developments in the field of information and telecommunications in the context of international security Kingdom of the Netherlands. https://unoda-web.s3-accelerate.amazonaws.com/wp-content/uploads/2015/08/NetherlandsISinfull.pdf [2016-9-19].

> Forum on Cyber Expertise (GFCE), which was launched during the fourth Global Conference on Cyberspace in The Hague, can play an important role in this regard.

Since the Internet has become a strategic asset for all Dutch, there is a need for extensive international discussions on relevant issues.

The Netherlands believes that the connection to cyberspace means that everyone is interrelated without affecting the same sovereignty. States should not take any action to influence the activities in such cyberspace. The attribute of transparency of the Internet suggests that it is vulnerable to malicious attacks. Some guidelines should be established to solve this problem, so as to ensure that the Internet is used for the common interests of mankind.

The duty of care is to identify what measures States can take to ensure that the territory is not used for unlawful cyber actions. As a result of differences in capability between States, measures should be taken to minimize the use of illicit technology and the implementation of illegal acts. This involves capability-building; In terms of accountability of cyber-attack, it is necessary to distinguish between the issues of accountability from being legitimate, accountability is to determine the State responsibility, taking counter-measures is a legitimate response, with some basic conditions being fulfilled. Counter-measures are an integral part of the existing international laws, and do not exclude peaceful settlement of conflicts. Both of counter-measures and peaceful settlement are important ways to guarantee compliance with the international laws. Counter-measures are subject to the principle of necessity and proportionality.

As shown above, the Netherlands concerns the following aspects in cyberspace security: first, the cyberspace security issue is dealt with in an international vision; second, cyberspace sovereignty is not recognized; third, capability building should be strengthened to prevent the occurrence of illegal acts in their territory; fourth, counter-measures are legitimate, but merely when following the principle of proportionality; fifth, governmental participation in Internet governance is opposed; but there is a need for the international community to jointly protect the security of the Internet.

8.2.25 Panama

Panama holds the idea that, as information and communication technologies are developing rapidly, all Panamanian people are increasingly in contact with communication technology in daily lives. It is a fact that the life of people is closely connected with the development of communication and information processing methods. The Government of Panama has acted in accordance with international principles, so as to adapt to the specific needs of the security institutions. To this end, the government has been making technical improvements to achieve more efficient and secure connectivity. In these improvements, the Government of

Panama has gradually developed a communication implementation plan, which includes contents of cyber, security and telephone technology. Relevant manufacturers confirm that these contents meet with international standards.

The Panamanian Government has established an infrastructure for the internal firewall platform to guarantee the security of the Internet, data and telephone information, and is linked to the national multi-service network. The Panamanian government uses data sessions based on security firewalls to ensure confidentiality and security of information. Panama believes that with an increasing number of communication solutions for fulfilling the security needs of security institutions, these institutions must be able to access tools that contribute to the harmonious development of the information field and take proactive and preventive measures.

As shown above, Panama's major concern in cyberspace security is mainly referring to international experience to address security problems of their own cyberspace, emphasizing on protecting the information from being stolen.

8.2.26 Peru

The Peruvian National Police regulates its enterprise data network through a variety of system security policies at all levels of organization and functional structure. In terms of information security, the enterprise data network has been outsourced through managed security services and run by a secure operation center. Role and Identity Management Projects are already in place, which will allow users to perform access controls, ensuring traceability and providing audit tools.

Precautionary measures taken to strengthen information security at the national level include: designating network administrators; training the staff in regard to information technology; software licensing of center servers of national police data; implementing "private cloud"; data backup; backup power systems (Uninterrupted power supply); upgrading power distribution boards and electrical connections; outsourcing peripheral security services (external) when the system is under attack or denies service; updating national police technology platforms and police information systems. National public safety is effectively improved by means of information integration; and interoperability between States is ensured by providing services, thereby facilitating international security.

Measures to be taken by the international community to strengthen global information security include: standardization of communications media, including the types of equipment and communication protocols; standardization of high-availability technical platforms to achieve interoperability of States in terms of international security; standardization of an information security mechanism; in the concept of "information field", each State involved in international security is exposed to risk factors and is possible to establish a common objective for combating and/or curbing a problem by establishing an automated information mechanism.

As shown above, Peru is mainly concerned with the following two aspects of cyberspace security: first, protection of cyberspace security of Peru with the police as the main force; second, enhancing international cooperation so as to cope with security risks in cyberspace with joint effort via standardized means.

8.2.27 Poland

Poland believes that cyber security is essential for maintaining economic growth and for maintaining the functioning of civil society. Cyber-attacks not only affect the private sector and public administration, but also affect the industrial automation system in critical infrastructure. Given the nature of these threats and the increasing reliance of industrial and commercial enterprises, administrative departments, and society on information technology, it is necessary to ensure coherence in information and telecommunications security systems. All stakeholders, including States, businesses and non-governmental organizations, must be involved and contribute to ensuring cyber security. Poland's cyber security system is based on institutional networks, with entities working in cooperation on civil and military levels and in areas related to cybercrime. The Polish government is stepping up its efforts to develop a national cyber security strategy and national cyber security laws. Key elements of the Polish cyber security system will include procedures, personnel and technology.

Poland believes that compliance with the international laws and international norms is a necessary condition for the maintenance of peace and security in cyberspace between States. Improving national capability is a key element for strengthening international cyberspace security. Expanding trust in cyberspace will have a positive impact on the relationship between countries in other areas.

Poland believes that human rights and fundamental freedoms in cyberspace and in the real world should be protected in the same way. Respecting the fundamental freedoms on the Internet is indispensable for a domestic society, sustainable growth, and prosperity.

Poland believes that further global development of confidence-building measures should be taken in cyberspace and be implemented at world, regional and national levels. The international community should encourage national capability-building around cyber security. Bilateral and regional cooperation must be deepened. The CEIBS cyber security platform, consisting of Poland, the Czech Republic, Slovakia, Hungary and Austria, is an excellent example of regional efforts. Through the international exercise in the field of cyber security, the nature of the threat and the means for coping with the threats can be better understood. The "lock" exercise held by "Network Europe" or the North Atlantic Treaty Organization falls within this situation. The significance of the participation of non-governmental organizations, industrial and commercial enterprises and academician stakeholders in international dialogues should not be underestimated.

As shown above, Poland is concerned with the following four issues on cyberspace security: first, the issue of cyberspace security is an issue at all levels of society and needs joint response from all levels; second, the States should comply with international laws and international standards, and do no harm to cyberspace of other countries; third, the basic freedom of access to the Internet should be guaranteed; fourth, it is encouraged in the international community to promote establishment of cyberspace trust measures.

8.2.28 Portugal

Portugal believes that progress in the field of information and telecommunications means increasing opportunities in the following aspects: the development of civilizations, cooperation among States, promotion of human creativity, and information flow throughout society. However, these technologies and means may be used to undermine international stability and security, and adversely affect the State's integrity in the civil and military fields.

Portugal believes that cyberspace security is of great importance and is increasingly important. The following aspects should be paid attention to:

(1) It is important to emphasize the progress made in the efforts to implement legislation on cyber security and integrity, including risk assessment approach adopted for this purpose, requiring appropriate technical and organizational security measures, and reporting on the security violations or lack of integrity that have significant impact on the operations of the service sector.
(2) The development of capability-building measures is very important. But there is objective difficulty in human resources.
(3) There is a need to facilitate access to knowledge and to promote collective training among all major stakeholders in the areas such as security.
(4) With regard to the protection of personal data and privacy, it is important to emphasize changes that have occurred, for example, it is mandatory to report on personal data violation events.
(5) In the conceptual context, it is necessary to reinforce the idea that relevant legislation should be derived primarily from the international laws.
(6) At the international level, with due consideration to a broader range of globalization, confidence must be strengthened and information sharing promoted, including combining a broad context of globalization, facilitating information sharing between all (public and private) stakeholders; committing to the completion of joint exercise participated by public and private entities and conducted in the border areas, and promoting technical standardization.

As shown above, Portugal is concerned with the following three aspects in cyberspace security: first, strengthening national capabilities in cyberspace security; second, domestic human resource construction; and third, enhancing mutual trust at an international level.

8.2.29 Qatar

Qatar holds the idea that information security is essential for national and global security and there is a need to continue to monitor existing and potential threats in the field of information security. To maintain information security, Qatar has developed a strategy to address the threat while fulfilling the need to maintain the free flow of information. Qatar has taken a series of measures to upgrade relevant technology, and to improve the legislation, supervision and law enforcement. Qatar also conducts coordination and cooperation on relevant issues at regional and international levels, as permitted by its domestic law. Qatar believes that the international community should continue its efforts to develop an international instrument that is binding in guaranteeing information security, thereby improving information security. Such instruments should provide the development of anti-hacking procedures so as to maintain the continuity of information systems.[24]

As shown above, Qatar mainly focuses on two aspects of cyberspace security: first, the State should establish responding measures for cyberspace security; second, the international community should have the legal binding force for cyber-attacks.

8.2.30 Republic of Korea

South Korea believes that[25] cyberspace offers unlimited opportunities for economic development and social development, as well as global prosperity. An open and secure cyberspace is essential for the increase of human achievement and the promotion of democratic participation. However, because of its nature of openness, anonymity, regardless of the States, cyber threats are bringing serious challenges to international security, such as cybercrime, cyber terrorism and cyber warfare.

In response to these challenges, the South Korean government announced in July 2013 comprehensive national cyber security measures, where measures are set out to address cyber-attacks and to strengthen the security of specific critical

---

[24]Q-CERT, Annual Reprot 2014. https://unoda-web.s3-accelerate.amazonaws.com/wp-content/uploads/2015/08/Qatar-IS.pdf [2016-9-19].

[25]The Republic of Korea. https://unoda-web.s3-accelerate.amazonaws.com/wp-content/uploads/2015/08/ROKISinfull.pdf [2016-9-19].

information infrastructure. After that, South Korea experienced a series of cyber-attacks, including the attack on nuclear power plant operators in 2014. In order to respond more effectively to cyber threats, South Korea promulgated a comprehensive plan in March 2015 to strengthen cyber security protection and set up the post of a President Secretary in cyber security affairs.

South Korea welcomed the conclusion of the 2013 report on the development of the field of information and telecommunications from the perspective of international security. The report confirms the possibility of applying international laws to States in cyberspace and looks forward to further discussion on how the agreed principles will apply to State conducts in cyberspace.

South Korea believes that[26] it is an important area of international cooperation to agree on a set of international norms and confidence-building measures and to build the cyber capability of developing countries and to promote cooperation among computer emergency response organizations. In this regard, the South Korean government is also committed to strengthening bilateral and trilateral cooperation with major States, and actively participates in regional and international forums on cyber issues such as the Association of South-East Asian Nations and the United Nations Group of Governmental Experts.

Korea believes that the injured State may act in accordance with the principles of national sovereignty and the principle of reciprocity; countering behavior cannot be infinite, and should be carefully implemented in line with the international laws; there is a need for an international organization to decide how to objectively judge the attribution of the cyber-attack, and to ultimately show the result to the international community; the international laws, such as the International Humanitarian Law and Countermeasures are applicable to international cyberspace.

As shown above, South Korea is mainly concerned with six aspects of cyberspace security: first, enhancing the State's response capabilities on cyberspace security; second, applying international laws to cyberspace; third, establishing a set of international norms and trust mechanisms by the international community; fourth, counter-measures being allowed with regard to cyber-attacks, but within a certain extent; fifth, the international community should have a standard and an institution for determining the attribution of an attack; sixth, the existing law being directly applied to cyberspace.

8.2.31 Russian Federation

Russia believes that, at present, most countries are very vulnerable to attacks. A practical solution should be found for the problem. The States should share their experience in coping with the issue, so as to benefit the international community's

[26]Republic of Korea. https://unoda-web.s3-accelerate.amazonaws.com/wp-content/uploads/2014/10/ROK.pdf [2016-9-19].

cyberspace security. The norms and regulations of international laws should be implemented to avoid causing conflicts with the use of information and communication technology, use of information and communication technology should be promoted for mere application for peaceful purposes, without interference in cyberspace affairs of other States. A trust system should be built at the international level in an institutionalized and universal manner, to be binding for the States. An international organization or a long-term organizational mechanism should be set to address cyberspace security issues; therefore, standards should be set to study and judge the evidence of a cyberattack; principles and norms should be established, so that States fulfill their responsibility within the region of jurisdiction. If the conflict can be resorted to the UN Security Council after the cyber-attack and let the Council decide, a lot of public conflicts will be avoided, and more room will be left for discussion.

Russia has mainly stressed the following three aspects: first, international methods should be adopted to deal with the risk in cyberspace; second, sovereignty exists in cyberspace, cyberspace affairs should not be interfered by another State; third, Article 51 of the United Nations Charter cannot be directly applied to the cyberspace.

8.2.32 Senegal

Senegal believes that the issue of cyberspace sovereignty is important, but many territorial-based principles cannot be applied; in the case of data, since the private sector has the information and the server is located abroad, it should be studied how the States may use sovereignty to enforce some rules on the private sector; if national sovereignty can be effectively applied, the government can force private enterprises to assist the States in combating terrorism, especially in developing countries and countries with fewer capabilities to find international solutions to transnational cyber-attacks, so as to ensure credible accountability and traceability, an international platform can be established to address the issue of traceability, to avoid the situation where a country claims to be attacked and starts fighting back after putting forward insufficient evidence; in armed conflict, the evidence should be sufficient; large-scale weapons of mass destruction and nuclear weapons have similar international decision-making platforms, which can help, in the event of a cyber conflict, establish a non-refutable evidence chain; The international community should help developing countries build national strategies and tools to combat cybercrime. Academic support is also required during helping developing countries build capability, so as to help these countries run autonomously and independently address their own cyber security issues.

Senegal addresses three problems in cyberspace security: first, cyberspace sovereignty is very important, and should be effectively applied to combat terrorism; second, an international platform should be built for determination of national cyber conflicts; third, help should be provided for developing countries to eliminate digital division.

8.2.33 Serbia

Serbia believes that[27] giving consideration to the significance of ensuring and developing cyberspace security, the Republic of Serbia has taken the field of cyberspace security as a strategic priority for the information society. Serbia's "Information Society Development Strategy for the Republic of Serbia before 2020"[28] (*Стратегију развоја информационог друштва у Републици Србији до* 2020) passed in 2010 announced that information security is one of the six priority areas. Serbia does not have a national strategy specifically for information security, but there are a number of other documents concerning this issue.

In January 2016, the Serbian Parliament passed the Information Security Act, which established the competent authorities for information security, responsible for developing regulations in accordance with national and international standards, working with other national authorities and conducting law enforcement inspections. This law also defines the important information and communication technology systems in Serbia. Thus, the operators must use appropriate technology and measures to ensure information security. These systems include: ① information and communication technology systems for public institutions; ② information and communication technology systems for handling sensitive personal information; and ③ information and communication technology systems in the areas of public interest (energy, transportation, gas, banking, health and other fields).

The competent authorities of Serbia carry out international cooperation, and give alert especially with regard to risks and events with one of the following characteristics: ① rapid development, which may become a high risk; ② beyond the national capability; and ③ that may affect more than one country.

The Information Security Act provides that a national computer emergency response organization is established within the Electronic Communications and Postal Services Authority; in addition, cooperation will be conducted with similar bodies in other countries. The law also provides for the cryptography safety and protection of electromagnetic compromising emanations.

The Serbian National Security Council and the Office of Confidential Information Protection (shortened as the Office of the National Security Council) are the departments of the Government of Serbia that are responsible for

[27]REPUBLIC OF SERBIA: "Developments in the field of information and telecommunications in the context of international security". https://unoda-web.s3-accelerate.amazonaws.com/wp-content/uploads/2014/07/Serbia.pdf [2016-9-19].

[28]Стратегију развоја информационог друштва у Републици Србији до 2020. Године. http://mtt.gov.rs/download/3/Strategija_razvoja_informacionog_drustva_2020.pdf [2016-10-6].

coordinating the implementation of national and European Union security policies at the national level. Part of the work of the department is to protect this confidential information by information security measures and coordinating the implementation of these measures in government institutions and other institutions, so as to protect confidential information. To that end, a decree on specific measures for the protection of confidential information in the information network system was adopted in 2011 (Official Gazette of the Republic of Serbia, No. 53/2011). The Information and Communication Technology Division of the Joint Services Authority of Serbia is responsible for activities related to information security protection, data protection and implementation of the prescribed safety standards of information systems of national institutions. The Serbian Academic Network is responsible for conducting computer security emergency response activities in educational and research institutions.

At the international level, since 2011, the Office of the National Security Council has been actively participating in the Security Sector Director Forum in South-Eastern Europe. One of the main objectives of the Forum is to strengthen information security and confidential information protection in the States of the region in accordance with international standards. The Office of the National Security Council is the chief coordinating body for the development of the concept of regional cyber defense within the framework of the security sector of South-Eastern Europe. The Office of the National Security Council has prepared and sent several related proposals for review, reunification and approval to other thematic working group members.

Serbia believes that States should cooperate in strengthening the security of global information and telecommunication systems, especially the maintenance of effective and targeted information against the exchange, warning and notification mechanisms of cyber security incidents. To this end, the States appoint coordinators and make the contact available to the public. Special attention should be given to the protection of critical infrastructures, especially when the relevant event affects more than one country. The States should also cooperate in knowledge exchange and education in this area. Considering that the risk of cyber-attacks increasing with more significant characteristics in an interconnected world, the international community should encourage cooperation and dialogue among States to promote the co-establishment of cyber security so as to contribute to international cooperation aimed at promoting cooperation in the field of information security. Common and effective cooperation will help to build a safer and more secure global ICT environment that will allow countries and citizens to stay away from the risks in the cyber world.

Serbia believes that, a state should have the corresponding capabilities in order to determine whether there is an attack, whether the attack is conducted through cyberspace, who the attacker is and who takes the technical responsibility and who takes the legal responsibility; therefore, help should be provided for each State to build such capabilities at the international level, so that each country has the most basic capability that can be recognized by the international community so as to discover the attack, and determine how the attack starts at the national level; there is no specific provision in international law providing that States are obligated to provide evidence of cyber-attacks; with regard to the legitimacy of counter-action, the Council made a political decision; the International Criminal Court made a legal decision; and these decisions are subject to the evidence of ICT use in a technical perspective; in terms of attack attribution, some criteria may be put forward to determine what kind of attribution is acceptable; the state should provide sufficient evidence for a legal institution to prove that a different country conducts an attack against the State, the evidence being recognized according to the international law, thus, it can be said that the country has tracked in a legal way; if a State discovers that its territory is used for an attack, the State should take actions and express the willingness to act, though the State may lack the capability to prevent the attack; in accordance with the International Humanitarian Law or the Law on Armed Conflict, civil-use infrastructure should not be attacked, unless it provides significant support to military activities. Therefore, it should be made clear that merely when the critical infrastructure suffers a serious threat or is involved in a military act. Cyberspace is not a human heritage, which is determined by the national sovereignty. It is something owned by a country based on its territorial jurisdiction. National sovereignty should weigh more than international law, for each country relies on its sovereignty to decide whether to accept certain treaties and conventions, and even the matter of whether to admit the International Court of Justice.

As shown above, Serbia's main focus on cyberspace security is in the following six aspects: first, to strengthen the construction of cyberspace security mechanisms in laws and institutions; second, to cooperate on cyberspace security at the international level; third, to depend on the capabilities to determine cyber-attacks, thus support for developing countries should be enhanced; fourth, accountability depends on basis more than political accusation; fifth, standards being set for the protection of infrastructure, clarifying civil nature; sixth, to recognize cyberspace sovereignty, denying the opinion that cyberspace is a global public area.

8.2.34 Spain

Spain believes that[29] information and communication technology provides important support for all societies around the world and is of increasing importance. But the globalization of such technologies poses serious risks and threats such as cyber espionage, cybercrime, hacking, and cyber war.

Cyber security is a strategic priority for Spain. As a result, according to the cyber security strategy of the European Union partners, Spain adopted a national cyber security strategy on 5 December 2013 to strengthen prevention, protection,

[29]Asunto: RES 69/28 "Avances en la esfera de la información y las telecomunicaciones en el contexto de la seguridad internacional". https://unoda-web.s3-accelerate.amazonaws.com/wp-content/uploads/2015/08/SpainISinfull.pdf [2016-9-19].

detection, analysis, response, recovery and coordination capabilities, so as to better respond to cyber threats. The strategy reflects a comprehensive approach to cyber security and establishes the National Cyber Security Council, an interdepartmental coordination system, to address crisis situations. The strategy sets out international cooperation measures and allows institutions and enterprises to participate, especially strategic institutions and enterprises. The main components of the strategy include education and awareness enhancing activities aimed at improving civil society's understanding of cyber security issues. In July 2015, the National Cyber Security Committee approved nine specific programs stemmed from the National Cyber Security Program to implement the national network security strategy.

Spain believes that[30] Governments should support and maintain an open, barrier-free and secure cyberspace while safeguarding fundamental values such as democracy, human rights and the rule of law.

Spain is actively involved in all strategic initiatives involving cyber security of the European Union, the Organization for Security and Cooperation in Europe, the North Atlantic Treaty Organization, the Council of Europe and the Organization for Economic Co-operation and Development. In 2015, Spain joined the "free online alliance" and the global cyber professionals' forum. Spain supports the outcome of the high-level meeting of the General Assembly, adopted in December 2015, on the overall review of the implementation of the outcomes of the World Summit on the information society. In addition, Spain is a party to the Budapest Convention on Cybercrime.

Spain also supports the recommendations contained in the report of the Group of Governmental Experts of the United Nations. Spain believes that the United Nations can play an important role in achieving an international consensus on cyber security, and therefore, supports institutional dialogue within the framework of the United Nations, supports institutionalized dialogues including other international forums, so as to promote regional cooperation and build global standards, best practices, national codes of conduct and confidence-building measures, ultimately ensuring peace and security for the use of information technology.

Spain believes that the WSIS process should be closely aligned with the 2030 sustainable development agenda, for the access to information and communication technologies has become a development indicator and is, as of itself, a vision. Spain supports to reach an international consensus on cyber security and believes that States should continue to consider how to interpret and apply the principles and norms of international law in cyberspace, especially the principles and norms involving the use or threat of use of force, international humanitarian law and the protection of the fundamental rights and freedoms of individuals. Spain supports the vision of the international community for the peaceful use of ICTs for the benefit of all mankind. Spain believes that the Charter is fully applicable in this regard. Measures taken in accordance with international law and timely, reasonable

[30]INFORME DE ESPAÑA SOBRE CUMPLIMIENTO DE RESOLUCION. https://unoda-web.s3-accelerate.amazonaws.com/wp-content/uploads/2014/10/Spain.pdf [2016-9-19].

and appropriate response to threats or attacks that may affect national security are inherent rights of States.

Spain believes that States should engage in effective cooperation to prevent the harmful practices in cyberspace, and that, in an informed manner, the territory is not allowed to be used for the internationally wrongful acts of the implementation of such technologies. The international community should take measures in the following four areas to strengthen global information security: ① confidence-building measures, including transparency, exchange of information and best practices; ② international law, the international community, and the United Nations in particular, should continue to consider how the principles and norms of international law should be interpreted and applied in cyberspace; ③ international cooperation, improvement in communication channels at the time of an incident, and construction of a stronger and more flexible mechanism for the cooperation between the police and judiciary; ④ capability-building incorporated in a bilateral form in the framework of international organizations, and to provide such support to countries that need to build capability.

Spain believes that the receiving countries should continue to be encouraged and assisted to carry out necessary capability-building and be assisted in the development of national laws determining cyber security standards.

As shown above, Spain is mainly concerned with the following three aspects of cyberspace security: first, improving the strategic position of cyberspace security in the State, and enhancing the ability to respond to cyberspace security; second, strengthen cooperation between the States to jointly cope with the threats brought by cyberspace security; third, assisting receiving countries to carry out construction of cyberspace security capabilities.

8.2.35 Sweden

Sweden believes that[31] while the development of cyberspace creates almost unlimited opportunities, it is necessary to properly address the security issues involving the use of information technology and telecommunications through international cooperation. In Sweden, the work on the national information technology security strategy is advancing with the times. The government is currently developing a strategy for cyber security. The Swedish Defense Commission has recently evaluated cyber security and cyber defense, emphasizing that Sweden needs to strengthen the overall cyber security capabilities.

Sweden participates in a variety of international cyberspace forums and actively makes contributions. Meanwhile, it also strives for bilateral and regional dialogue

[31]Submission by Sweden to UNGA resolution 68/243 entitled "Developments in the field of information and telecommunications in the context of international security". 2014-9-12. https://unoda-web.s3-accelerate.amazonaws.com/wp-content/uploads/2014/10/Sweden.pdf [2016-9-19].

on cyber issues, including the Nordic region of the Baltic Sea. Sweden is particularly concerned about the following issues: promotion of human rights in cyberspace; a multi-stakeholder governance model for Internet governance; the need to develop basic principles to guide international surveillance activities. Sweden advocates the development of a coherent cyber strategy for the European Union based on the fundamental values and benefits of the European Union.

The adoption of the comprehensive strategy for cyber security of the European Union in 2013 was a major progress. Sweden is one of the founding members of the "Online Freedom Alliance", which is committed to enhancing the freedom of the Internet around the world. Sweden has hosted the Stockholm Internet Forum for three consecutive years, a multi-stakeholder meeting aimed at deepening Internet freedom and global development. Sweden is one of the core sponsors of the Human Rights Council resolution 20/8 (2012), in which, the Council reaffirmed that the rights enjoyed by people off the Internet should also be protected on the Internet.

Sweden has issued a joint statement for three consecutive years in the First Committee of the General Assembly, noting that it is necessary to always address multiple perspectives of human rights and of the multi-stakeholder in the resolution of ICTs and international security issues. Sweden has also actively promoted the adoption of the initial set of confidence-building measures by the OSCE to reduce the risk of conflict arising from the use of information and communication technologies and enhance transparency, with emphasis on respect for and promotion of human rights.

Sweden believes that efforts should be made at the global level to develop core principles that guide the use of information and communication technologies and international relations in cyberspace. The international community, including all stakeholders, should be involved in effective cooperative efforts to strengthen cyber security. Such efforts could include the development of a voluntary set of rules for the conduct in cyberspace or international standards of conduct. Global actors should be committed to developing confidence-building measures to improve transparency and enhance predictability, thereby reducing misunderstandings and conflicts in cyberspace.

As shown above, Sweden is mainly concerned with the following aspects of cyberspace security: first, domestic cyberspace security strategic capabilities are to be enhanced in Sweden; second, the international community should work together to address the threat of cyberspace security; third, the multi-stakeholder Internet governance model is supported; fourth, human rights should be promoted on the Internet.

8.2.36 Switzerland

Switzerland believes that information and communication technology has become an indispensable driving force in social, economic and political activities. Switzerland is determined to seize the opportunities arising from the use of information and communication technologies. Considering the developments and challenges related to information and communication technologies, Switzerland is actively involved in the shaping of the information society in the form of implementing the "Swiss Federal Council's Information Society Strategy". However, the use of ICTs also makes functional deficiencies in information and communication infrastructure to be easily misused by criminals, intelligence, political military persons or terrorists. Interference, manipulation and specific attacks carried out through electronic networks are the risks that the information society must face. In this context, countries are increasingly involved in a series of regional and international policy discussions and debates on cyber security. As a result, the Swiss Federal Government established a Group of Experts in 2010 to review cyber security risks and improve the country's ability to respond to these threats.

On 27 June 2012, the Swiss Federal Government adopted a national strategy to prevent Switzerland from cyber risks and laid the foundations for a holistic approach. The strategy seeks to improve early detection of cyber risks and emerging threats, integrating infrastructure of Switzerland to be more capable of resisting cyber-attacks, and reducing cyber risks in the whole, focusing on prevention of cybercrime, espionage and sabotage. The strategy also mentions the need for a cyber security culture, shared responsibility, and a risk-based response approach. It also advocates coordination at the government level and development of national, public-private partnerships and international cooperation. The strategy includes 16 measures that should be in place in 2017. The Swiss Federal Government, in 2013, adopted a detailed plan for the implementation of the strategy.

The Swiss Government also established a Steering Committee, where the leading institutions responsible for implementing each specific measure attended. The mandate of the Steering Committee is to ensure a coordinated and targeted implementation of the strategy. At the operational level, the Government has set up a coordinating unit to support the work of the Steering Committee. The measures include risk and vulnerability analysis, analysis of threat conditions, continuity and crisis management and capability-building measures, as well as international cooperation and initiatives.

These 16 measures can be divided into four main areas: ① prevention (i.e., risk and vulnerability and threat analysis); ② emergency response (i.e., incident handling, positive measures and enforcement); ③ continuity (i.e. continuity and crisis management); ④ support processes (i.e., international cooperation, education and research, legal basis, etc.).

Foreign policy of Switzerland in the field of cybersecurity focuses on the development of responsible national codes of conduct, confidence-building measures and capability-building. Thus, Switzerland participated in various international processes. The Organization for Security and Cooperation in Europe (OSCE) has adopted confidence-building measures around cybersecurity. Switzerland considers this process to be of vital importance. In addition, the London process is another important process for Switzerland's participation. Switzerland also supported a series of projects aimed at capability-building.

Switzerland believes that all measures taken by the international community must strike a balance between security and human rights. The right people enjoy offline must also be guaranteed online. There is a need for further development of measures for confidence-building. The set of confidence-building measures adopted by the OSCE is essential for strengthening security. To carry out practical joint activities, and to enhance cooperation and improve transparency through the exchange of information helps to achieve the overall stability of cyberspace.

Switzerland is determined to cooperate at the international security policy level so as to respond to cyberspace threats together with other countries and international organizations. Switzerland is committed to monitoring and shaping relevant developments at the diplomatic level and promoting political exchanges within the framework of international conferences and other diplomatic initiatives. In this context, Switzerland participates in a variety of international processes aimed to develop the global mechanism. The OSCE has adopted confidence-building measures around cyber security, and Switzerland believes that this process is of the utmost importance. Thus, through the adoption of a "dual track", Switzerland will focus on implementing confidence-building measures and developing further measures.

Switzerland believes that the principle of sovereign equality and non-interference in the affairs of other countries is very important. The application of these principles is consistent with other principles of international law, such as International Humanitarian Law, International Human Rights Law, Customary International Law and the sovereign rights of other States. Sovereignty is the right of a State to control its territory. Therefore, the State has a duty to ensure that its territory is not used by non-State actors for international unlawful conduct.

States may, without their knowledge, have the possibility that their territories or cyber infrastructure under management are used for international wrongful acts. The principle of rationality should be designed, which does not require the territorial States to put an end to such action, but, which is the key point, make the best efforts to put an end to such action, even if it is unsuccessful; the principle of peaceful settlement of disputes must be taken into account. When a problem cannot be resolved, counter measures can be used as part of the response to international misconduct, but with the principle of proportional necessity being met. The first step of the counter measures is to trace the origin, including technical identification and legal traceability distinguished from each other. Tracing is the sovereign right of every state. This responsibility cannot be handed over to a third party. The evidence of traceability should be of a quality and should be deterministic, so as to be used as a basis for subsequent action.

As shown above, Switzerland focuses on five aspects of cyberspace security: first, strengthen the protection of cyberspace security at the strategic and institutional level; second, strengthen cooperation at the international level to jointly cope with the threat of cyberspace security; third, recognize sovereignty in cyberspace, emphasizing sovereign equality and non-interference, and the obligations brought about; fourth, the state should make efforts to limit its territory to be used in initiating international illegal action and publish relevant information, attaching little importance to the results; fifth, countering action is a reasonable way for response, as long as meeting the principle of proportionality.

8.2.37 Togo

Togo believes that the progress of information and telecommunications, though is a huge asset for national development, brings threats to national and international security. It is a virtual space that is often used by criminals or terrorists. Togo has also been confronted by this threat and has found criminal activities related to information and communication technology, ranging from cyber-fraud and other types of fraud, to child pornography and violations of people's freedom and integrity. In the era of proliferation of terrorism, the cyber and social media became the propaganda and recruitment platform for terrorist organizations. In addition, most countries are transitioning to an e-government, making the Togo government face major challenges. The functioning of the administration and civil and military security are likely to be compromised by cyber-attacks. Faced with this situation, there is an urgent need to take measures at the national and international levels to regulate the information and telecommunications sectors to ensure that they are not used for criminal purposes.

Togo has taken a number of measures for this purpose, including the promulgation of Decree No. 2011-120/PR on the system and the mandatory identification of subscribers to telecommunications services; the promulgation of Law No. 2012-018 on electronic communications and the amendments to Law No. 2012-018 and Law No. 2013-003; draft legislation on cybercrime, encryption, cyber security, personal data protection and electronic transactions. The purpose of these regulations is to ensure that all information and telecommunications activities are traceable and to establish a security mechanism to prevent fraudulent intrusion into information and telecommunications networks.

Togo believes that it is necessary to establish an institutional oversight framework, such as the Computer Emergency Response Organization, to be responsible for ensuring cyber security at the national level as a supplement to the postal and telecommunications regulatory authorities. There is also a need to strengthen the capability of the staff so that law enforcement agencies and public and private entities involved in ensuring cyber security can take effective actions to address threats in any form. In addition, international cooperation within the framework of the International Telecommunication Union and the United Nations also contributes to the improvement of information and telecommunications security.

As shown above, with regard to cyberspace security, Togo is mainly concerned with coping with the threat against cyberspace security by cyberspace legislation, mechanism construction, human force construction and other aspects.

8.2.38 Turkmenistan

Turkmenistan's domestic policy and foreign policy are based on neutrality and depend on the close relationship between national interests, global security and common progress. For Turkmenistan, a key factor derived from neutrality and international obligations is the peace-loving nature of its foreign policy. Turkmenistan, therefore, usually relieves all issues through political and diplomatic channels, mainly by the United Nations and other international organizations.

Turkmenistan has acceded to an international disarmament instrument that encourages the contracting parties to maintain global peace, harmony and security as its main objective. Turkmenistan attaches particular importance to the strengthening of international peace and security and calls for a reduction in the number of weapons, believing that with fewer weapons in the world, world development will be more stable and peaceful, and trust and understanding among nations and people will grow deeper.

As shown above, Turkmenistan has not yet formed an independent view on cyberspace security, but from the perspective of dealing with physical social problems, it will deal with cyberspace security issues from the perspective of international cooperation.

8.2.39 United Kingdom of Great Britain and Northern Ireland

The UK believes that[32] cyber security is an essential component of national and international critical infrastructures and is an indispensable basis for online economic and social activities. The actual threats and potential threats posed by cyberspace activities are of great concern. The United Kingdom has adopted a series of measures based on the United Kingdom National Cyber security Strategy, which was published in November 2011. The UK reviews the 2015 National Security Risk Assessment report, which confirms that cyber remains a top threat to national security. The UK will allocate £ 1.9 billion[33] over the next five years after allocating £ 860 million over the implementation of the last national cybersecurity strategy (2011–2016). The new national cyber security strategy will be released in 2016, including the establishment of a new national cyber security center.

[32]Response to General Assembly resolution 69/28 "Developments in the field of information and telecommunications in the context of international security". https://unoda-web.s3-accelerate.amazonaws.com/wp-content/uploads/2015/08/UKISinfull.pdf [2016-9-19].

[33]UK planning huge budget to fight cyber terrorism in the coming 5 years. http://news.xinhuanet.com/world/2015-11/18/c_128439327.htm [2016-10-6].

The United Kingdom recognizes that[34] international collaboration is at the heart of successful cyber security, and that it should first work with international partners to deal with cybercrime and major events, and then, it should focus on building cyber capabilities. The UK welcomes the first set of regional cyberspace trust building measures promoted by the OSCE.

The UK will continue to promote the establishment of a free, open, peaceful and secure cyberspace that will protect economic and social benefits and benefit all. The UK, through the Global Center for the Suppression of Sexual Exploitation of Children (WePROTECT) and other initiatives, takes the lead in dealing with cross-border cyber security challenges. The UK is also committed to sharing best practices internationally and ensuring that the global community is receiving assistance in expanding cyber security capabilities.

The United Kingdom continues to participate actively and constructively in international discussions on cybersecurity and considers that the consensus report of the recent panel of Group of Experts has made valuable progress in reaffirming that international law applies to cyberspace, and that States comply with international law, especially the provisions of the Charter of the United Nations as the basic framework for the use of ICTs by States. The UK welcomes discussions on future cyberspace confidence-building measures in the context of the Organization for Security and Cooperation in Europe and the organization of similar work in other regional organizations, and the UK looks forward to further involvement in strengthening the capability and international cooperation around cyber security.

The UK believes that the issue of responsibility attribution should be the responsibility of the state. National sovereignty decides the measures to take when being attacked, including counter-measures; Counter-measures are a transparent approach and must be proportionate; it should promote stability, not escalate, nor be a threat; the issue of controlling aggressive ICT tools is very complicated. These tools have both sides, and once fallen into the wrong hands, they can be used for malicious purposes; but we cannot allow them to damage our capability of self-defense in such a manner; development of a new defense system in the State should be allowed. It is very important to fight terrorism, as well as to exchange information and cooperate between countries; the responsible behavior and the act of the private sector should be included in the international norms, so that the relevant parties are allowed to respond to the requirements of the country to deal with public safety issues; transparency in international security issues is important; the States should be encouraged to share their favorable measures, and to encourage the States to perform transparency according to their cyber capabilities to disclose the cyber strategy of each State.

[34]Response to General Assembly resolution 68/243 "Developments in the field of information and telecommunications in the context of international security". https://unoda-web.s3-accelerate.amazonaws.com/wp-content/uploads/2014/07/UK.pdf [2016-9-19].

As shown above, the UK has the following concerns of cyberspace security: first, implement the national cyberspace security strategy, and stress the transparency of the States; second, strengthen international cooperation to deal with the threat of cyberspace security; third, recognize the application of international law in cyberspace; fourth, counter-action is legitimate, but needs to be used cautiously; fifth, control offensive ICT tools without affecting the legitimate use; sixth, include private institutions in the binding object of international regulations.

8.2.40 United States of America

As the inventor of the Internet, the United States of America has been in 20 years avoiding openly expressing its official position on the definition of the overall cyberspace in the United Nations. This may be, on one hand, out of its national security strategy, and on the other hand, because of the Anglo-American tradition of its case law. The United States from the domestic law to the government policy lacks a statutory definition of the Internet. However, by going through relevant American dictionaries, policies, and national strategy documents, there can still be found that it emphasizes some of the characteristics of the Internet.

According to comprehensive analysis in different aspects of the United States, it can be found that the United States, when defining cyberspace, has stressed on different occasions and by different people that **the cyberspace is to control the "nerve", infrastructure network, the virtual world and the global region**, which are one-sided definitions. Even if the above one-sided definitions are combined together, it still cannot include all the contents and elements of cyberspace, and the Internet. Therefore, only by sorting out all the elements of cyberspace, the basic position toward cyberspace, the policy to be implemented and the starting point of the means of the United States can be understood.

(1) In the National Strategy to Secure Cyber space[35] put in force in 2003, the follow definition is provided: cyberspace is "[the] nervous system-the control system of the State…composed of hundreds of thousands of interconnected computers, servers, routers, switches, and fiber optic cables that allow our critical infrastructures to work", which stresses that the cyberspace is a nerve controlling the state, so as to accentuate the outstanding importance of cyberspace.
(2) In the National Security Presidential Directive/NSPD-54/Homeland Security Presidential Directive/HSPD-23[36] signed on January 8, 2008, the following definition is provided: "Cyberspace means the interdependent network of information technology infrastructures, and includes the Internet,

[35]White House, and United States of America. "The National Strategy to Secure Cyberspace." https://www.us-cert.gov/sites/default/files/publications/cyberspace_strategy.pdf [2016-9-17].

[36]National Security Presidential Directive/NSPD-54/ Homeland Security Presidential Directive/HSPD-23. http://fas.org/irp/offdocs/nspd/nspd-54.pdf [2016-9-17].

telecommunications networks, computer systems, and embedded processors and controllers in critical industries", in which the emphasis is on the cyber infrastructure as an object of national protection.

(3) The report of Assuring a Trusted and Resilient Information and Communications Infrastructure[37] provided by the White House gives the following description of cyberspace: "National Security Presidential Directive 54/ Homeland Security Presidential Directive 23 (NSPD-54/HSPD23) defines cyberspace as the interdependent network of information technology infrastructures, and includes the Internet, telecommunications networks, computer systems, and embedded processors and controllers in critical industries. Common usage of the term also refers to the virtual environment of information and interactions between people", in which information and people are included to indicate that information and people should be included in the protection of cyberspace.

(4) In May, 2008, Gordon England, the U.S. Defense Secretary issued a memorial, in which the following definition is given: cyber space is "A global domain within the information environment consisting of the interdependent network of information technology infrastructures, including the Internet, telecommunications networks, computer systems, and embedded processors and controllers.", which emphasizes the cosmopolitanism of cyberspace and that the cyberspace belongs to a global region.

The United States believes that key infrastructure providing public services, such as the means of conveyance and transportation, etc. should not be attacked; but the attack on websites, and so on, will not affect international security. One website being painted or being destroyed will not cause great changes in the international security situation.

When cyber sovereignty is discussed, we should link it with our own management rules of ICTs within borders and clarify how international law applies to national use of ICTs instead of just national sovereignty. Meanwhile, attention should be paid to the exercise of jurisdiction (including the establishment of public policy and regulatory requirements), so that it is consistent with the international obligations of territorial States, including human rights obligations. The premise of non-external interference in the internal affairs of the State is to comply with the content of international law and to prohibit the State from coercive action. Because cyberspace behavior is governed by cyberspace sovereignty, the behavior of non-state actors should also be subject to cyberspace sovereignty. Therefore, it is the responsibility of the state to bear the legal consequences of non-state actors.

Peaceful settlement of disputes should not be emphasized blindly and without regard to the legitimate means by which States can deal with malicious attacks. The right to self-defense should comply with the principle of necessity and proportionality, and the international community should apply the principle of prudence.

---

[37]Cyber Space Policy Review. http://energy.gov/sites/prod/files/cioprod/documents/Cyberspace_Policy_Review_final.pdf [2016-10-6].

Any country when applying force to exercise their right to self-defense must be limited to some extent, so that the scope and extent of counter-measures meets with the attack.

The United States expresses its willingness to help developing countries by providing technical capability and knowledge in cyber security to enhance the cyber security capability building of developing countries. The United States is also willing to provide theoretical support and corresponding tools, and help other countries to improve the law, so that abuse of information and communication technology can be effectively eliminated. The United States is also willing to help developing countries to enhance public awareness.

The United States stresses three aspects of the cyberspace security: first, key infrastructure of States should not be attacked; second, cyberspace sovereignty exist, but it must bear responsibility and be bound by national law; third, cyber conflicts should comply with the principle of prudence, while allowing the states to have the right to use legitimate response means; fourth, the United States is willing to help developing countries to improve cyber security capability-building.

8.3 Laws and Regulation of Major States on Internet Management

8.3.1 Maintenance of National Security

1. The USA Patriot Act

The United States in 2001 issued the "Patriot Act"[38] (The USA PATRIOT: Uniting and Strengthening America by provided Appropriate Tools Requires to Intercept and Obstruct Terrorism), which clearly stated that the purpose of the legislation is to intercept and prevent terrorist activities. The Patriot Act greatly liberalizes law enforcement restrictions of law enforcement institutions and prohibits the dissemination of information involving information of political incitement, terrorism, provocation of national antagonism, national hatred and racial discrimination, which endangers national security and national dignity. The Patriot Act authorizes the Government to obtain personal information, including telephone, e-mail, medical, financial and other types of records, at any time without the supervision and permission of the judge, so that it may in fact be free from any constrain to monitor anyone. This Act reduces the restrictions on US foreign intelligence units, enhances the authority of the US Treasury to control and manage financial flow activities, especially for financial activities related to foreigners or political groups, and strengthens power of police and immigration management

[38]The USA PATRIOT: Uniting and Strengthening America by Providing Appropriate Tools Requires to Intercept and Obstruct Terrorism. https://www.gpo.gov/fdsys/pkg/CREC-2001-10-23/pdf/CREC-2001-10-23-pt1-PgH7159-3.pdf [2016-8-30].

units over the residence and expulsion of foreigners suspected of terrorist acts. This Act also extends the definition of terrorism, including domestic terrorism, and extends the scope of activities managed by the police.

2. The Terrorism Act of the UK

The Terrorism Act 2006,[39] issued by the United Kingdom in 2006, includes acts that seriously interfere with or disrupt the operation of electronic systems in the scope of terrorism and characterize computer hacking as a terrorist act, so as to combat cybercrime. The Act contains measures to prevent the return of Islamic extremists to the United Kingdom, unless they agree to be subject to surveillance and action restrictions. The Act also provides that unauthorized intrusion into nuclear bases, as particular regions, is considered a crime of terrorist acts. The Act also provides special powers to allow access to passports of the Islamic Jihad suspects, and the airline could be forced to provide passenger information for the British government. The Act also requires Internet companies to provide user data to the government. Under the Act, the British telecommunications companies and Internet service providers (ISP) must save relevant Internet data and other communication data details; and Internet service providers are required to retain the IP address of the Internet user.

3. Law of the Russian Federation On Mass Media

Early in the Yeltsin era in 1991, Russia enacted the Law of the Russian Federation ON MASS MEDIA,[40] which became the most important legal basis for the protection of the freedom of the press and the standardization of journalism. It was originally intended for "printing, audiovisual materials and other news for mass communication: regular printed publications, audiovisual, film archival material and other forms of regular mass communication", because the Internet at that time has not yet become the mainstream channel for news spreading. Along with the popularity of Internet application technology, the establishment of norms of the Internet in news communication has become a top priority. As of January 17, 2014, the law has been revised 30 times to include cyber communication in the mass media so that it is incorporated to be under jurisdiction of the law.

The Act mainly deals with information of terrorism, information endangering national security, spreading pornography and violence and other messages in harmful information, and combats cyber rumors and defamation, eliminates illegal Internet transactions and protects individual privacy. The law mainly prohibits the use of the mass media for criminal offenses, leakage of secrecy of special protection by the state or other laws, calls for the seizure of power, the change of the constitutional system and the integrity of the state by force, incitation of national, class, social and religious dissatisfaction and hatred, propaganda of war, obscene and

[39]The Terrorism Act 2006. https://www.gov.uk/government/publications/the-terrorism-act-2006 [2016-9-20].

[40]Law of the Russian Federation ON MASS MEDIA. http://www.policy.hu/myagmar/Russian_Mass_Media_Law_I.PDF [2016-10-7].

violent thought. It is prohibited to process newsletters of special media and secretly add news of adverse effects on the body and minds on television, video, film, documentary, art and computer websites and programs. It is forbidden to advocate the benefits of research and development, manufacture and use of drugs, hallucinogens and their substitutes on mass media and computer websites; news prohibited by other federal laws is not allowed for transmission.

4. Internet Code of Practice of Singapore

Singapore implemented the Internet Code of Practice[41] in November 1997, which stipulates that all Internet service providers are government-owned or government-based and comply with the Internet operating guidelines developed by the Media Development Administration. The Administration has the authority to order suppliers to shut down websites that are considered to endanger public safety, national defense, religious harmony and social morality. Information endangering public security and national defense, engulfing public confidence in the law enforcement sector, inciting or misleading some or all of the public, causing public hatred and defiance to the government, stirring dissatisfaction with the government, affecting racial and religious harmony, discrediting and ridiculing racial or religious groups, raising hatred among races and religions, promoting content of heretical or cult rituals, pornography and obscene content, hyping violence, vulgar pornography and terrorist means is prohibited on the Internet.[42]

8.3.2 Maintenance of the Social Order

1. Megan Meier Cyberbullying Prevention Act of the U.S.A.

The United States enacted the Megan Meier Cyberbullying Prevention Act[43] in 2009, which defines "cyber bullying" as "serious and repetitive malicious acts of any person transmitted by an electronic means in interstate or cross-border interactions for forcing, intimidating, harassing others or causing substantial emotional distress". In this definition, the term "transmitted" refers to the transmission of selected information between the points specified by the user, which does not change the form and content of the information when sent and received. "Electronic means" meaning any device that relies on electronic technology to receive information services, including e-mail, instant messaging, blog, website, telephone, and text message. The Act revises chapter 41 of the Penal Code, adding Article 881

---

[41]Singapore MDA:Internet Code of Practice. http://www.doc88.com/p-0116897120261.html [2016-10-7].

[42]Cyber information security of Singapore. http://news.cnwest.com/content/2012-12/27/content_8028700.htm [2016-9-21].

[43]Megan Meier Cyberbullying Prevention Act, H.R. 1966, 111th Cong. 2009. https://www.govtrack.us/congress/bills/111/hr1966/text [2016-9-120].

"cyber bullying" and imposing a fine or a term of imprisonment below two years, or both for cyber bullying.

2. Children's Internet Protection Act of the U.S.A.

In 2001, the United States enacted the Children's Internet Protection Act,[44] which regulates websites targeting children under the age of 13 and ordinary websites with children under the age of 13 involved, limiting the websites' acts of collecting online personal information of children under the age of 13, etc. and to monitor child pornography on the Internet, including virtual child pornography. The law requires schools and libraries receiving federal grants and libraries to install filtering software within the web server to ensure that the computers are not connected to obscene contents child pornography and other harmful contents when a minor is on the Internet. Otherwise, the school or the library cannot get federal government E-rate funds subsidies.

3. Act on the Protection of Physical and Mental Development of Children from Information Injury (Federal Act No. 89417-6)

Russia promulgated the Law on the Act on Protection of Physical and Mental Development of Children from Information Injury (Federal Act No. 89417-6) on June 28, 2012, which is commonly known as the "Network Blacklist Act".[45] This Act intends to shield websites, URL, and domain names of websites involving child pornography, drug abuse and manufacture, and suicide, etc. Under this Act, websites spreading child pornography, drugs and inducing children of self-mutilation are likely to be included in the blacklist and shutdown before the sentence of court; and websites spreading other prohibited information will be determined by the court whether to be shut down. The Act also provides that regulating authority will commission nonprofit organizations to supervise the websites publishing illegal information. If a website is found illegal, the nonprofit organizations will provide relevant information for the Russian Supervisory Commission, who should then warn the involved website. If the owner of the website does not respond within 24 h or does not delete the content, the network service provider (ISP) must take measures to shield the website. If the ISP does nothing, the web page will be blacklisted. Those who are not satisfied with being listed in the blacklist may appeal to the court within three months.

4. New Rules of Popular Bloggers of Russia

On May 5, 2014, Russia promulgated the "New Rule of Popular Blogger" (usually shortened as the "Blog Rules"), which clearly defines bloggers having more than three thousand daily visits on their pages as "popular bloggers" and must

---

[44]Children's Internet Protection Act. https://www.fcc.gov/consumers/guides/childrens-internet-protection-act [2016-9-20].

[45]Network Blacklist Act passed by Russian Federal Committee. http://news.xinhuanet.com/world/2012-07/27/c_112552785.htm [2016-9-17].

be registered at the Russian network regulatory department.[46] In addition, the “blog rules” apply not only to blogs or standalone sites, but also to social networking sites with more than three thousand followers. The Rules list popular bloggers as mass media, thus, the latter needs to meet the requirements of the law on mass media and be subjected to regulatory activities of the Russian network regulatory department, including prohibition of anonymity of information, use of website in criminal activities, publication and spreading of violence, cruelty and pornography, or various online information including foul language, and publication and dissemination of privacy of citizens, and so on. The Rules also allow the Russian government to install scanning software that can check any content on the web.[47]

5. Regulation of a Safe and Secure Internet Environment for Young People of Japan

Japan adopted in 2008 the “Regulation of Safe and Secure Internet Environment for Young People”, referred to as “Youth Network Restriction Regulation”, which specifies obligations of state and local public organizations, industry management associations, Telecom service providers, filtering software developers, web content service providers, civil society and minors guardians, etc. to guarantee safe and secure Internet activities for the minors, so as to control the spread of harmful information. The Regulation aims at protection of young people and enforces telecommunications service providers and other relevant agencies on providing network filtering services, and promotion and continuous upgrade of the filtering software, so as to ensure a safe Internet for the youth.

The Regulation states the following three types of harmful information: first, the act of direct and clear engagement, agency or induction of crimes or violations against the law, and the act of direct and clear publication of information inducing others to commit suicide; second, information involving obscene description of human sexual behavior or sexual organs or other information obviously producing sexual desire or stimulating sexual desire; third, thrilling description of murder, death penalty, abuse, and so on or other information of extremely cruel content. The Regulation stipulates that the site operator should immediately remove the bad information found, or a variety of methods should be adopted to confirm the age of the user. Green barrier services and terminals with filtering software should be provided for young people under the age of 18.

---

[46]Russia promulgated New Rules of Popular Blogger. http://news.sina.com.cn/m/2014-05-06/035730066703.shtml [2016-9-17].

[47]Responsibility of Internet Celebrities and Service Provider Clarified by New Law in Russia to Purify Cyberspace. http://www.npopss-cn.gov.cn/n/2014/0519/c219470-25036190.html [2016-9-27].

8.3.3 Guarantee for Cyber Security and Cyber Order

1. *Cyber-Crime* Convention of the European Union

The *Cyber-Crime* Convention,[48] which was drafted by the Council of Europe, is the first international treaty in the world to deal with issues related to Internet governance. It was officially opened for signature of member states and non-member states of the Council of Europe on 23 November 2001 and entered into force on 1 July 2004. As of October 2008, 46 countries, 46 states including most of the members of the Council of Europe and the United States, Canada, Japan, South Africa, have signed, 23 of which formally approved its coming in force. The main body of the Convention includes four chapters and 48 Articles, specifying the rights and obligations of the parties in the field of cybercrime from the aspects of substantive law, procedural law and jurisdiction. Article 1 to Article 10 of the Convention for the first time in the history defines the crime and the terms involved in cyber-crime; Article 14 to 22 provides procedural rules for the investigation and trial of cybercrime; Article 23 to Article 35 specifies the international cooperation matters such as extradition, evidence collection and liaison mechanism. This convention not only contributes significantly to international cooperation in combating cybercrime, but more importantly, has accumulated experience and set a model for the exploration of Internet governance through treaty law.

In 2003, the EU further adopted the Additional Protocol to the Convention on Cybercrime, Concerning the Criminalization of Acts of a Racist and Xenophobic Nature Committed through Computer Systems,[49] which aims to supplement the Cyber-crime Convention in accordance with the actual situation of the European Union, to monitor harmful information on racial discrimination and xenophobia, incitement to hatred, discrimination and violence on the Internet, and discrimination against race, color, descent and nation.[50]

2. Information, Information Technology and Information Protection Act of Russia

On 8 July 2006, the Russian State Duma adopted and promulgated Federal Act No. 149, the Information, Information Technology and Information Protection Act,[51] which was re-enacted in 2006 on the basis of the Information, Information and Information Protection Act of February 1995 in order to adapt to the new changes in the

[48]Cyber-crime Convention. http://www.europarl.europa.eu/meetdocs/2014_2019/documents/libe/dv/7_conv_budapest_/7_conv_budapest_en.pdf [2016-10-6].

[49]Additional Protocol to the Convention on Cybercrime, Concerning the Criminalisation of Acts of a Racist and Xenophobic Nature Committed through Computer Systems. https://ccdcoe.org/sites/default/files/documents/CoE-030128-AdditionalProtocol.pdf [2016-8-30].

[50]Zhang YJ (2011) Protecting the rights of minority by fighting against cybercrime—introduction and analysis of additional protocol to the convention on cybercrime, concerning the criminalisation of acts of a racist and xenophobic nature committed through computer systems. J South-Central Univ Nationalities (Humanities and Social Science) 31(2):124–127.

[51]Information, Information Technology and Information Protection Act of Russia. http://b2b.toocle.com/detail–6058251.html [2016-9-17].

field of information, and to better maintain the information rights of information subjects, especially the citizens, and to promote the application of information technology in various fields and protect information security. It becomes the basis of Russian information security legislation and is the basic law devoted to information security.

The Information, Information Technology and Information Protection Act establishes the basic model for the development of legislation in the field of information security, and adjusts various legal relations arising from the fulfillment of information collection, acquisition, transmission, production and dissemination rights, the use of information technology, and the implementation of information protection. The concepts including information, information technology, information systems, information and communication networks, information owners, information access, information privacy, information provision, information dissemination, e-mail, record information and information system operators are defined in this Act. The Act also gives due consideration to guaranteeing information rights of citizens and organizations such as access to information, privacy, etc. It gives emphasis that during the adjustment of information legal relation, the following principles should be followed: the information can be freely collected, acquired, transmitted, produced and disseminated through any legitimate means; only the federal law can provide information access restrictions; national institutions and local self-government agencies business information should go public and be accessed freely; private life of citizens shall not be violated. The legal relationships under the adjustment of the Information, Information Technology and Information Protection Act ranges broadly, significantly affecting Russian information security legislation and laying an important foundation for the legislation.

3. Commonwealth Consolidated Acts of Australia

In 2001, Australia promulgated the Commonwealth Consolidated Acts,[52] which prohibits the provision of interactive gambling services for clients in Australia and prohibits the provision of interactive gambling services for clients from designated countries in Australia. The Acts call for the establishment of a complaint system to deal with Internet gambling content information accessible in Australia, which is expressly prohibited. The Acts provide that the Australian police need to act against illegal Internet gambling content, including requiring Internet service providers to take filtering measures. The Acts also prohibit the publication of Internet gambling ads.

4. *Act on Promotion of Information and Communication Network Utilization and Information Protection* of South Korea

South Korea in 2000 promulgated the Act on Promotion of Information and Communication Network Utilization and Information Protection,[53] defining bad information in the information network communication in detail. The bad

---

[52]Commonwealth Consolidated Acts. http://www.austlii.edu.au/au/legis/cth/consol_act/iga2001193/ [2016-8-30].

[53]Act on Promotion of Information and Communication Network Utilization and Information Protection. http://unpan1.un.org/intradoc/groups/public/documents/APCITY/UNPAN025694.pdf [2016-8-30].

information includes information harmful to national security and national interests, disclosure of state secrets, defamation, rumors and other harassing information, harmful information such as obscenity, pornography, violence, contents violating the obligation to mark the harmful information for minors, speculation gambling, and betting crime, etc. The main contents of the Act include: first, using the “illegal communication” standard to replace the “improper communication” standard; second, authorizing the Minister of Information and Communications to issue orders to require network service providers to delete or block “illegal communication”, the network service provider refusing to obey such order will go through criminal sanction; and thirdly, the Information and Communication Ethics Committee (ICEC) may suggest that the Internet service provider (ISP) remove or prevent “illegal communication”, an ISP refusing to comply with the order will be subject to a criminal sanction; fourth, South Korea will begin to implement the Internet content grading system, and ICEC has the right to determine the grading criteria, procedures and application of the identification method of grading, and the right to directly determine and announce the level of a website; fifth, the ISP operating a website that is harmful for minors must be marked according to the provisions, otherwise, it should be punished; sixth, schools and libraries must install filtering software.

5. Specific e-mail law of Japan

Japan published in 2002 the specific e-mail law.[54] Specific e-mail is an e-mail sent for profit purpose of oneself or others without the consent of the recipient. This law stipulates that a specific e-mail sender must indicate the intention in the title, and their own real information (name, address, send and receive e-mail address and intention, etc.) in a specified location of the mail, and the sender shall not borrow other people’s name and e-mail address for forwarding. When the e-mail is for the first time sent to a group, there shall be a prompt for the recipient to confirm whether a message from the same address is wanted. If the message is rejected by the user, it is prohibited to be sent again. Violation of the above provision will be deemed as disturbing e-mail communication, relevant department may take necessary measures, the offender may be under a maximum penalty of less than one year and a fine of 1 million yen, a corporate legal person may be under a maximum fine of 30 million yen. Relevant institutions shall take the suggestions of the user on specific e-mails. In order to prevent specific e-mails from interfering with communication, the communication institution that conducts the e-mail service is obliged to develop and introduce new technologies, refuse to provide services for e-mails using false websites and sent to a large number of users.[55]

[54]Spam filled with temptation, special law promulgated in Japan to purify the Internet. http://japan.people.com.cn/2003/10/9/print/20031098 2155.htm [2016-10-6].

[55]Foreign Spam Regulations: Japan Spam Ruled by Law. http://news.sina.com.cn/w/2003-11-03/13091047696s.shtml [2016-9-21].

6. Spam Control Act of Singapore

In 2008, Singapore revised the Spam Control Act[56] to perform focused regulation of spam e-mail. This Act specifies that spam is commercial e-mails sent more than 100 times within 24 h, over 1000 times within 30 days or more than 10,000 times within a year, with the same or similar content.[57] The Act stipulates that, without permission, a company shall not send e-mail, text or multimedia information to the consumer, all advertising e-mail must be marked with the nature of advertising while being sent, and the sender's real e-mail address indicated, and the consumer does not have to pay to unsubscribe such type of mail. Consumers may claim damages for the junk e-mail sender who violates the regulations. The compensation is S $25 (approximately ¥128) for each spam e-mail and the maximum amount of compensation does not exceed S $1 million.[58]

7. Spam Act of Australia

In 2003, the Australian Federal Government took the lead in developing the Spam Act.[59] Since April 2004, any company or individual that sends a spam within Australia may be severely punished once discovered. The Act strictly delineates the scope of spam, by first strictly defining spam as commercial and second by defining the nature of being actively provided without permission of the user. Article 6 of the Act specifies commercial e-mails, such as offering goods or services, advertising or marketing goods or services, advertising or marketing for land or land proceeds, doing business opportunities or investment opportunities, advertising or marketing, etc., and clearly stressed the commercial nature of its information. The Act tends to protect the individual rights of citizens, that is, from 2004 onwards, all commercials entering the Australian Internet must first acquire the user's permission before entering the user's mailbox, otherwise it is illegal, and shall be pursued responsibly. Those who send spam once caught and convicted will be fined a maximum of $1 million.

The Act has a more extensive scope after adjustment, covering all spam involving electronic communications, including e-mail, text messages, MMS, instant messaging and fax, etc. Article 5 of the Act expressly states that the electronic information referred to in this Law refers to information used by the Internet or other registered operating services, which is sent to an electronic address to

[56]Singapore Spam Control Act 2007. http://www.lawgazette.com.sg/2007-8/feature2.htm [2016-10-7].

[57]China Court. Org. Singapore Law for Regulating Spam. http://old.chinacourt.org/html/article/200704/13/242472.shtml [2016-9-23].

[58]Singapore Put in Force A Series of Acts, Guaranteeing Internet Rights of Netizens to the Largest Extent. http://news.163.com/12/1227/18/8JOJ01MB00014JB5.html?from=tagtie [2016-9-21].

[59]Spam Act 2003. https://www.legislation.gov.au/Details/C2011C00080 [2016-9-21].

which an e-mail number is connected, an electronic information address, an electronic address of a telephone number and the like. The Act uses the looseness and strictness of the punitive measure, looseness referring to not specifying personal punishment, and strictness to a large amount of property penalty. Article 27 of the Act expressly provides that if an individual violates the provisions, only the provisions of civil penalties will be applied, without pursuing the criminal responsibility. For serious and repeating spammers, different degrees of penalties will be applied by the court based on the degree of violation against the law, with a maximum fine of $1 million per day.[60]

8.3.4 Data Safety and Privacy

1. Electronic Communications Privacy Act of America

The United States enacted the Electronic Communications Privacy Act of 1986[61] (ECPA) in 1986 to extend the original control over telephone cable monitoring (including electronic data transfer through computers). The Act prohibits any person from attempting or conducting or encouraging any other person to conduct the act of intercepting, using, disclosing any cable, verbal or electronic communication, or continuing to use and disclose information knowing that the information is obtained by intercepting or illegally disclosing the communications of others, or knowing that the information is prohibited by the criminal law. The above behaviors are defined illegal. Chapter 1 of the Act regulates the protection of cable, verbal and communication on transmission; Chap. 2 specifies the storage of electronic information in communications, in particular emphasizing the conditions of access to information stored in the computer; Chap. 3 mentions prohibition of monitoring or tracking of user information without permission, the user information including routing, positioning, signal and other information during the transmission of wired or electronic communication.

2. General Data Protection Regulation of the EU

On April 27, 2016, the European Parliament issued the text of Protection of Natural Persons with Regard of the Processing of Personal Data and on the Free Movement of Personal Data in the Process of Personal Data Processing Such Data, which is an alternative to the 95/46/EC Directive, also known as the General Data Protection

[60]Interpretation of Spam Act of Australia. http://www.chinaemail.com.cn/blog/content/2413/ [2016-9-21].

[61]Electronic Communications Privacy Act of 1986 (ECPA). https://it.ojp.gov/PrivacyLiberty/authorities/statutes/1285 [2016-9-21].

Regulation[62] (GDPR). 28 EU member states will turn the GDPR provisions into their national laws within two years. The Regulation will enter into force in 2018.

The overall direction of the new GDPR is to strengthen the personal data protection rights, so that the European people have a greater voice on the use of their personal data—and seek to simplify the process of business compliance. Regulations even include a specified management model, which gains the Regulation operability in enterprise internal control and compliance management. The object applicable also extends from the EU enterprises to all enterprises providing EU users with Internet and business services.

Key terms of GDPR include: ① penalty for violating the Data Protection Regulation may be up to 4% of the company's global turnover—for Google and other technology giants, the penalty will be billions of dollars; ② responsibility of data leakage extends to any data processor that is used by the data controller—and thus applicable to any third party providing certain types of services for processing data, which is more common in a cloud business model; ③ the so-called "forgotten rights" is written in the law, therefore, once someone does not want his/her data to be processed by a certain company, and "as long as there is no legal reason to retain the data", the data must be deleted, which has a significant impact on digital marketing; ④ if the company needs to deal with large-scale sensitive data or collect information from numerous consumers, the company is required to appoint a data protection officer, except for small and medium enterprises for which data processing is not core business; ⑤ in the event of serious data leakage, the enterprise or institution is required to inform the relevant state supervision institution immediately; ⑥ children are allowed to use social media merely under the consent of parents, each member state may set this article for children in a particular period from 13 to 16 years old; ⑦ a one-stop regulatory institution shall be established for data protection complaints to simplify the compliance process; ⑧ personal data portability rights should be guaranteed, so that personal data can be more easily transferred between different services.

3. Federal Data Protection Act of Germany

In 1995, Germany enacted the Federal Data Protection Act[63] and revised the Act in 2009 and 2015 respectively. The Act stipulates that the owner of information has the right to know which personal information is being recorded, by whom the information is accessed, and the purpose for acquiring the information. A private organization, before recording the information, must inform the information owner

[62]On the Protection of Natural Persons with Regard to the Processing of Personal Data and on the Free Movement of Such Data, and Repealing Directive 95/46/EC (General Data Protection Regulation). http://ec.europa.eu/justice/data-protection/reform/files/regulation_oj_en.pdf [2016-9-17].

[63]Federal Data Protection Act 2015 newest edition—BDSG2015. http://wenku.baidu.com/view/742095805901020206409c83.html [2016-9-21].

of the situation. Access to processing and use of personal information for advertising must be conducted with written consent of the information owner, if the information is wrong, the information processing party is obliged to correct it. Information acquired by illegal access or no longer needed must be deleted. If the information owner is hurt by illegal or improper access, processing, and use of personal information, the person causing the injury should take responsibility. If the law is violated, the violator will be fined between 50,000 and 300,000 Euros; if a profit is made in the violation, the fine should exceed the amount of profits. The law calls on public and private organizations to set up special information protection personnel, requires appointment of a "federal data protection and information freelance" inside the government to monitor acts of government institutions in the protection of personal data. The Federal Commissioner for Data Protection and Information Freedom is elected by the Bundestag, of which the office is in the German Ministry of the Interior. If someone believes that a government agency infringes its rights while collecting, processing or using its own information, he/she may complain to the Office of the Commissioner for Data Protection.[64]

4. Privacy and Electronic Communications Regulations of the U.K.

According to the EU Directive on Personal Information Processing and Privacy Protection in Electronic Communications (2002/58/EC), on 18 September 2003, the UK translated the Directive into the Privacy and Electronic Communications [EC Directive] Regulations 2003[65] to regulate privacy issues in the field of electronic communications in the UK.[66]

According to the provisions of the Regulations on public electronic communication service safety, public electronic communication service providers should take appropriate technical and organizational measures to ensure the safety of such services; the network providers should meet any reasonable requirements of service providers for the above purposes; the service provider shall inform the user of the nature of the risk, any appropriate measures that may be taken by the user to prevent such risks, and the likely cost of the user to participate in such measures; and, the service in addition to the costs of the user receiving and collecting information should be provided free of charge for the user.

In the case of communication confidentiality requirements, the Regulation provides that no person may use the network to store confidential information or use the network to obtain information stored on the user terminal equipment; that the user's terminal equipment may be required to obtain information about the

[64]Federal Data Protection Act of German Protects Information Security. http://media.sohu.com/20121224/n361396045.shtml [2016-9-21].

[65]Privacy and Electronic Communications (EC Directive) Regulations 2003. http://www.legislation.gov.uk/uksi/2003/2426/pdfs/uksi_20032426_en.pdf [2016-10-7].

[66]Privacy and Electronic Communications (EC Directive) Regulations of the UK. http://www.infseclaw.net/news/html/1082.html [2016-9-21].

purpose and access of the data storage, while denying the storage of and access to the data.

In the case of processing restrictions on traffic data, the Regulation provides that user-related traffic data processed and stored by a public communications provider should be cleared or modified so that it no longer constitutes personal information when it no longer needs communication transmission; in order to connect with the users cost payment, the public communication provider can process and store the traffic data it masters, and save the information for a specified length of period; if the traffic data processing and storage is to promote the electronic communication service marketing or to provide value-added service for the user, or a user associated with the traffic data has agreed with such processing and storage, or such processing and storage is carried out at a time required, the public electronic communication service provider may process and store the information.

In the case of processing restrictions on location data, the Regulation stipulates that the user's location data can only be processed without recognizing the user or with the consent of the user; prior to obtaining the consent of the user, the public communication provider must provide for the user associated with the data the type of location data to be processed, the purpose and time of the processing, and whether the data is sent to the third party for the purpose of providing value-added services and the user who agrees to the data processing should be available at all times through a simple method and be charged free for the withdrawal of such consent; location data can only be handled by a public communications provider or a third party providing value-added services and authorized individuals, and these processes are limited to the need to achieve these objectives.

In the User Directory, the Regulations provide that only when the user is informed at no charge the purpose of the use of a catalog containing his or her personal information and the information about the device, or when the user has the right to determine whether the personal data in the catalog is associated with the producer, the personal information of an individual user can be included in the catalog; when the data of an individual user is already included in the catalog, the user has the right to verify, correct or revoke the data at any time.

5. Personal Information Protection Act of Japan

Japan promulgated the Personal Information Protection Act[67] in 2003. The Act which prohibits the provision of personal information to a third party without the consent of the involved party (using restrictive principles); it is not allowed to obtain personal information by fraud or other means (collection of restrictive principles); within a necessary scope for achieving the goal, the information should be ensured to be complete and correct (material completeness and correctness principle); a person shall be informed immediately after personal information is obtained immediately (open principle); the necessary management measures shall

[67]Personal Information Protection Act (2003, No. 57). http://www.iolaw.org.cn/showNews.asp?id=12426 [2016-9-27].

be taken to ensure information security (safety protection principles); wrong information should, after the wrongness is learned from the involved person, be amended and rectified, and the involved person being informed of the amendment (the principle of personal participation); complaints should be handled by a system; and a self-regulatory system should be established (the principle of liability); use and profit of personal information shall not exceed the reasonable Scope of use (purpose clarification principle).

In addition, the law also restricts the server to collect information of Japanese citizens through foreign enterprises in a foreign country, and that foreign enterprises are required that they must have a Japanese agency in accordance with Japanese law to implement such operations.

8.4 Latest Progress of the Rule of Law System for Cyberspace Sovereignty

In June 2010, China published the white paper On Chinese Internet,[68] in which it is pointed out that the Internet is an important national infrastructure; that Internet within the territory of the People's Republic of China belongs to China's sovereign jurisdiction; and that China's Internet sovereignty should be respected and maintained. After that, the Chinese government has clarified the principle of cyberspace sovereignty in several domestic and foreign occasions. At the same time, China has established legislation on cyberspace sovereignty, so as to maintain cyberspace sovereignty in law enforcement and judicial practice and to respect cyberspace sovereignty in international cooperation.

8.4.1 Legislation Establishing the Principle of Cyberspace Sovereignty

On July 25, 2015, the National Security Law of the People's Republic of China[69] is enacted, wherein Article 25 states: the state establishes an information security system to enhance cyber and information security protection, improve innovation research and development and application in cyber and information technology, realize a safe and controllable information system and data for cyber and information core technology, key infrastructure and important areas, strengthen cyber

[68]White Paper on Chinese Internet (full text). http://www.scio.gov.cn/zxbd/tt/Document/1011194/1011194.htm [2016-8-30].

[69]National Security Law of the People's Republic of China, approved by vote of the NPC Standing Committee on July 1, 2015. http://www.gov.cn/xinwen/2015-07/01/content_2888316.htm [2016-9-1].

management, preventing, stopping and punishing cyber-attacks, cyber intrusion, cyber theft, illegal network-crimes such as dissemination of illegal information, safeguard sovereignty, security and developmental interests of the national cyberspace. This will be the first time for China to put forward the concept of cyberspace sovereignty in form of law, and clearly require safeguarding the national cyberspace sovereignty by the construction of cyber and information security system, strengthening the network information security capacity building and cyber information technology research and development, to combat cyber crime and other means.

On November 7, 2016, the 24th session of the 12th conference of the NPC Standing Committee voted to approve the Cyber Security Law,[70] of which Article 1 states: The Law is formulated so as to ensure cyber security, to safeguard the cyberspace sovereignty, national security and the societal public interests, to protect the lawful rights and interests of citizens, legal persons and other organizations, and to promote the healthy development of economic and social informatization. This law clarifies the maintenance of cyberspace sovereignty is one of the legislative purposes of the Cyber Security Law.

The Cyber Security Law although does not use the word "cyberspace", but according to the description, the content can be regarded as within the scope of cyberspace. In the law, the word "network" does not specifically refer to the Internet. Similarly, the network infrastructure does not specifically refer to the Internet backbone network. It is clearly stressed that the protection is for: "public telecommunications and information services, power, traffic, water, finance, public services, electronic governance and other important industries and fields, as well as other critical information infrastructures that once destroyed, losing function or leaking data might seriously endanger national security, welfare and the people's livelihood, or the public interest", which is exactly the content included in cyberspace.

The Cyber Security Law will come into effect on June 1, 2017. The law further defines the scope of key information infrastructure in maintaining the cyberspace sovereignty, stipulates the order of various types of activities on the network platform and protects corresponding data security and information security of the objects in the network.

[70]National Security Law of the People's Republic of China. http://www.npc.gov.cn/npc/xinwen/2016-11/07/content_2001605.htm [2016-11-23].

8.4.2 Strengthen Cyberspace Management Within Law Enforcement, Exercise Administrative Jurisdiction According to the Law

In February 2014, China established a central cyber security and informatization leading group, and a central cyber security and informatization office, so as to strengthen the administration of cyberspace. The law enforcement departments have introduced a series of provisions, such as "Interim Provisions for Development and Administration of Instant Communication Tools Public Information Services", "Rules for Interview of Internet News Information Service Unit", "Management Regulations for Internet User Account Name", "Internet information Search Service Management Provisions", "Notice on Strengthening the Risk Prevention and Education and Guidance of Bad Network Credit", "Provisions on Information Management of Mobile Internet Applications", "Several Provisions on the Restoration of Funds in New Types of Illegal Criminal Cases", "Notice on Further Strengthening Management to Stop False News", "Investigation and Punishment Approach for Online Food Safety Violations", "Internet advertising management Interim Measures", "Internet financial risk special rectification work implementation plan", "non-bank payment agency risk special rectification work implementation plan", "Internet broadcast service management regulations", "network performance management activities management approach". These regulations and provisions improve governance according to the law on cyber information, cyber finance, cyber services, cyber advertising, telecommunications fraud and other online chaos.

19 protected objects are listed in the Cyber Security Law, including personal information, critical information infrastructures, legal rights and interests, the information on the informant, reputation, business secrets, other networks, network, network products, network services, network infrastructure, online data, network information, privacy, user's personal information, user information, information obtained during their performance of duties, intellectual property rights, and important data; together with 17 managed objects, including program, public media, telephone network access formalities, electronic information sent by, critical information infrastructures, tools, instant messaging services, application software provided by, the publication of cyber security information, specialized cyber security products, network products, network services, critical network equipment, network access services, information distribution services, information published by users, and domain registration services; as well as 23 management subjects participating in the management, including governments and competent authorities, authorities legitimately bearing regulatory responsibilities for cyber security and their staff members, the public security authorities, public security bodies, the state, the State Council, the standardization administration of the State Council, the telecommunications authority of the State Council, other relevant departments under the State Council, competent departments of the State Council, other relevant authorities, society, the governments of provinces, autonomous regions

municipalities directly under the Central Government, governments at provincial level and above, network and IT authorities, competent authorities of local governments at county level and above, the relevant departments, staff members of the authorities, competent authorities, the authority that receives such report, and the government; and 4 roles for supporting the management, including certified organs, authorize cyber security service providers, competent organs, and professionals.

8.4.3 Cracking Down on Cybercrime in Jurisdiction and Exercise Jurisdiction in Accordance with the Law

In August 2015, China enacted the Ninth Amendment to the Criminal Law of the People's Republic of China,[71] improving penalties for the violation of personal information of citizens, illegal intrusion into the computer information system crime, destruction of computer information system crime, adding the crime of refusing to fulfill the obligation of information network security management, the crime of illegal use of information networks, crime of helping information cyber-criminal activities, and so on, and strengthening the efforts to crackdown on cybercrime. China's judicial organs provided judicial interpretations to provide a clear guide for punishing criminal activities to harm cyber security and improving the quality of criminal handling, the interpretations include "Interpretation on Several Issues of the Supreme People's Court and the Supreme People's Procuratorate about the Application of Laws in the Criminal Cases of Endangering the Security of Computer Information Systems", and "Provisions on several issues of the Supreme People's Court, the Supreme People's Procuratorate and the Ministry of Public Security in Collecting, Extracting, Reviewing and Determining Electronic Data in Criminal". The Cyber Security Law further enumerated 7 types of management bases: the laws, administrative regulations, national standards, industrial standards, the standard system for cyber security, code of conducts and articles of association; 6 categories of targets: malicious programs, information prohibited by laws/administrative regulations from publication or transmission, information concerning criminal activities, criminal activities, activities that impair cyber security; 4 kinds of control measures: to halt the transmission of information, such interim measures as network communications restriction in specific areas, to delete such information, and to block such transmission.

[71]The Ninth Amendment to the Criminal Law of the People's Republic of China (Document No. 30). http://www.gov.cn/zhengce/2015-08/30/content_2922323.htm [2016-10-6].

8.4.4 *Guarantee for Strengthening National Cyber Security in the Regulatory System*

According to other laws and regulations such as the National Security Law and the Cyber Security Law promulgated in 2015, China has built a cyber security system with Chinese characteristics and formed a cyber security system coordinated by central and cyber departments with other departments cooperating and doing their duties.

1. Institution of Overall Leadership

The National Security Law stipulates that the department of overall leadership of national security is the National Security Commission of the Communist Party of China, which is responsible for the decision-making and coordination of national security works, and which develops and guides the implementation of the national security strategy and relevant major policies and measures, coordinates major national security issues and important works, and promotes litigation of national security. It is also the overall leadership institution for cyber security.

2. Institution of Decision Arrangement and Overall Planning

The central and provincial cyber security and informatization leading group is responsible for national and local cyber security and informatization major decision-making arrangements. The State Council and the provinces, autonomous regions and municipalities directly under the Central Government are responsible for overall planning. Article 16 of the Cyber Security Law stipulates that: The State Council and the people's governments of provinces, autonomous regions and directly-governed municipalities shall make comprehensively plans; expand their input; support key industries and projects of cyber security technologies; support the research and development and application of cyber security technologies, spread safe and trustworthy cyber products and services, protect the intellectual property rights for cyber technologies, and encourage businesses, research institutions and colleges and universities to engage in national projects of innovation in cyber security technologies.

3. Institution of Coordination

The Office of the Central Cyber Security and Informatization Leading Group (National Net-Info Management Department) is responsible for "coordinating" cyber security and cyberspace governance. Article 8 of the Cyber Security Law provides that: The State network information departments shall be responsible for comprehensively planning and coordinating cyber security work efforts and related supervision and management efforts. Article 23 stipulates that: The State network information departments shall, together with the relevant departments of the State Council, develop and release a catalogue of critical cyber equipment and specialized cyber security products, and promote the reciprocal recognition of security certifications and security inspection results to avoid duplicative certifications and inspections. Article 39 stipulates that: The State network information departments shall comprehensively coordinate relevant departments in employing the following measures for critical information infrastructure security protection. Article 50 provides that: The State network information departments and relevant departments perform network information security supervision and administration responsibilities in accordance with the law. Article 51 provides that: The State network information departments shall do overall coordination of relevant departments to strengthen collection, analysis and reporting efforts for cyber security information, and follow regulations for the unified release of cyber security monitoring and early warning information in accordance with regulations. Article 53 provides that: The State network information departments coordinate relevant departments' establishment and completion of mechanisms for cyber security risk assessment and emergency response efforts, formulate cyber security incident emergency response plans, and periodically organizes drills.

4. Department of concerted efforts

Other departments of the State Council are responsible for the concerted efforts of cyber security. Article 8 of the Cyber Security Law stipulates that: The State Council Departments for telecommunications, public security, and other relevant authorities, shall be responsible for the cyber security protection, supervision and administration efforts within the scope of their responsibilities, in accordance with the provisions of this Law, and other relevant laws and administrative regulations. Article 15 provides that: The State Council administrative department for standardization and other relevant State Council departments shall, according to their individual responsibilities, organize the formulation and timely revision of relevant national and industry standards for cyber security administration as well as for the security of cyber products, services and operations. Article 32 stipulates that: In accordance with the duties and division of labor provided by the State Council, departments responsible for the security protection work of critical information infrastructure, are to separately compile and organize the implementation of critical information infrastructure security plans for that industry or field's critical information infrastructure, and guide and supervise security protection efforts for the critical information infrastructure operations.

5. Department of Local Responsibility

Local governments at all levels are responsible for cybersecurity-related matters in the region, including setting specific scopes and the security measures for the key information infrastructure, and organizing implementation of appropriate measures. Article 8 of the Cyber Security Law provides that: The cyber security protection, supervision and administration duties for relevant departments in people's governments at the county level or above shall be determined by relevant national regulations. Article 19 provides that: People's governments at all levels and their relevant departments shall organize and carry out regular cyber security publicity and education, and guide and stimulate relevant units to conduct cyber security publicity and education in an effective manner. Article 54 provides that: When the risk of cyber security incidents increases, the relevant departments of people's governments at the provincial level and above shall follow the scope of authority and procedures provided, and employ the following measures on the basis of the cyber security risk's characteristics and the harms it might cause. Article 56 provides that: Where, while performing cyber security supervision and management duties, relevant departments of people's governments at the provincial level or above discover that relatively large security risks exist online or they discover the occurrence of security incidents, they may, according to the scope of authority and procedures provided, conduct face-to-face talks with the legally-designated representative or main responsible persons for the operator of that network.

8.4.5 Government, Enterprise and the Public Join Efforts in Governance of Cyberspace

In the cybersecurity law, a total of 19 protected bodies are enumerated: the person whose data is gathered, the clients, legal persons, higher education institutes, citizens, the public, members, education training institutions, other organizations, enterprises, society, other persons, a particular individual, cyber security talents, relevant network sectoral organizations, minors, research bodies, users, and vocational schools; 31 categories were included in the management body, including persons responsible for security management, employees, digital information distribution service provider, individuals, personnel in critical positions, critical information infrastructure builders, critical information infrastructure operators, state organ government affairs network operators, members, foreign individuals, foreign institutions, foreign organizations, persons receiving public order management punishment and criminal punishment, persons responsible for cyber security, providers of network product, providers of network service, relevant network sectoral organizations, network operators, work personnel of cyberspace administration, the statutory representative of problem network operators, operator of the problem network, other direct responsible person of the problem network, application software download service providers, work personnel of relevant departments, relevant units, relevant industrial organizations, organizations, and specialized security management institutions; four types of obligations including individual, network operators outside of critical information infrastructure, whistleblowers, and organization. Counting relevant agencies of the management bodies and supporting the management, the law listed a total of 76 roles participating in cyber security activities.

The Cyber Security Law also enumerates 7 kinds of behaviors need to be regulated by the law: service activities, operations activities, supervision and management efforts, construction, usage, maintenance, and operation; 3 categories of monitoring focus, including cyber security incidents, risks, and threats; 7 items of a protection target, including safeguarding the integrity/confidentiality/availability of network information, forms a good environment, promoting widespread network access, raising the level of network services, cyber security, and network operational stability, and effectively responding to cyber security; 6 important works including cyber security guarantee system, cyber security strategy, cyber security policy, cyber security work tasks, cyber security measures, critical information infrastructure protection system; 9 measures to be taken, including monitoring, defending against, dealing with, industry self-discipline, electronic identify, emergency responding plans, providing truthful identity information, collection for cyber security information and warning information; 11 acts to be promoted, including security services, formulation of standards, stimulating the healthy development of the industry, innovation of technology, research and development of network technologies, technology application, openness of public data resources, to raise cyber security awareness and level, online data security protection and usage technology, and the utilization of new cyberspace technologies.

8.4.6 Improving International Cooperation and Respect for Cyber Sovereignty

In recent years, Chinese judicial organs continue to strengthen international cooperation and make joint effort to combat cybercrime. China has worked with Indonesia, Vietnam, Kenya, Cambodia, Laos, Singapore, Malaysia, Thailand, the Philippines and other countries to break several cross-border telecommunication frauds, based on respect for national cyberspace sovereignty, effectively cracking down on cybercrime.

8.4.7 Contents of the Cyber Security Law

Lang Sheng, vice chairman of Legislation Committee of the NPC Standing Committee, gave a lecture on the Cyber Security Law (Draft) of the People's Republic of China[72] on June 24, 2015 at the 15th meeting of the 12th session of the NPC Standing Committee. The Cyber Security Law includes 79 articles of 7 Chapters, mainly addressing the maintenance of cyberspace sovereignty and strategic planning, on the protection of network products and service security, on the protection of cyber security, on the protection of cyber data security, on the protection of cyber information security, on monitoring and warning and emergency response, and on the cyber security supervision and management system.

[72]Lang S (2015) Interpretation of the cyber security law (Draft) of the People's Republic of China. China Inf Secur 08: 52–55. http://www.doc88.com/p-7738264157865.html [2016-12-13].

1. On Maintenance of Cyberspace Sovereignty and Strategy Plan

Cyberspace sovereignty is the representation and extension of sovereignty in cyberspace. The principle of cyberspace sovereignty is an important principle of our country to be followed when maintaining national security and interests, as well as participating in international governance and cooperation. To this end, the Cyber Security Law has a legislative purpose to maintain cyberspace sovereignty and national security. Article 2 provides that: This Law shall apply with respect to the construction, operation, maintenance and usage of networks, as well as the supervision and management practices concerning cyber security within the mainland territory of the People's Republic of China. At the same time, in accordance with the principle of equal emphasis on security and development, there is a special chapter on the national cyber security strategy and cyber security planning in important areas, and specifies measures supporting cyber security.

2. Cyber Product and Service Security

To maintain cyberspace security, first, the security of cyber products and services should be ensured. The Cyber Security Law mainly specifies the following provisions: first, clarifying security obligations of the cyber product and service providers. Article 22 provides that: Providers of cyber products and services must not install malicious programs; when discovering that their products or services have risks such as security flaws or vulnerabilities, they shall immediately adopt remedial measures, and promptly inform users and report the matter to the relevant department according to regulations; second, summarizing practical experiences, and raising the safety certification and security testing system for the key equipment and special security products to law; Article 23 stipulates that: The critical cyber equipment and specialized cyber security products shall follow the national standards and mandatory requirements, and be safety certified by a qualified establishment or meet the requirements of a security inspection, before being sold or provided. Third, cyber products or services bought by a key information infrastructure operator need to go through a security check. Article 35 stipulates that: Critical information infrastructure operators purchasing network products and services that might impact national security shall go through a national security review organized by the state network information departments and relevant departments of the State Council.

3. Cyber Operational Safety

To ensure the safety of cyber operation, we must implement the responsibility of the principal of the network operator. Accordingly, the Cyber Security Law upgrades the existing cyber security level protection system to the law. Article 21 provides that: the state implements a tiered system of cyber security protections. Network operators shall perform the following security protection duties according to the requirements of the tiered cybersecurity protection system, to ensure the network avoids interference, damage or unauthorized access, and to prevent network data leaks, theft or falsification.

To ensure the safety of key information infrastructure, safeguard national security, economic security and protect people's livelihood, the Cyber Security Law provides a special section on the operation safety of key information infrastructure to implement focused protection. Article 31 provides that: The state implements key protection of public telecommunications and information services, power, traffic, water, finance, public services, electronic governance and other critical information infrastructure that, if destroyed, losing function or leaking data leaks, might seriously endanger national security, the national welfare, the people's livelihood and the public interest, on the basis of the tiered cybersecurity protection structure. The concrete scope of critical information infrastructure and security protection measures for them are formulated by the State Council. Section 2 of Chap. 3 of the Cyber Security Law, titled "Operational Security for Critical Information Infrastructure", provides the regulations for the development of security measures for key information infrastructure, the departments responsible for safety protection, the safety protection obligations of operators, and the supervision and support of relevant departments.

4. Cyber Data Security

With the development and application of cloud computing and big data technology, network data security becomes essential to the safeguarding of national security, economic security, protection of citizens' legitimate rights and interests, and promotion of data utilization. Thus, the Cyber Security Law regulates the protection of data security. First, Article 21(4) provides that the network operators should "Adopt measures such as data classification, back-up of important data, and encryption" to prevent cyber data leakage or theft. Second, Articles 40 to 45 provide the regulations to enhance the protection of personal information, prevent personal information data from illegal access, disclosure or illegal use. Third, Article 37 provides that: Personal information and other important data collected or produced by critical information infrastructures operators during their operations within the mainland territory of the People's Republic of China, shall be stored within the territory. Where due to business requirements it is truly necessary to provide it outside the mainland, a security assessment shall be conducted according to the measures jointly formulated by the state network information departments and the relevant departments of the State Council.

5. Cyber Information Security

The Decision of the Standing Committee of the National People's Congress on Strengthening the Protection of Cyber Information in 2012 (the "Decision") stipulates the principle of regulating cyber information dissemination activities. The Cyber Security Law adheres to the principle of the Decision, and further improves the relevant management system. First, establish the network identity management system i.e., the real name system specified by the Decision to ensure that cyber information can be traced back. Article 24 provides that: Network operators handling the Internet access and domain registration services for users, handling stationary or mobile phone network access, or providing users with information publication services or instant messaging services, shall require users to provide real identity information when signing agreements with users or confirming provision of services. Where users do not provide real identity information, network operators must not provide them with relevant services. Second, clarify the obligation of the network operator to dispose illegal information. Article 47 stipulates that: Network operators shall strengthen management of information published by users, and where they discover information of which the publication or dissemination is prohibited by laws and regulations, and they shall immediately stop dissemination of that information, employ handling measures such as deleting it, prevent the information from spreading, save relevant records, and report to relevant authorities in charge. Third, clarify prohibition of release or transmission of information prohibited by laws and administrative regulations. Article 48 provides that: Electronic information sent or application software provided by any individual or organization must not install malicious programs, and must not contain information that laws and administrative regulations prohibit the publication or transmission of. Fourth, the network operators are required to provide necessary support for maintaining national security. Article 28 provides that: Network operators shall provide technical support and assistance to public security bodies and national security bodies acting to maintain national security and investigate crime. Fifth, give the relevant competent authorities the right to dispose illegal information and block the dissemination of illegal information. Article 50 provides that: The state network information departments and relevant departments perform network information security supervision and administration responsibilities; and where discovering information the release or transmission of which is prohibited by laws or administrative regulations, the departments shall request the network operators stop transmission, employ disposition measures such as deletion, and store relevant records; for information described above that comes from outside mainland People's Republic of China, they shall notify the relevant organization to adopt technological measures and other necessary measures to block the transmission of information.

6. Monitoring and Warning and Emergency Response

To strengthen the construction of national network security monitoring and warning and emergency system, improve cyber security capabilities, the Cyber Security Law made the following provisions: first, require management to establish a sound cyber security monitoring and warning and information reporting system. Article 51 provides that: The State establishes systems for cyber security monitoring and early warning and information bulletin. The state network information departments shall do overall coordination of relevant departments to strengthen collection, analysis and reporting efforts for cyber security information, and perform unified release of cyber security monitoring and early warning information in accordance with regulations. Article 52 provides that: Departments responsible for critical information infrastructure security protection efforts shall establish and complete that industry or that field's cyber security monitoring and early warning and information reporting systems, and, report the cyber security monitoring and early warning information in accordance with regulations. Second, establish a cyber security emergency operation mechanism, and develop contingency plans. Article 53 provides that: The state network information departments coordinates relevant departments' establishment and completion of mechanisms for cyber security risk assessment and emergency response efforts, formulate cyber security incident emergency response plans, and periodically organize drills. Third, Articles 54 to 56 stipulate delivery of warning information and response to cyber security emergencies. Fourth, stipulate provisions of cyber control during the disposal of major social security incidents. Article 58 provides that: To fulfill the need to protect national security and social public order, and respond to major social security incidents, with the approval or by the decision of the State Council, temporary measures regarding network communications in certain regions may be taken, such as restricting it.

7. Another Important basis

The Cyber Security Law limits the emerging new type of cybercrime. Article 46 provides that: Any person and organization shall, when using the network, be responsible for their actions. They must not establish websites or new groups used to perpetrate fraud, impart criminal methods, produce or sell prohibited goods or controlled goods, or other such unlawful and criminal activities; they may not use the Internet to disseminate information concerning perpetrating fraud, producing or selling prohibited goods or controlled goods, or other such unlawful and criminal activities. These provisions not only shock and awe individuals and organizations performing fraud, but also clarify the inescapable responsibility of Internet companies.

The Cyber Security Law provides regulations for attacks of foreign people against critical information infrastructures within our territory. Article 75 provides that: Where foreign institutions, organizations or individuals engage in attacks, intrusions, interference, damage or other activities endangering the critical information infrastructure of the People's Republic of China, and legal responsibility will be prosecuted according to the law after causing serious consequences. The State Council public security departments and relevant departments may also decide to freeze the assets of said institutions, organizations or individuals, or take other necessary punitive measures. This provision demonstrates our firm determination to safeguard national cyber sovereignty.

Chapter 9
Scientific Basis for Maintaining Cyberspace Sovereignty

Abstract The cyberspace sovereignty involves four basic rights, the independence of cyberspace, the cyberspace equality, the self-defense rights of cyberspace, and the cyberspace jurisdiction. Among them, the independent right of the cyberspace is restricted by the centralized domain name resolution mode of the root domain in the Internet; the right of cyberspace equality in the Internet is restricted by the current situation of the jungle law in the Internet, such as the operation of the Internet, technology evolution and standard formulation; the self-defense rights of cyberspace is restricted by the fuzziness of the national boundary in the Internet.

Keywords The independence right of cyberspace · The right of cyberspace equality · The self-defense

Cyberspace sovereignty includes four elements: **information communication technology facilities** that support the existence of cyberspace; **data** to be generated, stored, processed, transmitted and displayed in an information communication technology system; **cyber roles** that transmit and process the data; and **control rules** determining principles of processing and transmitting the data. **Four basic rights: the independence of cyberspace**, that is, cyberspace infrastructure located in Chinese territory operates autonomously and cannot be interfered with by other countries; **cyberspace equality**, i.e., every country has equal governance status in international network interconnection; the state has **cyberspace self-defence rights** to protect their own cyberspace from being violated; **cyberspace jurisdiction**, i.e., the cyberspace constituent facilities and their data are protected by national jurisdiction. **Four basic principles**: **respect for** the cyberspace **sovereignty** of all countries, every country does not violate the cyberspace of other countries and does not interfere the cyberspace management of other countries; the cyberspace sovereignty of all countries has equal status in international cyberspace governance activities.

B. Fang, *Cyberspace Sovereignty*,
https://doi.org/10.1007/978-981-13-0320-3_9

9.1 Independence of Cyberspace

Independence of cyberspace is exhibited in the following aspects: networks of various countries can operate independently and do not stop service by interventions from other countries; national networks can interoperate with international networks but are not subject to international restrictions; without prejudice to the international interconnection, the state has the power to independently develop Internet policies. Hence, whether cyberspace is interconnected and whether its operational power is in the hands of the state itself when connected with others, should be the discussions focal point of the independence of cyberspace.

9.1.1 Independent Control Properties of General Networks

For geographically based networks, from the point of view of cyberspace, the cyberspace type can be divided into two categories, i.e., global interconnection and non-global interconnection. That is, one refers to cyberspaces formed by interconnection between domestic equipment and foreign equipment, and the other one refers to cyberspaces formed only by domestic equipment.

Cyberspaces formed only by domestic equipment will naturally not be controlled abroad. Even independent networks such as Internet of Things, sensor networks constructed in the territory by enterprises of other countries are naturally subject to the jurisdiction of the authorities, and the management of the authorities on this type of networks will not be interfered with by the outside. Therefore, networks of this type have natural independence.

9.1.2 Bipartite-Graph Network Form with Complicated Interconnection

If there are two networks, and there are many interconnection channels between the networks, then people can deem nodes in the two networks to be two graphs and that the interconnection between the two networks is just interconnection between points in the two graphs. Thus, the two interconnected networks may be called as "bipartite-graph interconnection mode".

Satellite network is a relay point constructed to support the interconnection between points on the ground. If the relay point is deemed as a line connecting two points on the ground, then the satellite network can be used to connecting two different networks in the territory in a mode of "bipartite-graph interconnection". This is a property inherent to satellites.

Although the satellite network can construct a "bipartite-graph interconnection" mode, it cannot interfere with the normal operation of other networks and cannot be easily suspended by an external technical means. Hence, it can be deemed that this kind of network which has a special mode and is helpful for interconnection of other networks has independence.

9.1.3 Independent Characteristics Brought About by the Harmony of Addressing and Interconnection in International Telecommunication Networks

International telecommunication networks are networks globally interconnected and independently operated in each country. These networks are constructed by various countries themselves and meanwhile interconnect with each other in accordance with standards. During the operation process of the telecommunication networks, a distributed management mode is adopted to conduct step upwards (outside) interconnection. In other words, the domestic communication is a set of systems, and addressing is performed directly according to a communication routing table. Along with the development in computing power, the communication routing table develops from the previous area routing table (in unit of area code, each area code is a complete internal routing table, and there is a routing table between the area codes) mode to today's national unified routing table mode (for example, there is no obvious area code system for mobile phones). The use of a unified national routing table mode is helpful for implementing flexible services such as "number portability", allowing users to realize "changing the network without changing the number, and changing the location without changing the number" and other wishes.

Foreign communication requires connection to the international exchange through "International Prefix Number" and then is exchanged to a corresponding country in accordance with the international protocols to enter the destination country, followed by addressing according to the routing mode in the destination country. In this system, the telecommunication network in each country pertains to domestic cyberspace, and the interconnection channel between various countries can be deemed as "International public domain", which is maintained by the countries together, and the public policy is developed by the International Telecommunication Union (ITU). In this case, the telecommunication network of each country is run independently and will not be interfered with in any form by another country. Thus, such networks have independence.

9.1.4 Particularity of the Separation of Address Resolution and Addressing in Internet

Internet is a network structure that is different from the international telecommunications network in management mode. The Internet does not use the digital directional address symbol mode. That is, unlike the telecom network for which directional addresses such as “International Prefix Number” and “Area Prefix Number” are contained in the digital addresses, internet addresses (IP address) do not contain any information of physical location. In addition, for the sake of convenience, similar to the telephone user name of the telephone network, the Internet is also designed to assign a corresponding easy-to-remember “domain name” to each IP address for people to remember, and similar to an information desk in the telephone network, the Internet has constructed a domain name resolution system to solve the automatic translation problem from domain name to the IP address. This convenience leads to people’s strong reliance, that is, people no longer remember the IP address but rely on the convenient resolution and addressing to realize access to an internet address. The resulting outcome is that the resolution system becomes an important part of the operation of the Internet, and if there is a problem with the resolution system, it is equivalent to the operation of the Internet having a problem. However, the internet domain name resolution system adopts a centralized resolution mode rather than distributed layer-by-layer resolution mode, which makes the entire Internet objectively subject to a concentration point of the domain name resolution system when it relies on this unified automatic domain name resolution system.

From the technical point of view, domain name resolution system includes a centralized mode and a distributed mode. The so-called centralized mode refers to the domain name resolution being handled by a unified resolution system which, like the global variables, needs to ensure that all domain names are absolutely not conflicted to each other. The current Internet root domain name system is this mode. The distributed mode refers to employing individual name resolution which, like a local variable, at first ensures that the names in their own areas do not conflict and then ensure that the global names do not conflict by adding an area prefix. The current postal address delivery system is this mode.

The reason why the Internet adopts a centralized resolution mode is because the Internet was originally the US domestic Internet and was designed according to the domestic management mode, so no one has questioned this more efficient centralized domain name resolution mode. Along with the United States inviting the world to access the United States Internet, the Internet gradually became international Internet, so in view of the logical structure, the international Internet can also be regarded as the United States Internet. That is why Professor Lv Shuwang from the Chinese Academy of Sciences said that the Internet was a “US network”.[1] From this point of view, the Internet’s sovereignty relationship has become complicated. As for carriers, the internet part located in territories of various countries is a cyberspace in the country where it is located, while from the perspective of the centralized domain name resolution mode, the internet should be a cyberspace of the US. This strange phenomenon led to struggles for sovereignty, and at least the Internet independence is objectively subject to the United States. This is also an important factor for the United States’ reluctance to accept cyberspace sovereignty.

---

[1]Lecture of professor LV Shuwang from the Chinese Academy of Sciences in Peking University. http://xsc.nuc.edu.cn/info/1011/2066.htm [2016-10-3].

Of course, the postal prefix of the postal address is named by the state itself. If there is a conflict, coordination between countries is necessary. It is like Korea (South Korea or North Korea), there is a conflict of names, and it is necessary to negotiate a solution to the conflict. The Internet Corporation for Assigned Names and Numbers (ICANN) has now played a role in avoiding the conflict in the naming of the Internet domain name system, and it is responsible for coordinating the naming of top-level domain names. For an international organization, this is the most appropriate approach. However, the current dilemma is that ICANN is subject to long-term control of the United States, and if its Internet policy conflicts with other countries, there is a lack of room for coordination. But only for the domain name naming system, this centralized naming model does not have a technical defect. The key is that the naming system and the resolution system should be separated, that is, the naming system adopts a centralized international organization management mode, and the resolution system may adopt a distributed national management mode, thereby giving sufficient operation room for independence of cyberspace of the countries.

9.1.5 Current Centralized Domain Name Resolution Mode

The current Internet domain name resolution system is step-by-step recursive resolution. But different from people's ideas, the Internet's resolution system is top-down approach rather than bottom-up approach, which forms a centralized resolution characteristic.

If a person wants to visit a website of the Chinese Academy of Engineering www.cae.cn, the access terminal will be provided with domain name resolution services by a recursive DNS called "recursive domain name resolution server". This terminal will query the IP address of www.cae.cn in the domain name resolution server. If the website has recently been accessed by a user sharing the recursive DNS with this terminal, it means that the recursive DNS also retains the IP address of www.cae.cn, so the recursive DNS can return the IP address directly to the terminal. If the IP address of this website is not in cache of the recursive DNS, the recursive DNS needs to first access a root domain name server to query address of a resolution server of the top-level domain .cn of this website. To ensure the reliability of the domain name resolution, the recursive resolution server sends a request to 13 root domain name servers at the same time, and preferably selects the first query result. The reason why 13 root domain name servers are adopted is because the size of the request packets specified by the protocol can only accommodate addresses of up to 13 root domain name servers. According to the principle of layer-by-layer resolution, the recursive DNS first obtains the IP address of the top-level domain .cn from the root server, and then obtains the address of the cae.cn resolution server from the resolution server dns.cn for .cn domain name, and then obtains the IP address of www.cae.cn from the domain name resolution server dns.cae.cn for .cae.cn.

Here, because of the top-down characteristic, the "fortress" of the entire resolution process lies in the root domain name resolution server. Although it appears that there are 13 root domain name resolution servers located in different countries, the primary root server is in the United States, and the remaining 12 servers need to accept synchronization of the primary root server, so the primary root server "A root" managed by Verisign is the "fortress" that controls the entire Internet. Therefore, the primary root domain name resolution server "A root" has the ability of paralyze a country's Internet, and it's controlled by the owner of the root domain name resolution server and its administrator.

From the viewpoint of hierarchical resolution, the root domain name resolver needs to have several next-level nodes to carry out the next-level resolution work, or a more specific resolution task, which is called top-level domain name resolution. After the Internet began to invite countries to access, national top-level domain names have been defined in the domain name system. Subsequently, in the designed recursive layer-by-layer resolution system, the national top-level domain names also bear the next-level resolution tasks.

At present, the Internet's root domain name system is managed by ICANN, and a "Top-level Domain Name Sponsorship Agreement"[2] was signed by ICANN and the top domain name managers. To clarify ICANN's jurisdiction over the domain name system, the agreement first defines a "legal" status of ICANN: "ICANN is a non-profit corporation formed on 30 September 1998 for the purposes of providing technical-coordination functions for the Internet in the public interest. Among ICANN's responsibilities is to oversee operation of the Internet's Authoritative Root-Server System" and "ICANN, to the extent it has the authority under its agreements and otherwise, shall cause the Authoritative Root-Server System to publish DNS resource records delegating the Delegated ccTLD to the nameservers recorded in the Authoritative-Root Database".

9.1.6 Impact of the Centralized Domain Name Resolution System on the Independence of Internet

The essence of independence of Internet is that a national network can run independently from outside control. However, the centralized domain name resolution system makes the entire Internet constrained by the main root domain name resolution server. Therefore, there are a "disappearance risk", a "blindness risk" and an "isolation risk" for countries other than the United States.

"**Disappearance risk**": If a country's top-level domain name is deleted from the primary root domain name server database, the country's top-level domain name space will be "erased" from the Internet's namespace, so that the international

[2]Model ccTLD Sponsorship Agreement-Triangular Situation. http://archive.icann.org/en/cctlds/model-tscsa- 02sep01.htm [2016-9-17].

community cannot find all the domain name spaces carried by the top-level domain name of the country, as the cyberspace carried by the country's top-level domain name is erased. As mentioned above, the resolution of Iraq, Libya's root domain names .iq and .iy were stopped respectively in 2003 and in 2004. Obviously, it is easy to dispel a country, as long as the top-level domain name of this country is deleted from the primary root domain name server database.

"**Blindness risk**": If the root domain name server refuses to respond to a request for domain name resolution of IP addresses from some country, it means that all users of the country can no longer visit the Internet, because the country's Internet users cannot get required domain name resolution results. According to an unconfirmed rumour, in the nineties of the last century, a resolution of IP addresses from Somalia was refused by the root domain name server. As compared with "disappearance risk", "blindness risk" has a larger impact on the country's Internet users, while "disappearance risk" only affects websites carried by the country's top-level domain name. However, the implementation of the "blindness risk" is more complicated than the "disappearance risk". It not only is necessary to ensure that all 13 root domain name servers and all their corresponding mirror servers refuse to perform resolution but also is necessary to ensure that it is possible to determine which IP addresses belong to this country.

"**Isolation risk**": If all the international entrances and exits of a country are blocked, according to the current domain name resolution system, the country's Internet domain name resolution process will be suspended because of failing to access the root domain name server, resulting in the country's Internet being paralyzed. As compared with "disappearance risk" and "blindness risk", it is very difficult to realize "isolation risk", because unimaginable resources are necessary to cut off the Internet access of a country. However, if the isolation is successful, the damage is the biggest, because though the "blindness risk" also affects an entire country, at least the Internet can be accessed through direct access to an IP address, but "isolation risk" cuts off the connection between a country and the outside to make the country an island.

9.1.7 Technical Means to Realize Independence Within the Internet

Some people think that since the root domain name resolution server is in the hands of the United States, and they cannot accept the US hegemony, how come they cannot rebuild their own Internet? In contrast, the international governance system formed by the telecommunication network can be harmonized by the International Telecommunication Union (ITU), and countries have not lost cyberspace sovereignty, for which the fundamental reason is that countries first build their own domestic telecommunications networks and then form interoperability through international cooperation. Hence, it was suggested that each country itself establishes an independent Internet and then interconnect with the international community or that respective countries access to the national network so that the resolution right of the root domain name can be retained in the hands of the country. Decimal network (IPv9)[3] invented and fully promoted by XIE Jianping from Shanghai Institute of Chemical Industry came up with this idea. Professor LV Shuwang also vigorously promotes the construction of “Chinese public network” to resist the “US network hegemony”.[4] However, if countries do not like the United States to control the Internet and form network hegemony, then what reasons will allow other countries to access their own Internet, accept their own network management, and recognize the country to form a new “network hegemony”? Especially, if other countries do not intend to re-build a new Internet and only to connect with their own network, then it is safe to say that the idea of building their own Internet may only result in becoming a self-built island. Obviously, it is difficult to get the sympathy out of the international community to deal with the inequality of today’s Internet world, with the approach of “to opposing US cyber hegemony”.

In fact, to solve the problem of independence, it is necessary to start from the technical system. This problem will be solved if the centralized domain name resolution system can be changed to a distributed domain name resolution system. In recent years, a new form of distributed information fidelity and delivery technology, i.e., the “block chain” technology can ensure accurate transmission of node information and ensuring that the node information will not be illegal tampering.[5] Image if each node is a top-level domain and is maintained by a corresponding country (for ccTLD: country code Top-Level Domain) or a corresponding enterprise (for gTLD: generic Top-Level Domain), then the address of the top-level domain name server can be exchanged through the block chain technology, which can also achieve the current purpose of domain name resolution. Internet users in various countries can first perform resolution through their own “area root domain name server”. Here, the “area root domain name server” is mentioned relative to the current root domain name server, which is, if it is in a country but bears the responsibility of root domain name resolution. The root domain name resolution server will use the block chain technology to exchange address with various top-level domain name servers.

The use of the distributed domain name resolution method avoids a bottleneck formed by the centralized resolution system, allowing the country’s independent operation rights from interference of any country or organization.

---

[3]Decimal network—developed and accomplished by XIE Jianping from Shanghai Institute of Chemical Industry. http://www.ccsa.org.cn/article_new/show_article.php?categories_id=73ca46f0-1b19-4d30-f550-44b1be116665&article_id=cyzx_173dae1a-c47b-e2c8-a140-466363d25c7c [2016-10-3].

[4]LV Shuwang: China does not have its own Internet, and it is a top priority to build public network home. http://news.jschina.com.cn/system/2014/12/27/023111503.shtml [2016-10-3].

[5]What is block chain? What can block chain technology do? http://www.qukuailianweb.com/164.html [2016-10-3].

9.1.8 Methods in Response to Three Domain Name Resolution Risks

1. Methods for solving the "disappearance risk"

The method for solving "disappearance risk" can only be obtaining the address of the top-level domain name server independent of the root domain name, which means that the top-level domain name owners not only inform the address of a server to the root domain name server but also inform the address of the server to more demanders, that is, inform the address of the server as much as possible in a mode of "not place all eggs in one basket", to ensure that the address of their top-level domain name server is not completely blocked.

Apparently, if "block chain domain name resolution system" is employed, it not only ensures that countries have a fair position, but also ensures that any single tampering cannot work, so that the removal of a country's top-level domain name cannot be technically realized.

"Autonomous root domain name resolution system based on national alliance" presented by academician FANG Binxing is a solution directed at "disappearance risk",[6] of which the basic idea is to construct a method of "peer-to-peer diffusion of domain name" by using an idea similar to "peer-to-peer route diffusion between autonomous systems", so that the top-level domain name owners not only report the address information of the resolution server to the original root but also report the address information of their top-level domain name servers to root domain name controllers of other countries. Meanwhile, for the respective national root domain name resolution system, the directly exchanged address information of a top-level domain name resolution server is used in preference to the information conveyed by the original root. Thereby, those countries that publish address information of their own top-level domain name resolution server will no longer be blocked by the international root domain name server. All this can be realized through the construction of national top-level domain name alliance. Members of this alliance negotiate a protocol of exchanging address information of the top-level domain name resolution servers and exchange corresponding address information of corresponding domain names via credible channels in an interconnected mode.

2. Methods for Solving the "Blindness Risk"

There are many ways to solve the "blindness risk", and the most popular method is to copy the domain name resolution data of the root domain name server and independently provide service to the outside. Since resolution servers that provide top-level services take different resolution policies, a root domain name server that

[6]Discussion of autonomous root domain name resolution system based on national alliance from viewpoint of cyber sovereignty of the State. http://news.xinhuanet.com/politics/2014-11/27/c_127255092.htm [2016-10-3].

provides resolution can be always found so that the country's resolution request will be answered. In practice, there are a variety of specific solutions.

(1) Google's recursive domain name resolution server. Google's "8.8.8.8" recursive domain name resolution server also provides a resolution mode of "recursive root" while providing recursive resolution and can directly provide a service of root-area resolution.[7]
(2) 360 company's emergency disaster recovery programs. 360 company's domain name backup program is also a "recursive root" backup mode, that is, recording a large number of real-time domain name resolution information, and after the root server refuses to provide services, directly providing results of the root region resolution that have been recorded.[8]
(3) Domain name rapid resolution solution presented by China Education and Research Network. China Education and Research Network (CERNET) takes a "camouflage root" mode, that hijacks all resolution requests for the root server, and directly answers by using the copied root zone information, thereby achieving an effect of rapidly providing domain name resolution.[9]
(4) Autonomous root domain name resolution system based on national alliance. In the program of constructing national top-level domain name alliance presented by academician FANG Binxing, super allies are set up in the alliance. Super allies not only exchange address information of their own top-level domain name resolution servers, but also provide resolution requests for each other so as to be capable of providing resolution services for each other when the international root domain name resolution server refuses to provide service to some ally.[10]
(5) Open Root Server Network. This is a mode of "open the roots", which, establishes a group of root servers operating independently to provide services, which also employs data of IANA root zone.[11]
(6) Yeti DNS Project. Yeti DNS Project, which China's institutions participate in, is also an "open root" mode. That is, a trusted root domain name resolution server is constructed to provide services and achieve the same resolution effect, but it is not subject to policy constraints from the root domain name resolution server.[12]

---

[7]Huang C, Maltz DA, Li J, et al (2011) Public DNS system and global traffic management// Proceedings INFOCOM, IEEE, 2615–2623. http://baike.baidu.com/view/5971613.htm [2016-9-25].

[8]DNS "paralyzing" continued: self-repair without affecting drowsing of websites. http://www.360doc.com/content/14/0123/16/8534868_347361717.shtml [2016-9-17].

[9]Domain name hosting and resolution services in education networks: To facilitate the rapid sharing of resources within the CERNET network. http://www.edu.cn/zxz_6542/20140424/t20140424_1104097_1.shtml [2016-9-17].

[10]Discussion of autonomous root domain name resolution system based on national alliance from viewpoint of national network sovereignty. http://news.xinhuanet.com/politics/2014-11/27/c_127255092.htm [2016-10-3].

[11]Open Root Server Network (ORSN). http://www.orsn.net [2016-9-21].

[12]Yeti DNS Project. http://www.yeti-dns.org [2016-9-21].

(7) "Global root" mode. To overcome insufficiency of the number of 13 root domain name servers, a logical root named Universal Anycast Root Server (UARS) is added to the current DNS system. By adding mirror images of 13 root domain name servers, it is possible to realize root zone resolution service in a specific area by using Anycast technology. For example, there are mirror image servers of F root, I root, J root,[13] and L root[14] in China, which can rapidly provide domain name resolution services for Chinese users.

All the above solutions basically physically decentralize the servers so that the dependency on the root servers is reduced to some extent. However, the root zone data still comes from IANA/ICANN and therefore essentially belongs to the root image. From the viewpoint of data sources, these solutions are still centralized in logic. Though they can effectively deal with "blindness risk", but they cannot deal with "disappearance risk".

3. Methods for Solving "Isolation Risk"

Methods for solving "isolation risk" are relatively simple. First of all, local resolution is preferred, that is, countries construct their own autonomous root domain name resolution systems (such as "area root" mode) to receive a resolution request from a domestic recursive domain name server, so that a resolution result of the top-level domain name is provided at first by the domestic root domain name resolution server (such as "area root domain name server") for each domestic resolution request.[15] Next, expand the number of connections with the outside world as far as possible, and especially in particular, pay attention to directional diversity of the connection channels. The so-called "directional diversity" means that multiple network channels connected to the outside do not intersect to the same point, so as not to be merged into one channel and attacked, and that if the countries are not in the same alliance, there will be no possibility of acting together. The purpose of directional diversity of the connection channels is to increase the difficulty of forming encirclement by attackers so as to break conditions for forming the "isolation risk" and allow a country's network channel to be always capable of being connected to the international community through some channel.

---

[13] Open DNS. http://www.doc88.com/p-6819957124082.html [2016-9-17].

[14] Introduction of L root image into China will further enhance experience of the Internet users. http://www.ch.21vianet.com/?p=2303 [2016-9-17].

[15] Discussion of autonomous root domain name resolution system based on national alliance from viewpoint of national network sovereignty. http://news.xinhuanet.com/politics/2014-11/27/c_127255092.htm [2016-10-3].

9.2 Cyberspace Equality

As far as cyberspace equality is concerned, the first thing is that the countries have the same rights in the international governance of cyberspace, but this is impacted by the "Stakeholders dominant mode" in the Internet field; the second thing is that countries should be equal in cyberspace, this is often subject to the right to speak brought about by the Internet market.

9.2.1 Importance of Cyberspace Equality

As one of the fundamental rights of a country, equality is an important symbol of having national sovereignty. Some areas are part divided from a country for historical reasons, but their relationship has not changed, such as Taiwan. Though such areas objectively have the military (the right of self-defense), "regime" (jurisdiction), and independent capacity (independence), such areas do not have sovereign status in the international community and cannot participate in international organizations of which the members are sovereign States. This shows that equality is an important attribute of national sovereignty. Therefore, the equality of cyberspace is an important area of cyberspace sovereign "wrestling".

The equality of cyberspace is particularly important in the case of uneven distribution of network resources. Inequality of resources can easily lead to unequal right to speak and then form resource allocation and use rules more favorable for powerful countries, which leads to a vicious circle of uneven development of the network field. China is a country with great potential for network development, also a country that has the largest market, but at the same time China is an underdeveloped network access country, so China needs to rely on the principle of international equity to protect the interests of the state, such as interests in domain name policy development.

9.2.2 The Internationalization of Internet Organizations Is a Manifestation of the Sovereign Equality of the Internet

In the Internet age, human society has many global problems, such as population problems, environmental problems, resource problems, drug problems, terrorist activities, financial crisis, etc. The emergence of these transnational issues calls for strengthening of the status and role of international organizations and international coordination, so that international organizations become the same important international community as countries, so as to realize the sharing and transferring of part of national sovereignty, making a country to not maintain monopoly of the dominant position in the international system.

Sovereign equality refers to the expression in form of one country with one vote in the international community, regardless of size of the country. The premise is that the Internet is internationally governed, that is, the governance is dominated by international organizations composed of sovereign states, which participate in decision-making links such as the development of public network policy and network development planning in a manner of reflecting interests of the countries. For example, the international telecommunications network employs a co-governance mode by the International Telecommunication Union (ITU-T) composed of sovereign states; likewise, the radio network also employs a co-governance mode by the International Telecommunication Union Wireless Organization (ITU-R) composed of sovereign countries.

As far as the Internet is concerned, because the Internet is evolved from the internet in the United States, in this evolution process, countries developed and constructed each country's internet under the premise of obeying the original system. Hence, the countries simply impose national sovereignty on cyberspace in their territorial jurisdictions and lack the voice of calling for participation in governance in the international community. For the United States, where the Internet is invented, in order to avoid the countries' voice asking for sovereignty in the Internet, the US government does not casually make a dominance of the Internet in this situation, but vigorously promote the mode of the "stakeholders" domination of the Internet. This obviously is a management mode based on the "jungle rule", but the strong are almost all US companies. Therefore, it is natural that the US government is strong in defending this rule.

The Internet is international, global and virtual, and Internet-induced legal issues are also international, so it is invalid if any one country tries to solve them through a unilateral act. Due to the coexistence of the multiple jurisdiction and multiple national laws, the international community tends to solve problems in cyberspace through international cooperation. If different countries fight separately by taking different jurisdictional standards, it will inevitably lead to conflicts and contradictions between different sovereign states. The international community has long carried out a series of international cooperation and achieved fruitful achievements. The Model Law on Electronic Commerce,[16] adopted by the United Nations Commission on International Trade Law in 1996, was the representative of the network legal norms. The promulgation of the law laid the foundation for the gradual resolution of the legal issues of electronic commerce, and which provided a framework and model text for the countries to establish their own e-commerce laws. In addition, the World Trade Organization (WTO), the World Intellectual Property Organization, the International Chamber of Commerce and some regional organizations such as the Organization for Economic Co-operation and Development

[16]UNCITRAL Model Law on Electronic Commerce. http://www.uncitral.org/uncitral/en/uncitral_texts/electronic_commerce/1996Model.html [2016-9-17].

(OECD) and the European Union have embarked on or have completed the development of international agreements or model laws on e-commerce and copyright.

The rapid development of the Internet requires the international community to accelerate the pace of cooperation to establish international uniform norms to reduce differences in national laws and promote the establishment of a new international information order. However, international cooperation must be based on the principle of sovereign equality, follow international law, fulfill international obligations, and do not interfere in the internal affairs of other countries, which is the only way to safeguard the common interests of mankind. International treaties should specify the principles of international law that should be followed in the global Internet information dissemination, such as the sovereign equality of the States in the exchange of information, the media should not be used to interfere in the internal affairs of other countries and settle disputes peacefully, and it should not be used for war and force threats, International legal cooperation, the prohibition of the dissemination of specific content information, the principle of freedom of expression, the respect for different cultures, the development of language diversification, etc.

9.2.3 Risks Brought About by Non-International Governance Modes

Since ICANN is a nonprofit enterprise registered in the United States and is under the jurisdiction of the US Department of Commerce, the public policy of the domain name does not operate based on a mode of cyberspace equality. If other countries want to change the IP of a top-level domain, they must file with the US Department of Commerce through ICANN, and the US government has no incentive to take care of the fundamental interests of each country.

There is a "blindness risk" in the internet of a country other than the United States. Because the operation of ICANN is not constrained by the international community, the root server may refuse to provide resolution service for a country's recursive resolution server, thereby disconnecting the country's access to the root domain name resolution server so that users in the country cannot access the Internet.

The top-level domain name of the internet in countries other than the United States runs a "disappearance risk". If the root domain name server removes information of a country's top-level domain name server without the approval of an international organization, it can cause the country's network to be no longer found by the international community.

ICANN, as a top-level domain name policy-making department, may not take into account some of the country's political and national interests, accepting some domain names provocative to a country's political or national attributes as top-level domain names, such as the use of words that oppose a religion or words of cults that are resisted by some countries as domain names, which is also behavior violating the principle of fairness, and there has been no restriction to this behavior so far.

9.2.4 Equal Interconnection Between Countries Is the Basic Requirement of Equality

The equality of cyberspace is an extension of the independence of cyberspace, which means that interconnection between networks of the countries, can be negotiated on an equal footing, and is not subject to privilege. At present, because some countries have an absolute advantage of the network resources, interconnection is liable to be constructed in a unilaterally favorable mode. The reality is that the access of the Internet in underdeveloped countries is constrained by large international telecom operators, such as Sprint, which dominates the international community. As a result, countries with a small internet scale often encounter unequal treatment when they access the Internet. Therefore, countries, especially with Internet power, shall not be detrimental to the interests of other countries in the management of their own cyberspace. The international dependence of the internet is very strong, and the relationship is very close. The strong countries on the internet should not force other countries to accept the internet polices they developed and should not directly damage the sovereignty of other countries. Historically, the United States mandated MSN to interrupt the service for five countries including Cuba and others of its service,[17] which in fact, is a challenge to the concept of equality of cyberspace.

9.2.5 National Cyberspace Immunity Based on Equality of Cyberspace

Cyberspace sovereignty must be at the expense of necessary compromise, so this is also a relative sovereignty. In the Internet age, the trend of sovereign immunity is more realistic. Hence, a state has the obligation to respect the independence of the other countries and to limit the supreme right of its own territory in accordance with international laws. In cyberspace, there seems no national boundary divided, but according to the international customary law, the online behavior in a country is still a national act. Judicial exemption, of course, should be enjoyed in a foreign cyberspace, which is doubtless.

[17]Microsoft cut off MSN service for five countries including Cuba. http://www.infzm.com/content/29199?depk3e [2016-10-2].

In international relations, the principle of exemption of state and its property is derived from the principle of national sovereignty. State immunity is an important issue related to the jurisdiction of the State's territorial jurisdiction, which generally refers to that the conduct and property of a State are not governed by the legislative, judicial and administrative aspects of other States. That is, without the consent of a State, the conduct of that State shall not be governed by the courts of the host country, and its property is not subject to the seizure and enforcement of the courts of the host country. This is jurisdictional immunity enjoyed by foreign countries. The issue of jurisdictional immunity involved by an international law can only occur between countries with equal relations. Study is necessary as to how to exercise the traditional national sovereign immunity theory in cyberspace. Obviously, coordination between restrictions and jurisdiction of state sovereignty in cyberspace is the key to solve this problem.

9.3 Self-Defense Rights of Cyberspace

The importance of the research of cyberspace self-defense lies in that we must profoundly understand the connotation and particularity of the right of self-defense, and to recognize the significance of safeguarding the right of self-defense, and definite responsibilities of the military to guarantee the implementation of the right of self-defense of a national cyberspace.

9.3.1 The Right of Self-Defense of Cyberspace Is an Extension of Cyberspace Independence

Self-defense rights of cyberspace mainly refer to having means of self-defense against any attack on their own network. Cyberspace is a sovereign domain, and when the national network has been violated, the national armed forces have the right to self-defense.

The security of cyberspace has attracted the attention of governments. In the United States, cyberspace strategy has become the third largest strategy after nuclear strategy and space strategy, becoming a new battle for international conflict. The United States has implemented the cyberspace security law, declaring that attack on the US Internet infrastructure is an attack on the United States, and the United States has the right to implement self-defense. The United States has established a cyber-warfare unit, which has the sense and ability of self-defense. The United States even declares that military strikes will be used when the national network is attacked.[18] Hence, the internet has become a battleground in the military field, which not just is an information means of supporting military competition in traditional fields. The realization of cyberspace self-defense cannot rely on other countries, and it is necessary to ensure that a country's network system is in a state of self-protection.

9.3.2 Particularity and Complexity of Cyberspace

Cyberspace has its own particularity and complexity. How to implement the right of self-defense needs to be carefully studied. As compared with traditional forms of national security, national security of the Internet age has new features, new threats and challenges. Under the powerful logic of the information revolution, the traditional geographical boundaries of regions become increasingly easy to penetrate and become blurred. It is often difficult to resist external affairs of a country outside the boundaries, and it is also difficult to confine internal affairs inside the boundaries of a country. Thus, it is necessary to expand the vision of national security from simple physical boundaries to cyberspace, and expand the Defense focus of national cyberspace security from management of opinion crisis to a comprehensive defense.

Interconnection of the Internet in the world makes the Internet have very special properties with respect to the physical community, which is completely different from the non-diffusing characteristic of the physical community. For instance, once the root domain name server is attacked, it will affect the normal operation of each country; if one domain name service provider website is attacked, websites relying on it to conduct domain name resolution will suffer, for example, on October 21, 2016, the Dyn domain name service provider was attacked, which lead to failure of Twitter, New York Times and other sites log in[19]; A site that is attacked against domain name by DDoS may evade attack by redirecting the domain name, but this will cause redirected third parties implicated in the DDoS attack[20]; a third country that has nothing to do with the conflict parties may also be implicated in a springboard-based attack.

[18]US strategic commander claimed that: Internet attacks on the United States will face military strikes. http://mil.eastday.com/m/20090516/u1a4375577.html [2016-10-3].

[19]US Internet large-scale paralysis, Twitter, New York Times and other sites were attacked. http://news.qq.com/a/20161022/016976.htm [2016-12-31].

[20]Historically, Google was attacked by DDoS because DDoS attacks between "PW" make the attacked "PW" redirect its domain name to Google's IP address.

9.3.3 Network Boundaries

The study of cyberspace self-defense should be carried out in a precondition of clarifying the utilization scope of the self-defense rights, that is, it is necessary to make it clear where the territorial cyberspace is, so it is necessary to clarify the boundaries of the network. Interconnection of the Internet makes attacks from outside on the territory easy. The form of attack can be either a cyber-attack or a spread of opinion attacking the government, intended to make social unrest. From this viewpoint, the cyberspace self-defense ability built by a country should be built based on setting "network boundaries", thereby having the ability to block attacks from outside networks and public opinion. Objectively, many countries have not yet realized that cyberspace has become a territory with a boundary and that territorial cyberspace and territory of a country need to be defended by the army. Of course, most countries do not have this ability, or are not aware of the need to build a cyberspace defense system to form a cyberspace self-defense system.

People should strengthen the awareness of network boundaries from the following aspects.

1. Prevent information penetration of foreign forces for subverting the power of a country

The international community should focus on the following facts. A small number of developed countries abuse their freedom of speech on the basis of free flow of information, use the Internet as a stage of military psychological warfare, manipulate the media, control public opinion, spread false information, undermine the psychological and spiritual environment of other countries, erode their traditional culture, morality, ethics and values, perform the psychological control of their people in order to achieve the purpose of intervening the affairs of other countries, undermining their political, economic and social system.

2. Prevent hostile forces such as foreign terrorism from using the Internet to impact social stability of a country

The international community should focus on terrorism, extremist religious and ethnic separatist forces which abuse freedom of speech, create false information on the Internet in the name of individuals or civil society, cross-border disseminate information contrary to the principles and norms of international laws and national laws in certain countries for purpose of creating social unrest and interfering with national stability.

3. Citizens' freedom of speech should be confined to the legal framework

National, organized or political abuse of freedom of speech is completely beyond the scope of giving citizens freedom of speech prescribed by Article 19 of the International Covenant on Civil and Political Rights,[21] so it should not be supported or even protected.

9.3.4 *Authorization to the Army to Defend the National Cyberspace*

To guarantee the self-defense of cyberspace, the army must be authorized to function accordingly.

Because countries lack the knowledge of cyberspace sovereignty, the application of national military in cyberspace is often limited to attacking the enemy's network facilities and protecting their own military network information systems, but the application is less used for purpose of protecting a country's critical information infrastructure. In fact, the US military force is used to protect important domestic information systems. The Einstein system[22] in the United States is a three-tier response system, the first layer is the emergency department of the application system itself; the second layer is the United States Computer Emergency Readiness Team (US-CERT)[23]; and the third layer is the Joint Task Force-Global Network Operations (JTF-GNO).[24] This shows that the US military has been authorized to function of protecting cyberspace sovereignty. Thus, both to clarify the role of the military in defending the national network infrastructure and important information systems, and to clarify how to defend or take over these systems in the event of a military conflict so as to play the role of the regular army, are significant blank fields that need to be solved in many countries.

The network information system is different from the traditional building facilities. The building can be protected from attack by means of external fortification. However, the extensive interconnection of the Internet makes it easy for an attacker to perform direct attack. Therefore, the network information system cannot be protected simply by setting a peripheral guard line, and it is further necessary to implement the protection measures deep inside the information system. However, it is unlikely that the army will go deep into all information systems. The only solution is to work like the Einstein system in the United States, so that the army

---

[21]International Covenant on Civil and Political Rights, Chinese and English versions. http://www.hrol.org/Documents/ChinaDocs/Obligations/2012-11/272.html [2016-9-17].

[22]Einstein Program for the United States Network Security 17. http://3y.uu456.com/bp_Og0oh8hxyn00kc51ztr7_1.html [2016-9-17].

[23]US-CERT. https://www.us-cert.gov/ [2016-10-3].

[24]Joint Task Force-Global Network Operations. https://en.wikipedia.org/wiki/Joint_Task_Force-Global_Network_Operations [2016-10-3].

and the information system managers perform protection together, thereby constituting a defense mechanism based on integration of military and civilian and coordination protection of the military and the local.

9.4 Cyberspace Jurisdiction

Cyberspace jurisdiction refers to the right of the state to have jurisdiction over its own cyberspace, including legislative power, administrative power, judicial power, resource allocation rights, etc.

9.4.1 Definition and Scope of Cyberspace Jurisdiction

Cyberspace jurisdiction is an integral part of cyberspace sovereignty, refers to the right that the composition platform of cyberspace and its data are subject to the country's judicial protection. The cyberspace jurisdiction determines the scope of network authorities of a country. The popularization and development of information technology, especially Internet technologies make the human society project activities in political, military, economic, cultural, social and other fields into the cyberspace. In the cyberspace, the artificial "virtual world" reproduces various social phenomena previously taking place in the real world. Cyberspace is virtually an extension of the real world, correspondence of all individual actors and their activities in the cyberspace can be found in the real world, and realistic actors and their behavior are also expanded in cyberspace. This change extends the territorial connotation that is the basis for the exercise of the jurisdiction of a country, so that the cyberspace as a "territorial network" of a country has become a newly extended space where the national jurisdiction can be exercised in addition to territorial land, territorial sea, and territorial airspace.

In the real world, national sovereignty needs to be used to maintain political security, military security, economic security, cultural security, social security, and all these security elements can be mirrored in cyberspace. Therefore, cyberspace jurisdiction is used to govern and manage the information and communication infrastructure located in the country, the data carried and the activities that occur in cyberspace so as to ensure the maintenance of many security elements.

Management of cyberspace objectively exists in every country in the world. Moreover, in general, relevant management means and laws and regulations are more perfect in countries and regions where the internet is more developed. At the level of concrete practice, all the countries around the world, without exception, effectively manage their cyberspace—from the network infrastructure to the network application, and the cyberspace are prevented from being compromised by bad influence factors.

9.4.2 Construction of Legal Norms of Cyberspace

The application of the state jurisdiction by the modern civilized government is based on the rule of laws, and the jurisdiction of cyberspace at first requires construction of a legal framework for cyberspace. The global flow of information brought about by the Internet breaks through the territorial boundaries between countries and creates a new space for mankind that impacts feasibility and applicability of traditionally geographically based laws. The new cyberspace needs to be regulated by new legal forms, and it is necessary to develop new rules that are different from traditional territorial jurisdiction to bind this new space.

For example, *the United States enacted the Computer Fraud and Abuse Act*[25] in 1986, which stipulates that "intentionally extort from any individual, firm, corporation, educational institution, financial institution, governmental entity, or legal or other entity, any money or other thing of value" is criminal behavior. In 2003, the United States issued the Controlling the Assault of Non-Solicited Pornography and Marketing or CAN-SPAM Act,[26] the following behavior should be punished in accordance with the rule: any person who intentionally accesses a protected computer without authorization in an interstate or foreign trade and transmits a large number of commercial electronic mails through the computer; transmits a large number of commercial electronic mails through a protected computer for purpose of spoofing or misleading recipients; intentionally transmits mails of which the header information is false; register more than 5 e-mail accounts or domain names using wrong identification information, and transmits commercial electronic mails through a variety of accounts; transmits a large number of commercial electronic mails to more than 5 e-mail addresses by impersonating an e-mail user or its legal successor.

Rating system is another effective measure used by the United States for the remediation and management of harmful information. The film rating system started earlier in the United States and has now become mature. In 1995, 39 companies including Microsoft, Netscape, America Online (AOL) announced a label format standard, i.e., the Platform for the Internet Content Selection (PICS), thus providing an effective filtering means and management solutions. This new platform for the Internet content selection realizes selection as to Internet content by inserting filter software between the information receiver and the information sources. PICS divides information on the Internet into four aspects—sex, violence, language and nudity, and the information of each aspect is divided into 0–4 levels.[27] Generally, each rating or classification system has its own hierarchical structure, and there is

---

[25]Computer Fraud and Abuse Act. http://www.infseclaw.net/news/html/?937.html [2016-9-25].

[26]The Controlling the Assault of Non-Solicited Pornography and Marketing or "CAN-SPAM" Act. http://www.magazine.org/sites/default/files/CONSUMER-CAN-SPAM.doc [2016-9-21].

[27]Zhang YR (2002) Inspiration to China from controlling of online information harmful for minors in the US. Juvenile Delinquency Prob 5:54–55. http://www.docin.com/p-1508725455.html [2016-10-4].

more detailed distinction inside each structure. There are mainly three aspects: content classification (soft pornography and hard pornography), audience classification (adult and child) and control hierarchy (code layer, content layer, physical layer). At present, hard pornographic material includes at least child pornography and obscene material. The distinction between soft pornography and hard pornography becomes an important criterion for dividing pornography and obscenity in most countries of the world, also forms the basis of legal regulation of pornography.[28]

In December 2005, the European Commission proposed a draft proposal to revise the "Television without Frontiers Directive, TVWF Directive",[29] which was renamed the Audiovisual Media Service Directive,[30] in the hope that by revising the directive, all media content areas can be covered, including telecommunications, radio, and Internet content. As prescribed by the Audiovisual Media Service Directive, the broadcasting of programs containing pornography or extreme violence is prohibited. This prohibition applies to all other programs that may harm minors unless the program is broadcasted at the time normally observed by the adult or taken protective technical measures.

The State Duma of Russia adopted the Law on the Protection of Adolescents from Harmfulness to Their Health and Development on December 21, 2010, and a revision of this law was adopted on July 11, 2012. In accordance with this Law, the Russian judiciary conducted classification on the internet sites, and a "time firewall" system was executed by relevant departments, that is, from 12:00 to 18:00 every day, some technical means were used to take special "information filtering" measures for internet users including minors to protect the teens from obscenity and porn sites. The bill also requires all Internet cafes in its territory to mandatorily install a filtering system aiming at preventing the minors from access to harmful information since September 1, 2011, and families of minors were also suggested to install this system.[31]

Russia promulgated the "Wi-Fi real-name system" on June 31, 2014, requiring that anonymous access to wireless network in public places should be no longer provided. After the adoption of the law, the Russian people must register the mobile phone number to use the public wireless network, and the companies controlling the access to network need to store the input personal information for six months.[32]

---

[28]Pornographic content control model in foreign internet. http://tech.sina.com.cn/roll/2008-02-28/0205588296.shtml [2016-9-21].

[29]Television broadcasting activities: "Television without Frontiers" (TVWF) Directive. http://eur-lex.europa.eu/legal-content/EN/TXT/?uri=URISERV:l24101 [2016-9-17].

[30]Audiovisual Media Services (AMS) Directive. http://eur-lex.europa.eu/legal-content/EN/TXT/?uri=URISERV:am0005 [2016-9-17].

[31]Russia: Establish a "information filtering" firewall. http://news.ifeng.com/gundong/detail_2012_12/28/20607648_0.shtml [2016-9-21].

[32]Russia requires a WiFi real name system. http://news.ifeng.com/a/20140809/41511186_0.shtml [2016-9-21].

Germany issued a "law of blocking webpage login" in 2009. According to the law, the Federal Criminal Police Office will establish a list of blocked sites and update daily. Internet service providers will block the relevant child porn pages based on this list.[33]

France enacted the Information Society Act in 2006, which clarifies the rights and responsibilities of everyone while protecting the freedom of online communication, protects citizens' rights of confidentiality of communication, property rights, privacy, image rights and security, implements standardized management on the Internet domain names, and improves security and reliability of e-commerce.[34]

Singapore issued the "Law of Network Behavior" in 1996, which explicitly defines "prohibited information", including information that is contrary to public interest, public morality, public order, public safety, national stability, or information prohibited by existing laws in Singapore; pornography, violence, racial discrimination and religious hatred are included in the prohibition of information.[35]

The Japanese government put forward a policy recommendation of "countermeasure against bad and illegal information online" in June 2005, mainly relating to the promotion of network filtering software and assisting self-discipline of the network providers. In terms of content rating standards, two evaluation methods are used for Japan's Internet content, namely, self-evaluation and third-party evaluation. Self-evaluation refers to that the creator of a site conducts a rating according to rating criteria and shows the rating results in the form of labels on webpages. Third-party evaluation refers to that rating of the content of a webpage is conducted by a third-party organization. The filter software carries out filtering based on the rating of the website according to different filtering conditions.[36]

Korea's legal system against online harmful information for minors adopts the combination of existing laws and specialized legislation. Specifically, the Korea's regulatory legal system against online information harmful for minors is mainly composed of two parts: the laws and orders. Based on three major laws of the Telecommunication Business Law, the Law of Promoting Utilization of Information Communication Network and the Juvenile Protection Act, and a series of laws and regulations including the Criminal Law and the Broadcasting Law, on the one hand, the Korean government has enacted legislation to regulate standards of obscenity, violence, and minor protection, and the regulatory authorities may recommend or order the network service providers to restrict or delete certain special operations or content in accordance with the standards, and the network service providers will be punished if they do not act in accordance with relevant

[33]German anti-child pornography law "law of blocking webpage login" officially entered into force. http://news.xinhuanet.com/world/2010-02/24/content_13038321.htm [2016-9-21].

[34]France implements standardized management on the Internet. http://news.nen.com.cn/system/2012/12/26/010178108.shtml [2016-9-23].

[35]Research on Governmental Governance of Public Opinion in Emergencies. http://3y.uu456.com/bp_14k0n8gg7y3xy6r95j74_17.html [2016-9-25].

[36]Japan promotes the use of mobile phone filtering software to purify the network environment. http://tech.sina.com.cn/t/2010-01-05/14483739295.shtml [2016-9-17].

requirements or refuse to meet the requirements; on the other hand, the regulatory authorities have the right to classify online information harmful for minors. If the regulatory authorities classify the content on some website as a special level or being harmful to minors, the website or publisher must place an appropriate logo and warning on the web and the published content, otherwise it will be punished.[37]

In 2008, Australia issued a new regulation regulating the network and mobile content, which requires a rating system for the network and mobile content like to that for films. In accordance with this new regulation, all content will be assessed and rated based on the requirements of users 15 years old or older. This regulation was made by the Australian Internet Industry Association, which represents the vast majority of major Internet content providers, covering only web content originating from Australia. This rule is intended to assist the minors and their parents in making informed choices, that is, making it clear what they are looking at, or what network and mobile content is not suitable for them to watch online.[38]

For a long time, the countries around the world often face and follow the cyberspace passively or act on the cyberspace using laws of the physical society, or corresponding management regulations are made directed against the existing problems. All these protrude the lag of the international community on cyberspace management. Particularly, some laws for the physical space cannot be directly applied to cyberspace. For example, the United Nations' law of armed conflict provides a principle of reciprocity and a principle of moderation etc. for conflict between States, but in cyberspace, it is impossible to make it as easy as the physical society who initiated the attack, what intensity of the attack, or what degree of the damage.

9.4.3 Protection of Political Security in Cyberspace

In cyberspace, each international actor has a new way of interacting. Because of the openness of cyberspace, actors in different levels, such as individuals, countries, interest groups, political parties, international organizations, etc., all can publish information in cyberspace and to use cyberspace to seek their own interests. Some actors can use the Internet to spread online speech or network works which are threats or potential threats to the state power in form of text, film, advertising, games and other ways, thus affecting the network audiences' thinking and behavior. This infiltration lasts for a long time and is imperceptible, and it can gradually infiltrate world view and values which have been set to the audience, so that the audiences gradually accept various political ideas advocated by the network media.

[37]Xu JY (2013) Study on Korea's legal system of supervising online information harmful for minors. Southwest University, Chong Qmg. http://www.docin.com/p-1518833237.html [2016-10-4].

[38]Australia publishes network and mobile content rating regulation. http://tech.sina.com.cn/roll/2008-07-17/0748736404.shtml [2016-10-3].

1. The countries protect the national political security in the form of legislation

Information that endangers national security refers to information that endangers national sovereignty, territorial integrity and security, divulges state secrets, splits the country, and subverts the regime. Most countries in the world have relevant penalties against "harm to national security".

In the United States, the information harmful to national security is divided into many aspects, of which "treason information" and "spy information" are more serious. For example, the United States in 2007 issued the Protect America Act of 2007,[39] allowing the US National Security Agency (NSA) to start a large-scale domestic monitoring plan; in 2008, the United States passed the Foreign Intelligence Surveillance Act of 1978 Amendments Act of 2008,[40] which allowed the US intelligence service to obtain authorization from the Foreign Intelligence Surveillance Court (FISC) so as to conduct electronic monitoring in a wider range to conduct all-round protection on the safety of the United States.

The *Le nouveau code penal*[41] divides information that jeopardizes national security into information that endangers national security, incites social unrest, incites racial discrimination, damages others' reputation, infringes privacy, etc. The "Anti-terrorism Law" in France expressly requires supervision of online browsing and dissemination harmful information such as incitement to religious hatred and terrorism. As expressly stipulated by this law, dissemination of terrorist propaganda and recruitment of extreme terrorists using the Internet can be banned, and the person who does this may be sentenced to seven years' imprisonment. In accordance with this law, relevant websites must delete terrorism information within 24 h since the information is online, otherwise the websites should be subject to seizure and severely punished in accordance with the law.[42]

Russia passed the Law against Retweets in 2014 to limit the spread of extreme or threatening statements. This law allows the government to hand down five-year prison sentences to people who re-disseminate extremist materials online, primarily aimed at punishing the "spread of extremist ideology".[43]

Japan has promulgated the "Specific Secrets Protection Act" which was much-criticized and questioned. This act specifies information that needs to be specifically protected in four fields of defense, diplomacy, anti-spyware and

[39]Protect America Act of 2007. https://www.justice.gov/archive/ll/docs/text-of-paa.pdf [2016-9-17].

[40]Foreign Intelligence Surveillance Act of 1978 Amendments Act of 2008. https://www.congress.gov/110/plaws/publ261/PLAW-110publ261.pdf [2016-9-17].

[41]Le nouveau code penal. http://www.360doc.com/content/13/1226/17/15261343_340313398.shtml [2016-9-20].

[42]France published the Anti-terrorism Law, which comprehensively guarded against terrorist activities. http://news.gmw.cn/2014-09/27/content_13392218.htm [2016-9-20].

[43]Everything You Need to Know About Russia's Internet Crackdown. https://advox.globalvoices.org/2014/07/06/everything-you-need-to-know-about-russias-internet-crackdown/ [2016-8-30].

anti-terrorism as “specific secret”.[44] Relevant documents of the act list a series of “specific secrets” regarding quantity and performance of weapons, ammunition and aircraft.

Singapore has promulgated the “Broadcast Law”, “Internet Operation Rules”, “Domestic security Law” and “Incitement Law”, and information that endangers national security is defined as internet speech and content which threatens public safety and national defense, shakes the public confidence in law enforcement departments.[45]

Greek criminal law defines information endangering national security as speech or information made or transmitted by any person in any form, which is harmful to public order and public safety.[46]

Governments also take full advantage of legislation, administration, justice, and even intelligence, from the point of view of safeguarding their national security, to protect their national security from violation in cyberspace.

2. The countries take means to control public opinion in the countries

What political security requires is that the country has the supreme power of exclusivity to dominate the political system and ideology related to its own interests in the international and domestic society. Whether a country’s political security is guaranteed is related to whether the state power can stably achieve the control and disposal of various affairs in the country. As the most important and most powerful actor in the international and domestic society, government is also the main promoter and user of the Internet and can use the Internet to promote its social system, ideology and values. Using cyberspace jurisdiction, the government can control the Internet to ensure that its openness does not conflict with the legitimacy of speech that involves national security and social stability. Every country needs to have the ability to regulate whether the Internet information is in line with national security interests and is not contrary to the national political system and ideology.

For example, in 2005, a video showing that a Korean was beheaded in Iraq was spread on the Internet, causing a strong social response. The Korean Ministry of Information and Communication required the Information and Communication Ethics Committee as the center to start 24-h emergency surveillance system and take immediate action to delete it immediately if relevant videos appeared on the Internet.[47] In the same year, Korea’s domestic media had a growing voice of

[44] Today’s hits: The Japanese House of Representatives forcibly passed the “Specific Secrets Protection Act”. http://news.163.com/13/1204/08/9F85M0JR00014JB5.html?f=jsearch [2016-10-3].

[45] HU Xing. Singapore published a series of norms and regulations to furthest protect network rights of the Internet users.

[46] Legal Daily: The law will not allow to discredit the country's freedom of speech. http://opinion.people.com.cn/n/2014/0514/c1003-25015157.html [2016-10-3].

[47] Korea will severely punish behavior of spreading the Kim Shou-day beheaded video on the Internet. http://news.163.com/2004w06/12592/2004w06_1087993998073.html [2016-9-17].

condemning Japan's "Takeshima Day" regulations,[48] and the Information and Communication Ethics Committee took measures to close Japanese network forums like "Dokdo is the Japanese territory".[49]

The Internet has, to a certain extent, eroded the state's ability of controlling public opinion. In the no-center or multi-center Internet world, states are no longer the only center of issuing information. Information can be released by various actors on the Internet, which weaken the country's dominance and control of public opinion. Information can be spread more freely across the national borders through the Internet, and it can also facilitate the implementation of transnational crimes committed by the international terrorists. Hence, each country has implemented a series of plans and actions for maintaining national security, aiming at counter-terrorism, coping with extremists.

The US Department of Defense set up the 67th cyber war brigade in 2006, which monitored online public opinion round-the-clock, "strived to correct the wrong message", guided the self-serving report, confronted anti-American propaganda.[50] The US Department of Homeland Security set up a "social network monitoring center" in 2009, which particularly searched for information on social networking sites such as Facebook, Twitter and My space, political blogs, and other sites, and established a monitoring list of online public forums, blogs, message boards, well-known social media, popular blog, and conducted timely detection and disposal of negative information related to the country.[51] The US White House also removed netizen's sensitive comments on official accounts of Facebook and Google+.[52]

The European Commission launched the 2015–2020 security plans. According to this plan, the EU will strengthen surveillance of cybercrime in five years, prevent the spread of extremist ideas on the Internet, prevent terrorists from gaining money through the Internet and crack down on illegal arms trade on the Internet.[53]

The British Home Office proposed "Monitoring Modernization Plan" in 2008, requiring monitoring and backup of all communication data on the British Internet

---

[48]Two islands and reef groups at North latitude 37°14′12″, east longitude 131°51′51″ were called "Dokdo" by South Korea called "Dokdo", and "Takeshima" by Japan, which currently are under the actual control of Korea, but Japan claims to have sovereignty over them.

[49]Self-immolation of Korean people to defend sovereignty. http://news.sina.com.cn/w/2005-03-19/03515400978s.shtml [2016-9-17].

[50]How foreign countries manage the internet. http://theory.people.com.cn/n/2013/0110/c143844-20160586-2.html [2016-9-17].

[51]Management of social networks in the United States. http://news.xinhuanet.com/world/2012-01/19/c_111452562.htm [2016-9-17].

[52]China Internet Space Research Institute. "Foreign regulation on Internet bad information—methods and technology" Chapter III Administrative constraints on the internet in the countries, 3.2 Endangerment of national security and national dignity, 3.2.1 the United States. Beijing: Law Press, 2016.

[53]EU new security plan against terrorist crime on network, National Internet Information Office of the People's Republic of China. 2015-05-03/ 2015-05-14. http://www.cac.gov.cn/2015-05/03/c_1115159504.htm [2016-8-30].

such as web browsing time and e-mail address.[54] In 2012, the British government has extended the right of Law enforcement agencies and intelligence departments to supervise the network communication.[55]

In France, radical websites are blocked, and sensitive information is deleted. Websites that support terrorism will be blocked in an administrative manner without the authorization of a pre-trial judge.[56]

The Australian Communications and Media Authority is responsible for the management of the Internet, radio, wireless communications and telecommunications throughout Australia. "Website blacklist" and filter software are used to block online content involved in racial hatred, terrorism and so on.[57]

9.4.4 Protection of Economic Security in Cyberspace

The economy involves the people's livelihood and the fortune of the country. The emergence of the virtual economy has greatly accelerated the economic operation rate, expanded the scale of economic operation, and accelerated the pace of economic globalization. Particularly, the virtual economy so far has been globalized, and the world economy is being integrated at an unprecedented rate and scale. The globalization of virtual economy is reflected in various fields such as finance, real estate, intangible assets and gambling industry, and it has a profound impact on the national economic security.

1. Financial internationalization

Financial markets include stocks, bonds, futures (e.g., large commodity futures such as grain, oil), options and foreign exchange. Under the influence of financial globalization, not only the capital gains of the whole world (now mainly developed countries and some emerging developing countries) have converged, but also the economic operation modes of all countries are basically unified, and goals and systems of relevant economic policies and regulatory systems also tend to be consistent.

2. Network economy

The global economic crisis that has happened since 2009 was caused by the subprime mortgage crisis in the real estate sector, and then extended to the US

[54]Britain protects cyber security by administrative means. http://www.hebdx.com/tabid/74/InfoID/9658/frtid/76/Default.aspx [2016-9-25].

[55]The UK strictly manages network communication tools, allows security departments to access data. http://news.xinhuanet.com/world/2012-06/13/c_123277623.htm [2016-10-3].

[56]France has shielded 60 websites involved in terrorism over the past year. http://news.xinhuanet.com/world/2016-04/16/c_128901973.htm [2016-10-3].

[57]Summary: Australia comprehensively manages and filter network bad information. http://news.xinhuanet.com/world/2012-06/10/c_112175263.htm [2016-10-3].

financial crisis and even the global economic crisis. In fact, the real estate is more damaging to the economy than financial assets in the economic downturn. With the global financial liberalization and the relaxation of capital market regulation, as well as the application of advanced communications technology, international capital flows more conveniently and faster. Real estate mortgage securitization makes the real estate market more closely related with the financial securities market. The flow of international virtual capital promotes the real estate markets in the countries quickly to globalization and internationalization, and their linkages are enhanced.

3. Financial virtualization

In addition to the financial markets and the real estate market, the price of virtual economy markets, such as intangible assets, the gambling industry is also part of the monetary performance of the commodity value. The abnormal rise in the price of virtual assets also has a close relationship with the funds. This correlation makes the stock market and the real estate, oil futures and the stock market, bond market, and even real estate, foreign exchange and the stock market, which are originally unrelated with each other, have a close relationship and put them together as a whole.

It should be said that the economic globalization since the 1980s was essentially the globalization of the virtual economy. The international flow of large-scale virtual assets has become the core of contemporary economic globalization. The development of the world's virtual economy has substantively changed the contemporary international economic relations, of which the leading content has gradually shifted from the trade and actual investment, to rapid flow of large-scale funds with virtual assets as the carrier. The international flow of virtual assets has deepened the economic ties of the world economy within the global system. It is the flow of virtual assets free from the traditional space and time constraints that makes the economies of the world intertwined, penetrated and integrated into the operating system of world economic integration. This cannot be realized by the globalization of real economy. It can be said that the essence of contemporary economic globalization is not the globalization of the real economy, but the globalization of the virtual economy.

The operating mechanism of the virtual economy is different from the real-world economy, and the transaction is rapid and concealed. Traditional borders are no longer effective boundaries to control finance and product trading, and hundreds of millions of even more large-scale financial products or virtual goods that form economic core can be transmitted across borders in an instant. As a result, traditional sense of control and dominance by the countries on industries are weakening. Financial tycoons can more conveniently walk in the international financial markets, opportunistic attacks on some country's financial markets to reap huge profits, endangering the country's economic security.

Economic security requires that the state, by its jurisdiction, maintains the normal order of production, distribution, exchange and consumption of its internal goods. Maintaining economic security is an important point of government management. The Internet forced the economic network and the electronic business. The openness of network facilitates the participation of all kinds of actors with financial means in the virtual economy. Virtualization and networking of financial and economic transactions are an objective reality that cannot be avoided in today's world and are a developing trend. The emergence of virtual economy poses a challenge to the country's economic security, which requires the state to exercise regulation of networking of the economic transactions and exercises the power to regulate the operation of ecommerce.

9.4.5 Protection of Cultural Security in Cyberspace

The most important traditional mediums of communicating culture and civilization include paper books, newspapers, verbal language, etc., which have the persistence and effectiveness of cultural transmission and flash dazzling light in the process of human civilization so far. The prosperity of culture is a strong symbol of a country, and is an important guarantee for the political stability and economic development of a country. The Internet is a major revolution in cultural transmission and provides a new way for the spread of culture. Because of the openness of the Internet, the state cannot conduct all-around screening and filtering on quality and content of all network culture products, which, to some extent, affects the country's management of the Internet culture.

1. Position and function of cultural security

Due to the openness of the network culture, coupled with the lack of effective guidance and supervision, vulgar, pornographic content emerged in large numbers. Particularly, due to a lack of self-control and distinguishing ability, teens with an immature world outlook and outlook on life are very vulnerable to bad culture. The negative impact of cyberculture has become a social problem.

(1) **Garbage information in network culture can easily mislead people**. In the vast network information flow, some content is not healthy, some content has low taste and low style, and some content is filled with violence, murder, pornography, obscenity, and some content is filled with feudal superstition, and some content is politically wrong even reactionary. The harmful information is mixed with each other, penetrating and pervasive.
(2) **Internet addiction, indifferent family**. Some students are addicted to online chats and dating, and they fall into the illusory emotional world and cannot extricate themselves; some students are obsessed with online games and are addicted to the Internet, bringing adverse consequences to the body.
(3) **Subtle cultural infiltration**. The influence of cyber culture on the thought of netizens is imperceptible. Because more than 90% of the current Internet information is in English, and there are many websites and information in Western developed countries such as the United States and Britain, they are the

first places visited by the netizens. It is precisely because Western developed countries led by the United States and Britain occupy absolute control of information resources on the Internet, which results in online information monopoly and dumping, thereby forming a substantively "cultural aggression". A large number of information attached with the Western values flow into China. Since some young people know little about the essence of traditional culture, national culture is far from being rooted in the minds of young people, and thus it is difficult for young people inundated with a foreign network information flow to generate immunity and recognition. It is a severe cultural test for young people who are advocating new knowledge and have active thinking but with an immature outlook on life, values and morality.

Cultural security has a unique position in the overall security of the country, is irreplaceable with respect to the military security, economic security, and is the political basis of social stability. The basic requirement of cultural security is to maintain the survival and development of national culture, and it is important content of cultural security to maintain the value function of national culture. Culture of any nation and country is formed by the people during a long-term survival and development, and it is a result and a historical accumulation, also a way of life, and a value system. Cultural security requires a country to choose the political system and ideology independently and to prevent other countries from imposing a political, economic and democratic model under the guidance of ideology on the country; it is required to protect people's cultural life in the country from infiltration by other countries, to protect their people's values, behavior, social system from interference, to maintain the national character of their culture, to maintain national self-esteem and cohesion; and it is required to be able to use necessary means to expand the cultural impact of their own country.

2. Government's Protection of Cultural Security

Cultural security requires the government to have the ability of mastering the right of self- development and leadership of culture. People transfer existence in the real world to the Internet and create a mirror image of the reality in the cyberspace. The progress of digital technology makes it possible to produce real products such as film and television works, books and construction in the real world into electronic products, and these electronic products are compatible with the Internet so that they are fast and conveniently disseminated widely in the cyberspace. The Internet as a new channel for the transmission of cultural products and new producers of cultural products also challenges the cultural security, which requires the government to develop rules and regulations on the culture transmission via internet and the production of cultural products.

For example, all countries take legal, administrative, self-disciplinary and other actions to protect the legitimate rights and interests of Internet users, especially minor netizens, and to limit the dissemination of obscene information.

As stipulated by Germany "Public Places Juvenile Protection Law", Internet cafe operators are not allowed to provide minors with game software that may endanger their physical and mental health. For any Internet cafe or individual who disseminates pornographic information, its responsible person will be punished in accordance with the German law for a maximum of fifteen years' imprisonment. As stipulated by the German government, all Internet cafe computers must set up pornographic information filters and website monitoring systems. If there are netizens secretly logging on "pornographic websites", the computer will issue a warning, and the person who does not listen to the warning will be fined and charged. In Germany, 90% of Internet cafes prohibit computer games, and only limited low-level computer games can be played in other Internet cafes.[58]

In May 2007, Netherlands Pan-European Communication Company signed an agreement with the Dutch National Police to "block" illegal websites based on a "blacklist" of child pornography websites. As long as a user logs on to these sites, the police's statement will appear on the computer screen: "You are trying to open a website which spreads content of sexual assault on children. This is crime." No matter how this statement box is clicked, it will not disappear, which can prevent users from browsing such sites.[59]

Internet Watch Foundation (IWF) is a semi-official Internet surveillance organization and industry self-regulatory organization established by the British network operator in September 1996. The main purpose of the Foundation is to monitor the illegal and unethical behavior of the Internet operators and to address the increasing criminal problems on the Internet, such as pornography, sexual abuse and racial discrimination, and is particularly committed to the settlement of child pornography. This Foundation works daily with the support of the British Ministry of Industry and Trade, the Ministry of the Interior and the British Urban Police, and its funds are mainly provided by private companies such as network service providers, mobile development manufacturers, information content providers and communications software companies.[60]

In view of the foregoing, Network culture as a cultural phenomenon reflecting the social ideology, has great impact, influence and penetration on the current and future human life. Network culture can provide a broad field, avenues and means for the development and prosperity of the country and the promotion of advanced culture. However, some decadent culture will be more quickly invasive and spread through network and therefore becomes a serious threat to the cultural security of a country. In coping with the challenges of cyberculture to national cultural security, all countries need to effectively use cyberspace jurisdiction and formulate effective measures to safeguard national cultural security.

---

[58]Germany: Precautions against the protection of minors from trespass. http://news.youth.cn/zt/hlw/ggcs/201007/t20100729_1302408_2.htm [2016-10-3].

[59]A major network service provider in Netherlands "blocks" child pornography websites. http://tech.163.com/07/0326/09/3AGH42UH00091KT0.html [2017-10-4].

[60]Internet Watch Foundation. http://wang283869.honpu.com/ [2016-10-3].

9.4.6 Exercising Administrative Supervision Authority in Cyberspace

Cyberspace jurisdiction is based on the supreme right of a State, that is, the state has the highest management authority over its own network system. A country has the right to decide its own network management mechanism, the right to decide business models, business content, penalties, etc. of the Internet operating subjects. Countries can establish a market access system for access to the network and punish network behavior violating the network provisions. Countries may have the ability to find unauthorized access networks, prohibit unauthorized subnet to access to network. Countries may restrict or prohibit provision of information services on the Internet in violation of stipulations, have the right to stop and punish illegal network acts, and punish illegal operators by ordering them to withdraw from the Internet market. For those who have already withdrawn from the domestic network market, the country may have the power to cease its continued provision of network services.

In fact, the governments of all countries have already stepped up their administrative supervision measures to restrict the Internet from various aspects and multidimensionality in accordance with their own national conditions, in the hope that they will achieve the purpose of monitoring and preventing illegal information and harmful information through administrative acts such as government supervision and administrative law enforcement.

In the United States, for example, the division of responsibilities of US government departments on network regulation is as follows: the Internet infrastructure and communication control are regulated by the National Telecommunications and Information Agency (NTIA) and the Federal Communications Commission (FCC); the functions of cyber security and crime prevention are handled by the Department of Homeland Security, the Federal Bureau of Investigation, the Central Intelligence Agency; the development of e-commerce is regulated by the Ministry of Commerce. Wherein, the Federal Communications Commission is directly responsible for the Congress and has executive functions in legislative, executive and judicial sectors, and has a tremendous impact on the development of the US telecommunications industry. FBI and National White-Collar Crime Center (NWCCC) jointly set up the Internet Fraud Complaint Center (IFCC). IFCC analyzes the data obtained from the FBI, NWCCC and other agencies, and then provides national investigative information and effective cyber-fraud information resources to regulatory agencies such as law enforcement, so as to facilitate the federal, state, and local law enforcement agencies to crack down on national cyber fraud.

Russia has built a network security protection system, which is dominated by the government and is widely involved in the community.

Russian Federal Security Council and Science and Technology Council established an information security branch which uniformly leads the national information security construction and planning.[61] Since 2008, the Russian government has set up special network regulatory agencies within the Federal Security Administration, the Federal Media and Culture Administration and the Ministry of Internal Affairs. Among them, the network monitoring center of the Federal Security Administration is mainly responsible for monitoring all the bad information on the Internet, especially information relating to national security of Russia, such as information regarding promotion of national opposition, religious disputes, terrorist activities, organized crime; the network monitoring center of the Media and Culture Authority is mainly responsible for monitoring the news media; the network monitoring center of the Ministry of Internal Affairs is mainly responsible for monitoring new media such as "Twitter" and "Facebook".[62]

The European Union established the European Center for Combating Cybercrime in 2012 to protect European companies and people who are threatened by cybercrime. The center was set up in the EU Interpol of the European Police Department in The Hague, Netherlands, and became the center of the European fight against cybercrime. The Center will focus on combating illegal activities of organized criminal gangs on the Internet, especially those including online credit cards and bank fraud, which will result in a large number of unlawful proceeds.[63]

Singapore Broadcasting Authority (SBA) is responsible for the management of network communication content. SBA has developed seven guiding principles in terms of network policy[64]: (1) fully support the development of the network; (2) emphasize public education, industry self-discipline, promote the establishment of actual websites, and regulate industries with a system which issues a certificate and reflects the public value; (3) the scope to be regulated is limited to information released to the public, and there is no intervention for e-mails and web chat rooms only for private communication; (4) the regulation focuses on information related to Singapore affairs; (5) focus on pornographic information that is easy to get on the web, and the focus of management is on influential websites that publish pornography; (6) necessarily regulate online services; (7) encourage industries and the public members to continue to provide feedback so that the regulatory frameworks can reflect and align with technological advances and social concerns.

---

[61]Russia set up "network police" K Department. http://media.people.com.cn/GB/17049808.html [2016-10-4].

[62]Russian control network rumors by means of many measures. http://news.xinhuanet.com/world/2012-05/04/c_111890033.htm [2016-10-4].

[63]European Union set up a center against cybercrime. http://news.163.com/12/0329/04/7TO2UEH000014AED.html [2016-10-4].

[64]Li J (2004) Review of Singapore 's network content control system—discussion about perfection of relevant system in China. Nat Sci Ed J Public Secur Univ 4(30):45–49. http://www.pkulaw.cn/fulltext_form.aspx?Gid=1509961106&EncodingName=%E9%97%81%E8%8D%A4%E5%96%96%E9%8F%81%EE%87%A2%EF%BF%BD%E5%BC%B2%E5%A9%B5%E5%AC%AB%E5%84%8C [2016-9-25].

Because the Internet provides cross-border services, there are different legal grounds for handling information inside and outside the country. Information within the territory should be handled in accordance with the national laws. About foreign information or services that are harmful to the country, considering that the country where the illegal information or services were put out will not act in accordance with the laws of the country that is harmed. It is likely that the output country refuses to stop the output, so the harmed country needs to have its own ability to block such illegal network information or services.

Chapter 10
Extension of Cyberspace Sovereignty

Abstract Cyberspace sovereignty is the extension of state sovereignty in the cyberspace. As people may focus on data, information release, electromagnetic transmission and information technology in the cyberspace due to different needs, corresponding views of sovereignty emerge, including data sovereignty, information sovereignty, electromagnetic space sovereignty, technological sovereignty and so on.

Keywords Data sovereignty · Information sovereignty · Electromagnetic space sovereignty · Technological sovereignty

Cyberspace sovereignty refers to the national rights of the jurisdiction over from the information and communication technology infrastructure to all human activities conducted on the facility. In this field, scholars also put forward some other views on sovereignty, including data sovereignty, information sovereignty, electromagnetic space sovereignty, technical sovereignty and so on. In general, data sovereignty refers to the ownership and disposition of data; information sovereignty refers to the right to publish information; electromagnetic space sovereignty refers to the control of electromagnetic space of the state; technical sovereignty refers to the autonomy, self-direction and independent development of technology. In any case, the above sovereignties are a part of cyberspace sovereignty, merely with special emphasis on specific scenes. Thus, sovereign forms such as data sovereignty, information sovereignty, electromagnetic space sovereignty, and technical sovereignty can be regarded as a subset or projection of cyberspace sovereignty.

B. Fang, *Cyberspace Sovereignty*,
https://doi.org/10.1007/978-981-13-0320-3_10

10.1 Data Sovereignty

10.1.1 Basic Concept of Data Sovereignty

Cyberspace sovereignty is aimed at all the facilities, data and related activities in cyberspace; and the object of data sovereignty is data, which is an element of cyberspace. Data sovereignty in a broad sense is the data as a field, and in a narrow sense is an object. The data involved in data sovereignty covers all types of information, including structured, semi-structured and unstructured data, covering almost any information or daily behavior recorded or produced by any actor. The cyberspace sovereignty and data sovereignty are inclusive, and data sovereignty is a subset of cyberspace sovereignty.

Some scholars believe that data sovereignty refers to the highest jurisdiction of a state over a variety of data including text, pictures, audio and video, code, procedures produced by individuals, businesses and related organizations within its jurisdiction of the territory ("territorial network") in the process of production, collection, transmission, storage, analysis, use and so on. The data here refers only to the unprocessed, meaningless data contained in cyberspace, and does not involve the information and communication technology system and meaningful information contents. If the data is understood as mineral resources, information is extracted from the raw materials and processed out of the finished product. Thus, data sovereignty is equivalent to the state's ownership of natural resources. In this sense, data sovereignty is more valuable than information sovereignty, because the state can have sovereignty over mineral resources, but in the market system, the state merely has allocation and income rights over the means of production and the products.[1]

Some scholars have pointed out, that while it is certain in the physical world that data in the territory of the state should be bound by the laws of the state, in the virtual world of the Internet, it is not so apparent. On one hand, due to the liquidity, decentralization, fragmentation characteristics of data, it is difficult to constrain data in a scope of the geographical space; on the other hand, the stakeholder model dominates because of the long-term avocation in the cyber space for equal participation of international organizations, enterprises, technical groups, forming a rejection of the government.[2]

10.1.2 Components of Data Sovereignty

Some scholars believe that data sovereignty is the essential attribute of the rights and interests of data information subjects. Its premise is cross-border circulation of

---

[1]Expert Opinion: Improve Legislation to Clarify Cyber Sovereignty and Control Data Sovereignty. http://opinion.people.com.cn/n/2015/0205/c1003-26511363.html [2016-9-22].

[2]Data Sovereignty: WHY and HOW. http://news.xinhuanet.com/local/2016-06/17/c_129070400.htm [2016-7-22].

data, because data crossing borders will be out of the control of state power, and the state sovereignty is certainly challenged.[3] In essence, the producer of data is naturally the owner of the data. The problem is that, after data flows, the issue of rights over the use of data arises. If the data is produced by an individual, it involves personal data right, i.e., the user's right of self-determination and self-control of the data. If a large number of personal data converge to form a big data, or the data is generated by a national behavior, the state owns the jurisdiction in the use of the data; and thus, the cross-border data flow involves national data sovereignty.

Data sovereignty includes both data ownership and data use jurisdiction. Data ownership refers to the exclusive rights of sovereign states to national data; data use jurisdiction refers to the right of the State to independently manage and use national data. Data sovereignty means that even if the data is transmitted to the cloud or remote server, it should be subject to its own control, and cannot be manipulated by a third party without permission.

10.1.3 Attributes of Data Sovereignty

Cai Cuihong asserts that data sovereignty has the following three basic attributes[4]:

1. The relativity of data sovereignty

This relativity is first reflected in the divergence of the academic community on the concept of data sovereignty. Some scholars are skeptical about data sovereignty, they consider that the concept of data sovereignty is only an illusion.[5] The relativity of data sovereignty is also reflected in its practical constraints. The relativity of national sovereignty is not controversial in the academia, because the exercise of national sovereignty must be subject to natural law and international law. The freedom and independence given to a state by sovereignty is also subject to the freedom and independence of other states.[6] Similarly, once a country embarked on the information superhighway, it must be bound by the rules of international information circulation. The realization of data sovereignty is also confronted with the constraints of vertical and horizontal aspects, the horizontal referring to the strength of a country's cyberspace and the power relationship with other countries, and the vertical referring

[3]Transborder Data Flow: An Overview and Critique of Recent Concerns. http://scholarship.law.wm.edu/cgi/viewcontent.cgi?article=1547&context=facpubs [2017-10-4].

[4]Cai CH (2013) Concept and Application Promise of Data Sovereignty in the Context of Cloud Era. Modern International Relations, 12. http://www.cssn.cn/zzx/gjzzx_zzx/201505/t20150512_1779952.shtml [2016-9-22].

[5]Phantom Data Sovereigns: Walter Lippmann, Big Data and the Fallacy of Personal Data Sovereignty. https://www.researchgate.net/publication/256054668_Phantom_Data_Sovereigns_Walter_Lippmann_Big_Data_and_the_Fallacy_of_Personal_Data_Sovereignty [2016-10-4].

[6]The Evolution Of State Sovereignty: A Historical Overview. http://uir.unisa.ac.za/bitstream/handle/10500/3689/FundaminaSnyman.finaal.pdf?sequence=1 [2016-10-4].

to the cyberspace rights relationship between state and supranational, sub-state and even individuals. The data sovereignty of the Internet age must be at the expense of the necessary compromise, and thus, is a relative sovereignty.

2. Interdependence and Legitimacy of Data Sovereignty

Some scholars emphasize the independence of data sovereignty, that is, an independent sovereign state can be completely independent in the exercise of possession and jurisdiction over their own data, and can exclude any external interference.[7] In fact, data sovereignty of the Internet age and the cloud era has evolved from independent to interdependent, that is, a country cannot be completely independent and completely autonomous in global cyberspace. The realization of data sovereignty needs to be supported by the law of mutual consultation between States, but also depends on international treaties and international organizations that achieve various jurisdictions. Adeno Addis argues that data sovereignty includes two conflicting national missions: globalization and political particularity,[8] wherein globalization is an important prerequisite for the development and integration of nations into the international community, and political particularity is an important guarantee for national security and interest. Globalization makes the interests of nations interrelated, as well as making the relevant data of each country inter-influence and to be interdependent, and the requirement for moderate cooperation. Moderate cooperation is put forward is determined by the characteristics of the information and the data. Under normal circumstances, information and data achieve a higher value after being shared. Therefore, from the perspective of global common interests and in the premise of ensuring national security interests, data sovereignty is interdependent and cooperative.

3. Equality of Data Sovereignty and Inequality in Fact

As an appeal, the data sovereign equality means that there is no external authority other than international law to determine the internal data of the sovereign state affairs. Independent sovereign states recognize each other's data sovereign equality, and independently manage domestic data related matters. Equality of data sovereignty is mainly reflected in the country's foreign sovereignty. Sovereignty is a hierarchical relationship between a sovereign state government and a subordinate body. And sovereignty means that other similar countries recognize this political entity, means a formal equal relationship, without the right and obligation of giving order and obeying.[9] In general, the equality of data sovereignty is the ultimate aspiration of all countries. However, in the real world, national data sovereignty is

---

[7]Cao L (2013) Data right research of cyberspace. International Review, 1: 57. http://www.docin.com/p-727785123.html [2016-10-4].

[8]Addis A (2004) The thin state in thick globalism: sovereignty in the information age. Vanderbilt J Trans Law, 37(1):2. https://litigation-essentials.lexisnexis.com/webcd/app?action=DocumentDisplay&crawlid=1&doctype=cite&docid=37+Vand.+J.+Transnat'l+L.+1&srctype=smi&srcid=3B15&key=4b1581e4c8e66a356dd206535cb3a4a1 [2016-10-10].

[9]Lake DA (2003) The new sovereignty in international relations. Int Stud Rev 5(3):303–323. https://quote.ucsd.edu/lake/files/2014/07/ISR-5-3-2003.pdf [2016-10-4].

faced with de facto inequality. This inequality arises from the hegemony of global cyberspace in some countries, and the differences in cyberspace and data technology. For some countries with relatively backward technology, although some data (especially untreated raw data) goes beyond their handling and interpretation, these potentially valuable data may be transferred under economic or political interests to another country, so that it is placed in a disadvantageous position in international competition, harming its sovereignty.[10] This creates a de facto inequality problem of data sovereignty.

10.1.4 Inevitability of Data Sovereignty

Since the birth of sovereign states, there is a natural law to maintain its authority and legitimacy. In the process of long-term competition with other public rights organizations, the sovereign state gained an absolute advantage and successfully monopolized the legitimate public rights. Data sovereignty in the cyberspace will naturally become a country's weapon to maintain the data resources. Data sovereignty is the new development of national sovereignty theory in cyberspace era.

David Lyon argues that as a sovereign state, there is natural control of data in its cyberspace, which is a natural manifestation of maintaining its authority, legitimacy and its sovereignty, which is also the regulatory inertia of the government.[11] Benjamin Forest argues that the state uses various strategies to expand its rights, control and influence; one of the important strategies is to maintain its authority through mastering information and knowledge about various subjects and regions within the state.[12]

10.1.5 Sovereignty Protection Value of Data

The massive data in the information age is an important strategic resource to support a country's national security and development.[13] Through the analysis of

[10]Addis A (2004) The thin state in thick globalism: sovereignty in the information age. Vanderbilt J Trans Law 37(1):2. https://litigation-essentials.lexisnexis.com/webcd/app?action=DocumentDisplay&crawlid=1&doctype=cite&docid=37+Vand.+J.+Transnat'l+L.+1&srctype=smi&srcid=3B15&key=4b1581e4c8e66a356dd206535cb3a4a1 [2016-10-10].

[11]Surveillance Society: Monitoring Everyday Life (Issues in Society) 1st Edition. http://pdfstores.download/ook/SurveillanceSocietyMonitoringEverydayLife.pdf [2016-10-4].

[12]Forest B (2004) Information sovereignty and GIS:The evolution of 'communities of interest' in political redistricting. Polit Geogr 23(4):425–451. http://www.doc88.com/p-6897792004645.html [2016-10-4].

[13]Guarantee Security of "Data Sovereignty". China Defense Newspaper. Ver. 4, 2012-9-17. http://www.gfdy.gov.cn/ edu/2012-09/18/ content_ 5029079.htm [2016-10-4].

the big data of the national cyberspace, we can understand the social welfare of the parties, and even understand the government's information and intelligence, thus exposing vulnerable points.

Data is the basis of state rights. Data is the carrier of information, and information is the object of interest. Joseph S. Nye argues that rights are experiencing a transfer from "capital-rich" to "information-rich"; "information force" is a force multiplier of American diplomatic power.[14] Alvin Toffler points out the three pillars of power, namely, violence, wealth and knowledge. The first two are low quality rights, and knowledge is a high quality right, it can add value to violence and wealth.[15] Therefore, the data and information widely found in all aspects of society will inevitably become an important source of social rights and become the commanding heights of national competition.

10.1.6 Protection of National Data Sovereignty and Personal Data Rights in Accordance with the Law

Article 37 of the Cyber Security Law of the People's Republic of China states that: Personal information and other important data collected or produced by critical information infrastructures operators during their operations within the mainland territory of the People's Republic of China, shall be stored within the territory. Where due to business requirements it is truly necessary to provide it outside the mainland, a security assessment shall be conducted according to the measures jointly formulated by the state network information departments and the relevant departments of the State Council. Where laws or administrative regulations provide otherwise, those provisions apply. This also reflects that it is not easy to transfer personal information and important data collected in China to outside the territory.

Russia has enacted the Personal Data Protection Act, which stipulates that all Internet companies that collect Russian citizenship information must store these data on Russian domestic servers. Apple, Google, Facebook, Twitter and other Internet giants in the future can only be the user's personal data storage in the Russian local headquarters, rather than its headquarters in the United States.[16]

The European Union issued *Data Protection Directive in 1995—Directive 95/46/EC on the Protection of Parties and the Free Circulation of such Data in*

---

[14]Joseph SN (2004) Power in the global information age: from realism to globalization. Routledge, New York 75. https://www.routledge.com/Power-in-the-Global-Information-Age-From-Realism-to-Globalization/Nye-Jr/p/book/9780415700177 [2016-10-2].

[15]Alvin Toffler. Power Shift: Knowledge, Wealth, and Violence at the Edge of the 21st Century. https://repositories.lib.utexas.edu/bitstream/handle/2152/25709/PowershiftbyAlvinToffler.pdf?sequence=5 [2016-10-2].

[16]Russian New Regulation that Civil Data Can Merely Be Stored in Servers within the Territory. http://www.isccc.gov.cn/xwdt/xwkx/09/871184.shtml [2016-9-17].

Personal Data Processing, which stipulates that personal data may not be transmitted outside the EU Country, unless there is sufficient level of data protection.[17] However, although the EU has data protection laws prohibiting the private sector from manipulating data illegally, the laws are helpless for the public sector (such as law enforcement department, security services, etc.) of certain third countries. These public sectors are granted access to the laws of the host country's data right. For example, the Internet used by Internet users in the EU were mainly provided by US companies, but after the 2013 "prism" incident,[18] the EU began to pay close attention to information security issues. July 12, 2016, the European Commission and the United States reached the European and American Privacy Shield Framework Agreement on European data flow to the United States, in which the United States promised of regular self-inspection by the Ministry of Commerce on their own companies, so as to ensure clear restrictions, security and oversight mechanisms when its access to EU public sector data is established, out of law enforcement and national security.[19]

The European Parliament announced the *General Data Protection Regulation*[20] (GDPR) draft on January 25, 2012, which was the *Directive on Personal Data Processing and Privacy Protection in the Field of Electronic Communications*[21] proposed by Viviane Reding, former European Commission of Justice, for superseding the "On the Protection of Natural Persons with Regard to the Processing of Personal Data and on the Free Movement of Such Data, and Repealing Directive" 95/46/EC, 1995, and the Directive 97/66/EC on "Personal Data Processing and Privacy Protection in the Telecommunications Industry", 1995, to become the basic law for the EU's telecommunications network privacy.[22] The content of this regulation indicates that personal data protection management is mentioned at an unprecedented height, even through the development of detailed management practices, so that it has internal control and compliance management operability within the enterprise. The object is also extended from the EU enterprises to the EU users to provide Internet and business services to all enterprises. For example, the directive stipulates that the service provider should inform the user of the nature of the information without the user's permission and specify that the service provider has the obligation to regularly consult the user to select the registration information;

---

[17]Reform and Inspiration of Data Protection Directive of EU. http://www.doc88.com/p-4327060656821.html [2016-9-17].

[18]CAICT. Introduction and Analysis of European and American Privacy Shield Framework Agreement. 2016-08-26 http://3g.ishuo.cn/doc/ywknnfqf.html [2016-9-25].

[19]EU-U.S. Privacy Shield launched. http://ec.europa.eu/news/2016/07/20160712_en.htm [2016-8-26].

[20]Wikipedia. General Data Protection Regulation. https://en.wikipedia.org/wiki/General_Data_Protection_Regulation [2016-9-25].

[21]EU Parliament and Committee Directive on Personal Data Processing and Privacy Protection in the Telecommunications Industry. http://www.wells.org.cn/Article/ShowDetail/430 [2016-9-25].

[22]Legislation of EU on Personal Data Processing and Protection. http://book.sina.com.cn/books/2007-03-08/2117211648.shtml [2016-8-26].

users of permitted information may not send such information to these users. On April 27, 2016, the European Parliament issued the General Data Protection Regulation[23] that has been under discussion for years.

Jan-Philipp Albrecht, a Green Party member who leads the European parliament in consultation, said in a statement that the law returns the control of citizen personal data to citizens. Without personal permission, companies are not allowed to disclose information collected for a purpose. The consumers must give a clear license for the use of their own data.[24] Andrus Ansip, vice chairman of the European Commission for Digital Unified Markets, commented, that the future of the European data must be built based on trust. With reliable data protection common standards, people can be sure to control their own personal information and enjoy the digital unified market. We should not view privacy and data protection as an obstacle to economic development. In fact, they are important competitive advantages. The agreement reached today has laid a solid foundation for the development of innovative data services in Europe. Our next step is to remove the unreasonable barriers to the cross-border data flow: local regulations and, in some cases, the law of a state may restrict the storage and handling of certain data outside its territory. Therefore, we should go further and build an open and prosperous data economy within the EU—with the highest data protection standards as the basis, and breaking those unreasonable obstacles.[25]

The US government can obtain any information stored in the US data center or the information stored by the US company under the Patriot Act, which not only does not require prior consent of the data subject, sometimes the data subject may not even recognize such access. The *US Foreign Intelligence Surveillance Act*[26] of 1978 (FISA) also gives the US government access to data that is deposited or processed by US cloud service providers. These Acts are also the reason why the US government does not consider the "prism gate incident" as violation against the domestic law.

After the "Prism gate incident", Germany and other EU countries began to re-examine the data protection related to the reform of relevant bills. German Chancellor Angela Merkel said that the US intelligence agency's activities in German territory must comply with the German law. Merkel said in an interview with German television that German Interior Minister Friedrich's visit to Washington in the United States was the "first step" to clarify the activities of the

---

[23]On the Protection of Natural Persons with Regard to the Processing of Personal Data and on the Free Movement of Such Data, and Repealing Directive 95/46/EC (General Data Protection Regulation). http://ec.europa.eu/justice/data-protection/reform/files/regulation_oj_en.pdf [2016-9-17].

[24]EU Finally Passed Strict New Data Protection Regulations. http://mt.sohu.com/20151217/n431657865.shtml [2016-9-17].

[25]Agreement on Commission's EU data protection reform will boost Digital Single Market. http://europa.eu/rapid/press-release_IP-15-6321_en.htm [2016-9-17].

[26]Foreign Intelligence Surveillance Act. https://www.fletc.gov/sites/default/files/imported_files/training/programs/legal-division/downloads-articles-and-faqs/ research-by-subject/miscellaneous/ForeignIntelligenceSurveillanceAct.pdf [2016-9-20].

US intelligence agency. It is now necessary to ascertain whether the US Intelligence Agency has followed German law in German territory in the past. Merkel stressed that Europe needs a unified data protection requirement. For example, the current Internet companies such as Google or Facebook should inform the European countries on who will transfer data to whom. On this issue, the European countries have not yet reached an agreement. “This is undoubtedly part of the European data protection agreement,” said Merkel. Germany is striving to promote a unified data protection requirement in Europe and shall reaffirm that desire at the next meeting of the Minister of Justice and Interior.[27]

10.1.7 Domestic and Foreign Consensus on Data Sovereignty

At the international level, the concept of data sovereignty can become one of the core fulcrums and principles of cyberspace governance and cyberspace order. When it comes to the debate on cyberspace sovereignty, countries share different views. In the debate on information sovereignty, countries have different interpretations of information because of different values. Due to the ideological factors, the understandings of the states vary on the importance of specific information and their relationship with national interests.

Data sovereignty is directed at the rights of unprocessed data, regardless of the ideology. The discussion of data sovereignty is only a game between the economic interests of the states. The needs of each country are roughly equal. Therefore, the western societies are more receptive to data sovereignty discussion. Of course, information technology powers do not need to rely on data sovereignty to protect them. But they can also understand or accept the weak states in information technology to put forward demands for protecting their domestic data from the perspective of sovereignty. Since data sovereignty can avoid the different understanding and differences of values of cyberspace sovereignty and information sovereignty, the international community is more likely to promote the formation of international consensus on the basis of the protection of data sovereignty and data itself, thus contributing to the international cooperation process and thus is realistic.

Therefore, it is also a viable path to promote the landing of cyberspace sovereignty from the perspective of data sovereignty.

---

[27]Merkel Emphasize Activities of US Intelligence Agency in Germany must Comply With German Law. http://news.qq.com/a/20130715/001106.htm [2016-10-4].

10.1.8 Methods of Protection on Data Sovereignty

In general, the protection of data sovereignty is mainly effective supervision on the whole process from the production to the use of the data. The protection of data sovereignty in the Cyber Security Law of the People's Republic of China is regulated at the legal level.

1. Data Production and Collection

Rigorous review of mobile terminal, operating systems and applications and hierarchical management systems should be implemented to prevent theft and surveillance of citizens' the privacy, business information and government security information.

Article 27 of the Cyber Security Law states that: Individuals and organizations must not engage in online intrusions, interfere with other networks' regular functioning, steal online data or other such activities harmful to cybersecurity; they must not provide software or tools for the specific use of committing network intrusions, interfering with the regular functioning as well as protection measures of network, steal online data or other such activities endangering cyber security; and where they clearly know that others will engage in activities endangering cybersecurity, they must not provide assistance such as technical support, advertisements and promotion, or financial support etc.

2. Transmission of Data

Enterprises involving Internet data transmission should be regulated through legislation. Illegal data exit related to national security, business operation and civil privacy shall be strictly controlled.

Article 37 of the Cyber Security Law states that: Important data collected or produced by critical information infrastructure operators during their operations within the mainland of the People's Republic of China, shall be stored within the territory. Where due to business requirements it is truly necessary to provide it outside the mainland, a security assessment shall be conducted according to the measures jointly formulated by the state network information departments and the relevant departments of the State Council. Where laws or administrative regulations provide otherwise, those provisions apply.

3. Storage of Data

All enterprises operating in their own countries must use the data centers in the state territory to store business data. The government may regulate data in the data center to ensure Internet security and data security.

Article 34 of the Cyber Security Law states that, In addition to the provisions of Article 21 of this Law, critical information infrastructures operators shall also perform the following security protection duties:... ③ Conduct disaster recovery backups of important systems and databases; ....

4. Analysis and Use of Data

On one hand, the government establishes a public data release mechanism to release data to the public, and support enterprises to carry out third-party services with government data. On the other hand, the government shall establish a desensitization mechanism for data relating civil life and national security, to ensure that the big data used in value mining at the same time will not suffer from privacy leaks.

Article 43 of the Cyber Security Law provides that: Network operators collecting and using personal information shall abide by principles of legality, propriety and necessity, disclosing their rules for its collection and use, explicitly stating the purposes, means and scope for collecting or using information, and obtaining the consent of the person whose data is gathered.

5. Regulating the use of Data Center

Data center is the destination of data collection and transmission, and the center is the core of data rights. Therefore, the management of the data center should be enhanced to prevent leakage of information.

Article 21 of the Cyber Security Law stipulates that: The State implements a tiered system of cyber security protections. Network operators shall fulfill the following security protection duties according to the requirements of the tiered cybersecurity protection system, to ensure the network avoids interference, damage or unauthorized access, and to prevent network data leaks, theft or falsification: ① Formulate internal security management systems and operating rules, determine persons responsible for cyber security, and implement cyber security protection responsibility; ② Adopt technological measures to prevent computer viruses, network attacks, network intrusions and other actions endangering cybersecurity; ③ Adopt technological measures for monitoring and recording network operational statuses and cyber security incidents, and preserve network logs according to regulations for at least than six months; ④ Adopt measures such as data classification, back-up of important data, and encryption; ⑤ Other obligations provided by law or administrative regulations.

10.1.9 Problems Confronting Data Sovereignty in Legislation, Administration and Implementation

Cai Cuihong analyzes the problems in the implementation of data sovereignty in legislation, administration and implementation.[28]

[28]Cai CH (2013) Concept and application promise of data sovereignty in the context of cloud Era. Mod Int Relat 12. http://www.cssn.cn/zzx/gjzzx_zzx/201505/t20150512_1779952.shtml [2016-9-22].

1. Decentralization of the acting subject's ability without being mastered

Many private and even individuals could cross-border transfer large amounts of electronic data, without being known by their sovereign national authorities. Michel Foucault questioned the concept of power-as-sovereignty and proposed two concepts, namely surveillance and discipline. He argued that in the case of the triangle of sovereignty, citizenship, and right, it is some mandatory form of surveillance and discipline that should be observed.[29] Thus, the realization of data sovereignty not only depends on surveillance of the sovereign state from the top to the bottom, but also depends on self-discipline of individual actors according to civil norms.

2. Uncertainty of Domestic Data

There is a problem in the applicability of the "people" or "territorial" principles in the field of traditional justice in data sovereignty. The "people" principle refers to determining the scope of right exercise based on data sources or data body. "People" refers to the object of generalization, which may also be things. "Territorial" principle refers to determining according to the geographical location of the data. There are also questions about the applicability of the principle of territory jurisdiction, the principle of nationality jurisdiction, the principle of protection of jurisdiction, and the principle of universal jurisdiction in criminal acts related to cross-border data flows.[30] There is also a view that the data in the cloud is randomly and constantly moving, and it is difficult to determine the storage location of a time-specific data. Therefore, there is uncertainty in how to confirm the existence of data sovereignty.[31]

3. Difficulty in Actual Operation Due to the Amount of Data

In the big data and cloud computing era, data is featured with numerous types and a large amount. However, the fact that the Internet address and physical address are not in one by one correspondence, makes cross-border data transmission following the principle of "prior consent" face enormous challenges. The amount of data also poses another dilemma of data sovereignty, that is, the state cannot fully

---

[29]FOUCAULT IN CYBERSPACE: SURVEILLANCE, SOVEREIGNTY, AND HARDWIRED CENSORS, University Of Cincinnati Law Review, 1997, 66: 187. http://scholarship.law.duke.edu/cgi/viewcontent.cgi?article=1552&context=faculty_scholarship&sei-redir=1&referer=, http://cn.bing.com/search?q=Foucault+in+Cyberspace:Surveillance,Sovereignty,and+Hardwired+Censors&go=%E6%90%9C%E7%B4%A2&qs=n&form=QBRE&pq=foucault+in+cyberspace:surveillance,sovereignty,and+hardwired+censors&sc=069&sp=-1&sk=&cvid=CB7E8C6191684A4A8FBA8C327634568D#search="FoucaultCyberspace:Surveillance,Sovereignty,andHardwiredCensors" [2016-10-4].

[30]Chang JL (2007) Trans-border data flow's influence on jurisdiction of developing countries. SAHG China J 4: 46–48. http://www.cnki.com.cn/Article/CJFDTOTAL-SAHG200704018.htm [2016-10-4].

[31]Data Export in Cloud Computing—How can Personal Data be Transferred Outside the EEA? The Cloud of Unknowing, Part 4. https://script-ed.org/article/data-export-cloud-computing-how-can-personal-data-be-transferred-outside-the-eea-the-cloud-of-unknowing-part-4/ [2016-10-4].

master its data; and it is also very difficult for a country to recognize partial ownership of data, for it indicates recognition of incomplete sovereignty.[32]

4. Technical Challenge Brought by the Characteristics of Cyberspace

The packet characteristics of Internet information transmission make the transmission path uncertain, and thus difficult to intercept. In cyberspace, not only the sovereign states find it hard to know a specific cross-border data transmission, the transmitter itself may not know, either. This shows the new direction of information security in the age of big data and cloud computing, that is, addressing the issue of cloud data leakage. This will be a problem for both the terminal user and the cloud service provider.[33]

5. Data Regulation and Open Balance

The maintenance of traditional national sovereignty increasingly depends on the influence and control of information and data. This determines that the sovereign state must fully maintain and explore its own jurisdiction in cyberspace and information space, so that the state is in a dominant position in the international and domestic relations. However, it is undeniable that cross-border data flows, where appropriate, can enhance inter-country communication and promote international cooperation, thereby improving the living conditions of mankind. At the same time, in the era of big data, appropriate openness of data can create new business models and employment opportunities for big data applications, and the openness brings new growth points to economic development. Therefore, the exercise of data sovereignty by a sovereign state does not imply complete control over data, but rather a reasonable balance between regulation and opening. This is also the objective of the EU to enact the data protection directive while proposing the open data strategy, that is, with big data as the driving force, support social innovation, which drives the development of intelligent economy, helps to get rid of the financial crisis and increase employment, so as to achieve a social governance strategy.[34]

---

[32]Forest B (2004) Information sovereignty and GIS: The evolution of 'communities of interest' in political redistricting. Polit Geogr 23(4):425–451. http://www.doc88.com/p-6897792004645.html [2016-10-4].

[33]Rajnish C, Rajshree D, Joy B (2011) A survey on cloud computing security, challenges and threats. Int J Comput Sci Eng 3(3):1227–1231. http://www.cssn.cn/zzx/gjzzx_zzx/201505/t20150512_1779952.shtml [2016-10-4].

[34]Cao L (2013) Big data innovation: research of open data strategy of the EU. Inf Stud: Theor Appl 4:118–121. http://wenku.baidu.com/view/8b32b5f7998fcc22bcd10d28.html [2016-10-4].

10.2 Information Sovereignty

10.2.1 Basic Concept of Information Sovereignty

Information sovereignty is a subset of cyberspace sovereignty, and it is also a subset of data sovereignty. The information sovereignty is only for the information contained in the cyberspace, reflecting the content of a certain meaning of the information itself, neither the information and communication technology system, nor the data itself. Information sovereignty is the embodiment of national sovereignty in the network information activities, referring to the state of any information in its territory of the manufacture, dissemination and trading activities, as well as the relevant organizations and systems, including protection, management and control, including the highest power, is part of the modern national sovereignty, but also the expression of the concept of the world of information. The information here mainly refers to the dissemination of content for information.

From a political point of view, information sovereignty is the highest right of the state to allow or prohibit the circulation of information in its field, including the right to develop and consolidate the national culture through domestic and international information dissemination, to safeguard the image of the country internationally and international information, as well as the right to share information space and resources on an equal footing. From the perspective of the law, information sovereignty refers to the country in the field of network information content of the autonomy and independence.

As with the connotation of national sovereignty, the information sovereignty is also reflected in both internal and external aspects, which embodies the highest right of the state to create, disseminate and trade any information in its field; what kind of procedures to participate in international information activities, and the right to information in the interests of other countries by taking measures to protect.

10.2.2 Three Basic Rights of Information Sovereignty

It is generally believed that the so-called information sovereignty includes three basic rights,[35] namely the right of control, the right of management and the right of resource sharing. The control of the contents and methods of transnational data flow will become the basic content of national information sovereignty.

1. The Right of Information Control

Information control is reflected in the effective control of the content and manner of cross-border data flows in sovereign countries. The so-called control is to

[35]Ren MY (2007) Studies in national information sovereignty in the context of internet. Hebei Law Sci 6:71. http://www.pkulaw.cn/fulltext_form.aspx?Gid=1510023824 [2016-10-4].

effectively master and control the object, limiting its activities within a normal range. The information control right in a broad sense refers to the right of a subject to take protective measures for information within its jurisdiction so as to ensure the confidentiality, authenticity and integrity of information. Information control right crudely means that a sovereign state prevents domestic information in the information network from being tampered with and destroyed, and resists erosion and destruction of harmful information against the state. In the network environment, right of information control includes two aspects: having independent information technology and information production system; and having the right to ensure that the national information and resources not being contaminated tampered with or destroyed and to resist the erosion of harmful information.

Some people think that in the Internet age, information control is a guarantee for a sovereign state in the network society to gain a foothold, development and growth. Without the right of information control, the backbone of politics and economy of a country will be invisibly controlled by one or more powerful countries.[36] In other words, as a country needs to protect its territory from being invaded through air superiority, a government usually needs "information superiority" to ensure the stability of its own regime.

2. The Right of Information Management

The right of information management is embodied in the administration of a country's information on the export and import of information, as well as in the field of information when a country has the jurisdiction of the jurisdiction within the country to grasp the information control, and maintenance of information security under the premise of the information field to take a series of measures for micro management. The right of information management is mainly embodied in the following aspects: first, the development of information laws and regulations, which is the reflection of national legislative power in the field of information; second, determination of national information development strategy, and effective production, storage, circulation and transmission of national information resources; third, the establishment of the domestic information market supervision mechanism, so as to manage and monitor the content and flow method of the domestic information output and foreign information input, which directly involves cross-border transmission of information, and of which the major function is to protect national information security and exclude harmful information endangering national sovereignty; and fourth, the exercise of jurisdiction over disputes in the field of information in accordance with certain criteria.

[36]Peng QW (2002) Inquiry into national sovereignty in information cyberspace. J Inf 21(5):98–100. http://xueshu.baidu.com/s?wd=paperuri:(0be165807de6e6065abca209ad810bb4)&filter=sc_long_sign&sc_ks_para=q%3D%E9%9D%A2%E5%90%91%E4%BF%A1%E6%81%AF%E7%BD%91%E7%BB%9C%E7%A9%BA%E9%97%B4%E7%9A%84%E5%9B%BD%E5%AE%B6%E4%B8%BB%E6%9D%83%E6%8E%A2%E6%9E%90&tn=SE_baiduxueshu_c1gjeupa&ie=utf-8&sc_us=10079513782599099702 [2016-10-4].

3. The Right of Information Sharing

The right of information resource sharing is the right to realize the information resources sharing of all humans based on international cooperation. In the network environment, information resource sharing is mainly reflected in the following aspects: first, sovereign countries have a relatively independent information industry market and higher information resource profits. The sharing of information resources is reflected not only in the sharing of information flow, but more importantly, in equal sharing of interests of the information economy brought about by the information market and the information industry. Second, maintaining the sovereign states right to speak and equal participation in the cyberspace, so that it can participate in the development of global network rules on an equal footing, which is the principle of national sovereignty equality in the context of the Internet as an important manifestation. Third, to maintain the sovereignty of the country in the online world of national character, that is, the network has a considerable number of information resources reflecting the traditional culture of the nation, value orientation, and social awareness.

10.2.3 Four Fundamental Elements of Information Sovereignty

It is generally believed that information sovereignty has four basic elements: autonomy, controllability, manageability, and standard setting.

1. Information technology autonomy

Information technology is the basis of informatization. Without information technology free of foreign control, one cannot speak of the protection of information security and information activities management; without relatively independent and more advanced information technology research and development systems, the state cannot be called an information sovereign state.

2. The possession and control of information resources

Information resources, materials resources and energy resources together constitute the three strategic resources of the national economic and social development. Ignoring the construction of national independent information resources, without sufficient control of information resources, the information sovereignty is out of the question.

3. Management Capacity of Information System

The information system is a network and a media for information transmission, exchange, sharing, and is a platform for achieving national information sovereignty. As the information system is open and is free to access, and a country cannot perform effective management of the information system, the information sovereignty will be harmed.

4. Development of Information regulations and Standards

With the increasing development of global informatization, either domestic or internationally, there have been many legal issues on information activities. Therefore, there is a need to adjust the legal relations in the field of information. In this process, the state has an inherent demand for information laws and regulations to enjoy information sovereignty.

10.2.4 Source of Information Sovereignty

1. Satellite Communication Triggered Conflicts for Information Sovereignty

In 1957, the former Soviet Union launched the first man-made earth satellite. A former Soviet scholar pointed out that the application of artificial earth satellites to international communications indicates that by means of artificial earth satellites Moscow television programs can not only spread to any corner of the former Soviet Union, but also spread abroad. Which was then considered a challenge to national information sovereignty, and those who feared that people could directly watch foreign programs through artificial earth satellites would face how they would take measures to exercise absolute control over the flow of information.

Based on the principle of national sovereignty, any State shall enjoy, within its own territory, freedom of public communication in accordance with its own constitutions and laws, and no other State may interfere with it. However, whether a country enjoys freedom of public communication in other countries, and especially whether it has the freedom to use international satellites for international direct television broadcasting, there have been heated debates in the international community. In 1968, the United Nations Committee on the Peaceful Uses of Outer Space established the Working Group on Satellite Direct Broadcasting, which began a special study on the issue. In this process, coinciding with the cold war, the former Soviet Union, Eastern Europe and the wider third world countries generally adhered that the direct broadcast of satellites should be based on respect for national sovereignty. They proposed to establish a strict "prior consent" system, which requires a State to have direct satellite broadcast to the country, subject to the prior consent of the State Party. The Western developed countries, led by the United States, stressed the importance of the free flow of information, arguing that all countries were free to broadcast directly to the satellite without the consent of the receiving country.

In the 1960s and 1970s, the United Nations had a heated discussion on information sovereignty. November 15, 1972, the United Nations Educational, Scientific and Cultural Organization (UNESCO) announced the *Declaration of Guiding Principles on the Use of Satellite Broadcasting for the Free Flow of Information, the Spread of Education and Greater Cultural Exchange*[37] pointing out that satellite broadcasting should abide by the sovereignty and equality of all countries and that each country has the power to decide what the content of the program is, which is transmitted through the satellite to its own territory. The Declaration declares that: "Article 2" ① Satellite broadcasting shall respect the sovereignty and equality of all States. "Article 6" ② Each country has the right to decide on the content of the educational programmes broadcast by satellite to its people and, in cases where such programmes are produced in co-operation with other countries, to take part in their planning and production, on a free and equal footing. "Article 9". ① In order to further the objectives set out in the preceding articles, it is necessary that States, taking into account the principle of freedom of information, reach or promote prior agreements concerning direct satellite broadcasting to the population of countries other than the country of origin of the transmission. ② In order to further the objectives set out in the preceding articles, it is necessary that States, taking into account the principle of freedom of information, reach or promote prior agreements concerning direct satellite broadcasting to the population of countries other than the country of origin of the transmission."Article 10. In the preparation of programmes for direct broadcasting to other countries, account shall be taken of differences in the national laws of the countries of reception."

On 10 December 1982, the United Nations General Assembly adopted a non-legally binding resolution, i.e., *Principles of the use of States of Artificial Earth Satellites for the use of artificial earth satellites for international direct television broadcasting*. This resolution, as a product of compromise between the parties, though does not include the expression "prior consent", stresses in paragraph 1 of the resolution that "the implementation of international television live activities using satellites should be consistent with the principles of national sovereignty and non-intervention and the relevant United Nations documents"; and states in paragraph 13 that "States that intend to establish or authorize the establishment of an international direct television broadcasting satellite service shall promptly notify the receiving State of this intention, for example, the right to seek, receive and transmit information and ideas. If any of the receiving States puts forward such a consultative request, the consultation shall be performed expeditiously". Therefore, the resolution is considered to accept the principle of "prior consent". It was for this very reason, the United States voted against the resolution.[38]

2. Rules and Laws involving Information Sovereignty

So far, even though the international community has not yet reached any legally binding treaty on the use of artificial earth satellites for international direct television broadcasting, with the rapid development of satellite communications and

[37]Declaration of Guiding Principles on the Use of Satellite Broadcasting for the Free Flow of Information, the Spread of Education and Greater Cultural Exchange. http://portal.unesco.org/en/ev.php-URL_ID=17518&URL_DO=DO_TOPIC&URL_SECTION=201.html [2016-9-17].

[38]Communication Freedom and Restrictions in International Law. http://www.calaw.cn/article/default.asp?id=9975 [2016-9-25].

Internet communications, it has already become an unchangeable objective fact that states transmit information crossing borders. Therefore, the crux of the problem is how to establish a set of universally accepted international standards that restrict the freedom of such communications and establish a corresponding international implementation mechanism.

Before the establishment of the above international standard and implementation mechanism, each country shall follow the *Principles Governing the Use by States of Artificial Earth Satellites for Direct Television Broadcasting,*[39] adopted by the United Nations General Assembly. The Declaration of Guiding Principles Governing the Use of Satellites for Information Free Flow, Education Communication and Cultural Exchange Development had been adopted by the United Nations Educational, Scientific and Cultural Organization in 1972. *The Declaration on Fundamental Principles concerning the Contribution of the Mass Media to Strengthening Peace and International Understanding, to the Promotion of Human Rights and to Countering Racialism, apartheid and incitement to war*, was adopted in 1978, and ensured that the public communication activities thereof complied with the principle and rules set by a series of international legal documents including the United Nations Charter and the *Treaty on the Principles governing the Activities in States in the Exploration and Use of Outer Space, including the Moon and Other Celestial Bodies*[40] (shortened as the Outer Space Treaty).

According to these principles and rules, the state's public communication activities, first of all, should be based on peaceful purposes, and shall not perform propaganda advocating wars; second, shall not be used to interfere in the internal affairs of other countries, in particular, shall not be used to organize and incite activities aimed at subverting the legitimate rights of other States; again, shall not be used to advocate racial discrimination, genocide, apartheid and religious discrimination, and discrimination against women. Violations against the above-mentioned principles constitute a violation of the obligations of an international law and shall be punished according to the international law.

Ukraine has enacted the corresponding law on information sovereignty—the *Law of Ukraine on Information,*[41] which states: "Article 53. Information sovereignty: Ukraine's information sovereignty shall be based on the national information resources. Ukraine's information resources shall include all information belonging to Ukraine, regardless of contents, form, time, and place of creation thereof. Ukraine shall independently form information resources and shall freely manage them, except in cases stipulated by the law and international treaties".

---

[39]Principles Governing the Use by States of Artificial Earth Satellites for Direct Television Broadcasting. http://www.un.org/zh/documents/view_doc.asp?symbol=A/RES/37/92 [2016-10-2].

[40]Treaty on Principles Governing the Activities of States in the Exploration and Use of Outer Space, including the Moon and Other Celestial Bodies. http://www.unoosa.org/oosa/en/ourwork/spacelaw/treaties/introouterspacetreaty.html [2016-9-17].

[41]The Law of Ukraine on Information. http://www.wipo.int/edocs/lexdocs/laws/en/ua/ua032en.pdf [2016-9-17].

"Article 54. Guarantees of Ukraine's Informational Sovereignty The information sovereignty of Ukraine shall be secured by: Ukraine's exclusive property right to the informational resources formed using state budget funds; creation of national information systems; establishment of procedures enabling other countries to access Ukraine's informational sources; use of informational resources based on equal co-operation with other countries."

10.2.5 Challenge Confronting Information Sovereignty

When the Internet enables the life, work, study, and communication of people to be achieved in a global scale and becomes an indispensable part of daily life, there is a reduction in the reverence and dependency of people toward the current social space featured by the national territory and national will. The information revolution is shifting the state-centered world into a network-centric world.

With the development of the Internet, the concept of information sovereignty has been challenged in practice. There has been a series of contradictions and conflicts arising, including the contradiction between "information sovereignty" and the globalization of transmission, the contradiction between "cultural sovereignty" and international cultural transmission, the contradiction between national control and preferences of citizens, the conflict between "information super powers" and the concept of information sovereignty of developing countries.

The *Position Regarding the World Summit on Information Society,*[42] published by the International Broadcasting Association on December 6, 2002, once again challenged "information sovereignty" and stated that some countries that have advocated controls over the free flow of information across national frontiers have tried to justify such controls on political grounds, regional value systems or national information sovereignty. Such controls are clearly in violation of the Universal Declaration of Human Rights.

Further, the characteristics of virtual space and global interconnection of the Internet are also a challenge against national "information sovereignty". Zhang Shu-tian from Shenzhen University proposed four possible characteristics of Internet erosion of national sovereignty (that is, erosion of information sovereignty) that form a factor of a threat to national information sovereignty.[43]

1. Virtual nature of the Internet and the Physical Borders of State Sovereignty

Transboundary access and arbitrary manipulation on the Internet result in threat of information sovereignty by the attempt of interference from other countries. The

---

[42]Position Regarding the World Summit on Information Society. http://www.itu.int/dms_pub/itu-s/md/03/wsispc2/c/S03-WSISPC2-C-0022!!PDF-E.pdf [2016-9-17].

[43]Information Sovereignty in the Era of Internet. http://doc.qkzz.net/article/d3692db5-245a-47e1-8eb1-61869e52b416_4.htm [2016-10-4].

Internet is a virtual space that does not have any territorial boundaries and is not subject to any physical space. Therefore, any action on the Internet may be transnational. People can arbitrarily cross the border of the countries to access the world's information. Americans believe in manifesting destiny and are keen on spreading the faith of "democracy and freedom". Such aggressive culture expands into the whole world in this era of globalization using the penetration of the Internet. On the contrary, the national sovereignty is established on the territorial space of the state, based on a certain physical space, and is subject to physical boundaries. The state can only exercise the highest right in the territory within the boundaries. Therefore, the virtual nature of the Internet makes it impossible for the people and behavior in cyberspace to correspond to the geographical position in the real world, which leads to the difficulty of exercising the traditional national jurisdiction, and the national jurisdiction cannot be smoothly realize the constrains to the Internet. Moreover, limited control measures taken by the state on the Internet may violate sovereignty of other countries due to the characteristics of the Internet without national boundaries.

2. Non-binding Feature of the Internet and the Supreme Property of National Sovereignty

The free spread of the Internet has greatly challenged the country's regulatory capacity and posed a great threat to the maintenance of the state. The Internet is a free and open system. As a place of communication of thoughts and speeches, it allows individuals to speak freely. The information on the Internet can flow freely between sites. At this time, although the state enjoys supreme sovereignty over the people and objects in the territory, real laws are based on the territories and it is difficult to regulate the cross-border behavior of the Internet users in the virtual space. The monitoring of the online behavior is costly and difficult. Thus, information that would otherwise be monopolized or controlled by the state could be easily acquired by the average person, which challenges national concepts established in the same area and having the same experience with the development of virtual space. In addition, the Internet has a strong interaction, as the audience of individuals has more choices and the freedom to accept information. Likewise the same Internet users can also cross the national boundaries to form a different community, which weakens the state's ability to control citizens, and the ability to control cyberspace information is also weakened, which weakens the effectiveness of the highest power of the state.

3. Openness of the Internet and the Closure of National Sovereignty

The decentralized control system of the Internet determines that the exchange of information on the Internet goes beyond the supervision of the state and constitutes an impact on state jurisdiction. In addition to the establishment of the Internet domain name resolution system, there is no central control mechanism for individuals on their Internet behavior. While the Internet is borderless and open, the country and the specific location of its Internet activities are difficult to determine.

Therefore, it is difficult for the country to control and manage individual online activities. In accordance with the principle of national sovereignty, sovereign States have jurisdiction over anything in their jurisdiction. In other words, theoretically, the State has the right to exercise jurisdiction over information transmitted to its territory and information transmitted from its territory, and that the State has the power to exercise jurisdiction over individuals who use network information within its territory. National sovereignty emphasizes the supreme right and external independence, and always stays wary of any violation and intervention from the outside; the state is also limited to the opening to the outside world, even if the national sovereignty and national interests are not damaged as premise. However, it would be difficult to effectively cope with the proliferation of harmful information if the Internet located in a territory cannot be clearly defined and adapted to the secrecy of national sovereignty.

4. Activity of the Internet and the Passivity of National Sovereignty

The breadth of Internet communication reduces the ability of sovereign countries to monitor network communication. In the traditional mass communication mode, the feedback mechanism of the audience to the harmful information is not perfect, let alone the audience directly involved in the dissemination of information. In the Internet communication mode, personal communication on the Internet is active, positive, the network of virtual space structure also hides the information release and the identity of the recipient. Any person can freely choose and obtain information according to their own will and preferences, but also can easily and spontaneously send the information they want to publish to the public. This information dissemination can be issued for the specific public, but also for specific people's release, or even completely beyond the control of the state, which may have a huge impact on the country and society. Thus, individuals on the Internet are both recipients of information and disseminators of information, and many terrorist organizations and anti-government organizations use the Internet to create chaos and to subvert the activities of sovereign states. In addition, the Internet (as a thought and view of the collision and exchange of places) user's involvement in related matters, reviews and discussions are always positive. On the contrary, the state sovereignty is passive. Under normal circumstances, the state will not take the initiative to emphasize national sovereignty. Merely when the state sovereignty is facing the risk or reality of being violated, the state will act to safeguard the sovereignty.

10.2.6 Protection of Personal Information

In the Cyber Security Law of the People's Republic of China, the protection of personal information has been clearly regulated as a key point. The Law mainly regulates collection, storage and processing of personal information and other acts, showing the authority of information sovereignty.

1. Articles Involving Collection of Personal Information

Article 22: Where network products or services have functions to collect user information, their providers shall express this to users and obtain the agreement from the users; where citizens' personal information is involved, they shall also obey the provisions of this law, as well as other relevant laws and administrative regulations, on the protection of citizens' personal information.

Article 40: Network operators shall strictly maintain the confidentiality of user information they collect, and establish and complete user information protection systems.

Article 41: Network operators must not gather personal information unrelated to the services they provide, and must not violate the provisions of laws, administrative regulations or the agreements between the parties to gather personal information.

Article 44: Individual or organization must not steal or use other illegal methods to acquire personal information.

2. Terms Involving Storage of Personal Information

Article 37: Personal information and important business data collected or produced by critical information infrastructure operators during their operations within the mainland territory of the People's Republic of China, shall be stored within the territory. Where due to business requirements it is truly necessary provide it outside the mainland, a security assessment shall be conducted according to the measures jointly formulated by the state network information departments and the relevant departments of the State Council. Where laws or administrative regulations provide otherwise, those provisions apply.

Article 42: Network operators shall adopt technological measures and other necessary measures to ensure the security of personal information they collect, and prevent personal information from leaking, being destroyed or lost. When the leak, destruction or loss of personal information occur, remedial measures shall be immediately taken, and provisions followed to promptly inform users and to make report to the competent departments according to regulations.

Article 43: Where individuals discover network operators have violated the provisions of the laws, administrative regulations or agreements between the parties to collect or use their personal information, they have the right to request the network operators to delete their personal information; where discovering that personal information gathered or stored by the network operators contains errors, they have the right to request the network operators to make corrections. The network operators shall employ measures for deletions and corrections.

Article 45: Departments, with duties of security safety supervision and management in accordance with law and their personnel, and their staffs must keep personal information, private information and commercial secrets, which they learn of in performing their duties strictly confidential, and must not leak, sell, or unlawfully provide it to others.

3. Terms involving use of Personal Information

Article 41: Network operators must not violate the provisions of laws, administrative regulations or agreements between the parties to use personal information; and shall follow the provisions of laws, administrative regulations or agreements with users to process personal information they have stored.

Article 42: Network operators must not disclose, distort or destroy personal information they collect, without the agreement of the person whose information is collected, personal information must not be provided to others. Except where it has been processed so that the specific individual is unidentifiable and cannot be recovered.

Article 44: Individual or organization must not unlawfully sell or unlawfully provide others with citizens' personal information.

10.3 Electromagnetic Space Sovereignty

Since the emergence of satellite radio, cross-border information dissemination has been formed. People began to explore whether the electromagnetic space can be used without restriction. As the electromagnetic space is still within the scope of the territorial air, the state has the capacity to control it. Thus, the concept of electromagnetic space sovereignty is proposed. Electromagnetic space sovereignty is essentially a subset of cyberspace sovereignty, and which is the result of a special concern for the particular area of wireless environment in cyberspace.

The *Principles of the use of States of Artificial Earth Satellites for the use of artificial earth satellites for international direct television broadcasting*, adopted by the United Nations General Assembly in December 1982, specifies that the State is responsible for the act of satellite television broadcasting conducted by a subject under its jurisdiction and itself. Even if the act is the behavior of the private sector or an individual, the states still must take responsibility. This is equivalent to specifying the supreme authority of a sovereign State for satellite television broadcasting messages in its territory. Accordingly, cross-border satellite television broadcasts must be either agreed on or arranged by both parties, which is a "prior consent" principle. Therefore, without the consent of the national government, input and output data to a state are interference in the right of self-determination of the state, and which is a violation of the sovereignty. This can be regarded as a practical application of electromagnetic space sovereignty.

In accordance with the rules established by the International Telecommunication Union, countries have absolute planning authority over their domestic electromagnetic spectrum; it is not allowed to occupy any broadcast band without permission. Foreign organizations are using uncertainty of the boundary of electromagnetic space and forcing through the physical boundary to a state from outside the territory to send short-wave signals carrying harmful information to the state, and the injured country usually copes with the interference with a corresponding high-power interference means, which is a manifestation of electromagnetic space sovereignty.

10.4 Technological Sovereignty

In 2014, an EU-sponsored organization published the report *Technological Sovereignty: Missing the Point,*[44] using the term "technological sovereignty". The report points out that the impact of the study of these technological sovereign proposals is still emerging. More and more literature examines the development strategy of "data localization", that is, "restricting the storage and movement/processing of digital data to specific areas, jurisdictions and businesses by law and guidelines." These proposals became concerned in early 2014, because they are part of the Internet rights act under discussion in Brazil. At present, the "term" of technological sovereignty is still vague. For example, "data sovereignty" has been used by European decision makers and defined as the power of states to use respective methods to control generation of data or to transmit data through domestic Internet. It is a subset of cyberspace sovereignty, and is a manifestation of local jurisdiction for cyberspace conquest.

Certainly, the concept of technological sovereignty and cyberspace sovereignty intersects. Technological sovereignty emphasizes the overall technology, instead of just cyberspace technology, while cyberspace sovereignty emphasizes all aspects of cyberspace rather than just the technical aspect. The starting point of technological sovereignty is that the state not only has to control the independent technology, but also has the right of control, the right of jurisdiction and the right to formulating standards over independent technology. For example, in terms of measurement, if a state does not have its own measurement system, it will lead to lack of foundation of the scientific research and defense technology, showing a lack of technological sovereignty.[45] Technological sovereignty is closely tied with national economy. The essence of technological sovereignty is to support national economic behaviors. Russian officials once questioned the Eurasian Economic Union that if the member states do not establish technological sovereignty, the alliance is not substantial.[46]

[44]Technological Sovereignty: Missing the Point. 2013-06-05. http://newamerica.org/cybersecurity-initiative/press-releases/technological-sovereignty-missing-the-point [2016-9-25].

[45]Scientific Developmental Trend from the Perspective of National Science and Technology. http://www.cas.cn/xw/kjsm/gndt/200906/t20090608_651526.shtml [2016-12-31].

[46]Russian experts: the Eurasian Economic Union lack of technological sovereignty is not substantial. http://kz.mofcom.gov.cn/article/ddgk/h/201409/20140900730542.shtml [2016-10-4].

Chapter 11
Conflicts of Cyberspace Sovereignty Concept

Abstract For a long time, the Internet has not been dominated by sovereign states, and its administration does not fall into the responsibility of the United Nations which represents sovereign states. Therefore, the proposal of cyberspace sovereignty has brought about a head-on conflict in the Internet field. The viewpoints of supporting and opposing the cyberspace sovereignty are both distinct. Of course, there are also opinions that are free from the intermediate state.

Keywords Supporting cyberspace sovereignty · Opposing cyberspace sovereignty
Paying little attention to cyberspace sovereignty

Western countries, represented by the United States, believe that cyberspace governance mainly refers to the governance at the technical level, and stress that the freedom of connection and that of information flow in cyberspace should not be hampered; however, China, Russia and some other countries hold that content regulation should also be one of the key points of cyberspace governance, and advocate cyberspace sovereignty.

This argument was fully exhibited in the World Conference on International Telecommunications (WCIT) held in December 2012.[1] The International Telecommunication Union (ITU), a specialized UN agency of information and communications technology, organized the member states to discuss the current International Telecommunications Regulations (ITRS)[2] and treaties of global telecommunications industry at the conference. Before the conference, Russia submitted to the Conference a proposal about Internet issues, wherein Russia suggested adding 5 definitions including "Internet", "Internet traffic", "Internet access", "Basic Internet infrastructure" and "National Internet segment" to the International Telecommunications Regulations, and adding special chapters and clauses to ensure that nations have equal rights in Internet management and allo-

---

[1]World Conference on International Telecommunications (WCIT-12). http://www.itu.int/en/wcit-12/Pages/default.aspx [2016-9-21].

[2]Draft of the future ITRS. http://www.itu.int/en/wcit-12/Documents/draft-future-itrs-public-zh.pdf [2016-9-21].

B. Fang, *Cyberspace Sovereignty*,
https://doi.org/10.1007/978-981-13-0320-3_11

cation of Internet resources, and emphasized to strengthen the government's role in the development and management of the Internet so as to improve the governments' rights in the distribution of Internet resources. UAE also submitted a proposal during the Conference, wherein the draft ITRS proposed by UAE integrated the content mentioned in Russia's proposal, and added additional contents about numbering, addressing, domain name and resource identification, as well as security and trust. This proposal was supported by Russia, China, Saudi Arabia and other nations.

The US Congress passed a special resolution so as to oppose ITU's involvement in Internet governance, and many western countries also explicitly opposed to bring Internet-related provisions into the revised ITRS. Google and other Internet enterprises even reacted intensely and firmly put themselves against ITRS' involvement in Internet governance for the reason as follows: ITU represents sovereign countries, so ITU's involvement in Internet governance means that national sovereignty will get involved in Internet governance. Google specifically established a website named "Take Action" before the Conference, and Google encouraged netizens all around the world to sign and support "a free and open Internet".[3]

Because of these complications, Hamadoun Touré, Secretary General of ITU, invited Fadi Chehade, the CEO of the Internet Corporation for Assigned Names and Numbers (ICANN), to make a speech at the opening. In his speech, Chehade emphasized that ICANN and ITU had clearly distinct but complementary roles, and that ICANN would like to cooperate with ITU on such a basis. Touré praised and supported in public the proposals from Tunisia and other countries, and he was in favor of adding political contents for ensuring human rights, such as the freedom of online expression and freedom of online association, to the technical and professional ITRS. In order to avoid conflicts, Touré incited the Secretariat to make the draft named as "Foster a favorable climate, realizing a greater development of Internet", hoping to meet the demands of all parties by compromising. Since the text of this resolution are relatively mild, there were not too many disagreements in the closing of that morning.

At the conference, the US said that many issues, such as cyber-security, the scope of application and so on, were unsolved yet, while these issues might affect the property of ITRS. America did not agree to put Internet-related content into ITRS. America stressed that resolutions related to Internet had been previously made in the ITU Plenipotentiary Conference, and that this subject might be discussed later by countries at the World Telecom Policy Forum 2013 and in the review process of the World Summit on Information Society of 2014 and 2015, but it should never be tried to put Internet-related content into ITRS.

Delegations of many western countries like the US, Sweden, the UK and so on, made statements and declarations, one after another, to express that they regret and

[3]Take action, a free and open web depends on me. https://www.google.com/intl/zh-CN/takeaction [2016-10-1].

could not accept the way of pushing through the resolution, and did not agree to talk about Internet issues in ITRS. However, UAE, Saudi Arabia, South Africa and other Arab and African countries stressed the significance of Internet to developing countries. Prior to this, China and Russia also made speeches to emphasize the necessities of mentioning Internet issues in ITRS. As a result, according to the Chairman's ruling, Internet-related contents were written into ITRS in the form of resolution. So far, the discussion about Internet at this conference has dramatically concluded. On December 13, due to irreconcilable divergences, the Conference passed the texts about human rights and Internet accessibility by show of hands.

11.1 Viewpoints Supporting Cyberspace Sovereignty

As for supporting the presence of cyberspace sovereignty, there are official opinions from governments, authoritative personal viewpoints, as well as specific practices of processing relevant issues from the perspective of cyberspace sovereignty. There are voices in support of cyberspace sovereignty coming from internationally all walks of life, and different periods, such as the voice from the international community, the voice from the countries in support of cyberspace sovereignty, and even the voice of individuals from the countries against cyberspace sovereignty.

11.1.1 Viewpoint in the Declaration of Principles of UN WSIS

Titled "Building the Information Society: a global challenge in the new Millennium",[4] the Declaration of Principles of UN WSIS published in December 2003 clearly stated: "Policy authority for Internet-related public policy issues is the sovereign right of States. They have rights and responsibilities for international Internet-related public policy issues". The Declaration stressed: "to prevent the potential use of ICTs for purposes that are inconsistent with the objectives of maintaining international stability and security."

[4]Declaration of Principles: Building the Information Society—a global challenge in the new Millennium. https://www.itu.int/dms_pub/itu-s/md/03/wsis/doc/S03-WSIS-DOC-0004!!PDF-C.pdf [2016-9-21].

11.1.2 Viewpoint of Hongyuan LI from the Party School of Songjiang District Committee, Shanghai (2008)

In August 2008, Li Hongyuan, from CPC's Party School of Songjiang District Committee, Shanghai, pointed out in his article, i.e. *On Cyber Sovereignty and New National Security Concept*, published on the periodical name The Public Administration & Law[5]: Cyber sovereignty is a natural extension of national sovereignty in the information cyberspace, and its main content is the jurisdiction exercised by the nations in cyberspace. In the network environment, since the behavior space of the citizens of a country has been newly extended, the concept of national sovereignty correspondingly has a new connotation. Cyber sovereignty is discussed analyzing the countries' form of taking national responsibilities during the process of maintaining cyber sovereignty and studying the methods of exercising and maintaining national sovereignty in the cyberspace. The fundamental rights of nations can be easily infringed in the network era. However, the rights are surely enjoyed by each nation according to its sovereignty, and the rights are indispensable and crucial for a country. If the country possesses sovereignty, it sure has some fundamental rights; the denial of the fundamental rights of a country is equal to the denial of its sovereignty.

11.1.3 Viewpoints Published by the US Air Force Law Review: CYBERLAW EDITION (2009)

In 2009, the US Air Force Law Review:CYBERLAW EDITION published a article written by a colonel Patrick W. Franzese, i.e. "Sovereignty in Cyberspace: Can It Exist?"[6] In the article, it is pointed out: "The academics and scientists looked at cyberspace in romanticized terms, seeing the promise it held for all of humankind. This belief naturally affected how people considered the issue of cyberspace and sovereignty, which resulted in essentially two competing theories in lieu of the national sovereignty concept. The first theory is that cyberspace is immune from state sovereignty. However, this theory ignores the fact that cyberspace needs the stability and regulation that state sovereignty provides, and states have a valid interest in exercising their control in cyberspace. The second theory is that cyberspace is a global commons. This theory, however, distorts the essence of a global commons and discounts the role states play in creating them".

---

[5]LI HY (2008) On the cyber sovereignty and the new national security concept. Pub Adm Law 8:115–117. http://www.cnki.com.cn/Article/CJFDTOTAL-XZYF200808038.htm [2016-9-25].

[6]Lieutenant Colonel PATRICK W. FRANZESE, CYBERLAW EDITION: "Sovereignty in Cyberspace: Can it Exit?", Air Force Judge Advocate General School The Air Force Law Review, 2009. http://www.thefreelibrary.com/Sovereignty+in+cyberspace:+can+it+exist?-a0212035708 [2016-9-24].

The article lists the following 5 reasons for the presence of cyberspace sovereignty.

(1) Some entity must control cyberspace for it to exist and function. Cyberspace requires a physical structure, because without it, users have no access. That physical structure, however, is terrestrially based and thus naturally falls under the purview of the state where those physical assets sit. Additionally, cyberspace itself requires regulation and oversight.
(2) Financial relationships in cyberspace need laws to govern those relationships and transactions. If cyberspace was immune from state sovereignty, any financial relationship established in cyberspace would be tenuous at best and fraught with peril for either side. The fact that business decisions are heavily influenced by the laws of a respective state evidences that cyberspace is not immune from state sovereignty.
(3) Objectively, content sent through cyberspace holds significance in the "real" world. While cyberspace ideally allows for the free flow of information, no "cyberspace exemption" shields information from the valid interests of the state where information is sent, received, or stored. For example, the United States, along with many other countries, has a state interest in preventing the possession and spread of child pornography; France has a state interest in blocking the spread of Nazi memorabilia; Australia has a state interest in protecting its citizens from defamatory statements. In each of the examples above, court systems decide that information accessible to the individual located in those respective states via cyberspace is subject to the laws within that respective state. Accordingly, a website located outside of France, which sells Nazi memorabilia, which people can access from France, is subject to the laws of France. While this area of the law is still developing, it demonstrates that states have the right to legally control the state interests in cyberspace.
(4) States increasingly need to assert their presence in cyberspace as a matter of national security. Whether by design or unawareness, many states connect to and operate some of their critical infrastructure in or through cyberspace. This has left those states, including the United States, increasingly vulnerable.
(5) Scientists who were promoting the early development of the Internet hoped to improve human beings through the Internet cooperation, and it is believed that there might no one to abuse the network. However, not everyone who uses the Internet today shares that same vision. Many of those users see the Internet as a means to gain an advantage over a competitor, or to disseminate a specific message of hate or violence. Consequently, much like the "real" world which requires state sovereignty to regulate, protect, and punish various actors, cyberspace needs this sovereign influence as well. Furthermore, since states currently exploit cyberspace as a means of gaining a strategic and military advantage over another state, states must exert their control as a matter of national security.

The result is that cyberspace is not immune from state sovereignty.

11.1.4 Viewpoints from the U.S. Senate Committee on Commerce, Science, and Transportation (February 2010)

On February 23, 2010, the U.S. Senate Committee on Commerce, Science, and Transportation submitted the report–Cyber Security: Next Steps to Protect Critical Infrastructure.[7] It is recognized in the article that cyberspace is subject to national laws. It is mentioned in the article: "Cyberspace is not a global commons. It is a shared global infrastructure. There is rarely a moment when a collection of bits moving from one computer to another is not actually on a network that someone owns and that is physically located in a sovereign state. The exceptions might be undersea cables or satellite transmissions, but the action still takes place on an owned facility where the owner is subject to some country and its law. At best, this could be a 'pseudo commons'. It looks like a commons but actually is not, as someone owns the resources in question and that someone is subject to the laws of some nation. Cyberspace is in fact a more like a condominium, where there are many contiguous owners."

11.1.5 Viewpoint of James Lewis from Brown University of U.S. (May 2010)

In May 2010, James Lewis from Brown University published his article Sovereignty and the Role of Government in Cyberspace[8] on The Brown Journal of World Affairs. In the article, he criticized Ira Magaziner's viewpoint that "Internet will be an environment or a world where private actors lead, not governments. The role of government in cyberspace should be minimal". Based on the reexamination of these concepts, he believes that the viewpoints of Magaziner are best seen as a product of their time rather than immutable characteristics of cyberspace. Ideology, culture, and business practices help explain the initial understanding of cyberspace and government's role in it.

[7]U.S. Government Printing Office. Cyber security: Next Steps to Protect Our Critical Infrastructure. Hearing, Before the Committee on Commerce, Science, and Transportation, United States Senate, One Hundred Eleventh Congress, Second Session. 2010-2-23. https://fas.org/irp/congress/2010_hr/cybersec.pdf [2016-9-6].

[8]Lewis JA (2010) Sovereignty and the role of government in cyberspace. Brown J World Aff 16 (2):55–65. https://www.brown.edu/initiatives/journal-world-affairs/sites/brown.edu.initiatives.journal-world-affairs/files/private/articles/16.2_Lewis.pdf [2016-9-25].

11.1.6 Viewpoints of Eric Talbot Jensen from Brigham Young University of America (2011)

On November 1, 2011, Eric Talbot Jensen from Brigham Young University of America published his article: Sovereignty and Neutrality in Cyber Conflict.[9] In this article, he points out: One of the most difficult issues in cyber conflicts is the application of territorial sovereignty and other geographic principles to an activity that defies the traditional notions of borders. The structure of the internet and the protocols by which it operates raise questions about the application of law of armed conflict provisions, such as the doctrine of neutrality, to cyber conflict. The traditional doctrine of neutrality is not applicable to the vexing problem of non-international armed conflicts, but it would be proved useful in preventing actions by both States and non-State actors that might tend to escalate the conflict. Some evolution would add clarity in the cyber age. The law of neutrality would also provide non-Parties an additional legal paradigm with authority to prevent cyber actions within their territories.

In 2014, Jensen also issued a book about cyber sovereignty: Cyber Sovereignty: The Way Ahead.[10] In this book, he points out: States have the right to develop their cyber capabilities to their own desires and resources. A state may choose to extensively develop its cyber capabilities and make them available broadly to its citizens as Estonia has done, or it can choose to close its cyber borders to outside influences as North Korea has done.

11.1.7 Viewpoint of Huang Huikang from the Chinese Foreign Ministry (January 2012)

On January 13, 2012, Huang Huikang, a Foreign Ministry official, made the following statement in an interview[11]: The first claim about network is cyber sovereignty, because it is the government's responsibility either to build and regulate the network or to crack down on network crimes, and the network is not a place which can be taken by whoever wants to. Though the network is virtual space, it must exist in real human society and within the territory of a nation, so the network is subject to the order of the country to which it belongs. Since each country needs to build an orderly network, the country has to regulate the network and balance the relationship between network regulation and network freedom so as to ensure

[9]Jensen ET (2012) Sovereignty and neutrality in cyber conflict. Social Science Electronic Publishing. https://ssrn.com/abstract=1952598 [2017-3-1].

[10]Jensen ET (2014) Cyber sovereignty: the way ahead. Social Science Electronic Publishing. http://www.tilj.org/content/journal/50/14JENSENPUBPROOF.pdf [2017-3-1].

[11]China News. Foreign ministry official: Network should be under the national sovereignty. http://www.chinanews.com/gn/2012/01-13/3604104.shtml [2017-3-1].

netizens' legal and free utilization of network. The viewpoint that network belongs to a virtual world is wrong, because the network can actually and objectively produce interest and legal consequences. As a result, the second principle is introduced: Relevant rules for the network under national sovereignty should be formulated and enforced, and an orderly network world needs to be established. Network is international, so network problems need to be solved through international cooperation despite the lack of border divisions at present. It is the basic principle for future Internet development and particularly for the formulation of future network rules to make sure that network convenience can be shared by the public through the promotion of common development. The UN works in the best interests of all countries, and which is also an appropriate platform for making relevant rules, therefore, we insist on strengthening, through the UN, the international legislation of network and the formulation of network rules.

11.1.8 Viewpoint of Fang Binxing from Beijing University of Posts and Telecommunications (April 2012)

On April 28, 2012, Fang Binxing, who is an Academician of the Chinese Engineering Academy and the former President of the Beijing University of Posts and Telecommunications, published on the third edition of Guangming Daily a article titled *It Is Extremely Important to Advocate Cyber Sovereignty* signed with the name "Wang Chonglun".[12] It is systematically brought up in the article the viewpoint of cyber sovereignty, and Fang believed that the proposal and advocacy of cyber sovereignty concept is of great practical significance to China. Firstly, it helps to ensure the feasibility and legality of national laws and regulations in the cyberspace; secondly, it helps to strengthen the international law status of China in the network era; thirdly, it helps to maintain the economic sovereignty of China in the network era; fourthly, it helps to provide legal basis for the military presence in the cyberspace; lastly, it helps to provide legal basis for building national information security defense.

Fang Binxing points out that China should positively advocate the presence of cyber sovereignty at the level of legal theories, and then vigorously promote the improvement of cyber sovereignty at operational level so as to gradually build a feasible national sovereignty system in the cyberspace and practically safeguard China's interest in cyberspace.

According to Fang Binxing, the following aspects are required for building the cyber sovereignty system: the first one is to define the scope of liability of cyber governance, wherein the scope of network liability is restricted by the location of physical devices which constitute the network infrastructure and are used for

[12] It Is Extremely Important to Advocate Cyber Sovereignty. http://politics.gmw.cn/2012-04/28/content_4054821.htm [2016-9-25].

providing network and information service; the second one is to build a neutral network infrastructure, wherein the international community should be supportive of entrusting the management of a root domain name resolution system to a neutral international organization which is recognized by all nations, and should make clear that each nation enjoys equal rights and obligations for the operation of the management right; the third one is to build an international arbitration organization for solving serious network conflicts so that the network of each country can be interconnected equally, and the situation, in which minority countries own network resources of absolute advantage and produce inequality of network rights by using the advantage, can be changed; the fourth one is to build a military mechanism for defending network security both by building a "network border defense" for defending "network territory" so as to block overseas attacks, and by making clear the role played by the army in protecting the nation's network infrastructure and important information system and making clear how to protect or take over these systems in case of military conflicts.

According to Fang Binxing, there is coast defense for the territorial waters, border defense for the territorial land and air defense for the territorial air, so there is supposed to be network defense for the network, which is crucial for national security. The advocacy of cyber sovereignty is in favor of gaining more support from the international community so as to form the justice strength for restricting the international network hegemony, as well as is beneficial for improving the guidance and education of netizens so as to form the concept of network border defense and safeguard national interests and social security.

11.1.9 Viewpoint of Guo Shize from the PLA of China (March 2013)

In March 2013, Guo Shize stated in his article Analysis of Cyberspace and Relevant Concepts[13] delivered on MILITARY ART that cyber sovereignty could be described to be "the state power to control the network resources and all software and hardware devices in its cyberspace, and the power of handling network affairs independently."

According to Guo Shize, cyber sovereignty should specifically include the internally superior right, the external right of independence, and the self-defense right to prevent aggression. The internally superior right means that the nation exercises its sovereignty so that all of the network-involving sections, information and devices within the country are subject to the management of the country; the external right of independence refers to the right to independently handle all of the domestic network-involving affairs in accordance with relevant rules of international laws and without being intervened by foreign forces, for instance, the country

[13]Guo SZ (2013) Analysis of cyberspace and relevant concepts, Military Art.

has the right to formulate network-involving policies, laws and regulations, build organizations and institutions and determine the operation modes according to its own will; the right of self-defense refers to the nations' right to build its national defense so as to prevent its cyberspace from being invaded, and the right to perform self-defense in case of cyberspace invasion.

11.1.10 Viewpoint of Andrew Liaropoulos from the University of Piraeus, Greece (March 2013)

In the 8th International Conference on Information Warfare and Security (ICIW) held in March 2013, Andrew Liaropoulos from the Department of International and European Studies of the University of Piraeus, Greece published his article: Exercising State Sovereignty in Cyberspace: An International Cyber-Order Under Construction.[14] In the article, he points out: cyberspace, in common with the other four domains (land, sea, air and outer space), is just a reflection of the current international system, and state sovereignty in cyberspace is needed to regulate the cyber domain and gradually reach an international cyber-order.

11.1.11 Viewpoints in the Report of Group of Governmental Experts on Developments in the Field of Information and Telecommunications in the Context of International Security (June 2013)

On June 24, 2013, the 68th session of UN General Assembly approved the Report of Group of Governmental Experts on Developments in the Field of Information and Telecommunications in the Context of International Security,[15] and it is pointed out in Article 20 of the Report from 15 nations: "State sovereignty and international norms and principles that flow from sovereignty apply to State conduct of ICT-related activities, and to their jurisdiction over ICT infrastructure within their territory." In 2015, the 70th session of UN General Assembly examined and approved the Report of Group of Governmental Experts on Development in the

[14]Liaropoulos A (2013) Exercising state sovereignty in cyberspace: an international cyber-order under construction?In: 8th international conference on information warfare and security. http://connection.ebscohost.com/c/%20articles/86139901/exercising-state-sovereignty-cyberspace-international-cyber-order-under-construction [2017-3-1].

[15]Item 94 of Provisional Agenda in the 68th session of UN General Assembly, Developments in the Field of Information and Telecommunications in the Context of International Security. http://www.un.org/ga/search/view_doc.asp?symbol=A/68/98&referer=/english/&Lang=C [2016-9-1].

Field of Information and Telecommunications in the Context of International Security,[16] and Article 20 in A/68/98 of 2013 was reiterated in Article 27 of the new report from 20 nations. At the same time, the following proposals for applying international laws to ICT were brought up in Article 28: ① States have jurisdiction over the ICT infrastructure located within their territory; ② In their use of ICTs, States must observe principles of international law, State sovereignty, sovereign equality, the settlement of disputes by peaceful means and non-intervention in the internal affairs of other States; States must comply with their obligations under international law to respect and protect human rights and fundamental freedoms.

11.1.12 Viewpoints in the Tallinn Manual on the International Law Applicable to Cyber Warfare (2013)

The Tallinn Manual on the International Law Applicable to Cyber Warfare[17] (Tallinn Manual 1.0 for short) published in 2013 is regarded as the classical principle of NATO countries, and is commonly recognized by NATO countries. In the Tallinn Manual, "Sovereignty over cyberspace" is right in Rule 1 in Sect. 1, Chapter I. Details given by Tallinn Manual are as follows:

A State may exercise control over cyber infrastructure and activities within its sovereign territory.

(1) This rule emphasizes the fact, although no State may claim sovereignty over cyberspace per se; States may exercise sovereign prerogatives over any cyber infrastructure located on their territory, as well as activities associated with that cyber infrastructure.
(2) The accepted definition of "sovereignty" was set forth in the Island of Palmas Arbitral Award of 1928. It provides that "sovereignty in the relations between States signifies independence. Independence in regard to a portion of the globe is the right to exercise therein, to the exclusion of any other State, the functions of a State".
(3) It is the sovereignty that a State enjoys over territory that gives it the right to control cyber infrastructure and cyber activities within its territory. Accordingly, cyber infrastructure situated in the land territory internal waters, territorial sea (including its bed and subsoil), archipelagic waters, or national airspace is subject to the sovereignty of the territorial State.

---

[16]Item 93 of Provisional Agenda in the 70th session of UN General Assembly, Developments in the Field of Information and Telecommunications in the Context of International Security. http://www.un.org/ga/search/view_doc.asp?symbol=A/70/174&referer=/english/&Lang=C [2016-9-1].

[17]The NATO Cooperative Cyber Defence Centre of Excellence, Tallinn Manual on the International Law Applicable to Cyber Warfare, 2013. http://csef.ru/media/articles/3990/3990.pdf [2017-3-1].

(4) Sovereignty implies that a State may control access to its territory and generally enjoys, within the limits set by treaty and customary international law, the exclusive right to exercise jurisdiction and authority on its territory. Exceptions include the use of force pursuant to the right of self-defense (Rule 13) and in accordance with actions authorized or mandated by the United Nations Security Council (Rule 18).

(5) A State's sovereignty over cyber infrastructure within its territory has two consequences. First, that cyber infrastructure is subject to legal and regulatory control by the State. Second, the State's territorial sovereignty protects such cyber infrastructure. It does not matter whether it belongs to the government or to private entities or individuals, nor do the purposes it serves matter.

(6) A cyber operation by a State directed against cyber infrastructure located in another State may violate the latter's sovereignty. It certainly does so if it causes damage. The International Group of Experts could achieve no consensus as to whether the placement of malware, which causes no physical damage, (as with malware used to monitor activities) constitutes a violation of sovereignty.

(7) If such cyber operations are intended to coerce the government (and not otherwise permitted under international law), the operation may constitute a prohibited "intervention" or a prohibited "use of force" (Rules 10 to 12). A cyber operation that qualifies as an "armed attack" triggers the right of individual or collective self-defense (Rule 13). Actions not constituting an armed attack but that are nevertheless in violation of international law may entitle the target State to resort to countermeasures (Rule 9). Security Council-mandated or authorized actions under Chapter VII of the United Nations Charter (Rule 18), including those involving cyber operations, do not constitute a violation of the target State's sovereignty.

(8) A State may consent to cyber operations conducted from its territory or to remote cyber operations involving cyber infrastructure that is located on its territory. Consider a case in which non-State actors are engaged in unlawful cyber activities on State A's territory. State A does not have the technical ability to put an end to those activities and therefore requests the assistance of State B. State B's ensuing cyber operations on State A's territory would not be a violation of the latter's sovereignty. Consent may also be set forth in a standing treaty. For example, abasing agreement may authorize a sending State's military force to conduct cyber operations from or within the receiving State's territory.

(9) Customary or treaty law may restrict the exercise of sovereign rights by the territorial State. For example, international law imposes restrictions on interference with the activities of diplomatic premises and personnel. Similarly, a State's sovereignty in the territorial sea, archipelagic waters or straits used for international navigation is limited under customary international law by the rights of innocent passage, archipelagic sea lanes passage, and transit passage, respectively.

(10) In the cyber context, the principle of sovereignty allows a State to, inter alia, restrict or protect (in part or in whole) access to the internet, without prejudice to applicable international law, such as human rights or international telecommunications law. The fact that cyber infrastructure located in a given State's territory is linked to the global telecommunications network cannot be interpreted as a waiver of its sovereign rights over that infrastructure.

(11) A coastal State's sovereignty over the seabed lying beneath its territorial sea allows that State full control over the placement of any submarine cables thereon. This is a critical right because submarine cables currently carry the bulk of international internet communications. As to submarine cables beyond the territorial sea, Article 79(2) of the Convention on the Law of the Sea limits the extent to which a coastal State may interfere with submarine cables on its continental shelf.

(12) Although States may not exercise sovereignty over cyberspace per se, States may exercise their jurisdiction vis-à-vis cyber-crimes and other cyber activities pursuant to the bases of jurisdiction recognized in international law (Rule 2).

(13) With regard to cyber infrastructure aboard sovereign immune platforms, see Rule 4.

(14) Traditionally, the notion of the violation of sovereignty was limited to actions undertaken by, or attributable to, States. However, there is an embryonic view proffered by some scholars that cyber operations conducted by non-State actors may also violate a State's sovereignty (especially the aspect of territorial integrity).

11.1.13 Viewpoints from Topi Tuukkanen of the National Defense University of Finland (2013)

In 2013, Topi Tuukkanen from the National Defense University of Finland published his article Sovereignty in the Cyber Domain[18] on The Fog of Cyber Defence, which is the periodical of the National Defense University of Finland. In this article, he points out: The Westphalian state system is challenged by cyberspace; the central concept of the system (sovereignty and its territorial manifestations) needs yet to be enforced in the cyber domain; nations need to monitor the on-going development trends—ideally also to influence them. Nations are recommended to establish a multi-national cross-scientific research program to consider the implications and challenges of cyberspace.

According to Tuukkanen, international legal scholars consider that the concept of sovereignty is challenged by the nature and characteristics of cyberspace. Due to

[18]Tuukkanen T (2013) Sovereignty in the cyber domain. Fog Cyber Defence 37–45. http://www.doria.fi/bitstream/handle/10024/88689/TheFogofCyberDefenceNDU2013.pdf [2016-9-25].

the structure characteristics of Internet, this challenge makes it difficult to exercise state sovereignty.

According to Tuukkanen, there seems to be a growing number of international legal scholars supporting the position that cyberspace is not a "fifth domain", so new norms of international law would be needed. On the contrary, states seem to agree that customary international law is in principle applicable to cyberspace although there may be a need for adaptation to the specific characteristics of cyberspace. Since Internet technologies offer anonymity and ubiquity, and the World-Wide-Web is an environment for connecting networks, telecommunication infrastructures, information systems and services, it seems to be logical to make cyberspace a "global commons" so that cyberspace in its entirety is not subject to the sovereignty of a single state or a group of states. Even if cyberspace in some circumstances may be considered as "global commons", the existing state practices point to the fact that the components of cyberspace are neither immune to state sovereignty nor to the exercise of jurisdiction. A clear example is the fight against cyberspace crimes. Furthermore, states regulate legally, functionally and technically the operations of Internet service providers and the telecommunication infrastructure utilities. Cyberspace is constructed by physical equipment, which is usually located within the territory of a state and is owned either by government entities or by enterprises, so the mere fact that a component has been connected to the World-Wide-Web, or Internet, is not to be considered a waiver from the state jurisdiction. Of course, the technologies, protocols, and properties pose challenges to the actual exercise of state sovereignty but that does not mean that the state could not overcome the challenges.

Tuukkanen believes that the principle of territorial sovereignty in cyberspace stems from the notion that the cyber infrastructure is located on the national land territory, on the territorial waters, in the national airspace, in a registered vessel or aircraft. However, there are several exceptions such as the diplomatic immunity. While cyber infrastructure falls under the jurisdiction and the state sovereignty, the same principle simultaneously protects states from the interference of other states, and, in case of this "protection", it is irrelevant whether the infrastructure is owned by governmental agencies or by private industries.

Tuukkanen concludes that the principle of state sovereignty and the right of a state to exercise territorial jurisdiction apply to the cyber infrastructure within the territory concerned. Moreover, the United States is also regulating the following cyberspace activities: activities initiated by individuals in the territory, or activities those appear within the territory, or activities those produce harmful effects on the territory. These legal constructs translate to similar conceptions in the technological domain: cyber event originating internally but terminating externally; cyber event originating externally but terminating internally; cyber event transiting. For cyber events originating and terminating internally are domestic issues to be addressed by national criminal legislation.

11.1.14 Viewpoint of Wang Yonggang from the Communication and Information Technology Commission of Construction Central (February 2015)

On February 5, 2015, Wang Yonggang from the Communication and Information Technology Commission of Construction Central delivered an expert opinion, i.e. *To Perfect Legislation, Make Cyber Sovereignty Clear, and Control Data Sovereignty*[19] on the Peoples Network, wherein cyber sovereignty refers to the generic term of the following rights owned by sovereign countries: the ownership and control power of Internet infrastructure and key hardware equipment; the independent intellectual property rights of Internet software technology; the speaking right to safeguard the state will and mainstream ideology in the field of Internet communication; the right to safeguard citizens' freedom of network communication and information security of the nation, organizations and individuals. Historically, the scope of national sovereignty is dynamic and developmental, because it varies and is expanded following the expansion of the space of human activities. National sovereignty expands from the primary land towards ocean, sky and outer space. When cyberspace appears, the national sovereignty will inevitably extend towards the cyberspace. "Territorial network" has already been a national sovereignty coordinated with land, ocean, sky and outer space.

According to Wang Yonggang, it was pointed out in The Internet in China (Full Text)[20] issued in China in June 2010: "The Chinese government believes that the Internet is an important infrastructure facility for the nation. Within Chinese territory, the Internet is under the jurisdiction of Chinese sovereignty. The Internet sovereignty of China should be respected and protected." In other words, the Internet sovereignty scope of China is just the scope of Chinese territory. Once the cyber sovereignty is made clear, it is possible to define the actors of network behaviors and illegal activities. For instance, individuals or groups of people who conduct network sabotage can be defined as hackers; network sabotage conducted by military can be regarded as armed attacks among nations.

[19] To Perfect Legislation, Make Cyber Sovereignty Clear, and Control Data Sovereignty. http://opinion.people.com.cn/n/2015/0205/c1003-26511363.html [2016-9-22].

[20] The Internet in China (Full Text). http://politics.people.com.cn/GB/1026/11813615.html [2016-10-1].

11.1.15 Viewpoint from Erin Jackson of the Netherlands (April 2015)

On April 15, 2015, Erin Jackson pointed out in the article Cyber Sovereignty: Centralized Authority in a Decentralized Domain?[21] published on a Dutch news website named "The Hague Institute": Since the Peace of Westphalia (1648) gave rise to the principle of non-interference of states, the concept of sovereignty has underpinned the international system in the digital domain, however, the concept of cyber sovereignty (the extension of State sovereignty into the cyberspace) is hotly contested.

Jackson points out, since the ambit of national sovereignty could previously be delineated on the basis of physical boundaries, the rapid expansion of information communications technologies and the Internet over the past few decades raises questions about jurisdiction over Net-based activity. Currently, the management of the web is based on a multi-stakeholder approach, involving the technical community, the private sector, governments and civil society. However, revelations by Snowden on American cyber espionage and global surveillance programs cast doubt over the security of private data, and this event has led some States to consider data localization (Brazil, Germany, and India for example), and others to place restrictions on freedom of the Internet within their borders.

As for the above problems, Jackson focuses on analyzing the standpoints of China, Shanghai Cooperation Organization and the UN. Jackson indicates that China strengthened its Internet firewall, and the firewall is even capable of blocking virtual private networks (VPN). In a statement to the UN General Assembly in 2013, the Chinese delegation on Information and Cyber Security elaborated on the idea of cyber sovereignty, stating that "countries should enjoy state sovereignty in information space. The governments are entitled to managing its network-related activities and have jurisdiction over its information infrastructures within its territory." Jackson mentions that the idea of cyber sovereignty was put forward by (members of the Shanghai Cooperation Organization) China, Russia, Tajikistan and Uzbekistan in 2011 in a letter addressed to the UN Secretary-General. Jackson indicates the working achievements of the Group of Governmental Experts on Developments in the Field of Information and Telecommunications in the Context of International Security, pointing out that the UN does not explicitly mention the expression "cyber sovereignty" but does state that state sovereignty applies to State conduct of ICT-related activities and to their jurisdiction over ICT infrastructure within their territory.

According to Jackson, ideological differences bring obstacles to the Internet, one aspect is the freedom of expression, and the other is that sovereignty may be used for restricting the free flow of information within the governments' jurisdiction. But

---

[21]Erin J. Cyber Sovereignty: Centralized Authority in a Decentralized Domain? 2015-4-14. http://www.thehagueinstituteforglobaljustice.org/atest-insights/latest-insights/commentary/cyber-sovereignty-centralized-authority-in-a-decentralized-domain/ [2016-9-21].

sovereignty is more than a mere prerogative, but also is a set of duties and responsibilities, so the governments need to be careful to master it. Anyway, there could be a centralized authority in such a decentralized domain. Countries need greater consensus on how to regulate cyberspace.

11.1.16 Viewpoint of Scott L. Malcolmson from the Carnegie Foundation of America (April 2016)

On April 3rd, 2016, Scott L. Malcolmson, a researcher from the Carnegie Foundation of America, delivered a article "An open and international Internet came to an end, but did it really exist ever?" on the British website The Guardian.[22] According to the article, under some circumstances, Internet sovereignty means that the nation protects the privacy of its citizens from the surveillance of international enterprises or the infiltration of other nations; however, in some other situations, Internet sovereignty also indicates that the nation is ensured to infringe citizens' privacy at any time and in any manner when it wants. It is inevitable that the nation has the last word as for how to make choices. Computer technology as well as the Internet, that appeared only after a long time, were rooted in national projects and shaped according to national demands. Moreover, since commercial Internet is largely dependent on advertising revenue and other retail forms, there has always been the logic of "localization" behind its huge scale. It is stated in the article that Internet is of great significance to the prosperity of national economy, which leads the nations completely back to the cyberspace.

11.1.17 Viewpoint of Fang Binxing from the Cyber Security Association of China (April 2016)

On April 27, 2016, Fang Binxing, Chairman of Cyber Security Association of China, made a speech titled On Cyber Security at the China-Russia Cyber Security Conference held in Moscow,[23] wherein the concept of cyberspace sovereignty was comprehensively explained. In Fang Binxing's opinion, the cyberspace is formed of four elements, i.e. platform, cyber role, data resource and data processing. In other words, the environment of cyberspace is an assembly of information and

---

[22]British Media. The Internet sovereignty concept of China represents the trend, the US can hardly dominate the network forever. http://www.cankaoxiaoxi.com/china/20160405/1118389.shtml [2016-9-17].

[23]China-Russia Cyberspace Development and Security Forum hosted in Russia by Cyber Security Association of China. http://www.wtoutiao.com/p/171M0Q7.html [2016-9-25].

communication technology systems, and these ICT platforms are the carriers of cyberspace; cyber roles take actions in the cyberspace on behalf of human beings; the forms of activities are data processing, storage and transmission for expressing users' intentions. Therefore, cyberspace is an artificial electromagnetic space with terminal, computer, network devices as platforms, wherein human beings can perform data calculation and communication so as to implement specific activities. In this space, people, devices and things can be organically connected to interact and generate corresponding contents, business, control and other information influencing our life.

At the same time, cyberspace sovereignty inherits the four basic elements of national sovereignty, i.e. "territory, resource, population and regime": wherein "territory" is embodied to be "territorial network" in cyberspace; "resource" is embodied to be "data" in cyberspace; "population" is embodied to be "cyber roles" in cyberspace; "activities" are embodied to be "data manipulation" in cyberspace. The so-called "territorial network" refers to the cyberspace carried by the ICT systems within the territory, and this artificial space is a natural extension of territory. The so-called "cyber roles" refer to the virtual network identities capable of taking active behaviors, such as network accounts, and are subjects of network behaviors. The so-called "data manipulation" refers to the behavioral process of storing, processing, transmitting and displaying data according to human will. Apparently, cyberspace sovereignty is a natural extension of national sovereignty in the cyberspace within its territory, namely, the country has sovereignty (the power to intervene in the data manipulation) over the ICT activities (specific to cyber roles), and ICT system per se (specific to the platform) and its data located in this space.

Fang Binxing provided a general definition of cyberspace sovereignty: the cyberspace sovereignty of a country is established on the ICT systems under the jurisdiction of this country ("territorial network"); its international interconnected domain boundaries are formed by the set of domestic network device ports which are directly connected to the network devices of foreign countries (boundary); activities of network users in the cyberspace are protected by the administration jurisdiction of the country to which the cyberspace belongs (population and regime). The platform forming the cyberspace and its data are subject to the judicial protection of the country (jurisdiction); each nation has equivalent governance status in the Internet interconnection (the right of equality); the operation of the cyberspace infrastructure located within the nation's territory cannot be interfered by foreign countries (the right of independence); the nation has the power as well as military capability of protecting its cyberspace from being infringed (the right of self-defense). Cyberspace sovereignty should be mutually respected among nations (respect for sovereignty); no attack on the cyberspace of other countries (mutual-nonaggression); no mutual-interference of cyberspace management affairs of other countries (non-interference of internal affairs of other countries); the cyberspace sovereignty of each country has equal status in international cyberspace governance (sovereignty equality).

Fang Binxing stressed again that cyberspace sovereignty should be imposed on network territory which needs to be protected by network boundaries. There is coast defense for the territorial waters, border defense for the territorial land and air defense for the territorial air, so there should be "cyber defense" for "territorial network". This is the precondition for cyber army to guard the "territorial network" and to resist the enemy overseas, as well as the first defensive line for maintaining the security of domestic network infrastructure, and also an important symbol for defending cyberspace sovereignty. Therefore, it is extremely crucial to maintain cyberspace sovereignty and establish network border defense.

11.1.18 Viewpoint of Hao Yeli from the China Institute for Innovation and Development Strategy (2016)

In 2016, Hao Yeli, Vice Chair of China Institute for Innovation and Development Strategy has given several speeches.[24] According to Hao Yeli, the resistance from the international community to cyber sovereignty reflects the interest demands of such three cyberspace actors as nations, citizens and the international community, which are specifically expressed in the following three aspects: the first one is to set the cyber sovereignty against the Internet spirit, holding that the exclusiveness of sovereignty is contrary to the interconnection of the Internet's spirit, and that the stress on cyber sovereignty will artificially produce new problems and result in Internet fragmentation; the second one is to set the cyber sovereignty against human rights, holding that Internet should support free speech, and that the intervention of sovereignty blocks free flow of information, wherein the firewall set by China became the focus of public opinion; the third one is to set cyber sovereignty against the multi-stakeholder system in that cyber sovereignty causes the fights for the Internet governance mode, wherein the multi-lateral governance dominated by governments may challenge the governance mode of multi-stakeholders.

According to HaoYeli, the above three major contradictions substantively reflect the conflicts among such three cyberspace actors as nations, citizens and the international community. These three actors start respectively from their own perspective, and generally ignore the other two actors; as a result, a currently non-compromising and irreconcilable situation is formed. To establish a new cyberspace order, it is necessary to inspect the overall situation from the perspectives of three actors and abandon single-point myth and binary opposition, so as to stand in the dimension of cyberspace Community of Common Destiny and scientifically master the unity of opposites of exclusiveness and transference from an overlook perspective. As a matter of fact, the balance and unification between development and security, freedom and order, openness and inclusiveness should

[24]Let the world understand China—Unity of opposites for network sovereignty under three perspectives. http://www.hbyjjx.com/keji/bhukb.html [2016-9-22].

be emphasized among such three actors as nations, citizens and the international community, so as to make clear that the demands of the three actors per se are opposite only when they are put into different categories, rather than absolutely conflicting and contradicting. However, what people eventually want is the overall balance under the big pattern, and the unity of opposites. Some conflicts may be resolved through the shifting of concept and perspective.

Hao Yeli brought up a theory of "Three Perspectives" starting from "Three points" of such three actors of nations, citizens and the international community and using "Three sides", including development and security, freedom and order, and openness and inclusivity for forming a complete and focused zone of mutual visibility, as a result, a stable triangle is obtained. In this triangle, cyberspace is divided into "Three layers", namely, the basic layer, the application layer and the core layer. The core layer contains national characteristics and the sovereignty exclusiveness; the application layer contains citizen characteristics and the sovereignty evolution; the basic layer contains international characteristic and the sovereignty transference.

As stated by Hao Yeli, the focus of sovereignty disputes used to be whether the cyberspace should have sovereignty, which is the evolution or extensibility of sovereignty; however, it is actually an undisputable fact that cyberspace has already become the fifth territory after land, sea, air and space. Instead of whether the cyber sovereignty is admitted, the divergence lies in the recognition of areas covered by sovereignty, which reflects different pain-spots of different nations about cyber security. The international community should respect and understand different concerns of different countries. Therefore, the key to the study is to specifically analyze the divisibility of cyber sovereignty by using a layered approach, so as to find the suitable region for sovereignty exclusiveness and transference. Traditional sovereignty is naturally exclusive, but the cyber sovereignty needs to be transferred in the age of globalization. The basic layer and the application layer have the open and shared transference, while the core layer has the inviolable exclusiveness. It is not allowed to challenge the core interests of sovereign nations by abusing the connectivity of Internet, or to shake the basic platform of "One net for the whole world" by using the exclusiveness of traditional sovereignty. The percentage relationship between transference and exclusiveness will be changed depending on whether the cyber sovereignty is respected by international rules.

11.1.19 Discussion About Cyber Sovereignty by Wikipedia (2016)

The latest definition of cyber sovereignty given by Wikipedia is as follows: ① Network Sovereignty[25] is the effort of a governing entity, such as a state, to create boundaries on a network and then exert a form of control, often in the form of law

[25]Network Sovereignty. https://en.wikipedia.org/wiki/Network_Sovereignty [2016-9-19].

enforcement, over those boundaries. In the context of the internet, the intention is to govern the web and control it within the borders of the state. ② Cyber Sovereignty[26] is a phrase used in the field of internet governance to describe governments' desire to exercise control over the Internet within their own borders, including political, economic, cultural and technological activities.

The above two definitions show that network sovereignty involve the problems of border and control, wherein network sovereignty is the control within the borders, and the control methods are mainly in the form of laws, but also include politics, economy, culture and technology. The governance methods ensured by network sovereignty ensures also include politics, economy, culture and technology.

11.2 Viewpoints Against Cyberspace Sovereignty

There are many kinds of starting points for opposing cyberspace sovereignty. Someone says that Internet is "a global commons" without sovereignty; someone holds that there is no "territorial network" for Internet, such as the Microsoft Azure which has been spread all over the world and created a system of its own; someone believes that Internet has no national boundaries, let alone territory or sovereignty; someone insists that Internet is dominated by the "stakeholder" rather than the government, and there is naturally no sovereignty; someone believes that the free flow of information will be affected in case of cyberspace sovereignty; someone regards Internet as a space for netizens, so the government has no authority over Internet and Internet has nothing to do with the government; someone thinks that cyberspace sovereignty cannot be endowed, otherwise, it may be used by the government for doing evil.

11.2.1 The Theory that Internet Is a Global Commons

Someone says that Internet is "a global commons" without sovereignty. For the pursuit of online enjoyment of unscrupulous, unrestraint and carefree behaviors, people having a good time on Internet firmly believe that Internet is a space in need of no regulation, so they call it "global commons".

In its National Security Strategy 2010,[27] the US used the concept of "Global Commons". According to the National Security Strategy of America, global commons "exist outside exclusive national jurisdictions, are the connective tissue

[26]Cyber Sovereignty. https://en.wikipedia.org/wiki/Cyber_sovereignty [2016-9-19].

[27]National Security Strategy (2010). https://www.whitehouse.gov/sites/default/files/rss_viewer/national_security_strategy.pdf [2016-10-5].

around our globe upon which all nations' security and prosperity depend", and utilizing global commons is an important goal of US national security strategy. The Global Commons does not involve land, nor belongs to affairs within the territory of a nation; it is also faced with security threats, but has no visible enemy or fixed component; to deal with the threats, it is necessary to use a wide range of military and non-military tools including political and diplomatic means, and to, at the same time, expand the cooperation with commercial, industrial and legal stakeholders. In 2010, Abraham M. Denmark stated in *Contested Commons: The Future of American Power in a Multi-Polar World*[28] that there were currently four global commons, i.e. ocean, sky, space and cyberspace, which were basically different from each other. According to some American scholars, Alfred Thayer Mahan, "Father of Sea Power Theory", may be the strategist who brought up the term "global commons" for the very first time; moreover, he used to describe the global ocean as "a broad highway and a vast commons".

As believed by people holding this viewpoint, Internet is a gift from America for the whole world, and the US government has declared that it would never intervene with the Internet, why would other governments want to butt in? In physical space, the behaviors of anybody will be marked by territory, and the territory per se is subject to the jurisdiction of sovereignty, so there is no question about sovereignty existence in physical space; however, due to its interconnection all over the world, Internet is different from the physical space. The light velocity rapidly shortens the geographic distance to be a global village, and causes regime overlapping and sovereignty coverage, thereby making jurisdiction non-operable. Therefore, if Internet is subject to the jurisdiction and domination of no single nation, no nation imposes its law over Internet, and Internet is regarded as international commons like high seas and outer space, everything will be fine for all.

International cooperation is needed for global commons. The fight against Somali pirates in high seas can be performed only with the negotiation of the international community, which is a real behavior of public power. Then, how to deal with the illegal activities within the "commons" of Internet? As a matter of fact, the international community would land, based on the reductionism, every illegal fact onto relevant space of law enforcement, rather than onto the space of "global commons" discussed by the whole world. As for various conflicts and crimes continuously occurring on the Internet, only the government has the power of regulation, but it is not realistic or fair to count on America alone, even if it were the international police, to solve all the problems on the global Internet. To perform effective regulation and build a harmonious, mutual-beneficial and interconnected Internet space, it is necessary to perform power division, which is dependent based on cyber sovereignty only. The fights against Internet crimes in various countries is essentially an extension of national sovereignty in the Internet space. It is a specific

[28]Denmark A, Mulvenon J (2010) Contested commons. In: Contested commons: the future of American power in a multi-polar world, pp 3–48. https://s3.amazonaws.com/files.cnas.org/documents/CNAS-Contested-Commons_1.pdf [2016-12-31].

manifestation of the state's will to impose on the Internet. If the government fails to get its legal hand into Internet, it will be impossible to settle the interest fights on the Internet.

The viewpoint that "Internet is a global commons" is wrong for the following reason: the viewpoint holder ignores that disputes also exist in the cyberspace, such as interest conflicts, seeking protection from a third party, crime fighting and so on. As the Internet is a gift to the whole world from America, does the Internet need America for law enforcement? At least the US government per se would not take the role of World Police for Internet in public. Of course, if the conflict on the Internet is reflected inside of the service provided by an entity, or if the conflict can be stopped when the service provider suspends the service, then the service provider does have the capacity to control the situation. For instance, detailed administrative provisions have been provided for Facebook so as to strictly control the speeches on Facebook. However, when the conflict cannot be solved by a service provider, who will come to help? For example, if the dispute inside of the enterprise goes beyond the handling ability of the enterprise, it is natural to turn to the government. For another example, if the dispute is between different service providers, who will be the arbitrator surpassing the service providers? In the case of the Eastern Court of Virginia, America ruling that Shanghai Meiya Company has to stop using the domain name "cnnews.com",[29] occurring in 2001, shows that the national sovereignty of America has naturally extended into the Internet space at the same time as it was imposed over the NSI Company (Company of Network Solutions) which is an American domain name registrar.

In the *Cyber security: Next Steps to Protect Our Critical Infrastructure*,[30] the Committee on Commerce, Science, and Transportation, United States Senate also recognized cyberspace merely as "pseudo commons", "rather than global commons". It is stated in the article: "Cyberspace is a "pseudo commons," more like a condominium or a shopping mall. It is a shared global infrastructure." "Cyberspace is not a global commons. It is a shared global infrastructure. Cyberspace is in fact more like a condominium, where there are many contiguous owners." "This ideology of a self-organizing global commons has shaped Internet policy and cyber security, but we must now recognize that this approach is inadequate. Two reasons: first, sophisticated intelligence and military services will overwhelm private efforts to secure networks; second, in the absence of government intervention, adequate security will not be provided."

The global village phenomenon caused by the Internet seems to be the geographic coverage brought by Internet particularity, but it is essentially the challenge

---

[29]Does Cnnews seem to be similar to CNN? Shanghai "Meiya Online" fought against CNN for its infringement accusation. http://www.people.com.cn/GB/channel5/569/20001018/277103.html [2016-9-19].

[30]U.S. Government Printing Office. Cybersecurity: Next Steps to Protect Our Critical Infrastructure, Hearing, Before the Committee on Commerce, Science, and Transportation, United States Senate, One Hundred Eleventh Congress, Second Session. 2010-2-23. https://fas.org/irp/congress/2010_hr/cybersec.pdf [2016-9-6].

of the new age and new technology to the law. In the past laws, troublemakers and sufferers are usually supposed to be in the same place and subject to the same jurisdiction. Due to Internet, it is possible that troublemakers and sufferers are in different judicial areas and even subject to different laws. Apparently, facing this challenge, people need to bring up new mechanisms so as to react actively, rather than allowing the chaos of Internet space. As political, military, economic, cultural, and social elements are loaded onto the Internet by nations, China initiated the action of "Internet+" that is highly dependent on the Internet, and the Internet will never be allowed to be a disorderly space.

In fact, as for different locations, there were agreements that both the location of the troublemaker and that of the sufferer have the right of jurisdiction. Since it has become a normal state in Internet crimes that the location of the troublemaker and that of the sufferer are different, the nation can provide "Internet Courts" so as to deal with trans-regional Internet crimes in a normal mode. Transnational crimes can be negotiated and disposed based on consensus of nations, or turned to the International Court according to international consensus. In other words, if the modes in physical society can be directly introduced into the cyberspace, the paradox of "global village" can be solved. Of course, if consensus cannot be reached because of ideological differences, then the only way is to establish the "National Firewall". It's like that, if one country is determined to support terrorism or is opposed to the forces of other countries, then other countries must defend by consolidating the frontier.

In a word, since network society is a mapping of physical society and there is no special exception, the opinion that Internet is global commons is untenable to deny the existence of cyber sovereignty. It is true that commons in physical spaces can generate corresponding network commons. For instance, servers may be established on pirate ships in high seas, and some countries may build Internet routing devices in space commons, without sovereignty jurisdiction, the only way to cope with these conditions is to cut off the connection with them.

11.2.2 The Theory that There Is no "Territorial Network" for the Internet

Someone holds that there is no "territorial network" for Internet, such as the Microsoft Azure Cloud which has been spread all over the world and created a system of its own.[31] If a regional cyberspace is established by an enterprise, then this cyberspace belongs to market behaviors, and is a virtual space built by the enterprise offering the facilities. This space is built by non-governmental behaviors and does not have common social properties, so the concept of "territorial network" does not exist at all. This space should not become the sphere of influence of

[31]Microsoft Azure. https://azure.microsoft.com/zh-cn/overview/what-is-azure/ [2016-9-19].

nations, because it cannot be divided by the nations in the same way as that for the natural spaces including the land territory, territorial waters and territorial air space. For western countries, private domains are sacred and inviolable, so is the space formed by servers, and no intervention from the government is allowed. Azure Cloud has spread all over the world, and its operation basis is the supposition that Internet is a global commons. As a result, Azure Cloud can be a Microsoft kingdom, and performs self-management just like a massive ship floating in high seas. In addition, all of Google's search engines all over the world have the function of filtering. Instead of being subject to judicial regulations, the basis of filtration is entrusted to a "Lumen" organization, and it's up to the "Lumen" organization to determine whether filtration will be executed. In this way, Google proves that it acts with self-discipline.[32] For another example, the appearance of Bitcoin apparently has nothing to do with the financial entities of any country. It came from and became popular on the Internet, and serves netizens; moreover, it has no national attributes, no regime property, or no subject of law enforcement, and no one has claimed to be the inventor of this system. This is also a reflection of the absence of "territorial network" or sovereignty.

As a matter of fact, the Cloud computing platform can make a Cloud entity very large by using its structure characteristics. It seems that a unified cyberspace is built, and overlapping is objectively formed in different physical spaces or different territories, but the existence of the concept of "territorial network" cannot be denied for this reason, because the government of any nation could shut down the ICT facilities within its territory. Given that Azure Cloud platform has the natural attribute of being transnational, it still can be divided and ruled according to the principle of "Reductionism". As a result, the government of a nation can perform administrative jurisdiction for the part of cloud computing platform constituted by the server within its territory, such as to propose demands from the perspective of commerce and industry, or even from the perspective of security.

The viewpoint that "There is no territorial network for Internet" is wrong for the following reason: the opinion holders ignore that the ICT carriers for forming the cyberspace exist within the territory, so the hands of law will naturally extend into this space via ICT facilities. From the perspective of protection, when it is necessary to turn to the government for protection, which government would be reliable, the regime to which the owner of the carrier assets belongs, or the regime of the asset location? The substance lies in that the intervention is meaningful only by the regime having effective compulsory means. Take the fight for domain name infringement as an example, if compulsory means exist in the domain name service sector, the regime of the country to which the domain name service sector belongs will have the capacity of intervention.

If, subject to jurisdiction, the government of one country orders Azure Cloud to shut down the part of computer system within its territory, does the cyberspace it is carrying not disappear consequently? If the carrier of cyberspace is stopped, then

---

[32]Lumen, About us. https://www.lumendatabase.org/pages/about [2016-9-19].

everything would be meaningless. Therefore, if the regime can force the platform carrying the cyberspace to stop, then it will have natural jurisdiction over this platform, and the jurisdiction will naturally extend to corresponding cyberspace. This is the reason for the correspondence between "territorial network" and "territory". It is like the case wherein no one is allowed to infringe a private construction but the law-enforcement department is allowed to enter for law enforcement according to sovereignty.

From the reductionist point of view, the cyberspace carried by the territorial ICT systems dependent is bound to be are subject to national sovereignty, and it cannot be a vacuum zone. The cyberspace hosted by the ICT systems located within the territory of the country is the country's "territorial network" and is protected by the state sovereignty. It is also stated in Tallinn Manual on the International Law Applicable to Cyber Warfare[33] published in 2013: "A State may exercise control over cyber infrastructure and activities within its sovereign territory", "States may exercise sovereign prerogatives over any cyber infrastructure located on their territory, as well as activities associated with that cyber infrastructure", "It is the sovereignty that a State enjoys over territory that gives it the right to control cyber infrastructure and cyber activities within its territory. Accordingly, cyber infrastructure situated in the land territory internal waters, territorial sea (including its bed and subsoil), archipelagic waters, or national airspace is subject to the sovereignty of the territorial State". In Cybersecurity: Next Steps to Protect Our Critical Infrastructure, the Committee on Commerce, Science, and Transportation, United States Senate also recognized that cyberspace is subject to the sovereignty control, and it is stated in the article: "Cyberspace is an artificial construct produced by machines. Those machines are all owned by individuals or organizations and all exist in some physical location that is subject to the sovereign control of some nation." The network security administration department of America is set up at the Department of Homeland Security, which proves from another aspect that America also believes that network security issues involve homeland security and Internet is an extension of homeland. This is the reason why the network security issues are directly assigned to the Department of Homeland Security, and it is shown that America also believes subconsciously that territorial network and territory are united.

In summary, all power comes down to means, and there will be no regulation without means. Therefore, it is untenable to deny the existence of cyber sovereignty by affirming that there is no "territorial network" for a country.

---

[33]The NATO Cooperative Cyber Defence Centre of Excellence, Tallinn Manual on the International Law Applicable to Cyber Warfare, 2013. http://csef.ru/media/articles/3990/3990.pdf [2017-3-1].

11.2.3 The Theory that Internet Has no National Boundary

Someone believes that Internet has no national boundary, let alone territory or sovereignty. Historically, the Internet is a gift to the whole world from America. The Internet was first operated in America, and then all nations around the globe accessed the Internet of the US, and made it evolve into the current international Internet. Of course, those who accessed the Internet are naturally subject to the administration of America. As a result, many people naturally believe that the international internet is the Americans' Internet, and is a form extending to all nations all around the world. In the treaties for nations accessed to America, sometimes there are even infrastructure provisions clearly indicating that it is not allowed to block information flow at the access side. As a result, many people believe that the network, which was built by Americans and had extended all over the world, is completely interconnected without national boundaries, and even hold that the firewall set in China is merely a very special case and is insufficient to deny the international internet's essence of no national border. Consequently, they think it is meaningless to discuss cyberspace sovereignty in the cyberspace without national boundaries.

In 1996, David Johnson and David Post from Electronic Frontier Foundation proposed that there can be no equipment capable of blocking some individual electronic signal from going in and out of a national border; moreover, the volume of information communication is huge and almost infinite while the filtration equipment is limited, so it is impossible to filter information.[34] Joel R. Reidenberg from the US Fordham University came up with a "permeable national border" on the basis that Virtual Private Network (VPN) needs to pass through countless networks and believes that assets can easily penetrate these networks. Even though nations can exercise cyberspace sovereignty, its power on the network is limited, so the existence of network weakens national sovereignty.[35]

In fact, whether the Internet boundaries exist is a problem of technical capacity. If there is the "territorial network", there will certainly be borders, and the differences only lie in whether to manage it or not, whether the nation could manage it, and whether the nation is capable of managing it well. www.uriminzokkiri.com, which is the official website of North Korea, is positioned in Shenyang of China. The visit to this website from South Korea will be hijacked by the warning website of South Korea (warning.or.kr), and the visitors will be warned that this website is a website of harmful information. IP addresses on North Korea's official website are not accessible in South Korea, and it shows that South Korea blocks the websites of North Korea by setting a national firewall at the national network boundary, rather than by domain name hijacking. Apparently, Internet boundary exists in South

---

[34]Law and Borders: The Rise of Law in Cyberspace. https://cyber.harvard.edu/is02/readings/johnson-post.html [2016-9-17].

[35]Reidenberg JR (2005) The simplification of international data privacy rules. Fordham Intl L J. http://heinonline.org/HOL/LandingPage?handle=hein.journals/frdint29&div=43 [2016-9-25].

Korea and is controlled; the controlling measures taken by South Korea within this boundary make it impossible for users inside of this boundary to log onto www.uriminzokkiri.com of North Korea. According to the information from OpenNet Initiative Bulletin,[36] ISPs in Bahrain, UAE, Qatar, Oman, Saudi Arabia, Kuwait, Yemen, Sudan, and Tunisia use McAfee and other Western-built automated filtering solutions to block the content deemed by its government as harmful information, and Israel, Germany and Belgium are also leading exporters of Backbone firewall technology. Because of these facts, the theory that Internet has no boundary collapses without being attacked.

The viewpoint that "Internet has no national border" is wrong for the following reason: the opinion holders provide a fallacious assumption, namely, the nation-to-nation Internet is directly connected, so there is no management entry point, and no way to find out the Internet borders and to execute management. On the one hand, the correspondence between border and sovereignty is not scientific. For instance, there is no border in the outer space, and it is impossible to directly exercise sovereignty in the outer space. But the outer space is at least jointly managed by the international organization formed by sovereign countries, so this is an indicator of sovereignty transference and reflects its sovereignty characteristics, and it is proved that the absence of borders is not a reason for ignoring sovereignty. Transportation networks (air transportation, sea transportation) are interconnected but still have borders and customs, which shows that interconnection, is not the requirement for giving up sovereignty. On the other hand, the Internet borders between nations are definite, and are formed by the set of ports of domestic routers in immediate connection with foreign network equipment; at the same time, there are facts showing that nations can managing them by taking necessary measures. Therefore, it is untenable to deny the existence of cyberspace sovereignty based on the theory that Internet has no national boundary.

11.2.4 The Theory that Internet Is Dominated by the Stakeholder

Someone insists that Internet is dominated by the "stakeholder" rather than by the government, so there is naturally no sovereignty. Western countries led by the US believe that the Internet belongs to the network builders, and is the result of the internet builders and other enterprises for the benefit of mankind. Enterprises that use the Internet as the survival basis will certainly do their best to promote the development of the Internet, and they will treat the Internet in a mental state of "stand or fall together". As a result, Internet should be continuously operated by

[36]OpenNet Initiative Bulletin. West Censoring East: The Use of Western Technologies by Middle East Censors. http://goodtimesweb.org/diplomacy/ONI_WestCensoringEast.pdf [2016-12-31].

relevant enterprises that construct, operate, manage and use the Internet in the form of "stakeholder", and governmental interference is not needed.

The US believes that "the process of multi-stakeholder has provided the flexibility and global scalability needed for coping with the challenge of Internet policies." In addition, John Forbes Kerry, Secretary of State, has clearly expressed his opinion on the mode of multi-stakeholder, and regards that the mode is crucial for Internet to maintain its global vitality. US Secretary of State Hillary Clinton stated the following content at the Freedom Online Conference: the United States supports the public-private collaboration that now exists to manage the technical evolution of the Internet in real time; the United States supports the principles of multi-stakeholder internet governance developed by more than 30 nations in the OECE in 2011; the position of America can be concluded by an American phrase, "If it isn't broke, don't fix it."[37] The US Congress even passed a special resolution to oppose ITU's involvement in Internet management. Google and other Internet enterprises are more firmly opposed to mentioning Internet management in ITR because ITU is on the behalf of sovereign countries and ITU's involvement into Internet management shows that national sovereignty will set foot in Internet governance.

As a matter of fact, international organizations of the Internet usually have no government background. This phenomenon was also very popular early in China, and this is one major reason for providing the China Internet Network Information Center (CNNIC) in the network center of the China Academy of Sciences, rather than in the government (e.g. the primary Ministry of Electronics, the Ministry of Information Industry, and the later Ministry of Industry and Information).[38] The main purpose of the "stakeholder" theory is to dominate the construction and operation of Internet, and avoid too much governmental interference of Internet affairs, so as to promote rapid development of global Internet.

Technically, the key role played by the "stakeholder" is understandable. In this way, since the Internet development mode is dominated by the great powers of information technology, "the law of the jungle" is objectively formed and dominates Internet technology evolution. However, it's already been an objective reality, and more countries need to be supported and gradually get involved. From the perspective of public policies, the development of Internet obviously cannot be dominated by non-government organizations with no administrative powers.

The viewpoint of "stakeholder-dominated" is wrong because of the following reasons. The first one is that the opinion holders counter-pose the stakeholder and the government. In fact, the government per se can also be the stakeholder; meanwhile, the government always can be the chief representative of the stakeholder because of the resources it masters. The second reason is that conflicts

[37]Secretary of Senate Clinton's Remarks at the Freedom Online Conference. http://iipdigital.usembassy.gov/st/chinese/texttrans/2011/12/20111209163103x0.5344769.html#ixzz4KZLXQOpR [2016-9-18].

[38]CNNIC had become an official public institution of Cyberspace Administration of China since 2014.

inevitable exist among stakeholders because the fundamental starting point of the stakeholder is the interests of their own, and sometimes one stakeholder may even damage the interests of others so as to sustain those of their own. However, the government's participation will balance the interests, and maximize the comprehensive interests of its own country. The third reason is that the stakeholder always starts from the perspective of interest maximization, and cares little about the function of "universal service", as a result, the interests of underdeveloped regions and information technology weak powers will not be taken into consideration when decisions are made, which makes it harder for information technology weak powers to catch up with the pace of modernization. The last reason is that the stakeholder does not have the qualification and capacity of formulating Internet public policies. It is definitely stated in the Declaration of Principles of the UN World Summit on the Information Society: "Policy authority for Internet-related public policy issues is the sovereign right of States. They have rights and responsibilities for international Internet-related public policy issues."

The US has a cyber army, which openly shows that national interests exist in Internet and need to be protected by the national army, rather than being handled by the stakeholder only. Of course, the cyber army of America is closely connected with enterprises; moreover, it is clearly expressed that America attaches great importance to and is highly dependent on stakeholders. However, it does not mean that the government has quit the exercising of rights in cyberspace. According to the Patriot Act of America, the law enforcement departments have been empowered to ask the US Internet Service Providers to provide intelligence cooperation, which shows that America has imposed national sovereignty over the Internet operation and Internet stakeholders.[39] In fact, from the perspective of protecting citizens' and netizens' interests, and from the perspective of protecting the legal rights of stakeholders of all nations, the biggest role can be played only by the exercising of national sovereignty. Therefore, the essence of denying cyberspace sovereignty because Internet should be regulated by stakeholders is still to exclude government involvement in global Internet governance.

11.2.5 The Theory of Free Flow of Internet Information

Someone holds that the free flow of information will be affected in case of cyberspace sovereignty. It is widely believed by western countries that Internet information should flow freely, and no one is expected to have the right to stop it.

On January 21, 2010, the US Secretary of State Hillary Diane Rodham Clinton made a speech[40] on Internet freedom at the Freedom Online Conference held in

[39]Wikipedia. Patriot Act. https://en.wikipedia.org/wiki/Patriot_Act [2016-9-21].

[40]Hillary Clinton's Historic Speech on Global Internet Freedom. https://techliberation.com/2010/01/21/hillary-clintons-historic-speech-on-global-internet-freedom/ [2016-9-21].

Washington D.C., wherein she brought up the concept of "Internet freedom", asserted that "The open form and free flow of information free from state sovereignty are values that deserve strong advocacy", and announced to make "the freedom to connect" as a basic diplomatic objective; America supports that people all around the world can enjoy this freedom, so it calls on other countries to do the same, and blames China, Burma, Cuba, Vietnam and Iran for their restrictions on Internet. However, while calling for Internet freedom, it also blames "WikiLeaks" as an act of theft.

"Internet freedom" obviously makes America's intention of preventing global information space from being restricted by a traditional sovereignty concept obvious. Its core is to expand the application scope of American sovereignty and develop the national interests of America, and which is an "enclosure movement" in cyberspace. The US government preached "Internet freedom", and further blamed other countries' behavior of restricting Internet freedom. This is substantively a hard sell of so-called "freedom" value to other nations of the world by its super-strong advantages in information technology, in its control power over Internet root servers, and in huge information industry and market. The US tried to perform online political propaganda, guidance on value and dissemination of ideas, and to master the jurisdiction of cyberspace, so as to further consolidate its advantageously dominating position in the global network field.

For holders of this theory, once cyberspace sovereignty exists, the Internet information freedom will be restricted by the legal systems of the sovereign countries in cyberspace, so the cyberspace sovereignty is unacceptable. As a matter of fact, the US took part in the UN's Group of Governmental Experts for Information Security and approved the UN viewpoint that national sovereignty is applicable to the ICT activities of nations, but they are afraid that restrictions in physical society on harmful information will be introduced into the cyberspace. Physical society is limited to a local area, and people may get used to local policy environment, so chances of penetration from outsiders are slim, which blocks the information dissemination plot of western world; on the contrary, since cyberspace has no geographic restrictions, western countries' strong desires for information dissemination are inspired, so they are strongly against nations' control of information from far away. Nowadays, the new worldview prevails that human rights surpass sovereignty, so the free flow of information is stressed more by western countries.

The opinion of "free flow of Internet information" is wrong for the following reasons: the opinion holders ignore the nations' determination to protect their own political and cultural security, for instance, Islamic countries will never allow their cultural and political foundations to be shaken by Internet. In addition, so long as there is no lack of relevant means in the cyberspace, governments of all nations will try their best to restrict the behaviors restricted by the governments in physical society, and they will never let their authority be challenged. According to Theresa M. May, who was Britain's Home Secretary at that time, in the past 5 years since 2010, the UK government had deleted altogether 75,000 pieces of information related to terrorism, 70% of which were relevant to ISIL (Islamic State of Iraq and the Levant), Syria and Iraq.[41] Apparently, it's up to the governments' public policy, rather than whether to give up sovereignty to decide the order to be followed by the free flow of information. The speech of removing harmful online information is essentially a reflection of playing the role of sovereignty.

In fact, there is no frontier defense among Schengen countries, and people are free to flow, but it does not indicate that there is only "EU sovereignty" and no national sovereignty. Instead, it is the decision made by sovereign countries according to their sovereignty. When America allows visa-free entry of citizens of a certain country, it merely shows that America is exercising its right to release, rather than losing sovereignty; in other words, America offers visa-free treatment to citizens of a region that is selected according to sovereignty. For the same reason, cyberspace sovereignty also exists objectively, and is independent of men's will. It only matters as for whether, when, how and why the country will exercise its sovereignty.

In the article, "Sovereignty in Cyberspace: Can it Exist?", the US Colonel Franzese stated: "While cyberspace ideally allows for the free flow of information, no "cyberspace exemption" shields information from the valid interests of the state where information is sent, received, or stored. For example, the United States, along with many other countries, has a stated interest in preventing the possession and spread of child pornography, France has a stated interest in protecting its citizens from defamatory statements. In each of the examples above, court systems ruled that information accessible to the individual located in those respective states via cyberspace is subject to the laws within that respective state. Accordingly, a website located outside of France, which sells Nazi memorabilia, that people can access from France is subject to the laws of France. While this area of the law is still developing, it demonstrates that states have valid interests in and legitimate control over what occurs in cyberspace." Clearly, it is totally up to the government to decide whether the free flow of information can be random and what the policies like for free flow of information. Therefore, it's merely wishful thinking to try to pursue unprincipled free flow of information by opposing cyberspace sovereignty.

11.2.6 New Sovereignty Theory of Cyberspace

In 1992, Howard H. Frederick stated in his article Computer Networks and the Emergence of Global Civil Society[42]: A new global civil society is formed in cyberspace, wherein this society has its own forms of organization, values and rules, and is totally separated from the government and owns the right of

[41]Speech Home Secretary Theresa May on Counter-terrorism. https://www.gov.uk/government/speeches/home-secretary-theresa-may-on-counter-terrorism [2016-12-31].

[42]Frederick H (1993) Computer networks and the emergence of global civil society. Global Net: Comput Int Commun 283–295. http://www.africa.upenn.edu/Global_Comm/Global_Society.html [2016-12-31].

self-governance. The article also emphasizes the novelty and independence of the cyberspace, and is skeptical of the national power in world. The article is worried that the intervention of national power may replace traditional jurisdiction of courts and that the determination and judgement by itself may replace those of the nations. This theory has seen the great role played by Internet in promoting national boundaries. A cyberspace with no national boundaries, infinite amount of information, and the freedom of transmission is changing the relationships among nations and people.

On February 8, 1996, John Perry Barlow, the famous Internet activist who was on the list of the Internet's Hall of Fame later, delivered his famous Declaration of the Independence of Cyberspace[43]: "I come from Cyberspace, the new home of Mind. On behalf of the future, I ask you of the past to leave us alone. You are not welcome among us. You have no sovereignty where we gather. We have no elected government, nor are we likely to have one. I declare the global social space we are building to be naturally independent of the tyrannies you seek to impose on us. Ours is a world that is both everywhere and nowhere, but it is not where bodies live. We are creating a world that all may enter without privilege or prejudice accorded by race, economic power, military force, or station of birth. We are creating a world where anyone anywhere may express his or her beliefs, no matter how singular, without fear of being coerced into silence or conformity. In our world, whatever the human mind may create can be reproduced and distributed infinitely at no cost. The global conveyance of thought no longer requires your factories to accomplish. We must declare our virtual selves immune to your sovereignty, even as we continue to consent to your rule over our bodies. Where there are real conflicts, where there are wrongs, we will identify them and address them by our means. We are forming our own Social Contract. This governance will arise according to the conditions of our world, not yours. Our world is different."

In 1997, Timothy S. Wu, Professor of Law School of Columbia University, published his article "*Cyberspace Sovereignty? – The Internet and the International System*"[44] on "*Harvard Journal of Law & Technology*", and he came up with the concept of "cyberspace sovereignty".[45] His main viewpoints are as follows: ① Some writers conclude that regulating cyberspace is really nothing new; others argue that cyberspace ought not to be regulated, or is impossible to regulate. Exponents of the latter view asserted that cyberspace should enjoy a kind of international sovereignty. Probably the most outspoken advocates of "cyberspace sovereignty" are the Electronic Frontier Foundation (EFF) and Wired magazine.

[43]Barlow JP (1996) A declarationof the independence of cyberspace. http://www.cs.cmu.edu/~ralf/cdoi.html [2016-9-25].

[44]Timothy SW (1997) Cyberspace sovereignty?—The internet and the international system. Harvard J Law Technol 10(3):647. http://jolt.law.harvard.edu/articles/pdf/v10/10HarvJLTech647.pdf [2016-10-5].

[45]The "cyberspace sovereignty" here refers to "virtual network sovereignty", i.e. the sovereignty belongs to the cyberspace itself, and the government has no right of regulation. It is later called as new theory of sovereignty.

David Johnson and David Post have recently presented a comprehensive argument for "cyberspace sovereignty".[46] ② Proponents of "cyberspace sovereignty" usually present a normative argument—that nations should respect the rules of cyberspace. However, they often make a descriptive, or predictive, statement as well: they claim that the "territorial" power of the world will, or already does, respect an emergent "cyberspace sovereignty". Such writers generally assert that state regulation of the Internet will be impossible or futile. If this assertion is correct, cyberspace sovereignty will be a reality. Moreover, it could be the case that states will simply choose, for self-interested reasons, not to regulate cyberspace.

Such a viewpoint that "Internet is a space for netizens, and has nothing to do with governments" is called as the new theory of sovereignty. According to the new theory of sovereignty, as in the real society, a "network society" is also gradually formed in the virtual space of network. This international society connected the whole world, and has its own governance rules, values and unique form. Besides, this international society is subject to the government of no sovereign country, and each Internet user is subject to its Internet Service Provider (ISP) only. If conflicts or contradictions occur among ISPs, mutual protocols will be used to coordinate and unify respective rules in the same way as coordinating pure technical standards. Conflicts among network members will be resolved by ISPs as the arbitrator, and the judgement will also be executed by ISPs.

The "new theory of sovereignty" is wrong for the following reasons: the new theory of sovereignty completely mixes the difference between ISPs' right to formulate industry ethics and technical standards, and the sovereign nations' right to formulate laws and exercise jurisdiction, and it overstates the restraint of technical standards on industry ethics. As we all know, America mainly cut in from non-governmental aspects when it was inviting the nations to access Internet in earlier time, and the US government did not show up for serious regulation of Internet. In early phase, academic staff and researchers of all nations joined the Internet camp as non-governmental individuals. At the same time, as business entities, enterprises found commercial opportunities, and joined the army of Internet construction. As factors of politics, military, culture, society and other aspects of nations are transferred onto Internet, the Internet construction and development of government behaviors gradually become subject behaviors, and governments gradually dominate Internet development. America also announced at the end of the 20th century to take back the ownership of Internet domain name administration, and entrusted, under the government supervision, specific administration to the non-profit institution ICANN. In 2011, Obama straightly pointed out in the preface

[46]Law and Borders: The Rise of Law in Cyberspace. https://cyber.harvard.edu/is02/readings/johnson-post.html [2016-12-31].

drafted for International Strategy for Cyberspace[47]: "The digital world is no longer a lawless frontier, nor the province of a small elite." He also admitted "Long-standing international norms guiding state behavior—in times of peace and conflict—also apply in cyberspace." The US may basically not intervene in Internet construction and operation, but it did not give up its sovereignty.

From another aspect, given that Internet is compared to market economy, the order of market economy is still maintained by the government, because the government can limit the floor or ceiling price of commodities, and restricting the production and circulation of a certain commodity. In other words, no market economy of western countries goes beyond the government administration, and the presence of a government cannot be denied for the fear of government's intervention into economy. The Monetary Quantitative Easing and Interest Float in America are government behaviors intervening market economy at crucial moments. Similarly, even though that government will exist in Internet, it does not mean that the government is to intervene in the free development of Internet. The government only takes Internet as the market economy and encourages its healthy development while ensuring its order. As a result, the affirmation that "There is no government business in Internet" is less and less objective; the belief that "The government is a lack of means for managing Internet" is even more unrealistic, especially after a series of rules and regulations are formulated by the government specific to Internet. From this aspect, the "new theory of sovereignty" in untenable at all and its essence depends on how the Internet is treated by sovereign countries.

11.2.7 The Assumption of Preventing Governments from Doing Evil

Someone thinks that cyberspace sovereignty cannot be endowed; otherwise, it may be used by government for doing evil. In other words, it is assumed that the government's motivation is to limit the development of network, so the government cannot be authorized. This theory came from a Scottish philosopher David Hume: "Every government member must be conceived as a scoundrel",[48] and is an extension of "Hume Assumption" into the cyberspace field. Moreover, the network real-name system was once implemented in South Korea, but then denied and abolished by the Supreme Court of South Korea for being a violation of the speech

[47]United States. White House Office, Obama B. International Strategy for Cyberspace: Prosperity, Security, and Openness in a Networked World. White House, 2011. Chinese translation of the whole text of International Strategy of Cyberspace by Obama Administration. https://www.douban.com/note/263597739/ [2016-9-24].

[48]Discussion on Political Obligation Theory of Hume. http://www.docin.com/p-783444901.html [2016-10-5].

and communication freedom as determined by the constitution.[49] This event causes people to believe that the real-name system implemented by the government not only is suspected of violating the privacy of citizens and the communication and speech freedom, but also bothers netizens with privacy leakage and network attack, which proves the possibility for governments to do evil from another aspect. Furthermore, the Patriot Act of America gives the US government the power to monitor for anti-terrorism and national security. Besides, since there was the case of the Pentagon Papers and the Watergate scandal, it is inevitable for the public to be suspicious of the US government's purpose of having the monitoring power.

The "assumption of preventing the government from doing evil" is wrong for its overgeneralization. The presence of national sovereignty cannot be denied because of the existence of national sovereignty enslaving the people; for the same reason, the presence of cyberspace sovereignty cannot be denied because some countries have adopted the means for limiting network development. The incident of Snowden, especially the surveillance of the whole world by the US National Security Agency, infuriated the nations of the world, which makes them believe that America is doing evil to the world. However, this still cannot deny the objective fact that the US has sovereignty. In fact, the will of national sovereignty is reflected in cyberspace just because the nations are capable of taking measures specific to cyberspace. These kinds of problems cannot be avoided by simply denying cyberspace sovereignty; instead, the role played by national sovereignty in the cyberspace should be emphasized, so that the nations are prompted to actively take responsibilities and obligations corresponding to cyberspace sovereignty.

11.3 Viewpoints that Cyberspace Sovereignty Can Hardly Be Determined

As for the cyberspace sovereignty, there are mainly two opposing kinds of viewpoints of being supportive or non-supportive, and there is also a "middle line". On one hand, many countries have a lack of corresponding national strength in information technology (e.g. the countries with backward information technology), and fail to enter into the extensive application phase of information technology, so they care little about the discussion about cyberspace sovereignty; on the other hand, some countries merely stress the cyberspace security while avoiding the problem of cyberspace sovereignty because they do not want to directly conflict with America (e.g. some NATO nations).

In addition, there are also some doubts about whether the cyberspace sovereignty can be extracted. In 2014, Patrick Schmitz from DePauw University of America

[49]Network Real-name System was abolished in South Korea. http://international.caixin.com/2012-08-24/100428234.html [2016-10-5].

issued his article Threats and Sovereignty in Cyberspace[50] on German Foreign Policy in the Cyber Age. It is stated in this article: The diversity of actors in the Internet has complicated the definition of state sovereignty beyond the realm of territories. If not compromising state sovereignty, it has, at the least, raised questions over how sovereignty manifests itself in a yet largely "ungoverned" virtual territory. The cyber age, therefore, presents new challenges for long-term governance.

11.4 Main Ideas of the International Community on Cyberspace Sovereignty

At present, main states have declared their opinions on cyberspace sovereignty, and the major representative viewpoints are as follows.

11.4.1 The Viewpoint from the UN's Group of Governmental Experts on Developments in the Field of Information and Telecommunications in the Context of International Security

In the UN's Report of the Group of Governmental Experts on Developments in the Field of Information and Telecommunications in the Context of International Security,[51] the term "cyberspace sovereignty" is not directly mentioned, but the de facto sovereignty of cyberspace has already been recognized. It is stated in the report that "State sovereignty and international norms and principles that flow from sovereignty apply to State conduct of ICT-related activities and to their jurisdiction over ICT infrastructure within their territory". From the level of terms, "ICT infrastructure" + "ICT-related activities" is right the cyberspace. Therefore, the above description is equivalent to the expression that "State sovereignty and international norms and principles that flow from sovereignty apply to the cyberspace of the State". According to the tendency, since the UN per se is formed of sovereign countries, it will certainly and actively promote the convention development and protection of cyberspace sovereignty worldwide from the perspective of maintaining interests of most countries.

---

[50]Patrick S (2014) Threats and sovereignty in cyberspace. German Foreign Policy in the Cyber Age. http://scholarship.depauw.edu/cgi/viewcontent.cgi?article=1019&context=studentresearch [2016-9-24].

[51]The UN Report of the Group of Governmental Experts on Developments in the Field of Information and Telecommunications in the Context of International Security. http://www.un.org/ga/search/view_doc.asp?symbol=A/68/98 [2016-10-2].

In view of relevant international conceptions derived from sovereignty and the UN Charter, on the basis of the working of previous "Group of Governmental Experts on Developments in the Field of Information and Telecommunications in the Context of International Security", and guided by No. 68/243(2013) Resolution of UN General Assembly, the expert group provided the following in-exhaustive viewpoints on how to apply international laws to ICT used by the nations: ① States have jurisdiction over the ICT infrastructure located within their territory; ② In their use of ICTs, States must observe state sovereignty, sovereign equality, the settlement of disputes by peaceful means and non-intervention in the internal affairs of other States, and other principles of international law. Existing obligations of international law are applicable for the use of ICTs by States. States must comply with their obligations under international law to respect and protect human rights and fundamental freedoms.

11.4.2 America Adopts Double Standards for Cyberspace Sovereignty

On the one hand, America insists on "global commons" and "Internet freedom" from the perspective of global hegemony, and opposes to the viewpoint of cyberspace sovereignty; on the other hand, America adopts super-strong measures to safeguard its cyberspace sovereignty and security from the perspective of maintaining national security. In some scenes, the US government pushes hard "the theory of cyberspace global common", and is against the Internet management of other countries according to state sovereignty. The reason is that these management measures partly block the movement of chasing western democracy as agitated by America, as well as corresponding anti-government activities. For example, America was against the opinion that Internet was publicly owned by the globe, and rejected to hand over the management right of global Internet; however, appealed by the whole world, America was forced to give up the administration over ICANN in 2015, but stressed that the principle should be followed that Internet is open, and emphasized that ICANN can only be privatized rather than being subject to the dominance of governmental or inter-governmental institutions.[52]

However, in some other scenes, America avoids or even opposes the "global commons theory", and is against the global publicity of Internet. One of the reflections of this standpoint is that the US government is against the popular "global commons theory" so as to prevent the long-term control of network by technical elites from threatening the security strategies of America. In the preface to International Strategy for Cyberspace, Obama points out: "The digital world is no longer a lawless frontier, nor the province of a small elite." This is equal to the

[52]Review: Happiness and concern of Internet domain name administration handover. http://news.xinhuanet.com/tech/2016-10/03/c_1119662321.htm [2016-10-5].

announcement that, in the cyberspace of information technology, "the time of lawlessness and being enjoyed by a small elite" is gone forever, and that it's time to take back civil rights. The second reflection of this standpoint is that the US government admitted in the International Strategy for Cyberspace that "Long-standing international norms guiding state behavior—in times of peace and conflict—also apply in cyberspace".[53] It is alleged in this document that America will determine a new international code of conduct though multilateral and bilateral cooperation. The third reflection of this standpoint is that America pointed out in The National Military Strategy of the United States of America, 2011: Redefining America's Military Leadership[54]: cyberspace is no longer equal to high seas and space as "global commons", and is classified as a globally connected space; after that, statements like "cyberspace is global commons" has never been mentioned in The 2015 National Security Strategy.[55] The fourth reflection of this standpoint is that, in the negotiation with "the Group of Governmental Experts on Developments in the Field of Information and Telecommunications in the Context of International Security" set up by the UN, America finally accepted the viewpoint "State sovereignty and international norms and principles that flow from sovereignty apply to State conduct of ICT-related activities, and to their jurisdiction over ICT infrastructure within their territory" in 2013. It means that America also shows the tendency of "cyberspace territory concept" at the legal level.

On February 23, 2010, the United States Senate Committee on Commerce, Science and Transportation submitted the report of Cybersecurity: Next Steps to Protect Our Critical Infrastructure.[56] It is mentioned in the report: "President Obama called cyberspace a strategic national asset. However, this very important point, critical to the challenge we're discussing here today, unlike the other strategic national assets, cyberspace is 85% owned and controlled by private companies and individuals. That means that no one—neither the Government nor the private sector —can keep cyberspace secure by themselves." "Cyberspace is an artificial construct produced by machines. Those machines are all owned by individuals or organizations and all exist in some physical location that is subject to the sovereign control of some nation." It shows America's acknowledgement of the use of national sovereignty and the cyberspace.

---

[53]International Strategy for Cyberspace. https://www.whitehouse.gov/sites/default/files/rss_viewer/international_strategy_for_cyberspace.pdf [2016-10-25].

[54]Mullen MG. The National Military Strategy of the United States of America, 2011: Redefining America's Military Leadership. Joint Chiefs of Staff, 2011. http://www.doc88.com/p-9793339390164.html [2016-9-24].

[55]National Security Strategy (2015). https://www.whitehouse.gov/the-press-office/2015/02/06/fact-sheet-2015-national-security-strategy [2016-10-5].

[56]U.S. Government Printing Office. Cybersecurity: Next Steps to Protect Our Critical Infrastructure, Hearing, Before the Committee on Commerce, Science, and Transportation, United States Senate, One Hundred Eleventh Congress, Second Session. 2010-2-23. https://fas.org/irp/congress/2010_hr/cybersec.pdf [2016-9-6].

It is pointed out in America's Cyber Future Security and Prosperity in the Information Age[57] published in 2011: "The cyberspace domain is often described as a public good or a global commons, but these terms are an imperfect fit. A public good is one from which all can be benefited, and none can be excluded, and while this may describe some of the information protocols of the Internet, it does not describe the physical infrastructure which is a scarce proprietary resource located within the boundaries of sovereign states. And cyberspace is not a commons like the high seas because parts of it are under sovereign control." According to this article, cyberspace is at best an "imperfect commons, or a condominium of joint ownership without well-developed rules." It is specially noticed in this article that cyberspace has the characteristic of reducing some of the power differentials among actors, and it is believed that this would provide a good example of the diffusion of power. At the same time, it is also admitted in this report that diffusion of power does not mean equality of power or the replacement of governments as the most powerful actors in world politics. However, it is emphasized in the report that the cyber domain does give much more power to non-state actors than in the past, and that the threats they pose are likely to increase.

Each level of the United States has recognized the existence of cyberspace sovereignty, but in some public places, America stresses that the UN's concept of cyberspace sovereignty is supposed to be effective only for "ICT infrastructure", rather than for network activities like online opinions. The definition of "cyberspace" by America mainly refers to the infrastructure per se; it may include data but not include activities. Apparently, the cyberspace of America is specific to the cyberspace formed by infrastructures. As a result, America takes the attitude of "Taking the same, removing the different", and strives to dominate and establish a self-beneficial international system of cyberspace sovereignty.

Cyberspace sovereignty is also an objective existence in the United States, but the United States maintains highly alert to the utilization of cyberspace sovereignty by other countries. This should be the reason why America is reluctant to accept cyberspace sovereignty. Since China is the main proponent of cyberspace sovereignty, America is highly suspicious of our intention, and affirms that our emphasis on "internet sovereignty" is for maintaining the power of information control so as to "maintain the Chinese Communist Party regime in the name of laws".[58]

---

[57]America's Cyber Future Security and Prosperity in the Information Age volume i. https://www.cnas.org/files/documents/publications/CNAS_Cyber_VolumeI_0.pdf [2016-9-6].

[58]U.S.-China Economic and Security Review Commission Staff Report: China and International Law in Cyberspace. http://origin.www.uscc.gov/sites/default/files/Research/ChinaInternationalLawinCyberspace.pdf [2016-9-24].

11.4.3 Viewpoints of the US Military

The US military formulates corresponding security strategy and action tactics according to the national cyberspace sovereignty viewpoints of America, and actively takes part in the national actions for safeguarding network security and sovereignty according to its obligations; moreover, it strengthens the network combat power, and enhances cyberspace strategic deterrence and actual combat capacity. In The Department of Defense Cyber Strategy,[59] the US definitely lists network as "the fifth battlefield" after ocean, land, space and sky, and actively initiates actual cyber war fares. Since the US army is playing a dominating role in NATO, the viewpoints of the US army will have substantial influences on NATO. As a military entity, the US army will be more likely to recognize the cyberspace sovereignty theory so as to find a reason for justifying the war, thereby making the cyberspace a glorious battlefield and maintaining its military hegemony in this battlefield.

1. JP-3-12(R) from the US Department of Defense Dictionary of Military and Associated Terms

In the US Department of Defense Dictionary of Military and Associated Terms —Joint Publication 3-12(R): Cyberspace Operation,[60] Cyberspace is defined as a global domain within the information environment, and one of five interdependent domains, the others being the physical domains of air, land, maritime, and space. It is stated in the article: Cyberspace can be described in terms of three layers: physical network, logical network, and cyber-persona. The physical network layer of cyberspace is comprised of the geographic component and the physical network components. It is the medium where the data travel. The logical network layer consists of those elements of the network that are related to one another in a way that is abstracted from the physical network, i.e., the form or relationships are not tied to an individual, specific path, or node. A simple example is any Web site that is hosted on servers in multiple physical locations where all content can be accessed through a single uniform resource locator. The cyber-persona layer represents yet a higher level of abstraction of the logical network in cyberspace; it uses the rules that apply in the logical network layer to develop a digital representation of an individual or entity identity in cyberspace. Apparently, the US army is aware of the human factor in cyberspace.

[59]The DoD Cyber Strategy. http://www.defense.gov/Portals/1/features/2015/0415_cyber-strategy/Final_2015_DoD_CYBER_STRATEGY_for_web.pdf [2016-9-21].

[60]Joint Publication 3-12(R): Cyberspace Operation. http://www.dtic.mil/doctrine/new_pubs/jp3_12R.pdf [2016-9-5].

2. Document from the US Naval Postgraduate School

In 2003, it was pointed out in Asserting National Sovereignty in Cyberspace: the Case for Internet Border Inspection,[61] a document of the US Naval Postgraduate School: National sovereignty is a fundamental principle of national security and the modern international system. The United States asserts its national sovereignty in many ways including inspecting goods and people crossing the border. However, most nations including the United States have not implemented any form of border inspection and control in cyberspace.

3. US Air Force Law Review

On November 20, 2009, cyber law was discussed by the US Air Force Law Review. It is mentioned in the remarks of Patrick Franzese, a colonel: "Cyberspace is not a common domains, and countries throughout the world can and should regulate the domain to prevent cyber-attacks. The United States can choose to take the lead in recognizing and establishing state sovereignty in cyberspace. By establishing state sovereignty in cyberspace, the United States, as well as every other state, will develop the framework to consider other cyberspace issues."[62]

4. The US Air Force Institute of Technology and Wright-Patterson AFB

In 2012, Kris Barcomb and so on from the US Air Force Institute of Technology and Wright-Patterson AFB delivered the article Establishing Cyberspace Sovereignty[63] at the International Conference on Information Warfare and Security (ICIW). It was stated in the article: In cyberspace, sovereignty is a more abstract notion because geographic boundaries in air, land and sea are difficult to define as data and applications increasingly reside in a global, virtual "cloud." Like cyberspace, the space domain is also relatively new, and its characteristics challenged traditional notions of sovereignty based on geography. Technological advancements outpaced the development of a legal framework for establishing internationally accepted practices in the domain, and the international community's understanding of sovereignty needed to mature to deal with the physical realities of space. Studying the emergence of space as a domain will help national leaders establish a concept of sovereignty in cyberspace. Once nations generally agree on the aspects of cyberspace where sovereignty might apply, they can then develop and employ means to protect those claims.

---

[61]Upton OK (2003) Asserting national sovereignty in cyberspace: the case for internet border inspection. Thesis Collection. https://www.researchgate.net/publication/235112846_Asserting_National_Sovereignty_in_Cyberspace_The_Case_for_Internet_Border_Inspection [2016-9-24].

[62]Recent Air Force Law Review Discusses Cyberlaw. http://seclists.org/isn/2009/Nov/90 [2016-9-24].

[63]Kris B, Dennis K, Robert M et al (2012) Establishing cyberspace sovereignty. Air Force Institute of Technology, Wright-Patterson AFB. http://www.igi-global.com/article/establishing-cyberspace-sovereignty/86074 [2016-9-24].

5. Lieutenant General Ronnie D. Hawkins

On January 13, 2015, the Lieutenant General Ronnie D. Hawkins delivered his opinion in Washington during a panel discussion with the local Armed Forces Communications and Electronics Association on the reorganization of Defense Information Systems Agency and the five "Cs" of the capabilities and services DISA provides.[64] Hawkins said: "The first C is "cyber", and when we start looking at what we have to do in defense of cyberspace operations, we've got to have the cyber sovereignty that the Department of Defense expects from us; the second C is "cloud" built by DISA; the third C is "collaboration", and we need the unified capabilities in the mobile and collaboration environments; the fourth and fifth Cs are command and control."

11.4.4 Viewpoints of the Internet Society

According to the Internet Society (ISOC): It is the foundation of internet to open the internet standards, because of which anyone can be allowed to establish a new online service that can be used by other internets even without anyone's permission. For the sustaining growth and development of Internet, the multi-participation by the government and regulators in the construction of Internet standard procedure and the openness of standard verification is very significant. The following 5 key principles should be followed: ① Respect for cooperation: the cooperation between standard organizations should be respected, and each organization should respect autonomy, integrity, procedure and intellectual property rules. ② Insistence of principles: seek for development through the principles of due procedure, broad consensus, transparent operation, balanced input and public participation. ③ Collective rights: the standards should be established on the technical basis as much as possible; should be beneficial for global interoperability, expandability, stability and flexibility; should be able to promote global competition; should be the corner stone of further innovation; should be helpful for establishing global community, thereby benefiting human beings. ④ Feasibility of implementation and deployment: plans that can be implemented according to justice terms should be formulated in defined order. ⑤ Voluntariness of use.

The Internet Society also believes that Internet-related government policies, business decisions and technical development choice influence the degree of the support or challenge to fundamental human rights from Internet. The advocacy for trust, open principles and the communication among stakeholders are important paths for promoting Internet to play its role in supporting human rights. The key factors are as follows:

---

[64]DISA Director Discusses Reorganization Efforts. http://www.defense.gov/News/Article/Article/603915 [2016-9-18].

(1) A framework supporting expression without borders. The key principle of Internet architecture has to be further protection of internet online freedom. It means that end-users can share information and thoughts across borders, and that there is no central authority, which is beneficial for Internet growth. However, situations exist in reality that information flow may be intervened and limited by government and internet intermediaries (such as internet service providers and social media platform), which sometimes limit and control some cross-national data streams or contents. Technology also plays its role in promoting human rights progress. On the basis of the advocacy of opening internet standards, both individuals and organizations all over the world are developing new technology and applications so as to promote basic freedom such as, information access and sharing (e.g. email, VoIP, live chat, video, blog), peaceful environments (e.g. social network, forum), and the acquiring of knowledge and culture content (e.g. Wikipedia).

(2) A new balance of online rights. The unique characteristics of Internet expanded the capacity and means for communication, creation, innovation and association, and resulted in the new situation of freedom, privacy and security of expression. According to Internet Society, security should not be sought at the cost of individual rights. Between security and network freedom, people should take into consideration the security that will not bring risks to online speech or online privacy. Some crucial challenges for internet and human rights include: ① Content filtering and screening. In the past few years, both democratic states and absolute states have made laws, usually according to the demands of national security, so that government institutions are authorized to punish online objections or to block the access to specific network content or services. It is encouraged by ISOC to develop technical and policy cooperation on the basis of international cooperation, so as to find a solution which will neither harm the overall stability and connectivity of the Internet, nor will harm human rights. ② Restriction or attenuation of encryption technology. One of the key ways for people to protect data is the encryption technology, which can be applied to a cloud, a hard disk, or the process of transmission. ISCO strongly advocates anonymous and ubiquitous end-to-end encryption, and it believes that individuals should have the ability of secret communication and anonymous network. This desire is accompanied by a series of difficulties: technical, economic and policy issues; moreover, more dialogue is needed between stakeholders for finding appropriate solutions for the problems. ③ Responsibilities of Internet intermediaries. More and more nations require and order online intermediary services—including the coordination of online communication, the promotion of network expression in various forms such as search engines, social networks and Internet service providers—to remove some content from their platforms. The legal liability policies of intermediaries affect the users' rights and interests including the freedom of speech, the freedom of association, and the right of privacy. Governments should ensure the system of liability so that companies will respect the rights of their users,

and principles such as transparency, proportionality, due process and accountability should also be supported by policy.

The guidelines provided by ISOC are as follows: ① Basic rights. The Internet is associated with opportunity, creativity, empowerment, knowledge and freedom. It has been built on these principles and its future success also depends on them. These principles are secured and consolidated by basic and fundamental rights. The rights people enjoy offline still apply online. ② Open connection. Connection does not ensure that one can freely innovate or freely share information and ideas. These capabilities need to be supported by the Internet environment and rely on the open and non-excessive restrictions on network activities. ③ Reliable Internet. Nowadays, it is difficult to fully participate in the world without an open, accessible and reliable Internet. As the Internet becomes more and more important, credibility will be more crucial for the users as for how to work, entertain, learn or arrange the finance, and even for their health care choices. ④ Technical restrictions. Internet access restrictions by technical measures may impair users' fundamental rights, and the Internet cannot be created as a space of equal opportunities. ⑤ Open dialogue. Open and inclusive dialogue should be encouraged, and the dialogue includes online privacy issues in such areas as national security, basic codes that all stakeholders must abide by, as well as the principles and fundamental rights set forth in international agreements.

11.4.5 Viewpoint of NATO

Tallinn Manual 1.0 is short for Tallinn Manual on the International Law applicable to Cyber Warfare[65] published in 2013. The NATO Cooperative Cyber Defense Center of Excellence invited dozens of international experts to compile this manual during the four years from November 2009 to March 2013 and published it.

It is stated in Chapter I of Tallinn Manual 1.0: in 1648 when sovereign nations were born, the control of information flow has become the most important characteristic of national sovereignty. Sovereignty means that the state has the right to control the network infrastructure and the cyberspace activities within its territory; the interference of one country in the network infrastructure of another country constitutes an infringement of the country's sovereignty. Tallinn Manual 1.0 affirms the existence of cyberspace sovereignty, elaborates its jurisdiction and the right of

[65]The NATO Cooperative Cyber Defence Centre of Excellence, Tallinn Manual on the International Law Applicable to Cyber Warfare, 2013. http://www.jku.at/intlaw/content/e275831/e275836/e276629/Tallinn_Manual_CW.pdf [2016-9-8].

self-defense, and tries to demonstrate the relationship among the sovereignty in existing international law, network infrastructure and cyber warfare.

Basic viewpoints of Tallinn Manual 1.0 are as follows: ① Existing international law can be applied to "cyber warfare"; ② Sovereignty exists in cyberspace, and it is recognized that one country can exercise its jurisdiction over network infrastructure and cyber activities within its sovereign territory; ③ When cyber-attacks are strong enough, the state has the right to exercise self-defense, and anticipatory self-defense is legal; ④ The cyber activities implemented in conflicts should now comply with the International Law of Armed Conflict.[66]

11.4.6 Viewpoint of UK

In 2013, the Defense Committee of England submitted Defense Committee -Sixth Report: Defense and Cyber-Security.[67] It is pointed out in 3. Military Activity in Cyberspace—Conceptual Framework[68] of this Report: "Whether the Armed Forces should engage in cyber warfare will depend on whether particular actions in cyberspace are considered to be acts of war." "As yet there is no internationally-accepted definition of a breach of sovereignty in cyberspace, nor is it clear what types of response would be deemed proportionate to particular types of breaches. Responses to cyber-attack would not need to be themselves in the cyber domain—they could be economic, judicial or of a conventional military nature." "The law of armed conflict applies as much to cyberspace as it does to any other domain of operation; cyber-attacks will be regarded as armed attacks, so no new legal code is needed to regulate military activity in cyberspace, the application of existing law and norms of behavior will serve us perfectly well." "One of the military functions the Armed Forces carrying out through cyber means is to deter attacks on UK national interests. With the borderless and anonymous nature of the internet, precise attribution (of attacks) is often difficult and the distinction between adversaries is increasingly blurred."

On April 7, 2015, the UK Oxford University published the book China and Cybersecurity: Espionage, Strategy, and Politics in the Digital Domain[69] written by Jon R. Lindsay and so on. It is stated in the book: "Cyberspace sovereignty" needs to be respected when cyber rules are provided. Cyber rules applicable for cyberspace are an essential reaction of the rules in the physical world, and it cannot

[66]NATO's cyber warfare manual: seeking legal basis for controlling cyberspace. http://www.chinanews.com/mil/2014/10-24/6712323.shtml [2016-8-30].

[67]Defence Committee—Sixth Report Defence and Cyber-Security. http://www.publications.parliament.uk/pa/cm201213/cmselect/cmdfence/106/10602.htm [2016-10-5].

[68]3. Military activity in cyberspace-conceptual framework. https://www.publications.parliament.uk/pa/cm201213/cmselect/cmdfence/106/10606.htm [2017-3-1].

[69]China and Cybersecurity: Espionage, Strategy, and Politics in the Digital Domain. http://www.ebooks.com/2543284/china-and-cybersecurity/lindsay-jon-r-cheung-tai-ming-reveron-derek-s/ [2016-9-19].

totally be separated from the development process of human and society. The spirit contained in most of the rules can be applied to network activities. For instance, the international law spirits of mutual non-aggression and peaceful co-existence should be reflected in the cyberspace. Sovereignty is the key to the rules of physical world, for instance, self-governance would be impossible without sovereignty, and there will be no power to provide cyber rules without cyberspace sovereignty. Just like international laws, the international rules for cyberspace should respect rather than opposing sovereignty. In short, people should provide cyber rules based on the respect for cyberspace sovereignty, not only in their own country, but also in other countries.

11.4.7 Viewpoints of Russia

In September 2011, Convention on International Information Security[70] was released at an "International Meeting of High-ranking Officials Responsible for Security Matters" in Yekaterinburg, Russia. The key provisions of the document have been condensed into a list of 23 fundamental issues of concern to Russia in information space.[71] Article 5, i.e. "The basic principles of the international information security", contains 21 principles that should be followed by member states in the information space, wherein the fourth principle is "Within the information space all member states enjoy a sovereign equality, have the same rights and obligations and are the equal subjects of the information space regardless of economic, social, political, or other differences", and the fifth principle is "Each member state is entitled to set forth sovereign norms and manage its information space according to its national laws. The information infrastructure located in the territory of a member state or otherwise existing under its jurisdiction is subject to the sovereignty and laws of such member state. The member states must strive to harmonize their respective national legislations, the existing differences shall not make barriers to the formation of a reliable and secure information environment". The information space and information infrastructure mentioned in these provisions are important components of cyberspace, in other words, it is pointed out in these provisions that the countries should exercise national sovereignty over cyberspace.

[70]Convention on International Information Security. http://archive.mid.ru//bdomp/ns-osndoc.nsf/1e5f0de28fe77fdcc32575d900298676/7b17ead7244-e2064c3257925003bcbcc!OpenDocument [2016-8-30].

[71]Information Space. Russia usually uses "information space" rather than "cyberspace" so as to underline the attributes of the activity.

In November 2011, an international cyberspace conference was held in London with the purpose of discussing international codes of behavior for cyberspace and promoting and establishing cyberspace behavior norms. At the conference, Russia stressed that cyberspace should also own national sovereignty, and that the preconditions of the rights and freedom of cyberspace should be the respect for relevant domestic laws.[72]

On October 4, an international cyberspace meeting was held at Budapest, Capital of Hungary, wherein the participants talked about the issues including economic development, social welfare, network security, network crimes and so on.[73] The topic of the meeting is the emphasis on the significance of openness and transparency, but Russia kept on underlining the necessities of respecting national sovereignty in cyberspace and the implementation of rules and regulations.

In 2014, Putin, President of Russia mentioned in a joint interview by the media of Latin America and Russia: "As for some widely mentioned network espionage events, these events not only reflect that some countries are hypocritical to their partners and allies, but also are infringements to national sovereignty, human rights and individual privacy".[74]

11.4.8 Viewpoints of Shanghai Cooperation Organization

On January 9, 2015, permanent representatives from China, Kazakhstan, Kyrgyzstan, Russian Federation, Tajikistan and Uzbekistan sent a letter to the Secretary General, which was an updated version of the International Code of Conduct for Information Security jointly submitted to the General Assembly in 2011 at its sixty-sixth session by China, Russian Federation, Tajikistan and Uzbekistan.[75] Subsequently, Kyrgyzstan and Kazakhstan joined in, and formed the six co-sponsors of the proposal.

The Code of 2015 further amended the Code of 2011 so as to take into full consideration the comments and suggestions from all parties. This norm stresses the international code of conduct such as "encouraging civilian application of information technology", "national sovereignty decides network policies", and "promoting globalization of information technology so as to close the digital divide" so as to establish an information environment that is peaceful, secure, open and

[72]China and Russia fight against Europe and America for cyberspace domination. http://news.xinhuanet.com/world/2011-11/02/c_122225934.htm [2016-10-5].

[73]International conference of cyberspace was held in Budapest. http://news.xinhuanet.com/newmedia/2012-10/05/c_131889095.htm [2016-10-1].

[74]Russia President Putin: Cyberspace espionage is actually aggression of sovereignty of other nations. http://world.huanqiu.com/exclusive/2014-07/5060472.html [2016-10-5].

[75]UN document A/69/723, Updated version of the International Code of Conduct for Information Security submitted by SCO members to the UN in 2015. http://infogate.fmprc.gov.cn/web/ziliao_674904/tytj_674911/zcwj_674915/P020150316571763224632.pdf [2016-9-21].

founded on cooperation, and to ensure that the use of information and networks facilitates the development and well-being of peoples and ensures international peace and security. Specifically, there are proposals from 8 aspects.

1. Encouraging civilian application of information

According to the SCO's International Code of Conduct for Information Security of 2015,[76] scientific and technological developments can have both civilian and military applications, and progress in science and technology for civilian applications needs to be maintained and encouraged; it is necessary to prevent the potential use of information and communication technologies for purposes that are inconsistent with the objectives of maintaining international stability and security and may adversely affect the integrity of the infrastructure within States to the detriment of their security; therefore, it is necessary to enhance the coordination and cooperation among States in combating the criminal misuse of information technologies, in that context, stressing the role that can be played by the United Nations and other international and regional organizations.

2. The application of sovereignty and international law

The Code of 2015 reaffirms that "policy authority for Internet-related public issues is the sovereign right of States", and believes that "States have rights and responsibilities for international Internet-related public policy issues"; it is necessary to develop a common understanding of how norms derived from existing international law relevant to the use of information and communication technologies by States will apply to State behavior and the use of information and communication technologies by States. To comply with the Charter of the United Nations and universally recognized norms governing international relations that enshrine respect for the sovereignty, territorial integrity and political independence of all States, respect for human rights and fundamental freedoms and respect for the diversity of history, culture and social systems of all countries.

3. To close the digital divide by transferring information technology

It is realized in this Code that the confidence and security in the use of information and communications technologies are among the main pillars of the information society and that a robust global culture of cyber security needs to be encouraged, promoted, developed and vigorously implemented. It is noted "that, given the unique attributes of information and communication technologies, additional norms could be developed over time", and the need for enhanced efforts is stressed so as to close the digital divide by facilitating the transfer of information technology and capacity-building to developing countries in the areas in which cyber security best practices.

[76]International Code of Conduct for Information Security. http://wcm.fmprc.gov.cn/preview/jks/zcwj/t858317.html [2016-10-6].

4. No threat to peace, non-interference in internal affairs, and the cooperation against terrorism

Not to use information and communications technologies and information and communications networks to carry out activities which counter to the task of maintaining international peace and security. Not to use information and communications technologies and information and communications networks to interfere in the internal affairs of other States or with the aim of undermining their political, economic and social stability. To cooperate in combating criminal and terrorist activities that use information and communications technologies and information and communications networks, and in curbing the dissemination of information that incites terrorism, separatism or extremism or that inflames hatred on ethnic, racial or religious grounds. To endeavor to ensure the supply chain security of information and communications technology goods and services, in order to prevent other States from exploiting their dominant position, including dominance in resources, critical infrastructures, core technologies, information and communications technology goods and services and information and communications networks to undermine States' rights to independent control, or to threaten their political, economic and social security.

5. To ensure both online and offline rights, and safeguard civil rights and morals

To recognize that the rights of an individual in the offline environment must also be protected in the online environment; to fully respect rights and freedoms in the information space, including the right and freedom to seek, receive and impart information, taking into account the fact that the International Covenant on Civil and Political Rights attaches to that duties and responsibilities for respect of the rights or reputations of others and for the protection of national security or of public order, or of public health or morals.

6. To equitably distribute resources, and play the same role

All States must play the same role in, and carry equal responsibility for, international governance of the Internet, its security, continuity and stability of operation, and its development in a way which promotes the establishment of multilateral, transparent and democratic international Internet governance mechanisms which ensure an equitable distribution of resources, facilitate access for all and ensure the stable and secure functioning of the Internet.

7. Full cooperation of governments and stakeholders

All States must cooperate fully with other interested parties in encouraging a deeper understanding by all elements in society, including the private sector and civil-society institutions, of their responsibility to ensure information security, by means including the creation of a culture of information security and the provision of support for efforts to protect critical information infrastructure; to develop confidence-building measures aimed at increasing predictability and reducing the likelihood of misunderstanding and the risk of conflict; to voluntarily exchange information regarding national strategies and organizational structures for ensuring a State's information security, and to exchange the best practice, wherever practical and advisable.

8. To settle disputes peacefully, and to encourage the UN to develop international law for information security

To bolster bilateral, regional and international cooperation, promote a prominent role for the United Nations in areas such as encouraging the development of international legal norms for information security, peaceful settlement of international disputes, qualitative improvements in international cooperation in the field of information security; and to enhance coordination among relevant international organizations; to settle any dispute resulting from the application of this code of conduct through peaceful means, and to refrain from the threat or use of force.

11.4.9 Viewpoints of EU, Japan and Other Developed Countries

On the one hand, these countries are generally subject to the basic cyberspace sovereignty ideas of America and are basically consistent with the US perspective in the discussion of the UN "Group of Governmental Experts on Developments in the Field of Information and Telecommunications in the Context of International Security". On the other hand, these countries are particularly concerned about the network security and sovereignty of their own; especially after establishing the national cyberspace security strategy, it is necessary to strengthen the strategic layout of cyberspace security from the level of sovereignty. Therefore, from the angle of tendency, these countries will gradually recognize and conditionally support cyberspace sovereignty, but they are slightly controlled by others and powerless in actions.

11.5 Main Intentions Against Internet Sovereignty

As for Internet, since the international community accessed the Internet of America at the very beginning, the governance mode is thereby established that the international Internet is controlled by America. Besides, the domain name resolution system adopted by Internet is centralized rather than distributed. It is inevitable that this centralized domain name resolution system has a concrete manager, who will certainly be the only authority in charge of the Internet center. The controller of the Internet center is in America, and the equipment is also in America, so the international Internet is objectively controlled by America. As a result, Internet is an exception of cyberspace, and Internet sovereignty is an exception of cyberspace sovereignty, so the Internet powers are extremely reluctant to accept and even resolutely object to the pursuit of Internet sovereignty in Internet by nations.

11.5.1 To Realize Internet Hegemony

The US and other Internet powers opposing Internet sovereignty advocate "global commons" and "Internet freedom", wherein the essence is against that the nations manage Internet of their own, and the main intention is to effectively get the control of Internet through the stakeholders so as to realize Internet hegemony.

Represented by America, the Internet powers advocate the governance mode of the "stakeholder" so as to maintain the mighty dominating mechanism of "law of the jungle". In the mode of the "stakeholder", the cyberspace governance is dominated by technical experts, commercial institutions and non-government organizations, government interference is not allowed, and even inter-state government organizations like the UN are excluded. Most of the stakeholders are members of Internet powers such as America, so the decisions of stakeholders usually are the results expected by America and other western powers.

In the name of private sectors and non-profit organization, the US has dominated for a long term the core technology and key resources of Internet. The Internet Corporation for Assigned Names and Numbers (ICANN) is in charge of the space allocation of IP addresses, the management of the system of Generic Top-Level Domain and Country Code Top Level Domain, and the management of the root service system, and can decide the "appearance" and "disappearance" of a certain website, computer and relevant equipment. Due to historical reasons, these powers are also subject to the US government for a long time. In recent years, some nations and organizations including Russia, China and developing countries have been calling for internationalization of ICANN regulations, and some countries wish that the UN could take over the right of management. In March 2014, Edward Snowden exposed the "PRISM". After that event, America has been and still is under tremendous pressure from the international community, so it announced to give up the regulation of ICANN but with some basic preconditions, which is to hand over the administration to a private institution following the principle of "multi-stakeholder" rather than a bilateral organization dominated by sovereign countries. Its purpose is still to exclude the role played by the government, and to promote the governance mode of stakeholders worldwide so as to replace the modes dominated by governments, thereby weakening government control.

11.5.2 To Pursue the Social Systems and Ideology of Internet Powers

America is so far one of the most powerful advocators of "Internet freedom". Due to different values, America and other western countries are against the role played by cyberspace sovereignty in dissemination of Internet information. It has always been proposed by western countries that human rights override sovereignty, and that freedom and other basic human rights of citizens are inviolable. In the cyberspace, western countries insist on network liberalism, and are against Internet administration by the country, holding that citizens' freedom to access information will be hindered to some extent. The US has always been publicizing "openness, transparence, human rights" of the Internet world. On February 15, 2011, during the political turmoil in the Middle East, Hillary made her speech titled "Internet Rights and Wrongs: Choices & Challenges in a Networked World" in the University of George Washington, and fully and exhaustively elaborated the America's policy of "Internet freedom"[77] by pointing out that the freedoms of expression, assembly, and association online together are called as the freedom to connect. Due to "Internet freedom", America is free from the restrictions of traditional sovereignty in the global information space, as a result, the application scope of American sovereignty is expanded, and "Internet freedom" objectively became an "enclosure movement" in cyberspace. On May 16, 2011, the US government issued the International Strategy for Cyberspace,[78] wherein Internet freedom is the core concept and an important component, and "Our international cyberspace policy reflects our core commitments to fundamental freedoms, privacy, and the free flow of information" is advocated. In the Cybersecurity Strategy of the European Union[79] issued by the European Commission in 2013, it is claimed that everyone is able to access the Internet freely and to the unhindered network content legally, and is believed that increased global connectivity should not be accompanied by censorship or mass surveillance.

In recent years, the focuses and standpoints of the reports on China by international network media are always oriented by the social systems and ideologies of Internet powers, and there are often comments "demonizing" China. Take New York Times as an example, among the 51 China-related passages randomly selected from the China-related reports on the website of New York Times in a period of 6 months from November 1, 2008 to April 30, 2009, 46% of the passages use biased nouns, 38% contain negative nouns, and only 8% of them adopts positive nouns, wherein the positive nouns are mainly concentrated on the economy development, and negative nouns are focused on political, military and social problems; besides, 16% of the

[77]Internet Rights and Wrongs: Choices & Challenges in a Networked World. http://www.alibuybuy.com/posts/55430.html [2016-9-19].

[78]The US International Strategy for Cyberspace (Chinese-English Bilingual). http://www.docin.com/p-706755166.html [2016-10-5].

[79]EU released Cybersecurity Strategy. http://www.scio.gov.cn/zhzc/8/5/Document/1432493/1432493.htm [2016-8-30].

passages deliberately emphasize the undisguised contents of "China Threat".[80] Apparently, Internet space is far from a free domain, and Internet has become a position for Internet powers to promote their social systems and ideologies.

11.5.3 To Destabilize the Social Order of All States

Statistics show that 94 of the top 100 websites with the largest visitor volumes on the Internet are located within Internet powers,[81] which makes it possible for Internet powers to screen and push out, according to their own standards, Internet information contents and transmission modes satisfying their standards of value, and to transmit to the audience the information in compliance with the national interests and values of Internet powers. For instance, on March 14, 2008, massive unrest has taken place in Lhasa, Tibet, and CNN and other western mainstream media violated the news principles of being truthful and objective, made a series of distorted reports on this event, and extremely smeared the image of our government by releasing false photos and passages and misrepresenting the truth.[82]

There is no lack of social unrest all around the world in history, and regime changes may also be caused thereby. However, due to historical reasons, the threshold was rather high, and it was really hard for it to happen. The occurrence of this reflected the universal desire of the people, and also proved it as an inevitable destination. However, following the rapid development of information, the threshold is greatly lowered, and the desires of the minority can kidnap the will of the majority, as a result of which the society is turned upside down. It leaves no chance for the government to make corrections, and can easily destroy the society, which is a violation of the basic law of "Historical Necessity". The so-called "Internet freedom" is playing the important role of "lowering the threshold", and it can easily cause social oscillation.

The London Riot in August 2011, as well as the social instability and regime changes in West Asian and North African areas in 2011 completely unmasked the Internet characteristic of being a "double-edged sword" of social media. Once it is used for malicious propaganda by ulterior force, such as producing false information, spreading dissatisfaction with the government, organizing protest and gathering activities and so on, the Internet will become a "source of rumor". Facebook, Twitter, YouTube or the like all belong to the "stakeholder" vigorously promoted by Internet powers, and Internet Powers can absolutely control the occurrence and development of

[80]Serious challenge from US Internet strategy and our countermeasures. http://theory.people.com.cn/GB/82288/143843/143844/17623412.html [2016-12-31].

[81]Legislation has to be subordinated to national strategic needs. http://news.163.com/14/0721/06/A1LJDVKL00014AED.html [2016-12-31].

[82]No foreign intervention in Tibet affairs. http://news.sina.com.cn/o/2008-03-28/090013648614s.shtml [2016-12-31].

the emergent mass incidents of all nations by using the mastered social media platform, thereby destabilizing the social order of other nations.

11.5.4 To Realize "Culture Hegemony"

Internet is "the fourth media" following the press, broadcast and TV, and provides for the Internet powers the communication route and medium that are efficient, all-weather, inexpensive, immediate and convenient, which objectively provides conditions for the expansion of American "culture hegemony" by virtue of Internet.[83] Numerous news, advertisements, online games, films and television and so on under the brand of Internet powers influence the thinking patterns and behavior modes of the network audiences of other nations, particularly those of adolescence, silence and peace. As a result, the network audience will gradually shield the original values, and be influenced by various cultural concepts of Internet powers. Once entering the Internet space, people actually enter into the culture environment designed by Internet powers. This kind of culture infiltration is somehow covert, and will not be exposed in a short period. However, as time goes by, this imperceptible impact will inevitably touch the foundation of traditional culture, ideology and values of other nations.

11.5.5 To Form Network Strategic Deterrence

Due to information technology advantages, the information goods and services of stakeholders enjoy vast accessibility and coverage degree all over the globe. At present, root name servers and other global Internet core infrastructures are in the control of Internet powers, and the main suppliers and application stores of global Internet infrastructure are absolutely dominated by Internet powers. Such an industrial strength enables Internet powers to control the Internet of other nations and to weaken other nations' cyberspace defense capability. The top-level domain names of Iraq and Libya disappeared from the Internet, which indicates that Internet powers in charge of stakeholders are capable of swinging the sword hung over all courtiers while there is no resistance.

[83]Severe challenges to China posed by American Internet strategies and the countermeasures. http://news.xinhuanet.com/politics/2012-04/11/c_122960620.htm [2016-9-24].

Chapter 12
Main Initiatives to Safeguard Cyberspace Sovereignty

Abstract The objective existence of cyberspace sovereignty is particularly prominent in cyberspace jurisdiction. Actions to govern cyberspace have been taken, mainly on legal norms, administrative supervision, industry self-discipline, technical support, military defense, international cooperation, social education.

Keywords Legal norms · Administrative supervision · Industry self-discipline Technical support · Military defense · International cooperation Social education

On December 27, 2016, the Central Network Security and Information Leading Group Office issued a "National Cyberspace Security Strategy".[1] Its strategic objectives are: "with the overall national security view as guidance, implement the innovative, coordinated, green, open and shared development concept, strengthen risk consciousness and crisis consciousness, comprehensively handle both domestic and foreign large pictures, comprehensively plan the development of the two great matters of security [internal and external security], defend vigorously, respond effectively, promote peace, security, openness, cooperation and order in cyberspace, safeguard the interests of national sovereignty, security and development, and realize the objective of building a strong cyber power"; its basic principles are: "respecting and protecting sovereignty in cyberspace, peaceful use of cyberspace, Governing cyberspace according to the laws, and comprehensively manage cyber security and development"; its strategic tasks are: "Resolutely defending sovereignty in cyberspace; Resolutely safeguard national security; Protect critical information infrastructure; Strengthening the construction of online culture; Attacking cyber terrorism, law-breaking and crime; Perfect cyberspace governance systems; Ramming cyber security foundation, Enhancing cyber security protection capabilities; Strengthening international cooperation in cyberspace".

Safeguarding cyberspace sovereignty and protecting cyberspace security are intended to manage all kinds of network activities within the sovereignty of our

[1] National Cyberspace Security Strategy. http://www.cac.gov.cn/2016-12/27/c_1120195926.htm [2016-12-28].

B. Fang, *Cyberspace Sovereignty*,
https://doi.org/10.1007/978-981-13-0320-3_12

country according to the Constitution and laws and regulations, and to take all measures including legal, administrative, economic, technological, military and diplomatic affairs to protect our information facilities and information resource security. Safeguarding cyberspace sovereignty and building a peaceful, safe, open, cooperative and orderly cyberspace, is intended to strengthen the legal norms to build the legal system of cyberspace; to strengthen administrative supervision, to build orderly, free and democratic cyberspace; to strengthen the industrial self-discipline to build an open but controllable and mutually prosperous cyberspace; to strengthen technical support to build a safe, reliable and stable available cyberspace; to strengthen the military security to build a peaceful, credible and transparently developing cyberspace; to strengthen the international cooperation to build a cyberspace with collaborative networking, sharing and shared responsibility; to strengthen social education, all-round to improve the level of cyberspace security education and resolutely defend the sacred position of cyberspace sovereignty.

12.1 Legal Norms: Construction of the Legal System of Cyberspace

Since China's official access to the Internet in 1994, the level of China's Internet governance and network development, social areas of adaptability and national policy environment are always closely associated. The road of network development and governance has distinctive Chinese characteristics. From the perspective of Internet awareness and network legislation, it can be divided into three stages: ① at the first stage before 2000, when focused on the attributes of information and communication tools, its main provisions were related to the computer Internet, regarding as a stage of the initial contact, the Internet promotion and trial governance; ② in accordance with the *People's Republic of China Telecommunications Regulations and Internet Information Services Management Measures* adopted on September 25, 2000 as a symbol, China began to focus on the network media attributes from the legislative level, and then with the Electronic Signatures Act adopted on April 30, 2004 and with the vigorous development of the subsequent e-commerce and social networking, further demonstrated the socialization attribute of the network, so it can be said that this is a cyberspace governance exploration stage as representatives of the department supervision and industrial self-discipline; ③ the establishment of the leading group of network security and information technology, on the 27th February 2014, opened a new stage of the overall planning, top-level design, managing network according to the rule of laws, the formal introduction of *Cyber Security Law* indicated that the legal construction of China's cyberspace entered the orderly stage of the top-level design, and the understanding of the network had changed from the virtual space to the integral part of the real society.

According to the statistics of the composition group of this book, by March 2016, China had issued 45 network-related laws and relevant decisions, 53 State Council administrative regulations, 58 judicial interpretations, 115 specialized ministry regulations in relation to network information, and 148 specialized local laws and regulations in relation to network information. It can be said that China has initially formed the network legal system covering network security, cybercrime, Internet information management, personal information protection, Internet industry management, telecommunications services, domain name management, e-commerce, network consumer protection, online games, network intellectual property protection, Internet infringement, electronic evidence and other areas.

The Electronic Signatures Act promulgated in 2004 (as amended by 2015), the *National Security Act* promulgated in 2015, the *Network Security Act* promulgated in 2016 and the proposed *Electronic Commerce Law* and a series of up-to-date legislation practices have shown that China's network legislation is in an accelerating stage but there are still some obvious shortcomings in the network security legal system, mainly in the following aspects: ① *Network Security Act* as the upper law has just introduced, the systemized architecture design, which has not yet been completed and supports lower law, which has not yet formed a response situation. ② Divided policies from various sources, decentralized legislation, departmental and local legislation with lack of coordination, result in difficulty in adaptation to the characteristics and rule of the legalized network. ③ Law enforcement capacity is lagging behind. ④ Legislation still has heavy management but light governance, and heavy duty but light right issues; and has lack of international vision, which is insufficient to effectively support China's participation in the Internet international affairs. ⑤ Network legislation extremely lacks talent, and the foundation of subject support is weak. ⑥ Compared with the actions to accelerate the practice of network security legislation to protect their own interests in some developed countries in Europe and the United States recently, China's network security legislation is still lagging behind, and the legal system has yet to be further improved.

From the point of view of safeguarding the sovereignty of cyberspace, the lag of China's cyberspace legislation has affected the effectiveness of claiming cyberspace sovereignty. In contrast to cyberspace governance and the construction of the network legal system in Europe and the United States and around the world, combined with the Chinese current judicial practice and legislative practice, the implementation of the network legislation system cannot be achieved in the short term. However, the acceleration of the process of the cyberspace security legal system's construction can help to improve the legal basis of the national cyberspace security as soon as possible. In theory, the cyberspace security legal system includes the basic contents of network subject, network behavior, network rights and obligations, and network legal liability. From the legislative contents, the cyberspace legal system includes the network special law and association law. The network special law mainly includes: cyberspace basic law, cyberspace security law, personal information protection law, e-commerce law, information and communication law, e-government law, network information service law, network social management law and so on.

The development of cyberspace has revolutionized the traditional legal system. Although China's cyber security legislation has made great progress in the past two decades, there are still large gaps between China and some developed countries in Europe and the United States. For example, there is a lack of the establishment and protection of new rights; punishment and relief cannot adapt the characteristics of the cyberspace era; there is no clear boundary between the state rights and the individual rights of citizens so that the relationship there between cannot be effectively balanced; the whole system needs to be further optimized.

In view of the above situations, facing to the network society, the practice of perfecting cyberspace security legislation should be: ① to establish a cyberspace legalization thought, and form structured innovation models of multi-participant, iterative optimization, cross-border inclusiveness and open sharing. ② To establish the basic principles of cyberspace legislation, such as the principle of cyberspace sovereignty, the principle of equal emphasis on cyberspace security and development, the principle of reunification of right and responsibility, and the principle of common governance. ③ To pay special attention to improve the National People's Congress of cyberspace security legislation, so as to promote personal information protection law, e-commerce law, e-government law, network information service management law, information and communication law, and law construction process related to network social management.

12.1.1 Network Management According to the Law to Construct Cyberspace Security Legal Framework System

"Decision of the Central Committee of the Communist Party of China on Several Important Issues in Promoting the Rule by Law"[2] adopted on October 23, 2014 proposed to strengthen the Internet domain legislation, and to improve the network information services, network security protection, network social management and other aspects of laws and regulations to normalize the network behaviors according to the law. The State Council "Guidance on Actively Promoting" Internet +"Action"[3] indicates to develop "Internet +", improving the Internet integration standards and laws and regulations, enhancing safety awareness, strengthening safety management and protection, to ensure network security; aiming at the new feature of the integration development of Internet with various industries, to speed up the legislative work related to "Internet +", to study, adjust and perfect the existing laws and regulations and policies that do not meet the "Internet +" development and management. In a speech at the symposium on cyber security and informatization work[4] on April 19, 2016, President Xi Jinping pointed out that it

[2]"Decision of the Central Committee of the Communist Party of China on Several Important Issues in Promoting the Rule by Law", Seeking Magazines. http://www.qstheory.cn/dukan/qs/2014-11/01/c_1113047776.htm [2016-9-24].

[3]Authorized Release: The State Council "Guidance on Actively Promoting "Internet +" Action". http://news.xinhuanet.com/politics/2015-07/04/c_1115815944.htm [2016-10-5].

[4]Full text of speech at the symposium on cyber security and informatization work by Xi Jinping: http://news.cctv.com/2016/04/25/ARTIa8u.THXqX8JF25uz6S7Yh160425.shtml [2016-8-27].

was necessary to speed up the process of network legislation, improve the supervision measures according to law and resolve the network risks. In July 2016 "National Informatization Development Strategy Outline"[5] further emphasized that it was necessary to perfect the informatized legal framework, to focus on network legislation and to speed up the establishment of the legal, administrative regulatory framework with the promotion of informatization development and the reinforcement of network security management as the goal, covering network infrastructure, network services providers, network users, network information and other management objects. In December 2016 "National Cyberspace Security Strategy"[6] proposed a goal of "promote peace, security, openness, cooperation and order in cyberspace,", in which "orderly" is interpreted as "the public's right to know, right to participate, right to express opinions, right of supervision and other such lawful rights and interests in cyberspace are to be fully protected, personal privacy in cyberspace is to be effectively protected, and human rights are to be fully respected. Domestic and international legal structures, standard and norms for cyberspace are to be established progressively, effective governance according to the law is to be realized in cyberspace, the network environment is to become honest, civilized and healthy, and the free flow of information is organically unified with safeguarding national security and the public interests."

The improvement of the cyberspace governance system and the governance of the cyberspace according to the law are meant to comprehensively promote the legalization of cyberspace, adhere to the law, and openly and transparently manage, govern, operate and use the network, allowing for the healthy operation of the Internet by the rule of law. Improve the cyber security laws and regulations system, build a good network order according to the law, protect the legal, orderly and free flow of cyberspace information, protect personal privacy, protect intellectual property rights, and effectively implement that there must be laws to go by, the laws must be observed and strictly enforced, and lawbreakers must be prosecuted. Enacted laws and regulations such as the Regulations on Network Protection of Minors, has clarified the responsibilities and obligations of all sectors of society, and clarified the requirements of network security management. Speed up the revision and interpretation of existing laws to make them applicable to cyberspace. Perfect the network security related system, establish a network trust system, and improve the network security management of the scientific and standardized level.

Specifically, it is necessary to sort out the existing rules related to cyberspace, so as to timely ban the outdated and undesirable regulations with obvious sectoral

---

[5] "National Informatization Development Strategy Outline" (full text) issued by Office of the CPC Central Committee and Office of the State Council: http://news.sina.com.cn/c/nd/2016-07-27/doc-ifxunyxy5687194.shtml [2016-10-5].

[6] "National Cyberspace Security Strategy" (full text). http://news.sina.com.cn/c/nd/2016-07-27/doc-ifxunyxy5687194.shtml [2016-10-5].

interests. The low-level regulations are needed to upgrade their level, and, for example, although the "Information Security Level Protection Management Policy"[7] issued by the Ministry of Public Security has played an important role on the security protection of China's computer information system, its legislative thinking stayed in the initial stage of network development and has been far from able of adapting to today's security demands on key information infrastructure protection, important information system security and infrastructure operations in national economic important areas. It should be necessarily adjusted based on concluding practical experience to be upgraded to the administrative regulations to raise the level of this law into the "Information and Communication System Security Regulations" enforced by State Council, promoting implementations of protection rules of cyberspace security technology systems. For the lack of legal protection, we should step up the development of appropriate laws and regulations, such as personal information protection law, e-commerce law, e-government law, network information service management law, information and communication law, and network social management-related laws.

12.1.2 *Prepare for Implementation of the* Cyber Security Law *to Solidly Construct an Upper Law System of Cyberspace Security*

Cyber Security Law is the basic law of cyberspace security management, which establishes the basic principles to ensure the safety of cyberspace, standardizes the top-level system design method such as strategic planning, as well as establishing and perfecting basic systems on network infrastructure security, network system operation security, network data security, network application security, personal information security and other aspects, and also clarifies the norms to be observed of construction, operation, use, protection, management, and network resource allocation, etc. of the infrastructure in the cyberspace (not just Internet). The law stipulates implementation methods necessary to be developing to the specific cyberspace business involved by the relevant network function departments, such as Internet, telecommunications networks, radio and television networks, Internet of Things, industrial networks, social networks and other departments to which the relevant departments can develop management approaches based on *Cyber Security Law*.

Combing the existing laws and regulations involving cyberspace, the laws and regulations to be retained, must be revised and converged in the framework of *Cyber Security Law*. The *Cyber Security Law* should play the role of the upper law

[7]"Information Security Level Protection Management Policy" noticed and issued by the Ministry of Public Security and other departments. http://www.gov.cn/gzdt/2007-07/24/content_694380.htm [2016-9-18].

on cyberspace, and the low provides basis of the upper law for the development of all the lower law.

In preparation for the implementation of *Cyber Security Law*, we should pay close attention to the development of laws and regulations supporting the network security, and timely introduce regulations supporting cyberspace security. The supported administrative laws and regulations may include: information and communication system security protection regulations, key information infrastructure security regulations, network security review regulations, minor network protection regulations, cloud computing and big data services regulations, industrial control system security regulations; and timely introduce regulations supporting cyberspace security.

12.1.3 Develop the Personal Information Protection Law *to Protect Personal Information Security of Citizens*

Personal information in the era of big data has become an important strategic resource. Driven by the interests, a variety of illegal collections, sales, thefts and other abuses of personal information behavior are repeated. Not only property damage may be caused to the Internet users, but also the safety of people's lives may be threatened. China's current laws have made great progress in protecting the rights of personal information. The "Decision of the Standing Committee of the National People's Congress on Strengthening the Protection of Network Information",[8] the "Criminal Law Amendment (9) of the People's Republic of China",[9] the "Residents of the People's Republic of China"[10] and the "Law on the Protection of Consumers' Rights and Interests of the People's Republic of China"[11] which was revised in 2013 have constructed the legal framework for the protection of personal information, including criminal liability, administrative liability and civil liability. Especially the "Criminal Law Amendment (9)" further reinforces the criminal law protection of the personal information. However, since China has not yet introduced a law systematically protecting personal information, basic rules of collecting, processing and using personal information are not systematically established, so that the personal information security environment has deteriorated.

[8] Authorized Release: "Decision of the Standing Committee of the National People's Congress on Strengthening the Protection of Network Information". http://news.xinhuanet.com/politics/2012-12/28/c_114195221.htm [2016-10-5].

[9] Authorized Release: "Criminal Law Amendment (9) of the People's Republic of China". http://news.xinhuanet.com/legal/2015-08/30/c_1116414724.htm [2016-10-5].

[10] "Residents of the People's Republic of China" (Full Text). http://news.sina.com.cn/c/2011-10-29/205123383476.shtml [2016-10-5].

[11] "Law on the Protection of Consumers' Rights and Interests of the People's Republic of China". http://www.gov.cn/jrzg/2013-10/25/content_2515601.htm [2016-10-5].

The early introduction of the *Personal Information Protection Law*, which specifically clarifies the rights of information subjects as well as rights, obligations and responsibilities of each information subject in collecting, processing, storing and using the personal information, very urgently protecting basic rights of individuals in the network era.

12.1.4 Develop the **E-commerce Law** *to Protect Security of E-commerce Transactions*

At present, most of China's e-commerce norms stay in the regulation level of the ministries and commissions of the State Council, and few correspond to the legal and administrative regulation level; there is a lack of overall models and norms in the principle of e-commerce, and no internal relation is between the single laws; the contents of the norms substantially focus on the site business, management, network communication monitoring and other aspects, in lack of substantive norms directly aiming at the e-commerce and the entire process of electronic transactions. As China's e-commerce legislation lags, the current e-commerce norms cannot meet the needs of the rapid development of e-commerce.

No transaction security means no sustainable development of e-commerce. It is necessary to introduce as soon as possible the *E-commerce Law*, providing the legal protection for the electronic transaction security. At the same time of the introduction of *E-commerce Law*, it is necessary to develop electronic transaction security management regulations, network payment security management regulations, cross-border e-commerce information protection regulations, civil credit information protection regulations and other supporting regulations.

12.1.5 Develop **E-government Law** *to Protect Security of E-government and Government Data*

The Law on Administrative Licensing,[12] adopted in 2003, is the earliest law on the recognition of e-government at the height of the law. Other rules on e-government are scattered in some departmental regulations, local regulations and rules, and other normative documents. Due to the lack of specialized laws governing the regulation of e-government, we have not yet established a complete legal system of

[12]Law of PRC on Administrative Licensing. http://www.gov.cn/flfg/2005-06/27/content_9899.htm [2016-9-18].

e-government, and the lag of e-government legislation has hindered the development of the e-government and the economic field dependent on the e-government.

In view of the characteristics of e-government, China should formulate the *E-government Law* or "E-government Regulations", and revise and improve the "Government Information Disclosure Regulation of People's Republic of China"[13] in the field of e-government, building the basic system such as informatization, paperless office, information disclosure, information sharing, information security and personal information protection and other aspects, achieving the open security management of the collection, storage, transmission, use, sharing of the government data, clarifying the boundary of scope and the manner of usage of the data sharing of the various departments, sorting out the obligations and rights of the data management and sharing of the various departments, to guide and advance e-government and to promote the innovation and entrepreneurial development relying on government data.

12.1.6 Develop **Network Information Service Management Law,** *to Regulate Management of Network Content Security*

In the current background of rapid revolution and development of the media integration and network communication, the "Internet Information Service Management Approach"[14] introduced by the State Council in 2000 has seriously lagged the management demands. Various departments have introduced information services management approaches in the relation to the network news, network audio-visual programs, online education, network medicine, online games, network culture, network publishing, network maps and other areas. Due to lack of superior law, there is no internal link between the regulations. Therefore, there is a need to make amendments.

On the basis of summarizing the legislation and enforcement experience of "Internet Information Service Management Approach", the *Network Information Service Management Law* should be introduced as soon as possible, to clarify the rights and obligations of each subject in the Internet information service market to promote the healthy and rapid development of the network information service market; to build supervision system and mechanism on the Internet information service to clarify limit of authority of the law enforcement departments to improve the legal responsibility system; to implement effective penalties to form deterrence at illegal and bad network information; to establish a multi-participatory mechanism

---

[13]Authorized release: "Government Information Disclosure Regulation of People's Republic of China". http://news.xinhuanet.com/politics/2007-04/24/content_6017637.htm [2016-10-5].

[14]"Internet Information Service Management Approach". http://www.gov.cn/fwxx/bw/gjgbdydszj/content_2263004.htm [2016-9-18].

to efficiently dock the government's regulatory enforcement and industry organizations, the public supervision and management.

12.1.7 *Develop* Cyberspace Information and Communication Law *to Protect Transmission Security of Cyberspace*

The legal systems of the traditional telecommunications field and the radio and television field are independent of each other, in fact, forming a mutual access and interoperable barriers. The three administrative regulations on "Regulations on Administration of Radio and Television"[15] promulgated in 1997, "Radio and Television Facilities Protection Regulations"[16] promulgated in 2000 and "Regulations on Telecommunications"[17] have been seriously lagging behind, which cannot meet the demands on the developing trends of broadcasting and television industry and telecommunications industry, and which further cannot adapt to the needs of triple play service. If the *Telecommunications Law* and the *Radio and Television Transmission Protection Law* are subsequently independently developed, the advancement of network convergence will be hindered at the legal level. To comply with the development of network integration, there is an urgent need to adjust the existing legal system. At present, there is no law in China that has a higher order and can regulate cyberspace of the triple play. Therefore, it is necessary to formulate a unified *Cyberspace Information Communication Law* to regulate subject, behavior, rights, obligations, responsibilities and so on in the cyberspace. Under the legal norms and constraints, it is possible to speed up the network construction including telecommunications networks, radio and television networks, Internet of Things, sensor networks and industrial control network and the formation of network resource distribution unified market, to protect the fair competition of market players in the cyberspace.

---

[15]Decree of the State Council of PRC (No. 228). http://www.sarft.gov.cn/art/2003/10/21/art_1602_26263.html [2016-9-18].

[16]Decree of the State Council of PRC (No. 295). http://www.sarft.gov.cn/art/2003/10/21/art_1602_26263.html [2016-9-18].

[17]Regulations of PRC on Telecommunications. http://www.scio.gov.cn/32344/32345/32347/33617/xgzc33622/Document/1452066/1452066.htm [2016-9-18].

12.1.8 Timely Introduce the Network Social Management Law

In today's times, the network has affected the social trends and development goals, and has had a profound impact on individuals, organizations and society. Network has constructed the new form of society, and the networked rapid spread characteristics have substantially impacted on the traditional coping styles. Although the network form of the social organization already exists in other time and space, the new information technology paradigm provides a technical basis for its infiltration and expansion throughout the social structure. The changes in the structure and behavior of the human society are obvious: many associations and community groups exist in the cyberspace, resulting in the great potential of social mobilization; the traditional communities move to the network, performing online and offline interaction; and some closed community activities do not open, not easily perceived by the outside. The socialization of various community groups brings difficulty to social management. It is necessary to attach importance to the basic research of the network society, timely introducing the network social management laws and regulations, such as "Network Social Organization Regulations", to correctly guide and standardize the healthy development of network society.

12.1.9 Form the System Framework of Cyberspace Laws and Regulations

From the recent construction of the legal system to safeguard the sovereignty of cyberspace, a legal framework with coordinated laws, regulations and rules should be established within five years.

1. Related Laws

It is necessary to consider the personal information protection law, network information service management law, e-commerce law as a first type of legislative planning; and consider an e-government law as a second type of legislative planning in the place of the cyberspace information and communication law such as telecommunications law and radio and television signal transmission law.

2. Related Administrative Regulations

It is necessary to consider the regulations on the protection of cyberspace security level, the regulations on the protection of key information infrastructure, the regulations on cyberspace security examination, the regulations on network protection for minors, the regulations on the protection of cyberspace defense, the regulations on the emergency response of cyberspace, the revision of "regulations on government information disclosure", the personal information cross-border transfer management regulations, the cyberspace basic resource management regulations, the cyberspace key infrastructure construction regulations, the e-government regulations as a first type of legislative planning; and consider the network social organization regulations, the cloud computing services regulations, the civil credit information protection regulations, the cross-border E-commerce information protection regulations, the electronic transaction safety management regulations, the internet security management regulations, the foreigners' personal information protection regulations, and the cyberspace public service market regulations as a second type.

3. Related Rules

It is necessary to consider to develop the department's regulations such as the cyberspace key equipment and cyberspace security dedicated product certification and testing methods, the personal information cross-border flow safety assessment approach, the key information infrastructure network security monitoring and evaluation methods, the cyberspace security monitoring pre-warning and information reporting methods, the cyberspace security incident emergency response and handling methods, the national cyberspace security incident emergency response plan, the cyberspace security violation penalty regulations, the cyberspace illegal personnel market ban regulations, the cross-border logistics service standards, the cyberspace transaction credit management methods.

12.2 Administrative Supervision: Construct Orderly, Free and Democratic Cyberspace

We should create "orderly" cyberspace, guarantee the legitimate rights and interests of the public in the cyberspace such as the right to know, participate, express, and the right to supervise, such that cyberspace personal privacy is effectively protected, and human rights are fully respected. Domestic and international legal systems and the standard norms of cyberspace are gradually established, such that the cyberspace can be effectively managed according to laws, network environment can display integrity, civilization and healthcare can be provided, free flow of information and national security being safeguarded, as well as public interests being organically unified. Therefore, it is necessary to protect the right to use the network according to laws, advocate network civilization, and build a good cyberspace order.

The protection of the right to use the network according to law is to respect the legitimate rights of citizens to use the Internet, to protect legitimate rights and interests such as the public's right to know, the right of participation, the right of expression and the right of supervision, to equally use the Internet to obtain knowledge, to guarantee the legal, orderly and free flow of network information, and to protect citizens' privacy and intellectual property rights in the cyberspace.

Advocating the network civilization is to encourage civilized integrity in the cyberspace, resist rumors and fraud; care for the healthy growth of young people, strengthen the protection of minors online, combat the spread of pornography, violence and other information; widely disseminated positive energy, inherit and promote the excellent culture of mankind, meet people's spiritual and cultural needs, play a guiding role in moral education, and construct the cyberspace to become a beautiful spiritual homeland.

Building of a good cyberspace order is to adhere to manage network according to the law, operate network according to the law and surf on the network according to the law, so that the network can be healthily operated on the track under the rule of law. It should improve the construction of legal norms of the network; clear the powers and responsibilities of law enforcement departments, strengthen the management of harmful information on the Internet, combat the spread of illegal information according to the law, and improve scientific and standardized level of the network security management.

12.2.1 Plan and Coordinate, Safeguard National Cyberspace Sovereignty, and Implement the Network Power Strategy

To safeguard the cyberspace sovereignty of the State and implement the network power strategy, it is necessary to strengthen the management of network by the law, to improve the administrative supervision system in the cyberspace management, and to exercise public power according to the law. It should coordinate the relevant departments to comprehensively promote the legalization of cyberspace. On one hand, it is necessary to clear responsibilities and obligations that should be borne by network users, network service providers, network infrastructure operators and other social aspects in cyberspace security management, clear network security management requirements and to urge the relevant units and individuals to fulfill the main responsibility; on the other hand, it is necessary to rationalize the system and mechanism of the law enforcement on the network, clear law enforcement subject and law enforcement authority, standardize the law enforcement procedures, adhere to legally, openly and transparently manage and govern the network, strengthen the refinement of the cyberspace management, and punish the network of criminal acts according to the law.

To safeguard the cyberspace sovereignty of the State and implement the network power strategy, we need strong network security capabilities for escorting, developing under the premise of the protection of national cyberspace security, and promoting national security with the healthy and flourishing development of cyberspace. To this end, from the height of national security and national development, we need an overall layout and co-ordinate the parties, effectively integrating and coordinating functions of domestic network security management departments, forming a resulted cyberspace management force from technology to content, from daily security to combating of crimes. We should establish the cross-sectoral, cross-industrial cyberspace security coordination mechanism, establish the work linkage mechanism such as Internet infrastructure management, content management, industry management and network crime prevention and combat, improve the linkage security mechanism integrated with the important industries, important areas and important information system, and build the national cyberspace security system.

To safeguard the cyberspace sovereignty of the State and implement the network power strategy, it is necessary to establish a comprehensive technical supporting development strategy to enhance China's hard power in cyberspace and to possess independent network core technology. To this end, it is necessary to stand in the height of national strategy, accurately grasp the strategic opportunities for the development of cyberspace technology, plan to develop a comprehensive information technology and network technology research and development strategy. We should select strategic areas and a priority direction in the relation to the overall situation and long-term development, make efficient and rational allocations and focus on tackling difficulties. It is necessary to increase investment for the key strategic major scientific and technological issues and key products, and to nurture scientific and technological strength and industrial strength of the national cyberspace security strategy. There are needs to build a national laboratory of the cyberspace, and to strive to achieve a major breakthrough in key technologies, through the guide and demonstration, leading research, development and overall upgrade of the domestic cyberspace technology.

To safeguard the cyberspace sovereignty of the State and implement the network power strategy, it is necessary to actively develop cyberspace security industry. To build a capital market policy supporting the development of enterprises, by focusing the advantages of resources onto the national enterprises through the market, it is possible to vigorously support and grow a number of key national enterprises, so that they become main bodies of technological innovation, main bodies of information industry development and main bodies of maintaining the network security.

12.2.2 Ensure a Safe and Managed Cyberspace

To protect the national cyberspace sovereignty, it is necessary to ensure a safe and managed cyberspace that can ensure universal access. It is necessary to protect the Internet freedom of speech, not sparse management, to create a safe and civilized network environment. We should resolutely crack down on the spread of rumors, obscenity, violence, superstition, cults and other harmful information in cyberspace; prevent, stop and punish any use of the network to commit the treason, the split of the country, the incitement to rebellion, the subversion or incitement to subvert the people's democratic dictatorship of the regime; prevent, stop and punish the use of the network to steal, to disclose state secrets and other acts endangering national security; prevent, stop and punish the foreign forces using the network to penetrate, destroy, subvert, split activities.

1. Carry Our Special Actions

It is necessary to effectively coordinate the relevant management departments of the state, continuously carrying out the special action to crack down on network rumors, obscene violence and other harmful information, and continuously cleaning up various types of illegal and bad information accumulated in the cyberspace. It is necessary to form an institutionalized cyberspace dynamic monitoring and management system, effectively renovating and cracking down on various cyberspace violations that endanger national security, affect social stability and damage to the interests of the masses.

2. Strengthen Security Management and Protection Work

It is necessary to clarify the management responsibilities, strengthen the technical capacity-building of management, build a full range of monitoring systems, and meet management demands directing to various types of new forms of network information dissemination. It is necessary to strengthen the protection of data resources, establish the big data security management system, implement data resource classification and grading management, and guarantee safe, efficient and reliable application to data. We should implement the big data security project, strengthen the security protection of the data resources in the collection, storage, application and openness and other aspects, strengthen the safety assessment and protection of all kinds of public data resources in public sharing and other aspects, and establish the credit mechanism of capitalization of Internet enterprise data resources and data use. It is necessary to strengthen personal data protection and crack down on illegal disclosure and selling personal data behaviors.

3. Universal Participation in Security Work

It is necessary to build an illegal information reporting system for national network and establish civil network obligations supervision team, forming a unified-powerful, national-linkage and efficient-disposal reporting mechanism. It is necessary to strengthen the publicity and guidance, cultivating a high degree of public awareness of the network security, civilized network literacy and law-abiding behaviors and habits. The enterprises, the public, third-party institutions and other forces should participate in cyberspace governance, achieving "a change from external network management forwards internal cyberspace governance".

12.2.3 Guarantee a Safe and Credible Cyberspace

To protect the national cyberspace sovereignty, it is required to ensure a safe and credible cyberspace supporting the society. We should take necessary measures to ensure the safety of key information infrastructure, and gradually realize the first assessments later use; strengthen the key information infrastructure risk assessment; strengthen security protection to the party and government organs and key areas of the site, so that grassroots parties and government organs construct, operate and manage by intensive mode; and establish an orderly sharing mechanism of the network security information of government, industry and enterprise, so as to give full play to the enterprises in the protection of key information infrastructure.

1. Network Security Review

It is necessary to vigorously promote the network security review system, strengthen the supply chain security management, promote the establishment of network security review standard specification systems, improve the review methods, and break through the safety review key technologies. Especially for important information technology products and services purchased by parties and government organs and key industries we should carry out security reviews, improve the safety and control of products and services, so as to prevent product service providers and other organizations using information technology to implement unfair competition or damage the interests of users.

2. Information Security Certification

It is necessary to perfect the information security certification and accreditation system, promote information security certification and accreditation system and capacity-building, strengthen the information security product certification work and promote social acceptance of the recognition of information security certification. It is necessary to strengthen the confidential network security protection, introduce a localized level evaluation index system, and promote progresses of widely using self-controllable safe and credible information technology products in the confidential information system.

3. Strengthen Capacity Building of Security Protection

It is necessary to strengthen security protection and supervision of the information systems, important information systems, confidential information systems of the government departments, and organize and carry out network security checks and risk assessment of government departments and key industries. It is necessary to improve and perfect the national network security system, and to establish key information infrastructure protection systems. It is necessary to perfect the important information system level protection mechanism and confidential information system grading protection mechanism. Focus on breakthrough information management, information protection, safety supervision and basic support key technologies, so that the central technical equipment can be safe and controllable while the operation of the network and information systems can be stable and reliable.

4. Disaster Backup

It is necessary to pay attention to the disaster backup construction of information systems to ensure the data security and service security of the information system. Basic information networks and important information system construction need to take full account of survivability and disaster recovery. Disaster backup construction should advocate resource sharing and mutual backup.

12.2.4 Guarantee a Safe and Controlled Cyberspace

To guarantee the national cyberspace sovereignty, it is necessary to ensure that an interoperable cyberspace can be safe and controlled, and by fully coping with the complex situation on the Internet, to take management tools to protect the security of cyberspace.

1. Strengthen Study and Judgement on Cyberspace Security Situation

It is necessary to strengthen the construction of national high-end cyberspace security strategy consulting teams and high-level thinking tanks, deeply study and judge the cyberspace security situation, fully recognize risks that the network security is facing, distinguish between potential threats and real threats, correctly understand the threat of evolution, master different levels, different angles of coping, and reduce excessive prevention regardless of the cost.

2. Improve Ability to Combat Crime

It is necessary to raise monitoring, early warning, reconnaissance and combat capability of the cyber terror and espionage activity, eradicate cyber violence information, and strictly prevent terrorists from using the Internet to promote incitement, organization and associations, collecting funds, recruit members, and train online. We should strengthen the network anti-terrorism, anti-spy, anti-stealing capacity building, and master abilities of strict law enforcement and prosecuting to crack down on cyber terror and cyber espionage activities. We should strengthen prevention and control against the cyberspace crimes, adhere to the comprehensive management, source control, precaution according to the law and other means to crack down on network fraud, network stealing, gun trafficking and drug trafficking, infringement of personal information, dissemination of pornography, hacking, infringement of intellectual property rights and other criminal acts.

3. Attention to Information Security Emergency Work

It is necessary to perfect the emergency response mechanism of network and information emergency events, improve the cyberspace security emergency disposal plan, strengthen cyberspace security emergency support service team building, improve the Internet network security emergency response capability and level, guarantee the Internet network security, and establish a sound command scheduling mechanism and information security notification system.

12.3 Industry Self-Discipline: Build Open, Controllable, Interoperable and Prosperous Cyberspace

To create "open" cyberspace, it is necessary to make the Internet technology cooperated with sharing and increasingly bridge the digital divide under the multi-stakeholders' joint efforts. We should strengthen the information technology standards, policies and open a transparent market, and promote product circulation and information dissemination more smoothly.

It is necessary to strengthen the cooperation and sharing of Internet technology. Multi-stakeholders need to strengthen the network communication, mobile Internet, cloud computing, Internet of things, big data and other areas of technology research and development, promotion and international technical cooperation to jointly solve the problem of Internet technology development and jointly advance the development of new formats and new industry, so that advanced Internet technology can be more extensively and safely applicable.

It is necessary to eliminate the international digital divide. Multi-stakeholders need to support the international community to strengthen network capacity-building, popularize information infrastructure and break information barriers so that everyone can equally use the Internet to acquire knowledge and information and the interoperable information superhighway benefits more developing countries.

12.3.1 Social Organizations Play Their Due Role

Social organization is a social group with specific functions established by people to achieve common goals. It is a non-profit organization set up by non-government institutions engaged in social welfare and mutual benefit activities other than the government administrative organs. It is also the "stakeholder" raised by the international community. One of its characteristics is: it is unofficial, which means that it does not represent the position of the government or the state; the second characteristic is: independence, it has its own organizational structure and management mechanism; it has an independent economic source, both in aspects of management and finance; it is independent of the government to a considerable extent; the third characteristic is: voluntary, so that the participation of members is not forced in the organization but completely voluntary. In addition, it has public welfare and so on.[18]

The mechanism by which social organizations play a role is different from that of government departments. It does neither use coercive means, nor is it for profit purposes. It operates through self-discipline and volunteer services and is an intermediate organization between government and market, assisting in coordination activities. Industry self-discipline, competition maintenance, industry management and many other functions should be achieved through industry associations rather than directly by the government. Social organizations are closer to the public, ways of service are more flexible, and innovation has a higher freedom.

Cyber Security Association of China (CSAC)[19] is a social organization for cyberspace security. It will mobilize all aspects of society to support the top-level design of cyberspace security in China, and at the same time to build an information exchange and cooperation platform for China's enterprises and research institutions engaged in cyberspace security, thereby enhancing the research, development and innovation ability of enterprises and research institutions and achieving independent cyberspace security technologies as soon as possible; it has organized social forces, especially through the production and research cooperation, to train and select high-level talent, providing a support for China's cyberspace security strategy and network security public policy, as well as the construction of law; it also strengthens cooperation with the international community, neighboring countries and developing countries, and actively participates in the development of international rules of cyberspace, creating a good international environment for cyberspace security in China.

12.3.2 Establish Collaborative Linkage Mechanisms

Attention should be paid to the establishment of collaborative mechanisms between social organizations. For example, Cyber Security Association of China, Cyber Research Institute of China, World Internet Conference Senior Advisory Committee, Internet Development Foundation of China, Network Culture Communication Research Association of China, Internet Association of China and

[18]Chen LS (2010) Study on the evolution path and construction strategy of political democratization in China—Based on the perspective of the relationship between government and civil society. Dev Res (12):125–127. http://www.wxphp.com/wxd_2y38x7qw2e1xkfw974n6_1.html [2016-9-24].

[19]Cyber Security Association of China. http://baike.baidu.com/item/%E4%B8%AD%E5%9B%BD%E7%BD%91%E7%BB%9C%E7%A9%BA%-E9%97%B4%E5%AE%89%E5%85%A8%E5%8D%8F%E4%BC%9A [2016-9-30].

other social organizations can jointly constitute a national core network group or federation supporting the social management of networks, forming a synergistic linkage mechanism and an effective collaborative linkage platform and space.

12.3.3 Self-Disciplined Organization and Industry

Key works that social organizations in the aspect of industry self-discipline should carry out can include the following points.

1. Enterprise Self-discipline

Social organizations should organize the industry self-discipline activities of domestic cyberspace security enterprises. Enterprises treat profit as priority, but the corporate social responsibility cannot be forgotten. Therefore, enterprises need to regard self-discipline to as the social responsibility. Social organizations should guide the member units to enhance the sense of social responsibility, consciously abide the state laws and regulations, to operate according to the law and operate with integrity, maintain fair and equitable industry competition order, and advance awareness and aspirations of the cyberspace security to the international arena.

2. Credit Rating

Social organizations should actively promote the cyberspace service (such as a web site) credit rating system. Follow the principles of government guidance, industry self-discipline, fairness and justice, and social supervision, strengthen our cyberspace service integrity system construction, and promote healthy and orderly development of cyberspace related industries. The main goal of the evaluation of cyberspace service credit is to build the credit management system of cyberspace related enterprises through the construction of cyberspace service credit databases and enhance the ability of enterprises to prevent credit risk.

3. Publicity, Education and Supervision

Social organizations should strengthen the integrity of publicity and education, and enhance the corporate sense of trustworthiness and integrity awareness of self-discipline, improve the credit level of cyberspace services, and promote healthy and orderly development of cyberspace-related industries. Social organizations should urge their members to clear their own illegal information.

12.3.4 Mobilize Members of Social Organizations to Actively Participate in Domestic Cyberspace Governance

Maintenance of network security is not just the government responsibilities, but also the responsibility of social organizations, or the responsibility of every netizen. We should actively promote the domestic industry in the process of cyberspace governance to play a good "industry self-discipline" role, consciously assume the responsibility of defending the national cyberspace security, guarantee the safe development of the "Internet +" actions, and build a trust system. We should guide the domestic industry to make plans for the government departments to strengthen exchanges and cooperation with government departments, and actively participate in the work of Internet governance.

1. Promote the Establishment of Cyber Security Industry Standards

It is necessary to establish industry standards, optimize the market environment, encourage network security enterprises getting bigger and stronger, and consolidate the industrial base for guaranteeing the national network security.

2. Organization of Cyberspace Security Certification

Using the Center for Excellence in Education (CEE) model, we will establish a network security certification and vocational training system in China, providing certification services, authorizing training activities, and rapidly expanding our talent to continuously improve the technology level and practical ability of existing employees.

3. Build Support Teams

It is necessary to organize and establish services in the country's network and information security experts support team, actively provide advice and assistance services for the government departments, and actively participate in the work of cyberspace governance.

4. Organize Volunteers

It is necessary to explore and establish a cyberspace security volunteer team to assist in the disposal of cyberspace security incidents, forming a situation where the whole society participates in the maintenance of cyberspace security.

5. Organize Cyberspace Security Training

We should organize an accreditation authorization mechanism of practicing qualification of vocational training lecturers and cyberspace security training lecturers; establish an accreditation authorization mechanism of training institutions and practicing qualification of lecturers; and organize the on-the-job training of conventional cyberspace security personnel and special security personnel (military and police).

6. Organize Social Education

It is necessary to promote enterprises to participate in social education and popularize cyberspace security knowledge: carrying out information security knowledge into the campus, into the Children's Palace, into the Science and Technology Museum activities, so that cyberspace security should be emphasis start with toddler. Carry out cyber security knowledge into the community activities, so as to begin to popularize cyberspace security knowledge from the common people, helping the masses to enhance self-proactive awareness, guiding net-users to safely visit Internet, and avoiding phishing sites, telecommunications fraud and other daily information security risks.

12.3.5 *Organize Members of Social Organizations to Actively Participate in International Cyberspace Governance*

Social organizations should play their special role, and actively mobilize their members to take the initiative to participate in international cyberspace management activities. In the international cyberspace management, the following work should be emphatically carried out.

1. Carry out International Exchanges and Cooperation

Social organizations should establish contact channels with relevant international organizations, and actively participate in international cyberspace governance organizations, such as International Organization for Standardization (ISO), International Internet Society (IOSC), Internet Engineering Task Force (IETF), Internet Corporation for Assigned Names and Numbers (ICANN) and other international affairs, and actively participate in international cyberspace security conventions, cyberspace security policy and standards development and other international affairs, and in the global cyberspace management system changes, issue the voice of China, come up with China's proposition and form China's influence.

2. Establish Contact with Other National Cyber Security Organizations

It is necessary to strengthen the exchange and cooperation with relevant enterprises, scientific research institutions and government agencies at home and abroad to jointly build a fair and just international order of cyberspace and establish a favorable environment and international environment to safeguard China's cyberspace security.

3. Strengthen Cooperation with the International Community, Neighboring Countries and Developing Countries

Through the "two-track" bilateral, multilateral cyberspace security dialogue and other international activities, a fair and just international order of cyberspace can be jointly built.

4. Participate in the "Multi-stakeholder" Governance Model

Cyberspace industry organizations should strive to play a good "stakeholder" role and promote its member units to join the "stakeholder" group in order to actively participate in the Internet governance work, reflecting China's demands in the Internet, commonly establishing a fair and just international order of cyberspace, sharing development opportunities, sharing fruits of development, fairly participating in cyberspace governance, protecting the core interests of our enterprises in the internationalization process, and building and maintaining a favourable environment and international environment of China's cyberspace security.

5. Expand International Market Space for Enterprises

The security enterprises should be led to go abroad, so as to promote the Chinese enterprise cyberspace industry organizations to lead the cyberspace security enterprises to go abroad, promote Chinese enterprises to actively participate in the development of international information technology standards to promote China's information security technology products into the international market, protect the core interests of Chinese enterprises in the internationalization process, and take responsibility for the bridging of the digital divide.

12.3.6 Organize Internet Content Industry to Strengthen Construction of Network Culture

Community organizations should organize the Internet content enterprise to develop positive and progressive network culture, vigorously cultivate and practice the socialist core values, spread positive energy, gather a strong spiritual strength, and create a good network atmosphere. It is necessary to organize and encourage Internet content enterprises to expand new business, create new products, build a network culture brand reflecting the spirit of the times, and constantly improve the network culture industry scale. It is necessary to actively promote the digitalized network production and dissemination of quality goods of the excellent traditional culture and contemporary culture. It is necessary to make full use of the advantages of Internet communication platform to promote the excellent cultural exchange between China and foreign countries, so that people from various regions could understand the excellent Chinese culture and the Chinese people could understand the excellent culture of various countries, so as to jointly promote the prosperity and development of network culture, to enrich people's spiritual world and to promote human civilization and progress.

The Internet content industry should strengthen the network ethics and network civilization construction, play a moral educational guidance role, and nourish the cyberspace and repair network ecology with human civilization excellent results. It is necessary to organize and construct the network environment having civilization and integrity, advocate civilized network operation and civilized Internet surfing, forming a safe, civilized and orderly information dissemination order. It is necessary to improve network civilization literacy for the youth, strengthen the protection of minors online, and create a good network environment for the healthy growth of young people.

12.4 Technical Support: Build a Safe, Reliable, Stable and Available Cyberspace

To create a "safe" cyberspace, it is necessary to effectively control the cyberspace security risks, complete and perfect the national network security system, so that the core technology and equipment is safe and controllable, and the operation of the network and information systems is stable and reliable.

The current objective situation is that China is a large importer of information technology, which is bound to form an asymmetry with the exporter of information technology. As the level of information and communication technology determines the maintenance capacity of cyberspace sovereignty, the key to reverse this asymmetry is to strengthen the building of independent technology, develop basic technology, general technology and disruptive technology, including an autonomy control capacity of core hardware and software and an autonomy building capacity of cyberspace defense systems.

12.4.1 Autonomy Control Capacity of Building Core Hardware and Software

In the independent research and development of core hardware and software, we should regard the government and the military sector as the starting point and the enterprise as the main body. With a combination of production, study, research and use, collaboratively tackle critical problems, pointing to the surface, advance overall, as soon as possible achieve core technology breakthroughs to strengthen the promotion of information technology and the localization of products. It is necessary to study and develop national information field core technology equipment development strategy. We should further clear the general ideas and methods of the independent information technology product development and application, and we should strive to master the core technology in our own hands, and truly grasp the initiative of competition and development.

1. Research & Development Capabilities of Key Infrastructure

Key infrastructure includes CPU, operating systems, industrial equipment, domain name systems, large databases. The autonomy and controllable key infrastructure is the cornerstone of the defense of cyberspace sovereignty. At present, the domestic key infrastructure core technology and products are controlled by others. On one hand, the key infrastructure is under a risk of a backdoor being implanted and other threats; on the other hand, there is a lack of independent infrastructure capacity, causing that China is very passive in the defense of cyberspace sovereignty. For example, the mainstream operating systems widely used by our users have a security problem of collecting system and user information by default, which seriously threatens the privacy and security of users; the domestic industrial control facilities are heavily dependent on foreign equipment, such that if there are hidden dangers, it is difficult to rely on autonomous technology; domain name resolution root servers are handled by very few countries, such that once our top-level domain name resolution services are cut off and our top-level domain names are written off, China's cyberspace will become an information island among the global Internet. In view of the above, We should be driven by the actual demand of the national key information system, to intensify the research and development efforts of the domestic CPU, the operating system and the industrial control system and gradually replace the foreign products in the government, the army and other departments to drive the market with demand, drive the innovation by the market, and gradually enhance China's independent research and development capabilities of key infrastructure.

2. Research and Development Capabilities of Core Software Products

The core software products include application software, office software, network software (such as browser and email) and other necessary daily software. Such software products have high popularity and large user groups. Core software and people's daily information processing activities are closely related. Once the backdoor is installed, it will cause serious risk of leakage. In the field of application software, China has had mature products. For the actual situation, when the government, military and other departments purchase and install core applications, the review and restrictive measures should be taken to promote the use of independent application software systems to gradually replace foreign software. It is possible to promote the development of domestic application software industry to form a virtuous circle, while protecting the government and the military software products without backdoor worries. In addition, it is also necessary to pay attention to software security to accelerate the popularization and application of trusted software products.

3. Internet Service Providing Ability

At present, foreign search engines, social networks, microblogging, blogs, cloud services, e-mail services, online games and other Internet services have attracted a very large scale of the domestic user base, and then have opportunities to understand strategy resources, such as China's mass users' identity information and activities. Based on these strategic resources a lot of valuable information and the situation can be analyzed, resulting in a very serious security risk. In order to solve this problem, the key solution is to strengthen the Internet service provider's own ability, develop the network basic service, enrich the cyberspace information content, establish the core competitiveness and attractiveness, and gradually reverse this asymmetric situation. It is necessary to implement the national big data strategy, establish big data security management system to support big data, cloud computing and other new generation of information technology innovation and application.

4. Assessment Capability on Supply Chain Risk

The computer and network hardware equipment, operating systems, compiler environment and application software commonly used in China's various industries are widely introduced overseas. Some of products are indeed irreplaceable domestically. But in the key link of the supply chain, China cannot be independent and controllable. The detection capacities of loopholes, backdoors and malicious behavior are limited, causing that China's computer and Internet systems are facing the risk of being monitored and controlled. In recent years, there have been many key aspects of the supply chain backdoor. The event which had the widest impact was that Apple's XCode integrated development environment was maliciously tampered, resulting in the information of about 100 million Apple mobile phone systems being stolen.[20] In view of this situation, it is necessary to investigate information equipment and software purchased and used by the government, military and other departments, and the risk assessment and compliance inspection can be provided for the involved product supply chain, so as to form an information system supply chain regulatory system to improve the risk assessment capability of information system supply chain security.

12.4.2 Autonomy Building Capacity of the Cyberspace Defense System

In the autonomous building of the cyberspace defense system, We should regard the military, the central network letter office, Ministry of Industry, Ministry of Public Security, Ministry of Security and other key departments as the starting point, to mobilize the domestic security enterprises and Internet companies to establish a defense system to achieve military defense. We should develop a development strategy of the national cyberspace defense system to strengthen the basic theory of network security and major issues of research; We should build a sound and

[20]Apple APP was "hacked" that hundreds of millions of users got infected. http://dzb.jinbaonet.com/html/2015-09/21/content_288917.htm?div=-1 [2016-9-30].

effective operation of the national cyberspace security technology support system, and strive to have core technology, platforms and facilities in our own hands; We should strengthen the network security standardization and certification work, making more use of standard norms of cyberspace behavior; We should do a good job on level protection, risk assessment, vulnerability discovery and other basic work, to improve the network security monitoring and early warning and network security emergency response mechanism.

Self-built cyberspace defense system needs to have four aspects of technical capacity that are the network security, the technical reconnaissance, the security management and the content control.

1. Cyberspace Security Technology Capability

All necessary measures should be taken to protect the critical information infrastructure and its vital data from attack damage. In order to form the capability of cyberspace security technology, we need to build the cyberspace security resource base, such as the national malicious code sample database, national cyberspace security vulnerability sharing platform, cyberspace security monitoring platform, cyberspace security situation sensing platform, cross-platform national level cyberspace shooting and other technical systems; build computer virus control system, cyberspace infrastructure protection system, computer network emergency response system and the national cyberspace strategy early warning system.

2. Technical Investigation Capability

The formation of technical investigation capabilities needs to build national intelligence analysis on threats, network big data analysis, cyberspace address tracing and other technology platforms; and to coordinate with cyberspace security technology platforms to jointly build an intelligence discovery system.

3. Cyberspace Security Management Capabilities

There is a need to adhere to technology and management, simultaneous protection and deterrence, focus on identification, protection, detection, early warning, response, disposal and other aspects, establishing the implementation of key information infrastructure protection systems. For the formation of cyberspace security management capabilities, there is a need to build a cyberspace security level protection verification platform, the Internet site filing and domain name management system, virtual identity management system, cloud computing platform security regulatory system, Internet of things open platform monitoring system, big data security regulatory system and other technical systems; to build the network security review technology system, cyberspace security inspection and supervision system, product and system security inspection and evaluation system, public key infrastructure and digital certificate authentication system, key management and authorization management infrastructure.

4. Cyberspace Content Security Control Ability

To form the cyberspace content security control ability, it is necessary to construct the domestic illegal IP blocking system, the cyberspace public opinion monitoring system, the cyberspace audio and video content monitoring system, the search engine management system, the network content service supervision technical system; and construct network public opinion control and early warning system.

12.5 Military Safeguard: Construction of Peaceful, Credible and Transparent Development of Cyberspace

To create a "peaceful" cyberspace, it is necessary to prevent information technology from being used to the purpose contrary to maintain international security and stability. It is necessary to commonly boycott cyberspace arms race, to prevent cyberspace conflict, and peacefully use cyberspace in line with the common interests of mankind. States should abide by *the Charter of the United Nations* on the principle of non-use or threat of use of force, to effectively curb the abuse of information technology; and to effectively prevent cyberspace conflict.

Having a cyberspace with peaceful development, both countries and the world are of great significance. Cyberspace should not be the battlefield of states and further should not become a hotbed of crime. States should work together to effectively control, prevent and oppose the use of cyberspace for terrorism, obscenity, drug trafficking, money laundering, gambling and other criminal activities. Whether it is commercial theft or a hacking attack on the government network, they should be resolutely cracked down on, based on relevant laws and international conventions. Maintenance of network security should not have a double standard, such that one country is safe while other countries are unsafe, or some countries are safe while others are not safe. Furthermore, a country is not supposed to sacrifice other countries to seek so-called absolute security by their own.

12.5.1 Construction of a Cyberspace Defense System Is an Inevitable Choice to Defend Cyberspace Sovereignty

Cyberspace is the new territory of national sovereignty. In the case that the concept of cyberspace sovereignty is universally accepted by the international community, the ability of guaranteeing cyberspace sovereignty becomes the key to the effective sovereignty of the state. To defend the cyberspace sovereignty, is to build cyberspace protection that adapts to international status and the network power, to vigorously develop the network security and defense means, to timely detect and resist network intrusion, and to cast and safeguard the strong backing of the national network security.

Sovereignty has territory, so there must be fortified fortification. Building a network border by military and civil society is not only an urgent task of China's current cyberspace sovereign security but also a cornerstone of long-term maintenance of cyberspace sovereignty. From the practice of world cyberspace sovereignty, a developing road of military and civilian integration is the only way to build the sovereign security power of cyberspace. In order to effectively cope with the challenges of cyberspace security facing the country, we must adhere to the principle of "combining military and civilian forces, combining peace and war, combining offense and defense and international cooperation", and adopt measures such as "military building civilian use, civilian building military use, military and civilian jointly building", forming a coordinated cyberspace sovereign security force.

The clear responsibility of the military to defend the national cyberspace sovereignty and critical information infrastructure is an objective needed to build a cyberspace defense system. China's reform has integrated the strength of the network warfare forces and improved the internal efficiency of the troops, but its mission is also limited to the protection of military tasks, including the protection of military command network security, the combat of enemy important information systems and information networks, and has not been imparted a responsibility to protect the vital information infrastructure of the country. It is difficult for the military to exercise the main force of the military in protecting the vital network information infrastructure of the country.

In the occurrence of major cyber security incidents involving national cyberspace sovereignty, under the framework of the National Cyberspace Security Emergency Response Command and depending on cyberspace sovereignty protection defense system with the military and civilian integration conformable to Chinese condition and security needs, it is important to recognize the need to establish a unified national network of a cyber security coordination mechanism in order to, co-ordinate the national political, military, economic, cultural, diplomatic and other forces, forming the overall force to effectively deal with network attacks from outside.

12.5.2 Military Power Is the Cornerstone of Defending Cyberspace Sovereignty

The army is not only the pillar of national security, but also the protection cornerstone of the cyberspace sovereignty. The practice of major military power has confirmed this point. The United States is the first country to put forward the concept of network operations. The United States not only pays long-term attention to the construction of network military force, but also carries out global network attack and defense actions. In the protection of national cyberspace sovereignty, the national armies of various countries have gradually formed completed cases from the cyberspace military theory to the building of the strength and then to the offensive and defensive actual combats, providing the world's research samples and learning paradigms for our network of military security.

In the United States, for example, most of the key infrastructure in the United States is mastered and operated by civil mechanisms, but up to 90% of the civil mechanisms do not have the ability to respond independently to cyber-attacks. Therefore, the United States built a Network Security Team system with government-led, military supported and civil coordination to protect the cyberspace security and sovereignty. In June 2009, the United States formally set up a Cyber Command,[21] commanding the US military network warfare actions. The United States focuses on the development of network warfare forces, researches and develops the network warfare weapons and equipment, and starts the "national network shooting range" project to strengthen the network army and network deterrent capacity-building. By 2011, the US military has developed more than two thousand kinds of network attack weapons,[22] the number of network warfare forces reaches nearly 10 million people[23] and there are three to five thousand network warfare experts.[24] Just after the "prism gate" exposure, Martin Dempsey, chairman of the US Joint Chiefs of Staff, said that in order to strengthen the US defense against cyber-attacks, the US plans to expand the cyber war command in the next four years to four thousand people, for which 23 billion US dollars will be invested.[25] In 2011, in "Cyberspace Action Strategy",[26] the US Department of Defense had definitely specified the network as a "fifth battlefield" following the sea, the land, the air and the outer space, and said military action would be taken to serious acts of cyber-attacks. The United States has also continued its cyber fire

[21]United States Cyber Command. https://en.wikipedia.org/wiki/United_States_Cyber_Command [2016-10-1].

[22]US military have developed more than 2000 kinds of virus weapons to strengthen the network warfare capabilities. http://www.china.com.cn/military/txt/2009-06/03/content_17881319.htm [2016-10-5].

[23]Cyberspace has become the US military new battlefield, the world's strongest with 100,000 hackers. http://www.china.com.cn/military/2013-03/06/content_28150970.htm [2016-10-5].

[24]US military forces is equivalent to seven 101 airborne divisions. http://news.xinhuanet.com/mil/2013-08/11/c_125148975.htm [2016-10-5].

[25]The network should not be a new tool for US hegemony. http://www.qstheory.cn/zxdk/2013/201315/201307/t20130729_253893.htm [2016-10-5].

[26]The United States "cyberspace action strategy" (Chinese translation). http://wenku.baidu.com/link?url=eER42eCg-_MGFZGsTw9xLtB4TgaABLwoHS6wOlFg68w4budNkAf0tWIAZ6UdKfF0upSzOjc4PGmTtF4R6Q3FZ8LRf2xcvhMLr77VEFF8qyq [2016-10-5].

exercises, such as "Cyber Storm"[27] dominated by the Department of Homeland Security and the "Silent Horizon"[28] dominated by the CIA.

12.5.3 Military Defense to Build Network Borders Is the Basis for Maintenance of Sovereignty

Network border defense refers to a set of network defense and attack countermeasures taken on the national borders of cyberspace to defend the national political, military, economic and cultural interests. The construction of national Internet borders is to ensure China's network security of the major basic projects, and to promote China's cyberspace sovereignty claims to further implement the major initiatives. At present, China's national border construction on the Internet already has the appropriate technical foundation and experience, while the successful practice of the United States can be used for reference.

The United States has repeatedly stressed that the freedom of the Internet does not mean not to set up national network boundaries to defend. As early as the Bush administration, the United States had used cyberspace as an independent field of operations, independent of land, sea, air and space, established network armed forces, developed network warfare weapons, and the "Cyberspace International Strategy" and "Cyberspace Action Strategy" clearly put forward to strengthen the network intelligence reconnaissance, active defense and offensive capacity of the building. The protection of the government network boundary by the United States is technically and dominantly based on its "Einstein" federal network security detection, response and recovery system,[29] with the Trusted Internet Connection (TIC)[30] joint implementation, being unitedly lead in the organization through the military and civilian joint cyberspace defense coordination agencies, regarding *Cyber security Information Sharing Act(CISA)*[31] and the military cyberspace warfare order as the yardstick to establish a complete network border protection system.

Facts show that building a national network border is the top priority of the maintenance of cyberspace self-defense rights and jurisdiction. Although the Internet is globally interoperable, the country's network boundaries are indeed objective. From reality, the network boundary can be determined by the "all domestic router ports that directly connected to the foreign routers". Based on the network boundary, building the national "network border" has an important real

[27]Cyber Storm: Securing Cyber Space. https://www.dhs.gov/cyber-storm [2016-10-5].

[28]CIA's 'Silent Horizon' Internet War Games. http://usatoday30.usatoday.com/tech/news/techpolicy/2005-05-26-cia-wargames_x.htm [2016-10-5].

[29]EINSTEIN. https://www.dhs.gov/keywords/einstein [2016-10-5].

[30]Trusted Internet Connections. https://www.dhs.gov/trusted-internet-connections [2016-10-5].

[31]S.754-Cyber security Information Sharing Act of 2015. https://www.congress.gov/bill/114th-congress/senate-bill/754 [2016-10-3].

demand, and based on the network border to further expand the construction of the country's "network defense system" has more important strategic significance.

"Network border" construction can prevent network intrusion, block harmful information, identify network identity, and clear cross-border e-commerce. The establishment of national cyberspace sovereignty in jurisprudence is bound to produce the corresponding network boundary; the establishment of network boundary defense facilities directly declares the existence of the network territory from the physical level. It is completely legitimate for China to implement effective sovereign control in the network territory. We should determine the "network border" status in the form of laws and regulations, and we should raise the network defense up to a position side by side with "border defense, coastal defense and air defense".

12.5.4 Attach Importance to Construction of Security Force System of National Cyberspace Sovereignty

The state should be based on the network border, from the view of "big state defense" to guide the construction of a new national "network defense" security system. Correspondingly the national important network security infrastructures should be brought into the construction system of the national "network defense", and the important network security information system in the cyberspace defense system should be brought into an operating mechanism having unified management and coordination.

For this reason, the first step is to establish the integration of the military and civilian network defense command system; the second is to build reserve a "Network Security Team"; the third is to build three levels of network defense systems, that is, the first line is involved in the government's relevant network security functions, the second line is involved in the network security force, the third line is involved in the active network forces; and the fourth is to set up a "central network defense joint command", which can full-time respond to the large-scale burst network attacks from outside, and which also can coordinate the handling of the domestic significant network security emergency in this framework.

The "Network Security Team" with military and civilian integration is constructed to form a peace-war combined cyberspace sovereignty guarantee system and mechanism. The network battlefield is different from the traditional space battlefield particularity: first, there are no obviously distinctive characteristics between the military and the people; second, combat weapons and production tools are fully universal; third, the important information system management rights usually belong to the government and enterprise. Therefore, there is a need to build a military and civilian "Network Security Team" under the national defense reserve system. In peacetime, the "Network Security Team" as a national defense reserve organization can organize the training, the management and the use; in wartime, the "security team" can be immediately converted into active service network warfare forces, responsible for anti-combat missions. The "Network Security Team" is dedicated to defending the government network and the national important network infrastructure, and military network warfare forces are dedicated to crack down on the enemy information system and defend the military command system. If necessary, the military network warfare forces could station on behalf of the military to the important national security interests of the information infrastructure, directly involving in coordinating and commanding the national Network Security Teams, both local and military.

The building of the core strength of a "Network Security Team" can be implemented in the "military building civilian use, civilian building military use, military and civilian jointly building" model. Herein, "civilian building military use" is to construct corresponding disposal agencies based on military, focusing on supporting local network security incident processing; "civilian building military use" is to construct corresponding disposal agencies based on the local, focusing on coordinating the demands of military; and the "military and civilian jointly building" is to build a formal "network defense reserve system" to the important information infrastructure sectors under the auspices of the military, forming an essential force for the protection of important information infrastructures.

Promote the "joint authority, joint communication (equipment), joint training, joint linkage, joint acting" world mode. Jointly establish enterprises and local network security agencies as the first echelon, the government network security functions as the second echelon, the military network security and network combat forces as the third echelon, forming the cyberspace sovereign security system with the military and civilian integration.

12.6 International Collaboration: Build a Collaborative, Interconnected and Shared Cyberspace

To create "cooperation" of the cyberspace, it is necessary to strengthen the role of the coordination of international organizations, improve the international network management system, and jointly safeguard the network security. Countries should cooperate more closely in areas such as technical exchanges, cyber terrorism and cybercrime defeat, and improve the multilateral, democratic and transparent Internet governance system, and gradually form a network of cyberspace destiny as the core of cooperation and profitability for every country.

Countries should work together to deepen international cooperation and jointly cope with the new threats and challenges facing the development and security of the international community in the spirit of mutual respect, mutual trust, equality and mutual benefit. Strengthen cooperation in the framework of the United Nations, ITU, Shanghai Cooperation Organization, BRIC countries and ASEAN Regional Forum. Advance the United Nations in promotion of the development of international information security legal norms, the peaceful settlement of disputes, promotion of the national cooperation etc., to play an important role. Strengthen coordination among relevant international organizations.

Common maintenance of network security is in line with national interests of states. Countries should work closely together to deal with increasing network threats such as hacker activities. We should actively cooperate with the international community in the field of information security and cyber security to strengthen cooperation and establish an exchange of communication channels to commonly deal with the threat of international information security. We should promote common initiatives to prevent and combat the criminal activities using the Internet and other information and communication technology. Strengthen the international cooperation in the computer emergency response and experience exchange and cooperation in the aspects of invasion of information sharing, joint response, personnel exchanges, technical equipment, information exchange and case investigation and etc.

Maintenance of the order of cyberspace must adhere to the concepts of the same boat, mutual trust and mutual benefit, and abandon the old concepts of the zero-sum game and the winner-takes-all. Promote the establishment of a multilateral, democratic and transparent Internet governance system, support the United Nations to play a leading role, and make efforts to achieve the common management of Internet resources and equitable distribution, ensuring equal participation of countries in the international Internet governance rights and ensuring the stable and safe operation of national networks.

To safeguard China's cyberspace security and sovereignty, China should actively participate in the activities of international organizations and strive to enhance China's international voice.

12.6.1 Actively Promote International Governance and Build a Cyberspace Fate Community

The Internet is the common home of mankind. Through the organization of the third session of the Wuzhen World Internet Conference, China has successfully set up a platform for global Internet sharing and put forward the "China program" of international governance of the Internet, and it is committed to jointly promote the healthy development of the Internet. China should continue to promote the Wuzhen World Internet Conference platform to promote the implementation of the "China program" of the international governance of the Internet. The principle of "respect for cyberspace sovereignty" is the starting point and fundamental goal of the Chinese program. The concept of "cyberspace sovereignty" is the core and soul of China's contribution. China always upholds the principle of sovereign equality established by *the Charter of the United Nations* as the basic criterion of contemporary international relations, which covers all areas of communication between countries and the principles and spirits of which should also apply to cyberspace. In the aspect of cyberspace governance, China should also actively promote the leading role of the United Nations in the connection with the international peace and security in the field of cyberspace; and promote the development of universal and effective cyberspace national codes of conduct within the framework of the United Nations, sharing network and information technology outcomes.

Cyberspace is the common space of human activities. The future fate of cyberspace should be grasped by the world. Countries should strengthen communication, expand consensus, resolve differences, deepen cooperation and achieve a win-win situation, and jointly build the cyberspace fate community as the core of the win-win cooperation. Based on mutual respect and mutual trust, respect for cyberspace sovereignty should be achieved, strengthening international cyberspace dialogue and cooperation, as well as the promotion of transformation of the global governance system of the Internet. China should actively deepen the bilateral and multilateral network security dialogue with each other, enhance mutual trust, and constantly expand the intersection of interests. Actively participate in global and regional network security cooperation, promote the Internet address, root domain name servers and other basic resource management internationalization, cooperate more closely in technical exchanges, combat cyber terrorism and cyber-crime and other areas and build a multilateral, democratic and transparent Global Internet Governance System.

12.6.2 Continue to Strengthen International Cooperation and Build an Interconnected, Cooperative and Shared Cyber Network

China should strengthen cooperation in the framework of the United Nations, ITU, Shanghai Cooperation Organization, BRIC countries and ASEAN regional forums. Promote the United Nations to play an important role in the promotion of developing international information security legal norms, the peaceful settlement of disputes, and the promotion of national cooperation, and strengthen the coordination between the relevant international organizations. China should actively cooperate with the international community to strengthen mutual cooperation in the field of information security and cyber security, establish exchanges and communication channels to jointly cope with the threat of international information security, fully respect the different concerns of various countries on Internet security, promote common initiatives and actively respond to cyberspace security challenges, jointly prevent and combat cyber-attacks, network theft, infringement of privacy, protect personal privacy and information security, and safeguard the legitimate rights and interests of citizens.

The use of the Internet to carry out propaganda war and psychological war has already been usual means by several extreme organizations. They not only build websites to launch seditious content, but also use the site to spread terrorist statements. Any terrorist organization in theory can be in the most remote corner to launch a network attack towards the most developed countries or regions to undermine people's normal life. This unequal attack can cause a wide range of indiscriminate damage with a very small price. In the front of this attack, each country is not an independent island. The United Nations Security Council has adopted resolutions 2129, 2178, which call on the international community to intensify its fight against cyber-terrorism. In the fight against cyber terrorism, China should promote the establishment of an anti-terrorism cooperation mechanism of international network, crack down on the use of information and communication technology and information and communication networks to engage in cybercrime and cyber terrorism, combat the spread of terrorism, separatism, extremism and incitement to national, racial and religious hostility, and do not provide a source of communication for the fear of information.

12.6.3 Actively Promote the Concept of Cyberspace Sovereignty and Advocate the Peaceful Development of Cyberspace

Cyberspace sovereignty carries the dreams and visions of the humans advocating the Internet global governance system reformation and promoting fairness and justice, which is also the Chinese program proposed to reshape the Internet international governance order, standing on the future of humanities high point against the unfair and unreasonable situation of the current Internet governance. China's efforts to reshape a new just and rational international order with the Internet as a starting point reflect the interests and aspirations of the vast number of developing countries and demonstrate the power of international morality. Especially in the development of network infrastructure, which is the largest information gap between the developing countries and developed countries, some of developed countries monopolize international cyberspace governance with the overwhelming advantage of infrastructure and technology, while China advocates the cooperation with the developing countries, reflecting the responsibilities and obligations of China as a big developing country.

China should actively promote the concept of cyber space sovereignty to the international community, so that more countries are aware of the importance of cyberspace sovereignty, and earnestly respect for cyberspace sovereignty without carrying out network attacks and interfering with the internal affairs on the network. We should support the United Nations to play a leading role in promoting the development of universally acceptable international agreements on cyberspace and international cyberspace anti-terrorism conventions, perfect judicial assistance mechanisms to combat cybercrime, deepen policy and legal, technical innovation, standards, emergency response, key information facilities protection and other areas of international cooperation. Build the World Internet Conference and other global Internet sharing and shared governance platform, and jointly promote the healthy development of the Internet. Through active and effective international cooperation, build a multilateral, democratic and transparent international Internet governance system to jointly construct a peaceful, safe, open, cooperative and orderly cyberspace.

12.7 Social Education: Improve Level of Cyber Security Education in All Directions

We should vigorously carry out the national network security publicity and education to run the network security publicity weak activities; promote network security education into the teaching materials, into schools, into classrooms, improving network media literacy, enhancing the whole society network security awareness and protection skills, reinforcing the abilities of identifying and resisting the network illegal information, the network fraud and other illegal and criminal activities; strengthen the network security professional construction to build first-class network security colleges and innovation parks, forming an ecological environment of personnel training and innovation and entrepreneurship; and make an effort to meet the needs of network security personnel, greatly improving the confidences of the whole society of network security awareness, basic protection skills and the use of network.

12.7.1 Adhere to Popularize Education and Strengthen Cyber Security Awareness

We should carry out a lasting, systematic awareness of education popularization activities and guide the public to safeguard the network security, which has strategic significance to achieve cyberspace security. It is necessary to gradually cultivate awareness of cyber security among all people, improve the network security skills, pay attention to privacy protection, strengthen legal awareness, enhance the ability to identify and prevent harmful information on the Internet, promote the formation of national good environment to build network security, network sharing of civilization, to create a good atmosphere in the Internet, civilized Internet, and provide network security guarantee for the social stability and long period of stability.

We should develop an education popularization program of China's network security awareness, and clarify the policy principles, the objectives, the key tasks, the implementation of programs and the resource security of the education popularization of network security awareness; establish a launch mode of network security popularization education with the multi-force cooperation of government advocacy, social promotion, enterprise implementation and university research, to complete the awareness popularization education from top to bottom, in an orderly manner. It is necessary to plan the launch form, the cooperation manner, the content and the coverage of the network security awareness popularization education, to ensure the formation of a systematic and continuous publicity and education force. Special attention should be paid to the network security awareness popularization education of children and adolescents, to provide protection for children and adolescents' safe, healthy and green online use, thereby ensuring the healthy growth of children and adolescents.

12.7.2 Cyber Security Begins at a Young Age While Studying Special Talent Mining and Training Methods

We should study the establishment of the mining and training system for the special talents on the network security, with the interest stimulation and individualized teaching as the main principle, to initially establish a discovery and training system for the "wizards" and "geeks" from the selection mechanism, training methods and other aspects, and particularly pay attention to the discovery and cultivation of young people; establish the discovery and cultivation system of cyberspace security young professionals with a virtuous circle, expand the influence of the cyberspace security technology on young people, attract young people to actively learn cyberspace security knowledge, and promote the generation of young professionals. The young professionals with great potential in the field of cyberspace security can be selected through the discovery system, the growth and talent of young professionals can be protected through the training system, and the effective operation of the discovery and cultivation system can be ensured through the development funds of young professionals, ultimately providing a youth talent pool for the team building of our cyberspace security personnel.

12.7.3 Pay Attention to Academic Education

We should set up a level of discipline of the cyberspace security and related professional, training and creating world-class network technology leading talents and high-level innovation teams.

The research on the academic education system of cyberspace security is the key to the cultivation of high-level innovative network security personnel, which is the foundation of the construction of national cyberspace security system. It is necessary to establish the academic education system of the cyberspace security, with a level of discipline of the cyberspace security as traction, open education and industry barriers, and construct a multi-mode and multi-track talent cultivation system with production, study and research cooperation from angles of the training objectives, training content and training methods. The academic education of cyberspace security includes three levels: undergraduate education, graduates education and doctoral education. It is necessary to set up systematic training objectives for professionals of different types, different levels and different technical fields; and with the "heavy foundation, wide direction" for the undergraduates and "guidance by classifications and training by tracks" for the graduates as a guideline, according to the personnel training objectives and expertise, establish scientific and rational curriculum system and training programs, explore a training model for the world-level leading talents and build a training base for the high-level innovative talents.

12.7.4 Strengthen Continuing Education

The establishment of cyberspace security personnel qualification system, is conducive to promoting and improving the quality and business level of the professional personnel; is conducive to unifying the business ability standards of network security professionals, and impartially evaluating the practicing qualifications of professional personnel, so as to rationally use professional and technical personnel; and is conducive to being in line with the international standards, promoting the process of global certification standardization, and competition for the speaking right of the international cyberspace security.

The vocational training system for cyberspace security is an important part of the cyberspace security personnel training system. Compared with the academic education, the vocational training has the characteristics of relevance and practicability, flexibility and diversity, skills and technical ability, continuity and persistence. These characteristics determine that the establishment of the vocational training system is able to rapidly expand the cyberspace security personnel and continuously enhance the ability and level of cyberspace security personnel.

Establish and improve the relevant policies, laws and systems, establish multi-party cooperation model including the government, the certification bodies, the training institutions, the universities, the research institutes and the enterprises, standardize the authorization system of the certification bodies and training institutions, improve China's certified knowledge system and training curriculum system, strengthen the infrastructure of China's certification bodies and training institutions and teaching staff, establish the joint certification model of the multi-party participation including China and foreign countries, actively promote the global standardization process of China's certification and training, seize the international speaking right of the cyberspace security certification and training, preliminarily construct the cyberspace security practicing certification and vocational training system with self-development and a virtuous circle, settling an important human insurance for enhancing China's cyber security defense capabilities.

12.7.5 Development of Specialized Education

The purpose of specialized education is to cultivate the specialized talents for the specific departments of the state, which has strong purpose and direction. In order to meet these specific needs, one is to establish a directed training system in combination with universities and enterprises, select appropriate universities, research institutions or enterprises to establish a scientific way of co-cultivation, design a specific curriculum system and practice internship mechanisms to strengthen the emergency network, network assessment, network management, network police, network warfare, network research, technology and other front-line team building; the another is to set up a low-academic but high-level special "technical school", using the characteristics of non-adaptability and specialization required by the specialized personnel to cultivate specialized personnel in network publicity, network assessment, network management, security and other aspects, like the training of "software workers".

Chapter 13
Conclusion

Abstract In order to promote the transformation of the global Internet governance system, President Xi Jinping proposed four basic principles – respecting cyber sovereignty, safeguarding peace and security, promoting open cooperation, building a good order. In order to build a community of common destiny in cyberspace, President Xi Jinping put forward five propositions: firstly, to speed up the global network infrastructure construction; secondly, to create an online cultural exchange and sharing platform; thirdly, to promote the development and innovation of network economy; fourthly, to protect the network security; fifthly, to construct the Internet governance system.

Keywords Respecting cyberspace sovereignty · Internet governance system
Four basic principles · Five propositions

In 2014, President Xi Jinping was the first in the international community to issue the voice of "respect for cyber sovereignty" which received the world's highest attention and positive response. As Internet is a national political, military, economic, cultural and social platform, the countries will not let the Internet become disorderly without management, endangering their own interests without a guard. Therefore, based on the principle of sovereign equality of the national cyberspace, the international governance of the global Internet will be the trend.

Respect for the maintenance of cyberspace sovereignty, the connotation of which is that: the cyberspace sovereignty is inviolable; the network affairs within national sovereignty should be decided by the people themselves; the countries have the right to learn from international experience in the view of their own national conditions, to develop cyberspace related laws and regulations and take necessary measures according to the law to manage national information systems and network activities within their own territory; to protect their national information systems and information resources from intrusion, interference, attack and destruction; to protect the legitimate rights and interests of citizens in cyberspace; to precaution, prevent and punish the propagation of harmful information to the

B. Fang, *Cyberspace Sovereignty*,
https://doi.org/10.1007/978-981-13-0320-3_13

national security and interests in their own network, safeguarding the cyberspace order.

In order to promote the transformation of the global Internet governance system, President Xi Jinping proposed four basic principles: firstly, to respect the cyber sovereignty, and to respect the rights of each country to choose their own network development path, network management model, Internet public policy and equal participation in international cyberspace management, without the network hegemony, without interfering in the internal affairs of other countries, and without engaging in, condoning or supporting the network activities harmful to national security of other countries. Secondly, to safeguard peace and security. Cyberspace should not become a national battlefield, and also cannot become a hotbed of crime, and the maintenance of cyber security should not have double standards, also cannot sacrifice the security of other countries to seek their own so-called absolute security. Thirdly, to promote open cooperation, adhere to the concept of the same boat, mutual trust and mutual benefit and abandon the old ideas of the zero-sum game and winner-take-all, advance the open cooperation in the Internet area, and promote each other to allow the cyberspace for complementary advantages and common development, so that more countries and people take the express of information age and share the development of the Internet results. And fourthly, to build a good order, the freedom is the purpose of order, the order is the protection of freedom, cyberspace is not "a land out of law", so we should adhere to the network management, operation and use according to the rules of law, to make the Internet run on a healthy track of law.

President Xi Jinping pointed out that the global Internet is interconnected and has become a common space for human activities, so the countries all over the world as a cyber space fate community, should strengthen communication, expand consensus and deepen cooperation. To this end, he put forward five propositions: firstly, to speed up the global network infrastructure construction, promote interoperability, and only when strengthening the information infrastructure construction, paving the road of information flow, and constantly reducing the information gap between different countries, regions and people, the information resources can fully flow. Secondly, to create an online cultural exchange and sharing platform to promote the exchange and mutual reference. The Internet is an important carrier of disseminating human excellent culture and promoting positive energy, culture will be colorful due to communication, and civilization will be enriched by mutual reference. Thirdly, to promote the development of network economy innovation and promote common prosperity, the key to solve the difficult problem of the world's economic recovery, is to adhere to innovation-driven development and open up a new realm of development. And fourthly, to protect the network security and promote the orderly development. The security and development are two integral wings and two driven wheels, the security is the protection of development and development is the purpose of security. The network security is a global challenge, no country can stay out of the place and survive, and to maintain the network security is the common responsibility of the international community. Fifthly, to construct the Internet governance system and promote fairness and justice. The international cyberspace governance should adhere to multilateral participation, multi-party participation, the government, international organizations, Internet companies, technology community, civil society, individual and other individual roles. The countries should strengthen communication and exchange, improve the cyberspace dialogue and consultation mechanism, study and formulate a global Internet governance rule, so that the global Internet governance system becomes more fair and reasonable and more balanced to reflect the wishes and interests of most countries.

The concept of the cyberspace sovereignty has long been a classic example in the telecommunications space, the participation of sovereign countries in the global telecommunications space governance has long been an example, and the cyberspace sovereignty in the management of Internet space of the countries also has a lot of practice, but for ideological reasons, the cyberspace sovereignty in the full implementation of Internet space will also have a long process. For the "Internet spirit of freedom" considerations, the western countries stand against that the governments of the countries apply their laws in the Internet information dissemination process, regardless of the fact that the countries have managed the Internet information dissemination in their cyberspace in accordance with the laws of their own countries. For military purposes, the US military recognizes the effectiveness of cyberspace sovereignty over the Internet, but limits cyberspace to the infrastructure and the data it carries to avoid the social attributes of its "space". Its purpose is to avoid that the human activities also belong to the category of cyberspace, so as to only locally admit the existence of cyberspace sovereignty.

Since cyberspace sovereignty is only conditionally recognized by Western countries, the management of sovereign countries still is excluded globally in the governance of the global Internet, and hope for the "stakeholders". The basic concept thereof is that Internet stakeholders rely on the Internet to survive, so they will fully maintain the healthy operation of the Internet, and actively promote the healthy development of the Internet. However, a simple truth is that the Internet is not only the source of corporate profits, but also should provide a universal service area, especially in the basic environment where the Internet has become an indispensable economic life, and at the same time, it further carries the national political, military, economic, cultural and social activities which are often not noticed by "stakeholders" with the interests first, and which are concerned and resolved only by the government. To this end, international organizations, Internet companies, technology communities, civil society, individual citizens and so on should take part in the Internet management under the auspices of the government as being the "multi-stakeholder", and there is need for the sovereign governments to develop the Internet public policy.

Considering that many countries are not aware of the importance of the Internet, and then do not realize the importance of participation in Internet governance, or they are accustomed to the United States and other Western countries dominating the Internet, thus abandoning the Internet governance aspects of the right to speak, therefore, the research and advocacy of the cyberspace sovereignty has become very important. Only by increasing the global Internet governance to the height of cyberspace sovereignty, will the international community take seriously what is a reasonable and legitimate model of global Internet governance, and will realize that a sovereign state cannot easily abandon the Internet's international voice, and will stand up to maintain the independence, equal rights, self-defense rights and jurisdiction of the Internet. This is also the important point of studying cyberspace sovereignty.

Of course, like the traditional sovereignty, the cyberspace sovereignty theory and practice will be dynamic, the connotation and extension of which are still changing, but the objective existence of which has become an international consensus. At some point, different countries may be only concerned about some of the content based on their own needs. For example, the EU countries are particularly concerned about the content of their data sovereignty, the United States pays special attention to the content of its right to self-defense, and some countries focus on the content of its information sovereignty. With the change in national demand, the focus will constantly change, leading to continuously derive a new extension required to research. Further, with the rapid development of technology, in turn, the traditional theory will be challenged. In terms of cyberspace sovereignty, the network territory is the cornerstone of cyberspace sovereignty, and the boundary is the definite condition of the network territory. However, Google claims to deploy thousands of hot air balloons at the atmospheric stratosphere (roughly one or two thousand meters high) emitting WiFi signals towards the ground, allowing netizens to connect directly to the world via mobile phones. This means that the concept of the boundary will be blurred. Although we can also clear the country's cyberspace (that is, the network territory), because of the fact that the infrastructure carrying the cyberspace is within the territory and cannot be changed, the ambiguity of the boundary may cause the difficulty of mapping between virtual life and reality, so that people will find that the domain of the network territory becomes increasingly difficult to confirm.

In addition, there are many issues to be further studied in relation to the applicability of cyberspace sovereignty. For example, what kind of principle should be taken for information that comes from other countries and flows through the local information infrastructure? Do you need to respect the information of other countries without infringement, or will it apply to the laws of the local state? As another example, a user of a country should comply with the country's laws and regulations to send and receive data on the country's platform; but which country's laws and regulations should comply, if he or she sends and receives data on another countries' platform? Is it the law of the user's country or the law of the country in which the carrier is located? These series of problems will need to gradually clear and be resolved as the connotation and extension of cyberspace sovereignty is deepened and evolved. Therefore, the theory of cyberspace sovereignty requires people to continue to study and enrich, and to adapt to the situation with continuous development and change.

The manufacturer's authorised representative in the EU is Springer Nature Customer Service Centre GmbH, Europaplatz 3, 69115 Heidelberg, Germany. If you have any concerns regarding our products, please contact ProductSafety@springernature.com

Printed and bound by CPI Group (UK) Ltd, Croydon, CR0 4YY
22/09/2026
02220985-0012